1985

IDRC-144e

SALUS: LOW-COST RURAL HEALTH CARE AND HEALTH MANPOWER TRAINING

An annotated bibliography with special emphasis on developing countries

Volume 5

Editor: Rosanna M. Bechtel

Abstracts written by: Rosanna M. Bechtel, Arna Blum*, Hope Cadieux, Amy Chouinard, Esther Ehrlich de Vries, Maureen Gadd*, Helen Hathaway*, Catherine Last*, Diana Manning*, and Jean Taylor*

Appropriate Health Resources and Technologies Action Group Limited, London, UK.

(This is the fifth in a series of annotated bibliographies on low-cost rural health care and health manpower training. These volumes are published irregularly.)

The International Development Research Centre is a public corporation created by the Parliament of Canada in 1970 to support research designed to adapt science and technology to the needs of developing countries. The Centre's activity is concentrated in five sectors: agriculture, food and nutrition sciences; health sciences; information sciences; social sciences; and communications. IDRC is financed solely by the Government of Canada; its policies, however, are set by an international Board of Governors. The Centre's headquarters are in Ottawa, Canada. Regional offices are located in Africa, Asia, Latin America, and the Middle East.

Bechtel, R.M.

IDRC, Ottawa, CA

IDRC-144e

SALUS: low-cost rural health care and health manpower training : an annotated bibliography with special emphasis on developing countries. Ottawa, Ont., IDRC, 1980.   194 p.

/IDRC publication/, /annotated bibliography/, /health services/, /public health/, /rural areas/, /paramedical personnel/, /vocational training/, /developing countries/ — /health planning/, /family planning/.

UDC: 016:613

ISBN: 0-88936-233-5

Microfiche edition available

Contents

Foreword

Health for all by the year 2000. This worthy aim, recently adopted by the World Health Organization, emphasizes the importance of appropriate health care delivery. Whether the aim is realistic or not, it implies that each member state of WHO is committed to providing health services to all segments of the population and that all people wherever they live have a right to enjoy good health, adequate medical care, and a long life. To meet this aim, each country must find its own way, taking into account its present health situation, the specific needs of its people, and its economic and social circumstances. The experiences of other countries in setting up health care delivery systems may not be directly applicable, but at the same time it is necessary to consider what others have done and to avoid "re-inventing the wheel." The planners and managers of health care delivery services must have rapid access to relevant experience and practice, the failures as well as the successes.

Many of the discussions surrounding *Health for all by the year 2000* have focused upon the need to make relevant information immediately available and the mechanisms to do it. WHO, in particular, is studying several information systems that might be set up with international cooperation to handle different aspects of the whole health picture. *SALUS: Low-Cost Rural Health Care and Health Manpower Training* may well become one of the components of such a system. Our efforts to involve other institutions, especially developing-country institutions, in the collection of material for the data base and in the provision of information services from it are already a step in this direction.

This volume of the bibliography sees some of the changes that were announced in Volume 4. For ease of reference, the mnemonic SALUS has been incorporated into the title. The abstracts are also considerably shorter than in previous volumes, for two reasons. First, shorter abstracts will lighten the workload of our small staff and will enable more than one volume, with more up-to-date contents, to be published each year. Second, the long abstracts, which were intended to be informative surrogates of the cited documents, are no longer necessary as we are transferring the documents themselves to microfiches. Where we have copyright permission, it will be quicker and cheaper for us to mail copies of requested documents in full as microfiches rather than as paper copies, which we have had to limit in the past to 30 pages. Coupons, which may be used to request documents not available locally, can be found at the back of the volume.

MINISIS, the package of computer programs used to compile SALUS, has attracted the interest of many institutions that have problems in processing their own bibliographic material. Several institutions, in developing and developed countries, have already signed agreements with IDRC for the use and modification of MINISIS for local conditions.

The SALUS machine-readable data base is written in ISO communications format so that it can be mounted and interrogated in different computers, but the widespread adoption of MINISIS should also make it easier for us to make both the data base and the microfiche file available to other institutions.

We would like to thank the staff of the Appropriate Health Resources and Technologies Action Group, Ltd., London, UK, for their contribution to Volumes 4 and 5. AHRTAG abstractors for this volume are listed on the title page. We also thank Mrs Esther Ehrlich de Vries for her abstracts and especially Mrs Anita Firth, whose assistance with the in-house production of this volume has been invaluable.

Rosanna M. Bechtel
SALUS Project Manager
Information Sciences Division
International Development
Research Centre

Abbreviations and Acronyms

ABU — Ahmadu Bello University, Zaria, Nigeria

ALERT — All Africa Leprosy and Rehabilitation Training Centre, Addis Ababa

ANM — Auxiliary Nurse-Midwife

APHA — American Public Health Association, Washington, D.C.

BCG — Bacillus Calmette-Guerin vaccine

CAHP — Coordinating Agency for Health Planning, New Delhi

CENDES — Centro de Estudios del Desarrollo, Venezuela

CENTO — Central Treaty Organization, Ankara

CFNI — Caribbean Food and Nutrition Institute, Kingston, Jamaica

CIDA — Canadian International Development Agency, Ottawa

CIIR — Catholic Institute for International Relations, London

CMAI — Christian Medical Association of India, Bangalore

CMC — Christian Medical Commission, Geneva

CPC — Carolina Population Center, Chapel Hill, N.C.

CSG — Capital Systems Group, Inc., Bethesda, Md.

CUSO — Canadian University Service Overseas, Ottawa

DANIDA — Danish International Development Agency, Copenhagen

DHEW — United States Department of Health, Education, and Welfare, Washington, D.C.

DMEIO — District Mass Education and Information Officer (India)

DPT — Diphtheria, Pertussis, Tetanus vaccine

Engl. — English

FAO — Food and Agriculture Organization, Rome

FP — Family Planning

Fren. — French

GPHCTC — Gondar Public Health College and Training Centre, Ethiopia

HSMHA — Health Services and Mental Health Administration, Washington, D.C.

IBRD — International Bank for Reconstruction and Development, Washington, D.C.

ICA — Colombian Agricultural Institute, Bogota

IDR — Institute of Development Research, Copenhagen

IDRC — International Development Research Centre, Ottawa

ILO — International Labour Organization, Geneva

IPPF — International Planned Parenthood Federation, London

IRHFP — Institute of Rural Health and Family Planning, Gandhigram, India

ITDG — Intermediate Technology Development Group, London

IUCD — Intrauterine Contraceptive Device

IUD — Intrauterine Device

KAP — Knowledge, Attitude, and Practice (Study)

KNIPOROS — Kenya-Netherlands-Israel Project for Operational Research in Outpatient Services, Kenya

LRCS — League of Red Cross Societies, Geneva

MCH — Maternal and Child Health

MEDLARS — Medical Literature Analysis and Retrieval Systems

MESH — Medical Subject Headings

NEAC — Nutrition Education Action Committee, Kingston, Jamaica

NIHAE — National Institute of Health, Administration, and Education, New Delhi

NTIS — National Technical Information Service, Washington, D.C.

OAS — Organization of American States, Washington, D.C.

OECD — Organization for Economic Cooperation and Development, Paris

OEO — Office of Economic Opportunity, San Francisco

PAHO — Pan American Health Organization, Washington, D.C.

Russ. — Russian

SIDA — Swedish International Development Authority, Stockholm

Span. — Spanish

TBA — Traditional Birth Attendant

UCLA — University of California, Los Angeles

UN — United Nations, New York

UNDP — United Nations Development Program, New York

UNESCO — United Nations Educational, Scientific and Cultural Organization, Paris

UNESOB — United Nations Economic and Social Office in Beirut, Beirut

UNFPA — United Nations Fund for Population Activities, New York

UNICEF — United Nations Children's Fund, New York

UNROD — United Nations Relief Operations in Dacca

USAID — United States Agency for International Development, Washington, D.C.

USGPO — United States Government Printing Office, Washington, D.C.

WHO — World Health Organization, Geneva

I Reference Works

2801 Bourre, A.L. South Pacific Commission, Noumea. *Annotated bibliography on medical research in the South Pacific: addendum no.3/ Bibliographie commentee de la recherche medicale dans le Pacifique Sud: supplement no.3.* Noumea, South Pacific Commission, Technical Paper No.142, Part 4, Jan 1976. 169p. Engl., Fren. See also entries 2102, 2114 (volume 4), and 2802.

This compilation is the 4th in a series of annotated bibliographies on medical research in the South Pacific. More than 300 references are taken from 150 medical journals, field reports by the South Pacific Commission, and documents from national health departments. These references are classified under the headings physiology, personal hygiene, treatment, diseases, surgery, gynaecology, and public health. Author and subject indexes are included. Abstracts are in the language of the original document (English or French). (RMB)

2802 Bourre, A.L. South Pacific Commission, Noumea. *Annotated bibliography on medical research in the South Pacific: addendum no.1.* Noumea, South Pacific Commission, Technical Paper No.142, Part 2, Jan 1973. 193p. Engl., Fren. See also entries 2102, 2114 (volume 4), and 2801.

This compilation is the 2nd in a series of annotated bibliographies on medical research in the South Pacific. More than 300 references are culled from 150 medical journals, field reports by the South Pacific Commission, and reports from national health departments. These references are classified under the headings physiology, personal hygiene, treatment, diseases, surgery, gynaecology, and public health. Author and subject indexes are included. Abstracts are written in the language of the original document (English or French). (RMB)

2803 British Life Assurance Trust Centre for Health and Medical Education, London. *Information.* London, British Life Assurance Trust Centre for Health and Medical Education. Engl.

Six times a year, the British Life Assurance Trust publishes this periodical covering the latest developments in health and medical education. The news section includes address changes, international conferences and courses, festivals, information services, general information, appointments, and abstracts of new publications. The section on research abstracts also contains an annotated bibliography, while the section on teaching and learning materials describes booklets and articles, catalogues, films, information services, mass media resources, tapes, and slides. Information on graphics, duplicating, filming, photography, printing, projection, and video is included in the section on equipment. Each issue closes with a feature on a library or resources learning unit, a centre for special problems, low-cost teaching aids, etc. (RMB)

2804 Bureau d'Etudes et de Recherches pour la Promotion de la Sante, Kangu-Mayumbe, Zaire. *Catalogue du Bureau d'Etudes et de Recherches pour la Promotion de la Sante. (Catalogue of the Bureau of Study and Research for the Promotion of Health).* Kangu-Mayumbe, Zaire, Bureau d'Etudes et de Recherches pour la Promotion de la Sante, n.d. 1v.(unpaged). Fren.

Catalogue items have been abstracted separately under entries 2326, 2386, 2590, 2591 (volume 4), 2806, 3144, 3170, 3172, 3253, 3278, 3285, 3319-21, 3334-35, 3337, 3341, 3347-50, 3352-63, 3377-78...

This catalogue contains titles and prices in local currency of the educational materials, such as books, brochures, flip-charts, and pictoral series, published in French by the *Bureau d'Etudes et de Recherches pour la Promotion de la Sante* (Zaire). Included are: manuals for nurses and teachers on infectious diseases, nutrition, pharmacology, pediatrics, obstetrics, and health education; health promotion materials for nurses, teachers, and students; and illustrated brochures on the new orientation toward rural and public health, maternal and child health, protection and education of youth, and health protection and environmental sanitation. A limited amount of this material is available in English. The catalogue also contains a currency conversion table and an order blank. (RMB)

2805 Carr, M. *Economically appropriate technologies for developing countries: an annotated bibliography.* London, Intermediate Technology Group, 1976. 101p. Engl.

This annotated bibliography contains sections on: agriculture (including equipment for food production, irrigation, crop storage and processing), livestock, animal feed, fishing, aquaculture, and fishing equipment; low cost housing and building materials; manufacturing of food, clothing, etc.; infrastructures of power sources, water supplies and sanitation, health, and roads and transport technology; handbooks, manuals, buyers' guides, and technical publications; and relevant bibliographies. There are author, country, and subject indexes. The health subsection contains 13 references. Only English material is included. (RMB)

2806   Centre pour la Promotion de la Sante, Kangu-Mayumbe, Zaire. *Centre pour la Promotion de la Sante. (Centre for Health Amelioration).* Kangu-Mayumbe, Zaire, Centre pour la Promotion de la Sante, n.d. 1v.(unpaged). Engl., Fren., German, Dutch.
See also entry 2804.
This brochure summarizes the purpose and activities of the Center for Health Amelioration (Zaire). The centre's efforts are concentrated in the areas of health promotion and health education, especially among young Africans. (RMB)

2807   Centro Panamericano de Ingenieria Sanitaria y Ciencias del Ambiente, Lima. *Bibliografia sobre abastecimiento de aqua y saneamiento en areas rurales. (Bibliography on water supply and sanitation in rural areas).* CEPIS Boletin Bibliografico (Lima), 3(1), Mar 1976, 25-50. Span.
This bibliography of selected holdings from the library of the *Centro Panamericano de Ingenieria Sanitaria y Ciencias del Ambiente* contains 178 entries in the areas of water supply, training, general information on water and environmental health, rural sanitation, and water and sanitation technologies. Documents in English, Spanish, and Portuguese are included and there is an author index. (RMB)

2808   Colombia, Ministerio de Salud Publica. *Boletin epidemiologico nacional. (National epidemiological bulletin).* Bogota, Ministerio de Salud. Span. Refs.
This triannual bulletin contains articles and copious statistical data on epidemiological problems in Colombia. Topics covered include infant and maternal mortality, prevalence of various communicable diseases, vaccinations, etc. A section entitled "Epidemiological Notes" deals briefly with worldwide outbreaks of disease and similar subjects. (RMB)

2809   Comite Regional de Promocion de Salud Rural, Guatemala. Hamlin de Zuniga, M. *Informador. (Informer).* Guatemala City, Catholic Relief Services--U.S.C.C., Office of the Regional Medical Consultant. Span.
The Regional Committee for Rural Health Promotion (Guatemala) publishes this short, monthly newsletter containing reports and articles on: rural health programmes, facilities, manpower, and methods; health education; community development; and local meetings and conferences. Educational material is often presented in the form of lively line drawings and comic strips. Although the emphasis is presently on Guatemala, contributions from readers elsewhere are solicited. (RMB)

2810   Darrow, K. Pam, R. *Appropriate technology sourcebook.* Stanford, Cal., Appropriate Technology Project, Volunteers in Asia, Nov 1976. 304p. Engl.
See also entry 1404 (volume 3).
Appropriate technology in health care constitutes 1 of about 20 subjects covered in this reference book; others

are agriculture, architecture, water supply, etc. Altogether they comprise citations for more than 375 publications from American and international sources. Each citation describes the type of document, the authors or editors, date of publication, price, and name and address of publisher. It also includes a critical annotation that often provides information on essential materials and production techniques. The citations are frequently accompanied by line drawings or photographs. A glossary of the technical terms, a sample page from an Indonesian village technology booklet, a list of appropriate technology periodicals, and a conversion table for metric and English measurements are also presented. (AC)

2811   de Benko, E. *Rural health in Africa: a selected bibliography.* Rural Africana: Current Research in the Social Sciences, Michigan State University, African Studies Centre, No.17, Rural Health in Africa (East Lansing, Mich.), Winter 1972, 118-131. Engl.
See also entry 3059.
Based on sociomedical literature of the last 10 years, this selected bibliography is intended to reflect the intricacies of rural health in Africa today. Approximately 200 citations are grouped under six titles: African folk medicine and traditional cures; child care, maternity, and family health; nutrition and food problems; epidemics, endemic diseases, and other disorders; mental health; and rural public health and modern medical services. (HC)

2812   Deblock, N.J. *Elsevier's dictionary of public health.* Amsterdam, Elsevier Scientific Publishing, 1976. 196p. Engl., Fren., Span., Ital., German, Dutch.
The book brings together for translators, authors, and readers 2 363 terms related to hospital administration and public health care, few of which can be found in a general dictionary. In the main section of the book, the terms in English are listed in alphabetical order, each followed by its equivalent in French, Spanish, Italian, German, and Dutch. No definitions or etymological data are given, but common synonyms and closely related terms in each language are listed in order of frequency of use. An index for each language, containing all the entries, is provided at the end of the dictionary. (DM)

2813   Harrison, E.A. USA, Department of Commerce. *Health care delivery: a bibliography with abstracts.* Springfield, Va., US Department of Commerce, National Technical Information Service, 1975. 137p. Engl.
One hundred and thirty-seven items on government-sponsored research and evaluation of rural and urban health care delivery systems were culled from the National Technical Information Services (NTIS) bibliographical retrieval system, Springfield, Virginia (USA). The items, which are not exclusively restricted to health care systems in the US, cover regional and community medical programmes, the economics of health care delivery systems, health maintenance organizations, emergency medical care, biomedical information systems, and ambulatory health care. Instructions on how to

obtain a customized on-line search from NTIS are included. (HC)

2814   International Association of Agricultural Medicine and Rural Health, Commission on Living and Working Conditions, Madrid. *Bibliographic index no.3.* Madrid, National Institute of Occupational Health and Safety, May 1977. 49p. Engl.

This bibliography is based on the response of over 30 developed and developing countries to a request by the Commission on Working and Living Conditions of the International Association of Agricultural Medicine and Rural Health for recent (post-1974) research publications on the subject of health in the agricultural sector and rural health in general. The citations are arranged alphabetically under the country of origin and are in the original language; there is neither a subject nor an author index and there are no abstracts. Articles on occupational hazards and the effect of environmental pollutants (especially pesticides) figure highly among the citations. (HC)

2815   Jordan, J.L. Council of Planning Librarians, Monticello, Ill. *Rural health care and international development in Africa; with additional reference to Asia and Latin America.* Monticello, Ill., Council of Planning Librarians, Exchange Bibliography No.1409, Dec 1977. 38p. Engl.

This English-only bibliography includes: 53 entries under health and development, examining health's role in economic and social development; 59 entries under integrated delivery of rural health care, concentrating on appropriate technology and community participation; 31 entries under health and population, emphasizing the relationship between health, fertility, and development; 38 entries under health planning, covering finance, systems analysis, operations research, measurement, modeling, and cost-benefit analysis; 39 entries under traditional medicine, dealing particularly with Africa and the integration of traditional healers into Western medicine; 18 entries under maternal child health, focusing on methods of low cost prenatal and postnatal care and the child survival hypothesis; 25 entries under training of health personnel; 25 entries under the economies of disease, excluding epidemiology; 5 basic sources in health economics; and 93 country studies grouped under Africa, Asia, and Latin America. Basic health issues and the bibliography's rationale are discussed in a brief introduction. (RMB)

2816   Malaysia, Ministry of Health. *Training programmes for para-medical and auxiliary staff.* Kuala Lumpur, Ministry of Health, Dec 1975. 26p. Engl.
Unpublished document.

This document provides briefs of 26 types of training for health-related work in Malaysia. Each page deals with one specific category of staff, giving the address of the current training centre or centres, entry requirements, duration and outline of curriculum, name of the examination body, type of certificate issued, and the form of study award available. Nine of the courses train post-

secondary school students as state registered nurses, public health inspectors, and specialized hospital and dental technicians. Eleven training programmes give registered nurses further qualifications for work within and outside hospitals. Seven programmes for auxiliaries include a rural nurse course to retrain midwife auxiliaries and a basic rural nurse course for young women with no previous experience. (JT)

2817   Medical Missionary Association, London. *Saving health.* London, Medical Missionary Association. Engl.

This quarterly publication carries articles from, and of interest to, those working in medical missions throughout the developing world. Different missionary hospitals and facilities are profiled and articles discuss common medical problems in environmental health, nursing, dental health, etc. A separate section lists urgent staffing needs by church denomination and country. (HC)

2818   Pibouleau, R.F. *Introduction to national and international exchange of knowledge and experience.* World Hospitals (Oxford, UK), 11(2 and 3), Jun 1975, 63-64. Engl.

Three obstacles to the international exchange of information are identified: confidentiality, language barriers, and insufficient knowledge of sources of information. Of these, the last is the most important. In this paper, a number of sources of information on the topic of planning and building health care facilities under conditions of limited resources are discussed. They include: MEDLINE--a computerized system for literature search giving immediate access to half a million references to articles in 2 400 medical journals throughout the world; bibliographic material put out by the German Hospital Institute of Dusseldorf, the British Department of Health and Social Security, the Swedish Institute for Hospital Care, and the Dutch National Hospital Institute (although more orientated toward the developed than the developing countries, the coverage of these bibliographies better fits the hospital field than does MEDLINE's); and a WHO series of publications issued at approximately yearly intervals on the planning, programming, design, and architecture of hospitals and other medical care facilities in developing countries. Developing countries are urged to open channels of communication by exchanging lists of publications put out by their ministries of health and public works and the inauguration of a specialized journal with an international orientation on the building of health care facilities under conditions of limited resources is recommended. (HC)

2819   Tichy, M.K. *Behavioral science techniques: an annotated bibliography for health professionals.* New York, Praeger, 1975. 119p. Engl.
381 refs.

The aim of this bibliography is to introduce professional health workers to relevant behavioural and social psychological literature on group dynamics and team functioning. The 1st section covers laboratory research on the external and internal factors effecting group performance and the results of group work. Each topic is introduced by a brief summary of the field followed by selected annotated references. The 2nd section is concerned with applied group dynamics covering general introductory literature, experience-based learning and therapeutic groups, team training, and evaluation. Each annotation in this section consists of an abstract and critique. The final chapter lists 381 references relevant to the subject, including those annotated elsewhere in this bibliography. In a brief introduction, the author discusses the impact of behavioural science on health care work and presents examples of successful collaboration between health personnel and behavioural scientists. (DM)

2820   Tichy, M.K. *Health care teams: an annotated bibliography.* New York, Praeger, 1974. 178p. Engl.
239 refs.

The purpose of this bibliography is to provide rapid access to literature on health care teams and groups, mostly in the USA, from several broad medical and behavioural science perspectives. The subjects covered include the functions and problems of existing teams, training for teams, and other related topics. Each annotation consists of a statement of topic (which is also listed under a topic index), an outline summary of the contents, and a critique. An additional alphabetical list of 239 relevant references, including those annotated in the main body of the bibliography, is provided at the end. (DM)

2821   Voluntary Health Association of India, New Delhi. *Catalogue of educational materials.* New Delhi, Voluntary Health Association of India, Apr 1977. 36p. Engl.
See also entries 3333 and 3484.

This catalogue of low-priced educational materials, collected from many sources and available from the Voluntary Health Association of India (VHAI), is intended for personnel in hospitals and rural health and development programmes. Individual entries are classified according to the expertise of the users for whom they are intended. In 16 alphabetically listed sections including environmental health, family planning, and nursing, the catalogue describes an assortment of educational materials such as pamphlets, charts, books, film strips, colour slides, and flash cards. The largest sections are those on child health (42 entries) and nutrition (39 entries); most of these materials are suitable for trained nurses, doctors, and other professionals, although several could be used by auxiliaries. A list of suppliers of health materials and information appears at the back of the book, followed by a list of the languages in which many of the catalogue entries are available, including Hindi, Nepali, Tamil, and other Indian dialects. (CL)

2822   WHO, Geneva. *World directory of schools for*

dental auxiliaries, 1973/Repertoire mondial des ecoles d'auxiliaires dentaires, 1973. Geneva, WHO, 1977. 379p. Engl., Fren.
See also entry 3302.

This bilingual directory is divided into two parts, dealing respectively with operating auxiliaries (personnel who perform a limited range of diagnostic, preventive, and curative services in dentistry) and non-operating auxiliaries (dental laboratory technicians, chairside assistants, etc., who do not independently carry out dental procedures). It contains available information up to 1973 on schools for each type of auxiliary. Each country or area is dealt with in a separate entry consisting of a table giving the names and addresses of the schools, their entrance requirements, duration of training, language of instruction, and other pertinent data. Following is a brief text that deals chiefly with curriculum content and projected job descriptions for graduates. Two annexes provide a summary of the information presented and a 3rd contains supplementary data on dental auxiliary training. This bilingual directory is intended to be a companion volume to the 1976 *World Directory of Schools for Medical Assistants.* (RMB)

2823   WHO, Geneva. *World directory of schools for medical laboratory technicians and assistants, 1973/Repertoire mondial des ecoles de techniciens et assistants de laboratoire medical, 1973.* Geneva, WHO, 1977. 567p. Engl., Fren.

This bilingual (French and English) publication is part of a series of world directories of institutions for the training of various health personnel; it aims to provide health administrators and educators with an informational basis for improving the education and training of laboratory auxiliaries in their own countries. The directory is divided into two parts, the 1st dealing with medical laboratory technicians and the 2nd with medical laboratory assistants. The medical laboratory technician is defined as a health laboratory worker with 10-12 years basic general education (including the study of mathematics, chemistry, physics, and biology) followed by 2-3 years of special training to enable him to perform either a general or specialized set of routine procedures under the supervision of a medical or scientific professional. The medical laboratory assistant is defined as a health laboratory worker with 6-8 years general primary education followed by 1 year of special training; his duties may include performing well-defined standard routine tests, undertaking the necessary clerical work in connection with the receipt of specimens, and the recording and reporting of results. Training institutions are listed alphabetically by country and then by city and the following information regarding them is set forward: name, address, year instruction started, admission requirements, sex and nationalities accepted, institutional facilities, language of instruction, duration of course, instructional hours, curriculum, name of diploma or certificate granted, whether the diploma or certificate is recognized by the national government, functions of the graduate, and the total enrollment, number of 1st year students, and number of graduates for the year 1973. (HC)

II Organization and Planning

II.1 Health Manpower

See also: *2829, 2883, 2896, 2898, 2931, 3012, 3231, 3232, 3235, 3236, 3241, 3253, 3304*

2824 **Barrientos Llano, G.** *Equipo de salud en el primer nivel de atencion. (Primary health care team).* Revista Cubana de Administracion de Salud (Havana), 2(1), Jan-Mar 1976, 11-23. Span.
16 refs.
Advancing medical technology in developed countries has resulted in medical specializations, auxiliary diagnostic apparatus, and impersonal and complex health care organizations, all of which have contributed to a reduction in physical illness but led to an increase in emotional and mental illness and a situation where the patient feels emotionally isolated from his doctor. In Cuba, community and family practices have been established to combat these negative aspects and the primary health care team is the 1st group of medical personnel to come into contact with the patient. The primary health care team is designed to deal with a specific problem and is usually composed of different types of doctors, nurses, and public health workers, as well as any necessary social workers, laboratory techni clans, administrators, etc. Each primary health team should then coordinate with other primary teams and secondary teams composed of more specialized hospital personnel within the polyclinics and the national health team. Although the Cuban health care system has succeeded in reducing infant mortality, controlling infectious diseases, and increasing life expectancy, the author criticizes health team members for not making a greater effort to visualize the function of the team as a whole and interact with one another, a fault that is particularly evident in the elitist attitude of doctors. (RMB)

2825 **Beaubrun, M.H.** *Mosaic of cultures.* World Health (Geneva), Dec 1977, 10-15. Engl.
Also published in Arabic, French, Italian, Persian, Portuguese, Russian, and Spanish.
A flexible programme for extending mental health services in Trinidad and Tobago involves restructuring of services, reallocation of facilities, and training a new corps of mental health officers for community care and preventive psychiatry. Each of the five very different cultural and geographical areas of the country now has its own team responsible for identifying special needs and developing services suited to its people. For example, alcoholism treatment is most needed for Indian groups

and the teams undertake suicide prevention work mainly among young East Indian girls who rebel against traditional demands for strict obedience to parents. Each team is led by a consultant psychiatrist and psychiatric social worker and includes mental health officers who are experienced nurses with additional psychiatric and social work training. These teams are allocated their own short-, intermediate-, and long-stay beds and can call on national alcoholism, child psychiatry, and penal services. They are supported by new legislation that authorizes the community work of mental health officers and provides easier admission and discharge of patients, at the same time offering better civil rights protection. A measure of the success of the new programme is the enormous increase in patient load as people who have never seen a psychiatrist come forward for treatment. (AB)

2826 **Biddulph, J.** *Health services for children in Papua New Guinea.* Papua New Guinea Medical Journal (Port Moresby), 15(4), Dec 1972, 206-214. Engl.
22 refs.
The author advocates for Papua New Guinea a streamlined health care delivery system based on the deployment of suitably-trained and supervised auxiliaries modeled on India's auxiliary nurse-midwives (ANMs). After training in diagnosis and treatment of common diseases, one ANM is able to provide health care to a population of 3 000 by visiting every household once every 3 months. The antenatal care provided by this worker in Papua New Guinea would focus on the identification of at-risk cases and the maintenance of overall maternal health; the child care would emphasize growth supervision, immunization, malaria prophylaxis, and the treatment of common conditions. Health education and home visiting would form an integral part of all care. A number of criteria for determining at-risk mothers and children are set down and considerable data regarding morbidity and mortality among mothers and children, utilization of health services, etc., are included. (HC)

2827 **Blumhagen, R.V. Blumhagen, J. Medical Assistance Programs, Wheaton, Ill.** *Training programs.* In Blumhagen, R.V., Blumhagen, J., Family Health Care: a Rural Health Care Delivery Scheme, Wheaton, Ill., Medical Assistance Programs, 1974, 83-84. Engl.
For complete document see entry 2890.
To staff a family health care scheme in Afghanistan, planners must determine what types of personality and qualifications are needed and what activities and respon-

sibilities will be expected of them in their work. They need to design a curriculum that will provide the necessary skills in clinical and field activities as well as information; therefore, existing institutions where skills are practiced are regarded as appropriate training centres. The students and all members of the family health scheme must take part in continued in-service training for a half day each week and they must also act as teachers to spread acquired skills and knowledge. Consequently, they must be highly motivated, since they will be placed in demanding but well-organized employment as soon as they are qualified. (DM)

2828   British Medical Association, London. *Primary health care teams.* London, British Medical Association, Board of Science and Education, 1974. 35p. Engl.
39 refs.
A panel appointed by the British Medical Association Board of Science and Education to consider functions and responsibilities of medical personnel concluded that the health team is the most appropriate means of primary health care delivery at home and abroad but that its composition should reflect the needs and resources of its particular situation. In developing countries, the primary health team should be composed of auxiliary health workers, including ideally one or more medical assistants, enrolled nurses, communicable disease auxiliaries, and laboratory auxiliaries, under the supervision of professional staff at the district hospital or administrative headquarters. An Institute of Health Sciences should be established at each regional centre to provide training for the full range of auxiliaries. Each grade should have a clearly defined job description, but there must be scope for promotion within a career structure separate from that of the medical professionals. The primary teams, operating from health centres, would each be expected to serve a population of about 10 000. Their influence could be considerably augmented by enlisting the services of the local apothecary, herbalist, village store-keeper, or indigenous practitioner, a possibility which merits research. (DM)

2829   Bryant, J. Rockefeller Foundation, New York. *Health and the developing world.* Ithaca, N.Y., Cornell University Press, 1969. 345p. Engl.
In 1964, the Rockefeller Foundation in cooperation with US AID convened an international committee to plan a study of health problems, services, and manpower in a representative sample of developing countries. A team of experts, of whom the author was one, visited 21 countries over a 2-year period and collected information from the ministries of health, universities, and personal observations. The 1st section of this book describes the background health and economic situation of each of these countries and problems of planning and management. A discussion of the structure of health services and health teams, as they are and as they should be, is followed by a detailed section on the education and attitudes of health personnel in each of the countries visited. Manpower education was the focus of the whole investigation, which also covered the economics of train-

ing medical personnel and how donor agencies may help. Finally, the findings and recommendations of the study are summarized. (DM)

2830   Darity, W.A. WHO, Brazzaville. *University Centre of Health Sciences, Yaounde: undergraduate and postgraduate training in health education; report on a mission 5-17 Jul 1974.* Brazzaville, WHO, 11 Sep 1974. 28p. Engl.
The purpose of this mission was to draft a plan for a regional health education centre to be located within the University of Yaounde, Cameroon. The mission involved: reviewing relevant courses and curricula offered by other departments, i.e., health sciences, social sciences, and education; reviewing available staff and other resources; suggesting a tentative course curricula for the programme; and reviewing and assisting the university in determining admission requirements, examinations, library facilities, and other prerequisites. The proposed centre will constitute a central training area administered by the university and directed by the *Centre de Sciences de la Sante* (Health Sciences Centre) as part of its ongoing programme, which will combine multidisciplinary academic experience with practical fieldwork leading to a bachelor or master's degree in health education. Included are: discussion of the basic, functional, and behavioural objectives of the programme; sample curricula; some course descriptions; enrollment projections; and a floorplan of the required facilities. (HC)

2831   Dickson, A. Commonwealth Secretariat, London. *Youth's contribution to health care: paediatrics in reverse?* London, Commonwealth Secretariat, May 1975. 30p. Engl.
29 refs.
Pre-World Health Assembly Meeting of Commonwealth Representatives, Geneva, Switzerland, 12 May 1975.
Many schemes already underway at Commonwealth schools and colleges provide opportunities for young people to offer their time and talents in community health service by doing work that could often be incorporated into the curriculum in the form of socially useful research projects. Medical training could be modified to include community health service or a period of work as health auxiliaries could be made a prerequisite for medical school applicants. Other academic disciplines can provide a fresh approach to practical health problems, as has been demonstrated by engineering students in the UK who have helped design new medical equipment. Although schools, clubs, and youth organizations provide a range of community health service schemes often aimed at helping other young people with problems such as drug abuse, there is potential for mobilizing a much larger cross section of the young for a wider range of responsibilities. (DM)

2832   Elliott, K. *Year of the health auxiliary?* In British Health Care Planning and Technology: Year Book of the British Hospitals Export Council,

London, Health and Social Services Journal/Hospital International, 1975, 79-87. Engl.
24 refs.

Health auxiliaries trained by short practical courses are now used in many countries as the most appropriate personnel for providing primary and preventive health care at the village level. A wide range of these workers, including traditional practitioners, can contribute to the health services in industrialized as well as developing countries, providing they are taught to take responsibility for some conditions and to recognize those that need referral. Specific diagnosis need not be necessary if appropriate training schemes such as the Medex programme's "clinical algorithm system" are devised by qualified physicians. An efficient referral chain may involve advanced radio or satellite communications, but in some countries where communications are poor and doctors few, health auxiliaries may have to take responsibility for most health care and health education with minimal supervision. (DM)

2833   Fulop, T. *New approaches to a permanent problem: the integrated development of health services and health manpower.* WHO Chronicle (Geneva), 30(11), Nov 1976, 433-441. Engl.
Also published in French, Russian, and Spanish.
WHO has devoted 30 years to identifying problems and possible solutions in the health sector; during this time it has noted the low priority accorded to health within most countries' socioeconomic development plans and resulting fragmented services and inefficient use of resources, personnel, finances, etc. It has also discovered that health personnel planning is often not linked with training and that training in turn is not related to job requirements. These findings have prompted WHO to elaborate a new concept of integrated development of health care services, encourage task-oriented education, and recommend use of new categories of health worker. In future, WHO should urge member countries to set up a permanent body for planning and overseeing integrated health personnel and services development. (AC)

2834   Gandji, F.A. WHO, Brazzaville. *Training of health teams for black African nations; a synthesis of sociophilosophical and sociopsychological factors involved.* Brazzaville, WHO, 26 Aug 1974. 38p. Engl.
16 refs.
The author analyzes the problems of building a health team in Africa and presents a profile of health personnel in Burundi, Niger, Dahomey, and Rwanda. He reviews the ratio of professional to nonprofessional health workers and covers the intricacies of human relations and leadership, including leadership and empathy, basic issues of human relationships, types of leadership, choice of a leadership pattern, the importance of recognizing and dealing with one's own feelings, and exploiting differences to strengthen personal influence. In the section on the development of a health team, he discusses integrated teaching in the medical and allied health fields; this covers: conditions created by the teaching staff, the importance of communication, and conditions

for the student's learning experience; the retraining and integration of existing health professionals into the new health team; and individual roles within the team. Methods for evaluation and the intercultural functions of the health team are the subjects of the section on problems of implementation and evaluation. There are some statistical data. (RMB)

2835   Kazmi, S.I. *Proceedings (in summary) of Health Auxiliary Teachers Workshop 21-23 Jul 1975.* Islamabad, Pakistan, Planning Commission (Health Section), Aug 1975. 19p. Engl.
Refs.
Health Auxiliary Teachers Workshop, Islamabad, Pakistan, 21-23 Jul 1975.
Recognizing the need for properly-trained auxiliary health workers for deployment in Pakistan's rural health services, teachers and planners met to discuss auxiliary nomenclature, existing situations, value, role and functions, categories and levels, basic qualifications, career structure, selection criteria, supervision, job descriptions, curricula, tutor training, legislation, and evaluation. It was agreed that the country's interests would best be served by three categories of intermediate-level auxiliaries: one, preferable female, for midwifery, preschool child care, and family planning; one for communicable disease control (including both health education and immunization); and a 3rd for primary health care (diagnosis and treatment). It is envisioned that the auxiliary will begin work under close and constant supervision, gradually take on more and more of the substitute role, and eventually qualify as a managerial, instructional, or technical (orthopedic, sanitation, etc.) specialist. An example of a methodology for evolving a curriculum design for an auxiliary training programme is included and a list of recommended teaching materials is annexed. (HC)

2836   Martin, G.E. *New roles for women in health care delivery: the Cameroonian experience; utilization of women in health care delivery in Cameroon and Africa.* In Health Resources Administration, Proceedings of the International Conference on Women in Health, Washington, D.C., Department of Health, Education, and Welfare, 1976, 123-127. Engl.
10 refs.
International Conference on Women in Health, Washington, D.C., 16-18 Jun 1975.
The role of professional, nonprofessional, and volunteer women in health care delivery in Cameroon is examined. The precentage of women in the medical profession (13.7%) is higher in Cameroon than in most other countries and increasing; the female-to-male ratio rose from 1:15 to 1:8 from 1969-1973. Women predominate in the nursing and midwifery professions where, because of the shortage of doctors, they are called upon to do much more than their traditional functions; these added responsibilities are now being recognized. Certain social factors make it possible for women to combine both motherhood and a career: couples can draw upon either the extended family or abundant, cheap labour for housekeepers and babysitters; maternity leave and bene-

fits are available; working mothers are allowed time to breastfeed their babies for up to 15 months; and students no longer need to discontinue their studies because of marriage and pregnancy. Even those women who work at home have an excellent opportunity to educate themselves and become health promoters through the numerous societies that constitute the Community Development Women's Programme. This federally-funded programme trains volunteer leaders to teach women about nutrition, hygiene, child care, money management, etc., with a view to encouraging them become more self-reliant and raise their living standards through group action. Unfortunately, the government has not yet seen fit to recognize the important professional and crucial nonprofessional contribution of women to health by placing one in a key administrative position; it is suggested that to do so would be appropriate. (HC)

2837   Moin-Shah. *Health care in Nepal.* In Ronaghy, H.A., Mousseau-Gershman, Y., Dorozynski, A., eds., Village Health Workers, Ottawa, International Development Research Centre, 1976, 25-29. Engl.
For complete document see entry 3250.
Nepal has adopted a 5-year plan (1975-1980) in anticipation of rapid health services expansion. As a preliminary step, a project to determine the country's health problems, needs, and resources has been undertaken by the Institute of Medicine, Tribhuvan University, Kathmandu. Its goals are to inventory health personnel, study health problems and needs as perceived by the people, identify health needs as perceived by professionals, and focus on an appropriate role for institutions. Several surveys have been conducted and preliminary results have been informative. The final results are expected to provide a baseline for health services expansion and the reorganization of the system. The system's new design is seen as a circle of concentric rings rather than a pyramid, the outer ring being formed by large numbers of lower-level workers who provide primary care, the middle by certified paramedical personnel who supervise the lower-level workers and provide secondary care, and the inner ring by holders of medical degrees (in rural areas), surgeons, and specialists who provide tertiary care. (HC)

2838   Raimbault, A.M. *Organisation pratique d'un enseignement de perfectionnement pour personnel paramedical dans une republique africaine, le Niger. (Organizing a refresher course for paramedical personnel in an African republic, Niger).* Paris, Centre International de l'Enfance, Sep 1972. 69p. Fren.
The *Centre International de l'Enfance*, Paris, was founded in 1947 to promote the study of problems in childhood, disseminate ideas about hygiene and puericulture, and train technical and specialist personnel in child health. Toward the last aim, the centre cooperates with national governments, WHO, and UNICEF and organizes refresher courses for workers in the field of maternal and child health; the steps involved in planning, implementing, and evaluating the centre's courses are presented with reference to a session for nurses that was conducted in Niger in February 1972. Background information on Niger, its health problems, and health resources is included. (HC)

2839   Ram, E.R. Christian Medical Commission, World Council of Churches, Geneva. *Integrated health services project, Miraj, India.* Contact (Geneva), 44, Apr 1978, 1-15. Engl.
Also published in an abbreviated version, *Services de sante integres: la project Miraj en Inde,* in Assignment Children (Geneva), 39, Jul-Sep 1977, 15-32.
A project for reorganizing and retraining health personnel in Miraj Taluka, Maharashtra, India, has resulted in less duplication of effort and greater health coverage of the area's 2 million inhabitants. The project was the result of cooperation between community representatives, public health employees, and project staff. It consisted of: training local village dais (traditional birth attendants) in the technique of hygienic delivery and the recognition of complicated pregnancies; training village health aides to gather health statistics, report outbreaks of infectious disease, monitor pregnancies, and distribute contraceptives and medications; training single-purpose health workers to provide basic services to a fixed population; and redistributing supervisory tasks amongst existing health professionals. Three years after the project's inception, a randomly-selected sample comprising 10% of the district's families was surveyed and the findings of the survey were compared with baseline data. It was noted: that the fertility rate had dropped from 152:1 000-102:1 000; that maternal mortality had decreased from 3.7:1 000-nil; that infant mortality had decreased from 67.6:1 000-23.1:1 000; that the incidence of scabies, diarrhea, gastroenteritis, and ascariasis had regressed by 60%; and that immunization coverage had risen from 85%-99.7% for smallpox, from 2%-85% for DPT, from 1.5%-83% for polio, and from 6%-55% for BCG. Details of the financing of the project are included. (HC)

2840   Sebai, Z.A. Baker, T.D. *Projected needs of health manpower in Saudi Arabia, 1974-90.* Medical Education (Oxford, UK), 10(5), 1976, 359-361. Engl.
Despite the lack of accurate demographic data (there has never been a census in Saudi Arabia), the authors attempt to estimate national health manpower needs by 1990. First, they recommend that Saudi Arabia give priority to planning new schools for training at least 300 health administrators, of whom there are only 16 at the moment. Also, support should be given to training rural health workers to serve in rural areas where doctors refuse to work. A special effort must be made to educate women; following present patterns, fewer than 25% of the jobs available for female health workers will be filled by 1990. Since Saudi Arabia has only one medical school at the moment, the authors also urge that present plans to construct two additional medical schools proceed as rapidly as possible. Even with three medical schools and expanded classes, it will still be necessary to educate students abroad to reach the 1990 target of 4 454 physi-

Low-Cost Rural Health Care and Health Manpower Training

cians. Finally, the authors suggest that a national health manpower plan based on accurate information be developed so that health planners can do their jobs more efficiently. (RMB)

2841   Singapore, Ministry of Health. *National survey of nurses and midwives.* Nursing Journal of Singapore (Singapore), 17(1), May 1977, 7, 41-42. Engl.

A survey of the employment status of nurses and midwives was carried out by the Singapore Ministry of Health in January 1976. A questionnaire was sent to 6 504 registered nurses and midwives, of whom 4 384 responded within 6 weeks. It was found that 89.8% of the respondents were working full time; that 87.2% of full-time workers were employed in the public sector, 11.1% in the private, 1.5% in nonnursing occupations; that 1.8% of the respondents were employed part-time; that 20% of the unemployed group was over age 55 years; and that domestic responsibility was a key reason cited for part-time employment or unemployment. Nurses valued opportunity for further training and experience and enjoyed considerable mobility within the field. It is recommended that training be geared to extending rather than limiting the nurses' career choices. It is also suggested that child care facilities might entice a significant number of nurses and midwives back into the workforce. (HC)

2842   Sudan,   National   Health   Programming Committee. *Social data.* In National Health Programme 1977/78-1983/84, Khartoum, Khartoum University Press, Apr 1975, 18-24. Engl.

For complete document see entry 2933.

The Sudanese public are concerned about the inadequacy of health service coverage and critical of the medical auxiliaries responsible for primary and nursing care. The poor quality of existing services results largely from the health workers' dissatisfaction with their status and working conditions and many workers leave government service to go into private practice. The nursing profession is particularly despised. In the north, it is still not respectable for women to seek employment outside the home and pay and conditions for nurses are bad. These prejudices are not so strong in the south, but the professional calibre of nurses is low. However, as more trainees (both male and female) are now recruited from higher educational levels, pay, attitudes, and career prospects for nurses should improve. In general, all health personnel require greater incentives, both material and psychological, to work in government service in the rural areas. Young doctors have indicated that they would be prepared to give up the chance of private practice for a government salary supplement, but they fear that they may be held responsible for the faults of the auxiliaries. Satisfaction of all health workers should improve when they see the national health programme in action and when their training and numbers are adjusted to implement the new policy. (DM)

2843   Takulia, H.S. Parker, R.L. Murthy, A.K. *Orienting physicians to working with rural medical practitioners.* Social Science and Medicine (Oxford, UK), 2(4), Mar 1977, 251-256. Engl. 21 refs.

In 1972, the government of India decided to enlist the services of full-time indigenous practitioners in the national health services. In a number of pilot areas, all indigenous practitioners were invited to register and to undergo 8-10 months of intensive training in treating minor ailments. In return, each would receive thereafter a monthly stipend from the government and the right to charge a fee per prescription dispensed from a national health service store. According to government estimates, these steps would bring some 250 000 registered medical practitioners (RMPs) into the national health infrastructure, providing medical relief to an additional 500 million people. In this paper, the government is lauded for taking such an unorthodox decision and the reasons behind it are discussed: the chronic shortage of doctors in rural areas; post-independence pressure from revivalists demanding involvement of indigenous medical practitioners; pressures by RMPs for recognition, licensure, and employment; a desire to protect the clients of RMPs; and above all, pragmatic considerations of efficient utilization of existing health manpower. Allopathic physicians are urged to participate in the experiment in an honest attempt to test its feasibility and some suggestions for familiarizing them in the theory and practice of indigenous systems of medicine are given. (HC)

2844   Thailand, Ministry of Public Health. *Training of health personnel under the responsibility of the Health Training Division, Ministry of Public Health.* Thailand, Ministry of Public Health, Health Training Division, Mar 1977. 6p. Engl.

The Health Training Division of Thailand's Ministry of Public Health plans to improve training programmes as part of the country's 1977-1981 5-year plan. The plan will affect training programmes for junior health workers, their supervisors, district health officers, and dental auxiliaries, among others. To double the present 5 647 junior health workers, who provide health education and some curative and preventive service in rural health units, health training centres in Chon Buri, Khon Kaen, Yala, and Pitsanuloke must turn out 1 000 workers annually instead of 500. The present 18-month course will be extended to 1 year of study and 1 year of field training. The Health Manpower Development Project, another facet of this plan, will revise the curriculum for junior health worker supervisors at Chon Buri and Khon Kaen health training centres and initiate an administrative training programme for district health officers. The Health Training Division also expects to double the number of dental auxiliaries who provide routine dental services to children aged less than 15 years. At present, 20 dental auxiliaries per year train at the Chon Buri School for Dental Auxiliaries, but when an additional school is completed at Khon Kaen health training centre, 40 will complete the 2-year post-high school course in 1978 and 200 per year by 1981. (HH)

2845   Viau D., A. Long, E.C. *Training of rural health workers in Guatemala and their relation to the health system.* Bellagio, Italy, Rockefeller Foundation Study and Conference Center, May 1977. 9p. Engl.
Society for Health and Human Values International Consultation on New Types of Basic Health Services..., Bellagio, Italy, 2-7 May, 1977.
Unpublished document.
In Guatemala, health auxiliaries are employed by the Ministry of Public Health and more than 12 church groups. Serving in government health posts are rural health technicians, auxiliary nurses, rural health promoters, and traditional midwives; all are trained by the government, but the last two are supported by the rural communities themselves. The present rural health programme concentrates on rural health technicians, but reassignment of tasks and the redevelopment of training curricula are underway in an attempt to prepare all auxiliary health workers to function as part of a health team. Auxiliary training will use stimulus-response methodology, the stimulus being the health problems of a community and the response the corresponding skills to be taught to each auxiliary; supervision will be provided by the ministry's public health doctors, nurses and sanitary inspectors stationed at health centres. To evaluate health auxiliaries as an integral part of the total rural health programme, a newly-designed information system is also being implemented. This system, in computer language, contains behavioural indicators of changes in the attitudes of auxiliaries and of communities as well as ecological indicators. It is capable of epidemiological surveillance and cost-effectiveness estimates and can assist decision-making for all levels of health manpower. (Modified author abstract.)

2846   WHO, Brazzaville. *African traditional medicine.* Brazzaville, WHO, Afro Technical Report Series No.1, 1976. 20p. Engl.
This report of the Regional Expert Committee on Traditional Medicine in Africa covers the present status of traditional medicine in Africa, the positive and negative impact of traditional medicine on health protection and promotion in Africa, the necessity and timeliness of integrating the activities of the traditional healers into health services, prerequisites for cooperation between traditional and modern medicine, utilization of plants and other products, and some practical ways of promoting integration of traditional medicine into health care delivery systems. Among the committee's recommendations were the following: that facilities be established for educating traditional practitioners in modern methods and modern health workers in traditional ones; that encouragement be given to the establishment of national associations of traditional healers with appropriate codes of ethics; that research projects into traditional medicine, including its metaphysical aspects, be launched; that the cultivation of certain medicinal plants in the villages be encouraged; that national herbaria be established; that local pharmaceutical industry based on the region's medicinal plants be developed; etc. It is also

suggested that the designation 'doctor' for a traditional healer be avoided as far as possible. (HC)

2847   Wintrob, R.M. *Toward a model for effective mental health care in developing countries.* Psychopathologie Africaine (Dakar), 9(2), 1973, 285-294. Engl.
In order to extend mental health coverage in the developing countries, a model that calls for a network of community mental health workers to perform primary psychiatric services is proposed. Mostly women with grown children, these workers would be respected members of their communities, willing to undergo a 3-6-month training course in a mental health facility, and available for visiting each of the households in their communities approximately once a week. On the job, they would identify specific mental health problems and discuss those requiring therapeutic intervention with the psychiatric nurse supervisor; once a course of treatment had been agreed upon, they would be responsible for explaining the treatment to the patient, administering it (in some cases), and monitoring the patient's progress. The psychiatric nurse supervisors, the secondary workers of the service, would serve as consultants to the community mental health workers and determine which cases required referral to the regional psychiatrist. The ratio of community mental health workers to psychiatric nurses would be 6-10:1 and the ratio of psychiatric nurses to regional psychiatrists would be 5:1; each regional psychiatric facility would serve a potential at-risk population of 100 000. The primary consideration in the selection of both psychiatric nurses and regional psychiatrists would be their commitment to the concept of a mental health service delivered primarily by non-psychiatrists. The model is currently being tested in Liberia. (HC)

II.2 Organization and Administration

See also: 2825, 2839, 2904, 2905, 2915, 2931, 2937, 2939, 2962, 2998, 3012, 3032, 3121, 3123, 3130

2848   African Medical and Research Foundation International, Nairobi. *Health education each day in the health centre.* AFYA (Nairobi), 2, Mar-Apr 1977, 54-59. Engl.
Also published as Chapter 8 in entry 1933 (volume 3).
Overcrowding and noise can severely reduce the effectiveness of health education in a health centre. Overcrowding is often the result of a conditioned dependence on health services that renders the patient incapable of self care; it can also be due to poor timing of clinics, poor screening of patients, or slack behaviour on the part of the staff. Excessive noise levels may originate in shouting and loud talk by the staff, or they may be the result of overcrowding, a badly designed or poorly-utilized building, or a lack of facilities for mothers with small infants or toddlers. A number of suggestions for reducing noise and overcrowding are set forward. They include: explaining, discussing, and placing responsibility for health on the patient; prescribing, insofar as possible, pills instead of injections, which tend to increase the

patient's dependency on forces outside himself; evaluating the quality of the health centre in terms of successful treatment, better community health, and patient satisfaction rather than numbers of patients seen; scheduling clinics to suit the patients' rather than the staff's convenience; encouraging staff to address each other and the patients in conversational tones; encouraging patients who must wait for extended periods (e.g., for prescriptions) to wait outside; and providing a place for toddlers to play. Some other suggestions for inserting health education into the day-to-day activities of the health centre are included. (HC)

2849 **Akerele, O. Tabibzadeh, I. McGilvray, J.** *New role for medical missionaries.* Science and Public Policy (London), Jun 1977, 267-275. Engl.
Originally published in WHO Chronicle (Geneva), 30(5), 1976.

Church-related medical programmes currently provide 15%-50% of most African medical services. The presence of these programmes is regarded: with embarrassment by some host countries, who should, in principle, provide health services for all; with suspicion by others, who suspect that church-related health services spring from ulterior motives; and with tolerance by others, who anticipate a medical vacuum should these programmes depart. Six countries (Botswana, Ghana, Lesotho, Malawi, Nigeria, and Zambia), however, have recognized the contribution of church-related medical agencies by setting up mechanisms for joint church/government planning of health services; two of these, Botswana and Zambia, have even adopted national health plans providing for an integrated effort by public and private sectors to fill the gaps existing in the health services network, particularly in rural areas. This paper reviews the role of church-related medical agencies in the light of current health needs, government efforts, and economic considerations and makes a number of recommendations for fostering more fruitful cooperation between missions and governments, including optimum use of existing resources, standardized training of the different categories of national health personnel, equal government and private pay scales, standardized equipment and drugs with emphasis on local suppliers, more government financing of the capital and recurrent expenditures of church-related health services, etc. (HC)

2850 **Arnon, A. WHO, Brazzaville.** *Report on a visit to Mauritius.* Brazzaville, WHO, Nov 1968. 14p. Engl., Hebrew.
See also entries 2339, 2354, 2363, 2513, 2666, and 2668 (volume 4).

A WHO consultant's report on the health services of Mauritius and recommendations for reorganizing them along the lines of the Israeli system are presented. In 1968, Mauritius devoted 11.69% of its budget to health services, but only 16% of those health care dollars went to preventive medicine. The government operated all the country's hospitals but maintained clinical, operative, diagnostic, and laboratory facilities at only two. Three specialty hospitals treated tuberculosis, mental illness, and leprosy. The public health service, the country's sole

preventive health agency, undertook prevention and control of infectious diseases, sanitation, medical services for schools, immunization, and family planning. Nongovernmental services included those offered by privately-owned sugar estates for their employees and 31 mother and child health stations maintained by the Sugar Industrial Labour Welfare Fund. Health personnel for the country's services comprised 172 doctors, 125 midwives, and 598 nurses. The author recommends establishing courses for midwives, providing comprehensive medical care, and remodeling social welfare centres into family care centres. For example, he proposes that the social welfare centre in Bambous be reorganized to provide health services for 727 local families. Changes in nursing education are recommended and possibilities for WHO assistance are suggested. Annexes to the report describe the existing medical services and provide a graphic representation of teamwork in comprehensive treatment. (EE)

2851 **Barbosa, F.S. de Carvalho, A.G. Lavor, A.C. Paranagua Santana, J.F.** *Atencao a saude e educacao medica: uma experiencia e uma proposicao. (Health care and medical education: an experiment and a proposal).* Educacion Medica y Salud (Washington, D.C.), 11(1), 1977, 26-40. Portuguese.

The authors propose the regionalization of Brazilian health services on primary (health posts and health centres), secondary (hospitals), and tertiary (specialized hospitals) levels and the integration of medical practice and instruction. They describe two experimental community health programmes carried out in the Planaltina health unit of Brasilia, where primary health care is provided by auxiliaries and in three rural health centres staffed by physicians, and secondary care is available in a 40-bed hospital. In view of the positive results of this project, a proposal is made for the extension of regionalized health services to a larger area in the capital region, which would then incorporate a specialized hospital capable of providing tertiary care. After the proposed health system is established, a new medical curriculum geared for the different levels would be implemented. (RMB)

2852 **Belmar, R. Sidel, V.W.** *International perspective on strikes and strike threats by physicians: the case of Chile.* International Journal of Health Services (Westport, Conn.), 5(1), 1975, 53-64. Engl.
51 refs.

The national health service (SNS) in Chile under Allende did not pay sufficient attention to planning or economic considerations and the resulting backlash from physicians seriously disrupted and discredited the system. Community participation was an essential component of the operation of 400 new health centres and locally trained volunteers had been recruited to assist professional medical staff and students in setting up and running satellite clinics. Within 3 years, the programme had reduced infant mortality and improved life expectancy. However, the new approach was opposed by most doctors and in particular by leaders of the *Colegio Medico* (Chilean Medical Association). Although 80% of physicians worked part-time for the SNS, most of their income came from private practice including a government subsidized fee-for-service programme. The success of the preventive measures, use of health workers, and community involvement of the new programme reduced the physicians' control over the health system and their income from private practice, but the chief reason for the opposition of the *Colegio Medico* was political. Illegal strike action was attempted and efforts made to disrupt and discredit the health service to reduce support of the Allende regime. Although doctors cannot be expected to be apolitical, the authors feel that resorting to illegal methods that threaten the health services and those who run them cannot be justified. (DM)

2853   Blumhagen, R.V. Blumhagen, J. Medical Assistance Programs, Wheaton, Ill. *Organization of family health.* In Blumhagen, R.V., Blumhagen, J., Family Health Care: a Rural Health Care Delivery Scheme, Wheaton, Ill., Medical Assistance Programs, 1974, 47-55. Engl.
For complete document see entry 2890.
The two essential features of a proposed family health scheme for Afghanistan are that communities and families be taught to care for themselves and that minimal medical procedures be provided to a maximum number of people. Initially, a large number of health subcentres will be established; these will eventually be part of a hierarchy of facilities and personnel. Key persons in this system are the family health workers (FHWs) who staff the subcentres, run periodic clinics in village buildings, and conduct field projects and home visiting with the help of locally-trained volunteer village health advisors (VHAs). At all levels of the hierarchy, most of the service is conducted through outpatient clinics, *triage* is practiced for maximum efficiency, and every opportunity is used for health education. Part of the staff's time is devoted to field work involving supervision of less qualified personnel, surveys, and immunization campaigns. To launch the scheme, the 1st step is the training of female and male family health workers and their immediate supervisors. (DM)

2854   Bryant, J.H. Christian Medical Commission, World Council of Churches, Geneva. *Five challenges to the churches in health work.* Contact (Geneva), 42, Dec 1977, 1-4. Engl.
12 refs.
Adapted from a presentation to the Board of Vellore Christian Medical College Seminar, New York, N.Y., Nov 1976; also published in French in Contact (Geneva), 33, Jan 1978, 1-6.
After outlining present patterns of disease, poverty, and health services in the developing world, the author identifies and discusses a series of health-related challenges that have special meaning for the Christian churches in terms of both their historic commitment to the neglected and underprivileged and their special resources. The 1st of these challenges is a reiteration of the church's age-old promise to serve the poor, despite health professionals'

orientation toward urban wealth. The 2nd challenge is to redefine development to reflect the dynamics of community life and social growth rather than economics alone. The author mentions certain minimum needs that must be fulfilled if a country is to be considered developed: disease control and primary health care, at least primary education, adequate and safe shelter, sufficient income to support a family, a safe environment that retains some of its natural beauty, political and religious freedom, and participation in the decision-making that determines one's future. Other challenges include promoting social justice, distributing health services equitably, and developing educational programmes for health professionals that lead to competence and commitment to serve the poor. The author cites examples of churches and church leaders who are responding to these challenges in innovative ways. (RMB)

2855   Chabot, H.T. *Chinese system of health care: an inquiry into public health in the People's Republic of China.* Tropical and Geographical Medicine (Haarlem, Netherlands), 28(2), Jun 1976, Suppl.2, S87-S134. Engl.
163 refs.
See also entry 2856; reprinted in monograph form, Amsterdam, Bohn, Scheltema and Holkema, n.d. 46p.
This literature review covers a wide range of documents, including Chinese press and scientific journals, studies by expatriates, and anecdotal accounts. In the introduction, the author discusses the relative reliability of his sources and problems of evaluating data from China. The 1st chapters provide background information, vital statistics, a description of health services and manpower in pre-revolution China, and a chart summarizing major historical events of the last hundred years. The chapter on medical policy from 1943-1972 deals with the development of the present system; this chapter is abstracted separately. The final section discusses those aspects of Chinese communist philosophy that have been central to the new approach to health, the influence of traditional philosophy, and the extent to which the Chinese experience is applicable to health services elsewhere. An epilogue poses a number of questions that future studies should consider. Of the 163 references provided, 14 are specially recommended for further reading. (DM)

2856   Chabot, H.T. *Medical policy between 1943-72.* In Chabot, H.T., Chinese System of Health Care, Amsterdam, Bohn, Scheltema and Holkema, n.d., S103-S112. Engl.
Reprinted from Tropical and Geographical Medicine (Amsterdam), 28, 1976, S103-S112; see also entry 2855.
The basic principles of health policy in China--emphasis on prevention, service to the common people, coordination of health campaigns with other programmes, and reconciliation of Western and traditional medicine--date back to the Communist enclaves of the preliberation period, but one of the keys to implementing the policy is a newcomer, the barefoot doctor. Introduced after the Cultural Revolution, the barefoot doctor has become the

primary health worker at the grassroots level. Selected by and from local production teams to staff basic health stations, barefoot doctors provide simple curative and preventive care and refer complicated cases to the next level in a comprehensive hierarchy of facilities. Within the hierarchy, doctors have a new role and their training has been decentralized and shortened with provision for continuing in-service education and a curriculum that includes both Western and traditional techniques. (DM)

2857   **Dinh-Thi-Cau.** *Mother and child welfare services.* In McMichael, J.K., ed., Health in the Third World: Studies from Vietnam, Nottingham, UK, Spokesman Books, 1976, 208-218. Engl.
For complete document see entry 2869.

Mother and child welfare services in Vietnam are organized in a four-tier system, parallel with other branches of health services. The National Institute for the Protection of Mothers and Newly-born is responsible for treatment at the highest level, scientific research and direction, undergraduate and postgraduate teaching, and popular scientific instruction. The institute also organizes meetings, special training tours, research, and technical supervision throughout the country. At the provincial and urban levels, the obstetric and gynaecology clinics of the large multidisciplinary hospitals assume the same role as the national institute and are responsible for the training of midwives. District and smaller urban centres oversee normal and complicated childbirth, provide instruction in contraception, and direct and control the work at commune level. Each commune serving 500-10 000 people has one or two maternity clinics directed by midwives, who undertake simple obstetric-gynaecologic care and promote family planning. Family planning itself is a domiciliary service carried out by mobile teams. These services are complemented by the Central Council for the Protection of Mother and Child, which coordinates health and welfare services, health education, and research by 40 000 *to tro san* (groups for mutual health in confinement) and 67 000 health education volunteers. (AB)

2858   **Ecuador, Ministerio de Salud Publica.** *Atencion de salud a nivel rural. (Rural health care).* Quito, Ministerio de Salud Publica, Direccion Nacional de Salud Rural, 1976. 44p. Span.
Convenio "Hipolito Unanne," Cuarta Reunion de Ministros de Salud del Area Andina, Bogota, Colombia, 1975.

This conference report discusses some of the health problems in rural areas of the Andean countries of Latin America. Resumes of the presentations of Bolivia, Chile, Colombia, Equador, and Venezuela are given, as well as statistical data on health manpower and the coverage and levels of health services and diagrams of the health administration and organization infrastructure of each nation. General considerations and recommendations are set forth, including the suggestions that rural health be assigned the highest priority, that trained health auxiliaries be used to deliver most health services, that the development of health services be coordinated with the development of other sectors, that closer ties be maintained between public health planners and teaching institutions, that social security benefits be extended to rural populations to help defray health costs, etc. A list of participants is included. (RMB)

2859   **Fendall, N.R.** *Medicine of poverty or what are people for?* In Report of the Fourth Commonwealth Medical Conference, Colombo, 1974, Vol.2, London, Commonwealth Secretariat, 1974, 1-26. Engl.
20 refs.
Fourth Commonwealth Medical Conference, Colombo, Sri Lanka, 1974.
Unpublished document.

Until health is seen as an objective and wealth as a means to achieve it, the knowledge and resources that could provide universal health will not be applied and medical services will continue to fight disease rather than promote health. In developing countries, health services should be organized for maximum effectiveness rather than efficiency or ideology. All possible sources of funds, private, public, and voluntary should be tapped and a suitable balance sought between primary and referral care. A hierarchy of facilities and personnel is the most effective organization providing that there is enough flexibility to permit improvement over time and that the most basic units of the service reach the target population. Priority should be given to farmers (the producers) and to heads of households (the providers and leaders). Professional and non-professional manpower are best kept as two distinct cadres to avoid upward creep among auxiliaries. In addition, greater use can be made of nurses, traditional practitioners (though only if thoroughly trained), pharmacists, and students. The standard of medical training should be maintained, but the curriculum broadened, with provision for postgraduate courses in appropriate fields; research should focus on the implementation of present knowledge rather than the acquisition of more. (DM)

2860   **Gandolfi, R.** *Approche medicale de la communaute mahoraise. (Medical approach of the Mayotte community).* Marseille, France, Universite d'Aix Marseille, 10 Mar 1975. 75p. Fren.
Thesis presented to the Faculty of Medicine, University of Aix-Marseille, 10 Mar 1975.

This detailed enquiry into the health profile and services in the French colony of the Comoro Islands (specifically the Island of Mayotte) covers the public health infrastructure and its personnel (including dental, laboratory, X-ray, and pharmaceutical services), organization of health services, curative services, control of communicable diseases, chronic diseases, nutrition and malnutrition, and mental illness. It is noted that the Islands, which are still at the economic subsistence level, have not yet invested heavily in Western-style, hospital-based curative medicine. A good, if impoverished, infrastructure in the form of a network of medical posts is in operation and it is hoped that future health care disbursements will be used to strengthen this system rather than the rudimentary hospital facilities. (HC)

II Organization and Planning

2861   Glass, R.I. *SANEPID Service in the USSR.* Public Health Reports (Rockville, Md.), 91(2), Mar-Apr 1976, 154-158. Engl. 12 refs.

SANEPID, an independent branch of the medical care system in the USSR, is devoted to the surveillance and control of preventable diseases. The service comprises a country-wide network of stations, each staffed by: sanitary physicians, i.e., graduates of traditional medical schools with some postgraduate training in public health or graduates of one of the country's 11 schools for public health specialists; workers with specialized training in the health fields (i.e., epidemiology, bacteriology, sanitary hygiene, etc.); and feldshers (paramedics). The stations monitor infectious diseases, child and adolescent health, food and water purity, and the specific occupational and environmental problems of a population of 150 000-500 000. The staff maintain close liaison with national and regional research institutes that advise on local problems. The station's director, the chief district sanitary physician, represents health services on his municipal governing council and approves new projects for safety. This model: provides independent and, consequently, enhanced status to both preventive medicine and public health personnel; concentrates responsibilities for occupational health, environmental health, etc., at the local level; and affords the district sanitary physician appropriate political effectiveness. (HC)

2862   Hospital Practice, New York. *In both Venezuela and Peru, 'simplified medicine' is goal.* Hospital Practice (New York), 11(10), Oct 1976, 152-166, 170. Engl.
See also entry 2699 (volume 4).

The practice of simplified medicine in Venezuela is described and compared with rural health care delivery in Peru; the two systems are similar, but Peru lacks the strong supporting infrastructure found in Venezuela. In both countries, primary health care for rural inhabitants is provided by auxiliaries working in dispensaries. In Venezuela, auxiliaries are local women who have been trained in practical obstetrics, gynaecology, pediatrics, oncology, cardiology, dermatology, and psychiatry at one of the country's 20 rural training schools. They treat prevalent illnesses using a composite of 32 drugs that include sulphadiazine, salicylic compounds, electrolyte tablets, potassium permanganate, antihelminthics, ascorbic acid, tincture of iodine, ferrous sulphate, B complex vitamins, antispasmodics, vaseline, merthiolate, chloramphenicol, tetracycline, ear drops, fungicides, expectorants, and vaccines. They are assisted by a 200-page manual that sums up their procedures and supported by weekly visits from a doctor nearby. Further technical support is available from a network of 20-80-bed health centres at the district level and large, fully equipped and staffed hospitals at the regional level. Parts of interviews with personnel at various levels within both systems are included. (HC)

2863   Israel, Ministry of Health. *Health and health services in Judaea-Samaria and Gaza-Sinai,* *1967-1976.* Jerusalem, Ministry of Health, May 1977. 49p. Engl.
Thirtieth World Health Assembly, Geneva, Switzerland, May 1977.
See also entries 2181, 2254, 2255, and 2256 (volume 4).

This report from the Ministry of Health of Israel covers the development of the health service infrastructure in Judea-Samaria and Gaza-Sinai from 1967-1976. Emphasis has been on the expansion of hospital and basic public health services, including a widespread network of maternal and child health clinics that have witnessed a substantial decline in infant mortality. Health personnel training, disease control, sanitation systems, housing conditions, nutrition, and educational services have greatly improved and health services have been extended to citizens of other countries despite the uncertain political situation in the Middle East. Recommendations made by the WHO special committee of experts in 1976 have been incorporated into the health planning process. Statistical data are included. (EE)

2864   Kherchi, A. *Approche de la medecine preventive au Maroc. (Approach to preventive medicine in Morocco).* Marseille, France, Universite d'Aix-Marseille, 21 May 1975. lv.(various pagings). Fren. 49 refs.
Thesis presented to the Faculty of Medicine, University of Aix-Marseille, 21 May 1975.

Morocco has adopted health services based on: a precise knowledge of the national health situation, resources, and needs; the utilization of modern methods of planning, such as statistics and health indicators; and continuous evaluation of the level of health. This paper explores the specific organization and actions that the government, in line with this policy, has devised to cope with these elements of preventive medicine: disease control (tuberculosis, malaria, syphilis, bilharzia, typhoid, cholera, meningitis, and trachoma), maternal and child health, health education, nutrition, mental health, community planning, water supply, ecological and environmental health, occupational health, and school health. Worthy of particular notice are the country's dispensaries; distributed throughout the rural areas in a ratio of 1:15 000 population, these facilities form the basis of the preventive health infrastructure. (HC)

2865   Kilama, W.L. Nhonoli, A.M. Makene, W.J. **University of Dar-es-Salaam, Dar-es-Salaam.** *Health care delivery in Tanzania.* In Ruhumbika, G., ed., Towards Ujamaa: Twenty Years of Tanu Leadership, Dar-es-Salaam, East African Literature Bureau, 1974, 191-217. Engl. 25 refs.

The history of health services in Tanzania has profoundly affected the new nation's progress; although the country has in principle decided to pursue preventive care, curative services have eaten up a large share of the health care budget. Efforts toward remedying this discrepancy were included in the 2nd national health plan (1967-1974) and will be emphasized in future. Thus far, preventive services have dramatically reduced smallpox and other infectious diseases and have been supported primarily by the self-help philosophy that prevades development in all sectors of Tanzania. In turn, self-help activities have been bolstered by the government, which provides some materials and funds for improving sanitation and water supply. Statistical data are presented to illustrate advances in services. (AC)

2866   Korea Health Development Institute, Seoul. *Maul Geon-gang Saup. (Community health project).* Seoul, Korea Health Development Institute, 1977. 1v.(unpaged). Engl.
The Korea Health Development Institute (KHDI) has developed a low-cost, integrated health care delivery system that it intends to demonstrate, with slight variations, in three different counties. The system will take the form of a three-tiered service and referral pyramid consisting, from top to bottom, of community health centres staffed by community physicians, primary health units staffed by community health practitioners, and primary health posts or village health posts staffed by community health aides or village health agents. System implementation will involve reorganizing and cross-training existing personnel, recruiting and training new categories of primary care personnel, renovating and building health care facilities, introducing innovative financial mechanisms, and encouraging the development of community decision-making bodies. In one of the three counties, a prepaid medical insurance scheme is to be attempted. This brochure contains summaries, complete with maps and diagrams comparing the old organization with the new, of the system as it is to be implemented in each of the three counties. (HC)

2867   Korea, Ministry of Health and Social Affairs. USA, Agency for International Development, Department of State. *Korea Health Development Institute.* Seoul, Ministry of Health and Social Affairs, 1976. 3p. Engl.
In 1976, the Korean Ministry of Health and Social Affairs established the Korea Health Development Institute comprising a board of directors, a president, and divisions for health projects, manpower development, planning and research, and general affairs. The determination of KHDI's basic goals and major policies, its budget, the appointment of its president and auditor, and its constitution are functions of the National Health Council. The KHDI itself is responsible for research and investigation into past and present public health systems and for designing, developing, implementing, and evaluating low-cost health care delivery demonstration projects. After assessing the long- and short-term needs of the health services, it must improve and maintain the health status of the community and train project personnel. The KHDI conducts or supports research in Korea and abroad on national health care delivery systems and, at the government's request, evaluates particular health service activities. The whole programme is supported by US AID. (HH)

2868   Kumar, S. National Institute of Health and Family Welfare, New Delhi. *Information and documentational needs for health and family welfare professionals.* New Delhi, National Institute of Health and Family Welfare, Nov 1977. 15p. Engl. National Workshop on Documentation in the Field of Health and Family Welfare, New Delhi, India, 2-6 Nov 1977.
In developing countries, there is a great need for the rapid dissemination of the medical knowledge accumulated during the 20th century. In response to this need, India is creating a health information system to collect, process, analyze, and transform information about organizing and planning health services, research, and training. Existing information facilities in postgraduate institutions of teaching, training, and research as well as medical colleges include the National Medical Library and the library of the All India Institute of Medical Sciences. Documentation services developed more recently include the Indian National Scientific Documentation Centre (INSDOC) and the newly-created National Institute of Health and Family Welfare (NIHFW), which proposes to act as a national centre to collect, compile, and disseminate practical health-related information. Documentation services initiated by the Documentation Centre of NIHFW include both anticipatory services such as an abstracting bulletin and bibliographies and responsive services such as document copying and a technical enquiry system. Nevertheless, vast amounts of Indian literature in health-related subjects remain totally uncovered and out of 175 Indian medical and health journals, only 45 are documented in *Index Medicus* and *Exerpta Medica*. Therefore, an active documentation-information system for India must acquire, analyze, and disseminate information both from India and from abroad. The National Documentation Centre must also provide translation facilities to make information from abroad available to users. The addresses of 27 important organizations in Southeast Asia concerned with health and family welfare are listed. (CL)

2869   McMichael, J.K. *Health in the Third World: studies from Vietnam.* Nottingham, UK, Spokesman Books, 1976. 342p. Engl.
Refs.
Individual chapters have been abstracted separately under entries 2857, 2870, 3002, 3150, and 3486.
The health achievements of North Vietnam's policy of self-reliance since 1945 are illustrated in this book by accounts from Vietnamese doctors, pharmacists, professors, research workers, journalists, and Ministers of Health. Their 1st-hand reports of the development of health services and the elimination of epidemics in North Vietnam, originally published from 1966-1972 in Vietnamese and French, are edited and combined, though many accounts are undated and some material is repeated. The 1st of the book's 3 main sections consists of 12 chapters on the organization and operation of the health services at all levels. These include a Health Minister's description of Vietnam's concepts in planning health services, a summary of past and present health personnel

training and the development of the rural health network, and journalists' descriptions of a a health centre and a hospital. Accounts of the organization of Vietnam's medical research, pharmaceutical industry, and traditional medicine are also included in this section. The 2nd part of the book consists of 4 chapters, written by doctors and professors, that describe the campaigns waged by the North Vietnamese against malaria, tuberculosis, trachoma, and leprosy. The emergency health services that coped with the recent war are discussed in the book's 3rd section and accounts of hygiene and epidemiology during the 1971 great floods follow. The final chapter elaborates the socialist basis of Vietnam's plans for medicine in the 15 years following the restoration of peace and an appendix recounts the editor's recent visits. (CL)

2870   McMichael, J.K. *Rural health network.* In McMichael, J.K., ed., Health in the Third World: Studies from Vietnam, Nottingham, UK, Spokesman Books, 1976, 69-77. Engl.
For complete document see entry 2869.
The rural health network in North Vietnam is based on part-time health workers in the villages, particularly auxiliary nurses, who are still working part-time in agriculture, paid locally, and assisted by unpaid volunteers. They refer patients with serious conditions to an assistant doctor from the commune health centre. The assistant doctors usually treat patients at home but may admit them to the health centre, which has 5-10 emergency beds, 5 maternity beds, and a pharmacy. The assistant doctor, an assistant pharmacist, a midwife, and a nurse make up the health centre staff. In the mountainous areas, the state provides medical care for minority groups, but elsewhere the communes finance their own health centres. Treatment is free and patients pay only for drugs. A general 50-l00-bed district hospital for each 100 000-200 000 people accepts referrals and administers national programmes. A local section of the Association of Traditional Medicine works closely with the district hospital and, in some places, organizes its own separate hospital. District, provincial, and national services are financed by the state. (AB)

2871   Milio, N. *Care of health in communities: access for outcasts.* New York, Macmillan, 1975. 416p. Engl.
Refs.
To make health workers aware of the effects of health care decisions on communities as well as the need for significant changes in the health care system, especially in the USA, the author examines the relationships between environment, health, and health care. He begins by tracing the important connections between people and their sociopolitical and ecological surroundings, comparing rich and poor nations and contrasting the rich and poor groups within these countries. The rest of the book focuses on the USA. First he discusses outcast groups such as minorities, the aged, women, and the poor and examines their access to health care services. An analysis of the health occupations, revealing the sickness and inpatient care focus of health activities, is followed

by a consideration of the political processes involved in health care decision-making. Short portrayals of the problems of health access of people in other countries appear as vignettes between several chapters in the USA section, under the heading "Images of Access," and illustrate the realities of health access for outcasts in India, Holland, Japan, and England. There are copious statistical data and the extensive notes section provides lists of references for each chapter. One of the 18 appendix tables summarizes the important facets of health services in 25 rich and poor countries. (CL)

2872   Peradze, O. WHO, Brazzaville. *Development of health services in Kenya.* Brazzaville, WHO, 18 Nov 1974. 6p. Engl.
As part of a WHO project for the development of basic health services in Kenya, an assessment of maternal and child health practices in rural health units was undertaken. The assessment revealed a need for a standardized set of MCH procedures, better preparation of health staff for the tasks they perform, and a more judicious distribution of tasks amongst health staff. Operational changes, consisting essentially of offering all MCH activities every day instead of on separate days and having all patients screened by the community nurse rather than seen directly by the medical assistant, were recommended and introduced in two health centres. To facilitate their introduction, the staff of the health centres were given inservice training as follows: the community nurse, in diagnosis and treatment of minor ailments and in clinical family planning methods; the medical assistants, in health centre administration and staff supervision; the health assistants, in health education, communicable disease control, general administration, etc.; the ungraded nurses, in giving injections, applying dressings, weighing children and pregnant women, and performing simple laboratory tests; and a new cadre of health worker, the statistical clerk, in record-keeping, filing, preparation of statistical reports, etc. These changes have proved popular in both clinics and have resulted in better coverage of the populations served. Future plans include the testing of this strategy in other areas of the country, the preparation of manuals for the operation of MCH services, the revision of the curriculum of the basic training of all health staff in order to make it more job-oriented, and the integration of other health workers (field nutritionists, family planning educators, etc.) into the basic health infrastructure. (HC)

2873   Riley, C. Sutherland, R.D. Commonwealth Secretariat, London. *Review of action taken following the Fourth Commonwealth Medical Conference: maintenance of medical equipment.* London, Commonwealth Secretariat, Nov 1977. 1v.(various pagings). Engl.
As a result of concern expressed by developing countries at the Fourth Commonwealth Medical Conference about the difficulties of maintaining and repairing medical equipment, the Commonwealth Secretariat commissioned two investigations into present arrangements for maintenance and repair in 1) Malaysia, Singapore, most Commonwealth African countries, and most

Commonwealth Caribbean countries and 2) Fiji, Papua New Guinea, Tonga, and Western Samoa. The findings and recommendations from both investigations are included. In almost all countries visited, facilities for the maintenance and repair of all hospital equipment, from beds to boilers, were poor or nonexistent. Reasons for this included lack of a hospital engineering service, lack of technical and professional personnel skilled in hospital engineering, inability to attract workers to hospital engineering due to low government salaries, use of foreign equipment and consequent inability to obtain spare parts, and lack of appreciation of and funds for preventive maintenance schemes. As a result of the two studies, the Secretariat recommended that governments take all possible steps to ensure that they have a properly planned and organized medical engineering service and career structure, medical engineering technicians be trained on a regional basis, and methods be established to facilitate the exchange of information in this area. (HC)

2874   Roemer, M.I. *Rural health care.* St. Louis, Mo., C.V. Mosby, Issues and Problems in Health Care, 1976. 121p. Engl.
Refs.
Although improved transportation has given the 53 million rural inhabitants of the USA greater access to health care than in the past, services still fall short of those enjoyed by their urban counterparts. This volume presents five papers on the problems related to rural health services delivery: the 1st explores the development of organized social efforts to tackle rural health problems on a nationwide basis from the time of the Civil War up to the present, the 2nd traces the growth of the public health movement in one rural county (1838-1949), the 3rd presents the diversity of organized health programmes as identified and analyzed in one rural county in 1952, the 4th constitutes an overview of rural health problems and attempted solutions as of 1968, and the 5th examines attempts by other nations, both developed and developing, to achieve a reasonable distribution of health manpower, facilities, and services. The epilogue briefly outlines recent health legislation that is of particular significance to rural areas: the authorization of professional standard review organizations, which will enable monitoring of the quality of work done by isolated rural physicians; the authorization of funds for stimulating and assisting the establishment of health maintenance organizations; the assumption of responsibility for neighbourhood health services by the Department of Health, Education, and Welfare; and the establishment of a network of health systems agencies to ensure that a given range of health services is made available to regionally-delineated populations. (HC)

2875   Roosman, R.S. *Public health care in Irian Jaya: an account of its policies.* Papua New Guinea Medical Journal (Boroko, Papua New Guinea), 19(4), Dec 1976, 196-204. Engl.
The history, resources, and problems of the health services in Irian Jaya (a province in Indonesia) are discussed in considerable detail and suggestions for their improvement are put forward. At present, the health services

include 9 district hospitals and 250 government- and mission-sponsored aid posts. Efforts to expand the services are hindered by geographical obstacles such as dense jungles, rugged mountains, and swampy lowlands that inhibit communication and transportation. Poor overland communication has made transportation to the interior expensive and coordination/supervision in a health network extremely difficult. Other obstacles to improved services include the low priority accorded health in the provincial budget, the tendency of government facilities to be concentrated on the coast, and the villagers' lack of understanding of Western medical concepts. (HC)

2876   Roze, D. *Approche sanitaire en Egypte. (Approach to health in Egypt).* Marseille, France, Universite d'Aix-Marseille, 10 Mar 1975. lv.(various pagings). Fren.
16 refs.
Thesis presented to the Faculty of Medicine, University of Aix-Marseille, 10 Mar 1975.
This enquiry into health services and health status in Egypt covers: the Ministry of Health, its organization, and dependent agencies (medical insurance, family planning, etc.); teaching hospitals; private medicine; army health services; present health status of the population (demography, mortality, morbidity, etc.); problems related to medical personnel; and the organization, administration, and content of medical education. The author notes that, despite a high ratio of physicians per population (1:1 800), the impact of medical services is considerably diminished by: the physicians' disinclination for rural service; a physician emigration rate of 27%; a shortage of nurses, midwives, nurses' aides, social workers, and technicians; and administrative complexities. (HC)

2877   Salazar Bucheli, J.M. *Reorganizacion del Sistema Nacional de Salud. (Reorganization of the National Health System).* Bogota, Instituto Nacional para Programas Especiales de Salud, Jan 1973. 82p. Span.
This Colombian government document presents the substance and history of Law No.85, which grants the president of the country extraordinary powers for the reorganization of the national health system and the Ministry of Health as well as any other necessary powers. The senatorial debates on the content of this law and its subsequent modifications are included. The restructuring of the national health system is meant to correct problems, particularly in the rural areas, concerning inequitable distribution of foodstuffs, water supply, garbage disposal, distribution of physicians and nurses, distribution and underutilization of hospitals, internal migration, etc. (RMB)

2878   Stephen, W.J. *Chilean health service.* Update (London), 12(12), 15 Jun 1976, 1409-1417. Engl.
12 refs.
Chile was the 1st South American country to introduce a national health service (the *Servicio Nacional de Salud*, SNS), financed mainly by direct taxation and

social security payments. During the Allende regime, efforts were made to extend the SNS to reach the rural population with preventive and other basic health care using auxiliary workers, but since the coup in 1973, these measures have been discontinued in favour of a variety of private curative services. The SNS persists but is grossly under-financed. Typically, the *consultorios*, neighbourhood health centres that form the basic unit of the SNS, are poorly equipped and short of nurses, midwives, auxiliaries, and social workers. Primary care is delivered by inappropriately trained and reluctant hospital specialists, who try to avoid the statutory 6 hours per week SNS service because it is of low status and poorly paid in comparison with private practice. It is unlikely that the Chilean SNS will be able to withstand its current deprivations. However, it could be argued that the decline of the SNS as presently organized is irrelevant to the major health problems of the country, which can only be solved by societal changes effecting such factors as nutrition, housing, and sanitation. (DM)

2879   Tandon, B.N. *Monitoring emergency nutrition programmes in India.* Food and Nutrition (Washington, D.C.), 2(2), 1976, 19-22. Engl.
Experience with the Special Child Relief Programme, an operation that provides emergency nutrition relief in 5 states of India, indicates that most of the problems associated with large scale emergency relief programmes can be overcome by means of an efficient monitoring system. The purpose of the monitoring system is to ensure maximum inter- and intragroup coordination, proper selection of the beneficiaries of the programme, continued training and supportive supervision of peripheral personnel, maintenance of supplies, and assessment of the benefits of the programme. The responsibility for monitoring is entrusted to a central committee whose function is to secure periodic feedback on all aspects of the programme and take corrective measures. Some specific actions initiated by the monitoring committee that have proven useful in the past are set down; the importance of collecting objective information on the benefits of the programme is stressed and it is suggested that these be expressed in terms of decreased mortality and morbidity due to severe malnutrition and improvement in the health of marasmic children. (HC)

2880   Vasco, A. Turizo, A. Pelaez, J.E. Correo, F. *Problematica de salud en las Americas; Colombia: sistemas de salud. (Health problems in the Americas: Colombian health care systems).* Revista Salvadorena de Hospitales (San Salvador), 5(2), May-Aug 1974, 198-211. Span.
The authors trace the history of health services in Colombia and the development of the health care system during the past century with a view to establishing the structure of a proposed national health service. After discussing the concepts of "system" and "health care system" and the characteristics of the latter, they examine the historical development of the institutional system in Colombia and features of the present health care system. It is concluded that the establishment of a government-controlled national health service based on ex-

isting institutions and personnel is not possible at the moment. (RMB)

2881   Vogel, L.C. Sjoerdsma, A. Swinkels, W. W'Oigo, H. Hyndman, G. *Operations research in outpatient services.* Amsterdam, Royal Tropical Institute, Medical Research Centre, Nov 1974. 13p. Engl.
Fifth International Public Health Seminar, Nairobi, Kenya, 17-24 Nov 1974.
From 1968-1974, the Kenya-Netherlands Project for Operations Research analyzed the outpatient services in Kenya and experimented with changes to maximize use of available health resources. Launched cooperatively between Kenya, Israel, and the Netherlands, the project aimed to improve efficiency of existing services and thus increase their overall capacity. During its 1st 6 years, the project tested the introduction of standardized drug packaging and prescription codes, the reallocation of duties among staff members, the reorganization of treatment departments, etc. These experimental changes were based on studies of outpatient clinic operations during which investigators attempted to identify current activities, possible alternatives, evaluation criteria, and outcome. A floorplan of a model clinic built as part of the project is included. (AC)

2882   Wade, M.A. *Approche sanitaire du Senegal. (Approach to health in Senegal).* Marseille, France, Universite d'Aix-Marseille, 15 Dec 1975. 115p. Fren.
39 refs.
Thesis presented to the Faculty of Medicine, University of Aix-Marseille, 15 Dec 1975.
This extensive enquiry into health status and health services in Senegal covers the organization and structure of the Ministry of Health, the curative and preventive infrastructures, the numbers and distribution of doctors and other health personnel, medical research, demography, epidemiology, the cost of health services, health planning and future trends, and traditional medicine. It is noted that curative medicine has persistently progressed at the expense of preventive medicine and that there is a great disparity between urban and rural services. It remains to be seen whether the current health strategies pledged to integrated health care, the universal right to health care, the improvement of basic services, and health education will be able to ameliorate this situation. On the positive side, however, the country's maternal and child health centres are reported to be fulfilling their preventive and educational role to the utmost and to be enjoying wholehearted and steadily increasing support from the population. (HC)

2883   Yepes Lujan, F.J. Agualimpia Montoya, C. Galan Morera, R. Jimenez Rozo, G. Paredes Manrique, R. Yepes Parra, A. Colombia, Ministerio de Salud Publica. Asociacion Colombiana de Facultades de Medicina, Bogota. Instituto Nacional para Programas Especiales de Salud, Bogota. *Niveles de atencion medica para un sistema de regionalizacion en Colombia. (Levels of medical* *care in a regionalized system in Colombia).* Bogota, Ramirez Antares, s.d. 55p. Span.

This proposal for a regionalized health care system in Colombia was formulated when government officials discovered in 1969 that it would be impossible to develop a plan of incentives for health manpower without a total reorganization of the existing health services infrastructure. The advantages of such a reorganization would be the more efficient use of resources, better quality care, greater coverage, improved working conditions, and the involvement of teaching institutions. The revamped system is described in terms of structure, function, and organization and the educational requirements and job descriptions of various categories of health personnel are briefly listed. The authors also discuss the necessary equipment and manpower for and the scope of health activities to be carried out at the rural, local, regional, and university levels. Some problems peculiar to urban and rural areas are mentioned. (RMB)

II.3 Planning

2884   Acton, N. Commonwealth Foundation, London. National Fund for Research into Crippling Diseases, Arundel, UK. *International Institute for Rehabilitation in Developing Countries, Teheran, Iran.* In Disabled in Developing Countries, London, Commonwealth Foundation, 1977, 136-138. Engl.

Symposium on Appropriate Technology and Delivery of Health and Welfare Services for the Disabled in Developing Countries, Oxford, UK, 26-30 Sep 1976.

For complete document see entry 3124.

Rehabilitation International advocates the establishment in Iran of an international institute to study the special problems of rehabilitation in developing countries. This institute will concentrate on services appropriate to less developed areas, organize demonstration projects, and train field workers and their teachers. It will also provide an information centre and advisory services. A 2nd centre will try to develop simpler technical aids under the guidance of the International Centre on Technical Aids, Housing, and Transportation, Stockholm. The institute should be in operation by January 1977. (HH)

2885   Ahmed, S. *Primary health care viewpoint of a country general practitioner.* World Hospitals (Oxford, UK), 11(2 and 3), Jun 1975, 108-111. Engl.

In addressing a congress of doctors and architects on the subject of planning and building health care facilities under conditions of limited resources, a rural practitioner from a developing country makes a number of pertinent suggestions. They include: seeking out competitive prices by investigating both eastern and western

economic blocs when shopping for medical equipment; encouraging local drug production on a mass scale; rejecting capital-intensive solutions, e.g., imported, disposable plastic appliances, in favour of labour-intensive ones such as hiring someone to sterilize reusable appliances; avoiding multistoried hospitals (unnecessary where land is available) in favour of single-storied ones so as to avoid expensive-to-maintain elevators; and making use of local rather than imported structural solutions. One such solution is that of the mud and wattle rondoval hut. Both builders and materials are readily available and the walls and ceilings can be rendered hygienic through the application of paint to which an insecticide has been added. Details regarding the construction, adaptation, and expansion of the rondoval hut are described and illustrated. A diagram of a simple water closet that uses less water than the traditional kind is also given. (HC)

2886   Alpers, A. Allbrook, D. McCall, M. Alexeyeff, S. Stanley, F. Armstrong, B. University of Western Australia, Perth. *Summary report of the Aboriginal Studies Group.* Perth, Australia, University of Western Australia, School of Medicine, n.d. 23p. Engl.

See also entries 0061 (volume 1), 2914, and 2915.

In 1970 and 1971, six researchers undertook a survey of the general problems of aboriginal health and welfare, traveling more than 8 000 miles to 31 communities where they talked with both aboriginals themselves and other Australians. No formal detailed analysis of disease problems was made, but available information was gathered to supplement the team's own observations. The team concluded that, although the disease patterns need to be scientifically investigated, the greatest need at present is positive strategies to meet major health hazards, which are intertwined with housing, educational, and economic problems. Not only is there a link between the disease and poverty found in most poor communities, but more specific interactions are evident – for example, chronic anaemia decreases energy and capacity to work and learn; illiterate young people despair of ever obtaining satisfying work and descend into alcoholism and prostitution. These interrelationships underline the importance of a coordinated plan and permanent coordinating body. Specific recommendations include increased numbers of itinerant public health nurses who have already proved their worth, the training of aboriginal health aides to assist in community health programmes, major improvements in educational policy and housing, and a shift from welfare-oriented programmes to consultive planning with aboriginal leaders, drawing on the indomitable spirit of the people. (AB)

2887   Bhatt, M.J. WHO, Brazzaville. *National health planning in Tanzania: report on a mission 1 Aug 1973-28 Apr 1974.* Brazzaville, WHO, 24 Jul 1974. 58p. Engl.

The purpose of this mission was to assist the government of Tanzania to formulate and implement a national health plan within the provisions of its national development plan. In keeping with the development plan, the health plan emphasizes preventive and rural health serv-

ices. It aims to achieve the following targets by 1980: to raise the number of rural dispensaries from 1 500-2 000 (1:6 000 rural population), to raise the number of rural health centres from 100-300 (1:50 000 rural population), to increase the number of hospital beds in proportion with population growth (3% per annum), to increase the number of medical aides from 600-3 000, to increase the number of medical assistants from 300-1 200 through the creation of an additional school, to increase the number of grade 'A' nurses from 526-1 300, to increase the number of grade 'B' nurses from 1 568-3 257, to increase the number of health auxiliaries ('sub-sanitary inspectors') from 300-1 000 through the establishment of two more schools, to increase the number of midwifery personnel from 727-2 000 (19 new schools for MCH aides envisioned), and to establish a comprehensive network of preventive services for implementation through the dispensaries and health centres. This report constitutes a detailed review of both existing and planned health resources, their geographic distribution and cost, and other miscellaneous features of health and health services in Tanzania. (HC)

2888   Bhatt, M.J. WHO, Brazzaville. *National health planning in the Gambia: report on a mission 19 Jun-23 Jul 1973.* Brazzaville, WHO, 24 Dec 1973. 54p. Engl.
44 refs.
A WHO consultant invited to study existing health facilities in the Gambia recounts observations and suggests that priority be given to organizing and managing health services and personnel training. Specific recommendations are that: the numerous single-purpose facilities be integrated into one basic health service; a basic service model be established as a demonstration and training centre; the health directorate be given authority to coordinate health action throughout the country; voluntary agencies be required to conform to the health policies of the government; job descriptions, standardized equipment, and standardized staffing patterns be introduced; auxiliary health personnel be provided with constant technical supervision and guidance; small clinical laboratories be attached to each health centre; training be job-oriented, etc. Appendices comprise an explanation of the purposes and makeup of the national health planning committee and other documents concerning the Gambia's National Health Plan. (HC)

2889   Bloem, K. Joseph, S. Wallace, N. Wray, J. *Appropriate technology in health in developing countries: proceedings.* Washington, D.C., National Council for International Health, 1976. 116p. Engl.
Working Conference on Appropriate Technology in Health in Developing Countries, Washington, D.C., 16-17 Dec 1976.
In 1976, representatives of various agencies concerned with appropriate health technology met to discuss physical and personnel resources in health, health service infrastructure and administration, the environment, food production and utilization, and obstacles and impediments to the development, implementation, and

evaluation of appropriate technology efforts in health. Participants were asked to consider each of these topics with respect to the major problem areas that are most amenable to an appropriate technology approach, the opportunities and problems related to integrating appropriate technology within an existing infrastructure, the best methods for developing communications between those concerned with intermediate technology in developed and developing countries, and the best methods for fostering collaboration between the 'developers' and the 'appliers' of intermediate technology. Reports of the panel discussions and the plenaries are set forward; no conclusions are drawn but a number of themes and issues that came up repeatedly are identified. A selected bibliography and a selected list of groups from various countries that are involved in the development of appropriate technology are appended. (HC)

2890   Blumhagen, R.V. Blumhagen, J. Medical Assistance Programs, Wheaton, Ill. *Family health care: a rural health care delivery scheme: final report with summary of experience and recommendations for a health care delivery system.* Wheaton, Ill., Medical Assistance Programs, 1974. 105p. Engl.
23 refs.
Individual chapters have been abstracted separately under entries 2827, 2853, 2891, 3193, 3221, 3222, and 3223.
This report summarizes experiences the authors gained in the Medical Assistance Programs (MAP) in Afghanstan during 2 years spent running a mobile clinic service and 4 years staffing and operating a base hospital, health centre, and associated satellite clinics in the Yakaolang area of Hazarajat. It also details a plan that could be implemented within the structure of the national health scheme. The 1st 5 chapters explain the plan's approach, which is to pursue achievable objectives with the active participation of the communities themselves and aim health care at the family as a whole rather than individuals within it. The following sections delineate the organization of family health, a plan of action including a sample work plan for the 1st year of the health centre programme, and an outline of methods, manuals, and standing orders. The next 5 chapters describe the roles of the various members of the health team and are followed by suggestions for the training of such personnel and evaluation of the programme. The report concludes with a bibliography and samples of the questionnaires and forms used in data collection. (DM)

2891   Blumhagen, R.V. Blumhagen, J. Medical Assistance Programs, Wheaton, Ill. *Priorities.* In Blumhagen, R.V., Blumhagen, J., Family Health Care: a Rural Health Care Delivery Scheme, Wheaton, Ill., Medical Assistance Programs, 1974, 33-45. Engl.
For complete document see entry 2890.
The 1st step in planning the Medical Assistance Programs' family health care scheme for Afghanistan was to set limited, achievable objectives. Planners selected a small number of priority measures that were

pursued with the funds available, easily understood by all people involved, evaluated, and built upon as the programme developed. They identified priorities from experience gained over 6 years in Hazarajat where MAP personnel had maintained records of mobile clinic activities, epidemics, child survival statistics, and special surveys. They also consulted village leaders and officials to decide strategies. Resulting plans were to concentrate on mass immunization, case-finding, treatment, follow-up, and health education to combat specific diseases and to enlist health workers in simple village clinics to provide services with the help of trained village volunteers. Another plan was to introduce sanitation and family planning programmes. These measures would require training programmes for workers, backup units for hospitalization, basic laboratory facilities, and methods and equipment for early care of priority conditions. (DM)

2892   Boeckler, M. *Planning and building of health care facilities in rural areas in view of climate, building material and building techniques.* World Hospitals (Oxford, UK), 11(2 and 3), Jun 1975, 218-224. Engl.

Some suggestions for planning and building health care facilities that are suited to the climate, economy, and culture of a developing country are set forward. In hot, humid regions, a cooling effect can be achieved by choosing a breezy site (such as a shore or hillside) with large shade trees nearby, constructing the walls of hollow concrete blocks, extending the roof to provide a shadow, whitewashing the walls to reflect the heat, and ensuring extensive cross-ventilation throughout the building. In regions with cool nights and hot days, heat from the day can be conserved in thick solid walls and naturally released during the night. Bats can be discouraged by leaving a space between the wall top and the roofing and putting windows in the roof (bats hate drafts and light) and termites can be deterred by building a concrete foundation or applying Dieldrin emulsion to the ground around the building. Economies can be gained by taking full advantage of locally-available materials such as wattle and daub, sun-dried brick, and 'stabilized earth'--a mixture of soil, water, and 5%-10% cement. In the planning of inpatient facilities, provision should be made for the relatives of the patients, who generally accompany and cook for them. Side and top views of a relatives kitchen in a hospital in Tanzania is included. (HC)

2893   Boyd, P. *Health programme of the Caricom Secretariat.* Cajanus (Kingston, Jamaica), 8(6), 1975, 370-379. Engl.

With the help of experts and funds from national and international agencies, the Caricom (Caribbean Community) Secretariat has devised a comprehensive programme to meet health priorities of member countries. Specific plans are being initiated to improve maternal and child health, combat diabetes, provide clean water, and improve food production and nutrition. Support services, which are an important part of the programme, include epidemiologic surveillance, health education in all schools and teacher training colleges, provision of laboratory facilities, reform of health legis-

lation, and research. In addition, a regional programme to repair and maintain equipment is planned. The mainstay of such programmes is auxiliary health personnel and, with generous funding from UNDP and UNICEF, a training scheme for health workers is under way in each member country and five regional centres are planned for more specialized instruction. Nursing education, which is now under review, may soon be coordinated with training of other health workers. (DM)

2894   Canadian International Development Agency, Ottawa. *Health guidelines.* Ottawa, Canadian International Development Agency, Jul 1976. 12p. Engl.

The Canadian International Development Agency (CIDA) offers expertise and equipment to support developing-country projects combatting major health problems in rural areas. It gives highest priority to projects that provide for the training of health auxiliaries, improvement of sanitation and water supply, health education, provision of basic equipment for treatment and prevention campaigns operable in field conditions, and construction of simple health facilities. Lower priority is accorded to projects in health planning and administration, hospital-oriented maternal and child health services, and training of health professionals. Construction of hospitals, provision of major equipment, and Canadian training for health professionals from developing countries, activities that CIDA has supported in the past, have proved to be a waste of resources. CIDA's special adviser for health provides guidance in all stages of project planning and evaluation and liaises with other aid and research agencies. (DM)

2895   Cheung, F.M. *Integrated view of community mental health.* Hong Kong, United Christian Hospital, n.d. 9p. Engl.

Unpublished document.

A community mental health programme should not only provide direct services for treatment and rehabilitation of the mentally ill but also promote mental well-being through education, research, and integrated social planning. This approach requires cooperation among community members, mental health workers, and policymakers. Research into the epidemiology of mental disturbance can throw light on the causes and possible methods of prevention or alleviation that might be undertaken by local people trained as community mental health workers. For instance, in Hong Kong, research shows that overall mental health could be improved by better sex education for the general public and by services that support people with marital problems arising from a combination of arranged marriage and cultural dislocation. The research effort must also monitor the impact of the mental health programme itself. Continuous evaluation of this type should help with the planning of environmental and institutional changes to promote mental welfare. (DM)

2896   Chorny, A. Novaro, S. Stulhman, L. Bernachi, M. *Metodo para el analisis y la estimacion de recursos humanos para los programas de atencion* *maternoinfantil. (Methodology for the analysis and estimation of the health manpower needs of maternal child health programmes).* Educacion Medica y Salud (Washington, D.C.), 10(3), 1976, 254-279. Span.

This methodology for estimating maternal child health manpower needs is the result of a joint PAHO/WHO project designed to help Latin American nations establish priorities and allocate available resources with the greatest possible efficiency. The method requires: a computer operating on FORTRAN IV; a team consisting of a planner, a statistician, and a computer programmer; and the sort of statistical data that are normally used by health planners. Depending upon the complexity of the problem, the process can be carried out in 1-3 months. The method is based on projected coverage, the organization of the health care system, and the type of care given by each level; it also takes into consideration geographical areas. Detailed instructions and diagrams for utilizing this method are given and its utility, advantages, and shortcomings, as well as its development and possible adaptation to other types of problems, are described. The results obtained in an experiment in maternal child health in Pernambuco, Brazil, are presented to exemplify the use of the method. Statistical data are included. (RMB)

2897   Christian Medical Commission, World Council of Churches, Geneva. *Position paper: declaration of the Africa Coordinators' Conference, Mombasa, Kenya, 18-21 Feb 1975.* Geneva, Christian Medical Commission, World Council of Churches, 1975. 3p. Engl.
Africa Coordinators' Conference, Mombasa, Kenya, 18-21 Feb 1975.
Unpublished document.

Mission health programmes in Africa must adopt new policies to serve the communities in which they operate and extend primary health care to all. Some essential changes are needed: personnel of the churches' national coordinating agencies must be recruited from the local populations and should receive in-service training, expatriate staff at church-related hospitals must be replaced by local personnel, health programmes must be expanded to peripheral populations, and primary health programmes must be cheap and locally sustainable. These changes may create a burden on local resources and mission services may need to seek government assistance. Where aid is forthcoming, the services should be seen as a joint endeavour with governments and at all times church personnel should cooperate with national medical services and seek suitable working relationships. (DM)

2898   Colombia, Departamento Nacional de Planeacion. *Politica de salud. (Health policy).* Bogota, Color Osprey, 20 Jan 1974. 317p. Span.

Chapter 1 of Part 1 of this study of Colombian health policy deals with health and development, factors influencing health planning and policy, the history of health services within the country, and the organizational structure and financing of existing health services.

Chapter 2 analyzes the health situation, including demographic statistics, health indicators, the demand for and the delivery of health services, and available health resources. In Chapter 3, policies and strategies are discussed. Chapter 4 covers methodologies for executing these policies. In Part 2, separate chapters deal with health promotion, preventive and curative medicine, health manpower training, research programmes, financing of health-related activities, health planning, and environmental health. An annex contains a health programming model. Statistical data are included. (RMB)

2899   D'Aeth, R.G. *Memorandum on health planning in Lesotho based on St. James Mission Hospital, Mants'onyane.* Mants'onyane, Lesotho, St. James Hospital, May 1974. 19p. Engl.
Unpublished document.

To extend the services provided by the St. James Hospital, Mants'onyane, Lesotho, a 10-year plan is proposed. It calls for the building of 3, and eventually 11, health centres to serve an 1 800 square mile area. Each centre will be staffed by 2 nurse practitioners, assisted at each clinic by 2 nurse-aides. A further 2-4 aides will be located in the surrounding villages to advise the local communities on nutrition and hygiene. St. James Hospital itself will have its 35-bed capacity enlarged to 137 and will accommodate a 2nd permanent doctor and visiting specialists. Provision will also be made for an airplane to transport doctors from the hospital to the rural clinics regularly and for an agriculturalist to improve local farming techniques. Appendices provide a comprehensive breakdown of the costs of the plan, including buildings and equipment, transport, salaries, and running costs. (DM)

2900   Das, R. *Planning India's food and nutrition.* Lucknow, India, Lucknow Publishing House, 1972. 187p. Engl.
29 refs.

This 4-part analysis of India's food and nutrition problems reveals that, although the green revolution has enabled India to increase food production to keep pace with population growth, under-nutrition and malnutrition are still widespread. Since the author aims to generate interest in the planning of food and nutrition policies among scientists, administrators, and planners, over half the book is devoted to planning strategy. Food production, food consumption patterns, and malnutrition are discussed, with short sections on environmental sanitation, parasitism, and social taboos affecting the nutritional status of local communities. Short-term solutions to India's food and nutrition problems at the national and local levels are described. A detailed analysis of long-term planning stresses the need for greater use of food science and technology and for nutrition education in planning solutions. A summary of the problems discussed offers recommendations for action, such as extending child feeding programmes and improving water supplies. Eighteen tables provide information and statistics on state-by-state estimates of food grain production, food consumption patterns in different states, etc. A selected bibliography includes 29 references. (CL)

2901   de Queker, P. *Bioclimatic approach to tropical architecture.* Kinshasa, B.P. 3258, 1975. 1v.(unpaged). Engl., Fren.
Refs.
Conference on Health Facility Planning and Design in the Developing Countries, New York, N.Y., 3-5 Dec 1975.
Unpublished document.

Buildings for the tropical environment should be designed to make maximum use of natural, rather than mechanical, means of temperature control. This calls for a thorough knowledge of the climatic conditions in a given locality and a few techniques for calculating human comfort needs at different times of the year. This paper indicates a number of climatic factors with which the architect must be conversant before attempting to design a building, a bioclimatic chart indicating the comfort zone for a lightly-dressed person doing light or sedentary work in the presence of a number of variables (shade, ventilation, etc.), and some simple calculations for measuring the protective value of certain design features (window orientation, shading devices, wall and roofing materials, cross-ventilation, etc.). Numerous charts and diagrams illustrating these techniques are included and an extensive bibliography on building in tropical climates is provided. Examples are taken from Zaire. (HC)

2902   Dwyer, J. *Nutrition education at the village level.* Food and Nutrition (Washington, D.C.), 2(2), 1976, 2-7. Engl.

A number of considerations that must be borne in mind when planning a nutrition education programme are identified. The 1st is that nutrition concerns fall under the jurisdiction of many international agencies and national ministries, none of which perceives the subject as lying totally within its purview; this can result in personnel from different ministries or sectors competing with each other for funds and duplication of some services while others are left undone. A 2nd difficulty arises from the fact that high level bureaucrats are often unaware of what, if any, staffing resources exist at the local level, their qualifications, their training needs, or what may reasonably be expected of them. Thus, workers may be assigned tasks that are beyond their capacity, a larger geographical territory than they can handle, or an unrealistic workload. A 3rd difficulty is related to the fact that rural people will generally not accept a new practice unless it is proved effective before their very eyes and within their economic means. This means that additional funds may have to be provided for models, demonstrations, and free samples. In the light of these considerations, it is recommended that planners give more attention to the specifics of local programmes and that nutrition education be made a carefully-coordinated effort on the part of the schoolteacher, the auxiliary health worker, the agricultural extension worker, and the community development worker. (HC)

2903   Ecuador, Ministerio de Salud Publica. *Plan nacional de salud rural. (National rural health plan).* Quito, Ministerio de Salud Publica, Direccion Nacional de Salud Rural, 1976. 1v.(various pagings). Span.

The 1969 prototype and subsequent revisions of Equador's national rural health plan are discussed in the 1st chapter of this 1976 version. Chapter 2 analyzes the prevailing health situation, including basic health indicators, the evaluation of present health conditions, and the definition of rural areas and their characteristics. In Chapter 3 the strategies, organization, future projections, and economic and manpower aspects of the national rural health plan are discussed. Chapter 4 describes activities carried out from 1972-1975 and Chapter 5 deals with general activities, such as nursing, supervision and future implementation, and university involvement and health manpower training. Annexes contain information on personnel recruitment and distribution, roles for the practice of rural medicine, a supervisor's guide and registration form, and architectural plans. Statistical data are included. (RMB)

2904   Ecuador, Secretaria Tecnica Ejecutiva de Politica Nacional de Alimentacion y Nutricion. *Ecuador: bases para la formulacion y desarrollo de la politica nacional de alimentacion y nutricion. (Equador: guidelines for the formulation and development of a national food and nutrition policy).* Quito, Secretaria Tecnica Ejecutiva de Politica Nacional de Alimentacion y Nutrition, May 1975. 1v.(various pagings). Span.
Convenio "Hipolito Unanue," Primera Reunion de la Comision Asesora Permanente de Alimentacion y Nutricion del Area Andina, Santiago, Chile, May 1975.

Equador's national food and nutrition plan presents separate strategies for the agricultural, fisheries, industrial, educational, health, social sciences, and research sectors. Existing special programmes in urban renewal, maternal child health, school health, health education, etc., are examined and evaluated. In order to achieve an acceptable nutritional status, a coordinated effort must be made by all sectors to identify desirable goals and formulate policies and alternative methods for attaining them. In addition, collateral studies should be carried out on: the eating habits of different social classes; the commercialization of food products; legislation concerning food supplements; the implementation of food quality control programmes; the training of nutritional personnel; the popularization of low-cost, balanced menu plans; increased national food production; the creation of new nutrient sources from local raw materials; and the reinforcement of existing special programmes. An annex contains a presidential decree concerning national nutrition policy. (RMB)

2905   Educacion Medica y Salud, Washington, D.C. *Novena Conferencia de Escuelas de Salud Publica de America Latina: informe final. (Ninth Conference of Latin American Schools of Public*

Health: final report). Educacion Medica y Salud (Washington, D.C.), 11(1), 1977, 60-71. Span.
Novena Conferencia de Escuelas de Salud Publica de America Latina, Rio de Janeiro, Brazil, 7-12 Nov 1976.
The Ninth Conference of Latin American Schools of Public Health (1976) focused on primary care and covered such topics as the definition of primary care, the extension of health services in Latin America, manpower training and resources, public participation, and the function of the school of public health in the development of primary care services. The recommendations by the conference participants for each of these areas are presented. (RMB)

2906   Elliott, V. *Priorities in appropriate technology in health in developing countries.* Washington, D.C., National Council for International Health, Dec 1976. 6p. Engl.
Appropriate Technology in Health in Developing Countries, National Council for International Health, Washington, D.C., 16-17 Dec 1976.
Unpublished document.
Appropriate technology is economically viable and adaptable to local circumstances, recognizes alternative means to the same end, enhances the self-respect and self-confidence of the users, and is cost-effective in social as well as economic terms. To fulfil these criteria, technological "hardware" must be supplemented with appropriate "software", i.e., systematic knowledge, experience, and organization. In the case of health programmes, problems must be correctly identified by those who will directly benefit from their solution and suitable methods of organization and evaluation developed. Relevant knowledge must include not only increased understanding of the mechanism by which new ideas become accepted but also identification of the circumstances in which innovations such as preventive measures are acted upon. Aid-giving countries can help the spread of appropriate technology in health care by supporting research, reducing legal barriers such as patent laws, and helping to establish adequate means of information exchange among all those involved. (DM)

2907   England, R. *Khon Kaen University Health Sciences Centre context study.* London, Llewelyn-Davies Weeks, n.d. 65p. Engl.
The Khon Kaen University Health Sciences Centre was proposed as part of Thailand's Third National Development Plan to train appropriate manpower and study the health problems of the northeast region. An initial survey revealed a disease pattern similar to that of most developing countries with some unusual illnesses arising from local customs. The survey team also investigated the utilization of existing health facilities and found that the rural population greatly prefer self-care or the services of private practitioners, especially traditional healers, to the government health centres, even though the latter are much cheaper. They want health care that is readily available, culturally sympathetic, and curative and are prepared to pay for it. Government health facilities would become more popular if they were convenient-

ly located and if a suitable balance were achieved between curative and preventive services. Changes in the laws concerning drug use, abortion, and health personnel are necessary and the training of all involved manpower requires reform. Efforts to educate traditional midwives about birth complications and contraception are already under way and should be expanded. Many of these changes could be brought about by a proposed Institute of Community Health and Population Sciences at the University, which would be responsible for research, health manpower training, health service planning, and the launching of specific health programmes. (DM)

2908   Feldstein, M.S. *Health sector planning in developing countries.* Economics (London), 37(146), 1970, 139-163. Engl.
34 refs.
A mathematical formula for planning in the health sector can be derived from input constraints, population constraints, tasks, benefits, efficacy of treatments, and desired outputs; its components can be easily applied to linear programming. The solution expresses the optimum level of particular health care activities and indicates the shadow prices of the constrained inputs, i.e., for all inputs with a binding constraint, the shadow price is positive; for all others, the shadow price is zero. The formula can be applied to disease control programmes in such a way as to remove the value judgments of planning officials and replace them with technical decisions based on epidemiologic and medical information. For example, applied to the tuberculosis programme in India, the equations indicate that optimum programmes at constraint levels imposed by allocating 10% of national health resources to TB concentrate on self-referral activities in persons aged 15-64 years and mass vaccination for those aged less than 15 years. Other examples are elaborated and the appendix presents equations used to calculate service outputs. (AC)

2909   Feuerstein, M.T. *Rural health problems in developing countries: the need for a comprehensive community approach.* Community Development Journal (London), 2(1), 1976, 38-52. Engl.
38 refs.
A comprehensive community campaign to tackle rural health problems has never yet been fully implemented, but partial attempts have been economical and effective. The essential features of this approach are that it is coordinated with other development projects as part of a national plan, it seeks to change the full range of background factors responsible for the major health problems, and it uses local resources and manpower where possible. To ensure community participation, the cooperation of local leaders must be enlisted and the programme must meet felt needs as well as long-term objectives. These aims should include improvement of women's health and education, not only because women are the mainstay of family health, but also because chronic ill health and ignorance prevent them from taking a more dynamic role in society. The disruptive effects of introducing changes can be minimized if the programme is compatible with local culture and the

indigenous medical system and if it involves many sections of the community simultaneously. It should also incorporate continuous research and evaluation, including base-line and pilot studies. The principles of this community approach should be taught to all health personnel. (DM)

2910   Gish, O. *Alternative approaches to health planning.* Assignment Children (Geneva), 33, Jan-Mar 1976, 32-51. Engl.
Efforts to provide equal access to health services for all citizens of developing countries are inhibited less by the traditional "curative versus preventive" orientation of health services than by the current "urban versus rural" dichotomy. In this paper, a number of suggestions for stemming the flow of funds to urban, hospital-based medical care and diverting it to rural, integrated health care are proposed. These include: focusing pre-planning studies on actual resource allocation and services utilization and not on epidemiology, since there is now in the Third World more information on disease patterns than is being utilized; calculating specific catchment areas for all types of facilities; expending the capital budget on new facilities and manpower training programmes that will favour the rural sector; concentrating manpower development resources on training numerous and inexpensive auxiliaries; incorporating innovative approaches to health care delivery into national policy; etc. Tanzania provides an example of the possibilities of population coverage through a relatively small financial outlay. (HC)

2911   Gish, O. Institute of Development Studies, University of Sussex, Brighton. *Health planning for women and children.* Brighton, UK, University of Sussex, Institute of Development Studies, IDS Discussion Paper, Apr 1974. 14p. Engl.
Study Seminar on the Participation of Women in Development: Implications for Policy and Planning, Cambridge, UK, 14-19 Mar 1974.
Health services in developing nations should give priority to the needs of women in their childbearing years and children aged less than 5 years, who together comprise 40% of the total population of Third World countries. In addition, health services planning should involve cooperation between the ministries of health and those of water, agriculture, education, etc., whose activities also affect health. Such coordination requires a shift in emphasis from town to countryside, which can only be accomplished by decreasing urban hospital building and increasing input into rural health services either from the private sector or through social reorganization. In making a 5-year health plan, data on expenditure and utilization of services must shape planning within a known recurrent health budget. Economic considerations also indicate that health manpower planning for national requirements should use large numbers of auxiliaries and medical assistants to improve health services. Maternal and child health services could follow the Tanzanian model, where a cadre of maternal and child health aids offer antenatal, maternity, and postnatal care at rural health centres. A decentralized system of

small maternity units involving hospitalization only for abnormal deliveries would relieve hospitals of normal deliveries and ensure better antenatal and postnatal screening. Generally, government policies should concentrate on preserving health and encouraging participation by village communities in health activities, as seen, for example, in the People's Republic of China. (CL)

2912   Golding, J.S. Commonwealth Foundation, London. National Fund for Research into Crippling Diseases, Arundel, UK. *Health care delivery for the disabled.* In Disabled in Developing Countries, London, Commonwealth Foundation, 1977, 40-44. Engl.
Symposium on Appropriate Technology and Delivery of Health and Welfare Services for the Disabled in Developing Countries, Oxford, UK, 26-30 Sep 1976.
For complete document see entry 3124.
Any policy for improving health care of the disabled in developing countries must emphasize preventive measures, methods for the early diagnosis of disabling conditions, and priorities in different types of care. Preventable disabling diseases include rubella, polio, leprosy, and kernicterus. Genetic counselling will also prevent some disability. Once children are born, early recognition of problems such as deafness is essential. Records of handicapped children should be kept so that vital early care can be initiated before irreversible conditions become established. Also, primary care personnel must have sufficient expertise to know if a serious injury requires immediate treatment. Finally, although medical care of the handicapped is important, it must take 2nd place to education. Good education will train the disabled, who are in any case debarred from unskilled labour, to help satisfy the developing country's need for skilled artisans and middle management. Because resources are limited, training should concentrate first on those who are easily employable and those who can work in sheltered workshops; these categories can become self-supporting. As the society grows more affluent, the severely disabled will get a greater share of its resources. (HH)

2913   Heredia, R. Vivas, A. Hernando Ochoa, L. *Modelo de simulacion para la evaluacion de los programas materno-infantiles en Colombia. (Simulation model for evaluating maternal child health programmes in Colombia).* Bogota, Corporacion Centro Regional de Poblacion, Apr 1977. 49p. Span.
Refs.
International Seminar on Evaluation of Child Health Services: the Interface Between Research and Medical Practice, Bethesda, Md., 1977.
The proposed simulation model was developed within the context of a larger model whose aim is to analyze and compare various policy alternatives that are open to the Colombian government in its efforts to promote social and economic development. The proposed simulation model is intended to provide the health planner or

administrator with a fine tool for evaluating maternal and child health programmes and for establishing standards of efficiency and effectiveness for them. It goes further than previous models in that it is concerned not only with the programmes' execution and impact but also with its justification and choice of design. This paper gives a detailed explanation (with diagrams) of the various stages and dimensions of the proposed simulation model and of the kinds of indicators it can be expected to generate; a short description of the larger model, *Sistema para el Estudio de las Relaciones Economicas, Sociales, y Demograficas* (SERES), is appended. (HC)

2914   Hetzel, B.S. *Health and Australian society.* Harmondsworth, UK, Penguin Books, 1974. 314p. Engl.
Refs.
Individual chapter has been abstracted separately under entry 2997; see also entries 2886 and 2915.
In an attempt to analyze the relationship between individual and community health, the author examines the environmental, sociological, cultural, and financial aspects of health care in Australia. After discussing some definitions of and different ways of measuring health status, he considers the relationship between health and environment, the impact of personal and social change on the individual's health, and the health of the Australian population as a whole, including morbidity and mortality. The special health problems of minority groups such as the aborigines and migrants are also cited. Integrating all these aspects of health, he proposes an overall strategy for health care services. First, he advocates a positive health policy based on prevention, the development of community health services, and increased health education for the people. Because of rising costs and increasing taxpayers' contributions to health care, he also supports a 1973 planning committee's recommendations for a compulsory health insurance plan, emphasizing that this plan is just one aspect of a complicated social system affecting health. Age-specific mortality data from five countries are included in an appendix, followed by detailed recommendations for further reading relevant to each chapter. (CL)

2915   Hetzel, B.S. Dobbin, M. Lippmann, L. Eggleston, E. *Better health for Aborigines?* Brisbane, Australia, University of Queensland Press, 1974. 309p. Engl.
Refs.
National Seminar on Health Services for Aborigines, Melbourne, Australia, 15-17 May 1972.
Individual chapter has been abstracted separately under entry 3001; see also entries 2886 and 2914.
These seminar proceedings contain papers covering: the sociocultural aspects of Aborigine health, with emphasis on alcoholism and petrol inhalation; the epidemiology of disease in Aboriginal communities; existing Aboriginal health services; new models for Aboriginal health services, some currently being tested; and Aboriginal attitudes to family planning methods. Each paper is

followed by a list of references and an abstract of the seminar discussion from each session is given. The main points of individual papers are summarized in the final section, which also discusses future planning of Aborigine health services and considers the recommendations of the seminar participants. A 17-page appendix gives detailed demographic and epidemiological data from state and Northern Territory health services and a selected bibliography includes 108 references. (CL)

2916   Honduras, Secretaria de Salud Publica y Asistencia Social. *Programa materno infantil: solicitud de ayuda a El Fondo de Poblacion de las Naciones Unidas. (Maternal child health programme: project proposal submitted to UNFPA).* Tegucigalpa, Secretaria de Salud Publica y Asistencia Social, Sep 1973. 1v.(various pagings). Span.
9 refs.
This project proposal presents plans for a 4-1/2 year maternal child health and family planning programme. A section of general information deal withs the project's justification, the attitude of the government of Honduras, present maternal child health strategies, etc. Other sections deal with the programme's objectives, working plan, budget, and the projected contributions of UNFPA and Honduras. Annexes contain information on health manpower, facilities and supplies, construction, family planning, the organization of the ministry of health, finances, training programmes, a health volunteer's job description, a mobile health unit project, etc. (RMB)

2917   Indo-Dutch Project for Child Welfare, Hyderabad, India. *Urban Indo Dutch Project for Child Welfare: questions and answers (a preparation for a dialogue with the communities).* Hyderabad, India, Indo-Dutch Project for Child Welfare, n.d. 15p. Engl.
See also entries 2918, 3016, 3017, and 3040.
A new scheme for urban community development is to be launched in Hyderabad by the Indo-Dutch Project for Child Welfare. Because the success of the project relies on the cooperation of an informed public, four teams, each composed of a community organizer and lady volunteers, are embarking on a programme of twice-weekly visits to the target areas to explain the aims and methods of the project. The teams will use this set of questions and answers to deal with a wide range of queries from individuals, local leaders, heads of institutions, and agency representatives. The questions and answers are arranged in five sections. The 1st covers general matters of policy, strategy and planning. The remaining sections concern the specific innovations of the project: preschool child education, an integrated health insurance plan, *Mahila Mandal*s (women's clubs), and *Vigyan Mandir*s (centres of learning for young people). The services proposed for each unit of 1 000 families are summarized in diagrams and a set of visual aids is in preparation to supplement this material. (DM)

2918 **Indo-Dutch Project for Child Welfare, Hyderabad, India.** *Indo-Dutch Urban Project for Child Welfare.* Hyderabad, India, Indo-Dutch Project for Child Welfare, n.d. 8p. Engl.
   See also entries 2917, 3016, 3017, and 3040.
The Indo-Dutch Project for Child Welfare, with the help of local government and voluntary agencies, has planned a range of services to improve the education, health, and nutrition of the 55 000 people living in an area of Hyderabad, India. The project is based on self-reliance and local initiative and leadership and all participants must contribute in cash, kind, or services. Preference is given to the poorer families and parents' participation is required. The proposals include a health assurance plan to provide comprehensive health care and health education for mothers and children. A creche and preschool group under the supervision of auxiliary nurse-midwives (ANMs) and mothers will provide day care with nutritious food for young children in a stimulating environment and child guidance for mothers. Centres of learning for 10-16-year-olds, equipped with recreational and skill-training facilities, will act as a base for self-improvement, self-employment schemes, and community services. Also planned are training centres for women offering a variety of educational activities. (DM)

2919 **International Secretariat for Volunteer Service, Manila.** *Mobilization of response structures from the grassroots towards health services: report of a workshop.* Manila, International Secretariat for Volunteer Service, Asian Regional Office, Jul 1974. 128p. Engl.
   International Secretariat for Volunteer Service Workshop on Mobilization of Response Structures from the Grassroots towards Health Services, Manila, Philippines, 8-11 Jul 1974.
   Individual chapters have been abstracted separately under entries 2999, 3115, 3128, and 3139.
A 4-day workshop on the role of volunteers in health services was held by the International Secretariat for Volunteer Service at the invitation of the Philippine Public Health Association. This workshop coincided with the First Asian Regional Conference of Public Health Associations and the Annual Convention of the Philippine Public Health Association; the three conferences were concerned with related topics and there was some cooperation between the organizing bodies. This report presents the proceedings of the ISVS workshop only. Papers presented at the meeting describing national health plans and individual health programmes in the countries represented are reproduced in full and the discussions, which were the focus of the workshop, are summarized. The delegates are listed under country of origin. (DM)

2920 **Jamaica Council for the Handicapped, Kingston.** *Proceedings of the Caribbean Regional Conference on the Handicapped Child.* Kingston, Jamaica, Caribbean Institute on Mental Retardation and Developmental Disabilities, Oct 1975. 171p. Engl.
   Caribbean Regional Conference on the Handicapped Child, Kingston, Jamaica, 12-15 Oct 1975.
The seven half-day sessions of the Caribbean Regional Conference on the Handicapped Child covered the establishment, as part of maternal and child health services, of: programmes for prevention of disability, early detection, and early intervention; special education programmes and facilities; social welfare services; and an overview of comprehensive services and planning. The final session consisted of two special reports, one on work provision for the profoundly retarded and the other on international resources for rehabilitation of the disabled. The proceedings publish the papers in full, summarize the discussions, and present the recomendations arising from the conference. A list of participants, including members of the conference committee and official representatives of the Caribbean Islands, is provided. (DM)

2921 **Jay, M.H. UK, Ministry of Overseas Development.** *Rural development in British aid policy.* Education Broadcasting International (London), 10(2), Jun 1977, 55-57. Engl.
Development policy in the 1950s and 1960s achieved overall growth of gross national product in the Third World but failed to benefit the poorest countries or the poor within each country. It is now recognized internationally that aid should be channelled into rural development, not only for humanitarian reasons, but also because land and labour are the major resources of these countries. An essential prerequisite for rural development is the establishment of a basic infrastructure including roads, extension services, marketing facilities, water supply, health care, and education. However, any innovation is likely to meet with a number of social problems, including political resistance within these regions to change in custom, as well as technical difficulties. To resolve these difficulties, Britain now sends a multidisciplinary project identification mission to confer with each host government to determine suitable uses for UK funds. The project design must ensure that the benefits reach the target population, but this depends on the efficiency and motivation of local institutions and personnel. Although British expertise may be involved in early stages of implementation, local people must eventually take over the work and host governments the responsibility for these programmes. It is too early to assess the success of British-funded projects of this type that are already under way in Gambia, Nepal, Sudan, and elsewhere, but at least the new approach to overseas aid is being put to the test. (DM)

2922 **Jazairi, N.T. Organisation for Economic Co-operation and Development, Paris.** *Approaches to the development of health indicators.* Paris, Organisation for Economic Co-operation and Development, OECD Social Indicator Development Programme Special Studies No.2, 1976. 58p. Engl.
   Refs.
   Also published in French as: *Differentes approches pour l'elaboration d'indicateurs de sante.*
After reviewing past development and uses of health

indicators to measure health care, the author discusses indicators that can be used to monitor mortality, morbidity, the quality of health care, health care delivery, and the integration of the disabled into society. Indicators of quality are more difficult to establish than those of mortality and morbidity, but the author recommends basing them on indices of hospital care, the application of preventive measures, state of pain or disability following standard accidents, correctness of diagnostic standards and clinical procedures, introgenicity, use of prosthesis, immunity against preventable diseases, screening procedures, quantity of care, quality of pharmaceutical products and laboratory output, and the patients' subjective assessment of quality. Indicators of health care delivery could be in terms of number and distribution of manpower and facilities and the utilization of services by rich and poor. Measuring the uptake of rehabilitation and employment schemes, income, housing, and quality of family life would help establish the final set of indicators. References are given to work undertaken in developing each type of indicator mentioned. (RMB)

2923   Jeffers, J.R. Korea Development Institute, Seoul. *Economic issues: Korea health planning and policy formation.* Seoul, Korea Development Institute, 1976. 135p. Eng., Korean.

An economist interested in identifying major health policy issues and solutions comments on various aspects of the Republic of Korea's health sector. First, he identifies and discusses major issues in health sector planning and policy-making, including the propositions that: outlays on health services encourage economic growth; private outlays on health services have aided Korea's economic growth during the past 20 years; the impact of outlays on health services seems to be greater at moderate or advanced levels of development than at low levels; the Korean government should exercise care in the allocation of health funds; the current health plan fails to reflect current demographic trends (e.g., the rural-urban drift); the current plan overemphasizes spatial, as opposed to community, allocation of services; the government should consider ways of regulating the private health sector in the interests of the population; and the government should increase the efficiency of the health industry before it increases the demand for health services by introducing a large-scale health insurance programme. In the 2nd part of the book, he elaborates and supports some secondary considerations related to production technology. The government is urged to declare a moratorium on the building of expensive, Western-style health facilities until those that exist start functioning at full capacity. (HC)

2924   Jorgensen, T.A. *Rural hospital in East Africa.* World Hospitals (Oxford, UK), 11(1 and 2), Jun 1975, 192-193. Engl.

The proper function of a rural hospital is to take care of patients who can only be treated in a hospital or who are too ill to cook their own food and keep themselves clean; the outpatient department should be reserved for those referred from lower levels of the health system for special

examinations and treatment. The optional size of the rural hospital is considered to be 90 beds. It should be equipped with an operating theatre, a laboratory, and perhaps an X-ray unit and be staffed by at least 1 doctor, 3-4 medical assistants, and 60 support staff. The number of rural hospitals that are required should be determined not by the number of beds per:1 000 people but by the accessibility of the available beds and by the local disease pattern. Having thus defined the functions and desirable features of the rural hospital, the author points out the relative contributions that doctor and architect can make in producing more practical, economical hospitals. The doctor can convey to the architect that, for example, lighting, ventilation, and door and passage dimensions are of more importance than quality or finishing of the building; the architect can make the doctor aware of relative merits of remodelling versus rebuilding, the importance of planning for extensions, the savings possible through the use of local building materials and techniques, and how to set up a proper budget. (HC)

2925   Kohut, M. WHO, Brazzaville. *Water supplies for small communities.* Brazzaville, WHO, 4 Jan 1971. 64p. Engl.
Unpublished document.

This report is the result of a survey of community water supplies in Tanzania undertaken to assist the government to develop a national community water supply programme. The findings cover: present planning, administration, and water supply policy; the influence of the present situation on public health; other organizations undertaking water supply activities; government investigations and surveys; subsidies to organizations interested in the promotion of water supplies; government research and training; contacts and specific activities; necessary improvements; priorities; and methods for improvement. The author recommends the creation of an advisory environmental health unit and a national environmental health institute, the implementation of demonstration projects for small rural water supplies, the improvement of water supplies in rural health centres and dispensaries, the development of a water testing kit, the establishment of national water standards and a national water supply policy, the enforcement of flouridation in public water supplies, and the incorporation of schistosomiasis control measures into water supply planning. He also lists the supplies and equipment to be requested from UNICEF. Annexes contain statistical data on water supplies, rural health centres, and boreholes in Tanzania. (RMB)

2926   Lancet, London. *Community health care-- Schumacher style.* Lancet (London), 2(8048), 1977, 1114-1115. Engl.
12 refs.

The provision of flexible community health care based on intermediate technology, as defined by Schumacher, will depend to a large extent on choosing the optimum size of community to be involved in the decision-making process. The critical size is probably much smaller than most people realize. A community of only a few hundred people can come to a consensus and responsibly select representatives to discuss health care that would be implemented either by the community itself or with outside help. In this way, varying levels of skill, education, material resources, and supportive technologies can be used to provide appropriate services. If the community is responsible for financing some of its immediate health needs, it will be more involved both in deciding priorities and in ensuring the programme's success. Such a scheme will require that knowledge and responsibility be shared between health professionals and those in need of their skills. (HH)

2927 Lechat, M.E. *Epidemiology of disasters*. Proceedings of the Royal Society of Medicine (London), 69(6), Jun 1976, 421-426. Engl.
Royal Society of Medicine Section of Epidemiology and Community Medicine Meeting, London, UK, 8 Jan 1976.
Despite the diversity of disasters, some generalizations can be made about their probable impact on health using epidemiological techniques. This information can improve the effectiveness of relief planning and evaluation, especially where there is adequate coordination and exchange of data among the agencies involved. When such agencies plan relief operations, determining what is not needed may be just as important as identifying requirements, if transport and resources are limited. For instance, surgical teams are often unnecessary because natural disasters tend to cause more deaths than injuries. Similarly, although communicable diseases are a major problem amongst survivors, they can usually be contained best by location and protection of vulnerable groups rather than by mass immunization. Acceptable calorie-rich local ingredients are usually preferable to expensive high-protein imports in food relief. Disaster epidemiology may also be used to evaluate relief measures and may bring to light unforeseen side effects, such as the association between powdered milk provision and vitamin A deficiency among children in the Sahel. Post-impact epidemiological surveillance, if carried out as part of a multidisciplinary study, could yield valuable information on the long term effects of both the disaster itself and of relief operations. Such an investigation might detect ill effects resulting from the withdrawal of emergency services or reveal opportunities for permanent improvements during reconstruction. (DM)

2928 Litsios, S. *Developing a cost and outcome evaluation system*. International Journal of Health Services (Westport, Conn.), 6(2), 1976, 345-360. Engl.
A basic strategy for evaluating health services in developing countries is presented. It is based on three major prerequisites: the employment of full-time evaluators at the national and regional levels, establishment of a firm link between evaluation staff and decision-makers, and establishment of effective feedback mechanisms to link local health personnel with evaluators. Once these conditions have been met, the strategy comprises steps to study national health plans and goals, accumulate standard designs and costs of health facilities as a basis for cost comparison, identify the characteristics of patients and

health services utilization, and research health system changes and measures and report their results. This strategy differs from traditional methodologies in the emphasis it places on guiding planned change through the generation of information of use to decision-makers. (HC)

2929 Lyengar, M.A. WHO, Brazzaville. *Health component in development planning*. Brazzaville, WHO, 1 Jul 1974. 53p. Engl.
From 1972-1973, a WHO consultant assisted the government of Sierra Leone to draw up a health services sectoral plan as part of the overall national development plan (1974/75-1978/79). His report contains a review of the project area and population, a history of general planning in Sierra Leone, an assessment of progress made in the health sector during the 1st 10-year development plan (1962/63-1971/72), and an account of the present health status of the population. He notes that, despite a lack of government support, the 1st plan did attain some of its objectives, such as an increase in hospital beds and rural health units and control of some major communicable diseases (sleeping sickness, yaws, and smallpox), and epidemic control measures were established. The new 5-year development plan calls for 1 MCH aide per:7 000 population, hospital facilities for as many complicated deliveries as possible (an estimated 24 000 per:year), an increase in the number of hospital beds from 0.8 to 1.0 per:1 000 population, additional Ministry of Health staff, specialist services in 1 hospital in each of the country's 4 provinces, 1 health unit per:chiefdom throughout the country (11 health units are to be upgraded to health centres and 1 health centre and 24 dispensaries are to be built), immunization (DPT, BCG, and malaria chemoprophylaxis) of specific target groups, improved residential accommodation for health centre staff, the reorganization and expansion of the statistical services of the Ministry of Health, a plan for the execution of water supply and sewerage systems, etc. Details regarding the phasing and budgeting of and the involvement of other sectors and international agencies in the plan are included. (HC)

2930 Mahler, H. *Health--a demystification of medical technology*. Lancet (London), 2(7940), 1 Nov 1975, 829-833. Engl.
Every country, industrialized or developing, should adopt a rational health policy aimed at providing effective medical care for the majority of people at risk as early, cheaply, and acceptably as possible. To do this, the health establishment must assess and describe available medical resources and target groups objectively so that the skills and knowledge necessary for effective action can be determined and so that resources can be assigned on a problem-solving basis. Unfortunately, this rational approach is seldom adopted, because the mystique of medical technology precludes consideration of important alternative approaches. The traditional awe with which the medical profession is regarded leads to groundless fears that any change will reduce the quality of the service and also results in the tendency for action to be taken at unnecessarily high levels of the medical

II Organization and Planning

hierarchy. Many tasks could be delegated from specialist to general practitioner, from general practitioner to nurse, or from nurse to mother without any loss of quality. For instance, the use of home rehydration kits by Mexican mothers to treat diarrheal diseases in children has proven to be just as effective as rehydration at a health centre and a great deal cheaper. National planning requires research into measures such as this that tackle clearly defined health problems under known local conditions. (DM)

2931 Mahmud, S. Fendall, N.R. *Health and integrated rural development.* Islamabad, Pakistan, Planning Commission, Aug 1975. 10p. Engl.
Pakistan's integrated Rural Development Programme, begun in 1972, is based on the philosophy that all aspects of rural life are interrelated and that no lasting progress can be made unless the various problems are attacked simultaneously. It calls for, on the one hand, restructuring the health care delivery system around a primarily agricultural thrust and, on the other, utilizing other disciplines to assist in the delivery of specific aspects of medical and health care needs. The following recommendations are concrete examples of the latter: introducing a health component into all rural development schemes that involve resettlement of a population, changes in cultural behaviour, changes in the environment, etc.; training agricultural workers to participate in the recognition, prevention, and treatment of nutritional deficiencies; training veterinarians in the basics of nutrition, dietetics, home economics, and the control of zoonoses; enlarging farmers' training centres to include a family health and home economics component for their wives; persuading public health engineering staff to accept responsibility for community education in their work; incorporating a functional health content into school textbooks; expanding the role of teachers to include the recognition, treatment, and prevention of common childhood infectious diseases; and utilizing the extensive networks of police stations, post offices, banks, etc., for the distribution of preventive medicines such as anti-malarials, iodized salt, etc. It is stressed that successful integration depends on mutual understanding between the various work sectors and workers and that this understanding is best inculcated during training; on the job, it can be encouraged through regular meetings of workers from all sectors to discuss common goals. (HC)

2932 Mante, K.S. *Interface between statistics and health planning.* Ghana Medical Journal (Accra), 14(3), Sep 1975, 206-208. Engl. 11 refs.
Health planning is often defined as the allocation of resources according to extrapolation of past performances, an assessment of present and future community needs and available resources, and educated guesses concerning influences beyond the control of the wielders of economic power. Evaluation of health activities is sometimes included. This paper discusses the role of statistics in health planning. Statistics are most useful in the extrapolation of past performances, which can usually be described in more or less precise numerical

language, but their use in other areas of health planning has major limitations. The author examines some of these problems, as well as the underlying assumptions in the use of statistics in health planning, and draws the reader's attention to system dynamics, a relatively new research technique that can be applied to studies in human ecology and other complex systems. (RMB)

2933 Mason-Browne, N.E. *Health in Belize: an emerging country.* Tropical Doctor (London), 7, Jan 1977, 25-27. Engl.
Health statistics indicate that two priorities for development in Belize (formerly British Honduras) are to widen the base of secondary industry and cultivate additional food sources for protein. Overall morbidity and mortality data compare favourably with other Latin American countries and the life expectancy beyond age 1 year is high at 71.2 years. The morbidity figures indicate that respiratory disease and diarrheal diseases constitute the major illnesses and they stem directly from the widespread poverty. Thus, the most important advances in health will be made only with an improved economic base supported by additional industry. Statistical data are included. (AC)

2934 McIntosh, C.E. *National food and nutrition policy and its effective implementation.* Cajanus (Kingston, Jamaica), 10(4), 1977, 195-205. Engl. 11 refs.
In the Caribbean, approximately 1.4% of all children are severely underweight, 12% are moderately underweight, and 40% are just below the desired minimum level; anaemia is prevalent among both women and children; food supplies are adequate but inequitably distributed; and the foodstuffs making the greatest contribution to total nutrient supply are imported. These factors all contribute to the need for a policy to bring food supply, food demand, and biological utilization of nutrients into a desirable balance. In this paper, the steps involved in formulating and implementing a food policy are discussed and these recommendations are made: that the implications of existing policies and programmes be scrutinized in the early stages of formulation; that project proposals be evaluated in terms of their implications for development such as effect on income redistribution, effect on employment, susceptibility to inflation, etc.; that the acceptability of the designated policy to the government of the country be taken into consideration; that implementation of the policy be expedited by the appointment of a food and nutrition projects administrator; that the availability of the required manpower be maximized by a more liberal immigration policy on the part of regional states; and that consideration be given to formulating a food and nutrition plan at the regional level. (HC)

2935 Ozguner, O. *Organization of design: phase alternatives in designing methods.* World Hospitals (Oxford, UK), 11(2 and 3), Jun 1975, 96-97. Engl.
Countries with limited resources tend to be characterized by a high rate of natural increase, a high

rate of internal migration, a society in which both the quantity and quality of needs are changing rapidly, and a dearth of statistical data on such subjects. Because of this, the architect of a new hospital or health facility cannot base his design on the conventional programme, i.e., the written form of the needs, because the needs are not actually known and cannot accurately be predicted. Guided by the concepts of growth, flexibility, adaptability, and uncertainty, he is asked to design a system that generates buildings rather than a finished product. In this paper, the extent to which structure, equipment, and space are amenable to these guiding principles is discussed and some suggestions regarding design are put forward. They include: spacing supporting structures as far apart as possible so that they will obstruct activity to the minimum; grouping inflexible, fixed elements (e.g., heavily-equipped service areas such as laboratories, operating rooms, laundries, etc.) in a central core; and providing for the expansion of those areas, patient rooms, waiting rooms, and outpatient facilities, which tend to grow more rapidly than others. (HC)

2936   Pan American Health Organization, Washington, D.C. WHO, Geneva. *Guide for the organization of health services in rural areas and the utilization of auxiliary personnel: recommendations of two working groups convened in Washington, D.C., Apr 1974.* Washington, D.C., Pan American Health Organization, Scientific Publication No.290, 1975. 65p. Engl.
Experiences throughout the world in establishing rural health services have provided some insights that seem generally applicable. These have been collated into guidelines and are presented in this joint WHO/PAHO publication. Major sections are an outline of methods, an analysis of activities and tasks, definition of a programme's infrastructure, and an explanation of the guide's concepts and terms. Within these categories, the roles of community, auxiliary, and health professionals are examined and the planning, organization, execution, control, and supervision of health services are detailed. Tables and figures present information on task delegation, resource allocation, teaching methods, etc. (AC)

2937   Pan American Health Organization, Washington, D.C. *Ten-year health plan for the Americas; final report of the Third Special Meeting of Ministers of Health of the Americas.* Washington, D.C., Pan American Health Organization, Official Document No.118, Jan 1973. 138p. Engl. Refs.
Third Special Meeting of Ministers of Health of the Americas, Santiago, Chile, 2-9 Oct 1972.
Part 1 of this conference discusses general concepts that must be considered in formulating a health plan for the Americas, including a definition of the concept of health, an operational nomenclature, ecology, maternal and child health, family welfare, population dynamics, food and nutrition, community participation, health manpower, profiting from past experiences, and finances. Part 2 sets forth recommendations on communicable diseases, malaria, chronic diseases, mental health,

maternal and child health and family welfare, population dynamics, nutrition, dental health, environmental health, occupational health and industrial hygiene, health aspects of regional development, animal health and veterinary public health, control of the use of pesticides, food quality control, drug quality control, traffic accidents, nursing, health laboratories, medical rehabilitation, health education, health and radiation, health service systems and their coverage, medical care and health systems, health administration and planning, information processing, statistics, research, health manpower, technology and teaching resources, legal considerations, and finances. Part 3 presents the goals of the 1971-1980 health plan, Part 4 the conference resolutions, and Part 5 the final declaration. Annexes contain lists of officers and participants and the agenda. (RMB)

2938   Parker, A. Newell, K.W. Torfs, M. Israel, E. *Appropriate tools for health care: developing a technology for primary health care and rural development.* WHO Chronicle (Geneva), 31(4), Apr 1977, 131-137. Engl.
Also published in French, Russian, and Spanish.
A proposal for the development of a WHO programme in health technology to complement existing WHO programmes in primary health care and rural development is outlined. Health technology is broadly defined as systematic application of knowledge in the health and related sciences to the solution of practical tasks; the aim of a health technology programme would be to assist countries in making informed choices among alternative health care technologies based not only upon technical factors related to their effectiveness and safety but also on economic, political, and social criteria. This means that a potential technology would be subjected to considerations such as its complexity (can it be applied by persons with limited training at the primary level?), its cost (does it absorb a disproportionate share of the health budget?), its inclusiveness (does it serve more than one purpose?), and its feasibility (can it be utilized in a situation lacking, for example, electricity or potable water?). The role of WHO in the identification and promotion of alternative health care technologies is discussed. (HC)

2939   Peru, Ministerio de Salud. *Plan nacional de desarrollo para 1977-78: plan operativo sector salud. (National development plan for 1977-78: health sector plan of operations).* Lima, Ministerio de Salud, Oficina Sectorial de Planificacion, 9 Jun 1977. 232p. Span.
In this plan of operations, the Peruvian Ministry of Health established certain guidelines, based on economic, social, and political considerations, that are obligatory for the public sector and recommended for the private sector. The plan describes and evaluates the national health situation and sets out health policies and programmes covering health services, finances, and resources for 1977 and 1978. It is expected that this plan will be reevaluated in terms of actual accomplishments versus proposed goals so that any necessary modifications can be made. Statistical data are included. (RMB)

2940 **Philippines, Department of Health.** *Proceedings and recommendations: sector on health and nutrition.* Quezon City, Philippines, Department of Health, Sep 1976. 1v.(various pagings). Engl. International Conference on the Survival of Humankind, Manila, Philippines, 6-10 Sep 1976. Unpublished document.

Participants at an international conference held in the Philippines in 1976 discussed primary health care, the national nutrition programme, and a management information system. They considered possible applications for telemedicine, auxiliary health workers, community participation, regular screening for malnourished children, the interaction of sanitation and nutrition, and food sources for vitamins. Conference recommendations included: initiating a system of telemedicine to link rural health centres with referral centres; establishing an evaluation centre to screen for schistosomiasis, tuberculosis, malaria, etc.; enriching foods such as salt and cooking oil to prevent nutritional disorders; utilizing coconuts to ease protein-calorie deficiencies; training village communicators as unofficial health workers; and planning radio broadcasts for a 4-year period to spread priority health messages. (AC)

2941 **Primary Health Care Programme Formulation Committee, Khartoum.** *Primary health care programme: eastern, northern, central and western regions of the Sudan, 1977/78-1983/84.* Khartoum, Khartoum University Press, May 1976. 251p. Engl. See also entries 2899 and 2942.

The national health plan originally implemented in the southern Sudan is applied to the rest of the country. Four sub-programmes were selected for priority consideration: the design of a health information system, provision of drugs and supplies, meeting health manpower and facility needs in these areas, and encouraging community development and self-reliance. These programmes apply to the whole country but must be adapted to local conditions. Consequently, this document provides: separate job descriptions and training procedures for workers in settled and nomadic communities, recommendations for design and equipment of primary health care units that conform to those of the national plan but with details that are region-specific, and proposals for community participation that involve liaison with existing village organizations of the area. After a summary of the plan, comprehensive appendices provide details of the information and referral systems to be adopted and costs of all the proposals. (DM)

2942 **Primary Health Care Programme Formulation Committee, Khartoum.** *Primary health care programme: southern region Sudan, 1977/78-1983/84.* Khartoum, Khartoum University Press, Feb 1976. 153p. Engl. See also entries 2899 and 2941.

Strategies for implementing a primary health care programme in the southern region of Sudan are described. A situation analysis based on existing records and brief field observation trips is followed by: an account of the proposed primary health care system; a study of manpower needs and methods of recruitment, training, placement, and supervision; an information system for record-keeping and programme evaluation, usable in the primary health units; a study of procurement, distribution, and costs of drugs and supplies; methods for encouraging community participation and self-reliance; and identification of those areas that would benefit from external assistance. The proposals are backed up by: job description outlines for all primary care personnel; specifications for design and equipment of health facilities; diagrams to illustrate administration, information, and referral networks; a summary of medical record-keeping procedures; and detailed analysis of costs. (DM)

2943 **Putsep, E.P.** *Some thoughts on scheduling, design and building of health centres and hospitals to be used for medical and paramedical teaching.* World Hospitals (Oxford, UK), 11(2 and 3), Jun 1975, 169-173. Engl. 24 refs.

Some considerations regarding the scheduling and design of the basic layout of a teaching hospital (medical or paramedical) under conditions of limited resources are set forward. There are three main phases in the process. The 1st phase involves determining: the hospital's relationship to existing and planned health care facilities; its responsibilities within the total health care network; its effect on existing hospitals, especially in terms of staff; and the advances in medical knowledge, medical technology, hygiene, and hospital administration that are relevant to its operation. This phase also includes the setting of two standards, or intensities, of medical care-- one for immediate and the other for later attainment. The 2nd phase involves transfering all units and departments as defined in the 1st phase into detailed spatial briefs. The final character, function, and size of the hospital and its initial and recurrent costs should be clarified at this point. The 3rd stage consists of developing the design in consultation with administrators, medical staff, and student union. It is stressed that there is no standard teaching hospital and that those that have been based on models from the developed countries have proven of doubtful value in the developing world. The planning of teaching hospitals should be based, rather, on a study of the latest trends in medicine, hospital organization, and technology but should be so simplified as to correspond to present manpower and financial resources. Some discussion of the limits to medicine, medical equipment, obsolescence, horizontal versus vertical construction, zoning, and the 'indeterminate' hospital is included. (HC)

2944 **Richter, H.B.** *Planning and building health care facilities in view of operational techniques: the supply system.* World Hospitals (Oxford, UK), 11(2 and 3), Jun 1975, 124-128. Engl. 17 refs.

The fact that hospital supply services have a higher cost coefficient per square metre than any other department except the surgical suite has prompted concern over the inappropriate and/or inadequate provision made for them during the planning stages. When setting up the supply services in a hospital in a developing country, two essential points should be kept in mind. The 1st is that since developing countries abound in cheap, unskilled labour, mechanical equipment should be kept to a minimum and subject to these conditions: there exists an adequate source of electricity, gas, oil, or water to power it; it can be simply and safely operated by unskilled hands; it is easily maintained; and a standby solution enables the department to function in the event of its breakdown. The 2nd point is that infection control assumes an even greater importance where unskilled labour takes the place of mechanization. In order to optimize infection control, hospital design should provide for: the separation of clean and soiled traffic; extensive utilization of contamination barriers; a shower at the exit of the laundry area; dressing rooms at the entrance to the central sterile supply room to facilitate gowning technique; smooth, washable walls and floors; laundry and trash chutes with smooth surfaces and perfectly-sealed doors; etc. It is further suggested that, because of economy in equipment, greater productivity, and safety through better control over unqualified staff, all sterilizing and food preparation functions be centralized; bed disinfection rooms, however, should be decentralized with one to a floor. (HC)

2945   Saied, A. *Politica y programas de salud de Panama. (Panama's health programmes and policy).* Panama City, Ministerio de Salud, Departamento de Impresiones y Publicaciones, 1974. 1v.(various pagings). Span.
Panama's Minister of Health discusses national health policies in terms of philosophy (health care is a right and a duty and should be available equally to everyone), general information, health status, organization of the Ministry of Health, human and material resources, finances, and legal considerations. National health programmes are presented, including basic health programmes in maternal child health, adult health, and environmental health and support programmes in community health education and administration of national and local health activities. Annexes include statistical data and reports on communicable diseases, community health services and community participation, and an integrated community health programme. (RMB)

2946   Shamsuddin, M. WHO, Brazzaville. *Development of basic services (North-Central State).* Brazzaville, WHO, 26 May 1972. 15p. Engl.
In 1966-1967, the author participated in a WHO project to prepare and implement a health development plan for northern Nigeria and train paramedical personnel. The principal health problems of the area included a shortage of health manpower and dispensaries, high infant and maternal mortality, lack of environmental sanitation, lack of health education services, and an incomplete system of data collection. Aspects of the proposed 4-year health development plan and its training and implementation facets are discussed. The author makes recommendations concerning the construction of rural

health centres, the operation of a demonstrative zone, health manpower, statistics, and the utilization of WHO personnel. (RMB)

2947   Sheriff, M.P. *Calculation, tendering, cost-control and organization of the building phase.* World Hospitals (Oxford, UK), 11(2 and 3), Jun 1975, 98-103. Engl.
Too often, when the building for a health facility in a developing country is ready for occupancy, one or all of the following situations have arisen: the original cost limits have been exceeded, the building fails to meet or exceeds the real needs of its users, and the building is too expensive to staff or maintain efficiently. In this paper, a number of suggestions for avoiding these outcomes are put forward. Those related to the design phase include: presenting the project in as much detail as possible; adapting the project to local environmental conditions, social expectations, and level of technical development; allowing for maximum use of standard components that the degree of industrialization of the country can afford; making all mechanical and electrical installations easily accessible and amenable to extension; and ensuring that the technical solution offered allows for quick and ordered system of erection. During the tendering phase, consideration should be given to on-going costs as well as basic costs and the different proposals should be carefully evaluated; discussion of the disadvantages of commissioning a building from an international firm is included in this section. The recommendations concerning the building phase include: drawing up a plan that clearly indicates the sequence of the different building trades to ensure that they do not interfere with one another and that damages incurred during construction are minimal, defining the obligations of the owner and the contractor as clearly as possible in the contract, and discussing the price of any change or extension with the contractor before giving an order to modify the plan. Finally, government bureaucracies are urged to expedite the approval projects, lest their inefficiency be the cause of additional costs and delays in much-needed health facilities. (HC)

2948   Shutt, M.M. USA, Agency for International Development, Department of State. *AID experience in the development and evaluation of integrated health delivery systems.* Washington, D.C., Agency for International Development, Technical Assistance Bureau, Office of Health, 1976. 16p. Engl.
Providing acceptable health services in developing countries requires preliminary assessment of available resources, ranking of priorities, and planning. The US Agency for International Development (AID) can support such studies prior to any radical modifications of the existing systems. The host country does most of the planning and provides basic local operation costs; AID helps with the costs of starting and evaluating projects and staff training. The agency is now involved with 25 systems in 23 countries and coordinates its work with the contributions of WHO, UNICEF, and other organizations. Its activities include implementing methodology

II Organization and Planning

39

for training health paraprofessionals and auxiliaries, developing information exchange and evaluation guidelines, surveying health delivery systems, and providing technical expertise in health and family planning. In addition, it offers consultative services at no cost by drawing on the resources of its own limited number of professionals. AID also relies upon other US organizations, professional and voluntary associations, and universities for expertise, while it is increasingly drawing upon experience of the developing world itself to help other countries. It is barely 5 years since the agency began looking at the feasibility of low-cost, integrated health care systems, but the demand for such systems is now great. AID support helps to minimize the political and budgetary risks to the developing world and at the same time assists in the development of practical and useful methodologies. Tables of AID projects are attached. (HH)

2949   Solomon, M.J. *Designing social projects without reliance on market demand.* In Sespaniak, L., Solomon, M.J., Preparing, Evaluating, and Managing Development Projects, Ibadan, University of Ife, May 1973, 11.13-11.19. Engl.
See also entry 2950.
To design projects to meet social requirements rather than economic demand, present and probable future needs must be determined and a study made of current efforts to meet them, because it is usually easier to modify existing systems than to start afresh. It is important at this stage to distinguish between real needs, such as new skills, and means to meet them, such as vocational schools. The latter are not real requirements and there may well be better alternatives. Also, the level of service needed must be defined with exact specifications both of quality and quantity. The desirable level usually exceeds the resources of the area, so a series of possible systems of varying sophistication should be worked out. For medical care provision these levels would range from the simple health centre, staffed by auxiliaries, to the well-equipped general hospital. Inputs and outputs must be clearly defined for each of these levels, an exercise that may stimulate a search for new alternatives. Having determined all possibilities, the planners must estimate the costs of each, not only the initial investment needed but also the yearly running expenses, before selecting the optimal system for implementation. (DM)

2950   Solomon, M.J. *Village health centre.* In Sespaniak, L., Solomon, M.J., Preparing, Evaluating, and Managing Development Projects, Ibadan, University of Ife, May 1973, 12.1-12.7. Engl.
See also entry 2949.
Leaders of a village of 25 000 people in the Western State of Nigeria requested a survey to assess health needs in the area. Ideally, such a study should identify health problems and felt needs of four categories of people: those who use the existing clinics, those who seek Western facilities outside the village, those who rely on tradi-

tional practitioners, and those who manage without recourse to any services. On the basis of this information, obtained from a specially designed questionnaire, detailed plans could be made for three levels of service, ranging from minimal improvement insufficient to satisfy the users to the type of service they would prefer. Reliable estimates of both capital and running costs are required for each level of service so that a realistic choice can be made. In the case of the Nigerian study, the cost of even the minimum level proposed exceeded the resources of the sponsors, so the plans had to be revised to consider methods of supplementing existing facilities rather than replacing them. Tables analyzing costs for the three levels of service and a sample health survey questionnaire are appended. (DM)

2951   Stewart, G.T. *Medicine and health: what connection?* Lancet (London), 1(7909), 29 Mar 1975, 705-708. Engl.
The priority goals for national health planning in developing countries must be: the application of proven preventive techniques in nutrition, maternal and child care, immunization, and epidemiological surveillance; improvements in housing, sanitation, and working conditions by local authorities, builders, and industry; and promotion of family planning. Each of these measures must include health education that uses the mass media, community organizations, and mobile education units to reach deprived groups. To meet these priority needs, the health budget must be suitably divided among preventive programmes, primary care, and secondary medical services. The latter may be improved by increasing the number of doctors in a developing country, but this expensive measure does not automatically contribute to the more important frontline and preventive services. To persuade doctors and nurses to join health teams with auxiliary workers, governments must introduce regulations and incentives and a period of service in a community health or primary care team should be included in all medical training. However, the provision of primary care alone is not sufficient to ensure the desired impact. The health service must be seen to be effective to participants, patients, and administrators alike. This can only be achieved by continuous evaluation of the work in relation to local needs, an assessment that is best carried out by the team itself. (DM)

2952   Stipek, J. *Facilities for outpatient care.* World Hospitals (Oxford, UK), 11(2 and 3), Jun 1975, 150-157. Engl.
19 refs.
Functional and architectural solutions to the various grades of outpatient services required in a developing country are discussed. These include: the health unit--a basic, permanent facility staffed by a local resident with elementary knowledge of nursing; the health station or subcentre--a facility staffed by nurses or health auxiliaries with accommodation for consulting, examination and treatment, beds for patients awaiting transport to the hospital, living quarters for staff, and space for equipment such as a diesel generator; the health centre--a facility staffed by a general practitioner and a health

Low-Cost Rural Health Care and Health Manpower Training

team and equipped to handle approximately 90 curative and 60 preventive cases per day plus a few inpatients; and outpatient clinics--facilities offering general and specialist services that may or may not be attached to a hospital. Some considerations specific to the construction of these facilities in a developing country are that: natural ventilation in health centres and subcentres should be ensured through a judicious choice of site, orientation, and architectural solution; health centres and subcentres should develop their own electrical power, water supply, and sewage systems rather than rely on local ones; construction solutions should differ in hot and humid as opposed to hot and arid zones (examples of each are illustrated); and structural solutions should aim for maximum flexibility so that their interiors can be altered extensively and as often as necessary at a minimum of cost and in a minimum of time. Proposals for the layout of the various facilities are set forward in 17 figures; examples are taken from Czechoslovakia and various developing countries. (HC)

2953 Sudan, National Health Programming Committee. *National health programme 1977/78-1983/84.* Khartoum, Khartoum University Press, Apr 1975. 204p. Engl.
  Individual chapters have been abstracted separately under entries 2842, 2954, and 2955; see also entries 2941 and 2942.
The National Health Programming Committee (CHP) reports its investigation into Sudan's health problems and proposes feasible strategies based on the national health policy and emphasizing preventive and social medicine, environmental health, comprehensive primary health care, improvement of existing curative facilities, and training of health manpower. The report is presented in two sections. The 1st summarizes the background socioeconomic, demographic, and health data used by the committee. It points out the present deficiencies within the health service, especially the inadequacy of medical record-keeping. The 2nd half of the report consists of the CHP's proposals. For each health problem, the report outlines: disease data, objectives, and strategy of the proposed campaign; costs in staff and services; expected benefits (social, political, and economic); and constraints (financial, institutional, and logistic). Comprehensive annexes provide the data on which the report was based and explain the methods adopted by the CHP to arrive at its conclusions and recommendations. (DM)

2954 Sudan, National Health Programming Committee. *Primary health care services--general.* In National Health Programme 1977/78-1983/84, Khartoum, Khartoum University Press, Apr 1975, 63-82. Engl.
  For complete document see entry 2953.
The aim of Sudan's national primary health care plan for 1975-1984 is to establish a service accessible to the entire population by setting up primary health care complexes, each consisting of 1 dispensary and 5 primary health care units (PHCUs) covering a total population of 24 000. The PHCUs are each to be staffed by 1 primary health

care worker (PHCW) selected from the local community by the Village Development Committee and trained to carry out simple preventive, promotive, and curative measures under the supervision of dispensary staff. The dispensaries are each to be staffed by 1 medical assistant, 1 nurse, and 1 cleaner. They will provide much the same services as the PHCUs but will also be responsible for supervision. The overall plan depends on good transport and communication facilities and the cooperation of local people who have been educated about the aims and limitations of the services. Other essentials are: early training, including reorientation courses for supervisory staff; job descriptions for all workers; details of recruitment, curriculum, educational objectives, in-service training provision, and systems for evaluation; estimates of required equipment and costs; and identification of intermediate targets for each province within the 9-year period. (DM)

2955 Sudan, National Health Programming Committee. *Development policy in health services.* In National Health Programme 1977/78-1983/84, Khartoum, Khartoum University Press, Apr 1975, 36-41. Engl.
  For complete document see entry 2953.
Health care planning in the Sudan involves decision-making at both national and regional levels: the priorities and budget for the current 5-year plan are determined nationally and specific proposals are drawn up by provincial and district committees and submitted to the Ministry of Health for approval. Decision-making bodies could be aided by the central information system that was developed after 1967, but at present medical record-keeping is inadequate and the system needs to be updated. The implementation of health plans requires the cooperation of the government departments responsible for construction, equipment, transport, water, and power, but lack of coordination among these agencies and shortage of resources, such as foreign currency, transport facilities, and trained health manpower, have combined to slow progress. (DM)

2956 Tribhuvan University, Kathmandu. *Rural health needs: report of a 1977 study in the primary health care unit (district) of Dhankuta, Nepal.* Kathmandu, Tribhuvan University, Institute of Medicine, Health Manpower Development Research Project, 1977. 36p. Engl.
This study of health needs and services in eastern Nepal was designed to provide basic information for planning the country's health care delivery system and for making the curricula of Tribhuvan University's various health personnel training programmes more need- and problem-oriented. The university's Institute of Medicine trained and supervised the survey team who interviewed selected households about their health status, practices, and utilization of government and private health resources. Additional information was gathered within health care institutions by interviews, work sampling, task analysis, and analysis of service records. Although the sample size was small and reporting of illnesses was relatively low, the survey showed that most sickness

needing care and most infant deaths could have been prevented. Even though almost all the time of health personnel is taken up with curative rather than preventive work, government programmes meet at most only 8% of the estimated need for curative services. The overriding factor determining low utilization rates in this district is distance; therefore wider coverage, enlarged and improved domiciliary services, and better understanding about health and maternity care are needed for the widely scattered population. (AB)

2957 USA, Agency for International Development, Department of State. *Guatemala: health services; proposal and recommendations for the review of the Development Loan Committee.* Washington, D.C., Agency for International Development, 3 Jun 1971. 1v.(various pagings). Engl.
See also entry 3415.

In 1971, the Agency for International Development (USA) assisted the government of Guatemala in a project to improve the quality of Guatemala's health care system. Section 1 of this document contains a project description and evaluation covering: the project's objectives; technical aspects, such as the rehabilitation of the auxiliary training school, the technical criteria for the construction and equipping of rural health posts, the radio network, the handling and delivery of medical supplies, maintenance, and technical assistance; training aspects, including the selection and training of teachers, medical assistants, medical maintenance technicians, auxiliary nurses, health promoters, and midwives and the funding of the training school; planning aspects; financial aspects, including alternative sources of funding; and the Ministry of Health. Section 2 deals with the project background, Section 3 with its economic and social evaluation, and Section 4 with problems and reliability of the construction schedule. In Section 5, the implementation plan is presented, covering such aspects as project execution, procurement and disbursement, reporting and evaluation, loan monitoring, and loan terms and conditions. Annexes contain various project documents. (RMB)

2958 Werner, D.B. Commonwealth Foundation, London. National Fund for Research into Crippling Diseases, Arundel, UK. *Health and human dignity: a subjective look at community-based rural health programmes in Latin America.* In Disabled in Developing Countries, London, Commonwealth Foundation, 1977, 75-96. Engl.
Symposium on Appropriate Technology and Delivery of Health and Welfare Services for the Disabled in Developing Countries, Oxford, UK, 26-30 Sep 1976.
For complete document see entry 3124.

Rural health programmes for Latin America should be decentralized and aimed at community self-sufficiency in costs and personnel, so that they can, if necessary, continue without the support of outside agencies. Projects should be open-ended to allow for evolution and growth and should involve the continuing education of local health workers in all aspects of community welfare.

Projects may, under certain circumstances, openly seek social reforms, but they can always promote social awareness by utilizing the often underestimated understanding, intelligence, and capabilities of rural villagers themselves. In order to maintain the respect of the villagers, local health workers must be allowed to diagnose, give initial treatment, and dispense drugs that are usually indiscriminately available on the black market. Directors, doctors, and other key personnel in any programme must adopt a humane and supportive role, always feeding back information on referral cases, for example, and generally encouraging the maximum range of skills in each worker. Outlines of trends and approaches to rural health programmes in Latin America are appended. (HH)

2959 WHO, Brazzaville. *Planification sanitaire a long terme pour la region africaine: 1975-2000. (Long term health planning for the African region: 1975-2000).* Brazzaville, WHO, 8 Oct 1974. 28p. Fren.

WHO recommendations regarding long-term (1975-2000) planning in the African region focus on health manpower development, environmental sanitation, epidemiologic surveillance and communicable disease control, and the strengthening of basic health services. Resolutions are expressed first in terms of overall objectives and then in terms of specific accomplishments within a time frame (e.g., pure water to be brought to 20% of the rural population by 1980, to 50% by 1990, and to 90% by 2000) or, in the case of health manpower development, specific personnel-to-population ratios (e.g., 1 doctor : 5 000-10 000 population, 1 nurse : 300 population, 1 midwife : 300 population, 1 auxiliary : 100 population, etc.). It is hoped that such projections will prove useful to governments in formulating their national health plans. A summary of current socioeconomic conditions in the region prefaces the recommendations. (HC)

2960 WHO, Brazzaville. *Technical operations in country health programming.* Brazzaville, WHO, 1974. 1v.(various pagings). Engl.
Workshop on Country Health Programming, Brazzaville, Congo, 4-22 Mar 1974.

These guidelines for conducting health surveys and formulating and implementing health strategies are designed to take into account the characteristics of a country's present socioeconomic system, the evaluation of the present and potential demand for health services, the structure and resources of the health system, and the attitudes of consumers and health workers. A two-phase operation is presented. The preparatory phase deals with information collection and analysis. The programming phase covers health survey methodologies, the formulation of health strategies and the analysis of their technical feasibility, a feasibility analysis of health development programmes, and the preparation, presentation, and handling of a country health programming document. (RMB)

2961   WHO, Geneva. *Something for all and more for those in greater need: a risk approach for integrated maternal and child health care.* WHO Chronicle (Geneva), 31(4), Apr 1977, 150-151. Engl.

Also published in French, Russian, and Spanish.

The 'risk approach' is a strategy advocated by WHO to make optimal use of existing resources for the benefit of an entire population. In the case of maternal and child health (MCH), the strategy involves: studying baseline data and the main factors influencing maternal and child health; identifying, according to local priorities, the main threats to maternal and child health; selecting indicators of the presence of these threats; developing a weighted scoring system for the most useful indicators; and developing a strategy of care whereby resources are allocated according to level of need. Since implementation of the strategy will necessitate contact, however superficial, with every mother and child in the relevant age group, community members (members of women's groups, schoolteachers, traditional birth attendants, or even mothers themselves) will need to be trained in screening techniques. Thus, while nominally directed at at-risk women and children, the approach should lead to greater awareness of health at the grassroots and improvement in both coverage and quality of health care at all levels. The strategy is to be tested in two pilot areas in Turkey. (HC)

2962   WHO, Geneva. *Report of the consultation on appropriate technology for health.* Geneva, WHO, Jan 1977. 28p. Engl.

A consultation to review the WHO Programme for Appropriate Technology for Health and initiate a series of short-term procedures in preparation for a longer term programme for 1978-83 emphasized the need to support appropriate technology as an integral part of health in rural development. The group selected for initial work four specific priorities for appropriate health technologies, including village obstetrics, oral rehydration, nutritional deficiency screening, and aspects of immunization technologies. At the local level, non-governmental organizations such as intermediate technology groups and the Christian Medical Commission could work especially effectively, whereas WHO could facilitate linkage among official organizations within regional and national contexts. WHO regional responsibility should lie with interdisciplinary primary health care groups, who can compile information on problems needing technological solutions for circulation by the WHO Interdivisional Coordinating Committee. The coordinating committee could stimulate mutual collaboration with other UN agencies through the Joint Services Group (JOSEG) and advise on contracting with the Appropriate Health Resources and Technologies Action Group (AHR-TAG). An annex to the consultation report identifies 27 detailed technological needs and the current state of corresponding new appropriate technologies as well as a large number of other potential areas for the programme's work. (CL)

2963   WHO, Geneva. *Disability prevention and rehabilitation.* Geneva, WHO, 28 Apr 1976. 69p. Engl. 79 refs.

Twenty-ninth World Health Assembly, Geneva, Switzerland, Apr 1976.

Individual chapter has been abstracted separately under entry 2969.

This report describes the global problem of disability and suggests a new policy and programmes for dealing with it. The operational definitions of disability, the magnitude of the problem, its causes and probable future trends, present rehabilitation services, and the role of WHO are examined. The report analyzes the motivation for and goals of disability prevention and rehabilitation, the programme objectives, the prevention of disability, and the organization and administration of coordinated national disability prevention services. Prevention is defined as social intervention to reduce the occurrence of impairment of physical or mental function as well as intervention in the health sector. Since present medical rehabilitation services are unlikely to meet needs in the foreseeable future, auxiliaries working at community level will be needed. A coordinated national approach combining prevention and rehabilitation within the framework of the general health services is recommended. Guidelines for planning, programming, and implementation are given. (HH)

2964   WHO, Geneva. Kleczkowski, B.M. Pibouleau, R. *Approaches to planning and design of health care facilities in developing areas. Volume 1.* Geneva, WHO, Offset Publication No.29, 1976. 145p. Engl. 8 refs.

Volume 1 of this series on approaches to planning and design of health care facilities in developing areas covers: legislation and administration for medical care facilities, with special reference to developing countries; the role of area-wide planning and functional programming in the planning process of medical care; rationalization of medical care buildings in developing countries; advanced building techniques and their utilization in developing countries; and the influence of climate on buildings. Statistical data, diagrams, and floorplans are included. Other volumes in this series will deal with prerequisites for planning, area-wide planning, tools for planning, planning of individual facilities, planning of parts of facilities, and building construction and operation. (RMB)

2965   WHO, Geneva. *Statistical indices of family health: report of a WHO study group.* Geneva, WHO, Technical Report Series No.587, 1976. 92p. Engl. 203 refs.

Also published in French, Russian, and Spanish.

A WHO study group surveyed recent developments and current activities in the measurement of family health, identified and evaluated indices of family health, considered the components of a family health data bank, drew up a list of research priorities, and recommended future activities. The indices of family health are classified as demographic, mental health, physical and organic health, social, and family planning; problems related to the measurement of each type are discussed and a proposed list of indicators appended. Some 15 recommendations for WHO action to stimulate interest among its member-countries in the development of indices of family health are set down. (HC)

2966   WHO, Geneva. *Application of systems analysis to health management: report of a WHO expert committee.* Geneva, WHO, Technical Report Series No.596, 1976. 69p. Engl.
WHO Expert Committee on the Application of Systems Analysis to Health Management, Geneva, Switzerland, 16-22 Dec 1975.
Also published in French, Russian, and Spanish.
WHO has, over the past 5 years, conducted successful research into the application of systems analysis to health administration. A 'systems approach' is defined as the perception of natural or man-made entities as sets of interacting parts; systems analysis consists of methods of making practical use of the knowledge of how these interacting parts operate, how they are managed, and how information flows through them. In general, systems analysis seeks to define the relationships existing in a system (and between other systems) and to calculate the effects of altering either the elements of the system or the ways in which they interact. The application of systems analysis is particularly useful in health management in that it provides for: consideration of all variables, over and above the biological and technical, that effect health intervention programmes; a planning approach that relates input to output; an emphasis on quantification; rigour in analytical methods; orientation towards health problems rather than categories of service; communication with key governmental decision-making centres that utilize comparable methods; etc. In this report, the history, accomplishments, and problems encountered during the application of systems analysis in a number of member countries are discussed and some recommendations aimed at helping national authorities to derive maximal benefit from the systems approach are set forward. (HC)

2967   WHO, Geneva. IBRD, Washington, D.C. *Health and rural development: main report, technical background papers, and summary.* Geneva, WHO, 1975. 3v. Engl.
This document was submitted to the World Bank (IBRD) as WHO's contribution to an assessment of the views and efforts of all UN and affiliated agencies in the field of rural development. The various chapters discuss: characteristics and dimensions of poverty in the Third World and some key aspects in the process of alleviating it; the rationale behind choosing priority fields of health intervention and selecting health inputs; priority fields of health intervention--nutrition, infectious disease control, reproductive health and fertility, and environmental sanitation; an operational definition of rural health development; WHO--its role, structure, and programming process; and future policies and programmes. Attached to the report are annexes that present the statistical data on which the analyses in the lst 2 chapters are based and background data on WHO's organization, programme structure, and 1975 expenditures on technical cooperation activities that are of benefit to rural populations. The report is accompanied by a series of technical background papers that justify the choice of, and analyze the major issues in, each field of intervention considered to be of high priority for rural development. (HC)

2968   WHO, Geneva. *Forward together: appropriate technology for health.* Geneva, WHO, n.d. 5p. Engl.
Also published in French and Spanish.
Recently WHO launched a programme dedicated to promoting appropriate technology in developing countries. From 1978-1983, the programme will be planning strategies to research equipment, tools, devices, chemicals, drugs, etc., that are effective, low-cost means to deal with health problems. Examples include: household treatment of diarrhea by oral rehydration; simple field methods of sterilizing medical equipment, diagnosing nutritional disorders, and ensuring vaccine efficacy; and effective but inexpensive two-way communications systems. (AC)

2969   WHO, Geneva. *Prevention of disability.* In Disability Prevention and Rehabilitation, Geneva, WHO, 28 Apr 1976, 34-41. Engl.
Twenty-ninth World Health Assembly, Geneva, Switzerland, Apr 1976.
For complete document see entry 2963.
A wide range of measures can be employed to prevent the onset or worsening of disability. Early intervention to avoid congenital disabling diseases can include genetic counseling, contraception and abortion, vaccination, education, and legislation to reduce accidents in the home, at work, and on the roads. Non-genetic congenital disorders related to maternal nutrition and communicable diseases can be prevented by health education, sanitation, attacks on biological vectors, and medical intervention to counteract the effects of malnutrition. Environmental factors also contribute to non-communicable diseases and social problems can cause psychiatric disturbances, alcoholism, and drug abuse. Since it is obvious that not all of the factors contributing to disability can be overcome, once an impairment has occurred it is vital to try to prevent any long-term functional limitation. Remedial actions include: early diagnosing of mental retardation, hearing, and visual problems; administering effective first aid; avoiding the infection of wounds; and giving adequate care to chronic cases. Even when long-term somatic or mental limitation has developed, disability can be avoided by medical, social, vocational, and educational assistance to help the patient achieve self-care, economic independence, and social integration. This type of rehabilitation requires the provision of training, simple aids, suitable accommodation, educational opportunities in line with those of the rest of the population, and education of society to accept the handicapped. In developing countries, some treatments will be too costly to be given priority and money should

be spent to prevent disability rather than to manage existing cases. (HH)

II.4 Geographic Distribution of Health Services

See also: 2851, 2878, 2883, 2910, 3012, 3129, 3214, 3436

2970   Calvert, P. *Doctors and the rural community.* Papua New Guinea Medical Journal (Port Moresby), 15(4), Dec 1972, 221-224. Engl.
To achieve more effective distribution of physicians in Papua New Guinea, the author proposes a plan for the establishment of rural hospitals that would serve a coherent community rather than a designated geographical area or a specific populaton. This strategy would maximize service accessibility, minimize language problems, and ensure a degree of economic and cultural uniformity among the patients. Moreover, the presence of a doctor at the community level would strengthen the morale of the auxiliary personnel by allowing them to take over much of the clinical work, preventive medicine, and training without lowering standards of care or efficiency. A number of measures for making rural service more satisfying to doctors are discussed, including the introduction of a postgraduate diploma in rural practice, which would have as a prerequisite at least 2 years rural service and evidence of original research into some aspect of rural health. Coursework would include such subjects as clinical ability in the absence of sophisticated diagnostic aids, personnel management, teaching methodology, etc. It is recommended that these and other methods aimed at decentralizing medical manpower be given highest priority. (HC)

2971   Chuttani, C.S. Bhatia, J.C. Dharmvir Timmappaya, A. *Factors responsible for underutilisation of primary health centre: a community survey in three states of India.* NIHAE Bulletin (New Delhi), 9(3), 1976, 229-237. Engl.
A community survey covering 10% of local village families was carried out in four community development blocks in three Indian states to study the utilization of government health care services provided through primary health centres and subcentres. Answers to interviewers' questions indicated that the responders' awareness of the existence of these health services decreased in direct proportion to the distance of their villages from the health centres and that their utilization practices followed the same pattern. About 51% of the villagers sampled who had used these services at one time or another were dissatisfied for a variety of reasons, including lack of medicines, treatment failure, and the impersonal behaviour of the medical and auxiliary staff. The authors point out that utilization of health centres might improve if the causes for patient dissatisfaction were removed, although no suggestions on how to make more people aware of their existence are made. Statistical data are included. (RMB)

2972   Good, B.J. *Professionalization of medicine in a provincial Iranian town.* Health Care Dimensions (Philadelphia, Pa.), 3, 51-65. Engl.
32 refs.
The conflict between traditional and modern practitioners in an Iranian town is described. In their attempts to monopolize the health care system, Western-trained physicians may eliminate an important segment, traditional practitioners, before they can replace them and adequately meet health care needs, especially in rural areas. This style of medicine professionalization also poses a serious threat to the development of innovative programmes for rural health auxiliaries, whose training is opposed by modern doctors on the grounds that such auxiliaries would be beyond their control. The author warns that these professional attitudes are a major obstacle to equitable distribution of health care services in Iran. (RMB)

2973   Heller, T. *Limits to health care planning.* Institute of Development Studies Bulletin (Brighton, UK), 8(1, UK), 1976, 17-20. Engl.
55 refs.
The effective pattern of health care in any country is determined by the struggle between market and central plan ideologies and not by the intentions of the health delivery planners. Redistribution of facilities in favour of the underprivileged is generally resisted by those with political and economic power, including most of the medical profession. In a market economy, plans to make young doctors serve in rural areas fail because such service for professional people is not part of the political consensus. Health personnel tend to migrate to posts with the highest rewards and often manage to leave developing countries, even in the face of emigration controls. Those who remain can maintain exclusive control over medical services by failing to provide training and supervision for auxiliaries and by supporting restrictive legislation. Even when health facilities are theoretically available to the poor, they are seldom used by those most in need because of their poor quality and cultural dissonance. The Chinese have overcome these problems by adopting an approach to health similar to their plans for other aspects of development: health care delivery is subject to local decisions, health personnel are treated no differently from other workers, and the service provided includes both well-accepted traditional methods and modern techniques of proven efficacy. However, the applicability of the Chinese system elsewhere is not yet known. (DM)

2974   Philippines, Department of Health. Development Academy of the Philippines, Quezon City. *Technical report: health facilities in the MBMR.* Quezon City, Philippines, Task Force on Human Settlements, Development Academy of the Philippines, Mar 1975. 37p. Engl.
A survey and report of the health facilities in the Manila Bay Metropolitan Region is set forth; it constitutes part of a wider investigation into human settlements and comprises data on the number and distribution of hospitals and rural health units. Most of the information was

taken from a 1973 annual report on government and private hospitals prepared by the Philippine Department of Health. Other sources included reports from the health planning division and the Bureau of Census and Statistics. The findings indicate the maldistribution of health services and provide a basis for planning more equitable delivery. Recommendations based on the findings include: the establishment of rural health units in municipalities not currently served by hospitals; the upgrading of provincial hospitals; the introduction of incentives, such as low-interest loans, for private hospitals, etc. (AC)

2975 Vargas Martinez, H. Gutierrez Saenz, R. Rodriguez A., C. *Distribucion de medicos en Costa Rica. (Distribution of physicians in Costa Rica).* Educacion Medica y Salud (Washington, D.C.), 10(3), 1976, 280-292. Span.

This article provides detailed information on the location of physicians in Costa Rica and their medical specialties; these data were obtained from a 1967-1975 survey. The authors emphasize the apparent correlation between the development of health institutions, the characteristics of health care provided, and the level of a nation's economic development. (RMB)

II.5 Financial Aspects

See also: 2885, 2899, 2923, 2944, 2947, 2948, 3026, 3062, 3066

2976 Abel-Smith, B. *Value for money in health services: a comparative study.* London, Heinemann, 1976. 230p. Engl.

This book is based on the assumption that a study of the market for health services and the way it operates in different cultures and at different levels of development is relevant to health planning today. The book begins with a description of the historical evolution of the organization and financing of health services in a number of different countries; it is shown that, as better techniques of individual treatment were developed, ways were sought to make them available to those who could not afford to purchase them on the open market. In some countries, medical charities arose and in others governments intervened; at the same time, workers and doctors developed simple, prepaid medical schemes that provided a precedent for compulsory insurance and national health services. The book goes on to explore: the case for free, or subsidized, health services; the effect of different ways of paying doctors on the quality and cost of medical care; the effects of the international drug companies on prescribing habits and the cost of medical care; the principles governing the efficient planning and utilization of hospital services; and value judgments in health planning. No one system of paying for health care is advocated over another; rather, the advantages and disadvantages of each are pointed out. Some guidelines to more cost-conscious planning for health in the developed and developing countries, respectively, are discussed and some changes in the attitudes, ethics, and commitment that are currently instilled in medical students are recommended. (HC)

2977 Binns, C.W. *Financing church related medical work in Papua New Guinea.* Papua New Guinea Medical Journal (Port Moresby), 15(4), Dec 1972, 242-245. Engl.

According to estimates of the World Bank, church-related agencies in Papua New Guinea received 10% of the medical work just prior to independence. Since this situation was likely to continue after independence, an inquiry into the financing of these facilities was undertaken. A survey of the major agencies operating within the country revealed that most were nearing a financial crisis: most were being forced to raise their salaries in order to compete with those of government; some had stopped providing food for patients; half were charging fee-for-service, which represented only a small percentage of the actual cost; and four had instituted health insurance schemes. All agencies were receiving some government assistance, which was used generally toward running costs and indigenous salaries. It is concluded that in view of the fact that the standard of care provided in rural areas by these agencies cannot be easily duplicated by the Ministry of Health, more government assistance to them could only be beneficial to the country. (HC)

2978 Chowdhury, Z. *Research: a method of colonization.* Dacca, Gonoshasthaya Kendra (People's Health Centre), n.d. 12p. Engl.
9 refs.
Modified version published in Bangladesh Times, 13-14 Jan 1977.

Much of the foreign medical aid now pouring into Bangladesh is of more value to the donors than to the recipients. This is especially true of research programmes. For instance, the proposed International Institute for Health, Population, and Nutrition Research will provide few opportunities for Bangladeshi scientists and will establish a United States monopoly over medical research in the country. Most of the funds will be devoted to salaries and benefits for the expatriate staff and opportunities for training and research will mainly go to foreigners. The activities of the Cholera Research Laboratory have shown that the areas of study are seldom of benefit to the local people, who are sometimes used as an experimental population for testing medications. Commercial factors also influence research topics and there is even evidence that mention of side effects from an injectable contraceptive were omitted in a report by the John Hopkins Fertility Research Project, presumably to hasten widespread use. Even the most well-intentioned foreign experts have an inadequate understanding of local needs and their recommendations are often inappropriate. For instance, WHO experts, while recognizing the need for health auxiliaries to provide primary care in rural Bangladesh, proposed an elaborate town-based 3-year medical assistants' training course for candidates with 12 years' formal schooling behind them, a system bound to produce an elite group with a preference for urban comforts. There are numerous other examples of the abuses of present medical aid to Bangladesh, but that does not mean that no aid is beneficial. It should be quite possible to distinguish between "invested" aid of this sort and appropriate aid by a rational assessment of proposals at the planning stage. (DM)

2979   Dunnill, P. Intermediate Technology Development Group, London. *Provision of drugs by appropriate technology.* Appropriate Technology (London), 4(2), Aug 1977, 16-17. Engl.
      See also entries 2980, 2982, and 2983.

The manufacture of drugs by hand or simple machines presents no insuperable technical problems to developing countries, although the production of basic chemicals and active ingredients that conform to high quality control standards is more difficult. Most raw material must therefore be imported at present. However, many other aspects of drug provision for the developing world, such as formulation, packaging, and storage to suit local conditions, could be undertaken on a very small scale in the recipient country if pharmaceutical auxiliaries were trained and equipped for these tasks. Carrying out these activities locally would reduce the cost of pharmaceutical imports, but still greater savings are possible if the government controls the range of drugs used, imports from the cheapest suppliers, and supports other appropriate technologies such as packaging, storage, and stock recycling methods that reduce secondary costs and wastage. Implementing the necessary reforms would also require government action to ensure the supply of small quantities of material to rural centres as well as control over imports and the development of new industries. Assistance with the various needed technologies could come from independent non-profit agencies such as the Intermediate Technology Development Group. (DM)

2980   Haslemere Group, London. War on Want, London. Third World First, Oxford, UK. *Who needs the drug companies?* London, Haslemere Group, n.d. 44p. Engl.
      150 refs.
      See also entries 2979, 2982, and 2983.

The abnormally high profits of the drug industry result from the monopoly power of multinational corporations. Patent protection and pricing policies keep drug costs to the consumer artificially high and prevent development of indigenous drug industries in the Third World using local raw materials. Despite these high profit margins, only 10% of the industries' income is used for research and development, compared with 20% for promotion and advertising, and much of the research effort is devoted to minor alterations of established drugs rather than genuine innovations. Only 1% of all money spent on medical research is used for work on the major diseases of developing countries and yet populations from these countries are sometimes used as guinea pigs for drug trials; unethical promotion techniques are common and potentially dangerous drugs are often available over the counter without warning notes. Many of these abuses could be eliminated by voluntary changes within the drug companies, combined with greater government control, but without nationalization. Safety standards

should be tightened up; prices should be brought down by restriction of patents and by pricing controls; marketing, or at least prescription, of drugs should be by generic rather than brand names; and advertising should be curtailed or replaced by a government-controlled information service for both doctors and patients. In the long term, Third World countries should cooperate with each other in drug research and manufacture. Important though these measures are to prevent misuse of drugs, only environmental change and education can tackle the underlying causes of disease. (DM)

2981   Lall, S. *International pharmaceutical industry and less-developed countries, with special reference to India.* Oxford Bulletin of Economics and Statistics (London), 36(3), 1974, 143-172. Engl. Refs.

Today's drug industry is characterized by a large number of small, locally-owned firms that supply a marginal proportion (10%-15%) of medical preparations and a small number of large, mainly international firms that control the remainder. The concentration of such a large proportion of the market in the hands of such a small number of companies has traditionally been tolerated not because of economies of scale (for drug technology is such that large firms have no special advantage over small firms) but because of the research and development (R/D) pursued by large firms. A close examination of R/D reveals, however, that most basic research is conducted in the public sector and that private R/D funds are largely devoted to market research, imitative research, and buying up small competitors' patents. The wastefulness inherent in private control of the drug industry, especially for the developing countries, is pointed out and six alternative models for managing the industry on a national scale are put forward. The most desirable of these would consist of moving in appropriate stages toward a socially-owned indigenous pharmaceutical industry that copies foreign technology, bans brand names, and markets the products through official agencies. Examples are taken from India. (HC)

2982   Ormerod, W.E. *How can drugs for tropical diseases be produced?* SCRIP (London), No.188, 10 Jan 1976, 9-12. Engl.
      See also entries 2979, 2980, and 2983.

Especially since the introduction of stringent safety measures following the thalidomide scandal, the enormous expense of developing new drugs deters the pharmaceutical industry from research into potentially unprofitable products such as those required for the prevention and treatment of common diseases of the Third World. It would ultimately be in the companies' interests to work in these areas, because it would improve public relations and ward off nationalization, but the losses incurred might not be offset by profits from other products. This problem could be overcome by establishment of a non-profit-making "sponsor," an agency that would identify needs and invite industry and research organizations to submit likely compounds to be screened under contract by a university department. The sponsor would take full responsibility for the product and would decide whether the benefits outweighed any toxic side effects, a risk that drug companies cannot afford to take. Should any profits result from sale of a drug developed in this way they could be divided between the contributing firm and the sponsor. Ideally both national and international organizations could act as sponsors using government or private funds, but the initiative could first be taken on a small scale by a university department. (DM)

2983   Segall, M. Institute of Development Studies, University of Sussex, Brighton. *Pharmaceuticals and health planning in developing countries.* In Two Papers on Pharmaceuticals in Developing Countries, Brighton, UK, University of Sussex, Institute of Development Studies, IDS Communication No.119, 1975, 3-19. Engl.
41 refs.
See also entries 2979, 2980, and 2982.

Great savings could be made in the health budgets of developing countries by the implementation of a rational pharmaceutical policy to ensure that priority needs are met as cheaply as possible and that optimal use is made of indigenous resources. Only those countries with an established fine-petrochemicals industry can manufacture the ingredients for most drugs, although there is probably potential for production of antibiotics and other useful chemicals by fermentation from agricultural resources. However, formulation and packaging could be carried out in developing countries from materials purchased in bulk. There are obvious savings to be made by importing drugs under generic rather than brand names from countries without patent laws, but quality testing is essential and must be carried out in the recipient country. To determine import requirements, drugs should first be classified according to therapeutic need and cost-effectiveness. Drugs for the prevention and treatment of common ailments of health centres are needed in large quantities and should be bought as cheaply as possible. A small range of these should suffice. At referral level, a larger number of more expensive drugs should be available, but in smaller quantities. A list of those pharmaceuticals that should be avoided for reasons of cost or ineffectiveness should also be compiled. This classification requires assembly of data on population, disease patterns, existing health services and future plans, and the current pharmaceutical position. To enforce national policy, a combination of educational and restrictive measures must be introduced, together with careful planning to overcome the formidable logistic problems that hamper distribution. (DM)

2984   Seoul National University, Seoul. *Chunseong health insurance program.* In Chunseong Gun Community Health Program, Seoul, Seoul National University, School of Public Health, Jul 1975, 69-85. Engl.
For complete document see entry 3147.

A survey conducted by the Chunseong Gun Community Health Program (Korea) in 1972 revealed that 80% of the local inhabitants wanted curative medical services in addition to the preventive services already provided. As

a result, the Chunseong Gun health insurance plan, run by local people with the cooperation of the programme members, was started in 1974 with an initial enrolment of 4 276. It provides two outpatient clinics staffed by doctors working part-time for the plan. Funded partly by a yearly premium and small fees for treatment, the plan receives 58% of its running costs from external sources. Thus far, the service has been underutilized, probably because surgery hours are limited, transport is difficult, pre-existing conditions are not covered by the scheme, and people are unaccustomed to a curative medical service they can afford. These problems should be overcome as the plan expands, acquires a more stable financial base, and employs a full-time physician. (DM)

2985   Sorkin, A.L. *Health economics: an introduction.* Lexington, Mass., D.C. Heath, 1975. 205p. Engl.
Refs.

This volume is an attempt to meet the needs of students of economics, public health, and medicine for a basic, up-to-date textbook on health economics. It focuses primarily on the economics of the health services industry in the USA with some coverage of the health problems in the developing world. The 1st chapter examines the distinctive economic characteristics of the health services industry as well as recent trends in expenditures, costs of medical care services, and mortality rates in the USA. Subsequent chapters analyze the demand for health services by summarizing and evaluating related studies, discuss the severity of physician shortages and the utilization of auxiliary health workers in both developed and developing countries, and examine hospital costs and the reasons behind their accelerating inflation. A health-related cost-benefit analysis is based on examples from both developed and developing countries. The interrelationship between health, population, and economic development in the developing countries is studied, as well as the relationship between health and poverty in the USA, with special emphasis on a few special federally-funded programmes such as the Neighbourhood Health Center Program and the programmes for American Indians. The final chapter deals with health insurance--both the existing private health insurance industry and the proposals for a public health insurance scheme. (HC)

2986   Taiyang Production Brigade Party Branch of Chishan County, Shansi, China PR. Chinese Medical Journal, Peking. *Uphold the party's basic line and do a good job in rural health revolution.* Chinese Medical Journal (Peking), 1(6), Nov 1975, 395-406. Engl.

Over the last 20 years, changes in the quality of life in Taiyang Production Brigade have been substantial; for example, life expectancy has increased 30 years, tap water has been made available to all members, waste disposal and composting have been introduced, etc. Some of these changes have resulted from a cooperative medical system initiated in 1956. This system in the early years offered medical treatment but not medications through a general fund; later, it incorporated a kindergarten and nursery and extended free comprehensive services to all children aged less than 15 years. Throughout the years, the service has expanded steadily despite reactionaries who oppose using the general funds for medical care. It now includes five barefoot doctors who are regularly provided with continuing education opportunities funded by the collective. (AC)

II.6 Cultural Aspects

See also: 2825, 2842, 2846, 2871, 2895, 2907, 2915, 3058, 3059, 3081, 3119, 3167, 3229, 3248

2987   **Abril, I.F.** *Mexican-American folk beliefs: how they affect health care.* MCN: American Journal of Maternal Child Nursing (New York), 2(3), May-Jun 1977, 168-173. Engl.

Because Mexican-Americans believe that a person without symptoms is healthy, they find the concept of prevention difficult to accept. Furthermore, they often poorly understand ideas about germs and contagion. They are likely to attribute disease to: exposure to the forces of nature, such as moonlight, eclipses, cold, heat, wind, sun, water, etc.; witchcraft or the evil eye; an imbalance of hot and cold in the body; dislocation of the internal organs; and strong emotions, such as anger or fear. Given these beliefs, health professionals who are treating Mexican-Americans must be willing to adapt, bearing in mind that their patients often prefer to consult family members before accepting therapy. Health workers who adopt a dictatorial manner will likely drive patients away. (HC)

2988   **Adams, R.N.** *Nutritional research program in Guatemala.* In Paul, B.D., ed., Health, Culture and Community: Case Studies of Public Reactions to Health Programs, New York, Russell Sage Foundation, 1955, 435-458. Engl.

For complete document see entry 3454.

Cultural differences between project staff and villagers threatened to abort a nutritional research project in one of the five Guatemalan villages where it had been introduced. The problems, according to an anthropologist who was sent to investigate, derived from some of the medical practices of the project, the villagers' fear of both Communism and the project motives, and the project staff's failure to appreciate their own cultural biases. Although the problems loomed large at times, the anthropologist was able to analyze their cultural and social bases and introduce remedial activities before the project had to be abandoned. For example, one problem was a belief that the food supplements were given to young children to fatten them up to suit the appetites of US consumers. The anthropologist discovered that fantasies about cannibalism were ancient and that the most effective way to deal with them was not to attempt their dissolution but rather to dissociate them from the project. (AC)

2989   **Aho, W.R. Minott, K.** *Creole and doctor medicine: folk beliefs, practices, and orientations to modern medicine in a rural and an industrial suburban setting in Trinidad and Tobago, the West Indies.* Social Science and Medicine (Oxford, UK), 11(5), Mar 1977, 349-355. Engl. 17 refs.

Based on interviews conducted during 1974-1975 with 77 mothers in Trinidad, data are presented on maternal beliefs about childhood illnesses and attitudes toward Western medicine. The hot-cold system of classifying illness and cure is described with several case histories of traditional treatment for the evil eye. Data from interviews with two traditional healers and two district health nurses are also included. The authors conclude that rural women use more traditional cures and are more distrustful of Western medicine than their urban counterparts and the implications for health educators and other health personnel are discussed. (Modified journal abstract.)

2990   **Armelagos, G.J. McArdle, A.** *Role of culture in the control of infectious diseases.* Ecologist (Wadebridge, UK), 6(5), Jun 1976, 179-182. Engl. 52 refs.

Technology, social organization, and ideology influence the incidence of infectious diseases and their impact on local ecology and disease transmission deserve greater study. For example, in the hill areas of Vietnam, the local population has customarily built homes on stilts--a custom that protects them from malaria-carrying mosquitoes. Similarly, social and occupational factors can determine disease patterns. Vietnamese hunting societies suffer from different diseases than do agricultural or urban peoples. Their population size is too small to support infections like measles and influenza, but they are commonly attacked by diseases that can be contracted from an animal host. Hunting exposes them to many animal species and the resulting epidemics seriously deplete their numbers and alter the social structure of the group. (DM)

2991   **Bonsi, S.K.** *Persistence and change in traditional medical practice in Ghana.* International Journal of Contemporary Sociology (Ghaziabad, India), 14(1-2), 1977, 27-38. Engl. 10 refs.

Although rapid social changes have challenged traditional medical ideas and practices in Ghana, indigenous medicine still persists in a form modified by Western medical concepts. Despite a continuing belief in divine or spiritual causes of illness, most healers are anxious to learn new ideas, new methods, and new herbal practices, as data from a sample of 150 traditional healers in southern Ghana show. Those who are interested can acquire new skills and knowledge at the Institute of Traditional Medicine, established after the political revolution of the 1950s, where the curriculum combines traditional herbal remedies with modern methods of preservation and administration of herbal preparations and the use of some Western medical technology. The objectives of the Institute reflect the attempts of traditional medical practitioners to lay the foundations for Western medical science within the established local system--attempts that have resulted in the organization, licensing, and standardization of medical practice. However, although traditional practitioners have been established as effective and reliable sources of medical care, this professionalization and its accompanying experimental clinical research and standardized drug manufacture could alienate the very traditions the institute is attempting to preserve. (CL)

2992   Carstairs, G.M. *Medicine and faith in rural Rajasthan.* In Paul, B.D., ed., Health, Culture and Community: Case Studies of Public Reactions to Health Programs, New York, Russell Sage Foundation, 1955, 107-134. Engl.
For complete document see entry 3454.

The author recounts his experiences studying and practicing in rural Rajasthan (India); he presents a series of case histories, during which he painfully learned cultural differences and the importance of respecting people, understanding their beliefs, and introducing changes by linking them with traditional techniques they are to supersede. During his stay, the author set up shop and let it be known that his services were available. His help was usually sought as a complement to traditional medicine whose practitioners inspired confidence by recognizing and catering to the psychological aspects of illness. (AC)

2993   Creyghton, M. *Communication between peasant and doctor in Tunisia.* Social Science and Medicine (Oxford, UK), 11(5), Mar 1977, 319-324. Engl.
16 refs.

The author explains some of the cultural attitudes and modes of unexpected behaviour that complicate communication between Tunisian peasants, especially women, and Western physicians. Since peasants tend to interpret a physician's behaviour in terms of that of the traditional practitioner, the author warns that doctors will have to be flexible enough to understand their patients' point of view if any meaningful exchange of information is to take place. (RMB)

2994   Dormaar, N.G. *Indian health in white man's society.* British Columbia Medical Journal (Vancouver, B.C.), 16(11), Nov 1974, 2p. Engl.

An informal comparison of 1 year's hospital admissions from an isolated Canadian Indian community and a mission school for Indian children revealed that the former group required 50 times more emergency hospital care. This disparity results not only from the poverty and poorer health of the Indian community but also from misuse of available facilities. Health care is often sought only when illness is so advanced that hospitalization is necessary. Government policies have deprived the Indians of both the means and the ability to make decisions about their own health needs. It is important therefore that multiservice centres should be controlled by local

tribes or by the Union of British Columbia Indian Chiefs and that the principal health practitioner should be a nurse employed by the consumer who is independent of government or doctor control. Her only guide should be the interest of the patient and she should have significant control over all available facilities, including the services of the doctor. In this way, some of the present fragmentation of health services could be overcome and Indians could regain their self-respect and powers of self-determination. (DM)

2995   Fonaroff, A. *Cultural preceptions and nutritional disorders: a Jamaican case study.* Bulletin of the Pan American Health Organization (Washington, D.C.), 8(3), 1975, 112-123. Engl.
30 refs.

Formal health education that disregards indigenous attitudes is unlikely to result in appropriate changes of custom; efforts to incorporate new beneficial practices into the traditional pattern altering only those beliefs and customs that are injurious can be much more effective. These were the conclusions of an investigation into the understanding of protein-calorie malnutrition by Jamaican women. Interviews were held with mothers who used Western medicine (group 1), those who used indigenous medicine (group 2), and some health workers, traditional and modern. All the interviewees believed that diet was a factor in marasmus (though few were aware that kwashiorkor had anything to do with nutrition), but group 2 mothers thought the major cause was a cold exacerbated by supernatural factors. Neither group perceived the disease to be a serious threat. From these discussions, it emerged that the traditional treatment of marasmus needs only a change in the emphasis put on diet to become effective. As the majority of Jamaican women probably practice traditional methods at home whatever they claim at an interview, health education should aim to modify rather than replace existing customs. (DM)

2996   Heggenhougen, H.K. Diamond, S. *Relevance of traditional medicine.* Kuala Lumpur, Institut Penyelidikan Perubatan, and Berkeley, Cal., University of California, International Center for Medical Research, Nov 1976. 36p. Engl.
44 refs.
Atlanta Symposium of the Albert Schweitzer Centenary, 1895-1975, Atlanta, Ga., 7 Apr 1975.
Unpublished document.

Any solution to the health problems of the Third World must combine traditional medicine's integrated methods with the technological achievements of the West. An example of such a synthesis between traditional and Western medicine is the Behrhorst Health Development Programme in highland Guatemala, established in 1962 to serve about 200 000 Cakchiquel Indians. In this programme, health promoters orient their work not to bureaucratic standards but to the social and cultural realities of their people. (CL)

2997   Hetzel, B.S. *Health problems of special groups.*
In Hetzel, B.S., Health and Australian Society,
Harmondsworth, UK, Penguin Books, 1974, 181-
222. Engl.
21 refs.
For complete document see entry 2914.
From 1965-1967, the infant mortality rate among Australian Aborigines was 6 times higher than that of the
rest of the population. Many children suffer from
malnutrition, recurrent gastroenteritis, and respiratory
infections. Further health problems result from the rapid
social change accompanying the clash of European and
Aboriginal cultures, including epidemics of adolescent
petrol sniffing and widespread alcoholism. A 1972 seminar recommended that future health care programmes
be planned in consultation with the Aboriginal community to ensure the preservation of Aboriginal dignity,
culture, and language. Similar cultural considerations
apply to the health situation of Australian migrants,
including Greeks, Italians, and Turks, who together
make up one fifth of the total Australian population.
Language difficulties and cultural isolation in migrants
are leading to emotional disturbances and underuse of
health and welfare services, in common with all Australian low-income groups. (CL)

2998   Hospital Practice, New York. *In Morocco
itinerant nurses hold the health care line.* Hospital
Practice (New York), 12(2), Feb 1977, 151, 157,
159, 161, 164, 168-170. Engl.
This informal review of health and health services in
Morocco is based on casual observation in a number of
cities and interviews with health personnel at all levels.
According to the Secretary General of the Ministry of
Health, Morocco's health problems are determined by
two factors. The 1st is that health problems are inextrica-
bly entwined with the problems of housing and education: urban medieval housing holds no provision for
sanitary waste disposal and wastes, in turn, pollute the
wells from which people drink; the majority of women
deliver at home with the assistance of the traditional
midwife and seek help in illness from the local *marabout*; and habits based on an ignorance of proper
nutrition, such as selling eggs in order to buy sweets for
children, are rampant. The 2nd determining factor is
Morocco's unfortunate medical hierarchy: private
practitioners catering to the rich draw salaries of $50 000
or more, while public health physicians and professors of
medicine make $7 000-$8 000. This discrepancy in pay
militates against recruitment for public health and
public health services must rely heavily on recent medical graduates, who are required to do 2 years of public
service, and polyvalent nurses. Since health personnel
are powerless to improve the conditions responsible for ill
health, they are left waging a defensive war against
disease. (HC)

2999   Jayatilaka, A.D. *Sarvodaya and delivery of
health care in Sri Lanka.* In International Secre-
tariat for Volunteer Service, Mobilization of
Response Structures from the Grassroots towards
Health Services: Report of a Workshop, Manila,
ISVS Asian Regional Office, Jul 1974, 46-55.
Engl.
International Secretariat for Volunteer Service
Workshop on Mobilization of Response
Structures from the Grassroots towards Health
Services, Manila, Philippines, 8-11 Jul 1974.
For complete document see entry 2919.
The *Sarvodaya Shramadana Sangamaya* began in
Sri Lanka in 1958 as a grassroots community develop-
ment movement. Based on Buddhist philosophy, its aims
are the "awakening of all" and the "sharing of services
arising from this awakening." The author suggests that
the public spirit the movement arouses could be tapped
for much needed improvement in the rural health services. At present, medical training is modeled on the
British system. There are few trained medical professionals and auxiliaries and 70% of the population rely on
the services of traditional practitioners. These indigenous healers, together with volunteer *Sarvodaya*
workers, should be trained in primary health care and
disease prevention and deployed in their home villages,
so that the major health needs of the rural population
may be met in the spirit of the movement. To achieve
this, the principles of *Sarvodaya* should be included
in the training of all health personnel, professional and
auxiliary. (DM)

3000   Kapur, R.L. *Mental health care in rural India:
a study of existing patterns and their implications
for future policy.* British Journal of Psychiatry
(London), 127, Sep 1975, 286-293. Engl.
Studies undertaken in three rural Indian communities
challenge the stereotyped notions that villagers are not
sophisticated enough to seek help for psychiatric
problems and that, when help is sought, it is generally
from the traditional healers. In the 1st study, all healers
were interviewed regarding the conceptual framework
within which they work, their methods of treatment, and
the type of complaints they handle. In the 2nd study, a
randomly-selected sample of adults was questioned to
determine who (if anyone) they would consult for four
striking, unambiguous psychiatric symptoms. The 3rd
study consisted of a population survey during which all
persons exhibiting one or more psychiatric symptoms
was asked whether they had consulted a healer for these
conditions. Three types of traditional healers were identified: *Vaids*, who practice an empirical system of
indigenous medicine; *Mantarwadis*, who cure
through astrology and charms; and *Patris*, who act as
mediums. It was found that a doctor was the preferred
healer, although a traditional healer might be consulted
simultaneously; the choice of healer was determined
more by the individual's reputation than by his
conceptual framework; choice of healer was not significantly influenced by the user's age, education, or income
category; and 59% of those exhibiting psychiatric symptoms had sought help from one or more healers. It is
concluded that making the villagers more aware of their
psychiatric problems is not an urgent priority and that
psychiatry should be introduced into the rural areas by
training popular healers, whether traditional or modern,
rather than primary health centre staff. (HC)

II Organization and Planning

3001 McConnel, F. Cawte, J. Kamien, M. MacPherson, P. Briscoe, G. Dobbin, M. *New models for Aboriginal health services.* In Hetzel, B.S., Dobbin, M., Lippmann, L., Eggleston, E., eds., Better Health for Aborigines, St. Lucia, Australia, University of Queensland Press, 1974, 143-184. Engl. Refs.

National Seminar on Health Services for Aborigines, Melbourne, Australia, 15-17 May 1972.

For complete document see entry 2915.

Experiences of Aboriginal health services in several parts of Australia show the need for Aborigine involvement at all stages in the delivery of health care. In Kimberley, Western Australia, a health centre's failure to influence Aborigine attitudes resulted in increased malnutrition, injury, and social decay since the granting of full drinking rights in 1971. This illustrates the need to arrest social and cultural disintegration among Aborigines by involving men as well as women and children in health programmes. The effects of social disintegration on mental and physical health led to a scheme in Bourke, New South Wales, to examine the health benefits of having a resident medical doctor trained in psychiatry and sociology living in an Aborigine community. The project affected the organization and functioning of that community by stimulating the formation by Aborigines of an Aboriginal Advancement Association, currently operating a medical benefits scheme and adult education classes. So far, these and other project observations suggest that most Aborigines benefit from community participation involving suitably trained medical personnel. Also, a comparison of Australian Aborigine health problems with those of American Indians shows that Australia could learn from past experiences of the American Indian health services. (CL)

3002 Nguyen-van-Huong. Nguyen-van-Dan. *Role of traditional medicine and pharmacy.* In McMichael, J.K., ed., Health in the Third World: Studies from Vietnam, Nottingham, UK, Spokesman Books, 1976, 188-207. Engl.

For complete document see entry 2869.

The Democratic Government of North Vietnam is attempting to unify modern and traditional medicine at all levels of the country's health services by integrating modern scientific medicine based on European experience, northern traditional medicine rooted in centuries of Chinese influence, and southern traditions indigenous to local Vietnamese tribal groups. Some of the logistics of integration have been delegated to the Society of Traditional Medicine, with its 11 000 practitioners, an estimated two-thirds of all traditional healers; the society has the task of gathering and synthesizing the stores of traditional knowledge and ensuring appropriate conditions for its members. To date, many local practitioners have been employed by the state in research institutions, hospitals, and health centres and more than 1 000 villages support traditional practices in their clinics. Training in traditional medicine is included as part of the curricula for all health workers and a number of doctors have already learned acupuncture and the use of traditional medicaments. The next steps are to justify traditional practices by clinical research and laboratory experiment and extend the pharmacopoeia, which is already the subject of much successful research and experiment. (AB)

3003 Ozigi, Y.O. *What is health and nutrition education?* In Ozigi, Y.O., Importance of Health and Nutrition Education in the Training of Rural Health Workers in the Northern States of Nigeria, London, Queen Elizabeth College, 1976, 26-41. Engl.

For complete document see entry 3245.

Health education should encourage self-help efforts that do not threaten the local culture or violate local customs. For this reason, health educators must understand the beliefs, customs, and politics of each area and present correct and relevant information with tact and sensitivity. Initially, they should enlist the help of local leaders to arrange a meeting to explain the need for health education and elect a committee to organize suitable activities. However, the educators' role extends beyond convening meetings and addressing formal community groups. They must befriend the local people, listen to their views, and learn the reasons for their customs. For instance, nutrition education requires a thorough knowledge of local techniques of food production, storage, and preparation, so that the advice offered can be realistic. Much of this communication can take place during informal encounters at clinics, markets, or in the home. However, health education need not be restricted to talk; there is wide scope for use of audiovisual aids in this work, including indigenous folk art. (DM)

3004 Pradhan, P. Development Research and Consulting Group, Pvt. Ltd., Kathmandu. *Rural health technology inventory in Nepal.* Kathmandu, Development Research and Consulting Group, 1977. 4p. Engl.

The results of a survey of the health technologies of 12 different ethnic groups in Nepal will be used to compile an inventory of existing traditional health care practices. Because such practices develop over generations among rural populations who have to maintain their own health, agriculture, and ecology, the author believes that they must have some scientific basis. The study will include mother and baby care, adaptation to high altitude living, treatment of common ailments, and water hygiene. For example, people living at high altitudes use salt and pepper in their diets to keep themselves physically fit. To ensure water hygiene, they avoid pond water and use running water only if it has not passed through a village. They also believe that copper vessels can clear polluted water. Consequently, the author maintains that these people are not entirely without health resources. (HH)

3005 Roodkowsky, M. *Development lessons learned in Ladakh.* Vectors (Cambridge, Mass.), Dec 1977-Jan 1978, 4-6. Engl.

In Ladakh, in the Indian Himalayas, Western medical personnel are not consulted by the local people because their practices are not compatible with indigenous attitudes towards health. Customarily, a sick person visits a traditional practitioner called a *la*, who decides whether the illness is physical or spiritual. In the latter case, a *lama* is consulted, whereas if the illness is physical, the patient visits the *amchi*, who heals using herbs or branding. *Amchis* are now being taught modern medicine in a study centre so that they can incorporate such knowledge into their own practices. An unrelated problem was caused by the emptying of latrines onto fields in May, when such fertilizer became a medium for hookworm. If people emptied the latrines earlier in the year, in the colder months, the waste would have more time to "cure" naturally and would therefore be less pathogenic. (HH)

3006 **Said, H.M.** *Integrated health education for life style acculturation.* Karachi, Hamdard National Foundation, 1976. 13p. Engl.
Ninth International Conference on Health Education, Ottawa, Canada, 29 Aug-3 Sep 1976.
In this paper presented to the 9th International Conference on Health Education, the author strongly criticizes Western medicine and its proponents for their failure to meet the health needs of traditional, rural Pakistan and the rural populations of other developing countries. The overly-rapid introduction of Western medicine and technology into Pakistan has led only to an artificially-accelerated urbanization and the creation of an affluent, Westernized upper class, of whom the modern physician, totally indifferent to the needs of his rural countrymen and concerned only with the pursuit of his Western life-style, is a typical example. This process is further aggravated by commercially-oriented corporations and pharmaceutical firms bent on creating markets for their products and by international aid organizations who automatically assume that the Western way is superior and therefore universally desirable. The author urges that, rather than a wholesale acceptance or rejection of Western medicine, an attempt should be made to integrate it into traditional patterns of health care, as in the People's Republic of China; the 1st step in this direction would be government recognition of and aid to traditional practitioners, regardless of objections from privileged professionals, because these practitioners provide the only medical care that is likely to be available to most rural people for a long time to come. (RMB)

II.7 Epidemiological, Family Planning, MCH, and Nutritional Studies

See also: 2839, 2869, 2900, 2902, 3196, 3291, 3339, 3402

3007 **Aall, C. Helsing, E.** *Sahelian drought: proposals for a supporting programme in Niger for food provision, nutrition rehabilitation, and malnutrition prevention.* Environmental Child Health (London), 29(6), Monograph No.37, Dec 1974, 303-329. Engl.
In 1974, the Red Cross proposed nutrition support for a population of 100 000-200 000 persons in drought-ridden Niger. Proposals that were the culmination of visits to the Sahel and discussions at national and international levels were aimed at the at-risk group: children aged less than 10 years and lactating and pregnant women. The major components of the proposals were to use local or regional foods with some protein-rich supplements, schedule and evaluate operations so that activities could be redirected if necessary every 6 or 12 months, and promote aims of self-sufficiency and self-reliance, realizing at the same time the long-term debilitating effects of the drought. Specific recommendations were to supplement every person in the at-risk group, vary amounts on the basis of need, and distribute rations comprising cereals (millet, sorghum, rice, and maize), red palm oil, and either fish protein concentrate or dried skim milk. Cost figures are estimated for 6 months using alternative programme plans. (AC)

3008 **Ademuwagun, Z.A. Familusi, J.B.** *Mother and child health in Africa: the role of health education.* Israel Journal of Medical Sciences (Jerusalem), 13(5), May 1977, 508-513. Engl.
24 refs.
Second Conference on Health Education in Africa, Yaounde, Cameroon, 23-25 Mar 1976.
In Africa, health education can contribute to the development and utilization of integrated MCH services. Health education must include all the means available, both conventional and unconventional, to generate community interest in adopting a particular pattern of health behaviour. The objectives of any broadly-conceived MCH health education project will be initially to identify the needs of the target population and the available facilities. The project must also collect information on sociocultural beliefs and practices, study other factors that may help or hinder projects, and define and overcome problems. Local leaders and the community as a whole should participate in problem identification and programme planning. Also, the health education project must approach not only the individual patient but also the total environment; to achieve this, it will therefore be necessary to involve planners, health personnel, and others in positions of influence, including traditional practitioners. Plans for control of prevalent communicable diseases, for example, must attack the overall background of deprivation. (HH)

3009 **Antes, E.J. Henry, S.** *Library services to small rural hospitals: a circuit librarian program: preliminary report.* Guthrie Bulletin (Sayre, Pa.), 46, Spring 1977, 188-194. Engl.
The circuit librarian programme was conceived to help the staff of small hospitals keep up-to-date with medical literature. The library collection of the Robert Parker Hospital, Sayre, Pennsylvania (USA) is larger and more comprehensive than that of any other hospital within a radius of 150 miles. When a 3-month feasibility study revealed that 6 hospitals within this radius were interested in the library's services, a programme was devised whereby a circuit librarian visits each hospital once a week to deliver documents and talk to individuals who are requesting information. After the programme had been in operation for 5 months, personnel at the hospitals were aware of who the circuit librarian was,

II Organization and Planning

when she could be contacted, and what services she offered; there was a substantial number of requests representing almost all the departments in the 6 hospitals; and users of the service appeared satisfied. Statistics for the 1st 2 months of programme operation, plus sample request, statistics, and evaluation forms, are included. (HC)

3010   Atlas, J. WHO, Brazzaville. *Development of basic health services in Kenya: nutrition.* Brazzaville, WHO, 27 Jul 1973. 1v.(various pagings). Engl.

The leader of the nutrition component of the WHO team for the development of basic health services outlines Kenya's problems and proposals in food production and nutrition. Observations are that Kenya comprises enough agricultural land for each person to have 1.5 hectares, but the land is used for cash crops and pasture as well as food and, although there are large numbers of livestock, they are kept for prestige and financial capital rather than food. The principal food crops are cereals, tubers, and beans and maize is the principal staple. Meat is seldom eaten in rural areas and other sources of protein, such as soybean and groundnut, are consumed in small amounts. Food consumption is inadequate in half of all rural families and in more than half during the preharvest season. Protein intake is inadequate for small children and thus the clinical signs of protein malnutrition are seen everywhere. Prophylaxis measures against goitre, which is endemic in many areas, have been introduced and studies of salt iodation levels were begun through the country. Other efforts have been devoted to training nutrition staff and coordinating nutrition activities; these are briefly outlined. (HC)

3011   Barrow, R.N. Puschel, J. Christian Medical Commission, World Council of Churches, Geneva. *Report on a visit to Brazil 19 Nov to 19 Dec 1973.* Geneva, Christian Medical Commission, World Council of Churches, n.d. 19p. Engl.

Representatives of the Christian Medical Commission (CMC) and the German Institute for Medical Mission on a 4-week fact-finding tour in Brazil in 1973 observed that the health services were largely curative and organized to suit health care providers rather than consumers, that facilities and personnel were too specialized and too expensive, and that they were inaccessible to deprived populations, such as the rural poor, migrants, and urban slum dwellers. The team concluded that the most acute health problems could only be overcome by major changes in government policy such as measures to limit urban migration, agricultural reform to provide cheap food for all, and better coordination of existing social services. However, some improvements could be possible through preventive community medicine. In particular, primary health workers could be trained by church organizations to provide preventive health measures. To this end, the three major Protestant church agencies operating in Brazil should share their experiences and resources more fully. Together they could plan projects that would expand existing community health facilities, provide training for village level health work-

ers rather than doctors, and link church-supported health services with other development programmes. (DM)

3012   Beaner, L.G. Anderson, M.L. USA, Department of Health, Education, and Welfare. *Syncrisis: the dynamics of health. XV: Tunisia.* Washington, D.C., U.S. Government Printing Office, DHEW Publication No.(OS)75-50, No.020, Jun 1975. 57p. Engl.
21 refs.
See also entries 1322, 1342, 1343, 1353, 1355 (volume 2), 1985, 1987, 1991, 2002 (volume 3), and 3181 for other volumes of this series.

Health in Tunisia is discussed in the light of a number of environmental, economic, social, and administrative factors. It is noted that, although the health status of the population has improved considerably over the last generation, a number of problem areas remain: a low level of environmental sanitation is responsible for a high level of under-five mortality and the prevalence of gastroenteric and parasitic infections; undernutrition and malnutrition represent serious problems to large numbers of the population, particularly infants, small children, and pregnant and lactating women; the health structure operates vertically, with little horizontal integration of activities; neither hospitals nor health manpower are spread equitably throughout the country; paramedical personnel (nurses, midwives, etc.) are underutilized, poorly paid, poorly supervised, and given limited responsibilities; maternal and child health centres are poorly organized and almost totally concerned with children to the exclusion of antenatal care, postnatal care, family planning, or health education; and health planning is seriously hampered by the lack of a data base. A review of foreign assistance in the health sector, and where it might be applied with the most far-reaching results, is included. (HC)

3013   Behar, M. Institute of Nutrition of Central America and Panama, Guatemala. *Correcting vitamin A deficiency.* Appropriate Technology (London), 3(3), Nov 1976, 15-16. Engl.

An unconventional but cheap and effective solution to widespread vitamin A deficiency has been developed in Central America. The Institute of Nutrition of Central America and Panama, with the assistance of a Swiss pharmaceutical company, has discovered a means of producing a stable concentrated pre-mix of industrially manufactured vitamin A and sugar. Although it requires highly sophisticated technology and skills for the initial production of vitamin A and the preparation of the pre-mix, the result could be added in measured quantities during batch production of local sugar mills. Virtually no labour is involved and the entire cost of prevention of vitamin A deficiency by this means is only US$0.05 per head per year. (DM)

3014   Breman, J.G. WHO, Geneva. *Smallpox: no hiding place.* World Health (Geneva), Apr 1978, 24-29. Engl.

In 1967, when smallpox was still endemic in countries

with a total population of over 1 200 million people, the WHO itensified smallpox eradication programme was mounted. It aimed to certify countries as smallpox-free by proving that no cases had occurred within their territories for at least 2 years. To be certified smallpox-free, the country had to submit a complete documentation of eradication activities and show that the national surveillance system was adequate to detect cases occurring within the previous 2 years. In addition, special field surveys were conducted to search out smallpox cases. This strategy rests on the assumption that, if cases existed, they would be near the last known outbreaks, they would come to the attention of the local health workers, they would leave pitting scars on the faces of the victims, and they would resemble chicken pox or other rashes with fever. Therefore, searchers went from house to house in villages where the last outbreak occurred, local health workers were questioned, preschool and schoolchildren were examined for facial scars, and persons with severe forms of chicken pox were investigated. In 1977, what may well be the last case of smallpox in human history was discovered in Merka City, Somalia. As a result, some 3 500 national staff and 24 WHO epidemiologists were mobilized for case detection. It is expected that Somalia, along with Ethiopia, Kenya, Djibouti, Democratic Yemen, and Yemen, will form in 1979 the last group of countries to be certified smallpox-free. For the first time, the eradication of a human disease will have been achieved--a milestone in the history of WHO and in the history of medicine. (HC)

3015   Brown, H.B. *Some aspects of food and nutrition in Haiti.* Cajanus (Kingston, Jamaica), 10(4), 1977, 206-214. Engl.
A high population density (490:km² arable land), low per capita annual income (US$35.00 among the rural peasants), and deficiencies in the quantity and quality of available food are all causes of Haiti's low nutritional standards. For example, a recent study of 857 rural children aged less than 5 years revealed that 13.6% were underweight; only 7% of children of regularly employed parents were classified as definitely or severely underweight, whereas 44% of children of unemployed parents fell into those categories. This link between poverty and malnutrition is only part of the economics of nutrition in Haiti. Another is found in the realm of food production, where farmers do not have the necessary capital to introduce better techniques and most of the improved, irrigated land is used to produce sugar cane and tobacco for export. Increased productivity in the rural sector, better distribution of national wealth, and a national food policy that balances the need for producing export crops with the need for increasing production of basic staples are called for. (HC)

3016   Butt, H.W. Indo-Dutch Project for Child Welfare,   Hyderabad,   India. *Nutrition programmes for children: suggestions to implement a practical programme.* Hyderabad, India, Indo-Dutch Project for Child Welfare, Sep 1975. 16p. Engl.
Andhra Pradesh State Level Conference on National Policy on Children, Hyderabad, India, 6 Sep 1975.
Unpublished document; see also entries 2917, 2918, 3017, and 3040.
Since food handouts are ineffective in the long run, the Indo-Dutch Project for Child Welfare nutrition programme seeks instead to tackle the problem of malnutrition by improving education, health services, and agriculture with the active participation of local families. The services of auxiliary nurse-midwives and teachers have been enlisted to initiate a wide range of projects including: nutrition and agriculture demonstrations; formation of *balwadis* (day care for pre-school children), creches, and *Mahila Mandals* (women's clubs); and specific agricultural development schemes. The latter have so far met with little economic success but have encouraged farmers to produce suitable ingredients for "Hyderabad Mix," a protein supplement prepared and packaged by *Mahila Mandal* members that has helped to eradicate the diseases of malnutrition from 7 000 children in the Chevella area during the 1st 3 years of the project. Future development of the nutrition programme will involve greater local initiative and leadership, especially among women, and establishment of links with money-earning projects to increase the income of rural families. (DM)

3017   Butt, H.W. Indo-Dutch Project for Child Welfare, Hyderabad, India. *Integrated approach for child welfare: the Chevella experiment.* Hyderabad, India, Indo-Dutch Project for Child Welfare, n.d. 12p. Engl.
See also entries 2917, 2918, 3016, and 3040.
The aim of the Indo-Dutch Project for Child Welfare (India) is to initiate a number of self-sustaining programmes in health, education, and agriculture over a period of 8-10 years. The 1969 pilot project resulted in a dramatic improvement in child health over the first 3 years and an increased demand for birth control. On the basis of this initial experience, a number of additional projects were started in 1972. The auxiliary nurse-midwives who manned the health centres were given further training to enable them to deal with routine work unaided, 1-month training courses were established for *dais*, and local mothers were recruited to help run preschool groups for children. The *Mahila Mandals* (women's clubs), originally formed to teach skills such as cooking and sewing, are now embarking on the production of handicrafts, food packets, and clothes for profit as well as for the children's groups. A variety of agricultural schemes have been attempted with mixed success. Cultivation of papaya and drumstick trees in the villages met with cultural resistance and some of the poultry farming schemes failed entirely. However, other food production projects are under way and, with the help of the nutrition demonstration units, acceptance of agricultural innovations is improving. (DM)

3018   Caribbean Epidemiology Centre (Carec), Port-of-Spain. *Leprosy control in Guyana.* Carec Surveillance Report (Port-of-Spain), 2(10), Oct 1976, 1-3. Engl.

II Organization and Planning

A domiciliary control programme for leprosy was introduced in the Georgetown area of Guyana in 1971. Its initial aim was to determine the prevalence of leprosy, the acceptability of domiciliary treatment, and the efficacy of domiciliary care compared to that provided in an institution. A number of skin clinics using hospital outpatient and health centre facilities were opened and anyone with a skin problem was urged to attend. Suspected leprosy cases were referred to a central clinic for treatment and records were maintained in all cases. An essential component of the programme was to preserve the liberty and anonymity of patients, and hence their motivation to continue, without exposing others to undue risk of infection. Rationalization for domiciliary care was based on two characteristics of leprosy: only 5% of the population are susceptible to the disease and chemotherapy progressively reduces infectiousness. Thus, patients may remain at home and in full employment, receiving regular treatment and supervision over a long period with minimal trauma for themselves and their families. (DM)

3019   Caribbean Epidemiology Centre (Carec), Port-of-Spain. *Marburg virus disease.* Carec Surveillance Report (Port-of-Spain), 2(10), Oct 1976, 3-5. Engl.
Marburg virus disease was first recognized in 1967 when an epidemic occurred in Marburg, Frankfurt, and Belgrade among laboratory workers who had been exposed to infected tissues of green monkeys imported from Uganda. The death rate was 29% of the primary cases, though none of the secondary cases died. Further outbreaks were reported in Southern Sudan and Zaire in 1975 and 1976. Laboratory studies have shown that the virus persists for a long time in the tissues of infected animals and may be excreted in urine and saliva. After an incubation period of 4-9 days, fever develops followed by gastrointestinal upset and a variety of other symptoms. Liver and kidney damage and *thrombocytopenia* occur and the only treatment possible is: maintenance of fluid, acid/base, and electrolyte balance; blood or plasma transfusion; and administration of antipyretics. Diagnosis from infected tissues is extremely dangerous and should only be carried out in high security laboratories. (DM)

3020   Caribbean Food and Nutrition Institute, Kingston, Jamaica. *Production of high-grade proteins from petroleum: a solution to the world food problem.* Cajanus (Kingston, Jamaica), 10(4), 1977, 215-218. Engl.
In this interview, Alfred Champagnat, recipient of the UNESCO science prize for his work on the biosynthesis of edible protein, discusses the potential of oil-derived proteins to compensate for world food shortages. He notes that a high-grade protein has been developed from petroleum-grown yeast. The protein is a tasteless, odourless, cream-colored powder and is currently used in Europe to fortify cattle feed. It meets standards for human nutrition set by the United Nations Protein Advisory Group and, when added to wheat flour in a ratio of 1:8, provides the full spectrum of amino acids found in meat. (HC)

3021   Caribbean Food and Nutrition Institute, Kingston, Jamaica. *Special issue: new foods.* Cajanus (Kingston, Jamaica), 9(2), 1976, 57-129. Engl.
The opening editorial comment of this special issue points out that new foods alone cannot eliminate hunger without social and political changes; the papers that follow describe some novel food sources, methods of food distribution, and basics of nutrition. Articles cover: new crops and farming techniques in the Third World; the possibility of using insects for food; nonagricultural sources of food, such as single-celled organisms, unconventional vegetables, and hydroponics; the probable impact of textured vegetable protein (TVP) production in Guyana; the effects of food processing on nutrients; and the importance of nutrition education in combatting world hunger. One paper, "Why turn waste into protein?" challenges the view that increasing food production by unconventional means can eliminate hunger on the grounds that food innovations usually benefit the rich not the needy. Many of the articles are reprinted from other sources and a collection of newspaper extracts on related topics concludes the issue. (DM)

3022   Central Treaty Organization, Ankara, Turkey. *CENTO Conference on Family Planning, Health and Demographic Statistics.* Ankara, Turkey, Central Treaty Organization, 1973. 198p. Engl. Refs.
Conference on Family Planning, Health and Demographic Statistics, Teheran, Iran, 12-16 Aug 1973.
This CENTO conference was convened to allow statisticians, family planners, physicians, statistics analysts, ministry of health officials from Turkey, Pakistan, and Iran, and a few professionals from the UK and the USA to discuss the application of statistical methods to population programmes. The report of the seminar contains: a keynote address detailing recent developments in the areas of data collection, data processing, analytic techniques, and the presentation of results; papers from Turkey, Pakistan, and Iran on vital statistics collection, training facilities for statistics personnel, and the current status of population and family planning statistics in their respective countries; three papers of an advisory nature dealing with the analysis of population data, ways of obtaining comparative data in family planning statistics, and the assessment of national health resources; and a discussion of areas for regional cooperation in the field of statistical activities. (HC)

3023   Chen, P.C. *Have we conquered the communicable diseases?* Medical Journal of Malaysia (Singapore), 31(1), Sep 1976, 1-4. Engl. 10 refs.
The author maintains that infectious diseases will never be completely controlled in Malaysia until all the people have access to clean water and have been educated to use it properly. Although some progress has been made in controlling air-borne diseases such as diphtheria and tuberculosis, the incidence of faecally-transmitted

diseases, particularly intestinal parasites, diarrhea, poliomyelitis, typhoid, and cholera has remained unchanged, because there have been few improvements in the field of environmental sanitation. Statistical data on water supply and toilet facilities in Malaysia are included. (RMB)

3024   Colombia, Comite Nacional de Investigacion en Tecnologia de Alimentos y Nutricion. *Bases para un programa nacional de investigaciones en tecnologia de alimentos y nutricion. 3 edicion. (Guidelines for a national research programme in food and nutrition technology. 3 edition).* Bogota, Ministerio de Educacion Nacional, Fondo Colombiano de Investigaciones Cientificas y Proyectos Especiales "Francisco Jose de Caldas," Comite Nacional de Invesigacion en Tecnologia de Alimentos y Nutricion, Serie Informes y Referencias No.12, Jul 1973. 75p. Span.
41 refs.

A special committee in Colombia has designed a programme to solve the problem of feeding the lower classes, who are generally malnourished because of a lack of food availability and consumer buying power. This document presents the background and details of the programme, including its objectives, restrictions, alternative strategies, methodology, necessary research, and establishment of priorities. Research projects to be carried out in food and nutrition technology are described and classified in order of importance. Recommendations to the industrial, agricultural, marketing, health and nutrition, and educational sectors are set forth. Annexes contain lists of problems involved in each alternative strategy and necessary research projects. Statistical data are included. (RMB)

3025   Condon-Paoloni, D. Cravioto, J. Johnston, F.E. de Licardie, E.R. Scholl, T.O. *Morbidity and growth of infants and young children in a rural Mexican village.* American Journal of Public Health (New York), 67(7), Jul 1977, 651-656. Engl.
33 refs.

The relationship between childhood illnesses and growth increments in length and weight was investigated in a 13-month birth cohort of rural Mexican children. Increments in length and weight for each year from birth-3 years were related to high and low frequencies of reported time ill during the same period. Seventy-two of the 276 children sampled had already been characterized as exhibiting growth failure in comparison to other members of their peer group and this was considered as a separate factor in the study. It appeared that upper and lower respiratory infection did not affect height or weight gain. A high frequency of diarrheal infection was found to reduce weight gain, although height gain was not affected. Relative to the total sample, the average child with chronic diarrhea achieved only 95% of expected body weight at age 3 years; a child with both growth failure and high diarrheal frequency reached only 90% of expected body weight at age 3 years. Statistical data are included. (Modified journal abstract.)

3026   Correa, H. *Measured influence of nutrition on socio-economic development.* World Review of Nutrition and Dietetics (London), 20, 1975, 1-48. Engl.
67 refs.

Detailed data from nutritionists' studies of how nutrition affects physical and mental capacities are combined with data and methods from the social sciences in an attempt to evaluate the influence of nutrition on socioeconomic development. By linking nutritionally determined physical and mental abilities with educational achievement, economic productivity, and interpersonal relations, analyses show that nutritional deficiency can detrimentally affect aspects of socioeconomic development. Malnutrition prenatally and during the first 2 years of life can lead to mental inadequacy as well as high infant morbidity and mortality. Evidence for this appears in data for 47 countries and shows the positive relationship between nutritional status and both IQ estimates and educational achievement. Further examples of statistical studies examine the relationship between nutrition and economic productivity by combining data on the nutrition-mental capacity relation with data on the connection between mental ability and economic performance. Estimates of the simultaneous effects of population, nutrition, health, and education on total production are presented using sophisticated models, including one based on the components of technological change. They show that calories *per capita*, as a determinant of the quality of labour, correlates significantly with production, especially in developing countries. (CL)

3027   Cowan, B. *Can severe childhood malnutrition be prevented?* In Getting the Most Out of Food: the Twelfth in a Series of Studies on the Modern Approach to Feeding and Nutrition, Burgess Hill, UK, Van den Berghs and Jurgens, 1977, 73-106. Engl.

In the catchment area of the Community Health Department of the Christian Medical College, Ludhiana, India, over half of 6 000 children aged less than 5 years did not attend a child health clinic in 1975, even though no child had to travel over 3 miles. Despite the fact that clinic workers seldom saw severe degrees of malnutrition, a field study based on data obtained by weighing children aged less than 12 months and measuring the upper-arm circumferences of children aged 14-60 months revealed 374 children with malnutrition. An analysis of 358 of these children, aged 7-60 months, showed that 39.9% had 1st degree malnutriton (70%-80% of Harvard standard weight), 32.7% had 2nd degree malnutrition (60%-70% of standard weight), and 24.4% had 3rd degree malnutrition (less than 60% of standard weight). Although 1st degree malnutrition, due mainly to a lack of supplementary feeding, occurred equally in males and females, rich and poor, and large and small families, severer malnutrition occurred more frequently in large, poor families with many females. Detailed analysis of the children with established malnutrition revealed an extremely poor clinical condition that was most resistant to treatment. This study implies that the children most needing clinical attention rarely attend and that concentrating preventive care on children less than 1 year could possibly prevent the severe degrees of malnutrition seen in the 2nd and 3rd years of life. This might be accomplished by encouraging *dais* to give intensive health education to the mothers of this small group. (CL)

3028 Crow, R. *Health care in the Turkana desert.* Nursing Mirror (London), 144(13), 31 Mar 1977, 62-65. Engl.

The author describes the desperate plight of the nomadic tribesmen of the Turkana desert in Kenya, who have perhaps the lowest standard of living in the world. Because of years of famine and low rainfall, malnutrition in this area is universal and there is a high incidence of hydatid cyst, parasitic diseases, spina bifida, fungus infections from thorn wounds, gangrene, tuberculosis, poliomyelitis, urinary tract infections, scorpion stings, hunter spider and crocodile bites, retained placenta, and battle wounds. Due to the nomads' fear of death and the complete lack of burial customs in their culture, the sick and injured are often abandoned and the only way to reach them is through the flying doctor services and mobile clinics. (RMB)

3029 Devadas, R.P. *Integrated role of nutrition in medicine--promotion of health and family planning and prevention of illness.* Indian Journal of Nutrition and Dietetics (Coimbatore, India), 19(9), 355-361. Engl.

The author discusses various aspects of nutrition in India. She recommends that nutrition education efforts be concentrated on mothers and young children, both at-risk groups, to encourage breast-feeding and promote desirable food habits and the use of proper weaning foods. Although complete nutritional surveillance of under-fives is the ideal, India's overworked primary health centres--the only contact with the medical system most villages have--are unable to carry out this task successfully; the author recommends the training of a nutrition auxiliary for every village. She also urges further training in nutrition for medical personnel, who tend to neglect the few opportunities for nutrition education they do have. (RMB)

3030 Devi, P.K. *Out of reach.* World Health (Geneva), Aug-Sep 1976, 26-31. Engl.
Also published in Arabic, French, German, Italian, Persian, Portuguese, Russian, and Spanish.

The poor health of women in India contributes to both infant mortality from low birth weight and maternal mortality from haemorrhage, post-partum infections, septic abortions, and tetanus. Malnutrition, anaemia, infections, and parasitic diseases are common and, although poverty is largely to blame for the poor state of women's health, many factors are involved. For example, a comparison of mortality and morbidity in different regions indicates that the death rate in Kerala is very much lower than in Uttar Pradesh though the average *per capita* income is the same. It seems probable that

Kerala's relatively high literacy rate, especially for women, contributes to the disparity. Other significant factors are transport and communication facilities and the availability and utilization of health services. To improve women's health, many experiments are now under way using village-level health workers. At present, the focus is on physical health, but such programmes should also consider the mental well-being of women. (DM)

3031 Duncan, J.W. *Planning of environmental health infrastructure and sanitary facilities in health institutions in Kenya.* World Hospitals (Oxford, UK), 11(2 and 3), Jun 1975, 204-206. Engl.

Visits were made to a cross-section of health institutions in four provinces of Kenya to collect information on their environmental facilities. The visits revealed that: some health institutions lack modern amenities and the capital to install them; maintenance is a major problem due to a lack of cleaners and other manual workers; a large number of dispensaries and health centres are being constructed on a self-help basis in an uncontrolled manner; rural water supplies are generally not treated; pit latrines--usually of good, solid construction--abound in almost all rural areas and towns; and, in almost all health centres, refuse awaits incineration in pits, where it gets scattered by dogs and pigs. It is recommended that: facilities constructed on a self-help basis be subject to national advice and inspection, construction of water seal latrines be encouraged in order to keep down flies and odours, water supplies be treated through slow sand filtration or chlorination, and refuse collection by donkey-drawn carts rather than by vehicles, which break down frequently, be encouraged. It is also proposed that a model environmental health project, consisting of a construction and maintenance team equipped with a drilling rig, be undertaken. The team would move from one location to another, constructing and maintaining cased wells and shallow boreholes, water-seal latrines, and elevated refuse depots. An estimate of the staff, equipment, and funds required for such a project is included. (HC)

3032 Fong, M.P. *Actions de medecine preventive chez l'enfant a la Reunion. (Preventive medicine for the child in Reunion).* Marseille, France, Universite d'Aix-Marseille, 10 Mar 1975. 56p. Fren.
38 refs.
Thesis presented to the Faculty of Medicine, University of Aix-Marseille, 10 Mar 1975.

Child health in Reunion is greatly influenced by a high rate of population growth (55% of the population is under the age of 20), an imbalance between population and production, a high rate of illegitimacy and parental irresponsibility, unsanitary living conditions, and a high incidence of malnutrition and infectious and parasitic diseases. The *Service Unifie de l'Enfance* (SUE) provides most of the preventive health care; this organization groups maternal and child health, school health, care of the disabled child, and juvenile social assistance with a view to monitoring the child in the continuity of his development from the prenatal period to adulthood. In this thesis, the facilities, resources, utilization, and quality of the SUE are examined within the social and economic context of Reunion. (HC)

3033 Frankel, S. *Working towards a village technology: recycling waste.* Papua New Guinea Medical Journal (Port Moresby), 18(1), Mar 1975, 21-31. Engl.

A digester system for recycling human waste was constructed for under US$1 000 at a district hospital in Papua New Guinea. The system consists of a sealed cement tank with a gasometer lid, a settling tank, and a shallow pond. The methane gas that collects in the lid is used for cooking, lighting, and refrigeration; the algae that develop on the shallow pond serve as food for ducks, fish, chickens, or pigs; and the remaining effluent is channeled onto gardens to keep them constantly fertilized. The hospital was able to power three stoves and one light, with gas to spare; to anticipate a yearly yield of 2 000 lbs. from its fishpond; to expect upwards of 200 table ducklings per year; and to enjoy the fruits of a flourishing garden. It is concluded that the returns on this moderate capital outlay, one that is within the means of the more sophisticated villages and all institutions, are impressive, particularly where there is a need to construct a waste system anyway. More detailed information regarding the construction and funding of such a system are appended. (HC)

3034 Frohlich, W. MacGregor, W.B. Francis, R.S. Rault, J. WHO, Brazzaville. *Development of health services.* Brazzaville, WHO, 30 Sep 1971. 14p. Engl.

The Seychelles are fortunate in that they are free from many tropical diseases and the worst forms of malnutrition. Endemic to the islands, however, are those diseases related to an insanitary environment--intestinal parasitism, gastroenteritis, and filariasis--and venereal disease. The prevalence rate for syphilis, judging from seropositive rates in primigravida, is 3.6%-3.8% and, for gonorrhea, 17.6%. It is expected that development in tourism will increase both the prevalence of the diseases and the possibility of the introduction of antibiotic-resistant strains. Examination of present venereal disease control reveals that laboratory and clinical facilities are unsatisfactory, that contact examination and treatment is nearly impossible, and that difficulties in procuring the reagents for serology are common. Other problems associated with communicable disease control in general are the curative orientation of the islands' health services, the dearth of trainees in the nursing and health inspector professions, and the lack of even one pediatrician, ophthalmologist, or ear, nose, and throat specialist. Some recommendations for increasing the number of nurses and health inspectors and for alleviating some of the other problems mentioned are given. (HC)

3035 Gideon, H. *Making the community diagnosis: the point of departure for community health programmes.* Contact (Geneva), 40, Aug 1977, 2-9. Engl.
Also published in French as: *Diagnostique communautaire,* Contact (Geneva), 31, Sep 1977, 1-8.

Community diagnosis is defined as a comprehensive assessment of the state of an entire community in relation to its social, physical, and biological environment. It is undertaken with a view to determining problems and setting priorities for planning and developing health care programmes for the community. There are five steps to conducting a community diagnosis: studying the available information about the area ('library reconnaissance'), visiting the area to determine the specific local situation ('field reconnaissance'), surveying the community regarding its basic demography and particular problems (sample demographic profiles and what can be deduced from them are included in this section), ascertaining community attitudes and behaviour through household interviews, and making the diagnosis. Suggestions on how to conduct each of these stages are given and a sample form for recording demographic data is included. (HC)

3036 Hamilton, P.J. Pan American Health Organization, Washington, D.C. WHO, Geneva. *Caribbean epidemiology centre.* In Research in Progress 1976, Washington, D.C., Pan American Health Organization, Department of Research Development and Coordination, 1976, 164-167. Engl.
For complete document see entry 2776 (volume 4); other chapters have been abstracted separately under entries 3069, 3082, 3465, 3476, 3495, 3497, and 3498.

In Trinidad, the Caribbean Epidemiology Centre (CAREC), a regional disease surveillance system established in January 1975, aims to reduce morbidity and mortality associated with communicable diseases. It acts as a regional centre for epidemiological surveillance, assists governments to develop effective national surveillance systems, serves as a specialized technical resource in the field of communicable disease control, assists in the development of laboratories, promotes collaborative relations between laboratories, provides selective diagnostic services, maintains facilities for the investigation of selected animal viruses, trains personnel for epidemiological surveillance and laboratory diagnosis, conducts laboratory and field research on diseases, provides facilities for visiting scientists, and researches virus diseases and their ecology. The centre publishes a monthly surveillance report that includes a digest of statistics. (HC)

3037 Hitze, K.L. WHO, Geneva. *Tuberculosis: a half-told story?* World Health (Geneva), Apr 1978, 19-22. Engl.
Also published in Arabic, French, German, Italian, Persian, Portuguese, Russian, and Spanish.

The history of tuberculosis control, from the discovery of the tubercule bacillus to the latest advance in drug therapy, is traced. Today, tuberculosis control consists of an inexpensive set of reliable diagnostic tools and effective preventive and curative methods that are, to a great extent, simple enough to be delegated to nonprofessionals. In 1964, a WHO committee on tuberculosis formulated the concept of the national tuberculosis control programme. The programme, defined as "the optimum set of activities leading to specific and systematic reduction of the tuberculosis problem within the resources available," meets the following qualifications: epidemiologically, it is countrywide and planned on a long-term basis; sociologically, it is adapted to and meets the needs of the population; operationally, it is integrated into and delivered by the general health services; and economically, it is planned and implemented within the resources available to the general health services. A number of countries have successfully implemented comprehensive national tuberculosis control programmes, but others, whether due to poorly developed basic health infrastructures or suspicion on the part of the authorities to the new, unsophisticated approach, have been reluctant to do so. It is suggested that, until these countries summon up the necessary will to apply themselves to the problem, global control of tuberculosis will remain a "half-told story." (HC)

3038 **Holdsworth, D.** *Traditional medicinal plants used in the treatment of malaria and fevers in Papua New Guinea.* Papua New Guinea Medical Journal (Port Moresby), 18(3), Sep 1975, 142-148. Engl.
16 refs.
Quinine, the specific treatment for malaria, is an alkaloid that occurs naturally in some plants. A study was undertaken to determine whether akaloids are found in the various plants used by traditional healers to treat malaria in Papua New Guinea. Senior high school students collected samples of the plants used in their villages for identification and testing. About half of the plants collected were for internal use; 42% of these were found to be akaloid positive and some were effective in the treatment of dysentery, coughs, headaches, and sores as well as malaria. It is hoped that further investigation into the composition of these plants will yield worthwile derivatives. The plants taken internally for malaria and fevers are listed along with their scientific and popular names, their preparation, and their usage. (HC)

3039 **Holland, W.W. Gilderdale, S.** *Epidemiology and health.* London, Henry Kimpton, 1977. 221p. Engl.
Refs.
Many different aspects of the contribution that epidemiology and its methods can make to health services and the improvement of health in general are presented in this compilation of essays by epidemiologists, social scientists, economists, and management experts. The various chapters treat: the five main epidemiological techniques--descriptive, case control, cross-sectional, longitudinal, and experimental--and how they can contribute to better health care in the modern Western context; a history of health improvement in the developed countries, a model for interpreting the active social processes involved in this improvement, and the application of this model to current health problems; the background,

structure, and development of Poland's integrated health services; cost and quality in health and their measurement (with reference to the British National Health Service); the organization of India's rural health system; the Health Services Development Research Project, West Azarbaijan, Iran; the experience of the Department of Social Medicine and Public Health, Singapore, in training medical students, practicing doctors, nurses, allied health personnel, and auxiliaries in epidemiology; the management process in health services (with reference to the British National Health Service); the role of epidemiology in health planning and ways in which the community physician can contribute to the process; and the contribution of epidemiology to health services management at microcosm (primary) institutions (hospital) and macrocosm (regional) levels. Each chapter is prefaced by an abstract. (HC)

3040 **Indo-Dutch Project for Child Welfare, Hyderabad, India.** *Abstracts of research on the health component.* Hyderabad, India, Indo-Dutch Project for Child Welfare, 1976. 48p. Engl.
30 refs.
See also entries 2917, 2918, 3016, and 3017.
The introduction to this collection of abstracts from the Indo-Dutch Project for Child Welfare outlines the origins, aims, and activities of the project since its inception in 1969. Designed for the child population of a limited area near Hyderabad, India, the project aims to bring together practicing child development workers, train additional personnel, and use local resources wherever possible. As part of the project, staff at Niloufer Hospital operated a mobile maternal child health clinic in selected villages and collected relevant information that forms the basis for the 30 papers abstracted in this booklet. Ten of the papers discuss child health services and the remainder present the results of specific surveys conducted by the staff, mainly concerned with assessment of malnutrition and the use of supplementary foods in treatment and prevention. Some additional information is given on the number of patients seen at the hospital and clinics, the staff at Niloufer, and categories of personnel in training. (DM)

3041 **Jamaica, Ministry of Health and Environment Control.** *Cornwall health programme in Jamaica.* Cajanus (Kingston, Jamaica), 10(3), 1977, 134-137. Engl.
A comprehensive health programme emphasizing maternal and child health, family planning, and nutrition is currently being introduced in the County of Cornwall, Jamaica. The programme's targets include: providing care for 90% of the area's pregnant women; providing postnatal care for 70% of the women; persuading one-third of the women aged 15-44 years to become family planning acceptors; providing preventive health services for 90% of all children aged less than 2 years and 70% of children aged 2-5 years; immunizing 80% of all children aged less than 2 years against smallpox, polio, diptheria, tetanus, and whooping cough; and monitoring the nutrition status of mothers and children and providing food supplements to 90% of children aged less than 2

years. The programme calls for the remodelling of 28 existing health centres and the addition of another 58. The health centres will be classified into four grades, according to the level of complexity of the services that they offer, and will employ a total of 1 500 professional and auxiliary workers. It is intended that this programme will have provided the necessary experience for the implementation of a nation-wide health service by the time it ends in 1980. (HC)

3042 **Jelliffe, D.B. Jelliffe, E.F.** *"Breast is best":* *modern meanings.* New England Journal of Medicine (Boston, Mass.), No.17, 27 Oct 1977, 912-915. Engl.
25 refs.
Reasons why breast-feeding is the recommended form of infant feeding for both rich and poor and developed and developing countries alike are documented in this paper. Despite the views that have been promulgated by the baby-food companies, human milk and cow's milk are dissimilar in almost all respects. The protective effects of breast milk against a range of infections have been shown to be due not to its cleanliness, as was previously thought, but to humoral 'host resistance factors' within it. Breast milk is the best prophylactic against food allergy, especially cow's milk allergy, during infancy. Modern studies have demonstrated that breast-feeding (with sucking throughout the 24 hours and without the inclusion of other food in the baby's diet) produces effective child-spacing through endocrinologic effects. Breast-feeding conserves resources at both the macro- and micro-economic levels in developing countries and certainly at the micro-economic levels in the developed ones. Finally, breast-feeding is conducive to early maternal neonate handling (the formation of intense attachment between mother and child) that may have implications for the later psychosocial development of the child. It is concluded that no single pediatric measure has such widespread and dramatic potential for child health as a return to breast-feeding. (HC)

3043 **Jelliffe, E.F. Caribbean Food and Nutrition Institute, Kingston, Jamaica.** *New look at multimixes for the Caribbean.* Environmental Child Health (London), 17(3), 1971, 136-150. Engl.
19 refs.
Multimixes are foods based on a staple ingredient consisting of either a cereal or one of the tuber-plantain-breadfruit group of vegetables. When combined with legumes, animal proteins, and dark green leafy vegetables, they provide a complete diet for infants and young children. In the Caribbean, the lack of essential amino acids in staple foods is one of the causes of juvenile malnutrition. Multimixes are carefully balanced to provide necessary combinations of vitamins, iron, or amino acids, particularly lysine and methionine. The ingredients are cheap and nutritious and contain none of the possibly harmful additives used in commercially prepared baby foods. The multimixes can, in some cases, be conveniently prepared for the whole family or the ingredients can be taken from the family meal before the condiments are added. Nutrition workers must advise mothers about the preparation and storage of seasonally available and culturally acceptable foods that can be used with the multimixes and the recipes, quantities, and cooking methods must be adaptable to home conditions. If possible, each mother should be seen individually to determine the vegetables she grows at home, her cooking methods and storage facilities, and her prejudices or misconceptions about food. Detailed cooking instructions and recipes noting the nutritional values of the foods are given in tables, a recipe section, and 4 appendices. (HH)

3044 **Jones, C.R. WHO, Brazzaville.** *Epidemiological surveillance in Mauritius: report on a mission 18 Nov-2 Dec 1974.* Brazzaville, WHO, 11 Apr 1975. 17p. Engl.
In the past 2 decades, Mauritius has made tremendous strides in communicable diseases control and surveillance, life expectancy has risen from 32-59 years, malaria has been eradicated, pulmonary tuberculosis has shown a steady decline, and immunization coverage has been greatly expanded. However, statistics show that improvement in some areas is still needed. Infant mortality is 60:1 000, venereal diseases are rampant and grossly underreported, and morbidity and mortality reporting in general is incomplete. Some improvements may derive from current projects to establish an extensive piped water system and sewage disposal, but additional improvements would be possible if an intensive health education campaign were launched to fight gonorrhoea and syphilis, if a more appropriate morbidity reporting form were introduced in hospitals and dispensaries, and if death certificates were required by law. (HC)

3045 **Levitt, S. Commonwealth Foundation, London. National Fund for Research into Crippling Diseases, Arundel, UK.** *Helping the handicapped child at village level.* In Disabled in Developing Countries, London, Commonwealth Foundation, 1977, 47-51. Engl.
Symposium on Appropriate Technology and Delivery of Health and Welfare Services for the Disabled in Developing Countries, Oxford, UK, 26-30 Sep 1976.
For complete document see entry 3124.
Because handicapped children tend to be retarded in other aspects of their development, stimulating environment is even more important for them than for the normal child. Restricted mobility due to physical or mental disability as well as malnutrition-related lethargy limit their perceptual experience, understanding of words, and social and emotional awareness. Although particular cases require expert help, there are simple exercises that can be initiated by parents, teachers, or health workers at home, in school, or in the community. The author suggests that village health workers be trained to advise and instruct parents and neighbours to assist in disabled children's primary development, once their emotional and motor abilities have been assessed. Active children will themselves demonstrate their potential to parents and teachers. (HH)

II Organization and Planning

3046   Llinares, V.M. Espana, Ministerio de Trabajo. *Agriculture, occupational medicine, and rural health.* Madrid, Ministerio de Trabajo, Instituto Nacional de Medicina y Seguridad del Trabajo, 1974. 43p. Engl.

The 1st of the book's three sections examines the world's growing interest in occupational hazards of agricultural work and rural life and devotes special attention to the work of the Japanese Institute of Rural Medicine. The 2nd section outlines Spain's efforts to protect its rural dwellers from infectious and occupational illnesses. These have included: standardizing preventive medical examinations; drawing up a table of occupational illness and hazards as a basis for compensation claims; legislating compulsory, periodic medical examination of those handling certain pesticides; establishing data collection centres in rural areas to monitor occupational risks; and organizing a mobile team composed of a doctor, a chemist, and an engineer to investigate new occupational hazards. The final section defines the place of occupational health within the medical curriculum, suggesting that last-year medical students be given a series of lectures on occupational and environmental health. (HC)

3047   Martin, A.E. WHO, Geneva. *Health aspects of human settlements: a review based on the technical discussions held during the twenty-ninth World Health Assembly, 1976.* Geneva, WHO, Public Health Papers No.66, 1977. 57p. Engl.
Also published in French.

Prior to the 1976 World Health Assembly, member states were sent a questionnaire and asked to contribute material describing the state of human settlements in their own countries. The responses indicated that developing countries emphasized problems of basic sanitation and nutrition while the developed countries were concerned about chemical and physical hazards and psychosocial problems. Consequently, the conference discussions covered a wide range of topics, including: nutrition; water supplies and sanitary disposal of excreta; the effects of housing structure on physical, mental, and social health; conservation, anti-pollution measures, and resource management; accident prevention in the home, on the road, and at work; health problems peculiar to slums, shanty towns, and squatter settlements; new housing and resettlement projects; transitional and temporary settlements (with reference to refugees, nomads, pilgrims, and migrant workers); and health education. The 255 participants agreed that health must be accepted as an integral part of planning and developing human settlements at the local, national, and international levels and that, in order to achieve this, health policies pertaining to the planning, management, and development of human settlements must be clarified and methods for making the health sector a partner in national policy- and decision-making must be identified. (HC)

3048   Maru, R.M. *Birth control in India and in the People's Republic of China: a comparison of policy evaluation, methods of birth control, and programme organization, 1949-1974.* Ann Arbor, University of Michigan, Department of Political Science, Mar 1976. 380p. Engl.
Refs.

China and India were chosen for this comparative study of birth control policies because of their demographic and economic similarities, their contrasting political systems, their recognition of the need to institute national programmes for controlling population growth, and the fact that, between them, they comprise over one-third of the world's population. The author endeavours to explain variations and similarities in their respective programmes through an analysis of leadership preferences and values, historical and ideological contexts, the structure and processes of the political decision-making systems, international environmental influences, birth control technology, and the elite perception of client response to policies. The various chapters analyze the factors that led to the adoption of national birth control programmes in both countries, trace the subsequent changing priorities of these programmes, discuss the status and popularity of different methods of birth control from the inception of the programme to the present, compare and contrast organizational features (i.e., the formal structures of the health and family planning organizations, including the training, distribution, and utilization of health and family planning manpower as well as organizational control), and explain the relationship between the birth control programmes and the political systems within which each developed. A distinction is made between aspects of the programmes that are deeply embedded in national political contexts and those that can be transferred to or adapted by other political systems. (HC)

3049   Masar, I. Christensen, S. WHO, Brazzaville. *Epidemiological services, Zambia. Report on a visit (10-20 Jan 1971).* Brazzaville, WHO, 3 Jun 1971. 11p. Engl.

In January 1971, WHO assisted the government of Zambia to investigate the possibility of collecting information on epidemiology and infant mortality. This report gives the results of surveys of existing health services, nutrition, morbidity, and mortality and these data are discussed. The authors recommend that: health services and resources be concentrated on epidemiology and the control of communicable diseases, laboratory facilities sufficient for accurate morbidity surveys be established, measures be taken to treat endemic goiter, and available information on nutrition and infant mortality be considered sufficient for accurate health planning. (RMB)

3050   Mata, L.J. Kromal, R.A. Urrutia, J.J. Garcia, B. *Effect of infection on food intake and the nutritional state: perspectives as viewed from the village.* American Journal of Clinical Nutrition (Bethesda, Md.), 30 (8), Aug 1977, 1215-1227. Engl.
53 refs.

A 1964-1972 study of mothers and children in a Guatemala highland village, where low income and deficient sanitation contribute to a high infection rate, showed that infection can affect a child's nutrition and growth from conception onwards. Weekly investigation of food intake, morbidity, and intestinal infection with parasites, bacteria, and viruses from birth-3 years of age revealed that infection caused extremely high morbidity among a sample of 45 children, particularly during the protracted weaning period (6-24 months). Fever and anorexia were particularly common during this time and infections such as diarrhea were principal causes of weight loss and impaired physical growth as well as secondary causes of malnutrition and death. Analysis of the dietary data from 30 fully weaned children showed very low calorie intakes but no protein intake deficit when values were calculated as functions of body weight. A strong inverse correlation between infectious diseases and calorie intake in the 2nd year of life pointed to infection as the most important single factor in malnutrition in the village. This implies that health and nutrition policies must include environmental intervention to reduce infection if food supplementation efforts are not to be entirely wasted. The failures of protein supplementation programmes in many parts of the world support this view. (CL)

3051   Mata, L.J. Kromal, R.A. Urrutia, J.J. Garcia, B. Institute of Nutrition of Central America and Panama, Guatemala City. *Antenatal events and postnatal growth and survival of children: prospective observation in a rural Guatemalan village.* In White, P.L., and Selvey, N., eds., Proceedings Western Hemisphere Nutrition Congress IV, Acton, Mass., Publishing Science Group, 1975, 107-116. Engl.
25 refs.

A high proportion of babies born in a Mayan Indian village in the Guatemalan highlands from 1964-1972 were of low birth weight: more than 30% were full term but small for gestational age (TSGA) and a further 7% were premature. Infant mortality was highest among the latter, but survivors from this group fared well in later years, whereas the death rate from the TSGA was persistently higher than that of surviving prematures as well as normal birthweight babies throughout early childhood. These findings resulted from a long-term survey of 465 babies born during the study period. Homes were visited weekly and numerous observations, mainly anthropometric, were made on both mothers and babies. These frequent measurements enabled monitoring of the children's growth rates up to age 6 years. All groups of children studied fell short of the standard growth curve, but the rates for low birthweight babies were consistently lower than for the others. The data revealed an association from low birthweight and abnormal maternal weight, height, age, and illness in pregnancy suggesting a link not only with the mother's ill health and malnutrition during pregnancy but with her nutritional status in early childhood. Hence an improvement in maternal environment by later marriage, increased child spacing, better socioeconomic status of women, and prenatal care could improve health, growth, and survival not only of immediate offspring but of generations to come. (DM)

3052   McDowell, J. UNICEF, Nairobi. *Food conservation.* In McDowell, J., ed., Village Technology in Eastern Africa, Nairobi, UNICEF Eastern Africa Regional Office, 1976, 22-27. Engl.
Regional Seminar on Simple Technology for the Rural Family, Nairobi, Kenya, 14-19 Jun 1976.
For complete document see entry 3090.

The application of appropriate food conservation technologies could radically reduce food losses in African villages. The required effective drying and moisture-proof, insect-proof, and rodent-proof storage containers can all be constructed by adapting traditional approaches using low-cost, readily available, rural materials. For example, solar driers of mud or clay with plastic covers dry food more effectively than indigenous methods and can be used to dehydrate vegetables to produce concentrated food for child feeding as well as dry foods for storage. Storage of grain can also be improved; although traditional African granaries are not usually able to keep food dry and free of insects and rodents, adaptations such as complete mud plastering, sealing with a lid, fitting of an emptying spout, and raising on wooden legs makes them into adequate storage places. Using insecticides to prevent infestation presents toxic and environmental hazards, so the potential for insecticide use in food storage at village and domestic level is very low. Instead, appropriate technology for pest control should include avoidance of infestation before storage, thus applying basic scientific principles at minimal cost. (CL)

3053   McDowell, J. *Development of high-protein/high-calorie biscuits in Uganda using indigenous protein sources.* East Africa Journal of Rural Development (Kampala), 6(1-2), 1973-1974, 97-110. Engl.

The steps taken to develop a low-cost children's food supplement in Uganda suggest an approach to producing similar products elsewhere. The criteria for the supplement are that it be small in bulk but high in both calories and complete protein. Local nuts and grains (groundnut, sesame, soya, finger millet, and wheat) can be ground to make flour and baked with fat, sugar, baking powder, salt, and water to form cookies or biscuits. Different combinations of ingredients and methods can be tried to produce final recipes that are nutritious, simple, and palatable. Four or five biscuits made from such recipes can provide 8-10 g quality protein and 200-300 cal; they also have a long storage life, are highly acceptable to children, can be adapted as a weaning food by crumbling and mixing to a paste with water, and can be used as a base for other locally needed vitamin and mineral supplements. (AB)

3054   McDowell, J. UNICEF, Nairobi. *Village technology component in primary health care systems.* Nairobi, UNICEF, n.d. 8p. Engl.
Unpublished document.

The concept of "health by the people" involves whole-hearted social participation in community action projects that apply appropriate technologies at village, community, and family levels to many basic health problems, including food supplies, housing conditions, water supplies, and sanitation. For example, appropriate village technologies for food conservation can salvage some of the developing world's food supplies presently vulnerable to mould, rodents, and insects; solar drying of fruits and vegetables to conserve vitamins and minerals can yield storable and easily transported products; appropriate village technologies for water storage can ease the burden of village women, who sometimes have to carry water from great distances; and appropriate low cost sanitation and home hygiene technologies can help to control gastroenteritis, diarrhea, and parasitic diseases. Technologies that the people can apply themselves to improve their own health and prevent their own illnesses are the only way to bring about better health for millions of the world's poor people. (CL)

3055 McDowell, U. UNICEF, Nairobi. *Community action: family health programmes delivering an integrated package; appropriate technologies for tackling malnourishment.* Nairobi, UNICEF, Sep 77. 15p. Engl.
Working Conference of the International Union of Nutritional Sciences, Hyderabad, India, 17-21 Oct 1977.
The alleviation of poverty-related malnutrition cannot wait for a more equal distribution of income. Appropriate technologies must be developed for low-income communities to make more food available, improve home hygiene, and conserve human energy. Technologies for increasing food supplies include effective food conservation such as solar drying and moisture- and pest-proof storage in scientifically improved granaries. Low-input farming technology based on ecological principles can maximize production without destroying the environment. For example, this type of farming returns all unharvested plant material to the soil and uses crop density and height variations to obtain optimum effects from solar radiation. A mixture of crops also provides a better balanced diet and insures against nutritional disaster following crop failure. However, although increased food supplies can partially alleviate malnutrition, improvement of home hygiene is necessary to prevent infections like gastroenteritis. Technologies to accomplish this include better house building using low cost cement and stabilized earth bricks, roof collection of water, and construction of fly-free latrines. Supportive technologies that conserve human energy include solar cookers, which reduce the energy expended in fuel collection and do not pollute the environment. (CL)

3056 McJunkin, F.E. USA, Agency for International Development, Department of State. *Water, engineers, development, and disease in the tropics: schistosomiasis engineering applied to planning, design, construction and operation of irrigation, hydroelectric and other water development schemes.* Washington, D.C., Agency for International Development, Jul 1975. 182p. Engl.
272 refs.
This publication identifies health-related environmental effects of water resources development in developing countries. It focuses primarily on the changes due to

relocation of water resources through lakes, canals, channels, irrigation, hydroelectric projects, etc. Based on the experiences of existing projects, it acknowledges the major health threats of schistosomiasis and filariasis and suggests measures for eliminating or controlling the parasites. Suggested engineering measures include disrupting the parasites' life cycle and creating an unfavourable environment for the snail hosts; chemical measures comprise disinfecting water and employing molluscides in infested areas. Notes on controlling aquatic plants, the construction of canal linings, and problems of reservoir development are appended. (AC)

3057 Menu, J.P. Dove, J.E. Noamesi, G.K. Dazo, B.C. WHO, Brazzaville. *Health component in South Chad irrigation project; feasibility study: report on missions (Sep 1972-Mar 1973).* Brazzaville, WHO, 1 Sep 1973. 116p. Engl.
In 1972-1973, WHO assisted the government of Nigeria to investigate the feasibility of an irrigation development project in a $100\,000^2$ hectare area south of Lake Chad. The WHO consultants helped to: survey the biological, ecological, and epidemiological situation in the project area; determine the impact of the project on disease patterns and control; assess the present health status and the possible effect of the project on future health conditions; advise on methods for reducing or eliminating health hazards and improving environmental health and sanitation within settlements; and suggest measures for providing safe domestic water supplies from boreholes, wells, and storage tanks. The report examines the existing situation in terms of medical services, communicable diseases, water supplies, and environmental sanitation and the anticipated impact of the project in these areas. The experts' recommendations for schistosomiasis and malaria control, water supplies, environmental sanitation, housing and village development, and health services are presented. Annexes include epidemiological data, water classification schemes, and traditional building techniques for village houses. (RMB)

3058 Mercer, H. *Investigacion social aplicada al campo de la salud. (Social research as applied to health).* Educacion Medica y Salud (Washington, D.C.), 9(4), 1975, 347-354. Span.
Historically, the relationship between social sciences and medicine has passed through three stages: social sciences as the study of culture, social medicine, and medicine as a social science. The author discusses these aspects and then briefly points out other alternatives based on the idea that health is a manifestation of the will of the people, dependent on sociopolitical factors that the social sciences can help to explain. (RMB)

3059 Messing, S.D. *Rural health in Africa.* East Lansing, Mich., Michigan State University, African Studies Centre, Rural Africana: Current Research in the Social Sciences, No.17, Winter 1972. 131p. Engl.
Refs.
See also entry 2811.
Rural Africana is a quarterly publication devoted to

current research into the problems of social and economic development in rural Africa south of the Sahara. Each issue focuses on a particular problem or area of research, presenting papers selected by a guest editor conversant with the subject and current endeavours in the field. This issue deals with health and the various papers in it treat such diverse aspects of the subject as: social problems in a small town setting that affect the development of health, the modern health care infrastructure, social structure and health care systems, movements of populations in relation to communicable disease, geographical variations in disease patterns, demographic research and training, nutrition and behaviour, traditional concepts of the etiology of disease, mental healing, and socio-psychiatric problems in a country in transition. A selected 200-item bibliography on rural health is included. (HC)

3060   Minde, K.K. *Children in Uganda: rates of behavioural deviations and psychiatric disorders in various school and clinic populations.* Journal of Child Psychology and Psychiatry and Allied Disciplines (London), 18(1), Jan 1977, 23-37. Engl.
21 refs.
A survey of psychiatric symptoms in Ugandan primary school children was undertaken to determine the viability of behavioural screening techniques, originally developed for European children, in an African context. The subjects of the study were children attending three primary schools in economically distinct areas, children who had been committed to a reform school, and attenders of a child psychiatry clinic. Teachers of all the primary and reform schools were asked to complete a symptom screening test and clinic personnel were asked to distinguish between children exhibiting organic and behavioural symptoms. Those children whose scores of behaviour suggested the presence of psychiatric symptoms were then assigned a clinical diagnosis and their parents were questioned according to a symptom checklist. Finally, child and family were interviewed in order to shed some light on the origin of deviance. It was observed that, while some specific symptoms were rarely encountered in Uganda, the majority seemed to possess transcultural relevance as evidenced by good correlation between teachers and parents in identifying disturbed children. Furthermore, factors (divorce, family breakup, etc.) associated in many cultures with psychiatric disorders were evident in the disturbed children in the study. It is therefore concluded that African children do show symptoms comparable to those in European countries, although in Africa the symptoms are seen merely as forms of nuisance that require punishment by an adult. A child psychiatrist, in order to have some impact on the population, would have to find and treat such children in the community. (HC)

3061   Mount Carmel International Training Centre for Community Services, Haifa, Israel. Israel, Ministry of Agriculture. *Course on rural community development: field work in Swaziland.* In Report of the Course on Rural Community Development, Haifa, Israel, Mount Carmel International Train-

ing Centre for Community Services, Jul 1975, 25-46. Engl.
See also entry 2569 (volume 3).
Eight 1975 graduates of a rural community development course held at the Mount Carmel International Training Centre (Israel) took part in a field exercise to collect socioeconomic data in a rural area of Swaziland. Ten Swazi rural workers acted as consultants and interpreters. Investigators surveyed the inhabitants of 12 scattered homesteads by means of 2 questionnaires and 4 personal visits. They found that sanitary facilities were generally lacking; there was no piped water supply and most water sources, including river water, were known to be infected with schistosomiasis. In spite of this, 11 of 12 families did not boil their drinking water. Other findings were that: maize porridge is the staple food; protein-rich food and milk are rare, although nuts, peas, and cereals provide some quality protein; food eaten by women during pregnancy appears to be of low-protein content; and the quality of available health care could be greatly improved--although 2 well-trained nurses see up to 100 patients a day, they are supported by a doctor only once a month. The recommendations of the group include improvements in agricultural practices, education, nutrition (especially during pregnancy), water supply and sanitation, and the utilization of existing health services. (EE)

3062   Muller, M. *Selling health--or buying favour?* New Scientist (London), 73(1037), 3 Feb 1977, 266-268. Engl.
The promotion of commercial preparations of baby milk to mothers in developing countries has provoked international public censure in recent years. Less well known are the methods used by producers of baby foods to influence the medical profession. One such company, the Philippine subsidiary of the US pharmaceutical firm Mead Johnson, offers a wide range of inducements to doctors and nurses to promote its products; in addition, its donations of free samples and equipment to nurseries, maternity hospitals, and clinics help to win the exclusive markets. A possible indicator of the success of these tactics is the company's leading position in the baby food market. There is also indirect evidence that medical advice is influenced by such promotional techniques. According to a survey in Manila, doctors are favourably disposed toward the milk companies and surprisingly ignorant of many aspects of breast-feeding. These and other abuses have recently been brought to light by a court case against the US parent company, Bristol Myers, on the grounds of fraudulent misrepresentation to shareholders of the firm's milk promotion in developing countries. This case has generated public concern about US milk industries' activities abroad and resulted in calls for US AID to launch a breast-feeding promotion campaign as a counter-means. However, the crucial issue remains the *modus operandi* of the pharmaceutical industry in countries like the Philippines. Greater reforms in such operations will be necessary before rational policies can be implemented to meet health needs. (DM)

3063 National Academy of Sciences, Washington, D.C. *Making aquatic weeds useful: some perspectives for developing countries.* Washington, D.C., National Academy of Sciences, 1976. 183p. Engl. Refs.

An introductory review rather than a technical treatise, this report is intended for those whose resources and interests could stimulate research on aquatic weed utilization. It examines methods suitable for developing countries to control and use the aquatic weeds that often hinder development efforts and harbour disease vectors such as snails and mosquitoes. Topics covered include use of herbivorous animals for weed control, the harvesting and uses of aquatic weeds, wastewater treatment using aquatic weeds (including such possible complications as the pollution of groundwaters and the creation of disease vector breeding grounds), and the nutritional potential of aquatic crops such as the Chinese water chestnut and water spinach. Most topics are discussed in terms of: specific techniques and their advantages, limitations, and special requirements; research needs; selected readings; and research contacts. Duckweeds and their uses are considered in detail in the 1st of 2 appendices, which are followed by summaries in Spanish and French. (CL)

3064 National Academy of Sciences, Washington, D.C. *Food science in developing countries: a selection of unsolved problems.* Washington, D.C., National Research Council, National Academy of Sciences, 1974. 89p. Engl. Refs.

This collection represents an extension of the National Academy of Science's search for ways of applying appropriate science and technology to problems of economic and social development, in particular, problems in food science and nutrition in developing countries. This compendium is directed especially to readers who cannot easily obtain international journals or travel to international meetings. It contains a total of 42 specific problems, each of which is split into sections consisting of the problem description, background information, possible approaches to a solution, and special requirements. A list of references and key contacts for each problem follows. The problems are organized into 4 main groups, the 1st of which (New Foods) contains 11 problems including 1 concerning local low-cost weaning foods. The 2nd group (Food Processing) contains 11 problems and the 3rd (Food Composition) 5, whereas the 4th and largest group contains 15 problems, each concerning nutrition and health. This final group includes 2 discussions of sociological aspects of food science and 2 problems in food and nutrition planning and policies. The remaining problems in this group are of a more technical nature and include some biochemical and microbiological aspects of food science. Finally, a separate list identifies 41 contributors, no individual authorship being assigned to the problems because of overlap and combination of contributions. (CL)

3065 Nightingale, K.W. *Health problems of a South African tribal homeland.* New Zealand Medical Journal (Wellington), 85(579), 12 Jan 1977, 18-21. Engl. 22 refs.

A doctor in a mission hospital in Kwa Zulu (Zululand) discusses malnutrition and disease in this South African homeland. Kwa Zulu is a rocky, hilly territory subject to drought in winter and torrential, eroding rainstorms in summer. In 1954, the Tomlinson Report stated that, if fully developed, it could support a population of 13 000; since then, there has been no significant agricultural development and the population has risen to 100 000. Up to 50% of the children seen in the hospital's clinics are under the third percentile (weight) and about 25% suffer from malnutrition. About half of the adult inpatients present a variety of conditions associated with malnutrition such as pellagra, osteomalacia, and scurvey. Other diseases that are seen frequently are tuberculosis, rheumatic fever, rhemuatic heart disease, typhoid fever, amoebic dysentery, hookworm, and other parasitic diseases. An investigation of 150 randomly-selected families in 1974 revealed that the average monthly income is R14.87 (the local poverty datum line is estimated at R103.99), of which R11.29 is spent on food. The farm produce of the families was investigated and concluded insufficient to provide more than a small proportion of an adequate diet. It is concluded that health problems in Kwa Zulu are directly related to socioeconomic status and that large scale agricultural aid and the introduction of irrigation schemes and drinking water supplies are urgently required if the people are to survive. (HC)

3066 Noguer, A. WHO, Geneva. *Malaria: cause for alarm.* World Health (Geneva), Apr 1978, 13-17. Engl. Also published in Arabic, French, German, Italian, Persian, Portuguese, Russian, and Spanish.

Two technological advances made the world eradication of malaria feasible after the Second World War: the discovery of DDT, a long-acting insecticide that continues to kill insects for several months after spraying, and the development of extremely efficient synthetic drugs (chloroquine, amodiaquine, primaquine, and pyrimethamine) for treating the human host. Malaria eradication strategy was based on interrupting the transmission of the disease by reducing the contacts between man and mosquito for long enough to insure the natural disappearance of the parasite from its human hosts. Rather than calling for the total annihilation of the mosquito population, the strategy aimed to reduce the density and life expectancy of the mosquitos that bit mankind by spraying people's homes. The simplicity of the strategy encouraged WHO to believe that a time-limited programme could be carried out for a relatively modest outlay. Thus, in 1959, WHO calculated the cost of world eradication of malaria at slightly over US$1 691 million. This estimate, however, fell considerably short of the real figure; from 1957-1976 in the Americas alone, over $995 million was spent. Countries became discouraged, health and socioeconomic priorities changed, and technical difficulties, such as the resistance developed by the mosquitos against DDT, have forced WHO to revise its tactics. A revision, approved by the 22nd World Health Assembly in 1969, recommends a more flexible, pragmatic approach to malaria control while retaining global eradication as the final goal. (HC)

3067 Nyirenda, F.K. *Underfive clinics: normal/underweight children.* League for International Food Education Newsletter (Washington, D.C.), Feb 1978, 3-4. Engl.

At an under-fives' clinic in Malawi, underweight children are treated in a separate group, not only because immunization is not always effective in malnourished children, but also because it allows clinic staff to instruct the children's mothers without embarrassing them. This grouping of children according to problem rather than location demonstrates that children living in towns and villages can be equally undernourished, a point that is not always clear to village women, who may think that a town child has access to better food. The approach also provides an incentive to mothers to work to have their children "promoted" to the normal children's clinic day, so that they can receive all the vaccinations. (HH)

3068 Oyemade, A. Olugbile, A. *Assessment of health needs of agricultural workers in Nigeria.* Public Health (London), 91(4), Jul 1977, 183-188. Engl. 12 refs.

A survey was carried out in Badeku (Nigeria) to identify the health needs of its 2 394 inhabitants. Interviewers questioned 178 heads of households regarding housing, sanitary facilities, and health knowledge and asked their wives about utilization of health facilities and fertility. The survey revealed that: housing was generally poor, inadequately ventilated, and polluted by smoke; 95.5% of all households dumped their refuse behind the houses or in the bush; 84.3% of all households defecated behind the houses or in the bush; all the households obtained their water from a communal well; over 90% of the children had never been immunized against tuberculosis, poliomyelitis, or measles and only 64.6% had been vaccinated against smallpox; although 85.7% of the women received their antenatal care in a health facility, only 10.6% delivered there; infant mortality during the 4-year period preceding the survey was 23%; and, although 51.7% of the men interviewed knew that drinking water from ponds or streams could be dangerous, only 7.8% associated any health hazard with indiscriminate defecation. It is concluded that any programme designed to improve hygienic standards in the area must be prefaced by an intensive education campaign on the causes and modes of transmission of disease. (HC)

3069 Pazos, A. *Sewage treatment with tower-like filters.* In Research in Progress 1976, Washington, D.C., Pan American Health Organization, Department of Research Development and Coordination, 1976, 340. Engl.

For complete document see entry 2776 (volume 4); other chapters have been abstracted separately under entries 3036, 3082, 3465, 3476, 3495, 3497, and 3498.

A project to study the efficiency of tower-like trickling filters under different loads and volumes of domestic sewage is currently underway in Guatemala City. The project involves the construction of a plant consisting of a primary settling tank, the tower-like filter, an Imhoff tank, and drying beds. The flow of the sewage through the plant will be controllable so that its biochemical oxygen demand, dissolved oxygen, total solids, settlable solids, bacterial and coliform content, etc., can be determined through testing at different rates. The process at work in the filters is known as 'biologic percolation.' (HC)

3070 Penchaszadeh, V. Marquez, M. *Investigacion en salud maternoinfantil y reproduccion humana. (Research in maternal and child health and human reproduction).* Educacion Medica y Salud (Washington, D.C.), 11(1), 1977, 41-49. Span.

Medical research has never received much support in Latin America and most existing research projects are biologically oriented. Consequently, research methodologies are not designed to take into account anything other than biological factors. The authors propose a new "tridimensional approach" to research in maternal child health that incorporates biological, psychological, and sociological aspects; they list specific topics to be studied using this method in the areas of public health, genetics, fetal growth and development, the newborn, childbirth, nutrition, child development, geriatrics, and fetal and infant deformities. The authors point out that research topics should be determined by the needs of the country rather than international criteria. (RMB)

3071 Percira, S.M. Begum, A. *Vitamin A deficiency in Indian children.* World Review of Nutrition and Dietetics (London), 24, 1976, 192-216. Engl. 119 refs.

This study examines the nutritional status of Indian children in terms of vitamin A deficiency and associated vision impairment and blindness. Surveys have revealed that millions of children are at risk because of malnutrition, early weaning, the dietary restrictions imposed on pregnant and lactating women, and chronic illness and infestation. When vitamin A deficiency is the only health problem, it is easily treated by massive doses of the vitamin given either orally or by injection, but when the condition is combined with other illnesses, treatment is much more complicated. Consequently, the authors conclude that a curative approach is much less effective than prevention of vitamin A deficiency, which can be carried out by giving massive doses of the vitamin to expectant and lactating mothers and to at-risk children, incorporating locally available carotene-rich foods into the diet, and fortifying other foods, such as sugar or tea. (RMB)

3072 Pielemeier, N.R. USA, Department of Health, Education, and Welfare. *Syncrisis: the dynamics of health. XIII: Botswana, Lesotho and Swaziland.* Washington, D.C., U.S. Government

Printing Office, DHEW Publication No.(OS)75-50, No.018, 1975. 136p. Engl.
Refs.
See also entries 1322, 1342, 1343, 1353-1355 (volume 2), 1985, 1987, 1991, 2002 (volume 3), and 3012 for other volumes of this series.

This volume is one of a series of profiles that describe and analyze the health conditions of a country and their impact on socioeconomic development. The three countries in question--Botswana, Lesotho, and Swaziland--have been grouped together because they share much in common: similar cultures and languages resulting from their Bantu heritage, similar institutions arising from their historical association with UK, a common pastoral tradition, and an economic dependence on South Africa. In addition, they exhibit similar disease patterns, nutrition deficiencies arising from a common corn-based diet, and demographic characteristics. However, because of distinct differences arising from varying endowment in natural resources, levels of political and economic development, and geographic location, each one is treated separately. These topics are discussed: health environment, determinants of health and disease, health care delivery system (including health manpower and training), and some country-specific subjects such as settlement patterns, housing, agriculture, land tenure, labour migration, etc. It is hoped that this volume will prove a valuable source of background information to those concerned with the health or the development of these three developing countries. (HC)

3073   Pio, A. Western, K. *Tuberculosis control in the Americas: current approaches.* Bulletin of the Pan American Health Organization (Washington, D.C.), 10(3), 1976, 227-231. Engl.
Also published in Spanish in *Boletin de la Oficina Sanitaria Panamericana* (Washington, D.C.), 80(4), 1976, 281-287.

Expected declines in tuberculosis indexes in the Americas have not materialized because of a considerable lag between the validation of new methods of control and their application. Early control measures focused on systematic X-raying of entire communities and hospitalization of patients in isolated, specialized institutions, both expensive methods that are only readily available in developed countries. In the mid-1940s, the discovery of effective antibiotic and chemotherapeutic agents and the scientific demonstration of the protective value of BCG vaccine made ambulatory treatment and prophylaxis possible. By the 1960s, in order to extend coverage to a greater part of the population, the idea of integrating tuberculosis activities into the general health services emerged, although, contrary to expectations, this idea has been more widely accepted in the developed, rather than the developing, countries. A recent survey of 19 085 health institutions in 16 different Latin American countries revealed that fewer than half of these had incorporated tuberculosis activities into their general routine; moreover, in 10 Latin American countries in 1973, an average of 70.8% of the tuberculosis budget in 1973 went for hospital beds while only 5.2% was spent on BCG vaccination, diagnosis, and treatment activities within the general health services. (HC)

3074   Prince Leopold Institute of Tropical Medicine, Antwerp, Belgium. *Disaster epidemiology: proceedings of an international colloquium, Antwerp, 5-7 Dec 1975.* Antwerp, Belgium, Prince Leopold Institute of Tropical Medicine, 1976. 219p. Engl., Fren.
International Colloquium on Disaster Epidemiology, Antwerp, Belgium, 5-7 Dec 1975.
Reprinted from *Annales des Societes Belges de Medecine Tropicale de Parasitologie et de Mycologie Humaine et Animale* (Antwerp, Belgium), 56(4-5), 1976, 187-403.

The introduction to the colloquium dealt with general aspects of disaster epidemiology and was followed by two half-day sessions on nutritional problems such as famine prediction, nutritional surveillance, and specific deficiencies. Contributors to the closing session discussed the role of international agencies in disaster relief and planning. Most of the 21 papers from the colloquium are reproduced in their entirety together with the resulting discussion and are followed by general comments and a summary of the conference conclusions in French. The items are entered in the language of presentation, either French or English, though session titles are also given in Dutch. Names and addresses of the 73 participants are listed. (DM)

3075   Retel-Laurentin, A. *Infecondite en Afrique noire: maladies et consequences sociales. (Infertility in Black Africa: diseases and their social consequences).* Paris, Masson, 1973. 188p. Fren.
518 refs.

Obvious differences in the fertility rates of various African ethnic groups have long puzzled anthropologists and medical personnel. This enquiry examines the phenomenon of infertility in Africa with a view to shedding some light on its origin and aetiology. Topics covered include: population density and geographical distribution of infertile societies; characteristics of African fertility and infertility from the beginning of the 20th century; African morbidity, with emphasis on sleeping sickness and venereal disease; the social determinants of low fertility during the colonization period; the marital context; and beliefs concerning abortion. The infertile society is characterized by a high level of totally sterile individuals, an "acquired sterility" amongst women aged 30-35 years, a high rate of fetal wastage, premarital sexual freedom and unstable marriages, and a rate of syphilis infection surpassing 10%. It is concluded that efforts to end the debilitating effects of infertility upon these societies will have to begin with a vigourous campaign against venereal disease. (HC)

3076   Ritchie, J. UNICEF, Nairobi. *Food preparation.* In McDowell, J., ed., Village Technology in Eastern Africa, Nairobi, UNICEF Eastern Africa Regional Office, 1976, 27-31. Engl.
Regional Seminar on Simple Technology for the Rural Family, Nairobi, Kenya, 14-19 Jun 1976.
For complete document see entry 3090.

The range of food available to low-income families in Africa is sufficient to maintain an adequate level of nutrition if properly used. Africa has many excellent vegetable foods that, either singly or combined, can rival animal foods in nutritional value. Therefore, appropriate technologies for child feeding should be based on the use of inexpensive local cereals, legumes, and vegetables. For example, supplementary and weaning foods could consist of simple nutritious mixes of local beans, roots or cereals, green leaves, and fruits rather than expensive imported breast milk substitutes or high protein baby foods. Western-type jars of strained infant foods can be replaced by convenience foods prepared by African mothers from peas, beans, groundnuts, or *sim-sim* by roasting, boiling, drying, and pounding to a flour. Protein-calorie rich biscuits can be made from any mixture of flours from pulses, oil seeds, and cereals with wheat flour, fat, baking powder, and sugar or salt and have proved highly popular in Uganda. Teaching improvements of accepted local dishes and cooking methods is more likely to improve nutrition than trying to introduce new ones and there is also a need for simple technologies to keep food clean and maintain a hygienic home environment, because much malnutrition is related to gastroenteritis and other infections. (CL)

3077   Rowland, M.G. Barrell, R.A. Whitehead, R.G. *Bacterial contamination in traditional Gambian weaning foods.* Lancet (London), 1(8056), 21 Jan 1978, 136-138. Engl.
12 refs.
See also entries 3078 and 3096.
A study of traditional infant weaning foods in a Gambian village showed that nutritionally inadequate gruels were frequently contaminated with bacteria. Regular observations of growth, dietary intake, and health status for each village child from birth revealed that, from the age of 3 months onwards, the body weight of the infants fell behind internationally accepted standards, their intake of breast milk decreased, and they were fed more supplementary foods. Diarrheal disease also appeared at age 3 months and was common by 6 months, so investigations were carried out at various stages during preparation and storage of traditional supplementary gruels to determine when bacterial contamination occurred. Viable counts of five bacteria, including *staphylococcus aureus* and *eschericia coli*, showed that bacterial multiplication in gruel during storage in a bowl increased rapidly after initial contamination of both freshly-cooked gruel and the empty bowl. Bowls of two commercial milk formula infant foods, when similarly tested, showed that bacterial levels were not much higher than in the gruel, regardless of whether the milk had been prepared with boiled or unboiled water. These findings indicate that microbiological contamination, contrary to expectations, is not confined to commercial baby milks and feeding bottles but is also found in traditional weaning foods and simple containers. Although one sure way of avoiding contamination is to give infants only freshly-prepared food, this would be time-consuming for the mother, so nutritionists should develop easy, quick, semisolid weaning foods based on local food resources. (CL)

3078   Rowland, M.G. Cole, T.J. Whitehead, R.G. *Quantitative study into the role of infection in determining nutritional status in Gambian village children.* British Journal of Nutrition (London), 37(3), 1977, 441-450. Engl.
21 refs.
See also entries 3077 and 3096.
Any programme directed at improving the nutritional status of a community must take local disease patterns as well as dietary inadequacies into account. This study attempts to quantify the contributions of different infections to the growth pattern and nutritional status of Gambian children in the 1st 3 years of life. The measurements of heights and weights of 152 children aged 6 months-3 years in Keneba, a rural Gambian village, show that by 1 year the average weight-for-age of the children is only 75% of the international Jelliffe standard. Relating these height and weight measurements to the disease prevalence of 9 categories of disease, including upper and lower respiratory tract infections, gastroenteritis, and malaria, shows that there is a highly significant negative relationship between gastroenteritis and both height gain ($P > 0.01$) and weight gain ($P > 0.001$). Malaria, though seasonally more variable, has a lower mean prevalence and shows a highly significant negative relationship to weight gain only ($P > 0.001$). Normal weight gain and even some catch-up growth could be possible after the age of 1 year in the absence of gastroenteritis, according to multiple regression analysis. These findings suggest that assessing nutritional status entirely on anthropometric measurements alone cannot give any indication of the relative importance of dietary and other factors, such as disease patterns, and that height and weight measurements need a supporting investigation into the quantitative role of these other health aspects. (CL)

3079   Sanchez R., H. Pereda F., C. Terra Institute, Madison, Wisc. Centro para el Desarrollo Rural y Cooperacion, Santiago. *Diferentes patrones para medir desnutricion infantil en zonas rurales de Talca. (Different methods of measuring juvenile malnutrition in rural areas of Talca).* Santiago, Centro para el Desarrollo Rural y Cooperacion, 1976. 109p. Span.
16 refs.
This extremely comprehensive study analyzes the results of a nutritional survey by 4 health professionals of 292 rural Chilean families carried out in October-November 1976. The nutritional status of children aged less than 6 years was measured using height/age, weight/age, circumference/age, and height/weight tests and the results compared to those of children from three control groups. Questionnaires were used to ascertain the children's socioeconomic status and whether or not the family was accustomed to make use of available medical services. The different levels of malnutrition present in the sample population as evinced by each test are discussed and the authors conclude that malnutrition tends to increase with age and occur more often in the children of unemployed agricultural workers than in the offspring of farm labourers and small farmers. Annexes describe in detail the questionnaires and the nutritional

measurement methods used. Statistical data are included. (RMB)

3080 Sandhu, S.K. *Health education in filaria control.* Journal of Communicable Diseases (New Delhi), 8(3), Sep 1976, 175-178. Engl.

In India, public education about the origin and transfer of filariasis is the most important element in programmes to control the disease. Without education, the people cannot avoid contact with the disease and cannot be effectively motivated to institute vector control measures. They will continue to harbour superstitions about the causes and ostracize the victims and their families. Through education they can gain an understanding of the relationship between poor sanitation and disease spread, the reasons for testing night blood samples, and the early symptoms of the disease. Aids for teaching them include mass media, posters, lectures, discussions, pamphlets, etc., but the most effective teaching method currently is to identify community leaders, concentrate education activities on them, and urge them to launch their own control campaigns. (AC)

3081 Sartorius, N. WHO, Geneva. *Compete or complement?* World Health (Geneva), Dec 1977, 28-33. Engl.
Also published in Arabic, French, Italian, Persian, Portuguese, Russian, and Spanish.

Convinced that delivery of services and research are complementary activities, the WHO Division of Mental Health is committed to research projects aimed at improving mental health care delivery. Research teams in Colombia, India, Senegal, and Sudan are cooperating to develop simple inexpensive methods for providing mental health care at the primary health level, methods that can be used not only by simply-trained health personnel but also by other workers such as traditional healers, police, and teachers. Other cross-cultural studies aim to evaluate the effects of socioeconomic, nutritional, and even climatic variations on specific diseases and treatments. One such large study involving 5-year follow-up of 1 200 patients with severe mental disorders showed that the prognosis was considerably better for patients in developing countries than for those in industrialized countries. This new knowledge is being used to dispel unfounded fears and encourage early treatment and further comparative research is exploring such variables as family structure in order to define better ways of service provision. Where obstacles to improvement of services are due to factors other than lack of knowledge, they must be removed by better coordination, direct strong involvement of different sectors contributing to mental health care, and appropriate political and administrative decisions. (AB)

3082 Schifini, J.P. *Stabilization ponds.* In Research in Progress 1976, Washington, D.C., Pan American Health Organization, Department of Research Development and Coordination, 1976, 343-344. Engl.
For complete document see entry 2776 (volume 4); other chapters have been abstracted separately

under entries 3036, 3069, 3465, 3476, 3495, 3497, and 3498.

Because of their relatively low cost, stabilization ponds are recognized as one of the most suitable approaches to sewage treatment in the developing countries. A study is underway in Chile to evaluate the efficiency of stabilization ponds (lagoons) under the climatic conditions prevailing in the city of Melipilla, their performance in comparison with that of conventional sewage treatment systems, and their load capacity. Three stabilization ponds have been built by the side of a conventional sewage treatment plant. Different loads and flow rates are being applied to the lagoons and the biochemical oxygen demand (BOD), the dissolved oxygen (DO), and total solids are being measured and correlated with sunshine hours and water and air temperatures. Preliminary results have shown marked reductions in BOD, fecal coliforms, and algae in the effluent when the three ponds operate in series; appropriate loading design parameters for such ponds operating at temperatures above 13 degrees centigrade have been developed. Further results from the study should shed light on the feasibility of implementing this treatment process on a wider scale. (HC)

3083 Schuenyane, E. Mashigo, S. Eyberg, C. Richardson, B.D. Buchanan, N. Pettifor, J. Macdougall, L. Hansen, J.D. *Socio-economic, health, and cultural survey in Soweto.* South African Medical Journal (Cape Town), 51(15), 9 Apr 1977, 495-500. Engl.

A random sample of 186 non-white families in Diepkloof, Soweto, South Africa, was studied during 6 months in 1975 to determine socioeconomic, educational, and nutritional status. The method was to interview the study population according to a standard questionnaire and collect anthropometric data for all available children and adults. In all, 208 preschool children, 315 schoolchildren, and 511 adults were weighed and measured. The following were among the study findings: 61% of the families had a mean income below the poverty datum line, 30.6% of the families with more than one working member were below the poverty datum line, 74% of the mothers interviewed had attended antenatal clinic, 28% of the mothers interviewed had not breastfed their infants, only 23% of mothers who were bottle feeding infants were cleaning the bottles properly, four common pediatric disorders were widely misunderstood, the prevalence of malnutrition rose from infancy through early childhood and reached the pinnacle among 10-12-year-olds. It is concluded that health education is not reaching the people and it is suggested that the radio and newspapers be used to disseminate health information. Four tables and three figures illustrate the results of the study. (HC)

3084 Sekou, H. *Sante et nutrition au Niger. (Health and nutrition in Niger).* Medecine d'Afrique Noire (Paris), 24(7), 1977, 521-525. Fren.

The experience of rehabilitating the drought-afflicted populations of Niger illustrates the importance of good management in the application of emergency relief.

Prior to 1974, piecemeal efforts on the part of various national and international relief agencies did not result in the desired health and nutrition improvements. In 1974, under government auspices, the agencies agreed to cooperate in a medico-nutritional programme aimed at nutritional rehabilitation, the prevention of malnutrition, the distribution of food supplements, the provision of preventive medicine and health education, and first aid. The programme was to be run as a government project, make use of existing facilities and personnel, abide by national health policy, and be administered by one organization, the *Office des produits Vivriers du Niger* (Niger Bureau of Food Supplies); it involved the deployment of 10 medico-nutritional teams during a 6-month period. The accomplishments of the teams during that period are deemed 'remarkable.' The extent to which they adhered to programme policy, however, varied with the team leader: where the leader was a doctor, curative medicine soon took precedence over nutrition activity and where the leader was a health administrator or a nutritionist, a good balance between medical and nutritional activities was achieved. Types and numbers of interventions performed during the programme are included. (HC)

3085 Seoul National University, School of Public Health, Seoul. *Basic health information provided by research activities.* In Chunseong Gun Community Health Program, Seoul, Seoul National University, School of Public Health, Jul 1975, 90-124. Engl.
For complete document see entry 3147.
The research findings of the Chunseong Gun Community Health Program (Korea) staff are outlined in summaries of 13 research papers on major public health problems. All the work was carried out by surveys within the community served by the programme. Child nutrition was investigated by an anthropometric survey and a study of weaning foods. Haemoglobin and haematocrit levels were measured in children and adults. Two papers examine parasite infestation and transmission and two others look at problems of water supply and sanitation. Aspects of fertility are investigated in a study of social factors influencing the use of contraceptives and as part of a long term project on pregnancy wastage. The remaining papers are concerned with the analysis of vital statistics, general health information, and medical care expenditure. Most of these papers have been published elsewhere in full, but two ongoing research topics on the utilization of the health infrastructure and the sanitary conditions of the Chunseong Gun community health service area have yet to be completed. (DM)

3086 Siegmann, A.E. Elinson, J. *Newer sociomedical health indicators: implications for evaluation of health services.* Medical Care (Philadelphia, Pa.), 15(5), May 1977, Suppl., 84-92. Engl.
33 refs.
Using traditional biomedical indicators, Ivan Illich, Victor Fuchs, and Rick Carlson have independently demonstrated the ineffectiveness of physicians in improving people's health. Rather than suggesting the

futility of medical care, however, this evidence may be taken to demonstrate the need for health indicators that are more sensitive than traditional ones like morbidity and mortality statistics. Indicators ought to: reflect the varying degrees of health that people experience; be reasonably objective, reliable, and obtainable; and be sensitive to variations in the social and physical environment, in personal health services, and in personal health behaviour. A number of indicators that meet these criteria have already been developed by the Committee on Sociomedical Health Indicators (USA). These include the sickness impact profile, the assessment of unmet needs, and an index of reproductive efficiency. The 1st defines illness in terms of health-related dysfunction rather than medical diagnosis; it takes as indicators some 300 sickness-related behaviours that are associated with 14 functions such as movement of the body, eating, usual daily work, etc. The 2nd is a method for evaluating health care delivery systems; it calculates the differences between actual and needed services. The 3rd indicator, reproductive efficiency, offers an alternative to infant mortality as a measure of health status. It is the percentage of pregnancies that produce normal, surviving children. (HC)

3087 Singapore, Ministry of Health. *Background.* Singapore Public Health Bulletin (Singapore), 28, Jul 1977, 6-12. Engl.
See also entry 3496.
This background paper describes a national health campaign against infectious diseases undertaken in Singapore in 1976, with special emphasis on veneral diseases, tuberculosis, food borne diseases, malaria, dengue haemorrhagic fever, and leprosy. The epidemiology of each of these diseases is briefly presented. The campaign's objectives were to promote early detection and treatment by educating the public on the symptoms and consequences of these diseases and to reduce their incidence by motivating the public to adopt preventive measures. Twenty-four government and private organizations combined their resources to sponsor a traveling exhibition on infectious diseases, a mobile X-ray unit, the production of publicity and educational materials, an essay contest and a drawing/poster design competition for schoolchildren, lectures and films, school surveys, and a weekend symposium for physicians. Statistical data are included. Appendices contain the exhibition schedule and a list of the educational and publicity materials produced. The results of the campaign are evaluated elsewhere. (RMB)

3088 Tribhuvan University, Institute of Medicine, Kathmandu. *Rural health needs: report of a study in the primary health care unit (district) of Tanahu, Nepal.* Kathmandu, Tribhuvan University, Institute of Medicine, 31 May 1977. 102p. Engl.
As part of a project aimed at assessing health needs and health resources in Nepal, a household survey and a study of health facilities were undertaken in the Tanahu District. For the survey, four groups of households were selected according to geographic location. Individuals in

II Organization and Planning

each household were interviewed and questioned about these topics: the age, sex, marital status, occupation, education, immunization, and long-term disability of household members; visits to health personnel during the past month; water supply and storage; latrines and drainage; births, including antenatal, natal, and postnatal care and the problems and cost of such care, within the past year; family planning knowledge and practice; illness in the household during the previous 2 weeks; type and cost of consultation with a practitioner (if any); and satisfaction or dissatisfaction with the treatment received. The study of health facilities was based on observation and interviews with 40 out of 100 health workers in a number of different health facilities in the district. The findings of the survey are set forward in 42 tables and indicate high levels of untreated morbidity and disability, an expressed preference for government provided health services, a significant reservoir of couples planning to adopt family planning (although the majority of the people are as yet unaware of any form of birth control), an almost complete preoccupation with curative care on the part of health personnel, etc. Questionnaires used in the interviews are appended. (HC)

3089   UNICEF, International Union of Nutritional Sciences, New Delhi. *Community action-family nutrition programmes: generation of interrelated activities: guidelines on policies and procedure.* New Delhi, UNICEF/SCARO, Oct 1977. 22p. Engl.

Working Conference of the International Union of Nutritional Sciences, Hyderabad, India, 17-21 Oct 1977.

This report summarizes common principles for community action programmes to improve nutrition in the 20 developing countries represented at the conference. It gives background information and guidelines for setting up programmes and training workers in health and development projects, using resources actually or potentially present in the community. The section on programmes covers: community participation and organization; the selection, training, and supervision of community workers; and the content of projects. It emphasizes the retraining, re-equipping and certification of traditional birth attendants and indigenous practitioners and the need for workers to be able to give simple curative care, including the administration of antibiotics and injections. The techniques of evaluation, especially of health status, reproductive patterns, and environmental health, and government prerequisites for managerial and administrative adaptation to the requirements of expanded local schemes are described. There is also a table of some activities that communities have carried out, indicating their purpose, necessary community action, further activities to be encouraged, and the role of outside participation. These activities include self-assessment, increasing food availability, improving utilization of family finances and the environment, controlling disease, child spacing, dietary improvement, and general education. (HH)

3090   UNICEF, Nairobi. McDowell, J. *Village technology in Eastern Africa.* Nairobi, UNICEF Eastern Africa Regional Office, 1976. 63p. Engl.

Regional Seminar on Simple Technology for the Rural Family, Nairobi, Kenya, 14-19 Jun 1976.

Individual chapters have been abstracted separately under entries 3052 and 3076.

This conference report is intended as a baseline document and reference source on the development and extension of technologies appropriate to rural villages in East Africa and other developing countries. It covers basic concepts of UNICEF's policy, social aspects of appropriate technology, and technical and health aspects of food production, food conservation, food preparation, and water supplies. A detailed description of a village technology unit designed to implement and demonstrate appropriate technologies is presented and ways of encouraging and coordinating village technology development are listed. The seminar's 11 guidelines and 14 conclusions are set forth as general agreements on possibilities for practical action. Lists of seminar participants and of papers presented are given in 2 appendices. (CL)

3091   Universite Catholique de Louvain, Brussels. *Annual report: July 1975-June 1976.* Brussels, Universite Catholique de Louvain, Ecole de Sante Publique, Centre de Recherche sur l'Epidemiologie des Desastres, 1976. 6p. Engl.

22 refs.

Also published in French; see also entry 3092.

The *Centre de Recherche sur l'Epidemiologie des Desastres* (Brussels) reports that its activites have been seriously threatened by shortage of funds. Although the centre has been able to increase technical and scientific assistance to various institutions, it has not hired sufficient staff to meet the full demands and has been forced to cut research methods and postpone projects in scientific documentation and visual aids for field training. Ongoing research includes analysis of nutritional data collected in Niger in 1974 and field missions carried out in 1975 to assist with disaster planning and surveillance in Tunisia, Peru, Haiti, and Guatemala. The centre was consulted by a number of international relief, research, and other agencies during the year on aspects of disaster preparedness and these consultations are listed. The report concludes with full references to publications and seminar contributions by centre members. (DM)

3092   Universite Catholique de Louvain, Brussels. *Annual report: July 1974-June 1975.* Brussels, Universite Catholique de Louvain, Ecole de Sante Publique, Centre de Recherche sur l'Epidemiologie des Desastres, 1975. 10p. Engl.

Also published in French; see also entry 3091.

This report summarizes the objectives of the Research Centre in Disaster Epidemiology (Brussels), its activities for 1974-1975, and its future plans. The centre's major research effort was devoted to the famine in Niger and the relief operations of the League of Red Cross Societies. Its scientists surveyed 4 000 children in the area to estimate malnutrition and determine priorities for short-term relief; they screened vulnerable groups for vitamin A, iron, and copper deficiencies and investigated the composition of relief foods and the problem of lactose intolerance. Staff also questioned Red Cross workers involved in the Niger relief operation about problems of recruitment, team organization, briefing, and communications. They planned to use all this information to prepare guidelines that could be integrated into development plans. Other activities included a survey to determine optimal equipment for relief, seminars on disaster topics, and provision of visual aids and information. The centre plans to extend its documentation service, training projects, and active participation in field operations. (DM)

3093 Venezuela, Ministerio de Sanidad y Asistencia Social. *Revista Venezolana de Sanidad y Asistencia Social: actas del XVIII Congreso Panamericano de Tuberculosis y Enfermedades del Aparato Respiratorio y VII Congreso Venezolano de Tisiologia y Neumonologia. (Venezuelan Journal of Health and Social Welfare: proceedings of the 18th Pan American Conference on Tuberculosis and Respiratory Diseases and the 7th Venezuelan Conference on the Study of Tuberculosis and Pneumonia).* Caracas, Revista Venezolana de Sanidad y Asistencia Social, 41(3-4), Sep-Dec 1976. 261p. Span.
Refs.
Eighteenth Pan American Conference on Tuberculosis and Respiratory Diseases and 7th Venezuelan Conference on the Study of Tuberculosis and Pneumonia, Caracas, Venezuela, 23-28 Jun 1974.
This issue of the Venezuelan Review of Health and Social Welfare contains the proceedings of the 18th Panamerican Conference on Tuberculosis and Respiratory Diseases and the 7th Venezuelan Conference on the Study of Tuberculosis and Pneumonia. Papers presented at these conferences cover such topics as: epidemiological surveys; the evaluation of immunization, BCG vaccination, and curative treatment programmes; the incorporation of outpatient tuberculosis treatment into the public health system; the performance and evaluation of selected drugs; and the training of professional and auxiliary health workers in tuberculosis control. Many papers contain statistical data. (RMB)

3094 Wen, W. *Child care in new China.* Assignment Children (Geneva), 39, Jul-Sep 1977, 115-118. Engl.
Child care in both rural and urban areas of the People's Republic of China is based on early immunization and continued surveillance throughout childhood. For example, in Peking, newborns receive BCG vaccinatons before leaving hospital and their immunization records are filed at the health station nearest their home. Upon discharge, they are visited at home by a doctor and a local health worker and, within the 1st month, are seen by their doctor 3-4 times. Thereafter, they continue to have regular checkups by health station staff until a school assumes responsibility for their health care. Basically,

the same process applies to rural areas, such as Kwanglung province, although the majority of the tasks are undertaken by the barefoot doctor. Some support is provided by doctors who visit regularly from pediatric and gynaecology departments in the nearest provincial hospitals. (AC)

3095 Werner, D. Hesperian Foundation, Palo Alto, Cal. Project Piaxtla, Ajoya, Mexico. *Project to facilitate community based rural health care in Latin America.* Palo Alto, Cal., Hesperian Foundation, 1975. 19p. Engl.
Unpublished document; see also entry 1658 (volume 3).
The key to rural health care in developing countries lies in helping local people to cope effectively with their own health needs. However, there is a great demand for further study of appropriate methods for providing the necessary basic knowledge and incentives and especially for the development of practical teaching and work materials. The intention of this project is to gain first-hand knowledge of primary health care approaches and methods presently used in 13 Latin American countries and incorporate this information into new handbooks and materials for community members. The main focus will be on rural areas, particularly on communities and programmes featuring a substantial role for village health workers and the involvement of lay community members. Detailed objectives of the project include gathering specific data on the capabilities of village health workers at different training levels and exploring factors affecting their competence. Training of health manpower and consideration of financial aspects relevant to adequate low-cost health care are further areas for examination. After preparations, low-key field work (involving short visits by three or four project members to rural health care projects) will consist of gathering and sharing specific ideas, methods, and materials rather than conducting elaborate evaluations. The information obtained will be used to revise the villagers' medical handbook *Donde No Hay Doctor* and prepare additional training and work manuals in Spanish and English. (CL)

3096 Whitehead, R.G. Rowland, M.G. Cole, T.J. *Infection, nutrition and growth in a rural African environment.* Proceedings of the Nutrition Society (London), 35(3), 1976, 369-375. Engl.
17 refs.
Symposium on Nutrition and Growth, 295th Scientific Meeting of the Nutrition Society, London, UK, 1976.
See also entries 3077 and 3078.
Studies of the interaction between infection and malnutrition in Ugandan children have shown that infection contributes greatly to muscle wasting and the consequent development of marasmus and can also make children more prone to kwashiorkor. Similar studies with rural children in Guatemala and the Gambia that attempted to quantify the effects of diarrhea and other diseases on physical growth have proven that diarrhea is another major health problem associated with protein-

calorie malnutrition. Thus, nutritionists planning preventive programmes must work within a wide public health framework involving factors other than diet alone. Furthermore, the physiological factors responsible for growth inhibition due to infection need additional study. These include the failure to absorb nutrients (as in the case of diarrhea) and reduced nutrient intake due to loss of appetite. In addition, infection can induce changes in hormone levels that tend to inhibit growth by lowering plasma insulin and raising plasma cortisol concentrations; the latter may lead to inhibition of the immune response and secondary, more serious infection. (CL)

3097   WHO, Brazzaville. *Control of cholera and other water-borne epidemics through the improvements of community water supply.* Brazzaville, WHO, 10 Aug 1971. 12p. Engl.
Abridged version of document WHO/CWS/71.1; also published in French.
This paper deals mainly with the reduction of biological hazards in water supplies, the maintenance of water quality, and the control of epidemics, with special emphasis on environmental improvement measures to control waterborne diseases. The author discusses water quality surveillance and health precautions in both rural and urban water supplies, especially under emergency conditions. (RMB)

3098   WHO, Brazzaville. *Community water supply; report on a seminar.* Brazzaville, WHO, 1 Jul 1971. 162p. Engl.
Seminar on Community Water Supply, Brazzaville, Congo, 21-27 Apr 1971.
Also published in French.
This 1971 seminar was organized by WHO to motivate the participants to plan, develop, and implement community water supply programmes in their own countries and to formulate guidelines for such programmes in Africa. Plenary sessions, working group sessions, and reports covered such topics as: planning, investigation, design, and construction of community water supplies; the financing and administration of community water supplies in developing countries; and future studies and training. It was concluded that planning for water supplies should be integrated into programmes for health education and environmental health on a national level. Annexes containing conference documents, a list of participants, and working group reports, as well as an evaluation of the seminar, are included. (RMB)

3099   WHO, Geneva. *Oral health surveys: basic methods.* Geneva, WHO, 1977. 68p. Engl.
With a view to encouraging dental health personnel in all countries to make standard measurements of oral diseases and conditions as a basis for planning and evaluating their oral health programmes, this manual provides a set of diagnostic criteria that can be readily understood and applied in all countries and information on means of obtaining practical assistance in planning surveys, summarizing data, and analyzing results. The four chapters discuss, respectively: the general principles of planning, organizing, and conducting oral health

surveys; procedures for collecting basic data on oral health status; procedures for the concurrent estimation of treatment needs and oral health status; and post-survey action and the preparation of survey reports. Forms for use in the basic oral health assessment and the combined oral health and treatment assessment are included and tables that can be prepared by WHO with data from them are appended. (HC)

3100   WHO, Geneva. Kohn, R. White, K.L. *Health care: an international study.* Oxford, UK, Oxford University Press, 1976. 557p. Engl.
This international study of the utilization of health care services was undertaken to improve understanding among and communications between health care planners and providers. The study was based on a household survey of almost 48 000 respondents representing 5 million persons in 12 samples from seven countries (Canada, USA, Argentina, UK, Finland, Poland, and Yugoslavia). The vast quantity of data gathered is organized into these categories: theoretical orientation and methods, determinants of health services use (predisposing and ennabling factors, morbidity factors, and health services resource and organization factors), use of health services (physician services, hospitals, medicines, dental services, vision services, and selected nonphysician health care personnel services), and summary and conclusions. Each chapter is prefaced by summary of its contents. (HC)

3101   WHO, Geneva. *Reuse of effluents: methods of wastewater treatment and health safeguards; report of a WHO meeting of experts.* Geneva, WHO, Technical Report Series No.517, 1973. 63p. Engl.
Refs.
Also published in French, Russian, and Spanish.
The WHO expert committee on the reuse of effluents was convened to review and evaluate: the extent of intentional or unintentional reuse of wastewater; the health hazards associated with the practice for agricultural, industrial, recreational, and domestic purposes; and the latest technologic developments in wastewater treatment. The committee agreed that water uses should be graded according to the degree of purity they require, a system that would rationalize allocation during water shortage. The importance of development quality standards to govern reuse is stressed and areas where further research is required are identified. (HC)

3102   Wicht, C.L. *Future geriatric needs in South Africa: hospital and teaching aspects.* South African Medical Journal (Cape Town), 51(13), 26 Mar 1977, 440-442. Engl.
Noteworthy factors in geriatric care, derived from experience in a geriatric clinic, are that: symptoms are often wrongly attributed to the aging process, the aged are often overtreated and subjected to unnecessary diagnostic procedures, and functional abilities of the elderly and social factors are important in planning comprehensive care for the aged. The combination of multiple pathology, functional derangement, and social factors necessi-

tates a period of aftercare that entails physiotherapy, occupational therapy, and the services of a social worker. Health students should be trained in gerontology and geriatrics during their undergraduate years. (RMB)

3103   Yassur, Y. Yassur, S. Zaifrani, S. Zachs, U. Ben-Sira, I. *Keratomalacia.* Israel Journal of Medical Sciences (Jerusalem), 8(8-9), 1972, 1192-1194. Engl.
14 refs.
Causes and Prevention of Blindness, Jerusalem Seminar on the Prevention of Blindness, Jerusalem, Israel, 25-27 Aug 1971.
The authors describe a survey carried out on Rwandan children, aged 6 months-16 years, that identified vitamin A deficiency in association with severe protein and calorie malnutrition as one of the major causes of blindness in developing countries. Dietary studies revealed a severe lack of animal protein and lipids. The majority of the children with eye disease also suffered from kwashiorkor. (EE)

3104   Ziegler, J.P. WHO, Brazzaville. *Epidemiological services, Federal Republic of Nigeria: report on a mission 25 April-9 May 1973.* Brazzaville, WHO, 30 Nov 1973. 22p. Engl.
Also published in French.
This survey of epidemiological services in Nigeria includes statistics of the incidence of smallpox, cholera, yellow fever, poliomyelitis, influenza, malaria, cerebrospinal meningitis, measles, trypanosomiasis, yaws, whooping cough, human rabies, tetanus, gonorrhoea, and other diseases. It is noted that successful smallpox and measles campaigns are being threatened by incomplete coverage during the maintenance phase, that deployment of two immunization teams (one for BCG and one for smallpox and measles) is wasteful of resources and confusing to the population, and that surveillance could be rendered more effective through systematic utilization of laboratory services. It is recommended that: stool specimens from all cholera suspects be sent to the laboratory for verification; smallpox vaccination be administered systematically to all children from birth; all pregnant women and young children be immunized, preferably with a concentrated, single-dose antitoxin, against tetanus; the two immunization teams be combined under one administration; and liaison between regional ministries of health be maintained through a periodic dissemination of epidemiological information in the form of a monthly bulletin. (HC)

III Primary Health Care--Implementation

III.1 Rural Inpatient Care

See also: 2885, 2892, 2924, 2935, 2943, 2944, 2947, 3115, 3121, 3140, 3156, 3433, 3435, 3478

3105   Belliger, P. *Design for a simple effective baby incubator.* Appropriate Technology (London), 4(2), Aug 1977, 14-15. Engl.
For over 3 years a Tanzanian hospital has successfully used five inexpensive baby incubators produced locally according to a design that is described and illustrated with a photograph and detailed construction diagrams. Simple instructions are given for forming the perspex canopy that is mounted over a baby tray and heating box constructed from thin sheet metal and plywood covered with laminate. Correct temperature is maintained by 4 electric light bulbs, 2 alight constantly and 2 regulated by a thermostat; humidity is provided by a tray of water heated by the bulbs; and circulation of air is by simple convection through insect-wire screened holes. The design incorporates safety precautions and recommendations are made for operating and cleaning the equipment. A simple phototherapy unit could be added and the whole device could be built even more cheaply from painted wood with a canopy of heavy clear plastic sheeting. (AB)

3106   Berg, D. *Approach to the rehabilitation of the injured.* Papua New Guinea Medical Journal (Boroko, Papua New Guinea), 19(4), Dec 1976, 212-219. Engl.
The Angua Memorial Hospital, Papua New Guinea, has established facilities to treat and rehabilitate accident victims. One of these is an orthopaedic clinic whose staff assess the injuries of more than 50 patients per week and record details for later epidemiologic studies. The clinic's work is complemented by a sheltered workshop that was built and equipped by the general public and private industry in Lae. It is a self-contained and self-sufficient unit that provides work for many of the hospital's long-term surgical patients. Other facilities include a paraplegic ward in the hospital and an artifical limb factory that has an associated exercise room. (HC)

3107   Calvert, P.F. *Realistic midwifery service for Papua New Guinea.* Papua New Guinea Medical Journal (Port Moresby), 17(4), Dec 1974, 356-359. Engl.
The author urges that all births in Papua New Guinea should take place in health centres because there is no reliable method for forecasting complicated deliveries,

midwifery units have demonstrated high standards of care with resulting decreases in maternal/neonatal morbidity and mortality, and midwifery units need not be expensive to build or maintain. An example of such an effective, low-cost unit is found in the Kapuna Hospital, where expectant mothers are accommodated in a simple building donated by local government council. The midwifery theatre and postnatal ward are housed in an inexpensive building that would be required even if the unit took only select cases; the furniture, including delivery beds, is made locally; patients supply and launder their own bedlinen, towels, diapers, etc.; food is provided and cooked by the patients' relatives; and grounds are kept up by trainees and patients' relatives. A trained nurse is always on midwifery duty, which she combines with other clinic and hospital work, and additional assistance is provided by the trainees who are rostered there. In addition to reducing maternal/neonatal morbidity and mortality, having the service open to all has permitted a full check on the general health of the mother and that of her other children, provided an opportunity for health education, and resulted in improved community/health centre relations. (HC)

3108   Catholic Institute for International Relations, London. *Turba rural health project, Hugeriah district, Yemen Arab Republic: programme description.* London, Catholic Institute for International Relations, May 1976. 23p. Engl.
The chief impact of Western medicine on Yemen has been to divert attention from the causes of disease. The few doctors and hospitals are overwhelmingly concentrated in the towns, but drugs are available without any control over the counter and village pharmacists often set themselves up as doctors. Most of the small number of rural health services are manned and funded by foreign agencies, but in recent years locally elected develoment boards have made attempts to construct health facilities and improve water supplies. Largely on the initiative of the Hugeriah Development Board, the Turba rural health project was started in 1970 in response to a serious drought. A hospital was established, with foreign staff and funds providing curative services but little public health work. In 1973, however, plans were made to introduce preventive measures, training of auxiliaries, and the construction of village dispensaries for health instruction and primary care. The dispensaries were to be controlled by elected local committees, but the Ministry of Health offered some financial support and approved schemes for full-time training of practical nurses and on-the-job training of village health workers. Foreign aid was to be phased out by mid-1977. In the

absence of any evaluation so far, the future of the programme is uncertain. (DM)

3109 Chamberlain, R.H. *Basic radiology: a worldwide challenge.* Journal of the American Medical Association (Chicago, Ill.), 214(9), 1970, 1687-1692. Engl.
One-hundred-and-nineteenth Annual Convention of the American Medical Association, Chicago, Ill., 22 Jun 1970.

The Technamatic Radiology System meets the needs of the developing world by focusing on X-ray examinations for conditions likely to be treated in small hospitals and health centres and combining the design of robust equipment with recommendations for film, chemicals, and trained personnel. At the centre of the system is a battery powered generator that can be easily recharged overnight from any of a wide range of energy sources. The operator need only decide on one of three voltage positions and a time setting. Other components of the system, such as a stripped-down X-ray stand, collimater, film cassette holder, and film processing aparatus, have been chosen or designed to limit all possible sources of mechanical failure or human error, including problems of climate, maintenance, and availability of spare parts. The system as a whole is designed to produce not only reliable equipment for most common radiological needs but also films of such high quality that doubtful cases can be referred to specialist centres when necessary. A clear, semi-pictorial technique book gives complete instructions. The cost of the system is less than the cost of a conventional X-ray unit plus generator. A target for areas served by regional health centres and small hospitals would be one Technamatic System with trained physician and aide per 25 000-50 000 population. Medical students and physicians should master routine use of the system with 3 months' training and technical aides can be trained with physicians in a 2-month course. (HH)

3110 Durham, L. *Lae sheltered workshop.* Papua New Guinea Medical Journal (Boroko, Papua New Guinea), 19(2), Jun 1976, 119-123. Engl.

The Lae sheltered workshop-cum-rehabilitation centre is affiliated with Angau Hospital, Papua New Guinea. The workshop provides occupational therapy for inpatients, permanent employment for a number of resident disabled, and an occupational regime for outpatients from nearby areas. The occupations and machinery available in the workshop are particularly suited to physical rehabilitation. Coathanger making, for example, necessitates a wide range of vigorous upper limb and trunk movements that are appropriate to strengthening and maintaining the musculature of paraplegics. A leg-operated mitre machine and a treadle sewing machine lend themselves to strengthening and increasing the range of movement of the lower limbs. The workshop is staffed by 1 occupational therapist and 1 assistant and has an average daily attendance of 35-40 patients; the sale of items produced in the workshop enables it to be self-sufficient. Future plans include expansion of the facilities to meet the needs of female

patients and the addition of a course to train others to carry on the programme. (HC)

3111 Jobson, K.F. *Introduction to rural practice.* Tropical Doctor (London), 7(4), Oct 1977, 157-160. Engl.

A brief survey based on the author's experience in a 93-bed rural hospital in Ghana is intended to give the doctor new to the tropics some appreciation of the problems and conditions there. The various surgical interventions performed in the hospital during a 1-year period included 198 laparotomies, 19 sigmoid resections, 138 herniorraphies, 7 aspirations of amoebic abcesses of the liver, 45 thoracocenteses, and 156 Caesarian sections. Medical diagnoses included, in descending order of frequency, malaria, upper respiratory infections, gastroenteritis, typhoid, skin diseases, intestinal parasites, anaemia, measles, and gynaecological complaints. Tropical diseases encountered included onchocerciasis, guinea worm, schistosomiasis, and snake-bite. In a section on surgery, a number of simplified procedures (e.g., symphysiotomy, bottle aspiration, auto-transfusion, etc.) that can be substituted for those requiring a more sophisticated infrastructure are suggested and, in a section on preventive measures, doctors are urged to do their part in ensuring that resources are distributed equitably among curative and preventive services. (HC)

3112 Mutiso, D. Brown, P. Kanani, S. *Design, building and operation of health and hospital care facilities in East Africa and examples from Kenya.* World Hospitals (Oxford, UK), 11(2 and 3), Jun 1975, 189-191. Engl.

As part of its development plan for 1974-1978, the government of Kenya has attempted to design a feasible, effective, and modern health system that will achieve greater penetration of the rural areas and cope with the needs of a growing population. Since there are far too few technical staff to contemplate a separate design solution for each of the increasing number of projects that such a system would require, the Ministry of Works has turned to the 'type design' or component solution. The component is defined as a unit of building that, with the least modification in construction, may be built anywhere in the country, either as an extension of an existing complex or, in combination with other components, as a completely new building. First applied to district hospitals, the type design solution was soon adopted for health centres as well and, with experience, underwent a few modifications: the components were less stringently designed for a particular function and more flexible and a model for a standard health centre--one that can be built up unit-by-unit from a dispensary, through a subcentre, to a full health centre--evolved. The advantages of this solution are that it allows for the phased construction of a health centre and for any intermediate modifications that become expedient. (HC)

3113 Sanders, R.K. Joseph, R. *Tetanus: successful treatment in a rural situation.* Tropical Doctor (London), 7(3), Jul 1977, 99-104. Engl.

Over 5 000 tetanus patients have been treated as part of

III Primary Health Care--Implementation

77

the routine procedures in a general hospital in Raxaul, Bihar, India. The treatment was designed to provide the best for the most with a minimal expenditure of time, material, and money. The authors discuss basic concepts in the management of tetanus, including drugs and dosages, seasonal variations, the adult and neonatal forms, prevention, assessing potential mortality, and nursing and general procedures. Tracheotomy is not recommended. (RMB)

III.2 Rural Outpatient Care

See also: 2864, 2892, 2917, 2952, 3017, 3067, 3089, 3105, 3112, 3244, 3260, 3406, 3425, 3429, 3430, 3446, 3472, 3486

3114   Alsing, B. Wachira, J. WHO, Brazzaville. *Development of health services.* Brazzaville, WHO, 16 May 1974. 12p. Engl.
As part of a project for improving rural health services and rural health training, the activities at Kendara Health Centre, Kenya, were reorganized: record-keeping, filing, and other administrative tasks formerly conducted by medical staff became the duties of a statistical clerk; antenatal, family planning, and under-fives' clinics were scheduled weekly instead of bimonthly; and routine tasks such as weighing, urine testing, and temperature recording were delegated to a nursing aid, freeing the community nurse for immunizing, advising mothers, etc. After the changes were implemented, the centre's workload decreased; observations were that nursing staff were able to manage antenatal care, deliveries, child care, and minor treatment, but they needed encouragement and guidance to keep up good nursing standards. Workers lacked discipline with regard to arrival at work and the medical assistants needed training in staff supervision. The centre's experiences will be used in the preparation of procedural guidelines and manuals for use in rural health centres and rural health training. Other aspects of the project are briefly described. (HC)

3115   Arole, R.S. *Comprehensive rural health project, Jamkhed.* In International Secretariat for Volunteer Service, Mobilization of Response Structures from the Grassroots towards Health Services: Report of a Workshop, Manila, ISVS Asian Regional Office, Jul 1974, 113-120. Engl.
International Secretariat for Volunteer Service Workshop on Mobilization of Response Structures from the Grassroots towards Health Services, Manila, Philippines, 8-11 Jul 1974.
For complete document see entry 2919.
The Comprehensive Rural Health Project, covering 30 villages in Jamkhed, India, was started in 1970. The area was chosen because the community welcomed the programme and cooperated at every stage, contributing land, facilities, and voluntary labour. The initial objectives were to reduce the birth rate from 40-30:1 000 in 6 years, cut child mortality by half, identify and treat cases of tuberculosis and leprosy, and provide basic field training for health professionals. About 70% of the effort was devoted to promotional and preventive work such as

family planning counselling, health and nutrition education, supplementary feeding for at-risk children, and immunization; the remaining 30% of the resources provided curative services by means of a central hospital and mobile clinic. The project relied heavily on cooperation and division of labour between members of the health team. For example, most of the promotional tasks were delegated to health auxiliaries and village health workers (respected middle-aged men and women from each community), because these people were closest to the local inhabitants. The health team visited each village once a week and screened the residents for health problems during systematic house-to-house visits. Thereafter, the bulk of the follow-up work was carried out by the village health workers under the supervision of programme staff. (DM)

3116   Banam, J. *Community support and active participation: the answer to rural development.* Madang, Papua New Guinea, Para-Medical Training College, Jan 1976. 18p. Engl.
Unpublished document.
Extensive use of medical auxiliaries is part of government policy for the health service in Papua New Guinea. Teams of auxiliaries staff rural health centres equipped with basic facilities for inpatient and outpatient care, a laboratory, and an operating theatre; these teams are headed by a highly trained paramedical, the health extension officer. In theory, the setup is effective, but in practice, it has many problems based on interpersonal communications. The health services planners are too remote from village life to appreciate the auxiliaries and villagers' points of view, the auxiliaries are often dissatisfied with their working conditions and are either too authoritarian or too apathetic to gain the respect of the villagers, and the villagers are distrustful of the auxiliaries and often uncooperative. Some improvements might be achieved by nonformal education carried out by highly motivated volunteers along the lines of the *Sarvodaya Shramadana* Movement in Sri Lanka, but basic requirements are that the volunteers first confer with village elders to determine the felt needs of the inhabitants, camp in the community, and work alongside the people to realize the projects' aims. Government policies should be made sufficiently flexible to provide support for these activities so that the efforts of the voluntary organizations may supplement those of the health service. (DM)

3117   Barnes, P.A. *Nursing among the Tibetans: 6,000 ft in hills.* Australian Nurses Journal (Port Adelaide, Australia), 8(8), Mar 1977, 8-10. Engl.
An Australian nurse recounts her experience in the Tibetan Delek Hospital, Dharmsala, India. The hospital depends upon donations from foreign charities for both income and supplies that do not always correspond to the hospital's needs. For example, tranquilizers and antidepressants have figured largely among the gifts whereas antibotics, sulphonamides, and antihelminthics are what are needed. The author notes that a 4-day course in antibiotics, locally purchased, costs the equivalent of 4 days wages, that 20% of the patients attending

the clinic are suffering from gastrointestinal disorders, that another 20% are suffering from the obvious effects of malnutrition (general weakness and debility, anaemia, kwashiorkor, retarded growth, rickets, poor eyesight, diseases of the skin and mouth, and general susceptibility to infection), and that more than 25% of the clinic attenders are victims of tuberculosis. She identifies priorities as immunization services, nutrition education, sanitary education, and a community health programme for tuberculosis case-finding and follow-up. (HC)

3118   Bomgaars, M.R. *Common problems of children as seen in rural clinics--and how they are managed: Lalitpur experience.* Kathmandu, Shanta Bhawan Hospital, 1974. 6p. Engl.
Unpublished document.
The high child mortality in Lalitpur, Nepal, is largely a result of malnutrition and gastroenteritis. Although adequate quantities of nutritious foods are available, local customs do not encourage their use and the symptoms of malnutrition are attributed to a spell cast by contact with an unknown pregnant woman. Hygiene is inadequate and diarrheal disease is treated by starvation and deprivation of water. The staff in the health service are well aware of these customs and consider education an essential part of their programme. Mothers are encouraged to use a weaning food composed of readily available local ingredients as a supplement to prolonged breast-feeding. Gastroenteritis is treated with a simple home-produced rehydration solution. Other priorities of the health programme are immunizations, early treatment of infections, and early referral of more serious cases. The success of the service depends on village women volunteers and medical staff who together staff the weekly maternal child health clinics held in each village. (DM)

3119   Brand, P.W. Commonwealth Foundation, London. National Fund for Research into Crippling Diseases, Arundel, UK. *Rehabilitation in leprosy.* In Disabled in Developing Countries, London, Commonwealth Foundation, 1977, 68-75. Engl.
Symposium on Appropriate Technology and Delivery of Health and Welfare Services for the Disabled in Developing Countries, Oxford, UK, 26-30 Sep 1976.
For complete document see entry 3124.
Leprosy rehabilitation is possible only if the patient obtains treatment, is accepted by society, and leads an active life. Because of the stigma attached to leprosy, the doctor must be approachable, tolerant, and discreet, so that patients will not be afraid to seek treatment. The patient himself must be encouraged to be adaptable, as society's attitudes will not change quickly and he is the one who will have to make the major adjustments. He can also learn to minimize the risk of further damage to his insensitive hands and feet from tight footwear or bandages, wounds and burns, repetitive stress (such as walking), and infection. He should wear shoes but change them regularly and avoid using great force with his hands. Damage from repetitive stress is more difficult

to prevent, but the patient can learn to watch for the danger sign of inflammation, avoid harmful ways of walking and working, and toughen up his hands and feet naturally by walking barefoot on grass, sand, or soft soil. Much destruction of limbs is caused by mismanaged infection. The wounded part of a limb must be effectively immobilized to stop the spread of infection; preformed splints for fingers, feet, and legs applied at home enable the patient to continue working. (HH)

3120   Cadotsch, A.F. *Entwicklungszusammenarbeit im Aufbau eines Basisgesundheitsdienstes. (Team work in building up a basic medical service).* Acta Tropica (Basel, Switzerland), 34(3), 1977, 189-203. German.
10 refs.
After discussing some of the health and socioeconomic problems of Peru, the author describes a programme instituted by a team of Swiss doctors to make medical care economically feasible for the Andean poor. Local auxiliaries are trained in preventive medicine and curative medicine is restricted to a massive tuberculosis campaign. Ideas, experiences, problems, and preliminary evaluations are presented and examined. (Modified journal abstract.)

3121   Cash, R.A. WHO, Brazzaville. *Organizing of rehydration centres in Liberia: report on a visit 26 Jan-8 Feb 1973.* Brazzaville, WHO, 3 Mar 1974. 10p. Engl.
In 1973, the author visited Liberia's health facilities to advice on establishing rehydration centres and training in the treatment of cholera and pediatric diarrhea. He noted that most of the country's large hospitals had been equipped with modern cholera units but that fluid therapy was not practiced in the rural clinics where most treatment of pediatric diarrhea is undertaken. Therefore, the author recommends that: oral rehydration therapy be extended to all health facilities, particularly health posts; the excellent facilities at the John F. Kennedy Memorial Hospital be used to instruct medical workers in rehydration therapy; instruction courses emphasize the similarity between diarrhea and cholera therapy; a simple, locally produced fluid be used in rehydration; a central government pharmacy and distribution system be established; and immunization against cholera be deemphasized in favour of long-term sanitation measures. A guide to the clinical evaluation and treatment of cholera and other types of gastroenteritis is appended. (HC)

3122   Chamberlin, R.W. Radebaugh, J.F. United Farm Workers of America, Sanger, Cal. *Delivery of primary health care--union style: a critical review of the Robert F. Kennedy Plan for the United Farm Workers of America.* New England Journal of Medicine (Boston, Mass.), 294(12), 1976, 641-645. Engl.
The primary health care programme developed by the United Farm Workers of America, an example of a consumer-controlled system, provides quality health care in clinics held at locations and times convenient to

III Primary Health Care--Implementation

patients and employs bilingual clinic personnel from the same worker background to bridge the cultural gap between provider and consumer. From its inception, the users, who are mostly poor Mexican fruit pickers, were involved in the decision-making. The project is funded by contributions from the growers and aims to cover health education and outreach services as well as clinical attention. The family health worker, who has little formal education, does initial screening, translates, provides health education, acts as a health advocate, and collects data on living conditions that can be used to enforce or improve sanitation codes. Other staff include former college students, doctors, and nurses. These clinics all do simple diagnostic tests, perform screening, use Denver Developmental Tests, and employ a problem-oriented record system. Because of their involvement in union activities, health centre staff have been successful in health education and in improving safety and sanitary conditions for workers. However, the consumer orientation causes problems for staff, resulting in a high turnover of personnel. Staff have little opportunity for continuing education or involvement in decision-making and work long hours for little pay. (Modified author abstract.)

3123   Clukay-Newton, A. *Rural health care thrives under hospital's prepaid plan.* Hospitals (Chicago, Ill.), 51(15), 1 Aug 1977, 45-48. Engl.
The Athol Memorial Hospital serves nine towns in Massachusetts (USA) with a combined population of 23 000, including many elderly and unemployed persons. Until recently, the high cost of medical care and the lack of public transportation deterred the population from seeking care except during acute episodes of illness. Now, through the introduction of a comprehensive, prepaid health care plan with a strong preventive bias, the hospital is providing more accessible, economical health care. The area's health resources (local practitioners, social services, etc.) have been coordinated, the hospital's outpatient service has been expanded, free transportation for outpatients has been made available, and home nursing care has been introduced. Government financial support was enlisted and nurse practitioners were hired as physician extenders. Consumer input to the plan was assured in the form of an advisory council that includes representatives from the nine towns and the area's social and welfare agencies. The council, which reflects the socioeconomic structure of the community, meets once a month and: makes recommendations regarding the functioning, policies, and programmes of the plan; identifies current health care needs; and handles grievances. After 4 years in operation, the plan has enjoyed steadily increasing popularity and among some groups has successfully reduced the need to use inpatient facilities by as much as 30%. The plan, which at present has a membership of approximately 6 000, will be self-sustaining at 10 000. (HC)

3124   Commonwealth Foundation, London. National Fund for Research into Crippling Diseases, Arundel, UK. *Disabled in developing countries.*

London, Commonwealth Foundation, 1977. 148p. Engl.
Refs.
Symposium on Appropriate Technology and Delivery of Health and Welfare Services for the Disabled in Developing Countries, Oxford, UK, 26-30 Sep 1976.
Individual chapters have been abstracted separately under entries 2884, 2912, 2958, 3045, 3119, 3131, 3134, 3140, 3141, 3149, and 3256.
The 25 papers from this symposium on the health care of the disabled in developing countries cover practical descriptions of the manufacture of aids for the disabled, various approaches to rehabilitation, and philosophical reflections on the effects of outside aid on rural communities, including the planning of health care delivery and its implications in developing countries. The care of particular groups, such as leprosy patients, poliomyelitis cripples, and handicapped children, is described and details of the functions of an international institute for rehabilitation in developing countries to be established in Iran are presented. The conclusions and resolutions arising from the conference are set forth. (HH)

3125   Cuba, *Ministerio de Salud Publica. Medicina en la communidad. (Community medicine).* Havana, Ministerio de Salud Publica, Centro Nacional de Informacion de Ciencias Medicas, Serie Informacion de Ciencias Medicas No.23, 1975. 47p. Span.
Segundo Forum Nacional de Higiene y Epidemiologia, Havana, Cuba, 1975.
According to the prologue, five papers from the 1975 Cuban Forum on Hygiene and Epidemiology have been included in this collection for the purpose of redefining the concept of community health and socialized medicine in proper Marxist-Leninist terms as opposed to improper capitalist ones. Topics covered include: the comments of a discussion panel on community medicine; the organization of the health care system; the polyclinic, present and future; experiments with a work-study programme and its effects on the University of Havana medical school; and the training of community health specialists. (RMB)

3126   Dissevelt, A.G. Korman, J.J. Vogel, L.C. *Antenatal record for identification of high risk cases by auxiliary midwives at rural health centres.* Tropical and Geographical Medicine (Haarlem, Netherlands), 28(3, Netherlands), Sep 1976, 251-255. Engl.
10 refs.
A patient-retained antenatal record intended for use by nurses and midwives in rural health centres has been designed to simplify recognition of high-risk cases. Measuring 21 x 30 cm, the card is divided into three sections: the left two-thirds is for the woman's previous obstetrical and medical history and the right one-third is for examinations and recommendations concerning her present pregnancy. Relevant questions for history-taking and examination are printed on the card and appropriate answer boxes are included. All boxes that indicate risk are shaded or printed in a different colour.

Low-Cost Rural Health Care and Health Manpower Training

On the reverse side, the card has space for information on four additional pregnancies. The record has been used for several years at a rural health centre at Masii, Kenya, and the midwives who use it unanimously support it. A sample of the record is included. (HC)

3127   Farid, M.A. *Health worker and the antimalaria campaign.* Papua New Guinea Medical Journal (Port Moresby), 17(1), Mar 1974, 74-77. Engl.
The author outlines a strategy for better coordination of anti-malarial activities in Papua New Guinea. This strategy is dependent upon the cooperation of health workers at every level: personnel at the central level define the role of each department or ministry in the antimalaria campaign, the head of the health services promotes malaria training for each category of health worker, the director of preventive medicine establishes and presides over an annual technical antimalaria meeting, the provincial health officer follows up the antimalaria campaign through monthly meetings with unit heads, the provincial epidemiologist supervises field work, and the peripheral malaria workers fulfill their duties under the supervision of health centre staff. In remote areas, the work of the peripheral malaria workers includes: generating self-help among the people by disseminating information on the symptoms of malaria, its treatment, and personal protective measures such as mosquito netting, joss sticks, etc.; promoting the distribution of antimalaria drugs through drugstores, grocery stores, community centres, etc.; and encouraging managers of private or state industry to initiate antimalaria measures. Since the success of the campaign depends on the effectiveness of the peripheral workers, they must be carefully selected, trained, and supervised. (HC)

3128   Gonasthasthya Kendra, Dacca. *Gonasthasthya Kendra P.O. Nayarhat District Dacca Bangladesh: progress report number 4, July 1973-April 1974.* In International Secretariat for Volunteer Services, Mobilization of Response Structures from the Grassroots towards Health Services: Report of a Workshop, Manila, ISVS Asian Regional Office, Jul 1974, 83-93. Engl.
International Secretariat for Volunteer Service Workshop on Mobilization of Response Structures from the Grassroots towards Health Services, Manila, Philippines, 8-11 Jul 1974.
For complete document see entry 2919.
Of the 50 staff members of *Gonasthasthya Kendra* and its 13 subcentres, 23 are paramedics and more than half of these are women, a situation that is unusual in Bangladesh. These women workers are especially good at making contact with village women in their homes and at clinics, an important 1st step towards the involvement of the female population in rural development. As part of the highly successful family planning campaign, they provide advice and the contraceptive pill directly to women at home; these household visits have improved acceptance and reduced the drop-out rate and now the family planning clinic deals only with complications. All the centre staff, including doctors and nurses, are involved in some field work, which helps to form a per-

sonal link between the health programme and the community. Thanks to their personal explanations of the health insurance programme, enrolment is on the increase and participants tend to make better use of the services offered because they no longer wait until conditions are dangerously advanced before seeking help. Other types of development work initiated by the centre include women's clubs offering vocational training and schemes for agricultural improvement, using "para-agros" (analogous to the paramedics). (DM)

3129   Hanjari, G.B. *Role of the health centre in the national health programme in Kenya.* World Hospitals (Oxford, UK), 11(2 and 3), Jun 1975, 198-203. Engl.
9 refs.
The author examines the customary definitions of the health centre concept and points out that, as with other concepts, Western health centres may not be readily adaptable to developing countries. Kenyan health centres, for example, rather than being merely buildings housing doctors, must offer both stationary and mobile services, often provided by health auxiliaries when physicians are unavailable. Since they must serve the needs of a variety of peoples, their form must be flexible enough to adapt to different cultures, i.e., a completely mobile unit for the nomadic Masai or a riverboat service in the Tana River District. Figures illustrate the movements of the ambulatory and the domiciliary patient and the related functions of the health centre as well as the relationship of the health centre to the rest of the community. Although peripheral to the national health system, health centres are the foundation of national health services. (RMB)

3130   Hart, R.H. *Maternal and child health services in Tanzania.* Tropical Doctor (London), 7(4), Oct 1977, 179-185. Engl.
The increasing cost and limited effect of mobile preventive services prompted Tanzania to put more preventive responsibilities into the hands of the maternal and child health (MCH) clinics offered by its rural health centres and dispensaries. In order to maximize their efficiency and coverage, these clinics were advised to offer one comprehensive daily MCH clinic in place of different services on different days and to exploit the drawingpower of the most popular service, curative treatment, by requiring all mothers and children to pass through MCH clinic before being seen by the medical assistant. Experience has shown that these changes are best introduced in three steps: making a comprehensive clinic out of one of the existing clinics by adding the missing services and asking mothers to bring all of their under-fives with them at each visit, starting the new comprehensive clinic on any remaining non-clinic days, and, once staff are familiar with the new pattern and have developed some degree of efficiency, requiring all mothers and children coming for outpatient treatment to pass through the MCH clinic. Flow through the clinic is streamlined by means of a series of stations for registration, weighing, examination/advice, immunization, and dispensing. Clinics where the new pattern has been im-

plemented have witnessed a noticeable increase in coverage and a more even distribution of the weekly workload. Further details regarding medical records, statistics collection, supplies and equipment, etc., used in the clinics are included. (HC)

3131   Hindley-Smith, R. Commonwealth Foundation, London. National Fund for Research into Crippling Diseases, Arundel, UK. Pan American Health Organization, Washington, D.C. *Preliminary report on a survey concerning the possibility of providing simplified rehabilitation services at the primary health care level in Latin America.* In Disabled in Developing Countries, London, Commonwealth Foundation, 1977, 131-136. Engl.
Symposium on Appropriate Technology and Delivery of Health and Welfare Services for the Disabled in Developing Countries, Oxford, UK, 26-30 Sep 1976.
For complete document see entry 3124.
A preliminary case-finding survey in Cagua, Venezuela, showed that volunteers are capable of identifying the handicapped and that many disability problems could be solved by contact with a social worker. If such workers made home visits rather than relying on contacts made through a clinic, they could not only tell patients about relevant, existing facilities but also inform the health authorities about gaps in their services. The methodology of this disability survey evolved on an *ad hoc* basis. Members of a young people's club made contact with about half the disabled persons interviewed by covering several streets in a house-to-house investigation, while the sanitary inspector similarly surveyed other streets. Between them they reached about one-fifth of the town's 6 000 people, identified 63 patients, and made appointments for all to attend the health centre to see the Venezuelan Director of Rehabilitation and the representative of the Pan American Health Organization who had arranged to interview patients about their problems. Visiting clinic staff interviewed those who did not attend (about 50%) in their homes. The data from a similar investigation of a remote community proposed for autumn 1976 will be used to refine the methodology. (HH)

3132   Islam, Z. Altmann, M. WHO, Brazzaville. *Epidemiological surveillance and immunization activities in Malawi: report on a mission 20 Apr-18 May 1973.* Brazzaville, WHO, 5 Sep 1973. 14p. Engl.
Immunization and disease surveillance activities in Malawi were reviewed during a 3-week visit to several of the country's health facilities. Immunization is carried out in child health clinics and, in some areas, by mobile units. The number of child health clinics has increased markedly from 1969-1972 as has the percentage of under-five population immunized by them: from 1:7%-7.3% for DPT, from 1.2%-5.3% for polio, from 4.6%-14% for smallpox, and from 0-.9% for BCG. The country's eight mobile units have covered two districts to date, boosting smallpox and BCG coverage in these areas to 86%. However, the occurrence of BCG ulcers in 12

children due to positioning of the vaccination, improper care of the site, and other factors indicates the need for further education of community and health staff. It is recommended that the mobile vaccination campaign be continued, that vaccination and surveillance activities in all health facilities be increased, that the performance and coverage of mobile and static vaccination activities be assessed on a regular basis, and that the presence or absence of certain communicable diseases requiring immediate action be reported on a weekly instead of a monthly basis. Statistical data on the reported incidence of some prevalent communicable diseases is included and sample reporting forms for assessing BCG and smallpox coverage in the field are appended. (HC)

3133   Kark, S.L. *Manpower and team work in community health care.* Jerusalem, Hadassah Hebrew University Medical Centre, n.d. 108p. Engl.
96 refs.
Unpublished document.
The author examines the concepts of community health care, primary health care, and community medicine and analyzes the kinds and functions of health manpower necessary for community health care. Separate sections are devoted to the physician, the traditional practitioner, the nurse, the intermediate level auxiliary health worker, the social worker, and the community health worker. He also discusses the ways in which the changing needs of the community can influence the composition and scope of the community health care team and cites as examples the teams operating in the rural Polela Health Centre (South Africa) and the urban *Kiryat Hayovel* neighbourhood of Jerusalem. The personnel and activities of each team are described in great detail. From the similarities and differences between the two types of health team, the author has developed a community health practice that combines community medicine with primary health care and incorporates a number of complementary skills. (RMB)

3134   King, F. Morley, D. Commonwealth Foundation, London. National Fund for Research into Crippling Diseases, Arundel, UK. *Appropriate technology for rehabilitation in developing countries.* In Disabled in Developing Countries, London, Commonwealth Foundation, 1977, 52-60. Engl.
Symposium on Appropriate Technology and Delivery of Health and Welfare Services for the Disabled in Developing Countries, Oxford, UK, 26-30 Sep 1976.
For complete document see entry 3124.
The handicapped child in the developing world needs prompt attention within his community before his condition becomes irreversible or generates secondary handicaps. It can be difficult for busy mothers to take children for regular outpatient treatment or stay with them in hospital. Therefore, necessary physiotherapy and mental stimulation should be given at home. Local workers and traditional healers with simple equipment and selected skills can do much to improve the living conditions of handicapped children and teach their families how to care for them. For example, in a relatively stable com-

munity in Imesi, Nigeria, the handicapped who were helped to survive (and some were compassionately allowed to die) were assisted by local health workers to find a place in society. In contrast, in Matero, Zambia, little support was given to parents of children with physical and mental abnormalities; the hospital, only 8 miles away, was not answering the problems of this community, even though hospital facilities included a physiotherapy unit and specialist doctors. (HH)

3135 Lasserre, R. *Centre de sante rural a Bali. (Rural health centre of Bali).* Acta Tropica (Basel, Switzerland), 34(3), 1977, 205-213. Fren.
The Mengwe rural health centre (Bali) was built and equipped for US$15 000 in 1974 by a non-sectarian medical relief organization. The centre has been so successful that it is completely accepted by the local community and is regarded by the Indonesian government as a pilot project. The author attributes its success to: the suitable, easily accessible location; the locally recruited, well trained, and sympathetic staff; the constant upgrading of staff medical skills; 24-hour availability of a doctor and nurse; and an adequate supply of drugs. The author feels that the impact of the centre on the community can best be measured by the high acceptance rates among the local population of the centre's special programmes, such as the child health clinic, the family planning programme, the antenatal clinic, and vaccination campaigns. The centre has also become involved in health education and environmental sanitation activities. (RMB)

3136 Morley, D. *Growth charts, 'curative' or 'preventive'?* Archives of Disease in Childhood (London), 52(5), May 1977, 395-398. Engl.
In developing countries, simple "preventive" growth charts for use by health workers with limited training are replacing the complex "curative" growth charts used by pediatricians for growth research and monitoring of children in industrialized nations. The new charts emphasize preventing malnutrition by maintaining adequate growth, which is assessed by the direction in which a child's curve is moving rather than its position on the chart. As the chart is the only record of a child's health in many developing countries, it includes additional information concerning parents and siblings, immunizations, reasons for special care, breast-feeding and weaning records, anti-malarial treatment, and childbirth spacing. Such charts can be kept by parents in the home, rather than at a health centre, since trials have shown that home-based record systems work well. The growth charts, which are marked with standard curves based on measurements from an International Children's Centre (ICC) study rather than on problematic Harvard or Jelliffe standards, use the 50th centile from the ICC standards for boys as the upper line and the 3rd centile for girls as the lower line. Separate lines representing the -3 standard deviation (SD) and -4 SD calculated for boys and for girls from the ICC standards are available on plastic sheets that can be laid over the growth charts to show the weight-for-age of children in a community as a whole. (CL)

3137 Morley, D. *Nutritional surveillance of young children in developing countries.* International Journal of Epidemiology (Oxford, UK), 5(1), 1976, 51-55. Engl.
Simple methods are now available for surveillance of the growth and nutrition of children in developing countries with few resources and the likelihood of recurring food shortages. For individual child surveillance, especially in the early months of life, the simplest nutritional index is weight-for-age, although this is subject to genetic variation, as studies of West African and English boys show. Simple weight-for-age charts based on standards from an International Children's Centre study, rather than on questionable Harvard standards, are of value in that they indicate the direction of growth in connection with the velocity of the child's weight gain. Health workers can use these charts to measure the change in weight of a population of children by marking normal local deviations from the standards on plastic overlay sheets. National surveillance of young children, who are the most sensitive indicators of poor nutrition in a population, is possible by this method, which has been used in Malawi. However, as the age of children in developing countries is often unknown, alternative measurements of nutritional status such as mid-upper-arm circumference are often necessary. The Shakir arm circumference strip, made from washed and coloured old X-ray film, is particularly practical for children aged 1-5 years, as use in Africa and India confirms. For children aged 5-10 years, pragmatic evaluation by health workers shows that nutritional assessment by arm circumference combined with height measurement using a QUAC stick is more reliable. (CL)

3138 Morou, M. *Development animation, a basic for community participation in health programmes.* Bulletin of the International Union against Tuberculosis (Paris), 49(1), 1974, 82-86. Engl.
Twenty-second International Tuberculosis Conference, Tokyo, Japan, 24-28 Sep 1973.
Niger's Ministry of Human Promotion, whose role is to design programmes in health, education, and welfare, coordinate activities, and motivate participants, has implemented a four-pronged strategy to involve villagers in development programmes. The strategy includes a continuous socioeconomic survey to identify priorities, training courses for village leaders to open dialogue between them and government officials, training courses for peasant animators to assess community perceptions, and reorganization of districts to encourage interaction among "animated" villages. Applied to the health sector, this strategy means first aid and health care training courses that are linked to results from the socioeconomic survey and are offered to two villagers chosen by each community. The courses run for 7-10 days, first covering traditional methods and concepts and then moving to newer knowledge. To date, the stragety's main problems have been due to inadequate supervision, evaluation, and continuing education opportunities for village workers. (AC)

III Primary Health Care--Implementation

3139 Nugroho, G. *Community participation in a community health programme and community health insurance.* In International Secretariat for Volunteer Service, Mobilization of Response Structures from the Grassroots towards Health Services: Report of a Workshop, Manila, ISVS Asian Regional Office, Jul 1974, 105-112. Engl.
International Secretariat for Volunteer Service Workshop on Mobilization of Response Structures from the Grassroots towards Health Services, Manila, Philippines, 8-11 Jul 1974.
For complete document see entry 2919.
According to the author, a community health programme should involve local people in planning, decision-making, implementation, and overall responsibility. In addition, the health worker who initiates the project should work with, rather than for, the community so that the programme can become self-sustaining, even though outside funds may be necessary at the beginning. Two programmes of this type have been started in Java. The programme at Solo is an insurance scheme set up by the local people with virtually no outside financial help. Initially, meetings were held in the target community to explain methods and goals and then a pilot project was started. After 6 months, it was evaluated and expanded to include new services and new areas. The other village programme is also financed and run by the local people under the guidance of a doctor. It emphasizes environmental health and has included some major agricultural and sanitary innovations. (DM)

3140 Oshin, T.A. Commonwealth Foundation, London. National Fund for Research into Crippling Diseases, Arundel, UK. *Rehabilitation aids for some physically handicapped in Nigeria; their improvisation and adaptation.* In Disabled in Developing Countries, London, Commonwealth Foundation,, 1977, 20-25. Engl.
Symposium on Appropriate Technology and Delivery of Health and Welfare Services for the Disabled in Developing Countries, Oxford, UK, 26-30 Sep 1976.
For complete document see entry 3124.
Because rehabilitation aids are in short supply in Nigeria, they must be largely improvised. The delivery delay of up to 6 months means that, on arrival, individually fitted calipers and spinal supports may already be too small for children crippled by polio. As a substitute, the Occupational Therapy Department of the University College Hospital, Ibadan, makes knee cages from local leather and iron and modifies ordinary shoes. Plaster of Paris is used for back supports or for whole-leg casts, which are completed with shoes made from old rubber tires. Modifications of existing designs make orthopaedic aids more suitable for local conditions and easier to use. A folding version of the traditional child walker permits storage in a small home and folding crutches facilitate traveling in taxis and on public transport. Other walkers give mobility to crippled and weak patients. Also adapted to home use is a rope and pulley circuit that mobilizes and prevents stiffness of the shoulder joint. Ropes are further used to help paraplegics raise themselves to a sitting position by pulling on a

knotted length tied to the end of the bed. Alternately, ropes tied overhead allow the patient to lift himself up. Workshops for making such simple aids should be held in all developing countries. (HH)

3141 Patil, N.M. Commonwealth Foundation, London. National Fund for Research into Crippling Diseases, Arundel, UK. *Rehabilitation in rural areas.* In Disabled in Developing Countries, London, Commonwealth Foundation, 1977, 63-68. Engl.
Symposium on Appropriate Technology and Delivery of Health and Welfare Services for the Disabled in Developing Countries, Oxford, UK, 26-30 Sep 1976.
For complete document see entry 3124.
Since 1972, the Medical Appliances and Rehabilitation Clinic Centre in Jalgaon, India, has been developing rehabilitation aids from low-cost, easily available materials. Disabled people in this district need both appropriate aids and helpful advice to counteract prejudice and misconceptions about rehabilitation. For example, traditional healers may advise parents that their child with polio cannot recover and therefore parents are reluctant to try therapy. Once it has been demonstrated that such children can be helped, calipers can be made locally from rust-proofed iron with blanket cloth and cotton rexin for the upholstery, chrome and hide for the shoes, and leather straps. Inner tubes used for hernia belts are well accepted by users, whereas commercially made sprung belts may be abandoned because they cause pain to villagers with poor musculature. This rubber is also used to cushion the edge of cervical collars made from plastic buckets and foam rubber and to make a seat suitable for paralyzed people in small crowded rooms, toilets, or bath places. Bamboo and rope form splints for fractures; posterior knee supports, hand splints, and crutches can also be improvised. Such aids look different from commercially manufactured equivalents, so clinics must persuade users that performance is more important than appearance. (HH)

3142 Pettit, J.H. *Simple pharmacopoeia for out-station skin clinics.* Tropical Doctor (London), 7(3), Jul 1977, 107-110. Engl.
Skin diseases account for approximately 20% of all cases seen in developing countries. In over 20 years of practice in the Middle and Far East, a physician has developed a basic pharmacopoeia consisting of simple, inexpensive medicaments for treating the majority of skin problems. This paper lists the various medicines, sets down the formulae for combining them into a number of prescriptions, and describes how they may be used in cases of varying severity of acne vulgaris, eczema, candidiasis, hyperkeratosis of the feet, impetigo and other pyodermas, pityriasis versicolor, pruritus, scabies, tinea, ulcers, urticaria, and warts. (HC)

3143 Rossler, H. WHO, Brazzaville. *Epidemiological services.* Brazzaville, WHO, 7 Nov 1974. 17p. Engl.
This report describes a WHO project to control commu-

nicable eye diseases in the Dodoma area of Tanzania by developing appropriate methodologies, integrating them into routine health services activities nationally, and training health personnel to implement them. The history of eye diseases, particularly trachoma, in Tanzania is traced. A pilot project tested screening and treatment methods and a trachoma and conjunctivitis treatment programme were undertaken after morbidity surveys revealed the areas of greatest prevalence. Coverage was later extended to other parts of the area by auxiliary health workers trained in diagnosis, treatment, treatment supervision, administration, and health education. The author concludes that the project successfully reduced the incidence of eye diseases to non-endemic levels but recommended that more consideration be given to whether or not an eye diseases auxiliary can function most efficiently alone or as part of a mobile health unit, that the project be extended to other areas of Tanzania, that eye examinations always be performed by an ophthalmologist, and that WHO continue to supply expertise and UNICEF drugs. (RMB)

3144   Rotsart de Hertaing, I. Courtejoie, J. Centre d'Etudes et de Recherches pour la Promotion de la Sante, Kangu-Mayumbe, Zaire. *Medecine a l'ecole: comment ameliorer les contacts entre les ecoles, les hopitaux et les dispensaires. (School health: getting the most out of hospital and dispensary contact with the school).* Kangu-Mayumbe, Zaire, Centre d'Etudes et de Recherches pour la Promotion de la Sante, Brochure Illustre No.4, n.d. 27p. Fren.
See also entry 2804.
At Kangu-Mayumbe, Zaire, medical staff, teachers, and the students themselves share responsibility for maintaining the health of the school-age population. The school health programme begins each year with a thorough examination of each student, including growth monitoring and screening for diseases, nutritional deficiencies, abnormalities, and incomplete immunization. A team of older students assists the nurses by weighing and measuring students, recording the results, testing eyesight, and regulating the flow of students from one step to the next; one or two nurses assisted by a team of students can, in this way, examine 120 students within 3 hours. At the beginning of each trimester, an intensive campaign against malaria and intestinal parasites is mounted, consisting of demonstrations on the symptoms, treatment, and prevention of these two diseases and mass administration of an all-purpose antihelminthic. In addition, students are taught how to recognize the presence of worms in their faeces in order to seek treatment as required. Throughout the school year, hygiene and disease prevention form an integral part of the school curriculum. Also, students are given the opportunity to learn by doing: illustrations show them digging latrines, using a microscope, and giving blood. (HC)

3145   Rowley, J. *"We have survived another year...."* People (London), 3(2), 1976, 17-22. Engl.
In the early 1970s, the University of Ghana Medical School undertook the Danfa Project, an ambitious programme of health research and planning in 200 villages with a total population of 50 000. The villages were divided into four groups. Villages in area 1 received comprehensive health and family planning coverage, health education and family planning services only were provided in area 2, family planning was offered only in area 3, and the 4th group acted as a control with no services offered. Demographic and disease data were collected from all villages. Despite some successes, such as increased family planning acceptance, after 5 years members of the project team voiced serious criticisms of the programme's aims and methods, maintaining that it was too narrow and too research-oriented to meet the felt needs of the communities involved. The project also failed to coordinate its work with other development services in sanitation and agriculture or encourage community participation. In response to these criticisms the project has initiated schemes in health education and care for volunteers, traditional midwives, and village leaders. The new aim of the project is to show the government what support a community needs for self-help by creating an ideal village with a women's group responsible for home management and child care, active health and development committees, and a health team that includes trained volunteers and traditional midwives. (DM)

3146   Sankale, M. Lauture, H. de Dieng, F. Borel, G. Wone, I. *Exemples d'une medecine rurale efficace: les postes de sante prives catholiques du Senegal. (Examples of efficient rural medicine: private Catholic health posts in Senegal).* Medecine d'Afrique Noire (Paris), 23(11), Nov 1976, 653-664. Fren.
Staffed by certified nurses, 41 private Catholic rural health posts deliver curative and preventive services that have been effectively adapted to Senegal's means. They focus preventive activities on maternal child health and invite mothers of children aged less than 5 years to attend monthly meetings during which their children's weight is recorded and lectures and practical demonstrations in food preparation, hygiene, nursing care, etc., are given. Some of the posts have inpatient facilities for nutrition rehabilitation; in these, mothers rehabilitate their children themselves, using food obtained from the local market. Other preventive activities carried out in one or more of the posts are distribution of food supplements, home visiting for antenatal care, malaria prophylaxis, training of indigenous midwives, vaccination, and classes in literacy, home-making, and agriculture. The posts obtain medicaments from national drug stores and charge a small fee-for-service. (HC)

3147   Seoul National University, Seoul. *Chunseong Gun community health program.* Seoul, Seoul National University, School of Public Health, Jul 1975. 130p. Engl.
13 refs.
Individual chapters have been abstracted separately under entries 2298, 3085, 3298, and 3308.
The Chunseong Gun Community Health Program was established by Seoul National University (Korea) with

III Primary Health Care--Implementation

the help of the provincial government in 1972. Its aims were to provide field training and research opportunities and set up a model community health programme for a typical area of rural Korea (population 13 000). Surveys were carried out to collect demographic, economic, and health data and the findings showed that more than half the prevalent diseases were preventable. Initially, the programme provided for public health services only. Later, through a health insurance scheme run by the community with the help of the school, the programme expanded to include a medical clinic. The local population has cooperated and community organizations have been explored as a means for health education. Recently, mothers' clubs have been formed to recruit local women to act as primary health workers. This last project and the insurance scheme are still at experimental stages but will be improved and extended as the health service programme expands. (DM)

3148   Sood, S.K. Varma, S.K. All India Institute of Medical Sciences, Department of Rehabilitation and Artificial Limbs, New Delhi. *Project report on rehabilitation of amputees of Indore district (Madhya Pradesh), India.* New Delhi, All India Institute of Medical Sciences, Department of Rehabilitation and Artificial Limbs, n.d. 3p. Engl. Unpublished document.

The Department of Rehabilitation and Artificial Limbs of the All India Institute of Medical Sciences in New Delhi and the Viklang Punarvas Committee of Indore undertook a campaign to rehabilitate amputees in Indore district, an area of more than a million people that has had no effective rehabilitation services. A variety of local agencies assisted with the initial census in 1975, which took 2 1/2 months. Those identified by the survey were invited to attend day camps at which their requirements were assessed. In 1976, a team of experts visited the area and equipped some 600 amputees with artificial limbs, tricycles, or bicycles and supplied about 90 of the handicapped with the means of making a living. The service, which was aimed at the rural and weaker sections of society, was paid for by public donations and offered free to the amputees. (DM)

3149   Varma, S.K. Shrivastava, N. Bole, S.V. Commonwealth Foundation, London. National Fund for Research into Crippling Diseases, Arundel, UK. *Artificial aids for the masses in the developing countries.* In Disabled in Developing Countries, London, Commonwealth Foundation, 1977, 36-38. Engl. Symposium on Appropriate Technology and Delivery of Health and Welfare Services for the Disabled in Developing Countries, Oxford, UK, 26-30 Sep 1976.

For complete document see entry 3124.

An estimated 6.7 million people in India need inexpensive artificial disability aids that have not yet been developed. The authors suggest that established centres undertake research into the design of cheap, easy-to-use equipment that can be made from available materials by local artisans. For example, a plank with castors can be

subsituted for conventional wheechairs, which are too cumbersome for village life. A folding commode also saves space. A cheap seat and table as well as a shoeless lower leg prosthesis have been designed to allow the handicapped to squat in the culturally-accepted manner. Other adaptations include a cosmetic hand and simple elbow joint instead of an expensive and elaborate upper limb prosthesis and a cheap hand splint made from an aluminum clothes hanger. (HH)

III.3 Mobile Units and Services

See also: 3129, 3132, 3446, 3477

3150   *Psychiatry in Vietnam.* In McMichael, J.K., ed., Health in the Third World: Studies from Vietnam, Nottingham, UK, Spokesman Books, 1976, 322-327. Engl.

For complete document see entry 2869.

A German professor of social psychiatry considers that psychiatry in North Vietnam is not only highly developed but sometimes even *avant-garde*, in shaip contrast to that of South Vietnam and most other Third World countries. Psychiatric services reflect the importance attached to humane care of the mentally ill, who in Vietnam suffer mainly from schizophrenia, war neuroses, hysteria, and depression, but not from paranoia and 'obsessional neuroses. Mental illness incidence is fairly high (1:100 population). Most patients are treated in their homes by mobile psychiatric teams that utilize help from families and fellow-workers. Drug therapy is the same as that used in Europe, with additional tranquilizing potions from traditional herbs. Seriously ill patients are referred to one of two open hospitals, where they live in well-structured groups with a high proportion of qualified staff, many of whom were recruited after heroic war-time service. No agitated person is immobilized, locked up, or put in solitary confinement; the principal therapy, established originally in emergency care of disturbed people in bomb shelters, is physical contact and "mothering"--an approach that meets the family-centred needs of the Vietnamese. (AB)

3151   Bisley, G.G. *Mobile eye units in Kenya.* Israel Journal of Medical Sciences (Jerusalem), 8(8-9), 1972, 1245-1249. Engl. Causes and Prevention of Blindness, Jerusalem Seminar on the Prevention of Blindness, Jerusalem, Israel, 25-27 Aug 1971.

Because of the acute shortage of skilled health manpower in Kenya, ophthalmologists have to rely more and more on paramedical personnel to staff mobile eye units. The mobile unit team, which consists of a medical assistant, an enrolled male nurse, and a driver, is supervised by an ophthalmologist and a lay administrator. As head of the team, the medical assistant has completed a 4-year training course, worked 1 year in a district hospital or health centre, and undergone a year of ophthalmic training. He plans the visits and oversees the care. Visits are well publicized beforehand and last about 3 days, during which schoolchildren are treated for conjunctivitis and trachoma and surgical treatment is offered. The major difficulty facing mobile eye units so far has been tracking down and treating the nomadic peoples of Kenya, who accept blindness with resignation and do not seem to realize that much of it is curable. A table shows costs, both capital and recurrent, for one mobile unit operating in Kenya for 1 year. (EE)

3152 Chatterjee, A. *Mobile eye hospitals and cataract surgery in India.* Israel Journal of Medical Sciences (Jerusalem), 8(8-9), 1972, 1239-1243. Engl.
Causes and Prevention of Blindness, Jerusalem Seminar on the Prevention of Blindness, Jerusalem, Israel, 25-27 Aug 1971.
After a brief discussion of the epidemiology of eye diseases in India, the author outlines some basic principles for the operation of a mobile eye clinic, including recommendations on contacts with local hospitals, basic minimum personnel, essential equipment, suitable locations, proper scheduling, supplying corrective lenses, medical records maintenance, and health education. The proper procedure for cataract removal under field conditions is described and some statistical data are included. The author strongly favours the continued operation of mobile clinics as the only means of reaching rural patients whose blindness can be cured. (RMB)

3153 Daberkow, S.G. *Location and cost of ambulances serving a rural area.* Health Services Research (Chicago, Ill.), 23(3), Fall 1977, 299-311. Engl.
27 refs.
A location model is used to determine the most efficient (i.e., least-cost) number and location of ambulance facilities in a rural area of California (USA). The model incorporates response time and service time standards into the analysis and indicates the trade-off between costs and various time standards. The financial feasibility of individual facility locations is then analyzed. The results show that for many rural areas it is only economically feasible to provide emergency medical transportation on a volunteer or part-time basis. (Modified author abstract.)

3154 Essex, B.J. Everett, V.J. *Use of an action-oriented record card for antenatal screening.* Tropical Doctor (London), 7(3), Jul 1977, 134-138. Engl.
An antenatal record designed to streamline and standardize the identification of patients at risk from complicated pregnancies has been developed and tested in Tanzania. The record indicates at a glance the patient's obstetric history, the presence of one or more risk factors, and the appropriate action for each factor detected. It also includes advice on preventing anaemia, malaria, neonatal tetanus, and malnutrition. The record was used to screen 13 410 attenders of 41 mobile antental clinics held in Dar es Salaam during a 6-week period. Of these, 1 267 (17.65%) were found to exhibit one or more risk factors, 81% of which were detected from the patients' histories or heights as indicated on their records. It was also found that when old and new antenatal cards were used on the same patients, the new card had a much

higher rate of risk detection than the old. In addition, when the new card was used by different health workers on the same patients, it elicited a much higher rate of agreement than did the old (95% as opposed to 68%). Parts of the card are reproduced in this paper and the factors deemed risk indicators in Tanzania are listed. (HC)

3155 Franken, S. *Function of a mobile eye clinic.* Israel Journal of Medical Sciences (Jerusalem), 8(8-9), 1972, 1243-1245. Engl.
Causes and Prevention of Blindness, Jerusalem Seminar on the Prevention of Blindness, Jerusalem, Israel, 25-27 Aug 1971.
After denouncing the harmful techniques of vagabonds posing as eye doctors in India, the author outlines the functions of a modern mobile eye unit, such as extending ophthalmic care to rural areas and training medical students in rural practice. Mobile unit staff also do preliminary work: finding suitable surroundings and buildings, cleaning them, setting up the necessary equipment, and publicizing the available services. They remain for about 10 days in each village, offering surgical treatment and dressing, examining schoolchildren, giving general check-ups, and encouraging elemental hygiene. (EE)

3156 Hopital Protestant de Dabou, Dabou, Ivory Coast. *Hopital Protestant de Dabou. (Protestant Hospital of Dabou).* Dabou, Ivory Coast, Hopital Protestant de Dabou, n.d. 12p. Fren.
Since 1968, the Ivory Coast *Hopital Protestant de Dabou* has been training young African men and women with primary school educations to provide high quality nursing care in a small hospital or rural setting. Though the 3 year course does not lead to state certification, the trainees are beginning to replace the expatriate professional staff and are also serving in other local hospitals and health programmes. The rural work for which the trainees are prepared is based on mobile clinics serving nine villages over a range of up to 120 km. At present, the overwhelming pressure for curative services from these villages makes adequate public health measures difficult to carry out, but the planned expansion of rural activities includes a 2nd monthly visit of the team for purely preventive health work. Other planned developments are short full-time courses in health education for village clinic helpers, a rural maternity training centre in an isolated village, and a nutrition/antenatal village project run along nutrition rehabilitation centre lines. A baseline survey will precede the initiation of this expanded programme. Appendices to the report include the curriculum of the training programme for nurses, a report on the mobile clinic work, and a resume of the projected programme for meeting public health problems. (AB)

3157 Nicholson, K.G. Renshaw, A. Metcalf, C.A. Rideout, J.M. *Simple method for measuring haemoglobin; evaluation in Andean rain forest.* Lancet (London), 1(8016), 16 Apr 1977, 836-837. Engl.

III Primary Health Care--Implementation

87

A new method for measuring haemoglobin, tested in Equador and suitable for use in other developing countries, consists of a blood-sampling and diluting device, known as the "swizzlestick technique", modified Drabkins reagent, and a colorimeter powered by a battery. During the test period, all equipment was carried in a rucksack and, after 15 minutes instruction, a nurse and an army sergeant with no previous medical experience were able to make satisfactory measurements. This method of testing was acceptable to both adult and juvenile patients and the authors feel that the system could be expanded to measure plasma bilrubin, urea, albumin, total protein, and glucose. Full technical details will be published later. (RMB)

3158   Venkataswamy, G. *Eye camps in India.* Israel Journal of Medical Sciences (Jerusalem), 8(8-9), 1972, 1254-1259. Engl.
Causes and Prevention of Blindness, Jerusalem Seminar on the Prevention of Blindness, Jerusalem, Israel, 25-27 Aug 1971.
In the state of Tamil Nadu, India, cataracts affect some 800 000 people, of whom only 40 000 can be operated upon annually due to a shortage of hospital facilities. In an attempt to reach more patients whose blindness could be corrected by surgery, volunteer physicians and other personnel have organized mobile eye camps where eye examinations and minor operations are performed free of charge. The author describes one such camp and traces the history of a typical cataract patient from admittance to discharge. Some camps also hold special sessions for nutritionally-related eye diseases, conduct large-scale examinations of schoolchildren, and provide corrective lenses for the vision-impaired. Tables showing complications and cost per patient are included. (RMB)

3159   Yoder, P.T. Christian Medical Commission, World Council of Churches, Geneva. *Awash community health services project, Ethiopia.* Contact (Geneva), 35, Feb 1977, 1-9. Engl.
Also published in French as *Services sanitaires de la communaute ethiopienne d'Awash* in Contact (Geneva), 27, Jan 1977, 1-10.
A missionary recounts his experiences in extending health services to the Afar, a nomadic tribe in Ethiopia. He notes that his 1st contact with them was 19 years earlier but that only in the last 3 has he realized his dream of a community health project. He discusses some of their customs, such as male and female circumcision, and explains some of the obstacles to providing basic health services. Many of the latter were a trick of fate--for instance, the project's cooperation with a smallpox eradication campaign backfired, annihilating credibility in one village and seriously deterring all future immunization activities. Project staff comprised the missionary director, his wife, two dressers, a cook, and an interpreter. Their health activities included maternal child health services, information gathering, and efforts toward improving sanitation and water supply. (AC)

III.4 Community Health Education

See also: 2821, 2836, 3003, 3076, 3139, 3144, 3209, 3219, 3248, 3254, 3278, 3285, 3286, 3301, 3307, 3321, 3333, 3334, 3341, 3354, 3356, 3358, 3359, 3361, 3362, 3363, 3371, 3382, 3406, 3461, 3465, 3483, 3484

3160   Ayonrinde, A. Erinosho, O.A. *Pilot experiment in preventive psychiatry in a rural community: the case of Igbo-ora in Nigeria.* International Journal of Health Education (Geneva), 20(2), 1977, 120-125. Engl.
9 refs.
An experiment was conducted in the rural town of Igbo-ora, Western Nigeria, to encourage the utilization of a new psychiatric facility. First, the attitudes of a few professional care agents (nurses, medical students, etc.) and community leaders (chiefs, clergymen, health visitors, etc.) were surveyed to identify areas of ignorance or prejudice regarding mental illness and its management; then the health workers and community leaders were exposed to psychiatric symptomatology and concepts of mental illness through a series of discussions. A 2nd survey of the respondents' knowledge and attitudes revealed that their ability to recognize persons exhibiting the symptoms of simple schizophrenia, paranoid schizophrenia, anxiety neurosis/depression, and alcoholism as mentally ill and advise the proper course of action in each case had increased. Moreover, referral of patients who had previously been treated by traditional healers or the church, as well as those who had only just begun to manifest symptoms of mental illness, to the new facility commenced immediately after the respondents were exposed to psychiatric symptomatology. It is concluded that a heightened awareness of the concept, etiology, and course of psychiatric disorders can lead to referral and utilization of psychiatric facilities. (HC)

3161   Brown, G.F. Canada, Department of National Health and Welfare. *Alternative approaches to health promotion.* Health Education, Department of Health and Welfare, Health Programs Branch (Ottawa),, 15(2-3), Jul-Dec 1976, 1-24. Engl.
72 refs.
Recent trends in health promotion have aimed at exploiting the positive control that individuals have over their own bodies; some of the most promising techniques include biofeedback, autogenic training, guided imagery, behaviour modification, hypnosis, etc. Such therapies derive from a holistic view of human beings and thus link human physiology with psychology. Although they have existed for many years outside the conventional medical care system, they are currently gaining favour and have joined the repertoire of techniques used in the self-care and self-help movements that have emerged since 1960. They have also been accepted in some health promotion programmes sponsored by conventional medicine. (AC)

3162   Chacko, A. *In the realm of health education.* Nursing Journal of India (New Delhi), 68(1), Jan 1977, 12-14. Engl.
The Church of South India, Bangalore, has evolved an effective outreach programme consisting of 2 rural

health centres and 11 subcentres. One of these subcentres serves 3 000 people in 7 villages; it consists of a small dispensary, inpatient facilities for 4 patients, a community kitchen, staff quarters, and a community centre and is staffed by an interdisciplinary team consisting of a pastor, a nurse, an agricultural extension worker, and a social worker. The most important function of the nurse is giving health education on an informal basis during cooking demonstrations and home visits and formally as a 4-6-month family education class for local mothers. Twenty mothers are recruited for each course and taught about family budgeting, simple household skills, nutrition, hygiene, etc., through discussion and demonstration. A nurse from one of the health centres has this advice to offer concerning teaching methodology: be brief--5-10 minutes per communication is sufficient; be simple--make one or two points only, so as not to confuse the audience with too much information; make extensive use of visual aids and actual utensils; and try to use local events to illustrate the talk so that it will be remembered. (HC)

3163 Crow, M.M. Bradshaw, B.R. Guest, F. *True to Life: a relevant approach to patient education.* American Journal of Public Health (New York), 62, Oct 1972, 1328-1220. Engl.

"True to Life" is a pulp confession magazine designed by the staff of a family planning programme in a large public hospital in Atlanta, Georgia (USA), to present family planning and sex education information to young, lower class women who read such publications regularly and trust them implicitly. The magazine contains the usual 1st-person stories, dramatic titles, titillating photographs, and personal advice columns, although it differs from commercial publications of the genre in its relative feminist position and its emphasis on presenting ways in which individuals can take control of their own destinies, including birth control, which is always pictured as a natural part of life. Sample plot outlines are included. A reader survey revealed that some 90% of the target population liked the magazine well enough to buy a 2nd issue, although its appeal to a better educated, more sophisticated audience was limited. (RMB)

3164 Fernbach, V. James, W. Mendel, L. Reader, G. Richards, R. Shehan, M. Skiff, A. Williams, A. *Concept of planned, hospital-based patient education programs.* Health Education Monographs (Thorofare, N.J.), 2(1), Spring 1974, 1-10. Engl. 16 refs.

According to several American studies, patients who have been adequately informed about their treatment participate in their own care, undergo fewer hospital or clinic readmissions, require shorter inpatient care, adhere to diets and follow physicians' orders more closely, and suffer less anxiety and stress. These findings indicate the importance of patient education, i.e., the educational experiences planned for the patient by professional personnel as a component of care. It should be integrated into all inpatient care and should be supported by adequate funds, top administrative personnel, health professionals, and professional staff with training in the

behavioural sciences and educational methods. Above all, its success depends on a change in the perception of the patient as a passive recipient of professional services. Guidelines for implementing a patient education programme and indications for further research into the cost-benefit of patient education programmes are included among the recommendations. (HC)

3165 Freydig, C.A. WHO, Brazzaville. *Health education in Mauritius: report on a mission 5 Jan-7 Feb 1974.* Brazzaville, WHO, 28 Mar 1974. 9p. Engl.

In 1974, a survey of health education activities in Mauritius revealed that the ministries of health, social security, and youth and sports, the primary school system, agricultural extension workers, the rural development programme, etc., were all engaged in health education. In addition, television programming included 1 hour per week of health education. Based on these findings, a plan was devised to increase the skills of existing field-workers and coordinate their efforts. It called for: quarterly meetings of personnel involved in health education; the inclusion of health education in all job descriptions; the strengthening of the health education component in nurse, midwife, and health inspector curricula; the formation of a joint committee of representatives from the ministries of health and education; the distribution of press releases and pamphlets following television broadcasts; the introduction of weekly 10-minute radio talks on health; and the development of education materials, a monthly newsletter, and a reference library for use by those involved in health education. A limited version of the programme for short-term application is also outlined. (HC)

3166 Fuglesang, A. Zambia, National Food and Nutrition Commission. *Communication with illiterates: a pilot study of the problem of social communication in developing countries.* Markedskommunikasjon (Oslo), 7(3), 1970, 24-99. Engl.

See also entry 1047 (volume 2).

An inquiry into basic questions about communicating with illiterates in Zambia suggests reasons why nutrition and other educational campaigns fail. Though illiterates are not inferior, their social environment has not encouraged them to develop certain mental processes that are taken for granted in communication among literate people. Thus, information presented in concepts and visual symbols that are easily understood by educated people often reaches illiterates as a stream of signals with no significance; conversely, feedback from illiterates may be incomprehensible to educators. A substantial portion of illiterates poorly understand concepts such as number, quantity, weight, spatial area, horizontal and vertical, etc., and have great difficulty, for example, visualizing and drawing a straight line to join two points. A small study of the comprehension of pictures by illiterates has demonstrated that photographs, whose background and extraneous detail are obliterated, are more easily understood than unaltered photographs and much more readily recognized than silhouettes or line drawings, which were the least understood. Further research is

III Primary Health Care--Implementation

needed to develop a physiology of the illiterate and a comprehensive understanding of communication. (AB)

3167   Haraldson, S.S. International School of Geneva, Geneva. *Role of education in preserving traditional cultures.* Geneva, International School of Geneva, Sep 1974. 10p. Engl.
19 refs.
International School of Geneva, 50th Anniversary Symposium, Geneva, Switzerland, Sep 1974.
Unpublished document.
Education for children in developing countries can help to improve the living standards and health status of the people by teaching new techniques of animal husbandry, hunting, fishing, and health care delivery. However, it is important to relate the course content to the child's traditional culture and background. To achieve this, schools can offer courses with a deliberate cultural bias and, for nomadic people, they can be mobile. If children with aptitude receive further training in fields such as health and education, with emphasis on the particular problems of their own people, some are likely to return to work in their own communities, although some exodus of educated young people from the community will inevitably occur. (HH)

3168   Isley, R.B. Martin, J.F. WHO, Geneva. *Village health committee: starting point for rural development.* WHO Chronicle (Geneva), 31(8), Aug 1977, 307-315. Engl.
16 refs.
Also published in French, Russian, and Spanish.
A project for activating village health committees in Cameroon was carried out over a 2-year period. First, four pilot villages were selected and a detailed survey of the inhabitants' knowledge, attitudes, and practices with regard to health was conducted. Next, male nurses were trained to help organize village health committees, assist them in launching their health work, supervise the work, and extend the programme to other villages. By the end of the 1st year, there were 11 village health committees in operation; by the end of the 2nd, 40 more. The committees chose their own priorities and, with help from the nurses, became familiar with the planning process. Nearly every village eventually completed one or more health promotion projects using local personnel and materials. One village constructed 45 latrines, protected four springs, and planned the construction of an emergency maternity clinic, the placement of a first-aid kit in every home, and the building of a piped water supply. The same village took steps to formalize a land claim with the government. (HC)

3169   Kingma, S.J. *Comprehensive rural health project, Jamkhed, India: progress report.* Contact (Geneva), 25, Feb 1975, 7-12. Engl.
See also entry 988 (volume 2).
After 4 years of operation, the Jamkhed (India) comprehensive rural health project now boasts a vigorous maternal and child health programme, has made significant strides in the area of family planning, and has established control of leprosy and tuberculosis. More-

over, it has embraced the entire target population (40 000) within its activities and is only 2 years away from self-sufficiency. Much of the project's success is attributed to its responsiveness to felt needs and its deployment of village health workers. When it became apparent that the area's highest priorities were not medical services but food and water, effort was directed toward community development schemes such as sheep-breeding, well-digging, road improvement, community kitchens, etc. Similarly, when it was realized that the cultural gap between the city-educated health worker and the illiterate peasant was severely hampering health promotion, the recruitment and training of village health workers was begun. These volunteers are generally illiterate, middle-aged women who are well-respected in their communities. In-service training in the health centre and the field prepares them to conduct health education, give health advice, screen children for simple ailments, distribute contraceptives, and report all births and deaths in their communities. Impressive statistics regarding family planning acceptance, immunization, child weight gains, etc., are cited to illustrate the impact of the village health workers on their communities. (HC)

3170   Lelo di Kimbi Kiaku, N.M. Vindu Kiama, M. Courtejoie, J. Rotsart de Hertaing, I. Bureau d'Etudes et de Recherches pour la Promotion de la Sante, Kangu-Mayumbe, Zaire. *Centre pour la Promotion de la Sante: experience pratique de Kangu-Mayumbe. 2 edition. (Centre for Health Amelioration: practical experience in Kangu-Mayumbe. 2 edition).* Kangu-Mayumbe, Zaire, Bureau d'Etudes et de Recherches pour la Promotion de la Sante, Brochure Illustre No.2, n.d. 47p. Fren.
See also entry 2804.
The structure and purposes of the Center for Health Amelioration (Kangu-Mayumbe, Zaire) are presented in this illustrated brochure. In response to medical, educational, and economic problems, the centre was founded in 1961 to sponsor health promotion activities, provide health education materials, and encourage health education outside the schools. The centre's history is traced from 1961 to the present and its three-part structure is outlined. The Bureau of Research Studies for Health Promotion studies, edits, and tests material on health education, social medicine, and nursing education and adapts it for use in an African setting. The teaching centre instructs health education auxiliaries and the production centre manufactures slides, posters, books, brochures, and other health education materials using simple, inexpensive techniques. An appendix describes the admissions standards, length, curriculum, and graduation requirements of the course for health education auxiliaries. (RMB)

3171   Locketz, L. Pan American Health Organization, Washington, D.C. *Health education in rural Surinam: use of videotape in a national campaign against schistosomiasis.* Bulletin of the Pan American Health Organization (Washington, D.C.), 10(3), 1976, 219-226. Engl.

A videotaped programme on schistosomiasis, coordinated with a wide range of other campaign activities, was shown at schools, clinics, and other gathering places in the rural Surinam district of Saramacca. The usual procedure was to have two showings, the 1st for teachers and the 2nd for pupils in grades 4-6. The children were then asked to answer simple questions about the disease in writing. Booklets were also distributed to teachers and children and in a number of instances follow-up activities such as classroom exercises and in one case an art contest were carried out. By and large, the tape was a success. Viewer attention was best when the audience was comfortably seated and undistracted. It was found that the viewing by itself was not enough to ensure basic understanding of the schistosomiasis problem. Writing about the event afterwards helped for it to be taken seriously, reinforced the information conveyed, and allowed children to relate the ideas presented to their own experiences. It also gave the campaign workers a basis on which to estimate the degree of success achieved. At the same time, follow-up projects such as the art contest enlisted the active participation of children, community members, and educators and added greatly to the overall educational effect. (Modified author abstract.)

3172   ma Lelo, N.M. Rotsart de Hertaing, I. Courtejoie, J. Centre d'Etudes et de Recherches pour la Promotion de la Sante, Kangu-Mayumbe, Zaire. *Education sanitaire: quelques principes de base. 2 edition. (Health education: some basic principles. 2 edition).* Kangu-Mayumbe, Zaire, Centre d'Etudes et de Recherches pour la Promotion de la Sante, Brochure Illustre No.12, n.d. 39p. Fren.
See also entry 2804.
The government of Zaire disseminates health information through schools and health facilities rather than a special information system. An obstacle to this method of health education, however, is posed by teaching and health personnel whose training, motivation, and workload often discourages them from becoming seriously involved in health promotion. This illustrated brochure explains to nurses, paramedical workers, and teachers why they are the logical purveyors of health education and gives them some basic information on the aims, content, methodology, and technique of imparting health education. (HC)

3173   Medis, L.P. Fernando, P.A. *Health education in emergency situations: a cholera outbreak in Sri Lanka.* International Journal of Health Education (Geneva), 20(3), 1977, 200-204. Engl.
In 1974, when a cholera outbreak threatened 220 000 people in Sri Lanka, health education activities were immediately launched to promote active participation of the community in the control effort. Each village was asked to set up a committee to take responsibility for planning and implementing the education programme; health workers, teachers, and volunteers were oriented in the causes and control of cholera; and leaflets, posters, press releases, spot announcements, slides, and banners were utilized to inform the public of the 10 basic points

of prevention (boil drinking water, protect food from flies, take lunch to work rather than eat in the canteen, avoid eating leafy green vegetables, etc.). Full details of the objectives, target groups, content, and methods of the programme are provided in a table. A post-campaign survey revealed a definite improvement in people's knowledge regarding the transmission of cholera and their behaviour regarding its prevention. Another survey to determine whether the health education activities contributed to a permanent change in people's attitudes and practices is planned. (HC)

3174   Mehra, J. UNICEF, New Delhi. *Localized production of communication materials: the Baroda Project.* New Delhi, UNICEF, Project Support Communications Section, Jan 1977. 65p. Engl.
Unpublished document.
Because locally-produced audiovisual teaching aids are more easily understood and accepted by rural populations, a UNICEF-supported project in Gujarat, India, to produce materials for field staff in nutrition, childcare, and hygiene involved cooperation among personnel at village, block, district, and state levels. The contributors included villagers, village health workers, governmental Integrated Child Development Services (ICDS) workers, Applied Nutrition Programme (ANP) workers, and UNICEF project support communications staff. The project's intended strategy, after a preliminary exploratory survey of food habits and nutritional status, consisted of six phases. The planning phase, involving the establishment of a "content resource pool," would lead to field-testing of prototype communication materials, followed by a production phase, when selected materials would be printed. After a training phase for users of the materials and an evaluation of their effectiveness, the project, if successful, could be expanded to other areas of the country. The project is at present at the production stage after a series of 11 tests to determine the level of acceptability and comprehension of the visual materials in the "content resource pool." The objectives, methods, results, and conclusions of these tests appear here in detail with illustrated descriptions of the communication materials that are at present in production. (CL)

3175   Ramakrishna, V. *Real challenge: a self-health system with genuine commitment.* International Journal of Health Education (Geneva), 20(1), 1977, 19-28. Engl.
20 refs.
In view of modern medicine's continuing failure to provide for the health needs of most of the world, the author believes that improvement in the health of the masses can only come about through political commitment. One way of manifesting such a commitment would be the mobilization of health and health-related industries (pharmaceutical, agricultural, etc.) and organizations (community, school, etc.) to cooperate in a system called "self-health." Self-health would enable the individual and his family to reinforce the positive features of their existing health beliefs and practices and acquire the latest essential knowledge and skills for the practice of self-health measures, as far as their resources allow. The

new system would be promoted by the health education specialist, whose role will require: a strong commitment to the self-health principle and a high degree of competence in educational planning, programming, and coordination; different types of training (pre-, in-service, and continuing) for both health personnel and citizens; serving as an agent for change in organization, system, and process; learning how to conduct action research; mobilizing and using human resources; and dealing with the uncertainty of the future. It will be, essentially, a role of pioneering, innovating, and planning. Examples of self-health in action are taken from the author's experience in India. (HC)

3176 Schweser, H. Blaize, A.A. Project HOPE, Washington, D.C. *Development of a health education department in a less developed Caribbean country.* Washington, D.C., People-to-People Health Foundation, Project HOPE, 1976. 70p. Engl.
74 refs.
The aim of the 1-year model health education programme launched in Antigua in 1974 by the Caribbean Community Secretariat in conjunction with Project HOPE was to mobilize the whole populace to tackle the causes of disease. Project HOPE provided an experienced health educator and two counterpart nurses were assigned for on-the-job training in the techniques of health education for community participation. The first 6 months of the programme were devoted largely to extensive publicity in the mass media to inform the general public about the campaign. This was followed by a series of 1-month campaigns on specific health issues such as refuse disposal, mosquito eradication, maternal and child health, and nutrition. Songs, films, and slogans were broadcast on radio and television, but much of the effort was aimed at schoolchildren. The department designed a special health curriculum for use in schools and organized an in-service course in health education for teachers. A range of teaching methods was recommended. A similar in-service training course equipped student nurses to introduce health education into their routine contact with patients. The pilot programme was proclaimed a success at the June 1975 Conference of Caribbean Health Ministers and Antigua must now decide whether to maintain a permanent Health Education Department. (DM)

3177 Schweser, H.O. Project HOPE, Washington, D.C. People-to-People Health Foundation, Inc., Washington, D.C. *Health education by agricultural extension workers.* In Schweser, H.O., Manual for Community Health Education for the Caribbean, Washington, D.C., People-to-People Health Foundation, n.d., 89-79. Engl.
For complete document see entry 3371.
Caribbean farmers should be encouraged to produce crops selectively in order to provide nutritionally adequate supplies of calories and proteins, because the author feels that the problems of rural life and agriculture are so closely linked that they require joint improvement programmes. By contributing to improvements in the

agricultural sector, for example, agricultural extension workers (AEWs) can help to reduce urban migration and the ensuing health problems of urban poverty and unemployment and decrease juvenile malnutrition, which will lower child mortality and encourage smaller families. AEWs can also promote the development of a national food and nutrition policy and educate for changes in political and economic attitudes towards nutrition and agriculture. Aiming at a balance between the biological needs of the population and the financial benefits of exports, they should promote strongly viable programmes of research on nutrition and the increased production, conservation, marketing, and distribution of foods. (HH)

3178 Schweser, H.O. Project HOPE, Washington, D.C. People-to-People Health Foundation, Inc., Washington, D.C. *Health education by social workers.* In Schweser, H.O., Manual for Community Health Education for the Caribbean, Washington, D.C., People-to-People Health Foundation, n.d. 113-120. Engl.
For complete document see entry 3371.
Caribbean social workers should be encouraged to promote a comprehensive approach to the provision of health, nutrition, and social services for the whole community, especially the preschool child. Social workers can train auxiliaries, including unemployed school dropouts, to manage programmes for small children and strive to improve available clinics, day-care centres, nursery schools, facilities for neglected children, and financial services for deprived families. They can also provide education for parents on home management, child care and development, health and nutritional requirements, and family planning and run classes for children who already look after younger siblings and function effectively as helpers and teachers. Special resources for rehabilitating the handicapped, the identification and support of high-risk groups such as migrants, and the development of volunteer and cooperative services are also part of the social workers' task. By alleviating stresses that lead to mental illness they can help to maintain the population in good health. (HH)

3179 Schweser, H.O. Project HOPE, Washington, D.C. People-to-People Health Foundation, Inc., Washington, D.C. *Where health education should be taught.* In Schweser, H.O., Manual for Community Health Education for the Caribbean, Washington, D.C., People-to-People Health Foundation, n.d., 162-240. Engl.
For complete document see entry 3371.
In the Caribbean, health education in the community, schools, hospitals, clinics, and the home can provide the impetus for a united attack on disease, poverty, illiteracy, and civic inertia. By working with existing adult groups, health education workers can gain the support of community leaders and children can be reached by school health committees working together with education and health departments. Public health nurses, sanitarians, nutritionists, and community development workers should be encouraged to participate in health education

programmes as well as parents and school employees. Because hospital patients are particularly receptive to health education and can take their knowledge back to their communities, hospital personnel should take every opportunity to counsel individual patients and their families and to foster an interest in community health education. They should also try to stimulate community interest in the hospital itself. Clinics could similarly publicize their activities, because they are ideal places for group instruction, especially in maternal child health care and family planning at prenatal and postnatal and child health clinics. Health workers and related personnel must then establish active home visiting programmes to make sure that recommended health practices are carried out. (HH)

3180   Schweser, H.O. Project HOPE, Washington, D.C. People-to-People Health Foundation, Inc., Washington, D.C. *Role and importance of health education.* In Schweser, H.O., Manual for Community Health Education for the Caribbean, Washington, D.C., People-to-People Health Foundation, n.d., 1-21. Engl.
For complete document see entry 3371.

In the Caribbean, a preventive approach to health is essential because of rising costs and the shortage of professional health workers, so that much of the responsibility for health care must be borne by the people themselves. To this end, a national health education service should be developed with proper administrative support to ensure cooperation, coordination, and integration of health education activities with plans for the whole economy, including those for housing and water supplies. Such a service could plan the education components of all health programmes, train staff in the health department and other agencies, help people to recognize and act upon community health problems, work with educational authorities to develop school health projects, and produce and distribute educational materials. Its staff should include health education specialists at all levels, who can identify and act upon all opportunities for health education and training, as well as specialists in other fields such as social sciences, communications, public health, and teaching. Because training of professional health workers is vitally important, each country will need to develop and use courses and teaching methods appropriate to its own problems. Physicians and auxiliaries will work together with an understanding of their complementary roles if they are trained together as a team and a national health council representing all community interests can facilitate information exchange. (HH)

3181   Schweser, H.O. Project HOPE, Washington, D.C. People-to-People Health Foundation, Inc., Washington, D.C. *Health education by teachers.* In Schweser, H.O., Manual for Community Health Education for the Caribbean, Washington, D.C., People-to-People Health Foundation, n.d., 57-82. Engl.
For complete document see entry 3371.
To provide health education in the classroom, elementa-

ry and secondary school teachers need training in teaching methods as well as instruction in both personal and community health. They should be encouraged to promote a clean environment within the school, provide a good example of personal hygiene, and counsel parents and pupils about the prevention and control of disease. Teachers can also take advantage of vision-screening tests to instruct children in eye care, of weighing and measuring to motivate them towards better eating practices, and of inspections for cleanliness to talk about health and social relationships. Older pupils can learn about accident prevention and first aid; they can also make sure that younger siblings are properly immunized. Instruction can be integrated with other subjects so that home economics teaches hygiene, social studies involve community and family health, physical education concentrates on individual health needs, chemistry includes the study of insecticides, and mathematics covers the statistics of disease. Health can also provide subjects for compositions and debate in language instruction. In addition, an imaginative teacher can turn every contact with local health services into a learning experience and involve the students in community health by visiting refuse disposal systems, hospitals, etc. (HH)

3182   Schweser, H.O. Project HOPE, Washington, D.C. People-to-People Health Foundation, Inc., Washington, D.C. *Health education by nutritionalists.* In Scheweser, H.O., Manual for Community Health Education for the Caribbean, Washington, D.C., People-to-People Health Foundation, n.d., 83-88. Engl.
For complete document see entry 3371.
To combat malnutrition in developing countries, nutritionists must teach people to choose a balanced diet, despite local customs and superstitions that are often detrimental to good nutrition. Also, people passing from a subsistence to a market economy do not always know how to get the best food value for their money, since they are easily tempted by expensive, widely-advertised foods. Therefore, before any other steps are taken, proper nutritional surveys should be carried out so that the government can prepare a sound nutritional policy. Applied nutrition programmes can be built around food production, nutrition education in schools, and consumer education aimed especially at mothers and housewives. As a 1st step, nutritionists should encourage increased food crop production and an increase in income from cash crops so that more food can be grown and bought by the family. They can also help with nutrition education for all levels of health workers and can promote nutrition programmes in family planning projects, work to improve nutrition education in schools, and produce material for mass education. In addition, they can organize voluntary nutrition clubs that emphasize food production and education; a principal target of these clubs should be housewives and mothers with small children. (HH)

3183   Schweser, H.O. Project HOPE, Washington, D.C. People-to-People Health Foundation, Inc., Washington, D.C. *Health education by veterinari-*

ans. In Schweser, H.O., Manual for Community Health Education for the Caribbean, Washington, D.C., People-to-People Health Foundation, n.d., 98-l03. Engl.
For complete document see entry 3371.

Veterinarians can help health education services in developing countries to educate the public by teaching advanced animal husbandry and disease control methods to livestock breeders, slaughterers, and others directly involved with animals. Improved livestock management will not only help control the more than 150 diseases transmissible from animals to man, it will also increase available protein by avoiding some of the present waste caused by seasonal underfeeding of animals and forced slaughtering of diseased stock. Veterinarians can spread their knowledge by promoting and organizing educational programmes for animal health assistants trained in animal production technologies relevant to the region. They can also encourage training in secondary schools, educate children about the dangers of catching diseases from pets, and work for the strengthening of laws prohibiting animals in urban areas. On a larger scale, they can inform governments of the need for research on animal diseases relevant to tropical husbandry, the expansion of food hygiene programmes, and the establishment of quarantine depots. (HH)

3184 Schweser, H.O. Project Hope, Washington, D.C. People-to-People Health Foundation, Inc., Washington, D.C. *Health education by community development workers.* In Schweser, H.O., Manual for Community Health Education for the Caribbean, Washington, D.C., People-to-People Health Foundation, n.d., 104-112. Engl.
For complete document see entry 3371.

The community development worker (CDW) must encourage community education, confidence, self-reliance, and mutual help. In his role as consultant and guide to the community, he should coordinate the activities of all the organizations working on similar health programmes. He can develop potential leaders by giving classes in self-help, project organization, and parliamentary procedures. He must also foster literacy as a means of disseminating health information, including news of successful health projects in other villages and procedures for drawing up intelligible programme proposals. The CDW can also organize group meetings to listen to health programmes on radio and television, show films, discuss current issues, and study special problems. In addition to arousing interest in better public health practices, he should ensure that new health standards established during mass campaigns are maintained. Children as well as adults must be taught the value of working for the community; preschool children could be reached by identifying parents who could initiate programmes for them. (HH)

3185 Schweser, H.O. Project HOPE, Washington, D.C. People-to-People Health Foundation, Inc., Washington, D.C. *Health education by voluntary organizations.* In Schweser, H.O., Manual for Community Health Education for the Caribbean,

Washington, D.C., People-to-People Health Foundation, n.d., 121-161. Engl.
For complete document see entry 3371.

Voluntary organizations can contribute to health education by sponsoring community campaigns to increase public understanding and awareness of health problems. Professional groups can lobby to influence legislators and government policies, pharmacological associations can educate the public about the use and abuse of drugs, and national chapters of international organizations concerned with the improvement of community life can promote public and community health activities. Labour organizations have a role to play in promoting family planning, protecting the female work force, and financing education campaigns. Civic groups and consumers' councils can influence the public to demand quality and safety standards for goods and services. Consumers also need a say in the development of public health services. Women's groups should be encouraged to help with health policy and decision-making by preparing women for leadership, educating them about their legal position on issues such as abortion and employment, and setting up homemakers' clubs that promote responsible parenthood. Religious groups are effective educators for all community problems; they can organize clubs, classes, and counselling centres on drugs and social diseases and help with fund-raising. Youth groups can support informal campaigns to spread information about their special problems such as social difficulties and unemployment. (HH)

3186 Simmons, O.G. *Clinical team in a Chilean health centre.* In Paul, B.D., ed., Health, Culture and Community: Case Studies of Public Reactions to Health Programs, New York, Russell Sage Foundation, 1955, 325-348. Engl.
For complete document see entry 3454.

To increase the outreach of health education activities, the director of a health centre serving underprivileged populations in Santiago, Chile, relieved nursing staff of their clinical duties and reallocated their time to home-visiting and education programmes. This change removed an important link in the existing doctor-patient relationships; the nurses had previously provided important details of therapy to the patients. They had also given information about the patients' socioeconomic status to the doctors, who were unwilling to undertake health education or take a genuine interest in their patients' well-being. The effects of the change were that health centre services deteriorated and use declined. The director maintained that the nurses' services improved community education and offset poor health centre performance. (AC)

3187 Spillmann, R.K. *Development aid through information: trying a new concept in Colombia.* Acta Tropica (Basel, Switzerland), 34(3), 1977, 215-227. Engl.

Two model projects that aim to help the poorest section of the population are currently being tested by a Swiss foundation, *Vivamos Mejor*, in Cali, Colombia. The 1st project was begun in 1973. Through four moveable information centres, specially-trained indigenous staff prepare a specific population for and conduct the presentation of an intensive, 3-hour programme of basic information on nutrition, hygiene, and birth control. Teaching methods utilized in the presentation include short lectures, slides, films, demonstrations, discussions, and a puppet show; the presentation is conducted 5 times a week until it has been seen by as many of the area's adult population as possible. The 2nd project, begun a few years later, involves the creation of centres where neglected or undernourished children are rehabilitated while their mothers, through work with centre personnel, obtain the knowledge necessary to provide a better home for the child and his siblings. Two such centres have so far been established. A preliminary evaluation of the 1st project in 1975 demonstrated that a population who had been exposed to the presentation scored significantly higher on a knowledge, attitudes, and practices test than did a population that had not. Already the programme has attracted considerable attention in Latin American countries and it is hoped that, once scientific evidence confirming its validity becomes available, it will provide a model for health education in other large cities in developing countries. (HC)

3188   USA, Agency for International Development, Department of State. Pan American Health Organization, Washington, D.C. *Pila Project: cassettes reach rural women.* Development Communications Report (Washington, D.C.), 28, Apr 1977, 1-13. Engl.
Summary of Colle, R.D., Colle, S.F.de, Communication Factor in Health and Nutrition Programs..., Ithaca, N.Y., Cornell University, Apr 1976.
As part of a Guatemalan experiment, taped cassettes containing 8-minute segments of novelas, music, and local interviews, including health and nutrition messages, were distributed to local *pilas* (community laundry centres). The messages were repeated many times and the women patronizing the laundries could take home special cassettes and borrow a tape-recorder to listen to selections they particularly liked. Although not many took advantage of this, 100 people in less than an hour were able to repeat a sentence about the innoculation of chicks given on one of the tapes and win a prize of a baby chick. A simple survey showed that the system was flexible and that the women enjoyed the programmes, which resulted in an immediate change in attitude and behaviour. The tapes were successfully produced and there were no equipment failures. It is hoped that the project will be able to continue without outside help. (HH)

3189   Valdivia Dominguez, A. *Stimulating community involvement through mass organizations in Cuba: the women's role.* International Journal of Health Education (Geneva), 20(1), 1977, 57-60. Engl.
One of the basic principles of Cuban health care system is that of community participation, especially at the primary services level. Mass organizations have cooper- ated in the conscious promotion of this participation, first by becoming involved in areas of environmental health, vaccinations, mass physical examinations, and health education programmes. Now they take part in all public health activities, with these specific aims: developing the health consciousness of the people; stimulating the active participation of the population in public health programmes; controlling the health of the people and detecting local health problems; suppressing the commercial blood trade, which has been replaced by a system of volunteer donations; strengthening the relationship between the health team and the public; and strengthening the people's confidence in their own analytical ability and in the public health services. The Federation of Cuban Women, a mass organization comprising nearly 75% of the country's women aged 14 years and over, has been the primary force for freeing women from their traditional restrictions and chanelling their energies toward the achievement of national goals, including those of the health sector. FMC members have been particularly active in the mother and child care programme, the antipolio vaccination campaign, blood donation campaigns, environmental sanitation programmes, and the fight against parasitic diseases. (RMB)

3190   WHO, Brazzaville. *Guide for development of post-graduate and undergraduate training in health education in the African region.* Brazzaville, WHO, 30 Apr 1973. 14p. Engl.
Also published in French.
The need for professional health educators in the African region has been stressed at many national and international forums. Two such educators are envisioned; a health education specialist at the master's level and a health educator with a bachelor's degree. The 1st, an individual with a recognized postgraduate degree in health education, will be charged with these tasks: educational programme planning, implementation, and evaluation; community organization and group work; evolving curricula and teaching methodology for training health workers in health education; mass communications and the use of indigenous educational methods; pretesting, production, and distribution of printed and other audiovisual material; behavioural studies, both diagnostic and operational; and health education in the national educational system. The 2nd educator, a graduate of a general science programme with special training in health sciences and community education, will be trained to implement educational plans at the intermediate or local level, train workers in the use of health education methods and media, prepare simple audiovisual aids, guide and assess educational work of field staff, plan the teaching of health education in the schools, and organize health education activities for students, teachers, and parents. This document indicates, broadly, the requirements, nature, and content of courses for training both educators. It also describes the organizational structure within which the educators will operate. (HC)

III Primary Health Care--Implementation

3191   **Yemba, K.P.** *How a rural dispensary became a development centre.* Appropriate Technology (London), 4(1), May 1977, 4-8. Engl.
First appeared in French in Zaire-Afrique, Dec 1975 as: *Comment faire d'un dispensaire rural un centre de developpement*, an English translation appeared in Contact (Geneva), 36, Dec 1976, 1-7.

In 1971, a male nurse in charge of the dispensary at Sadi-Kinsanga, Zaire, initiated a public health programme by encouraging villagers to participate in sanitation and health education projects such as cleaning individual plots, digging latrines, and maintaining safe water supplies. Although they were reluctant at first, the villagers later appreciated the benefits of such activities and, following their example, 10 neighbouring villages carried out similar programmes. In 1972, each village formed a development committee comprising four prominent village members to maintain environmental health standards. In addition to sponsoring such projects as the building by villagers of a mother and child health care and nutrition centre at Sadi-Kinsanga, these development committees began to include economic development activities in their programmes. For example, they introduced the cultivation of soya beans, the raising of rabbits and ducks, and a brick project to facilitate the building of more hygienic houses. To coordinate these activities, members of 50 different development committees set up a Local Welfare Council that now makes many decisions for the area concerned. (CL)

IV Primary Health Manpower--Training and Utilization

IV.1 Primary Medical Care
IV.1.1 Professional

See also: 2970, 2975, 3111, 3125, 3186, 3281, 3308, 3326, 3379, 3439, 3440

3192   Adetuyibi, A. *Specialist training and medical research in developing countries of tropical Africa: a case for the establishment of postgraduate medical schools.* Medical Education (Oxford, UK), 11(5), Sep 1977, 355-357. Engl.
Physicians from developing countries are still generally forced to go abroad if they desire specialist training. The cost is high in terms of finance, personal hardship, and loss of services to the home country. Moreover, the training that the physician receives is based on an environment and a disease pattern that are far removed from his own. For these reasons, it is generally agreed that it is in the best interests of the developing countries to train their specialists at home. However, the British-cum-American method--a combination of hospital practice and attendance at symposia, seminars, and private tuition courses sponsored by associations such as the British Postgraduate Medical Federation or the American Cardiac Society--cannot be duplicated in the developing countries for lack of extramural support. It would be possible, on the other hand, to organize institutional training on a 'crash course' basis, at least as a temporary measure. Specialist schools could be set up in teaching hospitals, staffed by teachers recruited from all over the world (if necessary) and made available to students from several countries. Such schools would provide, in addition to specialist instruction, meaningful research, sophisticated investigations, and highly-skilled curative services. Once specialists became available in sufficient numbers, the schools could be replaced by the 'learn-on-the-job' system described above. (HC)

3193   Blumhagen, R.V. Blumhagen, J. Medical Assistance Programs, Wheaton, Ill. *Role of the doctor.* In Blumhagen, R.V., Blumhagen, J., Family Health Care: a Rural Health Care Delivery Scheme, Wheaton, Ill., Medical Assistance Programs, 1974, 69-70. Engl.
For complete document see entry 2890.
In Afghanistan, where only a tiny minority of the sick have access to a trained physician, doctors must adapt to a new role as medical experts and team leaders. They must assign priorities, develop and implement plans, evaluate programmes, and supervise and train other staff. They must maintain standards in work and education, liaise between different categories of health work-ers, ensure staff discipline, check equipment, and oversee record-keeping. These tasks cannot all be accomplished by one person, so authority must be delegated to other members of the team whenever possible. Delegation is also important in diagnosis and treatment and *triage* should be practiced to ensure that patients are handled efficiently by appropriately trained staff. This new role requires an understanding of the local community, the health programme, and the limitations of resources and of the doctor's own capabilities. (DM)

3194   Bobenrieth, M. *New physician.* Bulletin of the Pan American Health Organization (Washington, D.C.), 8(3), 1976, 8-11. Engl.
The physician of the future must be prepared to take on a new role as leader of a completely integrated health team in a new system geared toward primary health care. As team leader, he will be involved in the planning and allocation of health resources within the framework of medicine as a social science that treats people rather than diseases. To this end, health care and medical education must be made more compatible, so that the physicians can break away from restrictive Western patterns and have their consciousness raised about their role in society. (RMB)

3195   Cordova, A. Galigarcia, J. *Place of social sciences in the medical curriculum: an integrated study plan for the teaching of medicine in the University of Havana.* Social Science and Medicine (Oxford, UK), 11(2), Jan 1977, 129-133. Engl.
The 6-year University of Havana medical school curriculum is outlined. As well as the expected medical sciences, it includes such topics as Marxism-Leninism, international and social conceptions of medicine, the development of a scientific way of thinking, disaster training, knowledge of public health organization and administration, general cultural education, and physical education and sports. (RMB)

3196   Dickinson, J. *Where shall John go? Nepal.* British Medical Journal (London), 2(6042), Dec 1976, 1364-1366. Engl.
Doctors interested in working in Nepal should realize that it is one of the poorest countries in the world and that funds for curative medicine are extremely scarce. They should also understand that opportunities for expatriates are limited unless they speak the language and are familiar with the wide range of indigenous health practices and beliefs. However, some doctors may wish to explore

the many research possibilities that exist due to the unusual patterns of disease. For example, infective hepatitis, so common among visitors to the area, is rare among inhabitants, although nonalcoholic cyrrhosis of the liver is observed; most forms of tuberculosis are prevalent, but renal TB is rare; and emphysema and chronic bronchitis are common, but coronary artery disease is almost unknown. The effects of altitude are also of interest. The major health problems, however, are the preventable ones of poverty, malnutrition, and ignorance and the most relevant form of research is the study of methods of providing low-cost health education and health care to remote traditional communities. Government policy for health delivery wisely relies on the extensive use of paramedicals. Doctors can contribute to this work by helping to train and supervise auxiliary workers and by giving due recognition to the value of their work. Six nongovernmental agencies that employ some expatriate doctors are listed with details of type of project and addresses. (DM)

3197   Federacion Panamericana de Asociaciones de Facultadas de Medicina, Bogota. *Proyecto de la Facultad de Ciencias Medicas, Universidad Central del Ecuador; documento de presentacion final. (Project of the School of Medical Sciences, Central University of Equador: final introductory document).* Rio de Janeiro, Federacion Panamericana de Asociaciones de Facultades de Medicina, Programa de Ensenanza de Medicina de la Comunidad, Mar 1974. 55p. Span.

In 1971, the *Universidad Central* (Equador) initiated plans for a project designed to familiarize medical students with the problems of community and rural practice. In accordance with a Ministry of Health directive, medical students would be integrated into the health care delivery system as soon as possible, so that they could learn by practical experience. This document presents background information on the school and the two rural communities participating in the project, outlines the students' curriculum, and discusses the planning and staging of the project and the necessary resources. Statistical data are included on the budget and required personnel and equipment. Information covered in the body of the document is condensed and presented again in 10 appendices. (RMB)

3198   Figueredo Gonzalez, R. Rodriguez Hernandez, P. Rodriguez Guerra, E. Cuba, Ministerio de Salud Publica. *Utilizacion de los estudiantes de ciencias medicas (fase 1) como trabajadores de salud publica en areas de la Habana metropolitana. (Utilization of first-year medical students as public health workers in metropolitan areas of Havana).* Revista Cubana de Administracion de Salud (Havana), 3(2), Apr-Jun 1977, 213-218. Span.

Since 1969, Cuban medical students have participated in work-study plans of various types and, in 1976, modifications were introduced into the medical curriculum to enable the 1st- and 2nd-year students to function more effectively in the new polyclinics. Students spent up to 3

months as members of a health team concentrating on either child health, adult health, or obstetrics and gynaecology and took part in the planning and evaluation phases of these programmes as well as medical activities. (RMB)

3199   Holst, H.V. Hofvander, Y. Vahlquist, B. *Joint training courses in nutrition, public and tropical medicine for work in Third World countries.* Tropical Doctor (London), 7(4), Oct 1977, 189-192. Engl.
15 refs.

In 1973, a 10-week training course was begun in Sweden for doctors and nurses intending to work in Third World countries. Subjects covered include: medical socioanthropology; nutrition; maternal health and family planning; child health and common diseases in children; practical laboratory training; hygiene (environmental and food); health planning and administration; medical training and health information; emergency assistance; common infectious diseases; tropical infectious and parasitic diseases; infections of the eye, ear, nose, throat and skin; vaccinations; practical pharmacology; parasitological laboratory training; infectious and parasitic diseases case studies; epidemiology and combat of tropical infections and parasitic diseases; and special training (as required). Emphasized throughout the course are the need to cooperate closely with local public health authorities and foster a spirit of self-help in the host country. So far, some 64 doctors, 160 nurses, and a few other categories of personnel have completed the course and their remarks concerning it have been highly favourable. Future plans call for the inclusion of more English content (the course is now given mainly in Swedish) in order to make the course available to Third World participants. (HC)

3200   Hunponu-Wusu, O.O. *Need for medical statistics in the training of health personnel.* Medical Education (Oxford, UK), 11(5), Sep 1977, 351-354. Engl.

A number of areas of community medicine in which the application of statistical methods has become a necessity are pointed out. They include: the study of specific rates (birth, death, and morbidity); the clinical trial of new drugs, vaccines, or techniques; the evaluation of health services and programmes; testing for factors that may influence health or disease (e.g., smoking, cancer); and the elimination of unprofitable fields of investigation through the conduct of pilot studies. Paramedical workers such as midwives should be aware of the value of the various specific rates and be able to collect accurate data in their day-to-day work. Health educators and administrators are therefore urged to see that statistical methods are introduced into the curricula of all community health personnel early in their training. Examples of the applications of statistical methods are taken from Nigeria. (HC)

3201   Hunponu-Wusu, O.O. *Defining the objectives of medical education in a developing country.* Nigerian Medical Journal (Ikeja, Nigeria), 5(1),

Jan 1975, 14-18. Engl.
10 refs.

A clear definition of the educational objectives of medical schools in developing countries is extremely important for planning, evaluating, and reducing the costs of medical education. Doctors in Nigeria should not be trained exclusively along traditional Western lines but oriented towards service in rural health centres as well as hospitals. The changing health needs and problems of each community must feature prominently in the formulation of educational objectives of all types (institutional, departmental, instructional, and behavioural). The resulting objectives should then be relevant as well as feasible, observable, consistent, and stated in measurable terms. Clear objectives will help to define for teachers and for undergraduate students themselves the aims of medical education in general terms, the knowledge students must acquire, and the responsible attitude that they must develop. The list of objectives adopted by the medical faculty of Ahmadu Bello University, Zaria (one of Nigeria's six medical schools), provides an example of this approach. (CL)

3202   Jibril, M.O. *Training in relation to future career: medical education in Zaria, Nigeria.* Tropical Doctor (London), 29(4), Oct 1972, 196-200. Engl.

The Ahmadu Bello University Medical School, Nigeria, trains all its doctors to head teams of specialized auxiliary health workers. The 5-year medical course covers the same academic subjects as most medical schools plus an intensive community health course. The 3rd and 5th years concentrate on clinical subjects at the main teaching hospital at Zaria, while the 4th year is a "roving" year spent in hospitals and institutions in urban and rural areas, where the students learn a variety of disciplines. In this year, a special course in leprosy is taught, as well as conventional courses in medicine, surgery, obstetrics, and gynaecology. The students, by moving from place to place, learn about patterns of disease and their management in the community. The small number of staff in the peripheral hospitals means that the student is given more responsibility and has the opportunity to perform treatment procedures and simple operations, thereby gaining the competence and confidence that will equip him to work single-handed. The student also visits health centres and sees for himself how useful the auxiliaries are. These visits will be extended to include student postings as medical auxiliaries in health centres in the future. The ultimate career structure of the type of doctor the school aims to produce would be improved if such doctors could advance as "general medical consultants"; the preclinical course might also benefit from some basic instruction in Nigerian dialects. (HH)

3203   Kawee-Tungsubutra. *Auxiliary health training and development of the Faculty of Medicine at Khon Kaen University, Thailand.* In Ronaghy, H.A., Mousseau-Gershman, Y., Dorozynski, A., eds., Village Health Workers, Ottawa, International Development Research Centre, 1976, 33-37. Engl.

For complete document see entry 3250.

The Faculty of Medicine at Khon Kaen University, Thailand, has altered the standard medical curriculum to suit the needs of the rural physician. The result is that the present curriculum has more clinical training and fewer details in subjects like anatomy. Now it includes sociology, economics, and psychology and emphasizes community medicine and integrated preclinical and clinical study. It supports specialty study in only those diseases that are common to the region and involves students in the villages from the 2nd year onward. Along with these changes to its medical curriculum, the faculty has set up a pilot project for village health workers. The project provides for students to undergo 2 weeks intensive training followed by regular supervision and refresher courses at 6-month intervals. The project participants will be evaluated yearly by means of a survey of patients and personal visits. (HC)

3204   Lobo, L.C. *Educational technology and health manpower development in Latin America.* Biosciences Communications (Basel, Switzerland), 1(2), 1975, 99-110. Engl.
13 refs.

In Latin America from 1960-1973, the number of medical students increased by a factor of 8.97 while the number of professors increased by only 2.94. The resulting shortage of teaching staff has led to a demand for a more efficient, individualized, and scientific approach to education. One such approach is that of 'education technology,' defined as a systems approach to the teaching-learning process centering around the optimal design, implementation, and evaluation of teaching-learning. It involves identifying the elements of the teaching-learning process, defining their relationships to one another, and devising curricula, strategies, and methods that optimize the learning outcome. This paper discusses how education technology is applied and what concomitant actions militate in favour of its success. Also, in the spirit of optimizing the learning outcome, a case for removing medical education from the teaching hospital to the community is made. (HC)

3205   Long, E.C. *Alternatives to traditional medical training in Latin America.* New York, Institute of International Education, Issues in International Education No.6, 1976. 7p. Engl.

The author advocates the substitution of a health team-community-preventive model of health care in place of the traditional Western doctor-nurse-hospital-curative model, which developing countries cannot afford. He notes several barriers to introducing this new model: the authoritarian physician automatically assumes leadership of the health team and often prevents it from operating to full capacity, the different training and goals of various health team members may conflict, traditional organization and attitudes inhibit sharing and cooperation, and the Western health care model is often considered the only acceptable standard. The author proposes two new approaches to the training of health care personnel. First, he suggests a number of ways in which non-medical personnel could be utilized to provide

IV Primary Health Manpower--Training and Utilization

health care, including primary and secondary school teachers, police, agricultural extension workers, veterinarians, pharmacists, mailmen, etc. Second, in addition to training traditional practitioners and health auxiliaries, he encourages the retraining and reorientation of Western-educated health professionals, although he recognizes the difficulty of persuading medical and nursing schools to change their curricula. (RMB)

3206 Loransky, D.N. Belyaeva, A. Zalessky, G. Fokina, O. *USSR: optimizing the teaching of health education in higher medical training institutions.* International Journal of Health Education (Geneva), 20(2), 1977, 98-102. Engl.

Health education has always been an integral part of physician education in the USSR; nevertheless, a recent survey of 469 6th-year students from five medical schools revealed that, while the students possessed a sufficient volume of knowledge in the field of health education, the majority were unable to apply it. An experimental training programme based on the findings of pedagogical and psychological studies and aimed at improving the teaching of health education in medical schools was therefore drawn up. The programme emphasized: the development of scientific thinking *vis-a-vis* situation assessment, goal formulation, strategy selection, etc.; the acquisition of cognitive skills by means of a specially-designed system of exercises (teaching aids); and the application of a problem-solving approach to real-life situations. The programme was implemented within the curricula of 211 students from the same five medical schools and the performance of these students was then tested and compared with that of a 235-member control group. The results of the test clearly showed the students in the experimental group to be considerably better prepared for health education activities than those in the control group. The conclusion that the application of techniques gleaned through the social sciences, especially psychology and pedagogy, to the training of physicians for health education is not only desirable but expedient. (HC)

3207 Michaelson, I.C. *Contribution to the teaching of ophthalmologists from a developing country.* Israel Journal of Medical Sciences (Jerusalem), 8(8-9), 1972, 1077-1078. Engl.
Causes and Prevention of Blindness, Jerusalem Seminar on the Prevention of Blindness, Jerusalem, Israel, 25-27 Aug 1971.

The author mentions the training programme carried out by the Hadassah Medical School (Jerusalem) for ophthalmologists from developing countries. This programme is especially designed to help the student overcome any cultural or social shock he might feel upon returning to his own country after long periods of training abroad. (EE)

3208 Phoon, W.O. *Education and training.* In Holland, W.W., Gilderdale, S., eds., Epidemiology and Health, London, Kimpton, 1977, 132-142. Engl.
13 refs.

The study of epidemiology is essential to the proper planning of health services and all health personnel should receive suitable epidemiological instruction. Medical students, for example, ought to be given a short, systematic course in descriptive, analytical, and experimental epidemiology plus a considerably longer one in the clinical or field context. Such training might comprise any or all of the following: follow-up of a patient and his family for 1 year following his discharge from the hospital; the study of the health parameters of a designated community of approximately 1 000 people; visits to community health facilities such as a sewage treatment plant, a tuberculosis control unit, a factory, a home for the handicapped, etc.; a course in a selected subject, such as occupational dermatitis or venereal disease, taught by a multidisciplinary team; etc. Some general suggestions regarding the epidemiological requirement of other clinical specialists, nurses, allied and auxiliary health personnel and health officials are given and the need to have courses taught by persons with extensive field experience is stressed. Examples are taken from the Department of Social Medicine and Public Health, University of Singapore. (HC)

3209 Schweser, H.O. Project HOPE, Washington, D.C. People-to-People Health Foundation, Inc., Washington, D.C. *Health education by doctors.* In Schweser, H.O., Manual for Community Health Education for the Caribbean, Washington, D.C., People-to-People Health Foundation, n.d., 23-32. Engl.
For complete document see entry 3371.

The author suggests that the best way to change doctors' attitudes toward health education and preventive medicine is to redesign the medical school curricula. Physician training should be community- rather than hospital-based, so that the student sees social and economic implications of disease for the individual, his family, and the community. Physicians should be taught to: alert medical workers, the public, and the government to the possibilities of preventive medicine; monitor television, films, and radio for misleading sensationalism; and produce their own programmes and articles on the prevention of social diseases. In addition, they should counsel and refer patients and organize health education activities in offices, hospitals, and schools using appropriate teaching aids. They should also try to influence government planning regarding major health problems and actively support public health priorities. Doctors must also learn to function as part of a health team. (HH)

3210 Sekou, H. *Formation medicale au Niger. (Medical education in Niger).* Medecine d'Afrique Noire (Paris), 24(7), 1977, 526-529. Fren.

In 1974, on WHO's recommendation, Niger opened a school of health sciences within the University of Niamey. The purpose of the school was: to train physicians, pharmacists, dental surgeons, and public health technicians with a view to fostering a team spirit among them; to participate in the continuing education and continuous evaluation of all health workers; and to conduct scientific and operational research into African pharmacopoeia and public health. The medical curriculum has been designed to produce a doctor well suited to practice in Niger. The integrated approach to medicine and patient care is emphasized at every stage. Theoretical and practical content are chosen to complement each other, e.g., pathology, treatment by system, and introduction to clinical practice are given in the same year and the student is encouraged to view the patient and his environment as one. In this paper, the health manpower situation in Niger is reviewed and the school's history, teaching capability, teaching methodology, and expectations are briefly discussed. (HC)

3211   **Smilkstein, G.** *Extramural training of medical students: lessons from Southeast Asia.* Journal of Family Practice (New York), 4(5), 1977, 873-876. Engl.
11 refs.
Medical schools in Thailand, Malaysia, and the Philippines have altered their curricula to include extramural programmes that take the student into the community. At Chaing Mai University, Thailand, a 5-week course in comprehensive health care has been introduced in the 6th (final) year. Students spend 10 days working as team members in a rural area, regularly discuss community problems, identify consultants and resources that might assist them in problem-solving, and report their team's project. At the Department of Social and Preventive Medicine, University of Malaya, 3rd- and 4th-year students may spend 2 1/2 weeks in a rural community investigating the inhabitants' health problems, apply social and preventive medicine to the care of one patient and his family, and/or work with district health agents and conduct a survey. At medical schools in the Philippines, extramural community health programmes have become permanent fixtures in the curricula and senior medical students at the Cebu Institute of Medicine rotate through four community service models guided by resident personnel. In the rural service model, they work with the health centre nurse practitioner and public health worker, delivering preventive and curative care; in the urban model, they cooperate with health personnel and government agencies, conducting health surveys, running neighbourhood dispensaries, and directing health education programmes; in the hospital-based model, they spend half their time with patients and the other half in public health practice; and in the community medicine model, students live in rural areas and study social and cultural influences on patient health. (HC)

3212   **Stillman, P.L. Gibson, J. Levinson, D. Ruggill, J. Sabers, D.** *Nurse practitioner as a teacher of physical examination skills.* Journal of Medical Education (Washington, D.C.), 53(2), Feb 1978, 119-124. Engl.
8 refs.
The author describes a highly structured, sequential, competency-based course designed to teach University of Arizona (USA) medical students the basic procedures for conducting physical examinations. Nurse practitioners function as key members of the instructional team by observing and supervising the students, teach-

ing them proper techniques, and providing remedial help if necessary. Each team of 2 nurse practitioners handles 6 medical students and frees the physicians who formerly taught these skills for other duties. An informal faculty survey revealed that the teaching staff rated students in the new course as more adept at physical examination techniques than earlier classes and the students themselves stated in a questionnaire that they considered the nurses better instructors than the physicians of previous years. The students' attitude toward nurse practitioners as future colleagues in their medical practices was also improved. A course evaluation questionnaire completed by the participating nurses showed that they responded favourably to their role as instructors. The authors discuss some of the problems involved in implementing such a course. (RMB)

3213   **Stillman, P.L. Sabers, D.L. Redfield, D.L.** *Use of paraprofessionals to teach interviewing skills.* Pediatrics (Springfield, Ill.), 57(5), May 1976, 769-774. Engl.
10 refs.
An American medical college has developed and tested a method of employing paraprofessionals to teach and evaluate interviewing skills. The college trained two mothers to supply, during interviews, consistent information on a child's medical problem and to rate student interviewers on their ability to obtain information (content) and relate to people (process). The mothers then met with student interviewers who watched their interview on videotape and received feedback on their skills. A few weeks later, the students repeated the process and scored significantly higher on the process of interviewing than did a control group. (HC)

3214   **Taylor, C.E.** *Doctor's role in rural health care.* International Journal of Health Services (Westport, Conn.), 6(2), 1976, 219-230. Engl.
13 refs.
A recent survey of rural interns in India revealed that physicians would be willing to work in the villages if better professional and personal conditions prevailed. They listed these obstacles to rural service: lack of drugs and supplies, and of opportunities for maintaining professional competence, professional advancement, postgraduate education, obtaining materials for personal study, consultation with other members of the profession, etc. These are legitimate concerns with readily available and effective solutions, for example, the development of a regionalized system whereby each medical college is responsible for supporting a number of health centres. Support could take the form of periodic seminars and refresher courses for health centre personnel, biannual visits of college staff to health centre physicians, circulation of library materials among health centres, and the relaying of information, through various media, from college to health centre. Another solution would be to recognize the special contribution of rural doctors by providing them with adequate rural allowances, inviting them to present papers at medical conferences, encouraging them to publish in medical journals, and offering an award for outstanding rural

service--symbols that would help raise the status of community medicine in the eyes of the profession and the public. (HC)

3215   Villarreal, R. Bojalil, L.F. Mercer, H. *Bases para el diseno curricular de la carrera de medicina. (Basis for designing a medical course curriculum).* Educacion Medica y Salud (Washington, D.C.), 11(2), 1977, 109-118. Span.

The medical curriculum of the *Universidad Autonoma Metropolitana* (Mexico) has been redesigned to reflect the process of social change taking place in that nation and make the course of study flexible enough to cope with different types of problems. The principles underlying the curriculum and course work are described against a background of historical analysis of the socioeconomic structure of education and health. (RMB)

IV.1.2 Nonprofessional

See also: 2816, 2827, 2835, 2842, 2843, 2844, 2845, 2847, 2862, 2936, 3045, 3128, 3169, 3202, 3203, 3205, 3297, 3332, 3344, 3373, 3379, 3392, 3394, 3395, 3396, 3398, 3403, 3404, 3459, 3464, 3490

3216   *Asistente de salud en Panama--panacea o paliativo? (Health auxiliary in Panama--panacea or palliative?).* n.p., n.d. 9p. Span.
Unpublished document.

On a par with the People's Republic of China, Venezuela, India, and other developing countries, Panama has had its own auxiliary dispensary and community health workers, whose training is described and whose performance is evaluated in this document. The author advocates a nomenclature based on each auxiliary's function rather than efforts to attain international equivalency; he defines these functions and then presents diagrams of health manpower hierarchies designed according to these criteria. He also outlines the structure of an auxiliary-based health care system and proposes a project to determine the optimal use of auxiliaries and methods for the continuous evaluation of their performance. He concludes that the health auxiliary is neither a panacea nor a palliative but can be a valuable member of the health care team. (RMB)

3217   Amidi, S. *Effectiveness of village health workers for primary health care in Southern Iran.* Courrier of the International Children's Centre (Paris), 27(2), 1977, 109-112. Engl.

In Kavar, Iran, 16 literate villagers were recruited for a 6-month auxiliary health worker's course covering practical sanitation, maternal and child health care, nutrition, first aid, and treatment of common symptoms. They were then posted to 16 villages where they worked under the supervision of physicians. Thanks to these village health workers (VHWs), attendance at the central Kavar Health Corps Station dropped and more patients visited village health clinics during the 1st year of the new programme. Infant mortality also dropped, as did the birth rate, because of the VHW's involvement in family planning programmes as well as in community sanitation projects to provide toilets and separate animals from living quarters. A table of statistics is included in the report. (HH)

3218   Behrhorst, C. International Medical and Research Foundation, New York. *Program description: Chimaltenango Development Program.* New York, International Medical and Research Foundation, Oct 1977. 11p. Engl.
International Medical and Research Foundation Symposium on the Community Health Worker, Warrenton, Va., 26-28 Oct 1977.
See also entries 0757 (volume 2), 1745 (volume 3), and 2466 (volume 4).

In Chimaltenango, Guatemala, the development programme recognizes the importance of community involvement by encouraging dialogue between the health services and the Indian people. Committees drawn from the community are encouraged to discuss the importance of social and economic justice, land tenure, and agricultural production, as well as health topics such as nutrition, family planning, self-healing, traditional healers, curative medical services, and public health. The committees consider the community's needs, establish priorities, and talk to agricultural extension workers (AEWs) or rural health promoters (RHPs) who can arrange a wide variety of activities, including the training of extra AEWs and RHPs where they are needed. The programme supplements its training of RHPs and AEWs with loans for land acquisition to combat prevailing poverty. The RHPs are encouraged to learn by observing and working with patients under the guidance of Indian and professional instructors with the emphasis on symptom treatment and recognition of common diseases covered in a simple manual. The AEWs are also local men and women trained in preventive medicine as well as agriculture; they work with "collaborators" who can then themselves become AEWs. The extension services and land distribution work require outside funding. (HH)

3219   Bennett, B.E. *Model for teaching health education skills to primary health practitioners.* International Journal of Health Education (Geneva), 20(4), 1977, 232-239. Engl.
8 refs.

The health education component of the health associate's course at the John Hopkins School of Health Sciences (Baltimore, USA) aims to teach the health associate, a sort of physician's assistant, how to: identify his role in health education; identify the steps in the health education process; make an educational diagnosis; understand the conceptual frame of health education and behavioural change; synthesize biomedical and psychosocial information into teaching material; understand the variables affecting people's attitudes, knowledge, and beliefs about various health care problems; identify what a patient needs to know regarding the problems discussed in the modules; and develop methods and plans that best meet the educational needs of the patient. To meet these objectives, health education sessions are sequentially arranged to flow with the curriculum; a module on teaching infant nutrition, for example, is presented concurrently with the study of child-hood. Only a small part of the teaching is didactic; students are given a chance to exercise their newly-acquired skills during their clinical practice, their 1-year assignment to a family, their community health research project, and the patient stimulation laboratory. All these methods, plus the criteria used to evaluate the performances of the student, are discussed in detail in this paper. (HC)

3220   Berggren, W.L. *Utilization of medical auxiliaries in a rural health program.* Industry and Tropical Health (Boston, Mass.), 8, n.d., 135-139. Engl.
10 refs.
The Albert Schweitzer Hospital, Haiti, has successfully employed medical auxiliaries to undertake several campaigns against major diseases in a poor agricultural district of 90 000 people. In the 1st campaign, a mass tetanus immunization programme, all routine tasks were taken over by literate but untrained day workers who, with experience gained on the job, relieved the medical staff of all but emergency procedures. The same auxiliaries later conducted a census and nutritional survey in the community; without the aid of professionals, they worked as a team to measure heights and weights of young children, record findings, visit homes, and provide nutrition education. With the assistance of local mothers, they set up village mothercraft and nutrition rehabilitation centres. Some of the same personnel were recruited for a tuberculosis screening and treatment campaign that involved skin and urine tests, collection and smearing of sputum specimens, home visiting, education, and follow-up. Thus auxiliaries, originally re-cruited to carry out the most menial of tasks in a straightforward immunization campaign, acquired a wide range of skills without any formal training and were able to provide a rural health service at minimal cost. The majority were employed on a day-work basis, maintaining their normal means of livelihood and their links with the local community, until they were sufficiently experienced to become full-time members of the health team. (DM)

3221   Blumhagen, R.V. Blumhagen, J. Medical Assistance Programs, Wheaton, Ill. *Role of the family health worker.* In Blumhagen, R.V., Blumhagen, J., Family Health Care: a Rural Health Care Delivery Scheme, Wheaton, Ill., Medical Assistance Programs, 1974, 71-73. Engl.
For complete document see entry 2890.
The family health care scheme for Afghanistan proposed by Medical Assistance Programs requires the retraining of specialized health auxiliaries to provide a large new corps of male and female multipurpose family health workers (FHWs). Women FHWs should act as auxiliary nurse midwives and male FHWs should be trained for sanitation and immunization programmes. The male and female FHWs would share responsibility for health and nutrition education, record-keeping, and diagnosis and treatment of common diseases according to specific guidelines laid down in a manual. The work would be

carried out in village clinics, homes, and community projects with the assistance of volunteer village health advisors (VVHAs) and the on-going supervision and training by staff at the health centre where the FHWs would spend part of each week. (DM)

3222   Blumhagen, R.V. Blumhagen, J. Medical Assistance Programs, Wheaton, Ill. *Physician's assistant.* In Blumhagen, R.V., Blumhagen, J., Family Health Care: a Rural Health Care Delivery Scheme, Wheaton, Ill., Medical Assistance Programs, 1974, 79-80. Engl.
For complete document see entry 2890.
Physician assistants are used in many parts of the world to reduce the physician's workload. In Afghanistan, they can be recruited from local persons with 6-9 years basic education and may be given 1-2 years clinical and on-the-job training that qualifies them to carry out physical examinations, history-taking, and screening. They can diagnose and treat some conditions and carry out simple surgical procedures, conduct surveys, and deal with administrative tasks such as record-keeping and equipment requisition. In all these duties, they should be able not only to take responsibility but also to recognize their limitations and seek help when necessary. (DM)

3223   Blumhagen, R.V. Blumhagen, J. Medical Assistance Programs, Wheaton, Ill. *Volunteer village health advisor and the family.* In Blumhagen, R.V., Blumhagen, J., Family Health Care: a Rural Health Care Delivery Scheme, Wheaton, Ill., Medical Assistant Programs, 1974, 75-78. Engl.
For complete document see entry 2890.
In rural Afghanistan, volunteer village health advisors (VVHAs) can greatly improve the influence of salaried health workers. Ideal VVHA candidates are people who are enthusiastic and considered authorities on health matters within the community. As the interface between the village and the health team, they must be accepted and appreciated by both. They receive no formal training but can learn by accompanying family health workers (FHWs) at clinics and on home visits. They can assist the FHWs by case-finding, record-keeping, providing follow-up care, and teaching families to understand disease, immunization, medications, birth control, and the functions of the clinic. Women VVHAs are particularly valuable as they can talk to other village women and advise on maternal and child care. They can also accompany female FHWs on their rounds and as chaperones can increase the FHWs acceptability in the community. (DM)

3224   Bollag, U. *Gesundheitshelfer; Kritische Wurdigung seiner Aufgabe innerhalb des Ernahrungsprogramms. (Health aide: critical evaluation of his performance within the nutrition programmes).* Acta Tropica (Basel, Switzerland), 34(3), 1977, 249-256. German.
13 refs.
Community health aides (CHAs), locally recruited and trained, visit Jamaican households and identify malnourished children by weighing them each month

and recording the results on Gomez weight-for-age charts. Since CHAs are often the family's only source of nutrition and health education, they must be taught to interpret these charts correctly. The trend in weight gain or loss is the clearest indication of a child's nutritional status and should be considered together with his maternal, perinatal, and neonatal histories. Many underweight children are also small for their age, but the author cautions that it is not unusual in Jamaica to find children suffering from obesity, another form of malnutrition. (Modified journal abstract.)

3225   **Byrne, K. Programa de Promotoras de Salud, Olancho, Honduras.** *Health promoter programme, Department of Olancho, Honduras, Central America: programme description.* Olancho, Honduras, Programa de Promotoras de Salud, May 1976. 41p. Engl.
Unpublished document.

In 1972, homemakers' clubs in Olancho, Honduras, began deploying village women as health promoters to tackle the diseases of poverty, ignorance, and insanitary conditions so common in the rural areas. The clubs (self-help women's groups) had emerged spontaneously in 1969 and engaged in consciousness-raising and community development. They had originally been funded by Caritas, who withdrew support in 1975 when the women showed increasing political awareness and militancy. However, the clubs continued and at present are the basis for the health promoter programme, now financed partly by Oxfam and partly by local fund-raising. Health promoters are unpaid volunteer women who are trained in simple curative and preventive medicine for 3 months. Their chief function is the education of women in the clubs, record-keeping, and primary health care; they dispense medicines and refer serious cases to paid medical staff. They meet each month to share experiences and evaluate their efforts and they elect group educators from their own ranks who assist the paid administrators in assessment and planning. The confidence of the volunteers was increased by the success of their health care work with refugee women after the hurricane disaster of 1974. Appendices to the report provide: detailed information on staffing, equipment, and funding of the programme; background statistics about Honduras; and notes on the common diseases. (DM)

3226   **Damena, G.G.** *Providing health services for rural populations in Papua New Guinea.* In Ronaghy, H.A., Mousseau-Gershman, Y., Dorozynski, A., eds., Village Health Workers, Ottawa, International Development Research Centre, 1976, 38-42. Engl.
For complete document see entry 3250.

Government policy in Papua New Guinea is to provide a health facility within 4 hours traveling time of every citizen. For this purpose, the government supports the training of aid post orderlies (auxiliary health workers) and the strengthening of the existing network of aid posts. Some problems in the present system are that: full-time aid post orderlies are classified as casual workers and do not have the benefits and advancement opportunities extended to other government employees; hospital and health centre orderlies enjoy higher salaries and better working conditions than do aid post orderlies; supervision of aid posts is deficient; reviews of the aid post system lag behind local development, so that some aid posts become redundant; and, apart from their salaries, the aid post orderlies receive no remuneration for food, housing, travel, etc. (HC)

3227   **Flauhault, D. International Medical and Research Foundation, Warrenton, Va.** *Respective roles of the community and of the health services in relation to community health workers.* New York, International Medical and Research Foundation, 1977. 12p. Engl.
International Medical and Research Foundation Symposium on the Community Health Worker, Warrenton, Va., 26-28 Oct 1977.
See also entries 3232, 3234, 3236, 3239, 3243, 3244, 3259, 3266, 3268, 3294, and 3398.

The roles of both the community and the health services in supporting the community health worker (CHW) are carefully defined. Community health committees can identify the most pressing local health problems, which are often better tackled by the coordinated efforts of the community than by the health services alone. Based on local needs, the community should then define the selection crieria for CHW candidates, set standards for remuneration and financial and manpower back-up, and support their efforts to change harmful local habits. In particular, the CHW needs the village chief's backing in his dealings with administrative authorities. The community should also share responsibility with the health services for evaluating the social as well as the technical capabilities of the worker. On the other hand, the health services must provide technical support and advice to meet the total health needs of the community rather than its felt needs alone, assign suitably-trained personnel for different types of tasks, and maintain appropriate standards for facilities and care. They should also have a say in the selection of candidates, since they will be responsible for their training and for providing referral services afterwards. (HH)

3228   **Geigy, R. Swiss Tropical Institute, Basel.** *Training on the spot: Swiss development aid in Tanzania, 1960-1976.* Acta Tropica (Basel, Switzerland), 33(4), 1976, 290-306. Engl.

A rural aid centre was set up by the Swiss Tropical Institute at Ifakara, Tanzania, in 1961 to provide training courses for a variety of health auxiliaries. It was constructed and staffed by the Swiss personnel and financed largely by Swiss government and industry. From the beginning, it worked cooperatively with a Capuchin Hospital and the Swiss Tropical Institute's field laboratory. Gradually, the training courses expanded and the centre was designated a field post for medical students from Dar-es-Salaam. In 1973, it became a medical assistants' training centre with facilities for 120 students and an associated outpost health centre. Although the Swiss still support the project financially, Tanzanians are now taking over both administration and teaching. Full responsibility will be transferred to the Tanzanian authorities in 1978. The success of this project and of development aid generally relies on the earned trust of the host country and the cooperation of the local community. (DM)

3229   Harrison, P. *Basic health delivery in the Third World.* New Scientist (London), 73(1039), 17 Feb 1977, 411-413. Engl.
Two health programmes recently established in Latin America attempt to provide primary and preventive care for under-privileged populations using minimally trained health promoters from the communities, as recommended in the UNICEF/WHO guidelines laid down in 1975. The problems encountered by these projects are typical of such work in all developing countries. The Module for Amplification of Coverage (MAC) system operates in an urban slum in Bogota, Colombia, and the Integrated Services Project is run by UNICEF in Puno, Peru. Both programmes rely heavily on the services of the promoters, who are trained briefly in first aid, midwifery, vaccination, sanitation, nutrition education, and methods of community self-improvement. Although refresher courses are held and, in the Puno project, the promoters are issued a simple instruction manual and kit of supplies, it seems unlikely that these people can cope with the work without a great deal of supervision. Their most difficult task is to motivate the local populace to undertake environmental improvements. Prevention is not obviously better than cure to very poor families when the costs must be borne by the community. Sickness is usually tolerated until it is far advanced and, when treatment is sought, traditional practitioners are preferred because their fees are low. Unfortunately, the services of the promoters are not free and the small payments required are sufficient to deter use by many of those in need. In general, basic health care programmes for the poor can never be fully effective unless they are backed up by a genuine redistribution of resources in favour of the under-privileged. (DM)

3230   Hernandez Elias, R. Marquez, M. *Docencia medica media en Cuba. (Middle-level medical training in Cuba).* Educacion Medica y Salud (Washington, D.C.), 10(1), 1976, 1-39. Span. 15 refs.
The background, evaluation, and prospects for training middle-level medical technicians in Cuba are reviewed, with emphasis on the relationships between the socioeconomic, education, and health sectors. Since the 1959 revolution, training policies have passed through three stages, progressing from the quantitative to the qualitative. The health and education systems and subsystems that have emerged as a result of changes in the social, political, and economic sectors are described; these have facilitated a new approach to teaching based on work-study programmes and integrated training in one of these basic disciplines: nursing, laboratory work, radiology, mental health, pathology, rehabilitation, public health, library science, sensory organs, pharmacology, dentistry, and medical electronics. Sample

curricula for laboratory technicians specializing in microbiology, clinical laboratory work, gastroenterology, and haematology are presented. (RMB)

3231   Jagdish, V. *Reorganization of health auxiliaries in India.* Baltimore, Md., Johns Hopkins University, School of Public Health, Department of International Health, Aug 1976. 8p. Engl.
A wide variety of single-purpose health auxiliaries have been used in India for 30 years, but a 1972 survey by the Kartar Singh committee revealed that rural people would prefer home visits from a single health worker who could provide them with all the services they need. The committee proposed broad spectrum health workers who would meet the health, nutrition, and family planning needs of their communities with the part-time assistance of trained local people such as *dais* and school teachers. Similarly, a single cadre of supervisory auxiliaries, the health assistants, would be established, 1 for every 4 health workers. The target for the Fifth Five-Year Plan is to provide 1 female and 1 male health worker for every 8 000 people and eventually there should be 1 health assistant of each sex for every 2 male and 2 female health workers. The success of the new system depends on the training of these auxiliaries, who must be prepared for effective work in difficult rural conditions and given opportunities for continuing education and exchange of experiences with other health personnel. Medical colleges could provide staff for auxiliary training at no extra cost and should prepare doctors for their supervisory role within the health team. (DM)

3232   Joseph, S.C. International Medical and Research Foundation, New York. *Community health worker in developing countries: issues in administrative structure, support, and supervision.* New York, International Medical and Research Foundation, 1977. 14p. Engl.
International Medical and Research Foundation Symposium on the Community Health Worker, Warrenton, Va., 26-28 Oct 1977.
See also entries 3227, 3234, 3236, 3239, 3243, 3244, 3259, 3266, 3268, 3294, and 3398.
The author reexamines certain aspects of the community health worker's (CHW's) relationship with the community he serves and the formal health services. Health services with scarce resources may be tempted to employ many part-time health workers who are poorly paid and lack full civil service status, but there are drawbacks to this procedure. Continuing service is unattractive without financial or career motivation and lack of compensation diminishes the CHW's status with the community and other health workers and may lead to corruption. If full pay is out of the question, the worker may be authorized to charge a fee or be funded by the community either in cash or in kind or from a village insurance fund. A more flexible approach to career advancement might involve replenishing the pool of workers, changing entry requirements, and reconsidering the extent of community involvement at various levels of selection. An appropriate balance of authority and control over CHWs

between the village and the health system is vital, because tension between the two is damaging to the CHW, who is in a weak position to counteract a village administration that is prepared to abuse the system. A community with an honest approach and a just health service are both required. In some instances, the other levels of the health service should exist primarily to support and supervise CHWs and this will require the difficult and costly remotivation of all health workers. (HH)

3233   Kane, R.L. *New health practitioners.* Washington, D.C., U.S. Department of Health, Education and Welfare, Public Health Service, DHEW Publication No.(NIH) 75-785, 1975. 156p. Engl.
Refs.
Conference on New Health Practitioners, Bethesda, Md., 14-15 May 1974.
Papers and discussions of papers presented at the 1974 Conference on New Health Practitioners are summarized in this monograph, the 1st in a series on the teaching of preventive medicine. Topics covered include community and preventive medicine, health services organization, and the training, utilization, licencing, and evaluation of new health practitioners (nurse practitioners and physician's assistants). Examples of job descriptions and legislation governing new health practitioners in the USA are appended. (HC)

3234   Kark, S.L. International Medical and Research Foundation, Warrenton, Va. *Functions of community health workers in community health care.* New York, International Medical and Research Foundation, 1977. 14p. Engl.
22 refs.
International Medical and Research Foundation Symposium on the Community Health Worker, Warrenton, Va., 26-28 Oct 1977.
See also entries 3227, 3232, 3236, 3239, 3243, 3244, 3259, 3266, 3268, 3294, and 3398.
The community health worker (CHW) has great potential as part of a health-centre-based health team whose work includes primary care and community medicine. The doctors and nurses who train CHWs should be aware of relevant developments in epidemiology and the behavioural sciences and experienced in community health field work. In addition to possible clinical duties, the CHW will monitor community health, gather data on demography and health characteristics for community diagnosis, and survey health related behaviour. By collecting information on health services performances and the community's role and expectations, the CHW can help to solve local problems. Therefore, to function effectively, he must also have the necessary skills to promote cooperation between community organizations and the health services and other agencies. (HH)

3235   Kilama, W.L. *Self-reliance in the development of Tanzania health services.* In Chagula, W.K., Feld, B.T., Parthasarathi, A., eds., Pugwash on Self-Reliance, New Delhi, Ankur Publishing House, Aug 1977, 83-102. Engl.

Twenty-fourth Pugwash Symposium on the Role of Self-Reliance in Alternative Strategies for Development, Dar-es-Salaam, Tanzania, 2-6 Jun 1975.
Since 1967, the Faculty of Medicine, Dar-es-Salaam University, Tanzania has trained students, pharmacists, laboratory technicians, and paramedical personnel at rural dispensaries and health centres to meet Tanzania's rural needs. The most important of these rural paramedics are the medical assistants, who work mainly in rural health centres. One rung below them on the health occupation ladder are the rural medical aids, who treat simple outpatient cases at dispensaries and participate in mass mobilization campaigns with the maternal and child health aids. Preventive and promotive health services are the province of the health auxiliaries, who, like both groups of aids, have primary school education. Village medical helpers, selected by their village, occupy the base of the occupational ladder and formally embody village dedication to self-reliance. Preventive services, introduced from 1969-1975, focus on maternal and child health and smallpox eradication and self-help projects such as health centre construction that enable the people to improve their personal and community health. Tables give data on aspects of health manpower, services, and expenditure in Tanzania. (CL)

3236   King, M. International Medical and Research Foundation, Warrenton, Va. *Community health worker: who should he be? What should he do? How should we educate and supervise him?* New York, International Medical and Research Foundation, 1977. 4p. Engl.
International Medical and Research Foundation Symposium on the Community Health Worker, Warrenton, Va., 26-28 Oct 1977.
See also entries 3227, 3232, 3234, 3239, 3243, 3244, 3259, 3266, 3268, 3294, and 3398.
To achieve a high standard of care, the training of the medical staff who teach community health workers (CHWs), the training manuals and teaching materials used, and the methods of evaluating these workers and their projects must be carefully judged and supervised. The CHW, because of his limited education, is not qualified to direct and design his own training. He therefore needs the fullest possible support from the medical profession, such as a regional centre to help with the training and organization of these workers. Because the success of a CHW is uniquely dependent on his relationship with his fellow workers and his community, there is a need for hard facts about the workers and their projects. Questions should be asked about the political and social standing of the CHW; information should also be gathered about the characteristics and skills of groups of CHWs and the effect of their projects on mortality and morbidity figures. Another topic to be considered is the full-time, salaried auxiliary, who is potentially able to provide better health care because of his more extensive experience. (HH)

3237   Lesotho, Ministry of Health and Social Welfare.
Village health worker in Lesotho: report of a workshop held on 26th-27th March, 1977 at Tsakholo Health Centre. Maseru, Ministry of Health and Social Welfare, Aug 1977. 77p. Engl. Workshop on the Village Health Worker, Tsakholo, Lesotho, 26-27 Mar 1977.

This report of a 2-day workshop on the village health worker (VHW) in Lesotho has been produced in response to the interest shown in the workshop by the participants and others concerned with improving health care at the village level. It begins with an explanation of the need for the workshop and describes the development of the workshop schedule. The three ongoing VHW programmes in Lesotho at Quthing, Scott, and Tellebong hospitals are compared and summaries of the workshop's three working sessions on VHW job descriptions, implementation of VHW programmes at village level, and the development of the organizational framework for a VHW programme are given. The controversial points from previous sessions are presented in the report of the final session and followed by some retrospective observations on the workshop's success. Looking beyond the workshop, chapter 4 of the report discusses ideas and recommendations for future programme development. Twelve appendices contain the workshop's schedule, programme summaries of ongoing VHW programmes, outlines and summaries for each of the working sessions, and a participant information form that the 69 listed participants each completed. (CL)

3238   Loftus, J. *Medicine man.* World Health (Geneva), Oct 1976, 17-19. Engl.
Also published in Arabic, French, German, Italian, Persian, Portuguese, Russian, and Spanish.

The government of Thailand has initiated a pilot project to extend primary health care services through village volunteers; early results have been encouraging. An example of the project in action can be seen in Ban Ka Choraj (in northeastern Thailand) where the villagers recently selected Liam Gansa-noi to attend a course for local health communicators. Liam has long been the village medicine man so he was also trained as a village health volunteer. The government project has not changed his role; it has enhanced his medical skills rather than supplanting them and has expanded his knowledge to include principles of basic nutrition, sanitation, midwifery, and family planning. He has always been trusted by his neighbours and now he has used his influence to upgrade sanitation and hygiene in his village. The initial success of this project and others like it may be reflected in Thailand's 4th Five-Year Development Plan, which is reputed to advocate the training of 24 000 village health volunteers and 200 000 local health communicators. (AC)

3239   Lolik, P.L. Bhachu, S.S. Anyudhi, R.K. International Medical and Research Foundation, New York. *Primary health care programme in the southern region of Sudan.* New York, International Medical and Research Foundation, 1977. 13p. Engl.

International Medical and Research Foundation Symposium on the Community Health Worker, Warrenton, Va., 26-28 Oct 1977.
Unpublished document; see also entries 3227, 3232, 3234, 3236, 3243, 3244, 3459, 3266, 3268, 3294, 3398.

A new primary health care (PHC) programme for the Sudan was drawn up in 1976 to provide more basic health services to the rural population. The backbone of this programme is the community health worker (CHW) aged 20-35 years, who must be literate with 6 years primary education and good standing in the community. Selection of candidates to attend a 9-month practical training course is made by a selection team of responsible community members and by oral/written examination in English. The course qualifies the CHWs to assist the village midwife, advise on maternal and child health care, control communicable diseases, and recognize common causes of sickness and give appropriate treatment. They must also be able to obtain information about local customs and habits, discuss problems with local leaders, apply and supervise appropriate methods of improving the village environment, register births and deaths, keep records and submit reports, and establish and maintain an inventory of equipment and supplies. After graduation, each CHW has charge of a PHC unit and is supervised by a medical assistant who is responsible for a PHC complex of 5 dispersed PHC units and 1 dispensary. A sample baseline study on social, economic, and health conditions was made in 1977 and similar studies are planned for 1979 and 1983 to permit evaluation of the impact of the PHC programme. (MG)

3240   Mackay, J. *Health auxiliary training in Papua New Guinea.* Appropriate Technology (London), 2(4), Feb 1976, 28-29. Engl.
The 1974-1978 national health plan for Papua New Guinea stresses the training and deployment of medical auxiliaries to staff the nationwide network of health centres and aid posts. The health extension officer (HEO) has both medical and administrative responsibility for a health centre that he runs with the help of maternal and child health nurses, hospital orderlies, and an aid post supervisor. At present, the only institute for training HEOs is the Paramedical College, Madang, which has a 3-year post-secondary school course. Several problems have been encountered with this training course: communication difficulties arise because students must use a language and mathematical concepts that are unfamiliar in the local culture; conflict exists between Western style medicine and deep-rooted traditional beliefs; there is a lack of suitable textbooks and other teaching aids, especially texts that emphasize common local conditions; and finally, because much of the training takes place in the well-equipped provincial general hospital, students may be inadequately prepared for their subsequent work in health centres with much less sophisticated facilities. To overcome the latter difficulty, a "health centre" ward has been simulated in the hospital and a post-graduate probationary year introduced during which 6 months are spent at an approved hospital and 6 months at a health centre. (MG)

3241 Mahmud, S. Fendall, N.R. *Primary health care in rural areas of Pakistan.* Islamabad, Pakistan, Planning Commission, Nov 1974. 26p. Engl.

Pakistan has opted for a rural health care delivery system that is based on the deployment of auxiliary health workers of three kinds: a midwifery, pediatrics, and family planning auxiliary; a communicable diseases auxiliary; and a medical care auxiliary. All three are to be trained in one institute, with the 1st year taken in common. The 1st year curriculum will include the bilogical sciences, nutrition, personal and domestic hygiene, and health education, plus information on health services, government, and political organizations. The 2nd and 3rd years will be devoted to clinical and practical work, with students being rotated through various outpatient departments and primary care institutions. Teaching methodology will emphasize schoolroom rather than university techniques--oral rather than written communication, reiteration of lessons, and closely-supervised fieldwork--and examinations will endeavour to test the students' functional rather than literary or academic abilities. The estimated yearly requirement of 3 000-3 500 auxiliaries will be drawn mainly from the pool of high school drop-outs (completed 2ndary schooling is not advocated as it tends to obscure the gap between a professional and auxiliary). It is emphasized that the auxiliary, whether deployed in an assistant or a substitute capacity, has at all times the 'right' to supervision by a professional. Job descriptions and suggested curricula for all three categories of auxiliary are appended. (HC)

3242 Mascareno Sauceda, F. Martinez Urbina, R. *Necesidad, utilizacion y capacitacion de personal auxiliar voluntario en programas rurales de salud. (Need for, utilization of, and training of volunteer auxiliary health workers for rural health programmes).* Boletin de la Oficina Sanitaria Panamericana (Washington, D.C.), 82(1), Jan 1977, 7-13. Span.

Because of the difficulties of persuading health professionals to practice in rural areas, Mexico has organized programmes for recruiting, training, and deploying volunteer auxiliary health workers in these parts of the country. In order to be selected for these programmes, candidates must have worked for some time in the health sector, attained respect and authority within their own communities, and demonstrated the ability and resources to carry out health activities. Formal education is not important. Their training covers hygiene, nutrition, immunization, first aid, environmental health, community development, group dynamics, agricultural practices, etc. After training, these auxiliaries are sent to rural health posts to either assist health professionals or work on their own, in which instance they refer complicated cases to the nearest rural health centre and sometimes prescribe medicines. (RMB)

3243 Morton, J. International Medical and Research Foundation, Warrenton, Va. *Community health worker in Norton Sound region.* New York, International Medical and Research Foundation,

1977. 12p. Engl.

International Medical and Research Foundation Symposium on the Community Health Worker, Warrenton, Va., 26-28 Oct 1977.

See also entries 3227, 3232, 3234, 3236, 3239, 3244, 3259, 3266, 3268, 3294, and 3898.

The Norton Sound Health Corporation (Alaska, USA) maintains a regional hospital and a series of village clinics, each staffed by a community health aide (CHA). CHAs are selected in consultation with their communities from candidates who are stable, teachable, and socially acceptable. They receive medical supervision from hospital physicians and administrative guidance from a nurse or physician's assistant who acts as coordinator/instructor assigned to each village. They also have contact with other health workers who specialize in eye care, mental health, and public health. An annual basic training course consisting of 2 weeks in the classroom and 1 in a hospital is supplemented by field training in medical procedures and clinic and record maintenance provided by the coordinator/instructor. Afterwards, the CHA may take written and practical exams that qualify her for a higher salary and advanced course work; for example, five CHAs have done a trial laboratory course that enables them to do white bood counts, routine urinalysis, culture for *gonococcus*, and smears for *trichomonas*. There are three levels of CHAs with progressively higher qualifications and responsibilities, such as running and maintaining general and special clinics, screening, immunizing, and keeping records. The 3rd level, that of community health practitioner, has not yet been reached by any student. The overall aim is to provide the maximum amount of cost-effective care and to this end a cost benefit analysis is planned. (HH)

3244 Mwabulambo, D.J. International Medical and Research Foundation, New York. Tanzania, Ministry of Health. *Village health workers scheme in Tanzania.* New York, International Medical and Research Foundation, 1977. 7p. Engl.

International Medical and Research Foundation Symposium on the Community Health Worker, Warrenton, Va., 26-28 Oct 1977.

Unpublished document; see also entries 3227, 3232, 3234, 3236, 3239, 3243, 3259, 3266, 3268, 3294, and 3398.

As part of its long-term policy of resettling dispersed rural populations in permanent villages, the Tanzanian government intends to provide each established village with a well-equipped dispensary. However, it is estimated that it will take 45 years to achieve this goal. As an alternative, simpler form of health delivery, village posts manned by village medical helpers (VMHs) were introduced in 1969 to provide health care in unserved areas. The government finances VMH training and outlines its form, but selection of candidates is made by the villagers themselves. The VMHs selected (one male and one female) are mature, literate, married persons who are permanent village residents. After 3 months of training at the District Hospital, the VMH returns to work in the village on a voluntary, unsalaried basis but is exempt from community tasks other than health care duties. The responsibilities of the VMH include running the village health post, treating minor ailments, and, of greatest significance, increasing local awareness of the importance of preventive medicine. Some 2 020 villages now have VMHs and it is expected that this figure will have increased to 5 600 by 1980, when all villages will have access to some form of medical assistance. (MG)

3245   Ozigi, Y.O. *Importance of health and nutrition education in the training of rural health workers in the northern states of Nigeria.* London, Queen Elizabeth College, 1976. 82p. Engl.
17 refs.
Unpublished document submitted to the University of London; individual chapter has been abstracted separately under entry 3003.
Rural health workers (RHWs) have been the backbone of the Nigerian health service since the colonial era. Recruits with 7-11 years schooling are given a 2-year practical training course before starting work in rural and urban dispensaries, health centres, and mobile health units. Despite the fact that they are usually the only "scientific" medical workers available, their salaries, promotion prospects, and conditions of service are poor. They also tend to meet with opposition from professional medical staff, although they are well accepted by local communities. Respected and influential among the people they serve, they are in an ideal position to provide health and nutrition education, but at present their training does not equip them for this work. The importance of preventive measures in general, and health education in particular, is recognized by the federal government and a federal health education unit has been formed, but the Third National Development Plan does not provide adequate resources for these areas. Specific health targets should be included in community development programmes and new types of health auxiliaries, similar to the "yaws scouts" used for the mass campaign of 1957-1964, should be trained for particular tasks such as health education. Not only rural health workers but all health personnel should be given formal instruction in health and nutrition education as part of their basic training. (DM)

3246   Papua New Guinea, Department of Public Health. *Syllabus: aid post orderly.* Port Moresby, Department of Public Health, Medical Training Division, Jan 1972. 8p. Engl.
The course content, student activities, and goals of a 2-year aid post orderly course in Papua New Guinea are delineated. The content covers elementary anatomy and physiology, common illness and health problems in the country, means of disease transfer and preventive and control measures, health education in hygiene and nutrition, epidemiology and surveillance techniques, structure of the national health programme, etc. The student activities are mainly practical and are linked with the goals. For example, during the unit on disease transfer, students view germs through a microscope and are expected to be able to explain the relationship of germs and disease and the role that disease carriers play in the spread of disease. Course policies are that not more than 40% of time during training will be devoted to

lectures and that specific tasks, such as preparing health education talks, cultivating nutritious foods, etc., are to be conducted at school, whereas others, such as sterilizing syringes, dispensing drugs, and examining patients are to be carried out at the aid post and hospital. (AC)

3247   Rifkin, S.B. *Issues and perspectives.* In Rifkin, S.B., ed., Community Health in Asia, Singapore, Christian Conference of Asia Committee on Health Concerns, Jun 1977, 125-143. Engl.
See also entry 2408 (volume 4).
Community health is a dynamic process involving essential resources such as food, income, education, etc., as well as health institutions. Because hospitals are service-oriented, they are in many respects poorly suited to be centres for developing community health programmes. The medical professional's advisory role in these programmes is hampered by the present type of medical education and by the community's own perception of the doctor as the supreme conveyor of health. In contrast, the community organizer who helps people create structures for solving their own problems must often keep a very low profile, because his work is seen as a threat to the government and powerful interests within the community. The village health worker can serve as a bridge between the medical staff and the people, but he belongs and is responsible to the latter. He must develop both technical skills and skills in communication, organization, and social analysis, if he is to be more than simply an extension of the existing inadequate system. (AB)

3248   Rifkin, S.B. Zambia, Ministry of Health. *WHO: How? (Helping people to develop community health programmes).* Hong Kong, Christian Conference of Asia, Jan 1976. 28p. Engl.
Unpublished document.
For the new health care priorities established by WHO in 1975 to be put into practice, health workers must learn to work with local people rather than for them. Helping workers make this crucial change in attitude was one of the goals of a training seminar for health auxiliaries in Zambia. The opening sessions were designed to encourage the participants to discuss problems arising from their own health work, recognize the value of the preventive approach, and work cooperatively in a team. These sessions were followed by visits to nearby villages to carry out community diagnosis, an exercise that involved much more than simple data collection. The auxiliaries learned to approach people with humility and respect, establish a dialogue with local leaders, identify both felt and unfelt needs, and recognize local resources. On the basis of this information, they were then able to plan a health programme, stating objectives, priorities, and constraints, with provision for evaluation and follow-up. The final session of the seminar was devoted to health education, which was defined as helping people to change bad health habits. The whole programme reflected an ambitious new approach to health auxiliary training that recognizes constraints likely to exist in this or any similar training situation: inadequate time and difficult transport, absence of pre-existing health

IV Primary Health Manpower--Training and Utilization

structures in the target communities, and lack of the follow-up that is essential for sustained change. (DM)

3249   Ronaghy, H.A. Najarzadeh, E. Schwartz, T.A. Russel, S.S. Solter, S. Zeighami, B. *Front line health worker: selection, training and performance.* American Journal of Public Health (New York), 66(3), Mar 1976, 273-277. Engl. 8 refs.

In 1972, staff from the Department of Community Medicine, Pahlavi University, launched a pilot project to train and deploy village health workers (VHWs) in the Kavar area of Iran. After undertaking background surveys, the planning team defined objectives for six areas of health, wrote a simple textbook in Persian, and designed a 6-month course for the literate but minimally educated recruits. Training time was divided among preventive medicine and health education (34%), basic health sciences and record keeping (15%), and treatment (51%). Each of the 1st graduates, 5 women and 11 men, was posted to a village in March 1974. Within 10 months, family planning acceptance had risen in the pilot villages from 8%-21%, improvements to water supply had been made in 50% of the villages, and more than half the residents had visited the VHWs' daily clinics. The positive response to the VHWs suggests that even greater environmental improvements would probably have been made had additional resources been available. Surprisingly, the acceptability of the health workers appeared to be independent of such factors as age, sex, or place of origin. Selection of candidates by village authorities was therefore not essential and in practice raised unforeseen factional interests. This was one of several ways in which the VHWs differed from equivalent foreign personnel such as Chinese barefoot doctors, on whom they had been modeled. (DM)

3250   Ronaghy, H.A. Mousseau-Gershman, Y. Dorozynski, A. *Village health workers.* Ottawa, International Development Research Centre, 1976. 48p. Engl.
Workshop on Village Health Workers, Shiraz, Iran, 6-13 Mar 1976.
Individual chapters have been abstracted separately under entries 2837, 3203, 3226, 3251, 3252, 3395, and 3403.

Reports from a workshop on village health workers have been abstracted in this document. They represent experiences in training and deploying village health workers in Iran, Nepal, the Philippines, Thailand, and Papua New Guinea. They exemplify the workshop, which was an open forum for problems, obstacles, and failures as well as solutions and achievements; salient points raised during discussions are included in a summary at the end of the report. (HC)

3251   Ronaghy, H.A. *Middle level health workers training project in Iran.* In Ronaghy, H.A., Mousseau-Gershman, Y., Dorozynski, A., eds., Village Health Workers, Ottawa, International Development Research Centre, 1976, 11-13. Engl.
For complete document see entry 3250.

Since October 1973, a school in Marvdasht, Iran, has been training middle-level health workers called *behdars.* The trainees are selected from among candidates with 9th-11th-grade education. The course lasts 4 years and consists of 1 264 hours of theoretical instruction and 3 504 hours of clinical experience. The latter includes supervised practice at the Red Lion and Sun Clinic outside Marvdasht, at the Ministry of Health clinic in the department of maternal child health and family planning (female students only), at a dental facility, and in a mobile clinic. Students participate in history-taking, giving injections, administering local anaesthesia, providing first aid and preventive care, conducting simple laboratory tests, diagnosing, and prescribing. In addition to their regular classroom and clinical work, in the 1st 1 1/2 years they make periodic field trips to nearby villages, where they survey health needs and attempt to improve sanitary conditions, and during the last year they begin work in their own clinics and supervise 3-4 village health workers. A refresher course in educational theory, techniques, and resources is soon to be offered to promising *behdar* graduates to prepare them to train village health workers. (HC)

3252   Ronaghy, H.A. *Village health workers in Iran.* In Ronaghy, H.A., Mousseau-Gershman, Y., Dorozynski, A., eds., Village Health workers, Ottawa, International Development Research Centre, 1976, 6-10. Engl.
For complete document see entry 3250.

In Iran, 16 barely literate villagers were selected on the basis of physical and mental fitness, motivation, and recommendation by village authorities for training as village health workers (VHWs). They took an intensive 6-month course at Kavar, the site of a health corps station, under a physician's supervision. They formed four groups working in rotation with station personnel who taught: maternal child health and family planning; sterile technique, injection methods, burn management, wound dressing, and other procedures; the indications, contraindications, dosages, and side effects of drugs; and history-taking, physical examination, and patient evaluation. Trainees made numerous field trips to learn practical methods for improving village hygiene and sanitation. Their coursework is designed to prepare them for working in a clinic, home visiting, and maintaining patient records and vital statistics. After graduation, they are visited once a week by a physician, attend monthly continuing education meetings at the health station, and undergo a 2-week refresher course each summer. After the first group of VHWs had been working 6 months, they had received 4 875 patient visits (out of a population of 9 152) and increased the family planning utilization rate by 12.5%. (HC)

3253   Rotsart de Hertaing, I. Courtejoie, J. Centre d'Etudes et de Recherches pour la Promotion de la Sante, Kangu-Mayumbe, Zaire. *Dispensaire et sa nouvelle orientation: les responsabilites nouvelles du technicien de la sante. (Dispensary and its new orientation: the new responsibilities of the health technician).* Kangu-Mayumbe, Zaire, Centre d'Etudes et de Recherches pour la Promotion de la Sante, Brochure Illustre No.24, n.d. 37p. Fren. 20 refs.

See also entry 2804.

A proposal for extending health services into the rural areas of Zaire is outlined. Its implementation would involve converting existing dispensaries into health centres offering a full range of services (maternity, laboratory, inpatient, etc.) to a defined population, multiplying the effort of the health centres through the establishment of subcentres that would deliver primary care through auxiliary nurses, and complementing the effort of the health centres and subcentres through the establishment of aid posts that would offer first aid and health promotion through local auxiliaries trained in some basic aspect of health care. The aid post auxiliaries would be chosen from among literate individuals recommended by local authorities. Their initial training would consist of 8 weeks in a health centre with 2-3 weeks of refresher courses annually, the curriculum would be based on the programme proposed in the World Health Organization's *Reference material for health auxiliaries and their teachers.* It is recommended that a category of auxiliary be created to correspond to each classical medical qualification, so that auxiliaries can be introduced at all levels of the health service. (HC)

3254   Schweser, H.O. Project HOPE, Washington, D.C. People-to-People Health Foundation, Inc., Washington, D.C. *Health education by auxiliary health workers.* In Schweser, H.O., Manual for Community Health Education for the Caribbean, Washington, D.C., People-to-People Health Foundation, n.d., 48-55. Engl.

For complete document see entry 3371.

Auxiliaries working in their own communities are particularly well placed for carrying out health education activities if they have the tact and patience to attempt to change people's attitudes. To help them in this task, their training should cover methods of communication that will be useful in their own particular societies. They should be taught by specialists, experienced teachers who use audiovisual materials to demonstrate communications techniques. Motivation, morale, and status are all important to the auxiliary's position as teacher. Supervisors can build morale if they stress guidance and encouragement. The supervisor will also choose the specific health education area an auxiliary will deal with according to individual skills and aptitudes. In addition to his initial training, in-service courses, refresher courses, and conferences will help to improve the auxiliary's teaching techniques; he can also learn on the job from senior auxiliaries and newsletters designed to keep those in remote areas in touch. Particular health education activities will include: publicizing the services available at clinics and elsewhere; teaching and demonstrations in the clinic, in homes, or wherever appropriate; distributing pamphlets; helping the community identify health needs and plan programmes; investigating homes with poor sanitation or no latrine; and notifying the appropriate health agency of such problems. Preventive activities will include: assisting with immunization campaigns; following up family planning drop-outs;

introducing new clients to the clinic; investigating reasons for broken appointments, especially those of maternal child health patients; and visiting discharged patients at home. (HH)

3255   Sethu, S. Ramasamy, T.P. Paul, M.P. *Report on the pilot study of multi-purpose health workers (male) in Athoor Block, Madurai District.* Bulletin of the Gandhigram Institute of Rural Health and Family Planning (Gandhigram, India), 10(2), Sep 1975, 1-26. Engl.

The Gandhigram Institute of Rural Health and Family Planning (India) launched a pilot project to determine whether a male multipurpose health worker could provide services already being provided by unipurpose workers in the rural areas. The operational objectives of the project were to determine how the various activities could best be accomplished and what problems might arise during widespread application. Other goals were to test two different patterns of work, design a suitable health record, and discover training requirements of multipurpose workers. Undertaken at the Athoor Community Development Block, the study integrated activities for malaria, smallpox, family planning, and vital statistics collection. It also incorporated health education and case-holding for India's leprosy and tuberculosis programmes. From May-October, 23 multipurpose health workers undertook the three phases of the study-- the 1st to conduct a baseline survey of all the households in the area, the 2nd and 3rd to provide services. The group was divided so that 9 workers each visited 40 households a day for the 6 working days and 14 workers each visited 60 households per day but limited activities on the 5th and 6th days respectively to smallpox and family planning. Performances for the two patterns of work were compared with each other and with performances of unipurpose workers. Results indicated that the multipurpose workers following the 2nd pattern of work outstripped those using the 1st and compared favourably with unipurpose workers. (AC)

3256   Sich, D. Commonwealth Foundation, London. National Fund for Research into Crippling Diseases, Arundel, UK. *How to reach the family: problems and ways to solutions in health care in developing countries.* In Disabled in Developing Countries, London, Commonwealth Foundation, 1977, 98-105. Engl.

Symposium on Appropriate Technology and Delivery of Health and Welfare Services for the Disabled in Developing Countries, Oxford, UK, 26-30 Sep 1976.

For complete document see entry 3124.

Frontline workers (FLWs) in Korea provide a two-way link between the community and an under-utilized formal health care system. After being instructed in the structure and functions of the health system, they can direct or accompany patients to the appropriate service; they can also disseminate information about nutrition and hygiene. Ideally, FHWs are middle-aged women whose opinions are already respected in the community and who are competent to introduce new ideas. If the

FLW first approaches mothers with young children, she can gradually influence the whole family. The success of the worker rests on her position as respected adviser and she must have the support of community leaders or the community health council as well as other members of the health service. (HH)

3257   Sich, D. Christian Physicians' Association, Kang Wha, Korea. *Importance of frontline workers as health work partners.* Kang Wha, Korea, Christian Physicians' Association, 1976. 8p. Engl. Annual Meeting of the Christian Physicians' Association, Kang Wha, Korea, Jan 1976.

Christian doctors in Korea concerned with the mental and social aspects of health must be encouraged to support the introduction into the health care system of frontline workers (FLWs), who can help to care for those who do not or cannot take advantage of organized medical services. For cultural as well as economic reasons, FLW trainees should be chosen from local villages. As natural leaders within their own communities, they can raise the health consciousness of their neighbours, provide health education, and organize self-help activities. They can also act as communications channels between the people and the health services, help the health team organize campaigns, and identify local disease and health hazards. FLWs may also have a few limited preventive and curative functions, but their main job is to provide a liaison with the community. The details of FLW schemes must be adapted to individual cultures and situations, but general principles for all programmes should include the selection of candidates with suitable social skills, qualities of leadership, and the ability to communicate; the creation of appropriate job descriptions and training curricula; and the provision of the proper mechanism for evaluating and adjusting the programme. (HH)

3258   Sich, D. *Health post project: philosophy and work strategies for program implementation.* Yonsei, Korea, Yonsei College of Medicine, Aug 1974. 35p. Engl. See also entries 2357 (volume 4) and 3289.

The Health Post Project organized by the Yonsei College of Medicine (Korea) is a field laboratory for training all levels of community health workers. Its objectives are to encourage community self-help by introducing family health workers (FHWs) and developing village organizations, set up home visiting schedules and clinics, and identify the villagers' potential to solve their own health problems. Although no new medical services will be introduced, it is hoped that the health status of the community will improve because of the FHWs' activities. The FHW should increase health consciousness and act as a communications channel between the people and the health services. Proper integration of FHWs into the existing system by referral arrangements and supervision is vital. The project is also concerned with redefining the activities of local health centres and designing new role models and service packages for doctors, public health nurses, and multipurpose workers. To provide comprehensive health care, the centres will be

staffed by either a public health nurse (PHN) with midwifery training or a physician; the professional will coach and supervise the multipurpose workers, who will do the same for the FHWs. The PHN will also attend deliveries and supervise maternal child health care programmes. Two multipurpose workers will oversee the FHWs, whose primary functions will initially be in maternal child health care and family planning. Later, other programmes can be included. (HH)

3259   Standard, K.L. International Medical and Research Foundation, Warrenton, Va. *Role of the community health aide in the Commonwealth Caribbean with special reference to Jamaica.* New York, International Medical and Research Foundation, 1977. 17p. Engl. International Medical and Research Foundation Symposium on the Community Health Worker, Warrenton, Va., 26-28 Oct 1977. See also entries 3227, 3232, 3234, 3236, 3239, 3243, 3244, 3266, 3268, 3294, and 3398.

In 1967, two Jamaican village communities collaborating with the Department of Social and Preventive Medicine, University of the West Indies, selected village residents for training as community health aides (CHAs) to work in health teams under the supervision of established health professionals. A 2nd pilot project for training CHAs was started in 1969. The success of the two programmes encouraged the Ministry of Health and Environmental Control to train and employ in 1972 about 300 CHAs to combat malnutrition in two Western parishes and subsequently to employ CHAs in all parishes throughout Jamaica. The CHAs, mainly mature women selected for their literacy and respected position within the community, were trained by senior nursing personnel for 4 months and 3 months respectively for the 1st two pilot projects. However, subsequent programmes used 2-month training courses with continuous assessment and by 1977 over 1 160 CHAs were working in Jamaica's health services. The aides, who give health education to the community, administer first aid treatment, encourage family planning, and check child immunization records, are supervised by public health nurses. Evaluation and feedback at seminars are an integral part of the training programme. Training and employment of CHAs for 1975-1978 cost about $7.4 million. (CL)

3260   Suyadi, A. Sadjimin, T. Rohde, J.E. *Primary care in the village: an approach to village self-help health programmes.* Tropical Doctor (London), 7(3), Jul 1977, 123-128. Engl.

A low-cost health insurance scheme became the starting point for a number of community self-help projects in a rural hamlet in Kalirandu, Indonesia. The scheme arose out of a felt need on the part of the villagers to reduce the economic burden of desired health services. Because physician-delivery primary care was too expensive, even for a cooperative scheme, it was decided to train village volunteers as primary health workers and use insurance funds to pay for medicines and referrals and to provide low-interest loans to participating families. The village health workers were gainfully-employed individuals who received 5-6 weeks training (2 sessions per week) before assuming responsibility for the health of 10-15 families in their neighbourhoods. Their duties included promoting village sanitation and healthier housing, recording all births and deaths, reporting any occurrence of unusual or severe disease, monthly weighing of all under-fives, family planning motivation, providing simple treatment services, and collecting monthly insurance fees. The enthusiasm of the village health workers was such that, when the novelty of performing these routine tasks wore off, they sought new activities: the formation of a family planning acceptors club, which raised the acceptor rate from 30%-70% of all eligible couples within a few months; a latrine promotion drive that tripled the number of sanitary latrines within 2 months; a food supplement programme for the most underweight children; a community-wide vaccination programme; a home garden programme; etc. The success of the scheme is attributed to the wide participation by the villagers themselves, not only in sharing the benefits but also in identifying and planning desirable projects. (HC)

3261   Swinscow, T.D. *Primary care: a look at Kenya.* British Medical Journal (London), 1(6072), May 1977, 1337-1338. Engl.
In many parts of Kenya, primary care is provided at health centres by registered clinical officers formerly called medical assistants. After 3 years training, they are required to spend 3 years in government service, during which time they may be posted to remote areas with poor facilities where their efforts may meet with cultural resistance. In these working conditions, apathy could easily set in but for a number of measures that provide support and incentives. For example, district medical officers are expected to visit health centres frequently, help improve facilities, and encourage reading and continuing education. The supporting services are aided by the African Medical and Research Foundation, which publishes literature for all health workers, both professional and auxiliary, and flies teachers and specialists to remote parts of the country to run additional training courses. After their 3 years in government service, some clinical officers leave to go into private practice, but many stay on because of the opportunities for advancement in the career structure. With practical experience behind them, clinical officers may be accepted to retrain as licensed medical practitioners and some of these, after further field work and training, become fully qualified medical graduates. (DM)

3262   Thailand, Ministry of Public Health. *Ministry of Public Health Village Health Communicator and Village Health Volunteer Scheme, 1977-1981: guidelines for development of the Village Health Volunteers Scheme.* Thailand, Ministry of Public Health, 1977. 8p. Engl.
In rural Thailand, village health communicators (VHCs) and village health volunteers (VHVs) form part of a proposed rural health care development plan. VHCs will advise on health matters, give out news, and collect medical data while organizing community activities.

VHVs will, in addition to the above duties, give first aid and treatment to relieve symptoms, sell home medicines, and deal with family planning. Both categories of workers will be volunteers, but incentives such as free medical care, certificates, first aid kits, etc., will be provided by the Ministry of Public Health and other funding bodies, including WHO and UNICEF. Each community will select its own VHCs and VHVs, who will be trained informally in small groups to meet the problems of individual villages. The VHC requires 5 days training, the VHV 15 days, which will be provided by government health staff with experience in primary health care; they will also supervise and advise the volunteers. The project will be evaluated every 6-12 months. By 1981, the whole country should be covered by the programme, which aims at providing 1 VHC : 8-15 households and 1 VHV : village. (HH)

3263   University of the West Indies, Department of Social and Preventive Medicine, Mona, Jamaica. *Alternatives in the delivery of health services.* Mona, Jamaica, University of the West Indies, Department of Social and Preventive Medicine, n.d. 244p. Engl.
Refs.
Seminar/Workshop on Alternatives in the Delivery of Health Services, Castries, St. Lucia, 8-12 Nov 1976.
The purpose of the workshop was to consider the extent to which community involvement and participation may contribute effectively to the provision and delivery of primary care, examine the unmet health needs of several communities in the Americas and the extent to which individuals in the community might be trained to meet these needs, and formulate guidelines and plans for training programmes and demonstrate from experience that auxiliary programmes are workable. Various papers presented at the workshop cover the community health aide programme in Jamaica, the training of 'health helpers' in the interior of Surinam, Venezuela's programme of 'simplified medicine', Colombia's programme for the training of *promotoras de salud*, and the deployment of nurse practitioners in Canada. In addition, the Cuban system is examined as an example of a health service with a strong, community-based orientation. Details of the development and implementation of these programmes/systems, including the curricula, job descriptions, and evaluation of the auxiliaries in question, are given and ways in which these experiences could be applied in another situation, that of the Caribbean Island of St. Lucia, are explored. The papers are reproduced in full while the discussions are summarized. (HC)

3264   Venkataswamy, G. *Training and functions of ophthalmic assistants.* Israel Journal of Medical Sciences (Jerusalem), 8(8-9), 1972, 1081-1082. Engl.
Causes and Prevention of Blindness, Jerusalem Seminar on the Prevention of Blindness, Jerusalem, Israel, 25-27 Aug 1971.
Although there are various schools for the training of optometrists and orthoptists as ophthalmic assistants in

India, their full employment is not possible because of lack of funds. There is as yet no special course for ophthalmic nursing, but even for nurses trained in ophthalmic hospitals there is acute unemployment. The hope is expressed that in the future related auxiliary personnel will be utilized to treat all types of eye diseases. (EE)

3265 Watts, G. *People's health in people's hands: a new community health worker every three minutes for the next three years.* World Medicine (London), 13(8), 1978, 19-23,65,67. Engl.

In accordance with an Indian Ministry of Health plan to train 1 community health worker (CHW):1 000 people, each primary health centre (PHC) serving 100 000 people or more must train 100 CHWs within 2 years. The course for CHW trainees, who are selected by the village *panchayat* or elected assembly, lasts 3 months, so by training in groups of 20, the goal will be achieved on schedule. About 40% of the trainees so far have been women, 70% of farmer stock with an average age of about 30 years. They receive payment during training but afterwards are paid only a small allowance and are expected to retain their everyday jobs. They combine a preventive with a curative role and receive a simple medical kit and manual. The manual for CHWs that has been translated into local languages contains sections on traditional medicine, which the CHWs will be encouraged to use as well. The Ministry's plan also aims to improve the standards of birth attendants or *dais* and to provide 1 male and 1 female multipurpose health worker : 5 000 people, although sufficient numbers cannot be trained until the mid-1980s. These multipurpose workers will replace the multitude of individuals now responsible for single programmes. The author points out that the problem of referral through health assistants, PHCs, and district hospitals has not yet been solved. (HH)

3266 Welty, T.K. International Medical and Research Foundation, Warrenton, Va. USA, Department of Health, Education, and Welfare. *Navajo community health representatives program.* New York, International Medical and Research Foundation, 1977. 8p. Engl.

International Medical and Research Foundation Symposium on the Community Health Worker, Warrenton, Va., 26-28 Oct 1977.

See also entries 3227, 3232, 3234, 3236, 3239, 3243, 3244, 3259, 3268, 3294, and 3398.

Elected Navajo Community Health Representatives (CHRs) function in 99 out of 102 chapters (the smallest political unit on the Indian reservation) and are trained at the Navajo Community College for the specific problems and priorities of the people they serve. The functions of the CHRs are varied and may shift from year to year. Basically, they are responsible for liaison between Indians and the health service and for the maintenance of health displays, bulletins, and reports in their chapters. They are involved in immunization, extensive programmes of health education, and specific local health schemes and they also cooperate with other health

and social workers. They are important as interpreters, patient advocates involved with patients' rights, and home help aides in coordinated home care plans, often also helping with emergency transport. In Tuba City, CHRs serve in the gastroenteritis and streptococcal programmes aimed at reducing the incidence of rheumatic fever and rheumatic heart disease. Because of difficulties in finding and following up cases of gastroenteritis, this special programme was broadened to deal with environmental health. The author suggests that the CHR programme could be improved by increasing salaries and career opportunities, providing vehicles with radios for the workers, and making schemes more adaptable to local conditions. (HH)

3267 WHO, Geneva. *Utilisation du personnel auxiliaire dans les services de sante ruraux: une experience au Zaire. (Use of auxiliary personnel in rural health services: an experiment in Zaire).* Bulletin of the World Health Organization (Geneva), 54(6), 1976, 625-632. Fren.

Also published in English and Russian.

Upgraded training for 35 auxiliaries in the regional health services, Kasango, Zaire, has reaped encouraging results. The auxiliaries were nurses who already had received some multipurpose, post-basic training and had been acting as doctor substitutes on an *ad hoc* basis; the purpose of training was to equip them with standard treatment procedures and to increase their self-confidence and status. The teaching method was to present standard procedures in the form of decision trees or flow charts that began with the patient's complaint and proceeded through a series of rational therapeutic decisions based on sequential collection of discriminating information. The auxiliaries were given a checklist to be countersigned by their supervisors when they completed the three defined levels (observation, execution, and competence) for each skill. Later, they received regular visits from their supervisor, who offered on-the-job guidance in problem-solving. Team spirit was promoted through regular meetings attended by all hospital or health centre staff; problems raised during these meetings were used as the starting point for refresher courses that the auxiliaries themselves were encouraged to prepare. (HC)

3268 Wood, C.H. International Medical and Research Foundation, Warrenton, Va. *Summary of the current state of community health workers in Kenya.* New York, International Medical and Research Foundation, 1977. 3p. Engl.

International Medical and Research Foundation Symposium on the Community Health Worker, Warrenton, Va., 26-28 Oct 1977.

See also entries 3227, 3232, 3234, 3236, 3239, 3243, 3244, 3259, 3266, 3294, and 3398.

In order to improve the distribution of health services in Kenya, several different outreach schemes involving a variety of community health workers have recently been started by voluntary agencies. For example, one hospital at Nangina started training public health aides in 1969 and another at Chogoria began training community workers in 1973 to extend hospital coverage. In 1973, a much larger governmental rural health development project initiated by the Ministry of Health began a major maternal and child health and family planning (MCHFP) programme, which aimed to provide MCHFP services from 400 delivery points throughout the country. This programme, which involves training a new cadre of family health field educators to work within the community, represents the largest input so far into the community health worker field, but another scheme involving experienced nurses working through missions has also been established. In general, though objective evaluation is needed, most schemes have shown that even if there are "felt needs" in a community, some outside input has been necessary to initiate discussions and activities. Only one programme has received direct financial support from the community. Most voluntary agencies have paid a regular minimum wage, but the government programme pays almost double this because it requires more staff training. Unfortunately, the higher salary decreases the ability of local communities to fund their own programmes. (CL)

3269 **World Neighbors, Oklahoma City.** *Volunteer health promoters.* Oklahoma City, Okla., World Neighbors in Action, 9(1E), n.d. 8p. Engl.
A rural area with a population of 29 000 in Central Java was chosen as the site for a pilot project in health and community development. For several years, a health centre in one of the villages had provided family planning, emergency services, health education, and a mobile clinic. Although relatively successful, the programme was run entirely on the initiative of health centre staff with little contribution from the local people. Now the emphasis of the programme is on health improvement by, rather than for, the people using a community-organized volunteer health team to link the villagers with the health services. These volunteers are selected from the local population on the basis of such qualities as personal motivation and ability to teach, learn, and lead. Volunteers are trained by health centre staff in weekly practical sessions and are each assigned a group of 15 households in their home village for which they are responsible. They are expected to act as an example in their own lives and to carry out simple household surveys, keep records, and confer with village leaders in planning community development. The volunteers also offer some simple curative services. The essential feature of the volunteer health promoter programme is that the workers are unpaid, so they offer their services to the community without charge; their only incentive is community improvement. For this reason and because they are familiar with the people, understand their needs, and operate on a small scale, they are easily accepted by their neighbours. (DM)

IV.2 Primary Nursing Care
IV.2.1 Professional

See also: 2816, 2838, 2841, 3199, 3205, 3212, 3308, 3317, 3318, 3323, 3337, 3376, 3399

3270 **Banerjee, A. WHO, Brazzaville.** *Development of health services in Zambia: nursing.* Brazzaville, WHO, 27 Mar 1974. 6p. Engl.
A new basic programme that includes public health content has been devised for Kitwe School of Nursing (Zambia). The 3-year programme expands the 1st year curriculum to encompass: microbiology, hygiene, preventive medicine, and sociology; experience in problem-solving for patients in hospital; visits to sites of social, occupational, or environmental significance; and field observation of community health nursing activities. The programme's 2nd year incorporates the study of mental health, public health nursing, and maternal child health and includes 6 weeks community nursing practice. The 3rd year consists of further community nursing practice, public health practice in the hospital, and an apprenticeship in assisting junior nurses. Classroom and field activities are planned to utilize team effort. (HC)

3271 **Beaton, G.R. McMurdo, J. Wilson, T.D. Nursing Association of South Africa, Pretoria. University of Witwatersrand, Johannesburg.** *Extended role of the nurse.* Johannesburg, University of Witwatersrand, 1977. 19p. Engl.
Conference on the Extended Role of the Nurse, University of Witwatersrand, Johannesburg, South Africa, 4-6 Aug 1977.
In South Africa, nurses could provide more primary health care if they had better training, recognition, support, and legal protection. Primary health care training should include, for example, competence in midwifery. Continuing education and a career structure are necessary to ensure adequate medical care and job satisfaction. The career structure should provide the opportunity to advance clinically rather than administratively. To adequately supervise and support the PHC nurse, doctors must be convinced of their value and function with them as a team in preventive and curative work; they must also act as teachers and come to terms with any financial threat the nurses may pose. Other nurses and allied health workers will also need to change their traditional ideas and there must be a clearer definition of roles and lines of authority. For example, investigations and treatments that the PHC nurse can order must be clearly stated. Legislative changes are necessary to allow nurses to prescribe medicines appropriate to their function. Other legal problems involve the issuing of sick certificates, the present fragmentation of control of health service staff, and the questions of protection and professional indemnity. Despite these problems, the PHC nurse can help to overcome the under-utilization and maldistribution of health workers. (HH)

3272 **Bergman, R.** *Nursing education and the evolving role of the nurse.* Tokyo, International Hospital Federation Congress, May 1977. 11p. Engl.
22 refs.
International Hospital Federation Congress, Tokyo, Japan, May 1977.
See also entries 2133, 2176, 2189, 2357, and 2470 (volume 3).
The nurse's role in today's health care system ranges

from direct practitioner in nurse-rich countries to teacher-supervisor of auxiliaries in countries with limited health personnel. Three major trends in nursing have evolved: the expansion of the nurse's traditional role, more extensive use of auxiliaries, and the development of a new kind of health worker--the physician's assistant. Some of these trends are questionable, according to the author, who opposes WHO support of minimally prepared auxiliary workers as primary health care workers and of the physician's assistant, arguing that the role of nurses should be expanded rather than new categories of workers created. Nurses have already proven suitable for comprehensive curative and preventive health care, especially in pediatrics. Examples can be found in Israel's collective and border settlements, where nurses function unofficially as nurse practitioners and in outpatient clinics. The author points out that many interpersonal, legal, and administrative implications connected with the scope of nursing practice will have to be more clearly defined and formalized. The evolving role of nurses in developing countries, where the ratio of all nursing personnel to population may be as low as 1:15 000, also demands the reevaluation of the nurse's function and international responsibility to see that the nurse's abilities are utilized in the most efficient manner. (EE)

3273   **Educacion Medica y Salud, Washington, D.C.**
Informe del Comite del Programa de Libros de Texto de la OPS/OMS para la Ensenanza de Enfermeria en Salud Comunitaria. (Report of the PAHO/WHO Textbook Programme Committee for Teaching Community Health Nursing). Educacion Medica y Salud (Washington, D.C.), 10(4), 1976, 371-388. Span.
9 refs.
First Meeting of the PAHO/WHO Textbook Programme Committee for Teaching Community Health Nursing, Washington, D.C., 31 Jul-8 Aug 1975.
In 1975, the PAHO/WHO Textbook Programme Committee for Teaching Community Health Nursing met to analyze nursing education in view of the nurse's expanding role in community health activities, make recommendations for new curricula, and evaluate recently published nursing textbooks in English, Spanish, and Portuguese. Concepts such as community, human health, community health, prevention, and community health nursing are defined and present tendencies in health care and Latin American health needs are discussed. Present methods and principles for teaching community health nursing are presented side-by-side with suggestions for a better oriented approach. Finally, the function and characteristics of a textbook and possible reference sources for community health nursing are examined. (RMB)

3274   **Hamunen, M. WHO, Brazzaville.** *Development of health services in Botswana: public health nursing and MCH.* Brazzaville, WHO, 20 Dec 1974. 11p. Engl.
A WHO nurse reports on a project in Botswana, during which she was based at the Francistown clinic and trav-

eled to other clinics and a local hospital to assess family health care. She notes with satisfaction that nursing services in Botswana are well-organized and functioning efficiently, that public health is already a part of the nursing curriculum, and that the Francistown clinic enjoys full technical and monetary support. She recommends that the Francistown clinic begin to train personnel, that the MCH and family planning content of the nursing curriculum be strengthened with emphasis on practical work in rural areas, that short public health seminars be organized for nursing and midwifery staff, that a comprehensive course on family planning be formulated, that a special seminar on health education in venereal diseases be offered to nurses, and that a course on teaching hygiene and nutrition be given to all public school teachers. Short accounts of health resources and health problems in Botswana plus the programmes offered in the Francistown clinic are included. (HC)

3275   **Heese, H. de V. Ireland, J.D. McWilliams, D.M.**
Health care of children: the potential role of the paediatric nurse associate. South African Medical Journal (Cape Town), 48, 1974, 1752-1758. Engl.
Biennial Paediatric Congress of the South African Paediatric Association (MASA), Pretoria, South Africa, 3-5 Apr 1974.
In 1973, Capetown's Red Cross War Memorial Children's Hospital enrolled five nurses in a pilot training programme for pediatric nurse associates (PNAs) organized by a pediatrician. The students' qualifications included a suitable personality for handling children and their parents, the ability to work independently, and a diploma or experience in pediatric nursing. At the end of the 4-month course, the candidates had to pass written, clinical, and oral examinations; they then had an additional 4 months practice in the hospital before further assessment. The course trained the PNAs to recognize and assess symptoms associated with each body system, the common important childhood diseases and their complications, and everyday problems of child care. In addition, the PNA provides health education, counsels parents, diagnoses handicaps, and deals with nutrition, immunization, and the general and legal aspects of the care of children. As part of a team working under the supervision of a medical authority, these nurses must also carry out certain tests and necessary procedures, give emergency treatment, and decide whether referral is necessary. (HH)

3276   **International Labour Office, Geneva.** *Employment and conditions of work and life of nursing personnel.* Geneva, International Labour Office, 1976. 108p. Engl.
International Labour Conference, Geneva, Switzerland, 1976.
This report was prepared by the International Labour Office in collaboration with WHO for circulation amongst member states as a basis for debate at the 61st session of the International Labour Conference. Some of the factors that prompted consideration of the employment and conditions of work of nursing personnel were

that: the growth of health services in both developed and developing countries has resulted in an enormous demand for nurses; the role of the nurse has undergone profound changes and is becoming increasingly important and complex; in almost all countries, nursing personnel are inadequate in numbers and qualifications to satisfy even the modest aim of 1 nurse:5 000 people; and, in almost all countries, the prestige of the profession is declining. Studies have shown that the last is related to both the economic and social situation of nurses and to their morale and the general conditions of the profession. For this reason, the report focuses on international and national standards regarding: the exercise of the profession; temporary and part-time work; standard hours of work, rest, and annual leave; overtime and exacting and inconvenient work schedules; remuneration, benefits, and welfare facilities; safety and health protection; social security; and career possibilities. One hundred and sixty-two conclusions are appended. (HC)

3277 **Kettle, B.E.** *Report of a study tour to Far East countries: Singapore, Hong Kong, Malaysia: Peninsular Malaysia, Sabah, Sarawak.* n.p., n.d. lv.(various pagings). Engl.
  Unpublished document; inquiries may be directed to the author at 19 Forth Street, St. Monans, Fife, Scotland, KY10 2AU.

In 1974, the authors set out on a study tour of the Far East to find ways of ensuring that Asian candidates for nurse training in the UK are fully aware of the different types of training available and their significance in the context of their own countries, explore ways of improving screening and selecting procedures so as to reduce multiple applications for training places and resulting frustration to applicants, gain an insight into the cultural and professional life in the students' home countries, and assess the needs of the trainees within their own societies. This report is based on interviews with medical, nursing, and training staff and visits to health institutions, schools, and schools of nursing. Each country is treated separately and discussed with reference to its general background, general education, health services, nursing services, nursing education, post-basic nursing education, employment possibilities, and problems associated with recognition of credits and/or having been trained in a foreign country; appendices include the curricula, admission requirements, and application forms of a number of nursing colleges in Australia and Hong Kong and some information regarding Chinese and Malay names and forms of address. The author recommends that a central admission centre for all applicants for nurse training in the UK be set up, that a list of suitable schools of nursing be compiled and supplied to the various overseas British Council offices, that English proficiency be tested in the country of origin and that testing facilities be periodically evaluated, and that schools of nursing be advised regarding the orientation and guidance of overseas students. (HC)

3278 **Khita, M.B. Courtejoie, J. Rotsart de Hertaing, I.** Centre d'Etudes et de Recherches pour la Promotion de la Sante, Kangu-Mayumbe, Zaire.

Educateur sanitaire: l'infirmier ou l'enseignant peut-il devenir un bon educateur sanitaire? (Health educator: can the nurse or the teacher become a good health educator?). Kangu-Mayumbe, Zaire, Centre d'Etudes et de Recherches pour la Promotion de la Sante, Brochure Illustre No.27, n.d. 63p. Fren.
  See also entry 2804.

Rather than create a special cadre of health workers for health education, Zaire has chosen to train public health nurses and teachers as auxiliary health workers. During the 1st year of training, student nurses learn how to plan a health education programme, give demonstrations using slide equipment, and approach the two most serious health problems--malaria and intestinal parasites; during the 2nd year, they study pathology and public health and practice giving health education during under-five activities; and during the final year, they examine the actual state of public health in the country, conduct public health research, undertake health inspections, and chair group discussions. Student teachers follow a similar programme. The proper use of other brochures in this series, both during training and in the field, is also explained. (HC)

3279 **Kierzkowska, S. Beltzung, I.C. WHO, Brazzaville.** *Enseignement infirmier. (Nursing education).* Brazzaville, WHO, 31 Oct 1973. 10p. Fren.

The curricula and facilities of 12 schools for nurses and nurse auxiliaries in Zaire are briefly described and evaluated. The 3-year course for nurse auxiliaries comprises 1 year of basic training and 2 years in hospital work, midwifery, or public health. It is becoming apparent, however, that 1 year of basic training is insufficient preparation for either the midwifery or the public health specialty; auxiliaries are tending to take the hospital option and then specialize. This phenomenon illustrates the need to key curricula to the job rather than to the traditional role of the nurse auxiliary and this point figures highly among the recommendations. Other recommendations are that some general (academic) subjects be dropped in favour of technical ones and that, in view of the dearth of doctors in the rural areas of the country, the training of the nurse be modified to include diagnosis, treatment, and all kinds of prophylaxis. (HC)

3280 **League of Red Cross Societies, Geneva. Indonesian Red Cross, Jakarta.** *Red Cross nursing and its relevance to Asian communities.* Jakarta, Indonesian Red Cross Society, 1975. 152p. Engl.
  Asian Red Cross Nursing Seminar, Jakarta, Indonesia, 11-15 Aug 1975.

Representatives of the Red Cross societies of 12 Asian countries attended a 5-day seminar in Jakarta in August, 1975, sponsored jointly by the Indonesian Red Cross and the League of Red Cross Societies, to discuss the future of the Red Cross nursing programme in these countries. Specific topics covered were the role of nursing in urban slum and rural areas and in nutrition, family planning, disaster preparedness and relief, and drug abuse programmes. Each session was introduced by one or more technical papers. The delegates were divided into

IV Primary Health Manpower--Training and Utilization

117

two groups for discussion and the report summarizes their findings together with the plenary sessions that followed. The full text of the papers presented at each session is published in an annex. The report also includes transcripts of speeches by visiting dignitaries and lists the overall recommendations of the conference. Details of the programme, field visits, an evaluation questionnaire, and a glossary of terms used are also given. (DM)

3281   Lekgetha, A.N. *Comprehensive health care system in Boputhatswana.* South African Journal of Nursing (Pretoria, South Africa), 63(8), Aug 1976, 19-20. Engl.

The introduction of a government-initiated comprehensive health care scheme in the Bantu homeland of Boputhatswana, South Africa, has necessitated the redefinition of the functions of the members of the health team. The responsibilities of the medical officer, for example, now include organizing the delivery system, delegating appropriate tasks to other members of the team, conducting and supervising clinical sessions, training, research, and public relations. The nurse has been authorized to take on a role that is more demanding both from a technical and an administrative point of view; for example, the South African Nursing Council in 1974 authorized qualified nurse-midwives to perform episiotomies, sutures, and similar procedures if a physician is not available. The nurse in charge of a clinic is considered to be the leader of the health team at that level and, as such, must act in a capacity similar to that of the doctor in charge of the district. More and more, the nurse is coming to be regarded as the co-therapist, rather than the handmaid, of the doctor and, in view of the increasing demand for health services in the homelands, it is expected that this trend will continue. (HC)

3282   McIntosh, C.A. WHO, Brazzaville. *Development of health services (nursing); assignment report.* Brazzaville, WHO, 5 Aug 1974. 8p. Engl.

In 1968, WHO initiated a programme in Malawi to assist with the development of public health nursing services. This report considers progress in nurse training, which covers enrolled level community nurses and the Zomba School of Nursing, registered nurses and midwives, other training programmes, overseas training of public health nurses, and standards and controls. The administration of district hospitals, rural health centres, and the maternal child health mini-plan is discussed. Conclusions and recommendations are included. (RMB)

3283   Nursing Journal of India, New Delhi. *Rural centre at Chhawla: a report.* Nursing Journal of India (New Delhi), 68(4), Apr 1977, 106-107. Engl.

Since 1946, the rural health unit in Chhawla (India) has served as a training centre for a national nursing college and has emphasized to students the importance of adopting approaches, techniques, and procedures that are suited to rural resources and conditions. The unit's regular staff, which constitutes 1 lady health visitor and 2 midwives, is augmented by teaching staff from the

college and is supported by staff from its parent health centre, Najafgarh. At Chhawla, senior students of the bachelor's programme are provided opportunities for making health assessment and planning, organizing, and conducting health care activities; students in the master's programme perform activities designed to prepare them for leadership positions in the rural community health service; nurse-tutors gain experience in providing community health nursing services and planning, implementing, and organizing learning experiences in community health nursing; and tutors for auxiliary nurse-midwives undertake advanced midwifery training. At the same time, staff and students cooperate to provide the population with comprehensive health care by visiting homes, offering health education, etc; they also participate in national health programmes and train indigenous *dais* in the rudiments of hygienic delivery. (HC)

3284   Pakshong, D.I. *Role of the nurse in community health.* Nursing Journal of Singapore (Singapore), 17(1), May 1977, 25-27. Engl.

The role of the community nurse in Singapore is too narrow to serve community needs and should be revised. Traditionally, nurses have been trained as single-purpose workers to serve specific population groups (pregnant women, newborn babies, TB patients, etc.). Thus, they have at times duplicated each others' efforts and have been unable to appreciate global health problems. They should be trained to assume various community health functions and some activities traditionally performed by doctors. Some steps in this direction have already been taken: many nurses are qualified as state registered nurses, midwives, and health visitors and some have received additional training in family planning, nutrition, BCG vaccination, gynaecological examination, etc. A recent decision of the government should allow nurses to further consolidate their role: polyclinics offering outpatient, maternal and child health, psychiatric, and dental services are to be introduced and they will provide ample community practice opportunities for nurses. (HC)

3285   Rotsart de Hertaing, I. Courtejoie, J. Centre d'Etudes et de Recherches pour la Promotion de la Sante, Kangu-Mayumbe, Zaire. *Infirmier et la sante publique: notions de prophylaxie et de lutte contre les maladies sociales. (Nurse and public health: notes on prevention of and the fight against communicable diseases).* Kangu-Mayumbe, Zaire, Centre d'Etudes et de Recherches pour la Promotion de la Sante, Brochure Illustre No.28, n.d. 29p. Fren.

See also entry 2804.

This illustrated brochure covers the practice of community medicine, communicable diseases and their prevention, opportunities for educating the public in the prevention of communicable disease, and the planning of a public health programme. Useful educational material from the same series is indicated along with the appropriate topic. (HC)

3286 Schweser, H.O. Project HOPE, Washington, D.C. People-to-People Health Foundation, Inc., Washington, D.C. *Health education by nurses.* In Schweser, H.O., Manual for Community Health Education for the Caribbean, Washington, D.C., People-to-People Health Foundation, n.d., 39-42. Engl.
For complete document see entry 3371.

Nurses work in all areas where health education is provided and, because of the respect in which they are held, have endless opportunities for such activities. They can encourage the acceptance and training of traditional healers, who can contribute to the success of health programmes. They also have an important role to play in the recruitment, training, utilization, and promotion of auxiliaries. They can promote, in practical ways, health education in schools and hospitals and encourage nursing personnel to participate in community activities. Orienting nurses and other personnel toward health education, whether in nursing schools or by in-service training, is particularly important. The author recommends the incorporation of principles, methods, and media of health education into the curricula of schools of nursing. Health education courses should aim specifically to give students practice in the actual methods of teaching, including field work and the use of audiovisual materials. (HH)

3287 Steiner-Freud, J. *Education for ophthalmic nursing in developing countries.* Israel Journal of Medical Sciences (Jerusalem), 8(8-9), 1972, 1089-1091. Engl.
Causes and Prevention of Blindness, Jerusalem Seminar on the Prevention of Blindness, Jerusalem, Israel, 25-27 Aug 1971.

Whereas many countries are training paramedical personnel other than nurses to provide ophthalmic care, the nurse with a broad background in all branches of medicine is the most suitable trainee. She has already had some experience in an eye clinic, an eye department, and public health nursing. She needs postgraduate courses to enable her to organize patient care in all areas of ophthalmic nursing, give first aid, and teach and guide staff and community. She should receive basic training in her home country and do postgraduate study abroad. To support her practice and that of other professional personnel, auxiliaries are needed. They can be drawn from the local population. (EE)

IV.3 Primary Family Planning and Midwifery Care
IV.3.1 Professional

See also: 2841, 3048, 3200, 3391

3288 Larsen, J.V. Baker, S.S. Baker, R. *Midwifery nursing associate: an experiment in a rural obstetric unit.* South African Journal of Nursing (Pretoria, South Africa), 63(11), Nov 1976, 7-8. Engl.
The Charles Johnson Memorial Hospital, a mission-cum-government facility, now provides care for some 110 000 people in the South African homeland of Kwa Zulu. In order to ease the heavy obstetric burden on the hospital's doctors (3 of whom delivered 2 726 babies in 1975), a postgraduate course for midwives was devised. The 3-month course, which consisted of formal lectures, clinical instruction, and inservice training, was designed to enable the midwifery nursing associate, as this new professional is now called, to: assess the antenatal patient, who may be visiting the hospital for the first time; detect risk factors during both the history-taking and the physical examination of the patient; assess the suitability of inducing labour and whether induction need be performed under medical supervision; look after patients with certain risk factors such as alo-pelvic disproportion during labour; perform vacuum extraction if necessary; conduct lumbar punctures on newborns and set up intravenous infusion where necessary; and take greater responsibility for teaching pupil midwives. Midwifery nursing associates are deployed both in the hospital and its clinics; they are regularly monitored by the senior medical officers who insist that adequate notes be kept on every patient. An evaluation of the programme, conducted 7 months after its inception, revealed that extremely competent antenatal screening by the midwifery nursing associates has resulted in a gratifying reduction in the perinatal mortality rate (31.1:1 000 as compared to 37:1 000). An outline of the course syllabus is included. (HC)

3289 Sich, D. Hopper, R.T. *Integrated rural MCH/FP services and the role of the midwife: the Kang Wha Health Post Project example.* Yonsei, Korea, Yonsei College of Medicine, 1976. 35p. Engl.
See also entries 2357 (volume 4) and 3258.

Health centre midwives in the Kang Wha Health Post Project (Korea) are responsible not only for midwifery and antenatal and postnatal care but also for maternal child health care, family planning, and administrative and supervisory duties. Each midwife in turn is supervised by the county health administration and supported by 1 family health worker (FHW) in each local village and 2 multipurpose workers attached to the centre. Except when she is conducting deliveries, she holds regular clinics at the health centre and gives weekly training and advice to support staff. Every pregnant woman should be seen once during the 1st trimester and twice in the last 6 weeks and, as well as conducting physical examinations, the midwife should discuss and advise on home delivery preparations, child care, and subsequent family planning. Problem cases are seen and referred independently. The actual delivery is the midwife's highest priority and she must also examine mother and baby within 6 weeks of birth. The midwife's family planning duties include counselling, loop insertions, and assisting a physician at sterilization operations. She must also organize vaccination programmes, advise on child health problems, maintain records and supplies, prepare an annual report, and oversee peripheral MCH/FP programmes. Her workload theoretically seems too heavy, but the project is still in its early stages and the client response is not yet complete. Appendices on evaluation frameworks for maternity care, child care, and family planning are attached. (HH)

IV.3.2 Nonprofessional

See also: 2835, 3048, 3169, 3200, 3241, 3268, 3393, 3401, 3403

3290   Arias Huerta, J. Keller, A. *Partera empirica: colaboradora potencial del Programa Nacional de Salud Maternoinfantil y Planificacion Familiar? (Traditional midwife: potential collaborator in the National Maternal and Child Health and Family Planning Programme?).* Salud Publica de Mexico (Mexico City), 18(3), Sep-Oct 1976, 883-892. Span.

Sixty traditional midwives were interviewed in 1974 by two nurses as part of a preliminary survey for a Mexican government project to determine the feasibility of incorporating traditional practitioners into the rural health care system, particularly in the area of family planning. After studying the midwives' sociodemographic characteristics, the number of births they attended, and their ascertainable medical and family planning knowledge and activities, health authorities concluded that any training given to traditional birth attendants was bound to benefit the rural population, especially if training efforts were concentrated on younger, literate midwives, who tended to be the most active, most familiar with local health services and therefore more likely to refer complicated cases, and most familiar with and more likely to recommend contraceptive methods. This training should emphasize pregnancy detection and complications, antenatal care, basic delivery instruments and hygienic techniques, detection and treatment of delivery and placental complications, care of the newborn, postpartum care, and contraceptive measures. (RMB)

3291   Benedetti, W.L. Caldeyro-Barcia, R. Centro Latinoamericano de Perinatologia y Desarrollo Humano, Montevideo. Oficina Sanitaria Panamericana, Washington, D.C. *Cuidados perinatales en las areas rurales de America Latina con referencias a algunos otros paises desarrollados y en desarrollo: revision bibliografica. (Perinatal care in rural Latin America, with reference to some other developed and developing countries: bibliographic review).* Montevideo, Centro Latinamericano de Perinatologia y Desarrollo Humano, Publicacion Cientifica No.713, May 1977. 85p. Span. Refs.

The relative benefits of institutional versus home childbirth are discussed with reference to Latin America. The advocates of systematic institutional delivery for all women argue that safe home delivery can only be achieved under conditions of adequate nourishment and hygiene that are almost nonexistent in Latin America. They propose the development of a national network of regional hospitals, each serving 30 000-100 000 people. The proponents of home delivery maintain that hospital delivery is costly, disturbing to the mother, and frequently a source of infection. They argue that normal deliveries can be safely conducted in the home by traditional birth attendants who have received some training in aseptic technique. In order to shed more light on the question, this document reviews: the Latin American statistical data regarding maternal, perinatal, and infant mortality; the type of personnel who currently attend births; literature of the past 12 years relevant to prenatal and perinatal care; recent innovative maternal and child health programmes; and the results of two studies undertaken by the Latin American Centre of Perinatology and Human Development, Montevideo, Uruguay, aimed at simplifying perinatal care. (HC)

3292   Chowdhury, S. Chowdhury, Z. *Medical highlights: the role of midwives and paramedics in voluntary sterilization programs.* Dacca, Gonosthaya Kendra (People's Health Centre), n.d. 16p. Engl. 18 refs.

Experience in *Gonoshasthaya Kendra* (People's Health Centre), Bangladesh, indicates that traditional midwives (*dais*) and paramedicals can provide birth control and sterilization services similar to those available from fully trained physicians. From August 1974-January 1976, 744 tubectomies were carried out by paramedicals and 342 by doctors at *Gonoshasthaya Kendra*. The infection rate was 5.37% and 5.84% respectively and all cases were successfully treated. The paramedicals proved to be as technically competent as doctors for this work and have often been more acceptable to villagers. With the help of *dais*, they can provide essential postoperative care that has been lacking in mass sterilization camps. Through weekly 1-hour classes, the *dais* can also learn administration of oral and injectable contraceptives, immunization, prenatal care, nutrition, and hygiene; these lessons are based on visual aids and practical demonstrations. The training enables them to provide health education and encourage women to practice birth control or accept sterilization. (DM)

3293   Indonesia, Department of Health. National Family Planning Coordinating Board, Jakarta. Indonesian Planned Parenthood Association, Jakarta. University of Indonesia, Faculty of Social Sciences, Jakarta. University of Indonesia, Faculty of Public Health, Jakarta. *Role of the traditional midwife in the family planning programme: report of the National Workshop to Review Researches into Dukun Activities Related to MCH Care and Family Planning.* Jakarta, Department of Health, n.d. 83p. Engl. 27 refs.

National Workshop to Review Researches into Dukun Activities Related to MCH Care and Family Planning, Jakarta, Indonesia, 31 Jul-2 Aug 1972.

This report of an indonesian workshop on *dukun* (traditional birth attendant) activities discusses the role and status of the *dukun* in the community (including the ceremonies she performs), her attitudes toward family planning and traditional methods of birth control, current *dukun* training and how it might be improved, the relationship between *dukun*s and health and family planning workers, her performance as a family planning worker, and strategies for improving her participation in family planning campaigns. In general, it is agreed that *dukun*s are persons of influence within their communities, that they are capable of communicating with women, and that they are still needed in MCH, especially in rural areas. Although, on the basis of available evidence, they are unlikely to make a significant contribution to the family planning effort, their training should be continued to avoid incurring their opposition to it. A participants' questionnaire is appended. (HC)

3294 Kagimba, J. International Medical and Research Foundation, New York. *Community based maternal and child health/family planning educator: a key person in the Chogoria community health project.* New York, International Medical and Research Foundation, 1977. 6p. Engl.
International Medical and Research Foundation Symposium on the Community Health Worker, Warrenton, Va., 26-28 Oct 1977.
See also entries 3227, 3232, 3234, 3236, 3239, 3243, 3244, 3259, 3266, 3268, and 3398.
In 1973, Chogoria Hospital (Kenya) established a community health project to provide dispensaries within walking distance of each local village, home visits by health teams, immunization coverage for young children, and family planning services. A cadre of maternal and child health/family planning health educators, well-respected women with 6 years of education, was selected by village dispensary committees and trained for 3 months. Their tasks included recruiting and counselling candidates for family planning, supplying mechanical forms of contraception, screening children in households for signs of malnutrition, giving lessons in baby care and food preparation, and checking childrens' immunization records. By 1977, 30 health educators had graduated from their 6-part course, which involved both theoretical and practical training in family planning, child care, and communication techniques. Since their posting to village dispensary teams, the number of family planning acceptors increased to 20% of women of child bearing age (compared to 5% in the rest of Kenya). (CL)

3295 Lubis, F. Budiningsih, S. Borkent-Niehof, A. Djunaedi, P.A. Universitas Indonesia, Jakarta. *Family planning project, Serpong, Indonesia: report of the course for traditional midwives in the Kecamatan Serpong.* Jarkarta, Leyden State University, Universitas Indonesia, Serpong Paper No.14, Sep 1974. 36p. Engl.
As part of a family planning research and training scheme in Serpong, Indonesia, a 5-month course was offered to traditional midwives or *dukun*s; the organization, aims, content, and methods of the course are the subject of this report. The instructors were local Western-trained midwives and auxiliary midwives. They were urged to: choose simple words in explaining complex concepts; exhibit patience in their dealings with the illiterate, elderly traditional birth attendants; and

appreciate the experiences of the 56 trainees. The trainees were divided into four groups according to residence so that they could come to classes together and be easily supervised. Content of the course comprised principles of hygiene, basic anatomy of the uterus and the physiology of childbirth, procedures for assisting the mother during parturition, care of the newborn and new mother, nutrition, and birth control. Many of the abstract ideas were presented through models, demonstrations, and examples from the *dukun*s' experiences. The atmosphere during the course was relaxed and some events suggested that better cooperation between the health centre and the *dukun* had resulted. A glossary, bibliography, and two tests used during the course are appended. (AC)

3296 Nicholas, D.D. Ampofo, D.A. Ofosu-Amaah, S. Asante, R.O. Neumann, A.K. WHO, Geneva. *Attitudes and practices of traditional birth attendants in rural Ghana: implications for training in Africa.* Bulletin of the World Health Organization (Geneva), 54(3), 1976, 243-348. Engl.
A survey of characteristics, attitudes, and practices of traditional birth attendants (TBAs) was carried out in the Danfa Project area of rural Ghana. The typical TBA was an elderly illiterate housewife or farmer who practices midwifery part-time; 48% were men who often practiced herbalism as well. The TBAs usually gave correct or neutral advice and, although they delayed in referring some complications to hospital, most saw the benefits of rapid referral for serious problems. They were supportive of family planning and very interested in improving their skills. However, a number of factors must be considered in organizing training programmes. Special adult educational methods must be employed. To achieve adequate coverage one must train large numbers of TBAs, who perform an average of only seven deliveries per year and who are widely scattered in remote rural villages. This poses formidable problems, especially in transportation and follow-up supervision. Combining TBA training with other village health programmes or community development projects could provide a solution. (Author abstract.)

3297 Sekou, H. *Medecine traditionnelle et la pharmacopee africaine: experience nigerienne de cooperation avec les guerisseurs. (Traditional medicine and the African pharmacopoeia: the Nigerian experience in cooperating with traditional healers).* Medecine d'Afrique Noire (Paris), 24(7), 1977, 517-520. Fren.
In Niger, traditional birth attendants have been trained to recognize the signs of complicated pregnancy and conduct normal delivery in a hygienic manner. Upon completion of a 15-day course in the nearest dispensary or maternity ward, these women receive a midwifery kit and a notebook for recording each birth attended. Once on the job, they are supervised by the dispensary nurse, who visits them once a month and replenishes their midwifery kits. Similarly, other village volunteers have been trained through a 10-day course to dispense simple remedies from the village pharmacy, facilitate the evac-

IV Primary Health Manpower--Training and Utilization

uation of seriously-ill persons, encourage village hygiene, and enlist village cooperation in mass campaigns. These measures have resulted in better care for the neonate, earlier evacuation of cases of complications due to pregnancy, and local mangement of some 50% of common ailments. In this paper, the possibility of harnassing the potential of yet another village resource, the traditional healer, is discussed: the demonstrated potential of this practitioner in cases of certain mental and psychosomatic illnesses is recalled and the advantages of bringing his practice under some form of scientific guidance is pointed out. (HC)

3298   **Seoul National University, Seoul.** *Mothers' club activities.* In Chunseong Gun Community Health Program, Seoul, Seoul National University, School of Public Health, Jul 1975, 86-89. Engl.
For complete document see entry 3147.
The mothers' club project of the Chunseong Gun Community Health Program (Korea) is an attempt to provide inexpensive simple primary health care using community volunteers instead of professionals. The programme trains mothers' club leaders to collect information on vital statistics and disease incidence, provide contraceptives, and assist with childbirth and emergencies using specially developed home delivery, first aid, and medical care kits. Other duties are to provide a health education service for the community. In 1974, the 1st 102 mothers' clubs leaders received an initial 2-day training, to be followed up with training twice a year and regular visits and spot checks by planning committee members. In 1975, the necessary kits had still not been designed and a training manual was needed, as were special medical records and evaluation forms. Plans have been made to prepare health circulars on hygiene, family planning, sanitation, and food to be distributed to all mothers' clubs. (DM)

3299   **Thapa, R. Nepal, Ministry of Health.** *His Majesty's Government's model of integrated community health programme.* Kathmandu, Ministry of Health, Department of Health Services, Sep 1977. 14p. Engl.
16 refs.
National Conference on Primary Health Care, Kathmandu, Nepal, 19-23 Sep 1977.
Unpublished document.
The government of Nepal's model of an integrated community health programme, based on evaluated pilot projects in Bara and Kaski districts from 1972-1975, aims to provide cost-effective door-to-door health service coverage for a maximum number of the population. After 6 weeks in-service training, village health workers visit neighbouring homes to distribute pills and condoms and provide family planning information. They also carry out nutritional surveillance of under-fives, give health education to mothers and traditional birth attendants, and act as liaison community leaders. By 1977, there were 800 village health workers, each locally recruited and supervised by a senior auxiliary health worker or health assistant in an integrated health post, but there are shortages of supervisors and limited supplies of

medicines, equipment, and transport facilities. Other problems include a lack of local participation in constructing health posts. Nevertheless, the plan's targets for 1977-1978 include the establishment of 50 new health posts and the programme urges coodination between health services and other basic development activities such as social services, road construction, and food production. (CL)

IV.4 Primary Dental Care
IV.4.1 Professional

See also: 3381

3300   **Hobdell, M.H.** *Suggestions for the organization and teaching of a Tanzanian school of dentistry, University of Dar es Salaam.* London, London Hospital, Department of Community Dentistry, n.d. 11p. Engl.
Unpublished document.
A new system proposed for Tanzania is designed to train dental auxiliaries, practitioners, and specialists to function as part of a dental health team; the courses involve alternating periods at a projected school of dentistry and at a field service centre. At each stage of the training, students may remain in practical field work until there is sufficient demand for more highly qualified staff. In this way, training costs are spread over a long period, the supply of personnel at each level can rapidly be adjusted to meet new demands, theory and practice are closely linked, and the workers themselves are provided with a satisfying career structure. The system requires a Dental Public Health Service Centre located in a projected school of dentistry but associated with other university departments that carry out epidemiological surveys, monitor performance of trainees, and help design and modify the students' curricula. (DM)

3301   **Schweser, H.O. Project HOPE, Washington, D.C. People-to-People Health Foundation, Inc., Washington, D.C.** *Health education by dentists.* In Schweser, H.O., Manual for Community Health Education for the Caribbean, Washington, D.C., People-to-People Health Foundation, n.d., 33-38. Engl.
For complete document see entry 3371.
Preventive measures are the most effective means of reducing dental disease problems in the Caribbean to a manageable level and dentists have the major responsibility for providing information and encouraging people to seek dental care. Patients are more likely to respond if they believe that care will be relatively painless and beneficial to both their health and their appearance. To bring about this change in behaviour, dentists and other members of dental and health teams should take every opportunity to educate individual patients, expectant mothers, school children, and industrial groups. Dentists should also work with education departments to develop dental health programmes in schools, look for oral evidence of diseases such as diabetes and vitamin deficiencies, and discourage the sale of products that disguise oral problems. An informed populace can influence the

spending of public health funds and will be more inclined to accept the use of dental auxiliaries. Recommended improvements in the quality of existing services, the education of dentists, and the rate of recruitment include the promotion of more dental health education concepts in the curricula of dental schools and the encouragement of student participation in field work in schools and other places. (HH) Y030IV.4.2 Nonprofessional

IV.4.2 Nonprofessional

See also: 2822, 2844, 3300

3302   **Bezroukov, V.** *Dental education in the developing countries and the role of WHO.* International Dental Journal (Bristol, UK), 27(1), Mar 1977, 18-24. Engl.
        16 refs.
        See also entry 2822.
Since 1958, WHO has called for the training of dental auxiliaries in developing countries to alleviate the shortage of professional dental personnel and provide oral health care for the masses. The organization has identified two major categories of dental auxiliaries: operating and nonoperating technicians. The operating technician is a high level auxiliary whose 3-year training course promotes skills in undertaking oral health education, diagnosing dental problems, performing preventive and curative dental services, and overseeing patient records, dental supplies, equipment repairs, etc. This category of personnel is widely known as a dental therapist and has been introduced into many countries throughout the world. WHO has provided support in the form of seminars on dental personnel training and stressed that oral health personnel development should be part of any plan for oral health services. (AC)

3303   **Taljaard, I. T.** *Dental education in relation to the needs of the South African community.* International Dental Journal (Bristol, UK), 27(1), Mar 1977, 2-9. Engl.
The government of South Africa recently adopted a national dental health policy of complete coverage by community dental health services (educational, preventive, therapeutic, and ancillary). Because of the shortage of dentists, it was decided to train a special category of auxiliary, the dental therapist, to take on the simple clinical procedures that form the bulk of the dentist's everyday duties. The dental therapist will be a secondary school graduate with 3 years training to prepare him to perform dental examinations of patients, scale and polish teeth, repair damaged teeth with direct plastic fillings, extract teeth and treat common oral diseases, recognize and provide emergency treatment for serious oral disease and conditions to be referred to a dentist, practice preventive measures on an individual and community basis, and offer dental health education to individuals and groups of people. A maximum of 5 dental therapists will work under the supervision of 1 dentist, either in hospitals, satellite clinics, or schools. The first 13 dental therapists will graduate from the Ga-Rankuwa Hospital near Pretoria in 1977; these facilities are to be expanded and others opened once the authorities fully appreciate the advantages of the scheme. (HC)

IV.5 Primary Laboratory Care

See also: 2823, 3230, 3338, 3345

3304   **Golgov, G.P.** WHO, Brazzaville. *Epidemiological services.* Brazzaville, WHO, 9 Jul 1974. 69p. Engl.
A WHO microbiologist reports on his activities as part of a project for the development of health services in Uganda (September 1971-June 1974). The activities included: conducting a survey of existing laboratory services; advising the Ministry of Health on the development, organization, and coordination of these services; preparing programmes for, and participation in, the training and supervision of laboratory personnel; and assisting in the epidemiological surveillance and investigations currently underway in the country. A three-tiered division of laboratory services, to be administered from within the preventive sector of the Ministry of Health, is proposed; the function of each level within the service and the kind and numbers of personnel required by each are outlined in some detail. (HC)

3305   **Lowry, G.F.** *Special unit and medical school laboratory technicians in New Zealand: a follow-up review and survey of training and qualifications, 1970-1975.* New Zealand Medical Journal (Wellington), 85(579), 12 Jan 1977, 12-15. Engl.
A 1970 survey was undertaken to ascertain the training opportunities and career prospects of laboratory technicians in New Zealand. A 1975 follow-up survey reassessed the number of technicians employed, their qualifications, and training course preferences. The 2nd survey revealed that the number of departments undertaking laboratory investigation had increased from 26-49 and the number of technicians employed from 150-290. Heads of departments and senior staff responsible for employment have indicated a high degree of satisfaction with technical institute courses and the certification authority's qualifying system in the field of technician training. (Modified journal abstract.)

IV.6 Primary Environmental Health

See also: 3098, 3375

3306   **Evans, J.H. Dixon, E.J.** WHO, Brazzaville. *Development of basic health services (training of sanitation personnel).* Brazzaville, WHO, 24 Mar 1972. 9p. Engl.
A 3-year course for public health inspectors at a Sierra Leone school of hygiene offers 2 years of classwork and 1 year of practical experience in sea and airport sanitation, pest control, health education, meat and food hygiene, waste disposal, disease control, disposal of the dead, labour control, building construction, veterinary control of food animals, village sanitation, sanitation of diamond and iron ore mines, storekeeping, and office routine. Refresher courses are offered to public health inspectors who are not graduates of the school. The facilities, staff, finances, and student selection proce-

dures of the course are described and the author's recommendations for improving the programme are listed. (RMB)

3307 Schweser, H.O. Project HOPE, Washington, D.C. People-to-People Health Foundation, Inc., Washington, D.C. *Health education by public health inspectors.* In Schweser, H.O., Manual for Community Health Education for the Caribbean, Washington, D.C., People-to-People Health Foundation, n.d., 43-47. Engl.
For complete document see entry 3371.

Public health inspectors (PHIs) can encourage community participation in environmental health programmes by organizing local schemes for refuse collection and street cleaning, publicizing available services and their costs, and teaching about the relationship between environment and disease. To educate and win public support for improving the environment, PHIs can organize programmes on radio, television, and in the press and sponsor film and slide shows, posters, window displays, and educational leaflets. The support of religious leaders, trade unions, and other officials will also influence attitudes and behaviour. Sanitation committees, youth clubs, and other local groups can actively participate in clean-up campaigns. PHIs should also follow up environment-related diseases and collaborate with health programmes such as latrine construction and control of zoonoses. In addition, they can promote environmental education programmes in the educational system, assist with in-service courses for all health workers, and work for new laws and regulations if existing legislation is inadequate. (HH)

3308 Seoul National University, School of Public Health, Seoul. *Training activities.* In Chunseong Gun Community Health Program, Seoul, Seoul National University, School of Public Health, Jul 1975, 45-55. Engl.
For complete document see entry 3147.

Field training at the Chunseong Gun Community Health Centre is an essential part of the master's degree programme in public health (MPH) offered by Seoul National University (Korea). First-year students spend at least 1 year at the centre during which they take part in the routines and carry out household and sanitation surveys. They learn about the major rural health problems of the area and the organizations responsible for public health services and they gain practical experience in data collection, record-keeping, and health services planning. Their training programme is constantly under review and their views are an essential part of the evaluation. For example, as a result of student opinion, the field period is to be extended to 2 weeks in the 1st year. Second-year MPH students undertake research at the centre. Along with MPH candidates, 4th-year nursing students practice in the centre and 4th-year medical students will soon join them. (DM)

3309 WHO, Brazzaville. *Deuxieme Reunion des Enseignants des Sciences de la Sante (Sciences de l'Environnement). (Second Meeting of Teachers of Health/Environmental Sciences).* Brazzaville, WHO, 2 Jul 1975. 68p. Fren.
Deuxieme Reunion des Enseignants des Sciences de la Sante (Sciences de l'Environnement), Brazzaville, Congo, 2 Jul 1975.
Also published in English.

Because the relationship between disease and insanitary conditions in Africa make it imperative that both health and environmental personnel know something of each other's disciplines, a meeting was convened to discuss ways and means of reinforcing the health content in the training programmes of environmental specialists and the environmental content in health manpower curricula. Among the means suggested were: creating a department of the environment within existing schools of health science, creating a department of sanitary engineering distinct from the department of civil engineering, and making some courses in sanitary engineering compulsory for civil engineers. It is noted that, although most countries presently offer programmes in sanitary engineering, it is not a popular profession due to its lack of advancement opportunities and its underutilization by the ministries concerned. Recommendations for action at the institutional, national, and international level stress the need to adapt training programmes to the specific needs of each country. (HC)

IV.7 Teaching Aids
IV.7.1 Rural Health Care

See also: 2821, 3144, 3172, 3174, 3188, 3273, 3484

3310 ACTION, Peace Corps, Washington, D.C. *Combatting Hansen's disease.* Washington, D.C., ACTION, Peace Corps, Jun 1976. 361p. Engl.

Based on field notes of Peace Corps volunteers, this book is an attempt to provide the foreign health worker in Korea with training and reference materials on Hansen's disease, or leprosy, in that country. The book treats: physiology of the skin, nerves, muscle, bones, joints, and eye; the induction and expression of the immune response and immunologic findings regarding leprosy; epidemiology of leprosy; classification, clinical course, and complications of leprosy; leprosy as a public health problem; leprosy-specific health education in Korea; methods of casefinding; diagnosis of leprosy--cardinal signs, symptoms, and examination and testing; patient management; cooperating institutions; and planning a leprosy control programme. (HC)

3311 Ajayi, V. *Guide to good health: a manual for rural workers.* Benin City, Nigeria, Ethiope Publishing House, 1975. 65p. Engl.

Intended for persons posted to rural areas in Nigeria, this manual discusses natural and acquired immunity, disease vectors and communicable diseases, and hygiene. The objective is to provide enough information about the spread and prevention of illness to preserve the good health of the reader. The explanations are simple and straightforward, but the language is sophisticated. Several nutritious recipes are included and a list of first aid gear is presented. (AC)

3312   Allard, H. Beaulieu, M. Collette, F. Cossette, G. Fortin, R. M'Vogo, R.B. **Cooperation Canada/ Tunisienne, Tunis.** *Manuel de pediatrie et soins. (Child welfare manual).* Montreal, Que., Hopital Sainte-Justine, Directeur des Projets Medicaux Canadiens en Tunisie, 1974. 779p. Fren. 15 refs.

This training manual-cum-handbook was compiled for the use of nurses specializing in pediatrics in Tunisia. Part 1 deals with prematurity, obstetric trauma, jaundice in the newborn, infections in the newborn, and congenital malformation and the physiology of digestion, digestive problems, dehydration and rehydration, and malnutrition. Definitions, descriptions, and procedures are set forward in point form. The 2nd part treats: pathology of the respiratory and nervous systems and the urinary tract; dermatology; pathology and trauma of the skeletal system; disorders of the blood, endocrine system, and connective tissues; parasitic diseases; and pediatric emergencies. The definition, etiology, symptoms, diagnosis, treatment, and possible complications of each condition are presented in a clear, concise manner. (HC)

3313   Arango G., J. Velez Gil, A. **Universidad del Valle, Division de Salud, Cali, Colombia.** *Instruccion programada: primeros auxilios en quemaduras: auxiliar de enfermeria. (Programmed instruction for auxiliary health workers: first aid for burns).* Cali, Colombia, Universidad del Valle, n.d. 16p. Span.

See also entries 1939-1947, 1961-1963 (volume 3), 3364, 3366, 3367, 3368, and 3369.

This unit in the programmed instruction series is designed to teach Colombian health auxiliaries: the differences between 1st-, 2nd-, and 3rd-degree burns; the proper treatment for each type; prohibited procedures; the diagnosis and management of shock; and advice to give parents in order to avoid household burns. Illustrations are included and each concept within the manual is presented in a number of fill-in-the-blank statements that the student is expected to complete correctly. (RMB)

3314   Brown, J.E. Brown, R.C. **Institut Medical Chretien du Kananga, Kananga, Zaire.** *Manuel pour la lutte contre la malnutrition des enfants: un guide pratique au niveau de la communaute. (Manual for the fight against childhood malnutrition: a practical guide for use at the community level).* Atlanta, Ga., Task Force on World Hunger, 1977. 123p. Fren.

This handbook for health workers in Zaire and the developing countries explains, in simple language, how to make use of sampling techniques and anthropometric measurements to determine the frequency of protein-calorie malnutrition in a community, discover the causes of protein calorie malnutrition through observation and the administration of a questionnaire, organize a nutrition education programme, and organize a nutrition rehabilitation centre. The nutrition education programme consists of an intensive, 2-3-month campaign during which a health worker residing in a

village monitors the weight of children at-risk from malnutrition and instructs their parents in food values, menu preparation, and cooking. The nutrition rehabilitation centre is a permanent feature associated with a hospital or a dispensary that offers treatment for severely malnourished children and nutrition instruction for their parents. The equipment, staff, budgeting, and administration of both the nutrition education programme and the nutrition rehabilitation centre are covered and some suggestions regarding teaching methodology are given. Additional information--how to take arm circumference measurement, how to judge the age of a child, menus and recipes, a sample schedule of discussions and demonstrations, sample health records and weight chart, etc.--is set forward in the appendix. (HC)

3315   Burgess, H.J. Burgess, A. *Field worker's guide to a nutritional status survey.* American Journal of Clinical Nutrition (Bethesda, Md.), 28(11), Nov 1975, 1299-1321. Engl.

This guide for conducting and analyzing a nutritional status survey of young children has been prepared specifically for health workers in developing countries who have little experience of survey methodology and no outside help. All or only portions of the guide may be used as local needs dictate. It provides an outline of necessary preparations, sampling, field organization, measuring techniques, and a recording form. To aid the statistical treatment and presentation of the data, a sample recording form is given together with coding instructions and output table layout. (RMB)

3316   Camel V., F. *Estadistica medica y de salud publica. (Medical and public health statistics).* Merida, Venezuela, Universidad de los Andes, 1970. 528p. Span. 45 refs.

Part 1 of this statistics handbook deals with research methodologies for planning medical research projects, collecting information, compensating for statistical error, selecting a sample population, and designing questionnaires. Detailed instructions are given for the processing and classification of information and the construction of graphs and tables. Methods for both descriptive and comparative analyses of data are presented. In Part 2, the author discusses the uses of public health statistics on demography, birth rates, mortality, morbidity, and resources and services. Part 3 deals with the three stages of public health programming. Copious statistical data are included. (RMB)

3317   **Cooperation Canada/Tunisienne, Tunis.** *Manuel de techniques pediatriques. (Manual of pediatric techniques).* Montreal, Que., Hopital Sainte-Justine, Directeur des Projets Medicaux Canadiens en Tunisie, Sep 1973. 139p. Fren.

This training manual-cum-handbook for pediatric nurses in Tunisia covers: hospital admission and discharge procedures; the measurement of vital signs (weight, height, temperature, blood pressure, etc.); bathing, carrying, and positioning the child for various procedures; X-ray; specimen collection; injection; perfusion and transfusion; oral and rectal administration of medicines and dosages; irrigation and drainings; ear, nose, throat, eye, and skin care; oxygen therapy; quarantine; special formulae (infant feeding); care of the newborn; care of the premature infant; infant resuscitation; tests and injections for diabetes; and surgical dressing. Procedures are illustrated by means of line drawings where necessary. (HC)

3318   Cooperation Canada/Tunisienne, Tunis. *Manuel de puericulture. (Child care manual).* Montreal, Que., Hopital Sainte-Justine, Directeur des Projets Medicaux Canadiens en Tunisie, 1973. 133p. Fren.
15 refs.

This training manual-cum-handbook compiled for pediatric nurses in Tunisia constitutes a guide to the development and care of the child from conception to adolescence. Topics covered include foetal growth and development, examination and care of the newborn, infant feeding, prevention of nutritional deficiencies (especially during weaning), accidents, physical and psychomotor development during each stage of childhood, and the physiological and psychological characteristics of puberty. Growth charts, diagrams of bodily proportions, and illustrations of motor development are appended. (HC)

3319   Courtejoie, J. Rotsart de Hertaing, I. Bureau d'Etudes et de Recherches pour la Promotion de la Sante, Kangu-Mayumbe, Zaire. *Petit aide-memoire therapeutique pour le dispensaire; quelques medicaments courants et leurs usages. 4 edition. (Therapeutic pocket-book for the dispensary; some common medicines and their usage. 4 edition).* Kangu-Mayumbe, Zaire, Bureau d'Etudes et de Recherches pour la Promotion de la Sante, Aug 1972. 103p. Fren.
See also entry 2804.

This short handbook covers some 80 antibiotics, diarrhea and malaria treatments, vermifuges and anthelmintics, local anaesthetics, sedatives, analgesics, muscle relaxants, heart medicines, diuretics, food supplements, expectorants, antacids, laxatives, urinary disinfectants, vitamins, insecticides, antiseptics, and uterine-contracting drugs commonly available at dispensaries in Zaire. Each drug is described; brand names are listed; instructions, dosages, possible side effects, indications, and contraindications are given; and remarks concerning additional treatment are noted. (RMB)

3320   Courtejoie, J. Rotsart de Hertaing, I. Bureau d'Etudes et de Recherches pour la Promotion de la Sante, Kangu-Mayumbe, Zaire. *Vers un eclairage nouveau de quelques problemes de sante: l'attitude des techniciens de la sante en face de leurs nouvelles responsabilites. 2 edition. (Towards a new light on some old health problems: the attitude of health technicians toward their new responsibilities. 2 edition).* Kangu-Mayumbe, Zaire, Bureau d'Etudes et de Recherches pour la Promotion de la Sante,

Brochure Illustre No.3, n.d. 27p. Fren.
See also entry 2804.

How to help health workers in Zaire adapt to new health technologies and the increasing emphasis on preventive medicine is the subject of this illustrated health education brochure. A checklist of medical priorities is presented with a questionnaire designed to help health workers establish which priorities are the most vital in their own communities. The questionnaire helps health workers to examine their attitude towards their role within the community and their understanding of their community's background and needs. (RMB)

3321   Dilamutung-a-Ngya, D. Rotsart de Hertaing, I. Courtejoie, J. Centre d'Etudes et de Recherches pour la Promotion de la Sante, Kangu-Mayumbe, Zaire. *Medicaments a la maison: quelques informations sur la pharmacie familiale et son usage. 2 edition. (Household medicines: notes on the home pharmacy and its use. 2 edition).* Kangu-Mayumbe, Zaire, Centre d'Etudes et de Recherches pour la Promotion de la Sante, Brochure Illustre No.15, n.d. 27p. Fren.
See also entry 2804.

This brochure for parents and health educators contains a list of common, safe, easily stored and administered drugs to be included in home pharmacies along with their principal indications, the form in which they are available, and their dosages for children and adults. Each drug is introduced to parents during sessions of an under-fives' clinic and accompanied by written instructions regarding its use, dosage, contraindications, etc., in both French and the local language. (HC)

3322   Essex, B.J. *Approach to rapid problem solving in clinical medicine.* British Medical Journal (London), 3(5974), Jul 1975, 34-36. Engl.

Flow charts based on specific symptoms provide a method of diagnosis that is accurate, repeatable, and rapid and requires only history-taking and clinical examination. Fifty-two of these diagnostic pathways, incorporating 130 common diseases of Tanzania, were constructed at the University of Dar-es-Salaam, primarily for use by health auxiliaries. They are region-specific and may not be applicable to areas with a different disease pattern. The charts were tested by a medical student on a sample of 1 249 hospital patients. In 94% of the cases, the results were in agreement with those of conventional examination by a doctor, but use of the charts reduced the time required to reach a diagnosis from an average of 13.7 minutes per patient to 1.9 minutes. Further trials carried out by rural medical aide students not only confirmed the speed and repeatability of this method but improved the students' accuracy from 70% by conventional techniques to 98%. Included in the charts are instructions for treatment or referral procedures so that the whole system of primary care can be speeded and standardized. (DM)

3323   Fountain, D.E. Johnson, R. *Infirmier: comment fair votre diagnostic. (Diagnoses for nurses).* Kinshasa, Societe Missionnaire St. Paul, 1975.

183p. Fren.

See also entry 570 (volume 1).

This detailed, comprehensive guide to diagnosis is intended as a textbook and an on-the-job reference tool for nurses working in rural health centres in Zaire. It presents the techniques involved in diagnosis, history-taking, physical examinations (male, female, and child), and laboratory tests. Information is presented in a simple, readable manner and many of the techniques and symptoms mentioned are illustrated by means of photographs. Each chapter is followed by a list of study questions and an extensive glossary of terms is appended. (HC)

3324   Ghosh, S. *Feeding and care of infants and young children.* New Delhi, Voluntary Health Association of India, 1977. 123p. Engl., Hindi.

22 refs.

First edition of this document published by UNICEF, SCAR, New Delhi, 1976.

This illustrated handbook, an adaptation of a UN Protein Advisory Group manual, provides practical information for doctors, nurses, auxiliary nurses, midwives, home economists, and those training village level workers in India about nutrition and nutritional disorders in infants, young children, and mothers. Three chapters covering maternal nutrition, anthropometric assessment of growth and nutrition in infancy and childhood, and the nutritional needs of children lead to 5 chapters concerned with feeding and food, including breast-feeding, weaning, substitutes for breast milk, and classification and processing of foods commonly grown and prepared in India. As the utilization of food by children is often severely impaired by infection and consequent malnutrition, the next 4 chapters deal with the major causes of morbidity and mortality, protein calorie malnutrition, deficiency diseases, and infections. Immunization against infections such as smallpox, typhoid, measles, etc., is covered in the next chapter and the features of effective under-fives' clinics and health and nutrition education programmes are described. A series of 8 appendices includes useful reference material on recommended food intakes at different ages, anthropometric standards, nutrient composition of foodstuffs, weaning foods, and measures. (CL)

3325   Godwin, P. *Language controls in writing for health workers.* Surabaya, Indonesia, Lembaga Kesehata Nasional, Jalan Inderapura, Mar 1973. 9p. Engl.

8 refs.

Unpublished document.

It is essential that the language of all literature for health workers be graded and controlled to ensure easy comprehension, especially when the material is not written in the mother tongue. To simplify English for this purpose, the author makes these suggestions: sentences should be kept short with few subordinate clauses, affirmative statements are usually easier to understand than negative ones, and the active voice is preferable to the passive. Outline form is a useful means of communicating concentrated information with few words. All nonessential discussions should be discarded, leaving only simple standardized sentence patterns, questions, and instructions. Although simplified English may be satisfactory for some health materials, in Indonesia and in many other countries, such literature should be translated into the vernacular wherever possible. These recommendations were made as part of an enquiry into the problems of language comprehension designed to assist translation for Indonesian health workers. A series of tests were carried out on a range of professional and nonprofessional health personnel to determine the readability of several medical books in English and Indonesian. A high proportion of testees needed help with their reading in both languages, but the results clearly showed the value of simplified versions to aid comprehension. (DM)

3326   Guilbert, J.J. WHO, Geneva. *Educational handbook for health personnel.* Geneva, WHO, Offset Publication No.35, 1977. 1v.(various pagings). Engl.

Also published in French as: *Guide pedagogique pour les personnels de sante.*

Guidelines for planning educational programmes for medical students are presented. They cover steps for setting educational objectives, concepts of teaching and learning, advantages and drawbacks of various teaching techniques, principles of evaluation, methods of testing, and design of an educational workshop. They were originally compiled from documents distributed at a workshop sponsored by the WHO African Region in 1969 and have since been revised based on comments from users. They are set forth in an unusual format that does not exploit traditional reading patterns or layout procedures. The end-product, as the author explains, "may irritate you and complicate your work until you get get used to" it. The author's objectives in book design are obscure, although they may be to emphasize the importance of setting educational objectives. In the author's words, "there must be a reason for it...even if I do not know it..." The text is interspersed with diagrams, charts, etc., that may be easily transferred to transparencies and a glossary and bibliography are included. (AC)

3327   Handa, B.K. *Rural latrines.* Nagpur, India, National Environmental Engineering Research Institute, 1976. 8p. Engl.

The hand-flushed, water-sealed, dug well latrine is advocated as the most suitable privy for rural villages in India for these reasons: it has a relatively large capacity, it is permanently placed, it is odourless and does not attract flies, it is inexpensive in comparison to a water closet, and its construction does not require any special equipment. The latrine consists of a brick shelter, a cement mosaic finish pan, a trap with a half-inch water seal, a connecting pipe, and a soakage pit; when the toilet is flushed, water and sewage drop into the soakage pit where the water is soaked into the soil and the sewage is digested anaerobically to become a rich humus. This illustrated booklet contains detailed instructions for constructing the latrine, an estimate of the cost of building latrines for family and school use, and advice regarding the required distance between latrine and well under various soil

IV Primary Health Manpower--Training and Utilization

conditions. (HC)

3328   Hay, R.W. Whitehead, R.G. Uganda, National Food and Nutrition Council. Medical Research Council, Kampala. *Therapy of the severely malnourished child: a practical manual.* Kampala, Medical Research Council, Child Nutrition Unit, 1976. 55p. Engl.
Available from TALC, Institute of Child Health, London.

This practical manual, primarily for use in Uganda, describes the special treatments and diets used for severely malnourished children in the Mulago Hospital Nutrition Ward, which operates in close collaboration with the Mwanamugimu Nutrition Rehabilitation Unit. The manual is divided into 9 chapters, interspersed with 9 "action sheets" that give simplified schemes of treatment for use in remote areas. The 1st 2 action sheets, concerning the establishment of a basic nutrition service, are followed by a chapter of text describing the general plan of the Mulago nutrition services and criteria for admission to the nutrition ward. Another action sheet summarizing the treatments appropriate to a range of malnourishment symptoms precedes a chapter on the care and recovery of the severely malnourished child and the preparation and administration of the special diets used at Mulago. Ingredients of one such diet are listed in action sheet 4 and sheets 5-8 give tables for calculation of the diet amount needed by a large weight range of children. Successive chapters deal with nursing severely malnourished children and assessing their recovery by weight curves and clinical factors, hospital medical care of malnourished children, and laboratory techniques such as detection of low serum albumin levels in malnourished children. Nutrition education for mothers of these children is described and a few final sentences cover post-therapy follow-up at a separate clinic. (CL)

3329   Hopwood, B.E. Lovel, H.J. Commonwealth Secretariat, London. *Wallo exercise: planning for rural health services in Africa.* London, Commonwealth Secretariat, 1975. 2v.(various pagings). Engl.

A hypothetical rural area in a typical African country is the context for an exercise in practical health planning designed for medical staff who may be involved in health services administration. Participants are expected to organize themselves into syndicates and produce proposals for the arrangement and distribution of health facilities, number and functions of staff, and methods for measuring the effectiveness of services. Data is given on the geography, demography, culture, economics, and communications of the imaginary Wallo area; also available are background data on the country including GNP per capita, salary scales, building costs, and drug prices and a report on health problems observed at a hypothetical dispensary. In addition to these background details, the participants' manual offers advice on how to run a syndicate, reach group decisions, and write a report. Further instructions for carrying out the exercise, including a breakdown of component sessions with recommended time allocation for each, are provided in the organizers'

manual, together with a comprehensive set of checklists of the factors that should be considered by the syndicates at each stage of planning and suggestions for evaluation. (DM)

3330   Houle, C.O. *Design of education. 1 edition.* San Francisco, Cal., Jossey-Bass, 1972. 323p. Engl.
A system of adult education that forms the heart of this book follows these steps: identifying a possible educational activity, deciding to undertake it, defining the objectives, designing a suitable format, applying the format to real life, putting the plan into action, measuring outcomes, and reappraising design. The steps, which incorporate a wide range of educational theories and practices, may be undertaken by an individual, group, or institution to cater to the educational needs of an individual, group, or mass audience. Specific examples of the system are presented corresponding to different combinations of teacher and student. A glossary and a bibliographic essay are included and subject and author indexes are provided. (AC)

3331   Hultberg, B. Longa, I. Lundin, B. Rau, B. *Manual for public health workers in Zambia.* Lusaka, Ministry of Health, n.d. 1v.(various pagings). Engl.

This manual was used in the 1st district public health coordinator training course for Zambian medical assistants. The 1-year course emphasizes the social, economic, political, and cultural environment of Zambia and the preventive approach to public health work in general and maternal and child health activities in particular. The manual covers: the calculation of vital statistics; epidemiology and related terminology; the causes, treatment, and prevention of infections that are acquired through the gastrointestinal tract, the skin and mucous membranes, and the respiratory tract; insect-borne infections (especially malaria); notifiable diseases; immunization schedules; antenatal, postnatal, and well-baby clinics; recommended midwifery procedures in the absence of a medical officer; staff relations; home visiting; the principles of health education; and some basic historical, economic, and sociological factors affecting health in Zambia today. Sample Ministry of Health reporting forms are included as required. (HC)

3332   John E. Fogarty International Center for Advanced Study in the Health Sciences, Bethesda, Md. USA, Department of Health, Education, and Welfare. *Barefoot doctor's manual.* Bethesda, Md., John E. Fogarty International Center for Advanced Study in the Health Sciences, 1974. 974p. Engl., Chinese.
Published in Chinese by the Institute of Traditional Chinese Medicine of Hunan Province, Sep 1970.

This manual-cum-handbook focuses on the improvement of medical and health care facilities in Hunan province's rural villages by means of local adaptation to meet the working needs of barefoot doctors. Separate chapters cover the human body, hygiene, diagnostic techniques, therapeutic techniques, birth control planning, diagnosis and treatment of common disorders, and Chinese medicinal plants. The manual's purpose is to integrate Western medicine with traditional Chinese medicine, prevention with treatment, and symptoms with disease. In the section on treatment, Chinese herbs and new therapeutic techniques are emphasized, along with the selective use of Western medicines, and acupuncture techniques are described in detail. The 7th chapter lists 522 medicinal herbs seen in Hunan province (with 338 illustrations) and offers several hundred tried and tested prescriptions based on their effectiveness, popular use, ease of preparation, and economy. There are numerous illustrations throughout the book, many labeled in Chinese and English, and charts are used extensively. Mass promotion of health is emphasized. (CL)

3333   **Laugesen, H. Voluntary Health Association of India, New Delhi.** *Better child care.* New Delhi, Voluntary Health Association of India, 1977. 48p. Engl.
See also entries 2821 and 3484.
This audiovisual teaching aid for health workers, produced in English and 14 Indian languages, contains a series of 50 pretested photographs of village women, children, and babies for use in child health education at the village level. Below each photograph are 50-100 words of text in clear, simple language. These pictures, in both black and white and colour, illustrate 12 simple rules for better child care. For example, one photograph shows a mother feeding supplementary soft foods to her 4-month-old child and another shows a mother washing her hands before preparing food. Photographs that assist in the diagnosis of malnutrition, anaemia, and vitamin A deficiency are included. The booklet's small size and plastic cover make it especially suitable for field use. A 2nd edition contains 4 extra pages explaining its use as a basic text for pamphlets, posters, and health talks as well as a visual and memory aid. (CL)

3334   **Lelo di Kimbi Kiaku, N.M. Rotsart de Hertaing, I. Courtejoie, J. Centre d'Etudes et de Recherches pour la Promotion de la Sante, Kangu-Mayumbe, Zaire.** *Vers intestinaux a l'ecole: prise de conscience du probleme par la jeunesse. (Intestinal parasites in schoolchildren: making children aware of the problem).* Kangu-Mayumbe, Zaire, Centre d'Etudes et de Recherches pour la Promotion de la Sante, Brochure Illustre No.6, n.d. 51p. Fren.
16 refs.
See also entry 2804.
In view of the prevalence of intestinal parasites among schoolchildren in Zaire, the government has produced a brochure on the nature and management of the problem in the schools. The brochure covers traditional and current beliefs regarding intestinal worms, various species of worms, the medicines available for treating each species and their relative costs, techniques for making health education lively and interesting for the students, and some studies on the effectiveness of health education on health behaviour and health status. The recom-

mended method of managing intestinal parasites consists of mass administration of an all-purpose worm medicine 3 times a year plus a vigourous campaign to elevate the level of hygiene in the school environment and increase the students' awareness of the problem and its prevention. Student participation in all phases of the campaign is encouraged. (HC)

3335   **Lelo di Kimbi Kiaku, N.M. Rotsart de Hertaing, I. Courtejoie, J. Centre d'Etudes et de Recherches pour la Promotion de la Sante, Kangu-Mayumbe, Zaire.** *On ne trouve rien au dispensaire...et pourtant, je suis malade. Quelques informations sur les maladies psychosomatiques. (They find nothing wrong with me at the dispensary...and yet I am sick. Some information on psychosomatic illnesses).* Kangu-Mayumbe, Zaire, Centre d'Etudes et de Recherches pour la Promotion de la Sante, Brochure Illustre No.16, n.d. 41p. Fren.
10 refs.
See also entry 2804.
Psychosomatic illness is frequently encountered in Zaire, especially among young people. The condition consists of a set of non-specific, or even specific, symptoms for which no organic cause can be ascertained; its origin is some anxiety-producing notion or circumstance such as fear of the supernatural, fear of cultural change, or problems of a financial, sexual, etc., nature. This booklet tells the health worker or the teacher how to recognize, understand, and manage psychosomatic illness. Treating patients by allowing them to talk out their problems is recommended. (HC)

3336   **Lund, J.** *Foundation for Teaching Aids at Low Cost, Institute of Child Health, 30 Guilford Street London WC1N 1EH.* Journal of Tropical Medicine and Hygiene (London), 80(4), Apr 1977, 88. Engl.
The Foundation for Teaching Aids at Low Cost (TALC) offers more than 40 sets of modestly priced film slides with scripts on the causes and treatment of childhood problems prevalent in the Third World. Subject scope ranges from nutrition, skin diseases, and child development through Burkitt's lymphoma, *cancrum oris,* measles, etc., to contraceptive devices, mental retardation, and communication and management. The slides are only part of the foundations' wares; it also provides weight charts (for overseeing child growth), inexpensive books, and free leaflets on current problems, such as bottle-feeding infants. Further information may be obtained by writing to the information and publicity office of TALC, c/o Institute of Child Health, 30 Guilford Street, London WC1N 1EH. (HC)

3337   **ma Yimbu Aliendihata, T.M. Rotsart de Hertaing, I. Courtejoie, J. Centre d'Etudes et de Recherches pour la Promotion de la Sante, Kangu-Mayumbe, Zaire.** *Infirmier face au malade: comment favoriser la guerison par un contact authentique. (Nurse-patient relationship: how to foster cure through direct contact).* Kangu-Mayumbe, Zaire, Centre d'Etudes et de Recherches pour la

Promotion de la Sante, Brochure Illustre No.30, n.d. 45p. Fren.

8 refs.

See also entry 2804.

This illustrated brochure can assist in the teaching of psychology, pedagogy, and African sociology. The 1st part is concerned with the nurse-patient relationship in general and covers: the rights of the individual, well or ill; the sick individual's perception of himself; the traditional explanation of disease; the traditional response of the sick person *vis-a-vis* the health worker; the phenomenon of transfer (of the patient's emotions onto the nurse); and the qualities of the good nurse. The 2nd part treats mental illness: the Freudian explanation of personality; the definition, cause, and various manifestations of neurosis; the psychological anamnesis; the traditional nomenclature, explanation, and treatment of mental illness; and the treatment of mental illness in the African *milieu*. The importance of treating the patient as part of a family, and not just as an individual, is stressed. (HC)

3338   Madeley, C.R. WHO, Geneva. *Guide to the collection and transport of virological specimens (including chlamydial and rickettsial specimens).* Geneva, WHO, 1977. 40p. Engl.

This booklet is intended to provide laboratories with a basis for developing their own guides to the collection and transport of virological specimens under local conditions. The book is divided into two parts, the 1st dealing with the handling of specimens taken from the patient for primary diagnosis and the 2nd with the processes involved in the exchange of specimens between laboratories. The 1st part covers these topics: the contexts in which the laboratory's resources are best applied--to detect the presence of viruses in the community, investigate the ecology and method of spread of a virus, evaluate levels of immunity in a community, answer specific questions regarding individual patients, etc.; general criteria regarding the choice of specimen and the time and method of collection; general principles regarding the transport (choice of container, temperature, etc.) of various kinds of specimens (blood and serum, cerebrospinal fluid, and smears); information that should accompany the specimen; information that should be labelled on the specimen; ensuring the safety of those handling the specimen, either in transit or in the laboratory; and special considerations for non-viruses that are traditionally handled in virus laboratories (chlamydiae, rickettsiae, and mycoplasmas). The 2nd part discusses the circumstances that may occasion an exchange of specimens between laboratories and the peculiar considerations regarding the preparation, packaging, labeling, and transport of specimens that a longer journey and, possibly, a more virulent content will entail. Formulae for transport media for virus specimens and chlamydiae are appended. (HC)

3339   McLaren, D.S. *Nutrition in the community.* London, John Wiley and Sons, 1976. 393p. Engl. Refs.

This text is intended to provide public health workers in both the developed and developing countries with complete and balanced coverage of the subject of nutrition in the world today. It is divided into five parts. The 1st, dealing with nutrition at the community level, presents an ecological approach to an understanding of nutrition, discusses the nature of 'community' and its relevance to nutrition, sets community nutrition in an historical perspective, examines the effect of population on food supply and vice versa, and discusses methods of collecting data on food consumption, nutritional intake, and the nutritional status of the community. The 2nd part, whose subject is malnutrition in the community, treats: the multi-factorial causation of malnutrition; the epidemiology of undernutrition; the epidemiology of overnutrition; nutrition, infections, and immunity; nutrition and mental development; and dietary toxins. The 3rd part covers various measures to combat malnutrition (nutrition policy-making and programme planning, nutrition rehabilitation centres, new sources of food, food mixtures, food fortification, nutrition education, etc.) and the 4th, the role of governments, the United Nations, and private organizations in combating malnutrition. The 5th part, which presents country experiences, contains accounts of food consumption, malnutrition, and the steps being taken to combat it in the Caribbean, Ethiopia, India, Philippines, the UK, and the US. (HC)

3340   Miles, D. Intermediate Technology Development Group, London. *Manual on building maintenance.* London, Intermediate Technology Publications, 1976. 2v.(various pagings). Engl.

Volume 1 of this illustrated maintenance manual deals with management. It covers such topics as financial control and objectives, costing, setting up a costing system, preparing the maintenance budget, maintenance plans and programmes, inspection, organizing maintenance, and administration. Sample checklists, job allocation sheets, and lists of items required for joinery and general repairs, painting and decorating, bricklaying and plastering, plumbing and drainage work, and electrical repairs are included. Volume 2 presents methods and materials for repairing and replacing foundations and walls and for plastering and rendering, painting, and roofing. The advantages and disadvantages of permanent versus temporary construction are discussed. (RMB)

3341   Nzita, M. Rotsart de Hertaing, I. Courtejoie, J. Centre d'Etudes et de Recherches pour la Promotion de la Sante, Kangu-Mayumbe, Zaire. *Sante de vos enfants: comment proteger la sante de vos enfants depuis la naissance jusqu'a leur entree a l'ecole. 2 edition. (Child health: how to protect the health of your children from birth to school. 2 edition).* Kangu-Mayumbe, Zaire, Centre d'Etudes et de Recherches pour la Promotion de la Sante, Brochure Illustre No.14, n.d. 51p. Fren.

9 refs.

See also entry 2804.

This illustrated brochure was prepared to assist parents in Zaire to protect the health of their preschool children. It deals with the chief causes of child mortality in Zaire, the purpose of the under-fives clinic, the role of medical and paramedical personnel in the under-fives clinic, immunization, care of the newborn, protecting the child from dangers in the environment, feeding the child, and care for the child in cases of disease or trauma. A sample growth chart and a schedule of vaccinations are appended. This brochure is also available in the local language. (HC)

3342 Papua New Guinea, Department of Public Health. *Standard management procedures for obstetrics and gynaecology in Papua New Guinea: a manual for nurses, health extension officers, and doctors.* Port Moresby, Department of Public Health, n.d. 45p. Engl.
Unpublished document.

This short handbook, prepared for professional medical staff in Papua New Guinea, outlines standard procedures and drugs likely to be used during the management of the three stages of labour and the treatment of some common complications of pregnancy. There are sections on ectopic pregnancy, abortion, convulsions, anaemia, labour, retained placenta, and foetal death *in utero*. The indications, contraindications, and instructions for carrying out vaginal examinations and using a vacuum extractor as well as the drug therapy for mild and severe salpingitis are also given. The use of a cervicograph is recommended for recording the obstetric history of the patient on admission, monitoring progress during labour, and alerting staff to possible problems. (JT)

3343 Piper, D.W. *Medicine for the paramedical professions.* Sydney, Australia, McGraw-Hill, 1970. 339p. Engl.

This illustrated reference book was compiled for use by lay or paramedical personnel such as nurses, technicians, social workers, physiotherapists, and dieticians. Although it assumes that the reader has some knowledge of anatomy and physiology, an explanation of each physical system appears at the beginning of the appropriate chapter. The chapters treat: common terms used in medicine; diseases of the cardiovascular, endocrine, respiratory, nervous, and haemopolitic systems; diseases of the gastrointestinal tract, kidneys, skin; diseases of bones, joints, and connective tissue; metabolic and deficiency diseases due to physical and chemical agents; infectious diseases; illness and emotions; common diseases of children; the use of radioactive isotopes in medicine; common symptoms in medicine; and medical and nursing care of the unconscious patient and the severely ill. Each chapter has been compiled by a specialist in the field and is followed by a list of references. (HC)

3344 Reilly, Q. *Health extension officer residency training manual.* Konedobu, Papua New Guinea, Department of Public Health, 1975. 113p. Engl.
See also entry 2623 (volume 4).

The 1st section of this handbook can be used by Papua New Guinea health extension officers as a training manual during their 1-year hospital residency; the 2nd part can serve as a reference manual during their 6 months' practical work in community health and health centre

management. The short clinical section lists the important skills that health extension officers must acquire while in residence in the fields of obstetrics and gynaecology, medicine, surgery, and child health. The remaining, major portion of the manual consists of 17 assignments in community health and health centre management to be completed while in training at a health centre. For each assignment there is a very detailed explanation followed by questions requiring written answers. Assignments cover the assessment of the health service, the creation of a work programme, the management of the aid post system, disease control (tuberculosis, leprosy, venereal diseases), community health nursing services, and administrative and management aspects of the health centre. The manual concludes with advice taken from ancient wisdom. (CL)

3345 Rogoff, M. *Laboratory assistant's manual: a guide for medical laboratory assistants.* Singapore, McGraw-Hill, International Health Services Series, 1974. 215p. Engl.

This manual is written specifically to help the laboratory assistant with little training who works in a simple laboratory in a developing country. It assumes that the medical officer of the health centre or rural hospital will supervise, advise, and order equipment and focuses on the practical procedures that can be undertaken with competence and accuracy by the assistant. After an initial introductory section that includes suggestions for setting up a temporary laboratory for field surveys or infectious disease control, the two main sections of the book deal with general laboratory procedures and the special procedures necessary for bacteriology, blood transfusion, and the examination of blood, faeces, urine, cerebrospinal fluid, and medico-legal specimens. Useful recommendations are also made for such special problems of rural areas as transport of vaccines and safe incineration of waste matter. The book's clarity of presentation, two-colour printing in both line drawings and text, short sentences, and careful limitation of vocabulary overcome many difficulties inherent in explaining technical processes. (AB)

3346 Ross, W.F. All Africa Leprosy and Rehabilitation Training Centre, Addis Ababa. *Guide to leprosy for field staff.* Addis Ababa, All Africa Leprosy and Rehabilitation Training Centre, Aug 1975. 67p. Engl.

This handbook for medical and paramedical personnel, a revision of *A Simple Guide to Leprosy*, deals with the diagnosis and management of routine leprosy cases in rural outpatient clinics but does not attempt to cover the whole field of clinical leprosy. It can be used in conjunction with an ALERT booklet on health education in leprosy and with two subsequent ALERT books on leprosy control activities and proper footwear for leprosy patients. This book aims both to provide beginners in leprosy patient care with a good foundation for learning practice under supervision and to enable experienced personnel with some skills in history-taking and clinical examination to diagnose and treat leprosy cases. Of the 6 main sections, the 1st 3 are general ones covering definition and description of leprosy terms, history and examination of leprosy patients, and description and classification of different kinds of leprosy. Three more specific sections deal with leprosy reactions and their management, drug treatment of leprosy, and management of complications other than reactions. Each section uses a vocabulary suitable for readers with English as a 2nd or 3rd language and contains numerous explanatory line diagrams and charts. A separate glossary explains 37 technical terms. A short section on the challenge facing leprosy field staff emphasizes, as does the whole of the book, the need to encourage leprosy patients to participate in their own care. (CL)

3347 Rotsart de Hertaing, I. Courtejoie, J. Bureau d'Etudes et de Recherches pour la Promotion de la Sante, Kangu-Mayumbe, Zaire. *Laboratoire et sante: techniques usuelles de laboratoire. (Laboratory and health: common laboratory techniques).* Kangu-Mayumbe, Zaire, Bureau d'Etudes et de Recherches pour la Promotion de la Sante, 1976. 155p. Fren.
See also entry 2804.

This laboratory technician's handbook covers more than 50 common tests of blood, urine and faecal samples, and fluids from the spine and body cavities, as well as bacteriological and immunological tests and techniques. The purpose of each test is explained, the necessary equipment and material are listed, the procedure is outlined step-by-step, and the possible results are discussed. The text includes many photographs and illustrations. Appendices contain a section on the use of the microscope, a list of abbreviations, and an index. (RMB)

3348 Rotsart de Hertaing, I. Courtejoie, J. Bureau d'Etudes et de Recherches pour la Promotion de la Sante, Kangu-Mayumbe, Zaire. *Tuberculose. 1 edition. (Tuberculosis. 1 edition).* Kangu-Mayumbe, Zaire, Bureau d'Etudes et de Recherches pour la Promotion de la Sante, 1976. 204p. Fren.
24 refs.
See also entry 2804.

This tuberculosis handbook for health educators contains general information on the incidence, diagnosis, prevention, and cure of the disease and outlines the role of health education in tuberculosis treatment and control. Included is a series of 69 illustrations, which are also available in the form of slides for public presentations, with instructions for using them as part of five detailed lessons on tuberculosis or a shorter, abridged lecture. Suggested teaching aids and sample questions are listed. Tuberculosis prevention measures and techniques, some statistical data, and discussion problems for schoolchildren and student nurses are summarized in the appendices. (RMB)

3349 Rotsart de Hertaing, I. Courtejoie, J. Bureau d'Etudes et de Recherches pour la Promotion de la Sante, Kangu-Mayumbe, Zaire. *Nutrition: l'education nutritionnelle dans la pratique journaliere. (Nutrition: nutrition education in daily practice).*

Kangu-Mayumbe, Zaire, Bureau d'Etudes et de Recherches pour la Promotion de la Sante, 1975. 287p. Fren.
52 refs.
See also entry 2804.

This manual for health workers concerned with nutrition education proceeds from a brief statement of the basic physiology of nutrition, through a section on the special needs of young children, to a discussion of the importance of weight monitoring in educating mothers about their children's health. There is an outline of a set of five talks on nutrition suitable for village audiences and a list of suggested teaching aids, recipes for cooking demonstrations, etc. Some 56 slides are available for use with these lessons. Appendices contain baby food recipes, weight tables, cautions about bottle feeding, methods of nutrition evaluation, and resolutions adopted during a 1973 conference on malnutrition. (Modified journal abstract.)

3350 Rotsart de Hertaing, I. Courtejoie, J. van der Heyden, A. Bureau d'Etudes et de Recherches pour la Promotion de la Sante, Kangu-Mayumbe, Zaire. *Sante meilleure: source de progres; notions de sante publique et d'education sanitaire. (Better health: a means of progress; ideas about public health and health education).* Kangu-Mayumbe, Zaire, Bureau d'Etudes et de Recherches pour la Promotion de la Sante, 1975. 268p. Fren.
Refs.
See also entry 2804.

The proposal that better health is essential to progress is the basic theme of this health education and public health handbook. Part 1 defines the purposes and areas of coverage of health education and public health, discusses the role of psychology in health education, outlines the teaching methodology of health education, and gives a resume of principles of hygiene and disease control. Part 2 presents practical methods of providing health education on these subjects: infectious diseases, parasitic diseases, malnutrition, contaminated wounds, hospital and dispensary procedures, school health, antenatal care, and child health. Many illustrations and photographs are included. (RMB)

3351 Rotsart de Hertaing, I. Courtejoie, J. Bureau d'Etudes et de Recherches pour la Promotion de la Sante, Kangu-Mayumbe, Zaire. *Malnutrition de l'enfant et ses consequences. (Childhood malnutrition and its consequences).* Kinshasa, Ministere de Sante, Brochure Illustre No.8, n.d. 63p. Fren.
21 refs.
See also entries 2326, 2386, 2590, and 2591 (volume 4).

This brochure was prepared in Zaire to inform citizens and health workers about the causes, consequences, and prevention of childhood malnutrition. The effects of undernourishment on growth, the development of the brain, and resistance to infection are emphasized and the need for improved sanitation is pointed out. The material is presented in simple, conversational style with new or unfamiliar concepts defined in the footnotes. Numerous excellent photographs, each with its own educational message, accompany the text. (HC)

3352   Rotsart de Hertaing, I. Courtejoie, J. Centre d'Etudes et de Recherches pour la Promotion de la Sante, Kangu-Mayumbe, Zaire. *Education nutritionnelle: quelques principes de base et recommandations pratiques. 2 edition. (Nutrition education: some basic principles and practical recommendations. 2 edition).* Kangu-Mayumbe, Zaire, Centre d'Etudes et de Recherches pour la Promotion de la Sante, Brochure Illustre No.7, n.d. 35p. Fren.
See also entry 2804.

This brochure is intended to assist health educators in Zaire to teach the fundamental principles of child nutrition to parents. It focuses on weaning, when the child is most vulnerable to malnutrition and infection, and emphasizes the importance of: prolonged breastfeeding; child spacing; introduction of solid foods in the infant's diet at the age of 6 months; protein supplements including meat, eggs, groundnuts, beans, and even certain insects and vermin; consumption of locally available sources of vitamins and minerals; and utilization of the "Road to Health" card. The message of the text is reinforced by photographs of healthy and malnourished children. (HC)

3353   Rotsart de Hertaing, I. Courtejoie, J. Centre d'Etudes et de Recherches pour la Promotion de la Sante, Kangu-Mayumbe, Zaire. *Tuberculose aujourd'hui: conceptions recentes de la lutte contre la tuberculose. (Tuberculosis today: recent concepts regarding the fight against tuberculosis).* Kangu-Mayumbe, Zaire, Centre d'Etudes et de Recherches pour la Promotion de la Sante, Brochure Illustre No.9, n.d. 35p. Fren.
16 refs.
See also entry 2804.

Zaire has mounted a campaign against tuberculosis based on these strategies: systematic vaccination of all newborns and children aged less than 15 years; early diagnosis of victims; simple, standardized treatment that can be administered on an outpatient basis; and an intensive educational programme. Treatment on an outpatient basis was chosen over inpatient care because: isolation of the patient does not reduce the risk of contamination, since the patient's potential for infecting others ceases soon after treatment is begun; outpatient treatment has been demonstrated to be as effective as inpatient treatment as long as dispensaries are kept adequately supplied with drugs; and outpatient treatment costs 20 times less than inpatient treatment. The success of such a campaign, however, rests on the participation of the people--their willingness to have their children vaccinated, to have their symptoms investigated, and complete their course of treatment--and for this reason the educational element of the campaign is crucial. This illustrated brochure explains in detail all aspects of the campaign and its underlying rationale. (HC)

3354   Rotsart de Hertaing, I. Courtejoie, J. Centre d'Etudes et de Recherches pour la Promotion de la Sante, Kangu-Mayumbe, Zaire. *Jeunesse et les maladies veneriennes: quelques informations sur la syphilis et la blennorragie. 3 edition. (Youth and venereal disease: some information on syphilis and gonorrhea. 3 edition).* Kangu-Mayumbe, Zaire, Centre d'Etudes et de Recherches pour la Promotion de la Sante, Brochure Illustre No.10, n.d. 27p. Fren.
See also entry 2804.

The fact that an estimated 50%-80% of all cases of venereal disease in Zaire occur in persons aged 15-24 years indicates the need for a sex education programme in the secondary schools. This brochure presents, in a simple, straightforward manner, information on the transmission, consequences, symptoms, treatment, and prevention of syphilis and gonorrhea that could form the basis for such a programme. (HC)

3355   Rotsart de Hertaing, I. Courtejoie, J. Centre d'Etudes et de Recherches pour la Promotion de la Sante, Kangu-Mayumbe, Zaire. *Don du sang: quelques informations sur le don du sang et la transfusion sanguine. 2 edition. (Gift of blood: information concerning blood donation and transfusion. 2 edition).* Kangu-Mayumbe, Zaire, Centre d'Etudes et de Recherches pour la Promotion de la Sante, Brochure Illustre No.13, n.d. 35p. Fren.
See also entry 2804.

This illustrated brochure explains, for the benefit of health educators and the public at large, these facts about the donation and transfusion of blood: why blood is required for clinics and hospitals throughout Zaire, who may give blood, what happens in the blood donor clinic, how the body replaces blood, and what sort of recognition is available to the blood donor. A number of anecdotes are cited to illustrate the dramatic results of a gift of blood and some aspects of the technique of transfusion and donation (blood grouping, blood storing, etc.) are expanded in the appendices. (HC)

3356   Rotsart de Hertaing, I. Courtejoie, J. Centre d'Etudes et de Recherches pour la Promotion de la Sante, Kangu-Mayumbe, Zaire. *Sang et l'anemie: qu'est-ce que l'anemie SS? Quelques informations sur l'importance du sang et les maladies qui peuvent l'abimer. (Blood and anaemia: what is sickle-cell anaemia? Notes on the importance of blood and blood-destroying diseases).* Kangu-Mayumbe, Zaire, Centre d'Etudes et de Recherches pour la Promotion de la Sante, Brochure Illustre No.19. n.d. 49p. Fren.
20 refs.
See also entry 2804.

This illustrated brochure deals with the functions and composition of blood; the determining of blood groups and their significance; the causes, symptoms, consequences, and prevention of anaemia; the definition, history, cause, mode of transmission, and treatment of sickle-cell anaemia; and the etiology and management of the anaemia due to scarcity of the enzyme G6PD (Glucose-6-Phosphate-Dehydrate). (HC)

3357 Rotsart de Hertaing, I. Courtejoie, J. Centre d'Etudes et de Recherches pour la Promotion de la Sante, Kangu-Mayumbe, Zaire. *Peut-on eviter les accidents? Quelques informations sur les accidents et leur prevention. (Can accidents be avoided? Notes on accidents and their prevention).* Kangu-Mayumbe, Zaire, Centre d'Etudes et de Recherches pour la Promotion de la Sante, Brochure Illustre No.20, n.d. 41p. Fren.
10 refs.
See also entry 2804.
Human failing is the cause of most accidents: those involving automobiles, for example, can generally be traced to driver error, the condition of the car, or the condition of the road. This brochure urges the people of Zaire not to accept this serious public health hazard fatalistically but to take positive measures to prevent accidents in the home, at work, and on the road. The "14 commandments of the good driver" are appended. (HC)

3358 Rotsart de Hertaing, I. Courtejoie, J. van der Heyden, A. Centre d'Etudes et de Recherches pour la Promotion de la Sante, Kangu-Mayumbe, Zaire. *Comment bien se nourrir? Mieux manger pour mieux vivre: quelques informations sur les meilleurs aliments. (How to eat well? Eat better to live better: notes on the best foods).* Kangu-Mayumbe, Zaire, Centre d'Etudes et de Recherches pour la Promotion de la Sante, Brochure Illustre No.21, n.d. 61p. Fren.
14 refs.
See also entry 2804.
This handbook for nutrition educators in Zaire covers necessary nutrients (protein, vitamins, minerals, calories, etc.) and their contribution to the human body, the sources of these nutrients, the types of food necessary for a balanced diet, nutritional requirements for adults and children, the economic aspects of nutrition, the consequences of malnutrition, and the consequences of overeating. (HC)

3359 Rotsart de Hertaing, I. Courtejoie, J. Centre d'Etudes et de Recherches pour la Promotion de la Sante, Kangu-Mayumbe, Zaire. *Medicaments et el tabac sont-ils dangereux? Quelques informations sur l'usage des medicaments et leurs abus: l'alcool, la drogue, le tabac.... (Are drugs and tobacco dangerous? Notes on the use and abuse of alcohol, drugs, tobacco...).* Kangu-Mayumbe, Zaire, Centre d'Etudes et de Recherches pour la Promotion de la Sante, Brochure Illustre No.22, 49 p. Fren.
15 refs.
See also entry 2804.
The harmful effects of alcohol, tobacco, and drugs are discussed in this handbook on addiction and the psychological basis for their appeal is explored. Abuse of intoxicants by young people in Zaire is widespread and generally associated with the problems of adolescence

and the breakdown of traditional family life. Prevention of abuse depends less on repression of the intoxicant by legal means than by action in the realm of mental health promotion. Means of encouraging young people to solve their problems in more constructive ways are suggested and a dialogue on alcohol is appended as a sample approach to health education. (HC)

3360 Rotsart de Hertaing, I. Courtejoie, J. Centre d'Etudes et de Recherches pour la Promotion de la Sante, Kangu-Mayumbe, Zaire. *Lepre aujourd'hui: conceptions recentes de la lutte contre la lepre. (Leprosy today: recent concepts regarding the fight against leprosy).* Kangu-Mayumbe, Zaire, Centre d'Etudes et de Recherches pour la Promotion de la Sante, Brochure Illustre No.23, n.d. 41p. Fren.
See also entry 2804.
The nature of leprosy and the campaign against it in Zaire is discussed in this informative handbook. Topics covered include: the epidemiology, symptoms, treatment, and prevention of the disease; common prejudices about lepers and their illness; and the essential elements of an educational programme on leprosy. A doctor-patient dialogue is appended as an example of how such a programme might be approached. (HC)

3361 Rotsart de Hertaing, I. Courtejoie, J. Centre d'Etudes et de Recherches pour la Promotion de la Sante, Kangu-Mayumbe, Zaire. *Pour une authentique education sexuelle: la sexualite et les problemes qu'elle pose aux jeunes. (Toward a meaningful sex education: sexuality and the problems it presents to young people).* Kangu-Mayumbe, Zaire, Centre d'Etudes et de Recherches pour la Promotion de la Sante, Brochure Illustre No.25, n.d. 52p. Fren.
22 refs.
See also entry 2804.
The aim of sex education is not merely to teach the mechanics of reproduction but rather to facilitate the passage of the individual from childhood to adulthood. This brochure discusses the purpose of, and proposes a content for, a sex education programme that is based on the needs of young people in present-day Zaire. It covers anatomy and sexual physiology, psychosexual development of the child in the nuclear family, sexual information required at each stage of development throughout childhood and adolescence, sex education in the family and the school, family planning, venereal disease, and mental health. It is hoped that this booklet will assist parents, teachers, health workers, and community leaders in their work with young people. (HC)

3362 Rotsart de Hertaing, I. Courtejoie, J. Centre d'Etudes et de Recherches pour la Promotion de la Sante, Kangu-Mayumbe, Zaire. *Pourquoi vacciner vos enfants? Quelques informations sur le role des vaccins dans la defense contre les maladies. (Why vaccinate your children? Notes on the role of vaccination in the defense against disease).* Kangu-Mayumbe, Zaire, Centre d'Etudes et

Recherches pour la Promotion de la Sante, Brochure Illustre No.26, n.d. 37p. Fren.

16 refs.

See also entry 2804.

This illustrated brochure is intended to assist health personnel, teachers, and other health educators in presenting the subject of vaccination. It covers the discovery of the principle of vaccination, the mechanism behind it, the principal vaccines and their mode of administration, vaccination schedules, the impact of vaccination on public health, and the importance of health education as a complement to vaccination. A sample dialogue on vaccination is appended. (HC)

3363   Rotsart de Hertaing, I. Courtejoie, J. Centre d'Etudes et de Recherches pour la Promotion de la Sante, Kangu-Mayumbe, Zaire. *Ma maison et ma sante: comment la maison peut-elle favoriser la sante? (My home and my health: how can the home foster health?).* Kangu-Mayumbe, Zaire, Centre d'Etudes et de Recherches pour la Promotion de la Sante, Brochure Illustre No.29, n.d. 49p. Fren.

9 refs.

See also entry 2804.

Environmental sanitation and health in the home are discussed for the benefit of both the public and town planners in Zaire. Topics covered include: community planning, design, and construction; protecting the home from animal and insect vectors (rats, mosquitoes, flies, etc.) and from the elements (orientation, materials, etc.); ventilation; human and household waste disposal and dangers of contamination; latrine construction; potable water; means of disinfecting contaminated water; hygiene in the home; domestic accident prevention; and the home medicine chest. Recommended procedures are illustrated by means of line drawings or photographs. (HC)

3364   Rubiano, L.M. de Universidad del Valle, Departamento de Enfermeria, Seccion Materno-Infantil, Cali, Colombia. *Primeros auxilios en hemorragias para promotoras rurales de salud. (First aid for haemorrhages for rural health promoters).* Cali, Colombia, Universidad del Valle, 1971. 18p. Span.

See also entries 1939-1947, 1961-1963 (volume 3), 3313, 3366, 3367, 3368, and 3369.

This unit of the programmed instruction series for rural health promoters, similar to the *Universidad del Valle* series for auxiliary health workers, deals with first aid for haemorrhages. Students are taught to distinguish between arterial and venous bleeding, control bleeding by direct compression of the wound or by applying a tourniquet, and identify and treat shock. The format of the manual is a series of self-testing, fill-in-the-blank statements. (RMB)

3365   Rubin, I.M. Plovnick, M.S. Fry, R.E. *Improving the coordination of care: a program for health team development.* Cambridge, Mass., Ballinger Publishing, 1975. 279p. Engl.

In this workbook designed to coordinate activities of health care workers, the health team becomes more than a popular expression; it becomes a problem-solving, co-operative unit that can work effectively if it is willing to do so. The workbook's core is seven 3-hour modules or sessions, during which the health team measures team effort, goals, and activities and eventually produces an atmosphere conducive to better cooperation. Additional modules that are optional cover introducing new members, sharing leadership, getting feedback, etc. Each module includes a list of desired outcomes and premeeting preparations, a flowchart of activities, and a detailed programme. (AC)

3366   Rueda S., B. Universidad del Valle, Departamento de Enfermeria, Seccion Materno-Infantil, Cali, Colombia. *Unidad sobre excretas para promotoras rurales de salud. (Waste disposal unit for rural health promoters).* Cali, Colombia, Universidad del Valle, 1972. 21p. Span.

See also entries 1939-1947, 1961-1963 (volume 3), 3313, 3364, 3367, 3368, and 3369.

Latrine and sewerage system construction are the subject of this programmed instruction unit for Colombian rural health promoters. Illustrations and construction recommendations are included. The students are reminded that contaminated water can transmit parasites and disease. Proper latrine maintenance and fumigation with inseticides as well as personal hygiene are stressed. This lesson follows the self-examination, fill-in-the-blank format of the rest of the series. (RMB)

3367   Rueda S., B. Universidad del Valle, Departamento de Enfermeria, Seccion Materno-Infantil, Cali, Colombia. *Unidad sobre parasitismo para promotoras rurales de salud. (Parasitic diseases unit for rural health promoters).* Cali, Colombia, Universidad del Valle, 1972. 36p. Span.

See also entries 1939-1947, 1961-1963 (volume 3), 3313, 3364, 3366, 3368, and 3369.

This programmed lesson teaches Colombian rural health promoters to recognize and control parasites and understand the mechanisms by which parasites enter the human body and cause disease. Parasites are classified according to their location inside or outside of the body: the latter include fleas and ticks and among the former are intestinal parasites such as worms, ascarids, hookworms, tapeworms, and amoebae. The life cycles of such parasites and their transmission to other human beings through contact or poor hygienic practices are discussed. The manual stresses the need for proper waste disposal and latrine construction, wearing shoes, washing hands before meals, avoiding contaminated water, control of flies and other pests, and careful preparation of food and meat. The symptoms of infestation--anaemia, intestinal obstructions, diarrhea, abdominal pain--are discussed. The rural health promoter is advised to assist her community to construct latrines and adopt hygienic practices. Anyone already infected should be sent to the nearest rural health post. (RMB)

3368   **Rueda S., B. Universidad del Valle, Departamento de Enfermeria, Seccion Materno-Infantil, Cali, Colombia.** *Unidad sobre basuras para promotoras rurales de salud. (Garbage disposal unit for rural health promoters).* Cali, Colombia, Universidad del Valle, 1972. 18p. Span.
See also entries 1939-1947, 1961-1963 (volume 3), 3313, 3364, 3366, 3367, and 3369.
After studying this programmed lesson, Colombian rural health promoters are able to instruct the families in their communities in proper methods of garbage collection and disposal. Topics covered are: the dangers of incorrect waste disposal, including pests and disease; the construction and maintenance of garbage containers; and methods of garbage disposal, such as burning and burial. The manual contains a series of self-testing, fill-in-the-blank statements. (RMB)

3369   **Rueda S., B. Universidad del Valle, Departamento de Enfermeria, Seccion Materno-Infantil, Cali, Colombia.** *Unidad sobre aguas de consumo para promotoras rurales de salud. (Potable water unit for rural health promoters).* Cali, Colombia, Universidad del Valle, 1972. 13p. Span.
See also entries 1939-1947, 1961-1963 (volume 3), 3313, 3364, 3366, 3367, and 3368.
After studying this programmed lesson, Colombian rural health promoters can teach the families in their communities about the importance of clean water. Topics covered include: the use and function of cisterns and wells; water-borne diseases such as diarrhea, typhoid, and parasitic infestations; the need for boiling water for 15 minutes to remove impurities; and the use of boiled water for drinking, meal preparation, and infant bathing. The format resembles that of the *Universidad del Valle* series for auxiliary health workers. (RMB)

3370   **Saunders, D.J. United Society for Christian Literature, London.** *Visual communication handbook; teaching and learning using simple visual materials.* Guildford, UK, Lutterworth Press, 1974. 127p. Engl.
This inexpensive handbook, well printed on sturdy paper and copiously illustrated with line drawings and diagrams, provides a clear, concise guide to audiovisual communication. In simple English, it explains how a teacher can best use a wide variety of equipment that can be devised from available low-cost materials. Initial chapters explain the particular contribution that audiovisual presentations can make and introduce general principles and their concrete application. For example, adaptations are suggested for materials used in teaching intelligent adult illiterates who have difficulties in understanding pictorial conventions such as perspective. The next 16 chapters each include a definition and description of a particular visual aid, a short discussion of its advantages and disadvantages, and explanations of how to make and use it well. These chapters discuss not only pictorial materials but also educational visits, model-making, drama and role playing, puppets, etc. Chapters on projection of slides and films discuss the selection and maintenance of equipment, alternative

sources of power, and other information of particular value to isolated or tropical health personnel--for example, using a dehumidifier made from rice to protect lenses from fungus. Final chapters show how several techniques can advantageously be used together and explain practical ways of evaluating one's own efforts. Project suggestions at the end of each chapter make the book useful as a training manual as well as a handbook for reference. (AB)

3371   **Schweser, H.O. Project HOPE, Washington, D.C. People-to-People Health Foundation, Inc., Washington, D.C.** *Manual for community health education for the Caribbean.* Washington, D.C., People-to-People Health Foundation, n.d. 261p. Engl.
267 refs.
Individual chapters have been abstracted separately under entries 3177-85, 3209, 3254, 3286, 3301, and 3307.
This wide-ranging manual covers in detail the contributions that health professionals, auxiliaries, and workers in related fields can make to the vital task of community health education in the Caribbean. It gives background information on community attitudes and the overall role of each type of worker and lists the actions that they can take to educate the people in better health practices. The contents are divided into five parts, which describe the role and importance of health education, health education by professional workers, allied disciplines and voluntary organizations, and situations where health education should be taught. (HH)

3372   **Swift, C.R. African Medical and Research Foundation International, Nairobi.** *Mental health: a manual for medical assistants and other rural health workers.* Nairobi, African Medical and Research Foundation, Rural Health Series No.6, 1977. 176p. Engl.
This handbook for East African medical assistants and other auxiliary health workers presents the subject of mental health in a clear and simple form. Divided into 23 chapters, which should be read in sequence, it begins with man's life cycle and personality development and introduces relevant terms. Considerations of stress and anxiety, causes of psychiatric illness, and psychiatric symptoms lead to chapters on patient evaluation, diagnosis, and neuroses. Problems of childhood and adolescence, personality disorders, and alcoholism and drug abuse are included in later chapters. Two chapters on organic brain disorders and epilepsy are especially important for medical workers and the book's longest chapter deals with the immediate management of common psychiatric problems in a series of charts. Legal aspects of admission procedures for patients with mental disease, mental health programmes, and prevention of mental illness are dealt with briefly in the final 3 chapters and some further reading is suggested. The book contains many expressive drawings accompanying the text, the language of which becomes increasingly technical as the manual progresses. (CL)

3373 Tanzania, Ministry of Health. *Practical proce-dures training book for medical auxiliaries in Tanzania.* Dar-es-Salaam, Ministry of Health, 1976. 67p. Engl.

This small booklet lists the practical procedures to be mastered by Tanzanian students in medical assistant (MA) and rural medical aid (RMA) training courses. A supervisor ensures that each procedure has been properly performed and all the required procedures in the book must be completed if the student is to qualify for these health posts. The 1st part presents procedures for five practical areas: nursing, the laboratory, the ward, the outpatient department and surgery, and obstetrics and gynaecology. For each area of activity, the numbers of times that each individual procedure should be performed by MA and RMA students are listed in two separate columns and there is a short list of procedures that they should observe as well. For example, in the nursing procedures section, MA students should take and record blood pressure 10 times, whereas RMA students need only perform this assignment 5 times, and all students should observe bedsore prevention routine. The rest of the book is simply a series of formats for recording observations and results collected during the completion of each of the assignments listed. (CL)

3374 Uberoi, I.S. Desweemer, C. Masih, N. Kielmann, A. Vohra, S. Foreman, A. Bohnert, S. Laliberte, D. *Child health care in rural areas.* Bombay, Asia Publishing House, 1974. 373p. Engl.

This manual is the result of the Rural Health Research Centre's (RHRC's) experience in training village health workers in Punjab (India). It provides a practical training guide and handbook for auxiliary nurse-midwives in rural primary health centres and subcentres. In response to users' suggestions and criticisms, the manual presents theoretical and practical aspects of rural child care in simple language with numerous line diagrams and charts. The text covers diseases control, immunization, assessment of children's health and care of the newborn, drugs, and treatment. A table of diseases and conditions that should be referred to a doctor appears in the final chapter. (CL)

3375 USA, Department of the Army. *Environmental health technician.* Washington, D.C., U.S. Government Printing Office, Department of the Army, Technical Manual No.8-250, 31 Jul 1974. 1v.(various pagings). Engl.

This US Army reference manual for environmental health technicians covers: the organization and function of the Environmental Health Program; basic statistics and chemistry; how to fill out reports; general control measures for disease prevention, including immunization, drugs, hygiene, and nutrition; control of infectious diseases; control of heat and cold injuries; classification of arthropods and control of parasitic diseases; rodent and snake control; pest control operations, surveys, chemicals, and equipment; water supply; food service sanitation; waste treatment and disposal; sanitary control of housing, special shops, and swimming facilities; and occupational hazards. Appendices include sam-ple checklists, questionnaires, and tests and mathemati-cal tables of equivalents. The manual contains copious illustrations and statistical data. (RMB)

3376 USA, Department of the Army. *Army medical department handbook of basic nursing.* Washington, D.C., U.S. Government Printing Office, Technical Manual No.8-230, Nov 1970. 1v.(vari-ous pagings). Engl.

This training manual instructs US Army medical corps-men, medical specialists, and clinical specialists in the nursing aspects of medical care; it also serves other army medical personnel as a handy reference tool. Separate chapters treat: anatomy and physiology; causes, symp-toms, and classification of disease and injury; pharma-cology and the administration of drugs; basic nursing procedures (including therapeutic, medical-surgical, and specialized procedures); outpatient medical care (routine general activities, immunization, minor surgery, etc.); obstetrical nursing care; emergency medi-cal care; administrative procedures; pediatric nursing; and geriatric nursing. Numerous illustrations of ana-tomical symptoms and the nursing procedures are included. The pediatric section contains a chart of normal childhood growth and development. (HC)

3377 van der Heyden, A. Courtejoie, J. Rotsart de Hertaing, I. Bureau d'Etudes et de Recherches pour la Promotion de la Sante, Kangu-Mayumbe, Zaire. *Malaria. (Malaria).* Kangu-Mayumbe, Zaire, Bureau d'Etudes et de Recherches pour la Promo-tion de la Sante, n.d. 125p. Fren.
See also entry 2804.

This malaria handbook is designed for use by health educators. The 1st section deals with the epidemiology of malaria, the life cycle and control of the *Anopheles* mosquito, and the detection and control of malaria. The rest of the book contains four detailed lesson plans, including a list of teaching and audiovisual aids and how and when to use them, lists of questions to ask during lessons and group discussions, and illustrations, also available as slides, to be shown to the audience. The 1st lesson is devoted to questions on the causes, symptoms, cure, and prevention of diseases so that the health educa-tor can ascertain the audience's general level of knowl-edge; the 2nd lesson covers the habits of the mosquito vector and the transmission of malaria; and the 3rd and 4th lessons present methods of malaria control. Some statistical data, health education problems for schoolchildren, and sample examination questions and answers on malaria are included in appendices. (RMB)

3378 van der Heyden, A. Courtejoie, J. Rotsart de Hertaing, I. Bureau d'Etudes et de Recherches pour la Promotion de la Sante, Kangu-Mayumbe, Zaire. *Vers intestinaux. (Intestinal worms).* Kangu-Mayumbe, Zaire, Bureau d'Etudes et de Recherches pour la Promotion de la Sante, n.d. 144p. Fren.
See also entry 2804.

This health educators' handbook on intestinal worms presents four lesson plans covering general knowledge,

IV Primary Health Manpower--Training and Utilization

hookworms (*ankylostomiasis*), roundworms (ascariasis), and latrine construction. The lessons are intended for use with some 68 slides that are included in the book in the form of black and white illustrations. Introductory material deals with the transmission and life cycles of intestinal worms, symptoms of infestation, and drugs and vermifuges used in treatment. Suggested teaching aids are listed. The appendices contain statistical data on parasitical epidemiology, health education problems for schoolchildren, sample questions and answers on intestinal worms, and the results of a mass campaign against intestinal parasites in children. (RMB)

3379 Vaughan, A.B. *Anaesthetics.* London, Oxford University Press, 1969. 306p. Engl.
This training manual is written specifically for fully trained medical auxiliaries in East Africa, but it could also be used by medical students and doctors who administer anaesthetics. Clearly written, the book contains explanations of practical procedures, illustrated with photographs and line drawings, and reflects awareness of the particular problems of developing countries by suggesting alternative procedures and by providing useful details, such as references to tropical diseases and explanations of older types of equipment that are still likely to be in use. The manual's five main sections explain the principles and the techniques of general anaesthesia, the techniques required in certain types of surgery and in the presence of common diseases, the methods of local and spinal anaesthesia, and essential procedures in emergency resuscitation, safety, and hygiene. Drugs are referred to by the name most commonly used, but a glossary gives trade and generic names as well as brief explanations of medical terms used in the book. Conversion tables and a list of equipment manufacturers are appended. (AB)

3380 Wachter, E. *Manuel d'education nutritionnelle des meres. (Manual of nutrition education for mothers).* Kinshasa, Ministere de Sante Publique, May 1973. 93p. Fren.
This illustrated manual is intended as a guide and reference tool for nutrition educators, mainly nurses, for use in their work with mothers in Zaire. It is organized into a series of 12 discussions, each of which is to be accompanied by visual equipment (a flannelography) and/or a cooking demonstration. In all, 22 recipes using locally available foods are given. Themes treated in the discussions include: disease prevention as the responsibility of the parent; the well-fed child (the 'road to health' card); foods for growth (protein), foods for resistance (vitamins and minerals), and foods for energy (carbohydrates); sources of protein; cost of various sources of protein; sources of vitamins and minerals; sources of carbohydrates; nutrition for pregnant and lactating women; the importance of breastfeeding; infant feeding from age 5-9 months; infant feeding from age 10 months on; improving the regular diet through the addition of soy products; nutrition and infection--preventing diarrhea; and the prevention and treatment of kwashiorkor and marasmus. Each discussion is presented in simple, question-and-

answer style and lists of the visual and cooking equipment required are appended. The manual is to be translated into a number of African languages. (HC)

3381 Watt, D.G. *Emergency dentistry: intended for those who must treat the occasional dental patient.* Weybridge, UK, Clausen Publications, 1975. 70p. Engl.
In under-developed regions of many countries, there is frequently a need for doctors and nurses without formal dental training to deal with pain, infection, and trauma of the mouth. Information enabling such people to diagnose common lesions and alleviate dental pain is presented here in technical language suited to the professional reader. The 1st 5 chapters progress from basic oral anatomy to detailed diagnostic procedures and descriptions of various universal pathological conditions including pulpitis and dental abscesses. Other infections described include those mainly seen in hot countries and associated with a dirty mouth, such as *cancrum oris*, the aetiology of which is believed to involve malnutrition. In the 2nd half of the book, wide-ranging chapters on trauma to teeth and adjacent tissues and emergency treatment of severe facial injuries are followed by more specific chapters on dental anaesthesia, tooth extraction, and post-extraction haemorrhage. The relevant drugs in dentistry are also considered and a chart gives dosages for adults, children, and infants. The book is amply illustrated throughout with clear line diagrams and occasional photographs, supplemented by charts where relevant. A list of dental equipment and materials is given in the 1st of 4 appendices, the others covering detailed blood data, methods for the prevention of tetanus, and emergency tracheostomy procedure. All major procedures and topics are included in an index. (CL)

3382 WHO, Brazzaville. *Printed eduation material; its preparation and testing: a guide for those engaged in preparing health education printed material.* Brazzaville, WHO, 16 Jul 1973. 9p. Engl.
Also published in French.
Pretesting can facilitate the production of effective and useful printed educational materials. In this paper, six steps in the pretesting of educational materials are identified and described. The 1st consists of stating the main purpose of pretesting, which may be one or all of the following: to test the material's format and design in attracting and holding the attention of the target group, test the message of the script in terms of its clarity to the target population, and observe the impact of the material on any individual or group as envisioned during its preparation. The 2nd step involves selecting, with the help of a statistician if possible, a representative sample of the target population. The 3rd step consists of choosing the appropriate tool--questionnaire, interview, or observation--for achieving the aims set forward in step 1; the 4th, of analyzing the data collected; the 5th, of modifying the material on the basis of the analysis in order to improve its educational value; and the 6th, of repeating the pretesting. The educational material will be ready for mass production when a substantial proportion of the

target group (about 80%-90%) easily understands its intended message. A questionnaire that was used to test leaflets on spraying in malaria control and some questions that can be used in the testing of pictures, posters, and exhibits are appended. (HC)

3383   WHO, Geneva. *Primary health worker: working guide; guidelines for training; guidelines for adaptation.* Geneva, WHO, 1976. 338p. Engl.
See also entry 1814 (volume 3); also published in French as: *Agent de sante communautaire.*
This document is a model for auxiliary training and reference materials; it has been drafted by WHO to be adapted by national, local, or regional personnel. It is divided into three guides: the 1st for primary health workers, the 2nd for their teachers, and the last for health administrators and teachers. The 1st .part is simply written and illustrated, covering communicable disease control, maternal child health, nutrition, first aid, sanitation, etc.; the 2nd consists of some suggestions for making the teaching/learning experience useful, realistic, and effective; and the 3rd presents ideas for adapting the 1st section to a country's national health plan, its primary health workers' job description, its health vocabulary, etc. The importance of having the manual adapted by people well acquainted with the local language, habits, and culture is stressed. (HC)

3384   WHO, Geneva. *Treatment and prevention of dehydration in diarrhoeal diseases: a guide for use at the primary level.* Geneva, WHO, 1976. 31p. Engl.
Simple technical guidelines for the prevention and management of dehydration due to diarrhea are presented in this handbook for primary health workers. Topics covered include: the five steps of diarrhea and its management--dehydration, rehydration, sustenance, cure, and prevention; how diarrhea can lead to death, especially in the case of young children; how to assess the degree of a patient's dehydration by his appearance, skin elasticity, radial pulse, eyes and fontanelle, and urine flow; the various forms of rehydration and how and when to apply them; how to tell whether rehydration is complete; conditions that might be causing or complicating dehydration; nutrition rehabilitation; medicines that should not be used in the treatment of diarrhea; and the five important lessons that every mother should be taught as part of the prevention of diarrhea. Annexes contain detailed instructions for conducting the various methods of rehydration (oral, nasogastric, intravenous, and intraperitoneal) and for making the oral fluid, plus a sample weight chart and a flow chart for the management of dehydration due to diarrhea. (HC)

3385   Wood, C.H. *Improved patient management in primary health care: the development of the flowchart approach for use by the health worker.* Nairobi, African Medical and Research Foundation, 1977. 10p. Engl.
Dr. Ben Essex has developed in Tanzania a method of rapid diagnosis of common diseases that can be used by intermediate level workers with 2-3 years vocational training. It employs decision theory and involves flowcharts based on epidemiological analysis of local complaints and diseases. The charts include 34 systems and 19 signs that lead to the recognition of 160 diseases. It has not yet been determined whether the charts can be modified for regions with different disease problems, how the method can be best taught, whether the approach can be adapted to deal with the management of diseases, and whether the system can be modified to suit village health workers. Dr. Essex claims that it is very difficult to modify the 53 flowcharts with their 150 internal linkings without disrupting the whole system. However, experience with a computer programme indicates that such modification may not be too complicated. A draft teaching manual assumes adequate prior instruction in medical sciences, natural history of common diseases, and physical examination. The student is not introduced to flowcharts until he understands their derivation and the need for them. The common charts can be memorized. There are no charts for the management of disease, but schedules taking a variety of constraints into account have been produced. There are now flowcharts for the diagnosis and management of obstetric emergencies. A further research proposal will take the work up to 1980 in its extension of the approach to other health care tasks. (HH)

IV.7.2 Family Planning and Midwifery

See also: 2821, 3336

3386   East-West Center, Honolulu. *Using folk media and mass media to expand communication.* Honolulu, East-West Center, IEC Newsletter No.20, Special Issue, 1975. 16p. Engl.
Inter-Regional Seminar-cum-Workshop on the Integrated Use of Folk Media and Mass Media in Family Planning Communication Programmes, New Delhi, India, 7-16 Oct 1974.
In 1972, UNESCO launched a campaign to incorporate folk art into educational broadcasts for rural populations. As part of this initiative, folk troupes from all over India were invited to attend a 10-day seminar/workshop in New Delhi in 1974 to explore the potential of eight varieties of folk form for rural family planning education. Each day began with lectures on aspects of folk art, the mass media, and education and then the artists attempted to introduce family planning messages into performances that were videotaped for evaluation by participants. Most of the delegates agreed that such efforts can not only make an easily understandable and entertaining contribution to rural educational broadcasts but also help to revitalize folk art itself, as long as a number of guiding principles are observed to ensure that the folk forms do not lose their originality and authenticity during adaptation and recording. The report includes comments from some of the participants and a supplement provides abstracts of the papers presented at the seminar. (DM)

3387 **Gally, E.** *Manual practico para parteras. (Practical manual for midwives).* Mexico City, Pax-Mexico, 1977. 559p. Span.

This manual for Latin American health workers with or without formal technical training emphasizes the provision of family planning and midwifery services within the rural community. The 1st part of the book discusses in detail the theoretical and practical aspects of birth control and provides guidelines for community education in sexual development, contraception, and planned parenthood. A chapter on the organization and content of family planning services also covers venereology, infertility, and psychosexual problems. The latter half of the book is devoted to antenatal care, mechanisms and management of normal and abnormal labour, and postnatal care. Detailed practical information is given concerning the anatomy and physiology of pregnancy and gynaecological abnormalities. Included are guidelines for history-taking, examination, diagnosis, medical referral, and medical treatment. The section on postnatal care deals with maternal, family, and child health, including nutrition, immunization, infantile illnesses, and child development. The author emphasizes throughout the wider role of the midwife as community adviser, health educator, and family planning promoter. The text is extensively illustrated with diagrams and photographs. (DM)

3388 **Khita, M.B. Rotsart de Hertaing, I. Courtejoie, J. Bureau d'Etudes et de Recherches pour la Promotion de la Sante, Kangu-Mayumbe, Zaire.** *Jeunesse et le probleme des naissances desirables; quelques informations sur les attitudes de jeunesse en face de la sexualite. (Youth and the problem of unwanted pregnancy; some information on the sexual attitudes of youth).* Kangu-Mayumbe, Zaire, Centre d'Etudes et de Recherches pour la Promotion de la Sante, Brochure Illustre No.11, n.d. 55p. Fren.
9 refs.
See also entry 2804.

This brochure contains suggestions for introducing secondary students in Zaire to the question of family planning within the context of a programme of sex education. Family planning is viewed as desirable from both individual and social points of view. Discussion focuses on the consequences of unlimited fertility at the family and national levels, the effects of unlimited fertility on economic development, male and female reproductive physiology, various types of birth control (natural, mechanical, and chemical) and the principles behind them, and different methods of birth control, their relative efficacy, advantages, and drawbacks. Reproductive physiology and birth control methods are illustrated by means of line drawings. (HC)

3389 **Rotsart de Hertaing, I. Courtejoie, J. Bureau d'Etudes et de Recherches pour la Promotion de la Sante, Kangu-Mayumbe, Zaire.** *Maternite et sante: notions d'obstetrique. (Maternity and health: obstetrics).* Kinshasa, St. Paul Missionary Society, 1976. 450p. Fren.

Refs.
This comprehensive, illustrated manual is intended for nurse-midwives and auxiliary nurse-midwives in Zaire. It is divided into two sections: the 1st discusses normal pregnancy from conception to childbirth and care of the newborn and the 2nd covers the recognition and management of abnormalities that may arise during pregnancy. Each chapter is followed by a list of review questions. Instructions for procedures such as episiotomy, manual extraction of the placenta, use of forceps, etc., and medications used in obstetrics, family planning, and health promotion are appended. (HC)

3390 **Rotsart de Hertaing, I. Courtejoie, J. Centre d'Etudes et de Recherches pour la Promotion de la Sante, Kangu-Mayumbe, Zaire.** *Pour que mon bebe naisse en bonne sante: quelques informations sur les consultations prenatales et leur importance pour la mere et l'enfant. (For a healthy baby: notes on prenatal consultations and their importance for the mother and child).* Kangu-Mayumbe, Zaire, Centre d'Etudes et de Recherches pour la Promotion de la Sante, Brochure Illustre No.18, n.d. 45p. Fren.
13 refs.
See also entry 2804.

Intended for health personnel in Zaire, this handbook explains basic precepts of antenatal care, including hygiene, nutrition, medical surveillance, prenatal examinations, indicators of high-risk pregnancy, and the integration of educational activities with prenatal consultation. Three prenatal visits and delivery in a health facility are strongly advocated for all mothers and the establishment of special villages near maternity facilities is recommended in order to accommodate mothers from far away. These villages, in addition to ensuring that mothers arrive at the maternity unit on time, provide an excellent opportunity for monitoring the general health of the residents and instructing them in health education. (HC)

3391 **Rotsart de Hertaing, I. Courtejoie, J. Centre d'Etudes et de Recherches pour la Promotion de la Sante, Kangu-Mayumbe, Zaire.** *Maternite et la promotion de la sante; le role de l'infirmiere-accoucheuse dans la medecine promotionnelle. (Maternity and health promotion; the role of the nurse-midwife in preventive medicine).* Kangu-Mayumbe, Zaire, Centre d'Etudes et de Recherches pour la Promotion de la Sante, Brochure Illustre No.31, n.d. 53p. Fren.
14 refs.
See also entry 2804.

The opportunities for health promotion afforded by maternal and child health activities are pointed out, for the benefit of nurse-midwives in Zaire, in this illustrated brochure. The prenatal consultation constitutes an occasion for promoting better nutrition and breast-feeding; the mother's stay in the maternity ward provides an opportunity for instructing her regarding proper care of the umbilical cord, vaccination, disease prevention, and child feeding; and the post-partum period is the ideal moment for encouraging her to adopt a method of birth control such as the IUD. The efficacy, advantages, and disadvantages of the IUD are discussed and instructions for its placement are given; educational dialogues one for use at each of the above-mentioned activities are appended. (HC)

V Formal Evaluative Studies

V.1 Health Manpower

See also: 3116, 3128, 3229, 3252, 3255, 3272, 3405, 3412, 3414

3392   Andreano, R.L. Cole-King, S. Katz, F. Rifka, G. WHO, Alexandria. *Assignment report: evaluation of primary health care projects in Iran.* Alexandria, WHO, Jun 1976. 44p. Engl.
See also entry 3472.
A WHO mission was invited to Iran in 1976 to evaluate rural health projects at Shiraz, Fars, and West Azerbaijan and the health component of the project at Lorestan, all of which used minimally trained front-line health workers (FLHWs). On the basis of their observations, interviews with involved personnel, examination of records, and calculation of the costs of implementing this type of programme on a large scale, the team concluded that a system of primary health care based on the experience of these projects could and should be developed for the whole country. The major defects detected by the team arose from faults in identification of priorities, in training of FLHWs, and in assessment and from lack of community participation. At least 1 project failed to carry out an initial study to determine needs and 3 of the 4 concentrated on curative measures to the neglect of family health, nutritional surveillance, and continuous follow-up of vulnerable groups. Training procedures that were partly to blame for these deficiencies should be revised both in content and in teaching method. The West Azerbaijan project successfully used female FLHWs for family health care and male workers for community health measures and their activities coordinated well with other health services, but in none of the projects was the local community involved in planning, selection of workers, or payment of FLHWs salaries, although the health facilities were welcomed. Evaluation should be an essential part of such projects and the team recommend that their own methodology be used to provide constant feedback on the effectiveness of the proposed nationwide programme. (DM)

3393   Cook, S. International Planned Parenthood Federation, Nairobi. *Family welfare educators.* In Cook, S., Report of an Evaluation of the International Planned Parenthood Federation Programme in Botswana 1969-1972, Nairobi, International Planned Parenthood Federation, 1973, 65-92. Engl.
For complete document see entry 3471.
Formal evaluation of the IPPF programme in Botswana indicated that: the 60 family welfare educators (FWEs) who had been trained from 1969-1972 were mainly engaged in conducting child welfare classes, assisting in clinics, and visiting local homes; their home visiting activities took up much less time than had been envisaged by the pilot programme initiators; and the drop-out rate was high for community development workers given additional FWE training. These findings were based on weekly reports from FWEs and research conducted at refresher courses. Recommendations are that: all future candidates be mature mothers with primary school education, a knowledge of English, and local village endorsement; they receive a month's pretraining experience in the local clinic to which they will be attached; and they be given flexible training carried out in rural development centres, supplemented by supervised practice in small rural or urban clinics, a probationary period, inservice refresher courses, and more frequent and systematic supervision. Statistics, research forms, details of methods, a course syllabus, and suggestions for future evaluation are appended to the report. (AB)

3394   Engler, T.A. *Evaluation scheme for polyvalent health assistants in a rural area of the Republic of Panama.* Bocas del Toro, Panama, Hospital de Changuinola, n.d. 10p. Engl.
Unpublished document; see also entry 3431.
The Integrated Health System, started in 1973 in Bocas del Toro, Panama, includes a method for evaluating the work of health assistants, who are auxiliaries selected from among the literate village men and trained to provide primary care at rural subcentres. Each of the three phases of the programme is being studied. The input phase, including recruitment, training, administration, and supervision, is assessed by means of surveys, medical records, supervisory reports, and accounts. Similar sources of data are used in the output phase to determine qualitative and quantitative specific achievements of auxiliaries. The wider outcome is assessed by surveys examining the impact of the programme on the community and the attitudes of health personnel to their work and to each other. This method of evaluation should be sufficiently comprehensive to cover all aspects of the programme including the specially designed administrative systems (to meet such needs as supplies, supervision, communications, patient referral, etc.) and the technical operational systems (which provide guidelines for division of labour among members of the health team). (DM)

3395   Farvar, M.T. *Health or development? Training of frontline health workers, particularly in Lorestan, Iran.* In Ronaghy, H.A.,

Mousseau-Gershman, Y., Dorozynski, A., eds., Village Health Workers, Ottawa, International Development Research Centre, 1976, 21-24. Engl. For complete document see entry 3250.

The experiences of the Selseleh Regional Development Project, Lorestan, Iran, reveal the problems that can arise from administrative and political inconsistencies. The project began training local people as frontline health workers, providing them with 2 months theory, 4 months supervised work in the health centre and field work in the villages, and 1 month common training with the other frontline development workers. From the outset, however, the project was foiled by overlap in administrative responsibility. The project fell within the Prime Minister's realm, whereas the health network fell under the jurisdiction of the Imperial Organization for Social Services. This meant that the physician/instructors were not subject to the project's policies and they disregarded community development aims. Thus, students imitated them, confined their work to treating scores of patients every morning in the health centre, and refused to move to the rural areas. A more successful element of the project, a pilot methane production plant, is also described. (HC)

3396 Khoo, O.T. *Capabilities of paramedical personnel.* Southeast Asian Journal of Tropical Medicine and Public Health (Bangkok), 6(2), 1975, 269-275. Engl.
10 refs.

In the developing world, paramedicals can provide efficient primary health care and reduce the number of people needing hospital treatment. For example, a survey of eight Indian hospitals showed that 40% of outpatients and 44% of inpatients were admitted for conditions that might have been prevented or treated by local paramedicals; as many as 67% of under-fives inpatients were in this category. In contrast, the medical auxiliaries of Chimaltenango, Guatemala, correctly treated 91% of local patients and 75% of their referrals to clinics and hospitals were resistant cases of diarrhea and pneumonia. Barefoot doctors in China can recognize 75 common diseases after 10 months training; their disease control activities have practically eliminated cholera, smallpox, typhoid, typhus, syphilis, and gonorrhea. Similarly, medical auxiliaries in the Belgian Congo help with the control of endemic disease, undertake research, and perform minor operations. (HH)

3397 Maru, R.M. *Health manpower strategies for rural health services: India and China, 1949-1975.* Economic and Political Weekly (Bombay, India), 9(31-33, India), Aug 1976, 1253-1268. Engl.
65 refs.

This paper compares the health manpower strategies pursued in India and China and brings out the implications of these strategies for the birth control programme. The key areas discussed are medical manpower training, redistribution of health manpower from urban to rural areas, and utilization of traditional medicine. The author points out that, while the broad principles of Chinese

rural health policy are relevant to India, the task of implementing egalitarian health policies through the existing elite system will not be easy. The Chinese experience suggests that neither a general commitment to socialism nor concentration of power in the hands of a small political-administrative elite can become an adequate mechanism for major social changes. Only a leadership determined to restructure both attitudes and power relationships within the political-administrative system will succeed. Such a restructuring must involve, among other things, de-bureaucratization and decentralization of power to the people. (RMB)

3398 Milio, N. International Medical and Research Foundation, Warrenton, Va. *Community health workers: evaluation of their impact on health.* New York, International Medical and Research Foundation, 1977. 26p. Engl.
55 refs.
International Medical and Research Foundation Symposium on the Community Health Worker, Warrenton, Va., 26-28 Oct 1977.
See also entries 3227, 3232, 3234, 3236, 3239, 3243, 3244, 3259, 3266, 3268, and 3394.

Examination of current approaches to evaluating the health impact of community health workers (CHWs) shows the need for new, alternative approaches that use an ecological framework to determine direct and indirect effects. Examples of typical approaches to evaluation examined here (including evaluations of paraprofessional tubectomy in rural Bangladesh and urban health promoters in Colombia) illustrate that non-physician practitioners are most commonly evaluated by comparing them to physicians. Measuring effectiveness in this way assumes that improved health necessarily follows health service delivery. This doubtful assumption also underlies these measurements of health outcomes as lives saved, acceptability to customers, and cost efficiency, as well as direct gross input-output measurements such as quantities of personnel or patients. These measurements often focus on social, demographic, and resource assessment of a population rather than on health-outcome oriented evaluation of CHWs' impact. All these inadequate forms of evaluation result from acquiescence to the political realities of organizational development and a poor understanding of the relationship between health service procedures and improved health. As an alternative, the author suggests that the fact that health, population control, housing, and income distribution are also dependent on rural development must be incorporated into evaluation methods used to measure the impact of CHWs. (CL)

3399 Palm, M.L. *Recognizing opportunities for informal patient teaching.* Nursing Clinics of North America (Philadelphia, Pa.), 6(4), Dec 1971, 669-678. Engl.
11 refs.

Health education has long been recognized as an independent function of nurses, occurring mostly during incidental, informal patient contacts, generally during regular care. Since previous studies have revealed that nurses are unclear about what constitutes patient teaching and how much of it they actually do, the author conducted a descriptive survey to determine whether nurses give top priority to patient teaching over physical care, supportive emotional care, or liaison activities in the nurse-patient relationship. One hundred and fifty-one registered nurses in a large midwestern (USA) hospital were presented with 22 written descriptions of patients with learning needs in nonemergency situations of direct nursing care with three distracting vignettes. The subjects could choose from four responses, one from each of the above-mentioned categories, and were not aware of the purpose of the study. Results revealed that 59% of the nurses sampled assigned top priority to patient education and 30% gave it second priority. There was some evidence of an inverse relationship between the nurse's educational background and the emphasis she gave to teaching activities and it was apparent that, while most nurses responded promptly to a patient's expressed learning needs, they rarely initiated teaching activities when the patient showed no interest. A sample vignette is included. (RMB)

3400 Pan American Health Organization, Washington, D.C. *Delivery of primary care by medical auxiliaries: techniques of utilization and analysis of benefits achieved in some rural villages in Guatemala.* In Medical Auxiliaries, Washington, D.C., Pan American Health Organizaton, Scientific Publication No.278, 1973, 24-37. Engl.
Twelfth Meeting of the PAHO Advisory Committee on Medical Research, Washington, D.C., 25 Jun 1973.
Six village projects run by various international, missionary, and private organizations in Guatemala prove that auxiliary health workers are both acceptable and economically feasible practitioners of primary care. The objectives of the programmes differ but all are supervised by a physician and rely on community participation. In some, the Primary Care Personnel (PCP) work part-time and are unpaid, but even the most expensive programmes are 75% less costly than a service manned by doctors and could be financed by the local community. Potential PCPs must be literate, motivated, and respected by their neighbours. Their training is entirely practical. INCAP provides trainee auxiliary nurses with a therapeutic guideline manual and then requires the students to practice the knowledge gained under constant supervision from a qualified PCP until their mistake rate is less than 5%. Once the mistake rate is down to 1%, supervision sessions are held once a week. This system ensures technical quality control, but community control is also necessary and in some programmes a community medical committee is responsible for selecting PCP candidates. Ideally, these committees help determine priorities and type of medical care and mobilize villagers to make use of the services; already in two projects the committees have extended their activities to other development work. The success of these PCP programmes is evident from the fall in infant mortality in the areas covered and the acceptance of PCPs by those communities. (DM)

3401 Rosenfield, A.G. *Auxiliaries and family planning.* Lancet (London), 1(7855), 1974, 443-445. Engl.
10 refs.
Family planning programmes have high priority in many countries, but auxiliaries and midwives may have to be used where there are too few doctors to deliver the services. A study in Thailand indicates that auxiliaries' medical care is competent, although they should always be able to refer problem cases. A medical checklist for the use of an auxiliary before prescribing the pill has been developed and, if given adequate training and practical experience, she can also insert intrauterine devices and perform pelvic examinations. In Thailand, when auxiliary midwives began to prescribe the pill, the acceptance of both the pill and other family planning services improved dramatically. In a preliminary study, the continuation rate also improved and there was no increase in short-term side effects or complications. (HH)

3402 Thomas, A. Kataria, M. *Manpower planning in inpatient units.* Nursing Journal of India (New Delhi), 68(2), Feb 1977, 54-56. Engl.
A study was undertaken in 33 inpatient wards in India to determine the nursing manpower needed in comparison with the nursing manpower available. A daily census of inpatients was taken over a period of 1 month; the patients were classified as completely dependent, partially dependent, or ambulatory according to their demands in terms of nursing time; and the seasonal variation in the number of patients was calculated through a retrospective study. It was observed that: the average number of patients needing nursing care in the units was 1 196 per day; on an average, 21.1% were completely dependent, 43.7% partially dependent, and 35.1% ambulatory; and the demand for nurse-days was maximum in the summer months, with wide variation in the workload from day to day, ward to ward, and season to season. Taking these variations into consideration, it was calculated that an average of 455 nurse days per day are needed in the 33 wards, whereas only 216 are available. This gap of 239 nurse days becomes 393 when the need to provide for days off, holidays, casual leave, and paid leave are considered. The fact that nurses are often observed performing non-nursing tasks makes the picture even more discouraging. Health administrators are urged to take steps to ensure effective utilization of existing nursing staff by identifying all non-nursing activities that could be delegated to non-nurses and all simple nursing tasks that could be delegated to auxiliary nursing personnel. Daily, monthly, weekly, and yearly assessments of nursing needs are also recommended. (HC)

3403 Zeighami, B. Zeighami, E. *Evaluation of Iranian village health workers efficacy.* In Ronaghy, H.A., Mousseau-Gershman, Y., Dorozynski, A., eds., Village Health Workers, Ottawa, International Development Research Centre, 1976, 14-20. Engl.
For complete document see entry 3250.

Three evaluation studies have been completed in the Kavar auxiliary project, Iran. The 1st study, conducted 6 months after village health workers (VHWs) began working in experimental villages, aimed to assess the VHWs' acceptability and its relationship to certain character traits. A selected sample of adults were asked whether they were satisfied with the VHWs' work and level of knowledge and whether they preferred a male or female VHW. The results indicated that villagers approved of VHWs, that they tended to prefer a VHW of the same sex but generally accepted an opposite-sex VHW, and that some older villagers were sceptical about the knowledge of younger VHWs. The 2nd survey was undertaken to assess whether the VHW had influenced the villagers' knowledge and practice of contraception. A sample of residents in the experimental villages were interviewed and their responses compared with those of a similar sample from a number of control villages in which family planning services were provided by a village midwife. Findings were that villagers who had access to VHW services scored much higher in both knowledge and practice of contraception than did those in the control villages. In the 3rd study, the entire populations of control and experimental villages were surveyed 15 months after VHWs set up practice; the goal was to assess objectively VHW impact by measuring and comparing mortality and birthrates. Although vital rates showed striking differences (e.g., the infant mortality was 124:1 000 live births in the control village as opposed to 60:1 000 in the experimental), the difference in fertility and crude birthrates was deemed not significant. All findings are discussed in some detail. (HC)

3404   Zeighami, E. Zeighami, B. Javidian, I. Zimmer, S. *Rural health worker as a family planning provider: a village trial in Iran.* Studies in Family Planning (New York), 8(7), Jul 1977, 184-187. Engl.

In 1975, a survey was conducted by Pahlavi University (Iran) to determine the effects of 16 rural auxiliary health workers, trained by a university project to provide curative, preventive, and health education services, on family planning knowledge, attitudes, and practices in the villages where they had been working for 14 months. A total of 1 308 men and women (more than half from 16 control villages served by traditional midwives) were interviewed using a questionnaire soliciting personal data and information on use and attitudes toward contraception and related social issues. The results indicated that 13% more eligible women in the project villages were using contraceptives, particularly oral contraceptives, which were the only ones the village health workers were permitted to distribute. Male workers were just as effective as female workers at promoting family planning, although cultural factors mitigated against this sort of activity. Contraceptive knowledge among the general population was also greatly increased in the project villages. The authors conclude that, while village health workers have a significant effect on contraceptive acceptance, acceptors are generally older women who have already had a socially acceptable number of children rather than young women wishing to limit the

size of their families. Statistical data are included. (RMB)

V.2 Organization and Administration

See also: 3431

3405   American Public Health Association, Washington, D.C. *State of the art study: findings from 180 health projects in 54 developing countries.* Salubritas (Washington, D.C.), 1(1), Jan 1977, 1-5. Engl.

The American Public Health Association's International Health Programs sent a detailed 57 page questionnaire to the directors of 384 health projects in developing countries in order to determine the present state of the work, identify trends and innovations, explain variations, and assess unmet needs. Information from 180 projects in 54 countries serving some 150 million people was received, a range that was wide though not entirely representative. Typically, the projects covered by the survey are rural, serve about 100 000 people, and were established in the 1970s. They are primarily service oriented, although nearly all conduct some sort of training, usually of auxiliaries and village health workers. Volunteer personnel are widely used and 8 out of every 10 projects have more than 2 volunteer health workers for every staff member. The services of traditional midwives are often enlisted, though seldom those of indigenous healers. The heavy reliance on auxiliaries is justified not only by the shortage of doctors but by the proven competence of these workers in conducting a wide range of tasks. The emphasis of the projects seems to vary with their location and funding. Despite recognition of the importance of preventive measures and general concern with health education, very little attention is given to environmental sanitation. Nutrition intervention is usually limited to child feeding programmes. Family planning, on the other hand, is a major activity and one in three of the projects takes the service direct to the people through household visits. The biggest deficiency revealed by the survey was the relative neglect of data collection and evaluation, particularly serious in view of the fact that many of these programmes are intended to act as models for future health service developments. (DM)

3406   American Public Health Association, Washington, D.C. *State of the art of delivering low cost health services in developing countries: a summary study of 180 health projects.* Washington, D.C., American Public Health Association, International Health Programs, Jan 1977. 62p. Engl.

A study of low-cost health care delivery systems was undertaken to identify innovative practices, developmental trends, and unmet needs in the field. The study was based on the responses of 180 projects in 54 countries to a detailed questionnaire covering these topics: project characteristics; population characteristics; areas of activity; range of services offered; goals, progress, and obstacles; health promotion; project planning and management; and data collection. It was noted that: the projects tend to be rural, serve a population of 100 000, and have been established during the 1970s; most projects rely on funds from fees, drug sales, and foreign official and non-official (churches and foundations) agencies; only half of the projects consider themselves fully matured; the populations served tend to be very poor; the most common services provided are health education, maternal and child health, treatment of the ill, nutrition, immunization, and training; although the projects recognize the seriousness of filth-borne diseases, only 4 out of 10 are attempting to improve environmental sanitation; 3 out of 4 projects are involved in the training of auxiliaries; administrative practices are characterized by incomplete plans, sketchy budgets, informal policies and procedures, centralized decision-making, and modest levels of funding; increasingly extensive use of community organizations and consumer involvement, however, is evident--over half of the projects make use of volunteers; and data handling procedures and evaluative practices are particularly weak. These observations are discussed in detail and some 40 innovations are identified, listed according to their areas of application, and briefly described. (HC)

3407   **Barkhuus, A.** *Consultants report on the health sector assessment: Haiti.* Washington, D.C., American Public Health Association, Jul 1974. 16p. Engl.

Three American consultants, who spent from 2-10 weeks studying the Haitian health sector, report their findings to the US Agency for International Development and proffer some solutions to the country's most urgent health problems. They observe that the health effort is hampered by a lack of policy at the central level, coordination at the intermediate level, and supporting structures at the peripheral level. They also comment that the malaria programme is inconsistently applied, government health services are poorly coordinated, nutrition services--one of the highest priorities in Haiti--are sustained by voluntary agencies, and successful pilot projects in MCH have been poorly supported. Based on their findings, the consultants recommend that a management study be undertaken in the malaria programme, a bureau of planning be established in the Ministry of Health to analyze the health sector and devise a suitable strategy, nutrition programmes be coordinated and eventually incorporated into a comprehensive delivery system, etc. (HC)

3408   **Basu, R.N.** *Evolution of smallpox eradication programme in India.* Indian Journal of Public Health (Calcutta, India), 20(2), Jun 1976, 52-61. Engl.

The history of smallpox eradication in India is traced from the end of the 19th century to the present and milestones in its evolution are identified. One of these was the launching of a nationwide eradication programme in 1962. The programme called for compulsory registration of all vital events in order to provide information about deaths from smallpox and the number of infants to be vaccinated, legal provision for compulso-

ry notification of smallpox outbreaks and compulsory vaccination (both primary and repeat), quality control of vaccine lymph at a central reference laboratory, and vaccination of 80% of the population within a period of 3 years. By 1963, despite country-wide programme implementation, pockets of endemicity remained. A joint government/WHO assessment of the programme revealed major problems resulting from poor supervision, faulty execution, and an unduly complex methodology. In 1969, the programme was reorganized with emphasis on case detection, immediate reporting, epidemiological investigation, and the prompt institution of containment measures. Mobile units were replaced by permanent ones and all health personnel were involved in casefinding and vaccination. Improvements in the programme since that time include the introduction of freeze-dried vaccine, which keeps better than vaccine lymph, and the replacement of the rotary lancet by the more efficient bifurcated needle. Efforts since 1973 have focused on the eradication of smallpox from the four states that were responsible for 92% of the total incidence in the country during the 1st part of that year and these are to be continued until total eradication is achieved. (HC)

3409   **Bicknell, W.J. Walsh, D.C.** *Caveat emptor: exporting the U.S. medical model.* Social Science and Medicine (Oxford, UK), 2(4), Mar 1977, 285-288. Engl. 14 refs.

Some of the shortcomings of the US health care delivery system are pointed out for the benefit of developing countries seeking to emulate it. Foremost among these is the fact that the system evolved within a context of almost limitless resources, totally independent of such concepts as disciplined planning and thoughtful investment. The system is, characteristically, hospital-based, technology-dependent, and oriented strongly toward research and specialization. The physician teaching environment has fostered a narrow, disease-focused, inpatient-based approach to medicine to the point that general practice and primary care have steadily lost their appeal to students on both professional and remunerative grounds. In 1973, only 20% of all physicians in direct patient care were in general practice, where an estimated 80% of the need is felt. Recent consumer movements have begun demanding basic, integrated, personal health services and a trend toward community-based, team-delivered health care is gaining momentum. These new delivery systems tend to cater to a defined population living within a circumscribed geographical area and to operate within budgetary constraints, not unlike their counterparts in the developing world. It is suggested that the USA has more to learn than to teach in the area of health care delivery. (HC)

3410   **Bridgman, R.F.** *Regional planning of health care facilities and regional collaboration between health care institutions.* World Hospitals (Oxford, UK), 11(2 and 3), Jun 1975, 65-67. Engl.

Regionalization is defined as a concept that aims to adapt an administrative structure governing a network

of interrelated institutions--in this case, health facilities-
-to local geography and population density on the one
hand and the prevailing problems of the region on the
other. Regionalization is characterized by a two-way
flow of patients, personnel, and services between its
centre and its periphery. Regional boundaries may or
may not coincide with state or provincial boundaries, but
they must correspond to economic ones so that this
two-way flow can take advantage of existing channels of
communication and so that intersectoral planning and
coordination at the regional level are made possible. In
this paper, the various aspects and advantages of regionalization of health facilities are reviewed and some impediments to it in the developing world are pointed out.
These last include the scattered nature of rural populations, the absence of good transportation facilities, the
lower rate of hospitalization utilization that make regional standards from the developed countries impossible to apply, and the lack of trained, experienced
administrators. Nonetheless, regionalization is strongly
advocated as a means of avoiding duplication of scarce
services, optimizing local-level facilities, and promulgat-
ing effective planning. (HC)

3411   Chen, P.C. *To serve all the people.* Medical
Journal of Malaysia (Singapore), 29, 1975, 237-
239. Engl.
The author discusses the factors that make it difficult to
provide effective health care for all the rural people of
Malaysia. Factors included are the scarcity of money,
the lack of trained health planners and managers and
alternative health care systems, professional resistance
to auxiliary health workers, and the difficulties of adapting Western technology to other cultures. (RMB)

3412   Cuba, Ministerio de Salud Publica. Rius, U.R.
*Cuba: la salud en la revolucion. (Cuba: health
after the revolution).* Havana, Editorial Orbe, Dec
1975. 177p. Span.
The 1st chapter of this 1975 report on health care in
Cuba deals with the beginning and characteristics of the
national health system, including the organization and
distribution of health services. Rural health and community medicine are covered in separate sections. Chapter
2 discusses health resources and contains statistical data
on hospitals, polyclinics, health centres, health manpower, and health care activities. The health status of the
country is the subject of Chapter 3, with separate sections and statistical data on demography, mortality,
maternal child health, infectious diseases, environmental health, dental health, and nutrition. Complementary
services, including statistics, laboratory services, and
research, are examined in Chapter 4. Chapter 5 presents
development perspectives, such as the 1976-1980 five
year plan and the national health sciences information
centre. The report is introduced by a brief geographical
description of the country. (RMB)

3413   Duton Coles, R. *Demographie et sociologie
medicale en Martinique. (Demography and medical sociology in Martinique).* Marseille, France,
Universite d'Aix-Marseille, 28 Feb 1975. 65p.

Fren.
42 refs.
Thesis presented to the Faculty of Medicine, University of Aix-Marseille, 28 Feb 1975.
Despite the fact that advances in the medical sector have
far outstripped either economic or social development,
Martinique still exhibits some characteristics of a developing country such as a population explosion and a
prevalence of malnutrition and intestinal parasitism. A
detailed analysis of resources reveals that: the number of
physicians is sufficient, but their distribution is poor; the
number and geographical distribution of hospitals is
adequate, but their level of equipment is uneven; the
number of hospital beds is adequate, but their designation is inappropriate (too many for surgery, not enough
for pediatrics, chronic care, etc.); rural dispensaries and
maternal child health (MCH) centres are suffering for
lack of staff and equipment; and service development is
continuing in the direction of specialized teaching hospitals rather than necessary MCH and preventive services.
The cost to a weak economy of such an orientation is
pointed out and a more appropriate allocation of
resources is urged. (HC)

**3414   Esquivel, R. Morales, E. Garcia, E. Ardito
Barletta, N. Fierro, J. Sabol, J.B. Panama,
Ministerio de Salud. Panama, Presidencia. Panama,
Presidencia. Panama, Presidencia. Direccion General de Planificacion y Administracion.**
*Estudios sectoriales: sector salud; diagnostico,
anos: 1960-1968. (Sectoral studies: diagnosis of
the health sector; years: 1960-1968).* Panama
City, Lemania, May 1970. 340p. Span.
This study of the health sector, one of a series of sectoral
studies, attempts to evaluate the health situation in Panama from 1960-1968 for the purpose of establishing a
national health system that will make better use of available resources, both public and private. Although health
conditions have greatly improved since 1960, these
problems persist: concentration of health resources in
urban areas, especially the national capital; lack of
health professionals and auxiliaries; scarcity of health
services; lack of coordination among health institutions;
emphasis on curative rather than preventive medicine;
inadequate data collection systems; and incomplete coverage of special programmes in tuberculosis, malaria,
mental health, occupational health, and nutrition. The
authors examine health plans and policies, general
characteristics of the country, health-related organizations, health indicators, health resources, special
programmes, and the health situation in each province.
Annexes contain definitions of selected health vocabulary and copious statistical data. (RMB)

**3415   Guatemala, Ministerio de Salud Publica y
Asistencia Social. Guatemala, Secretaria de
Planificacion Economica. Academia de Ciencias
Medicas, Fisicas y Naturales de Guatemala, Guatemala. USA, Agencia Internacional para el
Desarrollo, Departamento de Estado.** *Programa de
evaluacion del sistema de salud rural de Guatemala; plan y metodologia. (Programme of evaluation for Guatemala's rural health system: plan*

and methodology). Guatemala City, Academia de Ciencias Medicas, Fisicas y Naturales de Guatemala, 31 May 1976. 1v.(various pagings). Span. Refs.

See also entry 2957.

In an effort to improve its rural health care delivery system, the government of Guatemala made some fundamental changes, including the introduction of the rural health technician and the restructuring of the rural health post so that it could be run by this type of auxiliary. This document examines and evaluates the new system, its objectives and organization, and efforts that have been made to reinforce it. After background studies were completed, the system was first established as a pilot project and then introduced into all areas of health on a regional and national level; each of these steps is described, as well as the projects that were carried out during the 1st year. The themes of special studies are outlined, such as the community and the macroenvironment, the rural health system and the functions and activities of its indicators, support systems, the health information system, and economic aspects. Finally, the administration, organization, and budget of the system are presented. An annex contains resumes of reports by four working groups. Statistical data are included. (RMB)

3416   Guest, G. Titus, J.B. WHO, Brazzaville. *Development of basic health services.* Brazzaville, WHO, 9 May 1972. 11p. Engl.

From February 1968-August 1971, WHO and UNICEF provided Liberia with technical advice, equipment, and supplies to extend the country's network of rural health posts, train more health assistants to staff the rural health posts, strengthen auxiliary supervision mechanisms, organize malaria therapy, strengthen maternal and child health services, and improve basic sanitation. By August 1971, the number of rural health posts had been raised from 13-46, a 2-year programme for medical assistants had graduated five students, standard schedules of duties and equipment for use in county laboratories had been drawn up, and sanitary wells and latrines had been established in one area. Although considerable, these accomplishments were short of the project's goals, which covered a wide scope. During the project, the need for the following became apparent: an overall authority to be responsible for the supervision and support of basic health services, revised curricula for health assistants and medical assistants , more effort to staff health posts with mobile as well as stationary health assistants, and a committee of county medical officers to discuss regularly the rural health operations. (HC)

3417   Haraldson, S.S. *Evaluation of the Canadian Eskimo Health Service.* Gothenburg, Sweden, Scandinavian School of Public Health, 1974. 127p. Engl. 93 refs.

Unpublished document; individual chapter has been abstracted separately under entry 3418; see also entry 3419.

This report of a 1974 field study in Canada's Northwest Territories (NWT) aims to evaluate Eskimo health services by comparing the study's observations and findings to data collected in Alaskan Eskimo districts in 1971-1972 and in Greenland in 1975 and by examining cost-benefit analyses of individual health service components. The report discusses the motivations and aims of the study and describes the study methods and the territories' geographical and administrative situation. A chapter on NWT's health profile gives mortality, morbidity, and epidemiological data up to 1973 in graphs and tables and the following chapter provides a brief history of NWT's health services, lists the health service zones and districts, and describes in detail the organization of present services, including physical resources and the geographical distribution, qualifications, turnover rates, and training of health manpower. The next chapter, based on the author's field visits to the NWT, supplies extensive health and health-related information about Mackenzie, Inuvik, and Baffin zones. NWT's special health problems, such as alcoholism, malnutrition, and otitis media are considered, as well as environmental health and communications problems in the health services. Hard data on the economics of NWT's health services are followed by a long discussion chapter (annotated separately) that evaluates the present services and suggests priorities for action. (CL)

3418   Haraldson, S.S. *Evaluation of the Canadian Eskimo Health Service: discussion.* In Haraldson, S.S., Evaluation of the Canadian Eskimo Health Service, Gothenburg, Sweden, Scandinavian School of Public Health, 96-112. Engl.

For complete document see entry 3417.

In Canada's vast Northwest Territories (NWT), 40 nursing stations constitute the backbone of health services available to Eskimos, who comprise 3% of the territories' population. However, local village health aides, as used in Alaska, would be more economically appropriate and practically suitable than nurses for this remote area. Although Eskimos have previously not participated in planning and implementing health services, NWT's objectives for 1975-1976 include encouragement of training for northern residents in medical and paramedical fields, training and appointing of community aides to communities of 50-100 persons, and provision of prenatal, postnatal, and family planning services. Assessment of present health services by their coverage, diversity of services offered, and transportation available to patients and health personnel shows that planners should concentrate on developing reliable transportation and communication facilities in remote arctic places. However, despite recent expenditure by NWT on transportation facilities involved in reducing the high Eskimo infant mortality rate, *otitis media* and meningitis remain endemic among Eskimos and mortality and morbidity data compare unfavourably with the rest of Canada. Malnutrition cannot be considered a high priority problem of the Canadian arctic, though small nutritional deficiencies exist, but family planning is indispensable for the present increasingly urbanized settlement patterns of Eskimos. Community and town planning are also needed to maintain cultural traditions and self-respect through fundamental involvement and utilization of local people in all social services, including health. (CL)

3419 **Haraldson, S.S.** *Evaluation of Alaska Native Health Service*. Gothenburg, Sweden, Scandinavian School of Public Health, 1973. 48p. Engl. 44 refs.
Unpublished document; see also entries 2699 (volume 4) and 3417.

An evaluation of Alaska's Native Health Service, based on observations of health facilities and analysis of available statistics, aimed to study the adequacy and cost-effectiveness of existing programmes and review the area's current and future priorities. The present well-developed preventive and curative services, supported by extremely high per capita expenditure (US$700 per year), have brought about low infant mortality and reasonable life expectancy. As even greater expenditure on medical facilities is unrealistic, the next step in improving health should be to improve standards of living, housing, water supplies, hygiene, and nutrition. Such developments, however, are constrained by Alaska's climate, underpopulation, and meagre agricultural resources. Furthermore, Alaska's Indians and Eskimos are facing a new range of mental and social diseases, especially alcoholism, that are related to their rapid cultural and economic transition from nomadism and a self-sufficient household economy to a sedentary life and monetary economy. Therefore, priorities in health planning should now focus on solving sociomedical problems, integrating health services with other development projects, improving coordination between different health activities, and decreasing professional staff turnover by appointing medical assistants to permanent positions in remote areas. An appendix contains a report of a study trip to the Navajo Indian Reservation in Arizona. (CL)

3420 **Hyndman, G. Sjoerdsma, A. Woigo, H. Royal Tropical Institute, Amsterdam.** *Survey of the MCH clinics Jun 1974: a report for the Kenya-Netherlands Project for Operations Research in Outpatient Services*. Nairobi, Medical Research Centre, 28 Nov 1974. 1v.(various pagings). Engl.

In January 1974, the maternal and child health services of the Kiambu District Hospital, Kenya, moved to a new building with more space, a proper waiting area, more and better-trained staff, and a more streamlined procedure. Five months later, a survey was conducted to determine the effect of the new situation on clinic attendance, waiting time, service time, patient characteristics, etc., and to provide baseline data for future experiments. Data were obtained over a 3-week period through observation of patient flow through the clinic and a questionnaire. It was noted that all patients spent less time in the common waiting room than they had previously and total time spent in the clinic was reduced for all services except family planning; no significant changes in the numbers or characteristics of attenders were noted. Details of the new procedures, the study methodology, and the study findings are set forward. Interview

schedules and observer instruction sheets are appended. (HC)

3421 **Johnson, A.M.** *Health services and socio-economic development in Venezuela*. Newcastle-upon-Tyne, UK, University of Newcastle, School of Medicine, Mar 1975. 31p. Engl. 24 refs.
Unpublished document.

Health services in Venezuela are unequally distributed and concentrated in the lucrative private sector. Although there are 84 government organizations concerned with health, in the absence of a coherent national plan there is virtually no coordination among them. Rural areas are especially poorly served and the quality of existing provisions is so low that they are under-used by those in need. Most doctors find ways of avoiding the legal requirement of 2 years' rural service and prefer specialized medicine in private urban hospitals to general practice. In both urban and rural areas, more health auxiliaries recruited from local communities are urgently needed for primary care delivery. Their work should be reinforced by more effective health education based on proper research and planning. Greater use could be made of the mass media for this work, especially as the urban slum-dwellers are strongly influenced by television, which encourages them to spend money on luxuries rather than health. (DM)

3422 **Monckosso, G.L. Mousseau-Gershman, Y. Kelly, P. Devoto, R. Nchinda, T.C. International Development Research Centre, Ottawa. Dorozynski, A.** *Applied operational research: report of a seminar workshop*. Ottawa, International Development Research Centre, 1977. 27p. Engl. Refs.
Seminar-Workshop on Applied Research in Public Health, Yaounde, Cameroon, 6-11 Dec 1976.

Operations research is defined as "the application of scientific methods and techniques to the study of complex problems in a system with well-defined objectives and having economical and technical constraints, with a view to establishing priorities and taking appropriate decisions that will lead to achievement of the stated objectives through an improvement in the functioning of the system." Seventeen participants from different disciplines met in Cameroon to explore the potential of an operations research approach to matters concerning health. They proposed to show that the scientific approach to a research project is not necessarily very complex and can assist even the uninitiated in the orderly elaboration of a project. The participants were called upon to: select, by means of the nominal group method (a scientific way of achieving consensus), two of Cameroon's high priority projects; define the two projects with greater precision, placing their components within the framework of an operational plan and describing their implementation in step-by-step fashion; describe on paper a complete project in a form acceptable to research organizations and donor agencies; formulate the questions to be asked regarding the project; and elaborate the methodology for finding answers to these questions. This report summarizes the experience of the participants in arriving at a research proposal and reproduces in full one of the proposals: an evaluation of the training and utilization of nurses, midwives, and state-certified birth assistants who graduated from the National School of Nursing and Midwifery in Yaounde from 1972-1976. (HC)

3423   Ordonez Carceller, C. *Organizacion de la atencion medica en la comunidad. (Organization of medical care within the community).* Revista Cubana de Administracion de Salud (Havana), 2(2), Apr-Jun 1976, 141-151. Span.
17 refs.
The author states that health care objectives must be constantly redefined in order to satisfy the changing needs of the community; consequently, they tend to pass through four stages: 1) emphasis on the reduction of mortality and morbidity among users of the health care system, 2) the extension of this system to previous non-users, 3) the expansion of the system to include social and economic aspects, and 4) the attempt to satisfy public demands of what the system should provide. The author feels that the Cuban health care system has successfully evolved during the past 15 years to a most satisfactory stage incorporating all four of these objectives. He describes the basic elements of the present community health care system, which is based on a national hierarchy of primary care delivered by health teams in clinics, secondary or specialist care available in hospitals, and tertiary or highly specialized care that is only available in selected hospitals, i.e., open heart surgery or special burn units. All of these levels are linked to related community services in each region. The author also urges that health care personnel, teachers, and medical students be encouraged to participate in community health services so that they can keep abreast of community needs. (RMB)

3424   Pakistan, Planning Commission. *Health services in Pakistan.* Islamabad, Pakistan, Planning Commission, 24 Dec 1976. 35p. Engl.
Pakistan's health system, which reaches only 20% of the population, is limited by a number of factors: inadequate coverage of rural areas, inadequate expenditure on preventive medicine (only 23.72% of the population is availed of safe water supplies and only 6.46% of sewage disposal), costly concurrent expenditure on several vertical programmes, and a disproportionate output of doctors in comparison with other paramedical personnel (the ratio of doctors to paramedicals is 1:1). A new policy, which envisages a shift from the present doctor-oriented approach to a three-tiered system consisting of doctors, auxiliaries, and community health workers is soon to be implemented. The policy calls for the construction of a network of health centres and basic health units to form a link between the village and the modern health superstructure, the integration of all smaller unipurpose health units into this general health network, a stabilization in the yearly production of doctors, an increase in the capacity of existing nursing schools, and the inauguration of a number of training centres for

auxiliaries at the district level. In this booklet, the organization, administration, and manpower and financial resources of the health system are reviewed and the proposed structural changes are summarized, the responsibilities of the federal and provincial governments *vis-a-vis* the implementation of these changes are appended. (HC)

3425   Pakistan, Planning Commission. *Evaluation of project for establishment of 150 rural health centres.* Islamabad, Pakistan, Planning Commission, May 1976. 9p. Engl.
In 1962, the government of Pakistan sanctioned a scheme for the establishment of 150 rural health centres. The health centres were to be staffed by 46 persons (1 male doctor, 1 female doctor, 14 medical auxiliaries, and 30 other staff) and equipped with inpatient facilities, an operating theatre, and a laboratory. Each rural health centre was to supervise 3 subcentres and be responsible for the preventive and curative needs of a population of 50 000. By June 1975, 131 rural health centres had been established. An evaluation based on 17 of them revealed that: inpatient facilities were under-utilized--in most cases, bed occupancy was less than 10%; in roughly half of the centres, operating facilities were underutilized or not utilized at all; immunization services were reaching a bare 20% of the population served; and no health education, sanitation work, *dai* training, or home visiting was being conducted and a minimum of family planning was being accomplished. It is observed that the underutilization of inpatient facilities is due to the programme's inability to attract doctors. Despite the fact that the centres were generally constructed according to specifications, well-served by transportation and communications networks, and provided with 'elaborate' staff living accommodations, a great many of the professional posts (ranging from 33.3%-61% for male doctors and from 75%-84% for female doctors) remained vacant. It is concluded that, while every effort should be made to recruit doctors for rural service, any rural health scheme that depends heavily on them is bound to run into difficulties. (HC)

3426   Sekou, H. *Action de sante et prevention en zone rurale. (Health and disease prevention in a rural area).* Medecine d'Afrique Noire (Paris), 24(7), 1977, 530-534. Fren.
A review of health and health services in the rural department of Dosso, Niger, is followed by a brief description of six pilot projects that have recently been initiated there. Niger's classification by the UN as one of the 25 'least developed' countries is reflected in its health resources. In Dosso, 1 departmental health centre, 4 health centres, 18 dispensaries, and 2 maternities serve half a million inhabitants. The health worker:population ratio is 1:98 000 for physicians, 1:493 000 for midwives, 1:98 000 for state registered nurses, and 1:70 000 for auxiliary nurses. In addition to lack of funds, the health infrastructure suffers from the priority accorded curative medicine in the country's health budget, the absence of MCH services, the rivalry between the *Services des Grandes Endemics* and the public health sector for

scarce resources, and the absence of a national health policy. It is hoped that the six pilot projects described (MCH, latrine construction, tuberculosis control, utilization of horse and buggy transporation in the supervision of peripheral staff, refresher courses for nurses, and the training of traditional birth attendants and village health volunteers) will be adopted as means of strengthening existing facilities throughout the country. (HC)

3427   Srikantarumu, N. Baily, G.V. Nair, S.S. *Operational model of the district tuberculosis programme.* Indian Journal of Public Health (Calcutta, India), 20(1), Mar 1976, 3-8. Engl.

Operations research technique has been applied to India's district tuberculosis programme in order to point up deficiencies in its casefinding and treatment activities. An operational model, in the form of a flow chart, was drawn up and applied to data from the district's peripheral health institutions, through which the tuberculosis programme is implemented. It was noted that out of a total outpatient attendance of 474 848, only 4 620 sputa were examined and 480 true cases of tuberculosis diagnosed; of these, 75 died, 215 were cured, and 190 were either drug sensitive or drug resistant by the end of 1 year. When the number of cases found was compared to the number that should have been found according to previous studies of similar populations, the programme's casefinding was calculated to be functioning at 27% efficiency; based on the figures mentioned above, treatment activity was found to be functioning at 65% efficiency. Since maximum casefinding efficiency is considered to be 100% and maximum treatment efficiency is estimated to be 85%, it is concluded that there is an urgent need to improve casefinding activities through more thorough selection of candidates for sputum examination. Improvement in treatment activities will become more necessary as improvement in casefinding is achieved. The flow chart and the methodology for computing the values assigned to it are included. (HC)

3428   Stephens, B. National Institute for Research in Development and African Studies, Documentation Unit, Gaborone, Botswana. *Health information system for outpatient services based on family retained health records.* Gaborone, Botswana, National Institute for Research in Development and African Studies, Documentation Unit, Discussion Paper No.2, Feb 1976. 35p. Engl. Refs.

A simplified health information system designed to meet the needs of both patients and administrators was developed and tested in five outpatient units in Botswana. The system consists of: a comprehensive, patient-retained family packet of records; a simple, precoded register for recording service statistics in the clinic; and a clinic follow-up book in which the names of individuals are noted on the days when they are expected to return. A time-motion study and observation of experts and clinic staff revealed that: although record-keeping took 20%-30% of staff time, it was often coupled with another activity such as health education; having patients retain

their own records considerably reduced time spend in tasks associated with clinic-retained records; the patients appreciated having a health history that they could take with them; only a small percentage (.04%-2%)of all patients forgot or lost their cards; 85.7% of all follow-up patients returned voluntarily to the clinic and another 8.7% were traced and treated by clinic staff; and the new statistics register, by reducing the amount of writing, tallying, and recopying done in the clinic, was calculated to save the clinic 10 500 person-hours per year. Samples of health cards, the statistics register, and the clinic follow-up book are appended. (HC)

3429   Vogel, L.C. *Operations research in outpatient services: experiments in Kenya.* Nairobi, Medical Research Centre, 8 Aug 1973. 4p. Engl.
Ninth International Congress on Tropical Medicine, Athens, Greece, 14-21 Oct 1973.
See also entry 3430.

Efforts from 1968-1972 to improve the efficiency of the Machakos Outpatient Department (Kenya) were only partially successful; although they increased the medical assistant's efficiency, they introduced vulnerability into other parts of the department and did not appreciably reduce patient waiting times. Based on six week-long investigations of activities of the department, they included a study of current operations, introduction of changes to eliminate bottlenecks in patient flow, and evaluation of changes. The changes: shifted the medical assistant's clerical duties to a clerk; limited the range of drugs he prescribed to 10 types of tablets, 10 types of mixtures, and 2 types of penicillin injections; standardized prescriptions by age group, dosage, and duration of treatment; and reallocated physical space. Follow-up indicated that productivity of workers increased, prescriptions and cost of drugs skyrocketed, and the clerk served as a new bottleneck. (AC)

3430   Vogel, L.C. Dissevelt, A.G. Gemert, W. Christensen, S. Quadros, F.C. Royal Tropical Institute, Amsterdam. *Study of some operational aspects of the outpatient department of a district hospital (Machakos, Kenya).* Nairobi, Medical Research Centre, 1969. 55p. Engl.
See also entry 3429.

The 1st in a series, this two-phase study defined the objectives and methods used in later investigations of outpatient departments in Kenya; it was undertaken in 1968-1969 to focus on shortcomings in the Machakos Outpatient Department and recommend changes aimed at improving efficiency. During the 1st phase, investigators examined the operations of the different treatment stations within the outpatient department, i.e., the dressing room, injection room, pharmacy, etc.; during the 2nd, they analyzed the activities of the medical assistant. Data for the 1st phase were collected from December 4-10 and from December 16-21, 1968; every patient attending the department was given a card upon which socioeconomic data, diagnosis, treatment, waiting times, and number of attendances were recorded. The resulting information, combined with timed observations of the medical assistant's activities, provided the baseline for recommendations that included using a higher bench for the treatment of wounds and ulcers in the dressing room, introducing a code for diagnosis, designing a functional patient record, etc. (AC)

V.3 Planning

See also: 3145, 3405, 3422, 3425, 3473

3431   Johnson, A.M. *Integrated health services: the Panamanian experience.* Newcastle-upon-Tyne, UK, University of Newcastle, School of Medicine, 1976. 17p. Engl.
Unpublished document; see also entry 3394.
A 3-month study of the Integrated Health Service (IHS) of Bocas del Toro, Panama, revealed a considerable gap between theory and practice. The IHS was introduced to the area by the central government in 1973 to provide a comprehensive range of health services. According to the plan, the three hospitals of the area should supervise both health centres staffed by doctors and subcentres built in traditional style by local labour and manned by auxiliaries. However, construction, supervision, and the activities of the health team are seriously handipcapped by transportation and communications difficulties. In addition, there are cultural obstacles to the IHS approach. The Guaymi Indians, whose social system traditionally centres on small family groups, resist the wider community involvement necessary for improvement of public health. Indigenous culture has over several generations been disrupted by the United Brands Banana Company, the major employer, which has moved people into overcrowded housing, put a stop to subsistence farming, and provided curative services for the resulting diseases that encouraged a doctor-dependent attitude to health. At present, the IHS is overstaffed with doctors who are reluctant to join the health team. Meanwhile, the auxiliaries, with minimal back-up, are attempting to mobilize local health committees to take preventive measures. Their efforts will eventually be supplemented by health education radio broadcasts in local languages, but so far the auxiliaries' success seems to depend on personal motivation and their status within the community. (DM)

3432   Litsios, S. *Principles and methods of evaluation of national health plans.* International Journal of Health Services (Westport, Conn.), 1(1), 1971, 79-85. Engl.
The author presents a straightforward approach to evaluating national health plans based on the premise that the purpose of the planning process is to establish the health objectives that are desirable, the health objectives that are achievable, the health resources required to achieve them in an efficient manner, and the configuration of programmes best suited to achieve them. Seven questions have been formulated as a basis for determining whether or not a national health plan lives up to this premise: 1) does the plan clearly lay out long-term health objectives? 2) Is the plan's programming in agreement with these objectives? 3) Are programme objectives, activities, and schedules properly integrated with one another? 4) Were the major resource allocation alterna-

tives available for achieving desired health objectives considered? 5) Did the planning process adequately explore alternative programme configurations? 6) Have programmes been implemented according to the plan? and 7) Have the desired objectives been achieved? Each of these questions is discussed in detail and some of the factors that tend to impede or complicate the evaluation effort are pointed out. (HC)

3433   Roscin, A.V. *Some solutions to the problems of planning flexible and co-ordinated health care facilities under conditions of limited resources.* World Hospitals (Oxford, UK), 11(4), Autumn 1975, 243-245. Engl.
Resource constraints to the planning and construction of health facilities can be handled in two ways: construction plans can be brought into conformity with allocations and implemented immediately, or construction of the desired end product can be phased over a period of time. The 1st method tends to result in a facility that soon becomes obsolete, necessitating unjustifiable expense for reconstruction and modernization. The 2nd calls for a carefully thought out design that provides for the possibility of enlarging any hospital department without disturbing the functioning of the main body of the hospital. A design methodology that fulfills this requirement is currently being tested in Russia. An experimental hospital is being built on the modular concept (i.e., according to standard planning and construction elements) and is to be put into operation in two phases, first as a 360-bed and then as a 600-bed facility. If the experiment is a success, the modular concept may become the basis of health care facilities planning by the 1980s. Details of the modular concept as applied in the experimental situation are given. (HC)

3434   Sekou, H. *Sante et developpement au Niger. (Health and development in Niger).* Medecine d'Afrique Noire (Paris), 24(10), 1977, 639-645. Fren.
Due to a scarcity of health personnel and a disease profile typical of a developing country, health and development are complementary necessities in Niger; the author suggests, however, that curative medicine is usurping too great a share of the health budget and that a number of development schemes, while bringing a certain amount of prosperity, have engendered public health problems of their own. Examples of the latter are cited: a water management scheme has contributed to the spread of guinea worm, the vectors of malaria and bilharzia have flourished in ditches left by a construction project, and a mining development which employs former agricultural workers has resulted in numerous social problems associated with adaptation. It is recommended that existing health services be reorganized into an integrated basic health infrastructure, that health planning be made an integral part of development planning, and that all development projects be carefully scrutinized for their implications for health. (HC)

3435   Stipek, J. *Models for health institutions and hospitals to be planned and built under conditions of limited resources.* World Hospitals (Oxford, UK), 11(4), Autumn 1975, 240-242. Engl.

The transplant of sophisticated hospital models from the developed to the developing countries has too often resulted in inappropriately-designed facilities. For example, wards tend to be arbitrarily designated, leading to overcrowding in some and underutilization of others; pediatric facilities are not designed to cope with the largely infectious nature of their occupancy; space and facilities for mothers are virtually non-existent; and facilities for the maintainance of hospital buildings and equipment are lacking. Moreover, haphazard expansion of hospitals has led to physical arrangements that are sometimes exceedingly disorganized. In this paper, the need to maximize the potential of existing structures and facilities by rearranging them in a more functional manner is pointed out; at the same time, the necessity of drawing up a masterplan for future growth for all institutions is recognized. Doctors and architects are urged to cooperate in these two tasks and some guidelines are set forward to assist them. (HC)

V.4 Geographic Distribution of Health Services

See also: 3405, 3412, 3413, 3414

3436   de Kadt, E. *Desigualdades en el campo de la salud. (Inequalities in the health field).* In Livingston, M., Raczynski, D., eds., Salud Publica y Bienestar Social, Santiago, CEPLAN, Mar 1976, 27-63. Span.
Refs.

In this study, the author attempts to analyze the growing preoccupation with the unequal distribution of health resources from a public health as well as a sociological point of view. In the introduction, he criticizes health ministries for being more concerned with national averages than the protection of at-risk groups and warns that, until they recognize the link between health and environment, much of the money devoted to the health sector will be wasted. Sections 1 and 2 examine the concepts of "demand" and "health needs." In Section 3, he discusses the inequalities of access to health care in terms of urban versus rural, larger cities versus smaller ones, and rich versus poor within the same city. Section 4 deals with the inequalities of health status measured in terms of infant mortality and Section 5 concludes that different groups run different risks and therefore have different health care requirements. In Section 6, the author demonstrates that the types of problems common to the health field also occur simultaneously in other areas, thus proving that they cannot be solved without taking into account social and economic factors as well. In Section 7, he considers health planning processes and, in Section 8, the effects of professional attitudes and status on health care systems. Section 9 describes ways in which the community can organize to improve its own health care delivery system, particularly by the training and deployment of auxiliary health workers. (RMB)

3437   **Philippines, Department of Health.** *Social services development in the Philippines; technical report part II: health.* Quezon City, Philippines, Development Academy of the Philippines, Mar 1975. 66p. Engl.

One of a 4-part report on social services development in the Philippines, this publication examines the country's health services, proposes a model for the hospital system, and estimates costs for providing 1 hospital bed per:1 000 population. The distribution of the existing health facilities is presented and locations for new facilities are suggested. The data, which were derived from government sources, indicate that bed-to-population ratios vary from a high in Butanes of 6.76:1 000 to a low of 0.18:1 000 in Lanas del Sur. The target is to realize a 1:1 000 ratio within the foreseeable future and strengthen a network of services whose most basic unit, the *barrio* health station, serves each settlement and refers patients to the rural health unit. Other facilities within the network include community hospitals or health centres with up to 10-bed capacity, emergency hospitals, provincial hospitals, regional hospitals, and the Philippine National Institute of Health--the pinnacle of tertiary care. Statistical data are tabulated. (AC)

3438   **Reitzes, D.C. Elkhanialy, H.** *Black physicians and minority group health care: the impact of NMF.* Medical Care (Philadelphia, Pa.), 14(12), Dec 1976, 1052-1060. Engl.

For over 25 years, the National Medical Fellowships organization (NMF) has tried to improve medical care by and for American blacks and other minorities. Over the years, the corporation's efforts have focused on breaking down racial barriers to postgraduate training opportunities for blacks (1946-1959), supporting black physicians during postgraduate training through fellowships and scholarships (1952-1959), motivating young blacks toward medicine and financially assisting them as undergraduates (1959-1970), and supporting minority group medical students on the basis of financial need (1970-1973). In order to assess the impact of the NMF on blacks in medicine, a comparative study of NMF grant recipients and other black physicians was undertaken. Questionnaires were sent to all 471 NMF recipients (up to 1970) and to one-third of all other black physicians; 59% of the former and 30% of the latter responded. The results showed that a greater percentage of the NMF recipients had obtained specialty certification and hospital and faculty appointments; however, fewer of the NMF recipients in private practice (55% as compared to 76% of the other physicians) were serving blacks and only 38% (as compared to 36%) were primarily serving the lower classes. These findings indicate that the NMF was eminently successful in its efforts to improve the position of black physicians but that this has not resulted in better care for disadvantaged black communities. It is suggested that this last goal will have to be pursued directly. (HC)

3439   **Taylor, C.E. Alter, J.D. Grover, P.L. Sangal, S.P. Andrews, S. Takulia, H.S. List, M.S.** *Doctors for the villages: study of rural internships in seven*

Indian medical colleges. New York, Asia Publishing House, 1976. 197p. Engl.

This 5-year study was undertaken in India to identify the changes needed to attract young doctors into the rural health services. Data gathered by means of questionnaires and a battery of tests were amassed for 3 years from a total 1 480 interns. The findings indicated that interns were willing to practice in the villages if living conditions and professional standards existing there were improved. The main deterrents cited were the inadequate drugs, supplies, equipment, opportunities for professional advancement and postgraduate education, access to libraries and reference materials, etc. Recommendations based on the findings number more than 50 and include: upgrading primary health centres; maintaining a basic supply of specific drugs; standardizing forms, procedures, and nomenclature; entrusting medical colleges with planning refresher training; raising the status of community medicine and rural practice; etc. (AC)

V.5 Financial Aspects

See also: 3406, 3413, 3417

3440   Biddulph, J. *Crisis in medical manpower.* Papua New Guinea Medical Journal (Boroko, Papua New Guinea), 20(2), Jun 1976, 80-83. Engl.
Twelfth Annual Medical Symposium, Lae, Papua New Guinea, 1976.

The large number of foreign medical students in Papua New Guinea's medical schools combined with small 2nd-year classes and the high attrition rate of national students has resulted in the incredibly high cost of K250 000 per national medical graduate and a 25% deficit in the national health plan's projected number of national doctors for 1983. The 1st problem can be solved by enrolling more national students, the 2nd by either hiring foreign physicians or expanding paramedical training programmes. The author recommends the latter alternative because auxiliaries are cheaper to train, remain in the country, and are more familiar with the language and culture as well as the disease patterns and medical services. The successful implementation of different types of auxiliaries is discussed. (RMB)

3441   Cole-King, S. Institute of Development Studies, University of Sussex, Brighton, UK. *Health sector aid from voluntary agencies: the British case study.* Brighton, UK, University of Sussex, Institute of Development Studies, IDS Discussion Paper No.97, Jul 1976. 86p. Engl.
20 refs.

This report presents the findings of a study of more than 50 British voluntary agencies that support health projects in developing countries. The organizations are classified as relief agencies, development agencies, missionary societies, or advisory, coordinating, or research organizations. Their relationships with other voluntary and governmental organizations, especially those within the recipient countries, are outlined and their major sources of income stated. Their health aid is

divided into: primary, secondary, or tertiary health care; special health programmes (e.g., specific disease eradication campaigns); training programmes for health personnel; health-related aid (e.g., water and nutrition schemes), etc. Detailed information on financial aid is provided in tabular form. Health sector expenditures are expressed as a proportion of total aid and are broken down into commodity aid, support of expatriate medical workers, recurrent expenses, capital outlay, etc. The types of projects supported by major charities and their selection criteria, objectives, and evaluation procedures are discussed. An appendix presents the sources of data for the report and the problems encountered in collection and analysis. (DM)

3442   Gish, O. Walker, G. *Transport and communication systems in health services.* Tropical Doctor (London), 7(3), Jul 1977, 119-122. Engl.

The cost-effectiveness of utilizing various means of transportation in a number of health service functions is discussed. These functions include supportive visits to peripheral basic care units, ambulance evacuation of patients, vertical health programmes, primary health care, delivery of supplies to peripheral units, and specialist clinic rounds on a scheduled basis. Of these, the visits to basic care units is deemed to have the highest cost-benefit ratio because it increases the effectiveness of care provided by basically-trained peripheral workers and can be combined with referral clinics, the delivery of supplies, and patient evacuation. The utilization of transport, especially aircraft, for ambulance or primary care purposes is difficult to justify, since the former is extremely expensive per evacuation and the latter is far less cost-effective than the provision of care from fixed clinics. For most visits, light pick-up trucks or vans are adequate. Utilization of light aircraft should be restricted to supportive visits to fixed units that could not be as effectively reached by land vehicles. Although their effectiveness is difficult to quantify, radio communication systems can serve to increase the morale and hence the effectiveness of peripheral unit staff. The estimated cost of setting up a radiocommunication system is quoted and a number of manufacturers of appropriate radio equipment are listed. (HC)

3443   Green, L.W. *Potential of health education includes cost effectiveness.* Hospitals (Chicago, Ill.), 50(9), 1 May 1976, 57-61. Engl.
47 refs.

An American physician discusses some of the benefits of institution-based health education, including: a reduction in broken appointments, overbooking, and waiting time leading to increased patient satisfaction; fewer malpractice suits, which often stem from patient dissatisfaction with the information they receive; more accurate, speedier diagnoses due to informed history-giving and earlier recognition of symptoms on the part of the patient; improved patient compliance with medical regimens; better utilization on health services e.g., a reduction in unnecessary use of emergency facilities; increased consumer participation in programme planning and other aspects of hospital planning and management; and reduced morbidity and mortality. Each of these benefits is illustrated and supported by recent relevant studies. (HC)

3444   Heller, P.S. *Issues in the costing of public sector outputs: the health and medical services of Malaysia.* East Lansing, Mich., University of Michigan, Center for Research on Economic Development, Feb 1975. 85p. Engl.
30 refs.
Unpublished document.
This study describes Malaysia's medical care delivery system and compares its health costs, health inputs, and demographic characteristics with those of other developing countries. A description of the cost accounting and budgeting system of Malaysia's Ministry of Health, a discussion of the issues that arise in costing health institution outputs (e.g., the cost of providing a service via a paramedic in a health centre versus the cost of providing the same service via a physician in an outpatient facility), a brief illustration of some of the applications of cost estimates, and 18 tables of data are included. The author hopes that the methods proposed for cost estimation prove useful to health planners. (HC)

3445   Rawitscher, M. Mayer, J. *Nutritional outputs and energy inputs in seafoods.* Science (Washington, D.C.), 198(4314), 21 Oct 1977, 261-264. Engl.
Energy used by US ships to harvest different varieties of seafood can vary by a factor of more than 100 when the content of edible protein or the line weight of the seafoods are compared. This energy difference has no relationship to the nutritive value of the food. When protein yield is compared, the energy to harvest some seafoods is in the same range as that needed to grow field crops. There is also a large increase in energy consumption after processing, partly because of the small percent of the live weight used for human food. Consequently, it is recommended that greater use be made of fish with low harvesting energies. (Modified journal abstract.)

3446   Walker, G. Gish, O. *Mobile health services: a study in cost-effectiveness.* Medical Care (Philadelphia, Pa.), 15(4), Apr 1974, 267-276. Engl.
23 refs.
Two mobile and four stationary primary health services in Botswana were examined and compared with regard to their cost-effectiveness. One mobile service used a truck and the other, a Cessna-185 light aircraft to deliver services. Costs were calculated per patient-contact and per effective patient-contact based on observation (for the mobile services) and clinical records analysis (for stationary clinics). The results showed that the fixed services generated an average cost per patient-contact similar to that for the truck-operated mobile unit but less than half that of the other mobile service. However, the mobile services were far more costly per effective patient-contact (8-14 times). (HC)

V.6 Cultural Aspects

See also: 3417, 3468, 3473, 3480

3447   Dennis, C. *Western medicine and traditional medicine in an African tribe.* Survival International Review (London), 1(15), Mar 1976, 28-33. Engl.
24 refs.
In Botswana, traditional Tswana medical beliefs and practices still persist side by side with Western medicine. The Tswana believe that death and illness are caused by supernatural intervention or human sorcery (also affecting cattle and crops) and isolate the sick to protect both them and the immediate environment. Thus, the functions of traditional medicine are protective as well as curative, productive (e.g., rain-making), and destructive (sorcery). Although *dingaka* (priest-doctors) counteract this sorcery by bone-throwing divination and herbal medicines, they acknowledge ultimate healing power from a supreme being. This religious aspect facilitated the acceptance of early Western medicine as practiced by missionaries, as did the established Tswana use of outside *dingaka*. However, despite British attempts to replace basic tenets of traditional Tswana beliefs with nonspiritualistic Western medical concepts that resulted in the displacement of herbalists by hospital-centred medical facilities, bone-throwers still flourish in Botswana and fill a basic psychological need. The author points out that a basic knowledge of predominant cultural factors, with the realization that Western medicine is not always most appropriate, is a vital prerequisite for the successful development of medical facilities in tribal societies. (CL)

3448   Furlong, E. *Training course for staff working with Asians.* Nursing Times (London), 73(12), 24 Mar 1977, 428-429. Engl.
A community nurse describes a 5-week (2 hours:week) course designed to help British health workers understand the cultural backgrounds of their Asian patients. Topics covered included: basic information about overseas patients, the local Asian community, countries of origin of the major groups of foreign patients, reasons for emigrating, religions; names, family life, and marriage, and the role of their women in the family; diet and dietary customs, birth and child care customs; hygiene, clothing, hair, make-up, attitudes to sickness and death; the language barrier, languages spoken, and special linguistic problems and how to deal with them. Impressed by the success of this course, the author recommends that similar courses be given to other health workers. (RMB)

3449   Imperato, P.J. *Indigenous medical beliefs and practices in Bamako, a Moslem African city.* Tropical and Geographical Medicine (Haarlem, Netherlands), 22(2), Jun 1970, 211-220. Engl.
16 refs.
In Bamako, Mali, four stages of modernization can be discerned from the people's use of health services. They range from complete reliance on modern medicine to total dependence on traditional practices. At present, the predominant pattern is to seek modern treatment as a

complement to traditional practices, after a traditional practitioner, such as a healer, herbalist, diviner, *soma*, or *marabout*, has diagnosed the supernatural cause. Because traditional therapies vary for each patient, the modern practice of prescribing similar treatments is difficult for the people to accept. However, the main attraction is that the traditional practitioner offers treatment that is attuned to the patient's beliefs about disease--the important phychological element of health care that has been bypassed in modern health care planning. (AC)

3450   Kleinman, A. *Cultural construction of clinical reality: comparisons of practitioner-patient interactions in Taiwan.* Bethesda, Md., John E. Fogarty International Centre for Advanced Study in the Health Sciences, Nov 1975. 76p. Engl. 23 refs.
Harvard Seminar on Implications for Health Care of the Cross-cultural Study of Health, Illness, and Healing, Boston, Mass., 25 Nov 1975.
Some insight into popular attitudes towards the variety of health practitioners operating in the private sector in Taiwan emerges from a medical anthropologist's study of shamans (folk healers), Chien interpreters (fortune tellers), Chinese-style doctors, Western physicians, and patients in a poor area of Taipei City. The investigation, conducted by interviews and direct observations of consultations, showed that the people had differing expectations for each type of healer and that the practitioners conformed to these expectations. The shamans go into a trance, ascribe supernatural causes to the clients' misfortunes, and prescribe charms or remedies. The Chien interpreters not only foretell the future but offer advice on how to cope with bad fate. Chinese-style doctors base their practice on taking the patient's pulse and prescribing traditional medications. They ask few questions and do not inform the client of their diagnosis. Similarly, Western doctors seldom explain their actions to their patients. Payment is for treatment rather than for consultation, so many unnecessary drugs and dangerous injections are given and little attempt is made by doctors to understand popular beliefs about illness or to provide health education. All these deficiencies are accepted by the general public as aspects of the autocratic doctor-patient relationship, but people are much less satisfied by Western medical services than by those of the shamans and even Western practitioners themselves sometimes turn to traditional remedies for their own problems. (DM)

3451   Lelo di Kimbi Kiaku, N.M. Rotsart de Hertaing, I. Courtejoie, J. Centre d'Etudes et de Recherches pour la Promotion de la Sante, Kangu-Mayumbe, Zaire. *Sante et tradition: proverbes et coutumes relatifs a la sante. (Health and tradition: proverbs and customs related to health).* Kangu-Mayumbe, Zaire, Centre d'Etudes et de Recherches pour la Promotion de la Sante, Brochure Illustre No.17, n.d. 59p. Fren. 16 refs.
See also entry 2804.

The customs, beliefs, and proverbs that form part of traditional medicine in Zaire are examined in this pamphlet. Traditional practices are classified and explained whenever possible within their cultural context. The authors stress the need to retain traditional medicine as a complement to modern, materialistic medicine because of its value in treating psychosomatic illness. (HC)

3452   Marriott, McK. *Western medicine in a village of northern India.* In Paul, B.D., ed., Health, Culture and Community: Case Studies of Public Reactions to Health Programs, New York, Russell Sage Foundation, 1955, 239-268. Engl.
For complete document see entry 3454.
Personal relationships in village India are governed traditionally by caste and kinship and relationships with outsiders tend to be fraught with distrust. This is one of the major reasons why modern medicine has had so little impact on rural inhabitants. Its practitioners have not adapted their style and delivery of services to suit the traditional structures. They could learn many lessons from the indigenous practitioners who are operating lucrative businesses that satisfy their patients. One lesson is the traditional practitioner's recognition of family members as important participants in patient care; another is the recognition of the respect paid to devoted healers who do not request payment and the application of the you-get-what-you-paid-for adage that is central to villagers' beliefs. (AC)

3453   McClain, C. *Adaptation in health behavior: modern and traditional medicine in a West Mexican community.* Social Science and Medicine (Oxford, UK), 11(5), Mar 1977, 341-347. Engl. 10 refs.
A study was undertaken in the small suburban community of Ajijic, Mexico, to determine the health perceptions and behaviour of traditionally-oriented and modern-oriented persons. This particular community was chosen because its cultural institutions and distinct self-identity extend back to pre-conquest times; at the same time, its proximity to a major urban centre, Guadalajara, makes it subject to a continuous modernizing influence. Forty-one mothers of families were interviewed and classified as traditionally- or modern-oriented. They were then questioned regarding both modern and traditional diseases, utilization of modern health facilities, ongoing illness episodes, etc. An analysis of the responses indicated that traditional women were heterogeneous in their health behaviour, experiencing illnesses, seeking practitioners, and using medicines from both systems. Modern-oriented Ajijicans, on the other hand, were less familiar with traditional diagnostic categories, experienced fewer traditionaly-derived illnesses, and did not consult traditional practitioners at all. This acceptance of the behavioural aspects of the modern medical system, however, was not accompanied by an understanding of its theoretical and cognitive features in either group. It is concluded that, because doctors and pharmacists do not communicate diagnostic or etiological information to their clients during consultation and treatment, these

156

more esoteric components of the modern medical system remained effectively hidden from lay people of both traditional and modern orientations. (HC)

3454 Paul, B.D. *Health, culture and community: case studies of public reactions to health programs.* New York, Russell Sage Foundation, 1955. 493p. Engl.

Individual chapters have been abstracted separately under entries 2988, 2992, 3186, 3452, 3481, and 3487.

A collection of articles on public response to health programmes, this book examines social and cultural obstacles to improved health. Through case studies, it documents Western biases and underlines the dependence of health programmes on the health workers' understanding and respect for their patients. Some of the articles assume the right of Western health workers to change and replace existing cultures, whereas others urge health workers to work within cultures in an attempt to incorporate new health-supporting habits. Examples have been taken from South Africa, Canada, Peru, India, China, Puerto Rico, USA, Chile, Brazil, Mexico, Guatemala, and the Pacific Islands. A subject index is included. (AC)

3455 Pillsbury, B.L. *"Doing the month": confinement and convalescence of Chinese women after childbirth.* Social Science and Medicine (Oxford, UK), 12(1B), Jan 1978, 11-22. Engl.
40 refs.

Traditional beliefs regarding confinement and convalescence after childbirth continue to find adherents among Chinese women of both rural and urban and Western and socialist ways of life. The custom of 'doing the month' involves an extremely restrictive set of prescriptions and proscriptions that a woman departs from at the risk of future illness or misfortune. They include: refraining from washing and any contact with water and wind, following a 'hot' diet to remedy pregnancy-induced 'hot/cold' imbalance, and observing taboos based on the belief in the polluting powers of the placental blood. In this paper, these practices are analyzed according to their empirical and theoretical bases and their efficaciousness is assessed in the light of modern Western medical and nutritional knowledge. It is observed that certain aspects of 'doing the month,' such as getting rest, avoiding exposure to drafts, and increasing the consumption of protein ('hot' foods) are undoubtedly positive. Others, such as the prohibition against bathing, may have been functional in an earlier period with a considerably higher infectious disease level but appear unwarranted in today's improved health environment. Nonetheless, it is concluded that, since 'doing the month' is an integrated health behaviour whose components are not easily disassociated one from the other, it should be respected by health professionals. The study is based on interviews in Mandarin Chinese with laypersons, herbalists, and physicians in Taiwan and with physicians and laypersons from the People's Republic of China. (HC)

3456 Ram, E.R. Datta, B.K. *Medical care for the rural people and its relationship with income and educational levels.* NIHAE Bulletin (New Delhi), 9(3), 1976, 221-228. Engl.

In Miraj Taluka (India), a study was undertaken to determine which type of medical practitioner was preferred for major and minor diseases, respectively, and how utilization of medical services correlated with patients' distance from the facility, educational level, and income level. The medical services available to the 216 225 Taluka inhabitants included 3 primary health centres, 11 subcentres, 5 ayurvedic dispensaries, 1 allopathic clinic, 34 private allopathic practitioners, 14 nonresident allopathic doctors, 25 resident and 8 nonresident RMPs, 15 resident and 9 nonresident ayurvedic doctors, and 3 resident homeopathic doctors. A random sample of 3 606 households (7% of the total) was interviewed and these findings were recorded: 80.3% consulted a practitioner for major illnesses, 72.5% consulted a practitioner for minor illnesses; for major illnesses, 67.2% consulted allopathic doctors, 24.9% RMPs, and 7.8% ayurvedic doctors; for minor illnesses, 30.9% consulted allopathic doctors, 29.3% ayurvedic, and 39.6% RMPs; in cases of major illnesses, 32.2% got medical help within 1 km of their homes; in cases of major illnesses, 61% got medical help within 1 km of their homes; 23.1% of the households that spent no money on medical care were entirely composed of illiterate members; and of those households in the lowest income group, 16.1% spent no money as compared to 8.1% in the highest income group. It is concluded that: more households seek help in cases of major illness than minor illness; in cases of major illness, families tend to seek help from allopathic doctors, no matter how far away; the average annual expenditure on medical care is 2.9% of family income; and expenditure on medical care is directly affected by educational and income status. (HC)

V.7 Epidemiological, Family Planning, MCH, and Nutritional Studies

See also: 3040, 3132, 3187, 3188, 3217, 3292, 3315, 3408, 3427

3457 Addy, D.P. *Infant feeding: a current view.* British Medical Journal (London), 1(6020), May 1976, 1268-1271. Engl.
79 refs.

A 1974 report on infant feeding practices in the UK recommends that breast-feeding be strongly encouraged for at least 2 weeks and preferably for the baby's first 4 months. A number of studies carried out in the UK and elsewhere revealed an association between bottle-feeding and a wide range of disorders including infections, cot deaths, obesity, and chemical disturbances such as hypocalcaemia. The high solute concentration of cow's milk probably contributes to the latter by putting too great a strain on the infant's kidneys. The high infection rate is probably attributable in part to the risk of contamination in the preparation of bottle feeds and also to the absence of the passive immunity conferred by breast milk. The adverse effects of artifical feeding in infancy may be long-lasting and there is statistical evidence that bottle-feeding may predispose individuals to diseases such as ulcerative colitis, coronary heart disease, and obesity in later life., In view of this overwhelming evidence in favour of breast-feeding, it is recommended that maternal allowances be adjusted to permit working mothers to spend more time breast-feeding their babies. (DM)

3458   Adriasola, G. Juricic, B. Mujica L., H. Mena G., P. Moliha C., R. Marchant, L. *Influencia del control prenatal sobre la morbimortalidad materna y perinatal. (Influence of prenatal care on maternal and perinatal morbidity and mortality).* Boletin de la Oficina Sanitaria Panamericana (Washington, D.C.), 83(5), Nov 1977, 413-424. Span.

A 2-stage evaluation of the maternal child health care provided by hospitals in Chile's national health service was carried out in 1972. Health indicators used to measure the quality of care included: physical examinations; gynaecological examinations; mother's age, weight, and blood pressure; place of delivery; etc. In the 1st stage, the prenatal care received by a group of patients with high maternal and infant mortality and morbidity proved unexpectedly superior to that received by a control group of healthy mothers and children; however, the authors attribute this to the fact that women with complictions are more likely to seek medical care. A 2nd comparison of the care received by women in provinces with the highest and lowest maternal and infant mortality and morbidity yielded the expected result: better antenatal care resulted in lower morbidity and mortality. (RMB)

3459   Alban Holguin, J. *Seminario sobre atencion de la salud en areas rurales. (Seminar on health services in rural areas).* Bogota, Federacion Panamericana de Asociaciones de Facultades (Escuelas) de Medicina, Jun 1975. 57p. Span.

Seminario sobre Atencion de la Salud en Areas Rurales, Bogota, Colombia, Ruben y Caracas, Venezuela, Sabanitas y Panama City, Panama, Quirigua, Chimaltenango, y Antigua, Guatemala, 2-11 Sep 1974.

Representatives from 8 Latin American governments and 10 medical schools visited 6 innovative programmes in 3 countries to observe them in action, study their financing and their organizational structures, analyze the coordination between the programmes and other health services, and assess their suitability for application in other countries. The programmes visited were: Programme for Training Paramedical Personnel for Work in Rural Areas, Quirigua, Guatemala; Community Medicine Programme, San Carlos University, Chimaltenango, Guatemala; Programme of Integrated Medicine, Colon Province, Panama; Community Medicine Programme, University of Panama; Simplified Medicine, Ministry of Health and Welfare, Venezuela; and Community Medicine Programme, University of the Andes, Merida, Venezuela. This report contains a brief introduction to the health problems of rural Latin America, a summary of modern thought regarding possible solutions (health services pyramid, team approach, etc.), and descriptions of and comments on the 6 projects visited. The need for better communications between health services administrations and training facilities is stressed. (HC)

3460   Aly, H.E. Moussa, W.A. Maksoud, A.A. Gharib, N. Farahat, S. Egypt, Ministry of Public Health, Nutrition Institute. *Effect of supplementary feeding on health and growth of infants and young children of low-socio-economic group in Egypt (1975-1976).* Astra Protein Letter (Molndal, Sweden), 5(1), Apr 1977. 8p. Engl.

Fish protein concentrates (FPC) could be a valuable supplementary food for young children in Egypt if introduced into the weaning diet on a large scale. Staff at the Nutrition Institute, Cairo, studied the effects of a formula containing 10% FPC mixed with local foods on a group of children aged 4-24 months from poor families attending the Institute's outpatient clinic and compared the children with a control group provided with a diet based on wheat-soya blend (WSB). Some children from each group received the weaning food as a supplement to breast milk; the others were wholly dependent on the prepared mixtures. The growth of each child was followed for at least 6 months and, although the breast-fed babies fared best, all thrived normally. Children with severe protein-calorie malnutrition recovered rapidly on either of the weaning foods, but FPC feeding caused a significantly higher weight gain, though the infection rate was the same as for the WSB-fed group. FPC was well accepted and mothers had no difficulty preparing it properly. These results suggest that FPC could make an important contribution to the weaning diet in Egypt, especially as it could be produced locally on a large scale from the rich fish reserves of the Mediterranean, Red Sea, and Lake Nasser. (DM)

3461   Anaise, J.Z. Zilkah, E. *Effectiveness of a dental education program on oral cleanliness of schoolchildren in Israel.* Community Dentistry and Oral Epidemiology (Copenhagen), 4(5), Sep 1976, 186-198. Engl.
22 refs.

A study was undertaken in Israel to examine the effect of a dental education programme on children's toothbrushing behaviour and to determine the relative merits of individual versus group instruction. A total of 175 randomly-selected children aged 11-14 years was divided into 2 experimental groups and 1 control group. The experimental groups received a lecture covering the main aspects of dental hygiene followed by individual and group instruction, respectively, in toothbrushing technique. Each child was assigned a patient hygiene performance (PHP) score at the outset and after lapses of 1 week, 1 month, and 2 months. Then the two groups were each divided into subgroups; one received refresher lectures and demonstrations at 2-month intervals and the other did not. Ten months later, all the children were again tested for PHP. Improved oral cleanliness during the first 2 months of the experiment was observed in both experimental groups regardless of the method of instruction used; however, only those children who had received both individual instruction and periodic reviews of the programme were able to maintain toothbrushing skills up to the end of the study. It is concluded that indiviaul instruction combined with reviews of the educational programme have a positive effect on skill maintenance that is greater than the effect of either alone. (HC)

3462 **Berggren, W.L. Berggren, G.M.** *Changing incidence of fatal tetanus of the newborn: a retrospective study in a defined Haitian population.* American Journal of Tropical Medicine and Hygiene (Baltimore, Md.), 20(3), May 1971, 491-494. Engl.

Over a 30-year period, the incidence of neonatal tetanus in a 10 m^2 area of rural Haiti declined from 25%-0% and infant mortality declined from 49%-5%, according to a retrospective survey carried out in 1968-1969 by the Community Health Department of the Albert Schweitzer Hospital. Local census takers, trained by the authors, questioned mothers aged 15-60 years about all the live children ever born to them. Although 1 143 of the 7 248 children were said to have died of neonatal tetanus, deaths from the disease had fallen dramatically since the 1940s. The improvement resulted from various health schemes introduced during the period, starting with the training of village health workers in 1948. With the opening of the Albert Schweitzer Hospital in 1956, a number of curative and preventive measures were established. These included improved training and equipment for traditional midwives, prenatal education for mothers about care of the umbilical cord, treatment and immunization of babies, and the production of an educational film for mothers about tetanus. A campaign to immunize all pregnant women with tetanus toxoid was started in 1961, but the elimination of the disease was only achieved when the immunization programme was extended in 1968 to cover all women aged more than 10 years. (DM)

3463 **Binns, C.W.** *Food, sickness and death in children of the highlands of Papua New Guinea.* Environmental Child Health (London), 22(1), Feb 1976, 9-11. Engl.
17 refs.
Tenth International Congress of Nutrition, Kyoto, Japan, Aug 1975.

A survey of child health and nutrition among the Enga people of Papua New Guinea revealed a high incidence of malnutrition. Growth rates were abnormally low from the age of 4 months and one third of the 1-4-year-olds weighed less than 80% of the standard for their age. These findings were based on nutritional surveillance by health auxiliaries of 83% of the children from an area of population 10 000 and examination of sample groups of those attending maternal child health (MCH) clinics. The health workers also collected information on diet, disease, and deaths by regular interviews with local clan leaders and with mothers attending the MCH clinics. They found that there was a significant association between malnutrition and incidence of respiratory and gastrointestinal diseases and that 73% of all child deaths occurred in the malnourished group. However, mortality among children attending MCH clinics was only half that of the others, although there was no significant difference in their weight. Clearly the MCH clinics are valuable for the treatment of the disease, but major improvements in child health require changes in infant feeding practices. The chief weaning food is the sweet potato, which is too bulky to provide adequate nourishment even though it is supplemented by prolonged breast-feeding. (DM)

3464 **Bollag, U.** *Is the community health aide in Jamaica well prepared for the detection of protein-energy-malnutrition?* Courrier of the International Children's Centre (Paris), 27(4), 1977, 338-346. Engl.

In Jamaica, a Young Child Nutrition Programme (YCNP) employing community health aides uses Gomez weight-for-age charts that can be misleading because they are based on the Harvard standard rather than readily available local data. Weight-for-age charts can be useful for assessing general states of health or adequate growth but should not be used for detecting malnutrition unless their accuracy is unquestionable and unless notes on maternal, perinatal, and postnatal clinical signs of malnutrition are included, as well as additional anthropometric measurements. Measurement of malnourished children in the YCNP by a physician revealed that most of these children were underheight as well as underweight and that weight must be assessed in relation to factors other than age in order to provide a true picture of under- or over-feeding. In fact, half the children measured at random at three child welfare clinics in Kingston were overweight, especially those in the 0-6 months age group, due perhaps to faulty parental attitudes towards fat babies and the habit of offering both breast milk and supplementary milk. The author suggests that commuity health aides be trained to teach nutrition and demonstrate hygienic preparation of local foods instead of concentrating on techniques of anthropometric measurement. (HH)

3465 **Caribbean Food and Nutrition Institute, Kingston, Jamaica.** *Evaluation of the effects of nutrition education in nutritional status.* In Research in Progress 1976, Washington, D.C., Pan American Health Organization, Department of Research Development and Coordination, 1976, 63-64. Engl.
See also entries 1045 (volume 2) and 2776 (volume 4) for complete document; other chapters have been abstracted separately under entries 3036, 3069, 3082, 3476, 3495, 3497, and 3498.

A study was undertaken in Lambs River, Jamaica, to assess the specific contribution of nutrition education to the improvement of nutritional status and to develop a model nutrition education programme. Socioeconomic and anthropometric data were collected from the Lambs River and a control area during the 1st 6 months of the project. Then a nutrition education programme conducted by technically trained government personnel (nurses, teachers, agricultural extension workers, etc.) and village-level volunteers was initiated. Some months later, change to nutritional status was assessed using these parameters: anthropometric data on the under-five population; nutrition knowledge and practice, especially in relation to the production and use of local foods; and breast-feeding practices. The results showed no significant change in the nutritional status of under-fives in either the experimental or the control area; improvement in the experimental area, however, was evident in a community-wide awareness of the programme and what it was doing, the increased cultivation of kitchen gardens, the greater extent and duration of breast-feeding, acceptance of the use of multimixes in infant feeding, and increased purchase of milk. It is concluded that nutrition education by local-level volunteers is feasible if supported by technical personnel but that in instances of extreme poverty, nutrition education without accompanying steps to make more food available is unlikely to produce significant improvement in nutritional status. (HC)

3466   Carpentier, J.C. Johnson, B.A. Aromasodu, M.O. WHO, Brazzaville. *Development of basic health services in Nigeria, Federal.* Brazzaville, WHO, 26 Feb 1974. 11p. Engl.
Since 1967, the government of Nigeria has, with WHO assistance, been working on a project to establish a national health system with special emphasis on malaria epidemiology and control. Steps were undertaken to enumerate and coordinate the health services of each state and their malaria control measures are listed. The author concludes that, although the incidence of malaria is steadily decreasing, the project has not yet achieved its goals; he recommends the establishment of a planning unit in the Ministry of Health for better long-range planning, a special projects department within the malaria control unit, and closer connections between government and WHO staff. (RMB)

3467   Chen, P.C. *Sociocultural influences on vitamin A deficiency in a rural Malay community.* Journal of Tropical Medicine and Hygiene (London), 75, 1972, 231-236. Engl.
13 refs.
In June 1970, the author conducted a dietary survey of 20 randomly selected households in a rural West Malaysian village, clinically examined 31 primary schoolchildren, and questioned 53 heads of household and 7 traditional practitioners or *bomoh*s to determine the incidence of vitamin A deficiency among the population and whether or not indigenous practices tended to promote or prevent it. More than half of the children examined showed signs of vitamin A deficiency and the dietary investigation revealed that the normal diet of rice and fish, with vegetables and fruit served on the average of once a week, provided only 0.8% of the recommended daily intake of vitamin A. The native aversion to specifically those fruits and vegetables most rich in vitamin A was only partially balanced by the consumption of fish and any other available liver as an indigenous cure for night-blindness and Bitot's spots.

The author recommends that the rural population, beginning with a few less conservative families, be encouraged to consume and cultivate more vegetables and continue their intake of all types of liver. Statistical data are included. (RMB)

3468   Chen, P.C. *Indigenous Malay psychotherapy.* Tropical and Geographical Medicine (Haarlem, Netherlands), 22(1), 1970, 409-415. Engl.
Indigenous Malay psychotherapy is examined in the context of the cultural background of rural patients and traditional Malay medicine to measure its effectiveness in the treatment of neuroses and anxiety and to see whether or not it can be substituted for more sophisticated Western psychiatry. The author feels that traditional psychotherapy is very effective in the treatment of minor illnesses because: the patient expects to be cured; the traditional practitioner (*bomoh*) is adept at finding satisfying explanations that fit into the patient's concept of the universe and the causes of sickness; the *bomoh*'s rituals jolt the patient out of his routine, keep him busy, and strengthen his sense of self worth; and the required participation of the patient's family and social group place him under a personal and social obligation to be cured. However, the author is not certain that traditional healers are equally effective at treating severe psychotics, who presently form the bulk of the caseloads of Malaysia's few Western-trained psychiatrists. A case history of a successful *bomoh* diagnosis and exorcism is included. (RMB)

3469   Chile, Ministerio de Salud Publica, Programa de Extension de Servicios de Salud Materno Infantil y Bienestar Familiar. *Investigaciones en el campo de la salud materno infantil, 25 areas PESMIB 1973-1976 (resumen y conclusiones). (Research in the area of maternal and child health in 25 PESMIB areas from 1973-1976; summary and conclusions).* Santiago, Ministerio de Salud Publica, Dec 1976. 99p. Span.
From 1973-1976, Chile's Ministry of Public Health programme for extending maternal child health and family health services was implemented in the 25 areas of Chile where maternal and child health was considered most at-risk. During the same period, the programme's evaluation unit studied: infant and maternal mortality before and after the implementation of PESMIB; sociodemographic and health characteristics in the 25 areas; operational efficiency, perceived morbidity, and utilization of the MCH services; role of the nurse, midwife, and auxiliary nurse in the delivery of MCH services; knowledge, attitudes, and practices related to pregnancy, delivery, postpartum, and infant care; patient satisfaction with the MCH services; maternal fertility; and rates of continuance among birth control acceptors in one of the 25 areas (Santiago south). This document presents the objectives, methodology, relevant findings, and conclusions of these studies. (HC)

3470   Colombia, Ministerio de Salud Publica. Instituto Nacional para Programas Especiales de Salud, Bogota. Asociacion Colombiana de Facultades de

Medicina, Bogota. *Estudio sanitario de comunidades rurales: informe general. (Health studies of rural communities: general report).* Bogota, Instituto Nacional para Programas Especiales de Salud, Serie 3, No.4, 1973. 1v.(various pagings). Span.

The Colombian Ministry of Health initiated a 1970 study to investigate the poor health coverage, the high incidence of disease, and the low socioeconomic status in rural areas and determine the most effective way of utilizing the country's limited research resources. This 1st volume covers the general methodology of the resulting 1972 survey, including questionnaires and operations control, the information processing system, the results from the test area, administrative organization, and national results. Local leaders were asked to describe their community's geographic situation, accessibility, demography, schools and health institutions, public services (water, electricity, sewage), and community organizations. The results for each section of the country are presented separately and include an alphabetical list of each community surveyed plus a descriptive analysis of the statistical data obtained. Appendices contain sample questionnaires, definitions of terms, and lists of survey organizers and participants. (RMB)

3471 Cook, S. International Planned Parenthood Federation, Nairobi. *Report of an evaluation of the International Planned Parenthood Federation programme in Botswana 1969-1973.* Nairobi, International Planned Parenthood Federation, 1973. 233p. Engl.

31 refs.

Individual chapter has been abstracted separately under entry 3393.

In 1972, following a 3-year pilot project undertaken in cooperation with the IPPF, the Botswana Ministry of Health launched a nationwide integrated MCH/FP programme. This programme is based on the use of family welfare educators (FWEs), who are literate women recruited from their communities to undertake activities in child health, family planning, nutrition, community development, agriculture, and first aid. At the beginning of the programme, a formal evaluation of the achievements of the pilot project was commissioned. Service statistics (personal and contraceptive data on FP acceptors), a follow-up study of acceptors, and an assessment of the fieldwork and training of the FWEs was conducted. Recommendations arising from the findings called for more careful selection of FWEs to reduce attrition, a probationary post-training period before registration, better supervision, more home visits, and some changes in FP policies. The report contains statistical tables, a bibliography, and 28 appendices that include the FWE training syllabus, copies of questionnaires, report forms, and correspondence with the FWEs, analyses of data, comments on problems encountered in the surveys, and suggestions for future research. (AB)

3472 Farvar, M.T. Razavi-Farvar, C. Centre for Endogenous Development Studies, Tehran. *Lessons of*

Lorestan. Ceres (Rome), 9(2), Mar-Apr 1976, 44-47. Engl.

See also entry 3392.

The Lorestan project began in 1974 as an attempt to develop a deprived rural area using local human and natural resources by enlisting the participation of the local people. The 1st stage of the project consisted of inconclusive studies by expatriate researchers followed by disorganized field work by a number of splinter groups. The health group, headed by doctors with an overly professional outlook, set out to recruit and train 35 front-line health workers. Training consisted of classroom and clinical teaching in an urban health centre with brief field trips to villages for observation. The result was that the trainees acquired the elitist tendencies and curative bias of the Western medical professional with no understanding of the causes of disease, of indigenous herbal medicines and their uses, or of the potential of the population for self-care. The field work was greatly improved during the 2nd phase of the project in 1975, when efforts were made to unite the splinter groups, reexamine priorities, involve more women, and transfer decision-making power to the local people. (DM)

3473 Gordon, G. *Evaluation of a nutrition programme in Northern Ghana.* In Getting the Most Out of Food: the Twelfth in a Series of Studies on the Modern Approach to Feeding and Nutrition, Burgess Hill, UK, Van den Burghs and Jurgens, 1977, 9-38. Engl.

This evaluation of the failure of a nutrition education programme in northern Ghana shows the dangers of imposing child feeding patterns without detailed knowledge of the dietary practices and socioeconomic situation of the local population. The traditional childhood diet consisted of a main meal of milled dough and soup, although some nutritional compensation was provided by the fact that infants were rarely weaned before the age of 9 months. In an attempt to improve the nutritional status of young children, nutrition education clinics and visiting social workers encouraged increased consumption of protein-rich foods and earlier supplementary feeding. To evaluate this education's effect, researchers visited 301 mothers with 498 children, some of whom had received nutrition education, and compared data on nutritional knowledge, dietary practices, nutritional status of children aged less than 5 years, and infant and child morbidity and mortality in both high and low-income compounds. Although nutritional knowledge generally improved after education, low-income mothers did not have the resources to practice it. Furthermore, the nutritional status of the sick children of mothers exposed to nutrition education was actually worse than that of the sick children of uneducated mothers; reasons included the bacterial contamination of suggested food supplements and the diminished supply of mothers' milk because of earlier weaning. In addition, the recommended porridge contained less iron than traditional 1st food, thus exacerbating anaemia caused by diarrhea. Consequently, infant and child morbidity and mortality were greater in children of mothers receiving nutrition education. (CL)

3474 Habicht, J.P. Reyna-Barrios, J.M. Guzman, G. Gordon, J.E. *Health services in field study of malnutrition: professional content, operational expediency, ethical considerations.* Guatemala City, Instituto de Nutricion de Centro America y Panama (INCAP), n.d. 35p. Engl.

17 refs.

Unpublished document.

This field study was originally designed to assess the effects of improved nutrition on the mental development of children in rural Guatemala by comparing results when 2 villages were provided with supplementary food and 2 similar control villages were not. However, it was ethically impossible to carry out this investigation without introducing some curative services to meet the felt needs of the people in all 4 villages, so ambulatory medical clinics were established in each community. These were staffed by auxiliary nurses whose 18-month training equipped them to carry our history-taking, diagnosis, and treatment according to therapeutic guidelines and to select patients for referral to a supervising physician who also analyzed the nurses' records for errors. With experience, the auxiliary nurses provided satisfactory services and became sufficiently acceptable to introduce more important but less popular preventive measures, such as immunization, encouragement of breast-feeding, and referral of children to the supplementary feeding station. The study showed that preventive measures are the most cost-effective means of improving health and nutrition, but changes in sanitation and hygiene are slow and require mass education. Fortnightly morbidity surveys produced a wealth of data for the study team, but effective quick action using the data for such purposes as epidemic control proved difficult, until responsibility for decision-making was suitably allocated among staff members. (DM)

3475 Joseph, S.C. *Protein-calorie malnutrition in West African children.* Rocky Mountain Medical Journal (Denver, Col.), 71(7), Jul 1974, 403-405. Engl.

20 refs.

A study of 162 consecutive pediatric admissions to the Yaounde Central Hospital, Cameroon, showed that significant undernutrition was a common finding irrespective of admission diagnosis. Of the 23 children primarily admitted for protein-calorie malnutrition (PCM), 35% suffered from kwashiorkor, 22% from marasmus, and the remainder from an intermediate form. Typically, virtually all cases were complicated by infections, anaemia, and diarrhea, conditions that must be treated simultaneously. This is difficult in hospitals that are short of staff and medicines and overcrowded so that children are constantly exposed to further infections. Hospital admission is thus an inadequate measure for combatting PCM. Although hospitalization for severe malnutrition will probably remain necessary for the foreseeable futgure in Cameroon as in other developing countries, far more effective is prevention by improved child care, early detection and outpatient treatment at health centres, or long-term rehabilitation by maternal education. Where possible, hospitals should set up separate nutrition rehabilitation units for affected children, so they may be isolated from sources of infection and so their mothers can participate actively in feeding and educational programmes. (DM)

3476 Kennell, J. Klaus, M. Pan American Health Organization, Washington, D.C. WHO, Geneva. *Have modern health practices removed the safeguard of bacterial interference, shortened breast-feeding, and increased infant malnutrition?* In Research in Progress 1976, Washington, D.C., Pan American Health Organization, Department of Research Development and Coordination, 1976, 36-37. Engl.

For complete document see entry 2776 (volume 4); other chapters have been abstracted separately under entries 3036, 3069, 3082, 3465, 3495, 3497, and 3498.

Observations in Guatemala indicate that early weaning is gaining popularity among low-income urban and rural populations. A study was undertaken to determine whether a change in hospital routine might foster a return to prolonged breast-feeding. An experimental group of mothers were allowed to hold and suckle their naked newborns for up to 45 minutes in a private room and to have contact with them for 5 additional hours per day during their stay in hospital. The control group of mothers had contact with their babies according to usual hospital routine, i.e., a glimpse at birth, identifications at 8-12 hours, and a 20-30-minute feeding every 4 hours thereafter. Babies of both groups are to be monitored up to 12 months of age for patterns of growth, duration of breast-feeding, and morbidity. Results to date indicate that mothers in the experimental group breast-fed for an average of 90 days longer than mothers in the control group and that their babies tended to develop fewer illnesses. If it can be demonstrated that this short period of early physical contact increases the length of breast-feeding, then great benefits can be expected from a simple procedure that can be provided at no cost. (HC)

3477 Khanjanasthiti, P. Nanna, P. Sakdisawat, O. Palpai, P. Kes-kasem-sook, P. *Health care delivery method for infants and preschool children.* Journal of the Medical Association of Thailand (Bangkok), 60(4), Apr 1977, 177-183. Engl.

A method of delivering health care with projected maternal child health coverage of 60% was tested in three Thai villages. In the two experimental villages, a mobile team from the local health centre made regular visits to the village meeting place and offered an integrated health care package including immunization, growth monitoring, antenatal care, family planning, health education, and treatment for simple conditions. The only extra cost of the service was transportation for the health centre staff; additional clinical assistance was supplied by a village volunteer. The authors observe that coverage of the target population in the experimental villages varied from 74.74%-88.17%, all the child attenders from the experimental villages completed the immunization schedule prescribed by the Ministry of Health, the incidence of protein-calorie malnutrition (PCM) dropped 24% after 2 years and 42% after 4 1/2 years among the children of the experimental group as compared to the control children, and improvement in nutritional status was noted in 45% of the experimental children suffering from PCM and in none of the control children. The authors conclude that this method reaches an acceptable percentage of the target population but that its effect on nutritional status takes 2-4 years to be felt. (HC)

3478   Larchet, M. Cosnard, G. Joullie, M. *Centre de Rehabilitation Infantile et d'Education Nutritionnelle de Ouahigouya (Haute-Volta). (Child Nutrition Rehabilitation and Education Centre, Ouahigouya, Upper-Volta).* Medecine Tropicale (Marseille, France), 37(3), May-Jun 1977, 255-274. Fren.

The nutrition rehabilitation and education centre at Ouahigouya, Upper Volta, treats young victims of protein-calorie malnutrition and instructs their mothers in the cultivation and preparation of nourishing local foods. The centre is staffed by 1 nurse, who conducts consultations and administers medical treatment, and 2 health monitors, whose main responsibility is education. Treatment consists of feeding the children a stew that is prepared by the mothers under conditions similar to those found in their villages. A study was undertaken to determine some characteristics of 435 children who were admitted to the centre during a 1-year period and the effect of treatment on 390 of them. It was observed that 55% of all the children admitted to the centre were aged 6-12 months. Of the 390 children whose progress was studied, 6 reached the norm upon discharge from the centre, 87 (27%) experienced weight gains of 10% or more of the norm, 131 (40%) experienced weight gains of 5%-9% of the norm, and 93 (28%) left with weight gains of 5% or less of the norm. Sixteen children (5%) actually lost weight and 27 (7%) either died or were considered therapeutic failures. The outcome of treatment seems not very impressive until one considers that the purpose of the centre is not to effect total recovery but to show mothers how to achieve it. Out of 64 children who could be traced after discharge from the hospital, 55 (42%) were regularly attending child welfare clinics and the nutritional status of 49 of them was improving. It is suggested that, in view of the young age of most of the children admitted to the centre, mothers be urged to supplement breast milk with solid food from the 6th month. (HC)

3479   Leclercq, L. Oanh, B.X. *Estimation d'une fonction de la demande de sante a Kinshasa. (Estimating the function of the demand for health services in Kinshasa).* Cahiers Economiques et Sociaux (Kinshasa), 14(1), 1976, 72.5-90.5. Fren.

A model for estimating the effect of a number of variables on the demand for health services was developed and applied to data from a previous study of 1 476 households (0.9% of the total population) in Kinshasa, Zaire. The variables chosen were income, level of education, sex, age, marital status, and level of urbanization; the demand included both the demand during acute episodes and the demand for non-urgent or preventive care,

though the former would naturally be much less amenable to the influence of variables than the latter. It was hypothesized that *per capita* expenditure on medical care would increase with revenue, level of education, age (to a point), and urbanization and decrease with marriage. Statistical analysis indicated that only three of the variables--income, education, and marital status--significantly influenced the demand for health services and all three influenced it in the manner expected. The study confirms the 'elasticity' of the demand for medical services, indicating that equal access to medical care has yet to be realized. (HC)

3480   Leeson, J. Frankenberg, R. *Patients of traditional doctors in Lusaka.* African Social Research (Lusaka), 23(6), 1977, 217-234. Engl.
14 refs.
See also entries 1453 and 1709 (volume 3).

The authors examine the reasons why people seek care from traditional and modern practitioners and postulate that most patients are "cured" whatever treatment they receive but that the cure is not the only consideration in choosing a therapist: convenience and the desire for an explanation, particularly if cure is delayed, contribute as well. Investigators sought characteristics of 1 919 patients receiving services from a modern (private) doctor in a Lusaka (Zambia) suburb and 1 123 patients attending traditional practitioners (*ng'anga*s) to determine their reasons for choosing one or the other. Medical records, often very incomplete, from the doctor's office were studied and the patients seeking traditional care were interviewed. The findings of this survey suggested that: young children commonly were taken to the modern doctor, rarely to the traditional practitioner; mental disorders were confined to the *ng'anga*s' practice; and genitourinary ailments, especially infertility, were much commoner in the *ng'anga*s' caseloads. It was revealed that two-thirds of their patients had gone first to a modern medical agency and many of them had been ill for a long time. Four major reasons were cited for attending a *ng'anga*: failure elsewhere, personal preference, convenience, and a desire to know the cause. (Modified author abstract.)

3481   Lewis, O. *Medicine and politics in a Mexican village.* In Paul, B.D., ed., Health, Culture and Community: Case Studies of Public Reactions to Health Programs, New York, Russell Sage Foundation, 1955, 403-433. Engl.
For complete document see entry 3454.

A social research group from the USA launched a project in Mexico to study the inhabitants of a rural village; at the villagers' request, the group opened a medical clinic as part of the project. The clinic operated with limited success for 2 months and then abruptly came to a standstill. Its activities were discredited in the community by several powerful persons, including the local *curandero*, who viewed it as a threat in some way to their position. Rumours were spread about the physician and about the psychological testing programme that was being administered to the children at school. As a result, the clinic closed, the school prohibited psychologic testing on the premises, and the research group completed their study through home visits. (AC)

3482   McDowell, J. UNICEF, Nairobi. *Kayunga Nutrition Scouts Project: an outline of a successful nutritional surveillance/prevention project in Uganda.* Nairobi, UNICEF, 29 Sep 1977. 6p. Engl.
Working Conference of the International Union of Nutritional Sciences, Hyderabad, India, 17-21 Oct 1977.
Unpublished document.

Whereas systems of nutritional surveillance that rely on mothers bringing children to clinics for routine checks have failed to reach the majority of children in rural Africa, a community-based project in southeast Uganda has shown that mass preventive surveillance can be effectively accomplished locally at very low cost. This surveillance and prevention project, initiated in late 1975 in Kayunga, used 12 teenage "scouts," selected by the community and trained for 6 weeks in the recognition and treatment of malnutrition, to patrol about 400 households. Making visits by bicycle, they assessed the nutritional state of young children by mid-upper-arm circumference measurement and gave advice to mothers on nutrition, general child care, and domestic sanitation. A meeting of the area's elders chose a management committee for selecting and recruiting scouts and appointed a respected elder as project manager. Though two scouts were dismissed by the committee, the scouts' work resulted in a drop in the number of malnourished children in the area from 7.4% of children in May 1976 to 5.0% in June 1977, with no cases of clinical kwashiorkor or marasmus seen from April-September 1977. The project also aroused community interest in the need for better water supplies and sanitation and increased people's willingness to contribute their labour for improvement schemes. The community now bears the total cost of the project, which is about US$5 000 annually. For this amount, 5 000 children are covered by a complete surveillance and prevention system at minimum cost to the central government. (CL)

3483   McNaughton, J. *Applied nutrition programmes: the past as a guide for the future.* Food and Nutrition (Washington, D.C.), 1(3), 1975, 17-23. Engl.
14 refs.

The applied nutrition programme (ANP) is an educational programme aimed at showing rural communities how to grow and use the foods needed to improve their diets and training the necessary teaching personnel. ANPs were launched during the late 1950s and, by 1966, were operating in 56 countries with the support of various international agencies. Since then, FAO, UNICEF, and WHO have jointly organized a number of technical meetings and seminars on the subject of planning and evaluating ANPs and reports of these meetings and seminars have been widely circulated; from subsequent assessments, however, it appears that these reports did not reach those who might have benefitted from them,

for programmes are still hampered by the same shortcomings. These include: confusion about the data needed for baseline surveys; vague plans of operation; over-optimistic goals; failure to suit training to programme needs; poor coordination between activities of different disciplines; inadequate staffing and financing; failure to involve village communities in programme planning; a tendency to use international experts as project staff and, consequently, a failure to train counterparts; failure to link production activities with the country's agricultural plans; etc. In this paper, assessments of ANPs in Latin America, Africa, and Asia are reviewed, the underlying reasons for their poor implementation are examined, and a number of general recommendations for improving them are put forward. (HC)

3484   Mehra, S. Voluntary Health Association of India, New Delhi. *Pretesting of "Better Child Care' booklet.* New Delhi, Voluntary Health Association of India, May 1977. 15p. Engl.
See also entries 2821 and 3333.

A 1976 pretesting of *Better Child Care*, a Voluntary Health Association of India teaching aid booklet for village women, showed that most photographs illustrating proper health practices were understood by the pregnant women, mothers of young children, and older women interviewed in the states of Uttar Pradesh, Gujarat, and Tamil Nadu. These illiterate village women were asked by female interviewers what they saw in each photograph and their responses were classified. In Uttar Pradesh, the results of 510 responses to 34 photographs showed that only 4 photographs did not convey the intended message and village health workers thought that the booklet was effective and appropriate, a conclusion supported by a separate readability test on the text. The Tamil Nadu and Gujarat pretest, which collected 410 responses to 35 photographs in each village, found little difference in the ability to recognize the photographs between the people of Tamil Nadu, who had had considerable health education, and the population of Gujarat, who had not. Misconceptions were analyzed to help health workers recognize areas of possible misunderstanding. (CL)

3485   Mora, J.O. Amezquita, A. Castro, L. Christiansen, N. Clement-Murphy, J. *Nutrition, health and social factors related to intellectual performance.* World Review of Nutrition and Dietetics (London), 19, 1974, 205-236. Engl.
44 refs.

The preliminary findings of a 1-year investigation into the relationship between malnutrition and cognitive ability are presented. The subjects of the study were pairs of siblings aged less than 5 years from a disadvantaged *barrio* in Bogota, Colombia. The sample comprised 186 well-nourished and 192 malnourished children, 218 of whom were enrolled in a food supplementation programme. Anthropometric, health, and psychological measurements were made at the beginning and the end of the year. Information on the medical history of the subjects and the sociocultural characteristics of their families was also obtained, so that the effects of malnutrition on intellectual performance might be isolated from the effects of social and health factors. At the end of the year it was observed that all children participating in the food supplementation programme had experienced significant improvement in physical growth and supplemented, in contrast to non-supplemented, malnourished children showed significant increments in intellectual performance. It is concluded that findings appear to justify a prospective study of physical and cognitive development in which observations would begin in the prenatal period. (HC)

3486   **Nguyen-xuan-Nguyen.** *Campaign against trachoma.* In McMichael, J.K., ed., Health in the Third World: Studies from Vietnam, Nottingham, UK, Spokesman Books, 1976, 244-249. Engl.
For complete document see entry 2869.

The high incidence of trachoma in North Vietnam (in colonial times 65% for the whole country and 90% for parts of the delta region) has been markedly reduced over a 15-year period, with the virtual disappearance of the most serious forms of the disease. This improvement has been brought about by better living conditions and by the long-term programme of the Ministry of Health's Institute of Ophthalmology and Trachoma. The latter covers 4 stages: (1) epidemiological research and organizational preparation; (2) mass therapy and prophylaxis; (3) treatment of *sequelae*; and (4) total eradication. In the preparatory stage ending in 1960, more than 400 experimental and screening stations were set up and 32 mobile anti-trachoma teams were trained, each with 2 assistant physicians and 5 nurses. The 2nd and 3rd stages saw the establishment of a permanent network of village stations, district dispensaries, and provincial centres, coordinated by the national institute and staffed by hundreds of physicians and assistant physicians specializing in ophthalmology, thousands of nurses for anti-trachoma work, and tens of thousands of propagandists for anti-trachoma hygiene. Eight million people have been treated, 4 million completely cured, and hundreds of thousands of complex eye operations have been carried out on entropion and trichiasis. The institute has undertaken research into improved operating and treatment techniques and has developed a palmatin ointment from *Fibraurea tinctoria* that satisfactorily replaces expensive imported antibiotics in the treatment of trachoma. (AB)

3487   **Oberg, K. Rios, J.A.** *Community improvement project in Brazil.* In Paul, B.D., ed., Health, Culture and Community: Case Studies of Public Reactions to Health Programs, New York, Russell Sage Foundation, 1955, 349-376. Engl.
For complete document see entry 3454.

A joint agricultural, educational, and health project that promised coordinated community development for a rural population in Brazil suffered from administrative breakdowns and succeeded only in demonstrating the deleterious effects of power struggles between project staff and community leaders. The goals of the project were to involve the community in improvement

programmes and entrench changes so that better hygiene, farming, teaching, etc., would outlast the project. The plan was to create a representative community council for decision-making and provide financial and technical assistance from outside. The community council comprised landowners, tenants, migrant workers, and housewives and reflected the socioeconomic spectrum in the community but not the political realities. Powerful members of the council were at times outvoted by the group and they resented the project coordinator's increasing authority. On the other hand, the project coordinator was over-zealous; he assumed too much power and encroached on the decision-making process of the council. Tension grew and eventually a minor incident caused a major blowup and ended the project. (AC)

3488   **Pinto, V.A. WHO, Brazzaville.** *Water supply and sewerage, Lesotho.* Brazzaville, WHO, 28 Jul 1971. 21p. Engl.

This report by a WHO expert covers both water supply and sewerage in urban areas of Lesotho and rural sanitation. The author suggests that more detailed surveys of the urban situation be undertaken as soon as possible, that the necessary personnel for conducting these surveys be trained, and that the services of the currently employed water engineer be retained. In the rural sector, he recommends the appointment of a special health inspector tutor to advise the government, the training of more health inspectors and health assistants, the addition of latrine construction to other water supply activities, increased cooperation among government ministries, and the establishment of water quality control facilities. An annex contains a list of government officials the author met during his 1971 visit. (RMB)

3489   **Rao, N.P. Vijayaraghavan, K.** *Spin-off benefits in nutrition programmes.* Indian Journal of Medical Research (New Delhi), 64(8), Aug 1976, 1107-1118. Engl.

The National Institute of Nutrition, India, evaluated the nutrition component of the India Population Project and found that nutrition supplements were distributed efficiently and were beneficial not only to the target population but also to other young siblings and to the overall image of use of the maternal child health services. The evaluation was undertaken in two phases--the 1st to determine the consumption pattern, use, and acceptability of supplements offered at existing subcentres and the 2nd to measure the supplements' impact on the subcentres' MCH services. In the 1st phase, investigators contacted 200 women who either were receiving supplements themselves or had children who were doing so. The sample represented eight villages located within 7 km of the subcentres providing supplements. In the 2nd phase, investigators interviewed 6 auxiliary workers and 247 villagers--54 of whom were from outside the supplemented catchment area. Findings from the 1st phase indicated that the mode of distribution was efficient, that 81.9% of mothers (and 63.3% of children) receiving supplements shared them with other members of their families, that 75% of the other members sharing supplements were aged 2-6 years, and that the supplements were consumed more quickly than was planned by programme personnel. Second-phase findings were that 95% of respondents in the project area and only 57% of nonproject area respondents knew of the existence of their subcentres, the auxiliary nurse-midwife in the project area had a much better image than did her counterpart in the nonproject area, and women in the project area utilized antenatal and other maternal child health services more willingly than did those in the nonproject area. (AC)

3490 **Rebello, L.M. Verma, S.P.** *Basic health worker and his recipient group: a diagnostic study for health education in malaria.* Social Science and Medicine (Oxford, UK), 2(1), Jan 1977, 43-53. Engl.
18 refs.

The success of the maintenance phase of the Indian malaria eradication programme depends upon how scrupulously the basic health worker (BHW) detects and treats cases and how willing the community is to report fever and accept treatment. In the Pataudi Block, Haryana State, 100 males and 100 females were interviewed regarding: the role and credibility of the BHW; their perceived threat of malaria; their awareness of the cause, transmission, and prevention of malaria; and their participation in surveillance activities. The respondents were interviewed individually in their homes or place of work. Results of the interviews revealed that: the BHW is well known in the community; his treatment/advice regarding malaria is preferred to that of any other practitioner; reporting is high (85%) in cases of ongoing fever but low (34.5%) in cases of fever between the BHW's visits; the perceived threat of malaria is considerable but declining; two-thirds of the respondents relate malaria to a mosquito bite; the activities of the maintenance phase of the malaria eradication programme (reporting fever, giving blood, and accepting treatment) are regarded as only marginally preventive; and 88.5% of the respondents have no reservation about having their blood tested, even though the results of the test are never communicated to them. It is concluded that the BHW should modify his enquiry so that the people understand that they are to report cases of fever that occurred since the last visit and not only cases of ongoing fever. He should also increase his effort to revisit those who were out during the first visit and start communicating the results of the blood tests to the individuals in question. The organization, content, and activities of a recommended malaria education programme that is to be carried out at the individual, school, and community levels are outlined. (HC)

3491 **Rey, M.** *Place of measles and its prevention among public health priorities in tropical Africa.* Children in the Tropics (Paris), 104, 1976, 3-10. Engl.

The author strongly urges that mass vaccination campaigns be used to control measles, which, with a death rate of 10% among children, is one of the four main infectious causes of infant mortality in tropical Africa. Because measles is so closely linked to malnutrition and often triggers kwashiorkor in infected children, it is 1 000 times more deadly in Africa than in industrialized nations, where living conditions and nutritional standards diminish its impact. Since living conditions and nutrition in Africa cannot be sufficiently improved in a short enough time, the author stresses that immunization, despite its expense, is the only effective weapon against measles. Although he admits that the results of some mass campaigns have been disappointing due to poor coverage, improperly administered vaccinations, inactive vaccines, and ineffective vaccinations given to infants aged less than 6 months, he cites the 85% reduction in measles-related morbidity in the Ivory Coast, the 75% reduction in Cameroon, the 60% reduction in Senegal, and the virtual eradication of the disease in the Gambia as examples of what can be accomplished by a properly-conducted mass campaign. Consequently, he suggests that priority be given to measles, poliomyelitis, and tetanus in Africa, because they can all be controlled by vaccination. (RMB)

3492 **Romano Santoro, J. Carlos Soares, F. Barros Filho, A.A. Daneluzzi, J.C. Garcia Ricco, R. Barbieri, M.A.** *Antencao a infancia em servico communitario ligado a universidade. (Child care in a university-related community service).* Educacion Medica y Salud (Washington, D.C.), 11(1), 1977, 50-59. Portuguese.

After discussing health policies and the role of medical schools in teaching and research, the authors briefly trace the development of the pediatrics curriculum in the Ribeirao Preto medical school and the associated child health programme in Pradopolis (Brazil). The socioeconomic and demographic background of Pradopolis is presented and various aspects of the programme, including goals, routine activities, and training opportunities for physicians and auxiliary health workers, are described. Because of the difficulties encountered in implementing the programme, such as the passivity of the population and the paternalistic attitude of programme promoters, the authors conclude that health programmes cannot be imposed from above. To be effective, they must conform to local socioeconomic and cultural conditions, which are generally the cause of health problems in the first place, and medical schools must learn to take these factors into account when planning their curricula. (RMB)

3493 **Salfield, J. Gibbs, J. Gobius, R.J.** *Problems associated with the treatment of malnutrition in the field.* Papua New Guinea Medical Journal (Port Moresby), 17(2), Jun 1974, 177-182. Engl.

From May 1972-May 1973, three Papua New Guinea villages participated in a special programme of the Catholic Mission Station (Bongos) to improve child nutrition. A nurse from the mission clinic visited each village monthly to give home cooking and infant feeding demonstrations with the assistance of an experienced health education orderly. In May 1973, the weights of 310 children aged less than 5 years were plotted on a graph and compared to those of 307 children plotted in 1972. Although individual increases in weight were recorded for 20% of the children who had received the benefit of the monthly home visits, the numbers of children with weights below 60% of the standard did not differ appreciably. The authors conclude that efforts undertaken in the health sector without simultaneous action in other sectors of the economy (agriculture, food production, etc.) will never solve the problem of malnutrition. They suggest that the government follow the multifactorial approach set forward in its own *Report of the Nutrition Policy Conference* (1972). (HC)

3494 Santos, A.T. *Review of schistosomiasis control in the Philippines.* Southeast Asian Journal of Tropical Medicine and Public Health (Bangkok), 7(2), Jun 1976, 319-321. Engl.

Schistosomiasis, which infects more than half a million people at an estimated cost of $14.5 million per year, is one of the major public health problems in the Philippines. Based on a successful pilot project, a disease control programme involving ecological and chemical methods of snail eradication, environmental sanitation, health education, and case detection and treatment has been adopted for nationwide application. In order to offset the expense of this approach, members of other government agencies (Public Works and Communications, National Irrigation Administration, Agriculture and National Resources, etc.) have been involved from the beginning and the help of various international agencies has been enlisted. After 4 years of great expense and effort, however, the programme has succeeded in reducing the snail population by 85% but not in interrupting the transmission of the disease to man. It is concluded that an even more comprehensive, long-term programme is required. The new, revised 10-year programme will limit its membership to agencies that can truly contribute to the control effort, assign full-time technical staff to the National Schistosomiasis Control Commission, provide adequate funds for control in the budget of each member-agency, and establish a clear-cut definition of the responsibilities of each member-agency. It was due to begin in 1976. (HC)

3495 Schneider, R.E. Shiffman, M. Pan American Health Organization, Washington, D.C. WHO, Geneva. *Development and evaluation of measures to reduce food waste caused by intestinal diseases.* In Research in Progress 1976, Washington, D.C., Pan American Health Organization, Department of Research Development and Coordination, 1976, 24-25. Engl.

For complete document see entry 2776 (volume 4); other chapters have been abstracted separately under entries 3036, 3069, 3082, 3465, 3476, 3497, and 3498.

A study to assess the impact of chronic calorie malabsorption due to gastrointestinal disease on health, food waste, productivity, and costs is currently under way in two Guatemalan communities of 960 and 980 inhabitants respectively. In the study, investigators: evaluated the villagers' status of health, nutrition, sanitation, and economics; conducted d-xylose absorption tests on all the men at regular intervals; and

monitored the actual waste of ingested food for a subgroup of villagers. They found that 56%-64% of all persons undergoing detailed malabsorption tests lost 200-300 calories:day--a loss representing 5%-6% of the daily cost of the diet regularly consumed by these individuals. After initial investigations, an improved water supply and a sanitary education programme was introduced in one of the communities and plans are to assess the impact of this intervention. (HC)

3496 Singapore, Ministry of Health. *Evaluation.* Singapore Public Health Bulletin (Singapore), 18 Jul 1977, 25-36. Engl. See also entry 3087.

The effectiveness of the 1976 Singapore national health campaign on infectious diseases is evaluated by means of a pre- and post-campaign survey of a sample of schoolchildren and servicemen, a count of those who attended the exhibition on infectious diseases and the lectures and film shows, and a monitoring of the incidence of infectious diseases and the attendance of suspected cases at government institutions. While public knowledge about infectious diseases was apparently somewhat improved as a result of the campaign, it appears to have been most effective in encouraging patients with venereal diseases to seek treatment. Incidence patterns of other diseases remained unchanged. It is suggested that the activities initiated during the mass campaign be continued whenever possible. Statistical data are appended. (RMB)

3497 Urrutia, J.J. Pan American Health Organization, Washington, D.C. WHO, Geneva. *Corn fortification: a field demonstration.* In Research in Progress 1976, Washington, D.C., Pan American Health Organization, Department of Research Development and Coordination, 1976, 10-11. Engl.

For complete document see entry 2776 (volume 4); other chapters have been abstracted separately under entries 3036, 3069, 3082, 3465, 3476, 3495, and 3498.

Laboratory tests have shown that cornmeal can be fortified and made nutritionally comparable to meat by adding certain nutrients. A test of fortified cornmeal (7.82% soybean flour, 0.12% lysine, and .06% A, B-1, B-2, niacin, and iron) was conducted in an Indian village in the Guatemalan highlands. From June 1972-May 1975, investigators monitored the health of pregnant women, infant and child morbidity and mortality, and foetal and child growth. Data were compared to baseline data that had been collected during an 8-year period before the study. Findings were that infant mortality had decreased 50%, morbidity during weaning had declined by 33%, and children aged 3-5 years demonstrated better growth patterns. Although change in foetal growth was observed, the fortification of corn proved to be very beneficial to children's health. (HC)

3498 Wey Moreira, B.H. Vieira, S. *Prevalence of dental caries in permanent teeth of white and black schoolchildren in Brazil.* Community Den-

tistry and oral Epidemiology (Copenhagen), 5(3), 1977, 129-131.
Engl.
18 refs.
See also entry 2776 (volume 4).

In order to compare the incidence of dental caries in white and black schoolchildren in Piracicaba, Brazil, 1 284 children aged 7-12 years were examined. The student t-test methodology for analyzing the examination results is described. The t-test revealed that white students in these groups had at least 5% more caries than black students: at age 7 years, both sexes of white children had a higher incidence of cavities; at age 8 years, both sexes; at age 9 years, males only; at age 10 years, both sexes; at age 11 years, males only. The results are presented in tabular form and the accuracy of the methodology is discussed. (Modified journal abstract.)

3499   WHO, Geneva. *Tuberculosis control: a review of recent programmes in Cuba.* WHO Chronicle (Geneva), 30(12), Dec 1976, 501-505.
Engl.
Also published in French, Russian, and Spanish.

Because the tuberculosis control programme set up in 1963 was not completely successful, a new programme was established in Havana, Cuba, in 1970 and by 1973 its services had been extended to the whole country. The main characteristics of the new programme include permanent and full integration into the general health services, case-finding by means of direct microscopy of smears and by culture examination of sputum from patients with respiratory symptoms lasting more than 3 weeks, fully supervised intermittent chemotherapy of ambulatory patients, complete BCG vaccination coverage of neonates and schoolchildren, payment to all patients under treatment of 100% of their wages, availability of hospital beds for inpatients when necessary, and periodic supervision of the base units by regional, provincial, and national levels of the health care system. Several aspects of the programme are discussed in detail and its progress up to 1974 is examined. WHO advisers stress the need for continuing evaluation. Some statistical data are included. (RMB)

3500   Yokogawa, M. *Programme of schistosomiasis control in Japan.* Southeast Asian Journal of Tropical Medicine and Public Health (Bangkok), 7(2), Jun 1976, 322-329.
Engl.
14 refs.

The schistosomiasis control programme in Japan emphasizes the elimination of the snail host by using pesticides and lining irrigation ditches in rice fields with concrete. Land reclamation activities have also helped to destroy snail breeding habitats. Nationwide environmental sanitation measures include providing uncontaminated water supplies, constructing latrines, encouraging children to swim in swimming pools rather than rivers, switching to chemical fertilizers in place of human excrement, and controlling animal hosts, especially cows, dogs, and rats. A comprehensive epidemiological surveillance system and integrated health education programmes have led to early detection of the few remaining cases of infestation. The author adds that increasing industrialization and improved living standards have decreased the risk of exposure to schistosomiasis for most of the population. (RMB)

Author Index

(figures refer to abstract numbers)

A

Aall, C., 3007
Abel-Smith, B., 2976
Abril, I.F., 2987
Academia de Ciencias Medicas, Fisicas y Naturales de Guatemala, Guatemala., 3415
ACTION, Peace Corps, Washington, D.C., 3310
Acton, N., 2884
Adams, R.N., 2988
Addy, D.P., 3457
Ademuwagun, Z.A., 3008
Adetuyibi, A., 3192
Adriasola, G., 3458
African Medical and Research Foundation International, Nairobi., 2848
Agualimpia Montoya, C., 2883
Ahmed, S., 2885
Aho, W.R., 2989
Ajayi, V., 3311
Akerele, O., 2849
Alban Holguin, J., 3459
Alexeyeff, S., 2886
Allard, H., 3312
Allbrook, D., 2886
Alpers, A., 2886
Alsing, B., 3114
Alter, J.D., 3439
Altmann, M., 3132
Aly, H.E., 3460
American Public Health Association, Washington, D.C., 3405, 3406
Amezquita, A., 3485
Amidi, S., 3217
Ampofo, D.A., 3296
Anaise, J.Z., 3461
Anderson, M.L., 3012
Andreano, R.L., 3392
Andrews, S., 3439
Antes, E.J., 3009
Anyudhi, R.K., 3239
Arango G., J., 3313
Ardito Barletta, N., 3414
Arias Huerta, J., 3290
Armelagos, G.J., 2990
Armstrong, B., 2886
Arnon, A., 2850
Arole, R.S., 3115
Aromasodu, M.O., 3466

Asante, R.O., 3296
Asociacion Colombiana de Facultades de Medicina, Bogota., 3470
Atlas, J., 3010
Ayonrinde, A., 3160

B

Baily, G.V., 3427
Baker, R., 3288
Baker, S.S., 3288
Baker, T.D., 2840
Banam, J., 3116
Banerjee, A., 3270
Barbieri, M.A., 3492
Barbosa, F.S., 2851
Barkhuus, A., 3407
Barnes, P.A., 3117
Barrell, R.A., 3077
Barrientos Llano, G., 2824
Barros Filho, A.A., 3492
Darrow, R.N., 3011
Basu, R.N., 3408
Beaner, L.G., 3012
Beaton, G.R., 3271
Beaubrun, M.H., 2825
Beaulieu, M., 3312
Begum, A., 3071
Behar, M., 3013
Behrhorst, C., 3218
Belliger, P., 3105
Belmar, R., 2852
Beltzung, I.C., 3279
Belyaeva, A., 3206
Ben-Sira, I., 3103
Benedetti, W.L., 3291
Bennett, B.E., 3219
Berg, D., 3106
Berggren, G.M., 3462
Berggren, W.L., 3220, 3462
Bergman, R., 3272
Bernachi, M., 2896
Bezroukov, V., 3302
Bhachu, S.S., 3239
Bhatia, J.C., 2971
Bhatt, M.J., 2887, 2888
Bicknell, W.J., 3409
Biddulph, J., 2826, 3440
Binns, C.W., 2977, 3463

Bisley, G.G., 3151
Blaize, A.A., 3176
Bloem, K., 2889
Blumhagen, J., 2827, 2853, 2890, 2891, 3193, 3221, 3222, 3223
Blumhagen, R.V., 2827, 2853, 2890, 2891, 3193, 3221, 3222, 3223
Bobenrieth, M., 3194
Boeckler, M., 2892
Bohnert, S., 3374
Bojalil, L.F., 3215
Bole, S.V., 3149
Bollag, U., 3224, 3464
Bomgaars, M.R., 3118
Bonsi, S.K., 2991
Borel, G., 3146
Borkent-Niehof, A., 3295
Bourre, A.L., 2801, 2802
Boyd, P., 2893
Bradshaw, B.R., 3163
Brand, P.W., 3119
Breman, J.G., 3014
Bridgman, R.F., 3410
Briscoe, G., 3001
British Life Assurance Trust Centre for Health and Medical Education, London., 2803
British Medical Association, London., 2828
Brown, G.F., 3161
Brown, H.B., 3015
Brown, J.E., 3314
Brown, P., 3112
Brown, R.C., 3314
Bryant, J., 2829
Bryant, J.H., 2854
Buchanan, N., 3083
Budiningsih, S., 3295
Bureau d'Etudes et de Recherches pour la Promotion de la Sante, Kangu-Mayumbe, Zaire., 2804
Burgess, A., 3315
Burgess, H.J., 3315
Butt, H.W., 3016, 3017
Byrne, K., 3225

C

Cadotsch, A.F., 3120
Caldeyro-Barcia, R., 3291
Calvert, P., 2970
Calvert, P.F., 3107
Camel V., F., 3316
Canadian International Development Agency, Ottawa., 2894
Caribbean Epidemiology Centre (Carec), Port-of-Spain., 3018, 3019
Caribbean Food and Nutrition Institute, Kingston, Jamaica., 3020, 3021, 3465
Carlos Soares, F., 3492
Carpentier, J.C., 3466
Carr, M., 2805
Carstairs, G.M., 2992
Cash, R.A., 3121
Castro, L., 3485
Catholic Institute for International Relations, London., 3108
Cawte, J., 3001

Central Treaty Organization, Ankara, Turkey., 3022
Centre pour la Promotion de la Sante, Kangu-Mayumbe, Zaire., 2806
Centro Panamericano de Ingenieria Sanitaria y Ciencias del Ambiente, Lima., 2807
Cesar Daneluzzi, J., 3492
Chabot, H.T., 2855, 2856
Chacko, A., 3162
Chamberlain, R.H., 3109
Chamberlin, R.W., 3122
Chatterjee, A., 3152
Chen, P.C., 3023, 3411, 3467, 3468
Cheung, F.M., 2895
Chile, Ministerio de Salud Publica, Programa de Extension de Servicios de Salud Materno Infantil y Bienestar Familiar., 3469
Chinese Medical Journal, Peking., 2986
Chorny, A., 2896
Chowdhury, S., 3292
Chowdhury, Z., 2978, 3292
Christensen, S., 3049, 3430
Christian Medical Commission, World Council of Churches, Geneva., 2897
Christiansen, N., 3485
Chuttani, C.S., 2971
Clement-Murphy, J., 3485
Clukay-Newton, A., 3123
Cole, T.J., 3078, 3096
Cole-King, S., 3392, 3441
Collette, F., 3312
Colombia, Comite Nacional de Investigacion en Tecnologia de Alimentos y Nutricion., 3024
Colombia, Departamento Nacional de Planeacion., 2898
Colombia, Ministerio de Salud Publica., 2808, 3470
Comite Regional de Promocion de Salud Rural, Guatemala., 2809
Commonwealth Foundation, London., 3124
Condon-Paoloni, D., 3025
Cook, S., 3393, 3471
Cooperation Canada/Tunisienne, Tunis., 3317, 3318
Cordova, A., 3195
Correa, H., 3026
Correo, F., 2880
Cosnard, G., 3478
Cossette, G., 3312
Courtejoie, J., 3144, 3170, 3172, 3253, 3278, 3285, 3319, 3320, 3321, 3334, 3335, 3337, 3341, 3347, 3348, 3349, 3350, 3351, 3352, 3353, 3354, 3355, 3356, 3357, 3358, 3359, 3360, 3361, 3362, 3363, 3377, 3378, 3388, 3389, 3390, 3391, 3451
Cowan, B., 3027
Cravioto, J., 3025
Creyghton, M., 2993
Crow, M.M., 3163
Crow, R., 3028
Cuba, Ministerio de Salud Publica., 3125, 3412

D

D'Aeth, R.G., 2899
Daberkow, S.G., 3153
Damena, G.G., 3226
Darity, W.A., 2830

Kumar, S., 2868

L

Lall, S., 2981
Lancet, London., 2926
Larchet, M., 3478
Larsen, J.V., 3288
Lasserre, R., 3135
Laugesen, H., 3333
Lauture, H. de, 3146
Lavor, A.C., 2851
League of Red Cross Societies, Geneva., 3280
Lechat, M.E., 2927
Leclercq, L., 3479
Leeson, J., 3480
Lekgetha, A.N., 3281
Lelo di Kimbi Kiaku, N.M., 3170, 3334, 3335, 3451
Lesotho, Ministry of Health and Social Welfare., 3237
Levinson, D., 3212
Levitt, S., 3045
Lewis, O., 3481
Lippmann, L., 2915
List, M.S., 3439
Litsios, S., 2928, 3432
Llinares, V.M., 3046
Lobo, L.C., 3204
Locketz, L., 3171
Loftus, J., 3238
Lolik, P.L., 3239
Long, E.C., 2845, 3205
Longa, I., 3331
Loransky, D.N., 3206
Lovel, H.J., 3329
Lowry, G.F., 3305
Lubis, F., 3295
Lund, J., 3336
Lundin, B., 3331
Lyengar, M.A., 2929

M

M'Vogo, R.B., 3312
ma Lelo, N.M., 3172
ma Yimbu Aliendihata, T.M., 3337
Macdougall, L., 3083
MacGregor, W.B., 3034
Mackay, J., 3240
MacPherson, P., 3001
Madeley, C.R., 3338
Mahler, H., 2930
Mahmud, S., 2931, 3241
Makene, W.J., 2865
Maksoud, A.A., 3460
Malaysia, Ministry of Health., 2816
Mante, K.S., 2932
Marchant, L., 3458
Marquez, M., 3070, 3230
Marriott, McK., 3452
Martin, A.E., 3047
Martin, G.E., 2836
Martin, J.F., 3168
Martinez Urbina, R., 3242
Maru, R.M., 3048, 3397
Masar, I., 3049
Mascareno Sauceda, F., 3242

Mashigo, S., 3083
Masih, N., 3374
Mason-Browne, N.E., 2933
Mata, L.J., 3050, 3051
Mayer, J., 3445
McArdle, A., 2990
McCall, M., 2886
McClain, C., 3453
McConnel, F., 3001
McDowell, J., 3052, 3053, 3054, 3482
McDowell, U., 3055
McGilvray, J., 2849
McIntosh, C.A., 3282
McIntosh, C.E., 2934
McJunkin, F.E., 3056
McLaren, D.S., 3339
McMichael, J.K., 2869, 2870
McMurdo, J., 3271
McNaughton, J., 3483
McWilliams, D.M., 3275
Medical Missionary Association, London., 2817
Medis, L.P., 3173
Mehra, J., 3174
Mehra, S., 3484
Mena G., P., 3458
Mendel, L., 3164
Menu, J.P., 3057
Mercer, H., 3058, 3215
Messing, S.D., 3059
Metcalf, C.A., 3157
Michaelson, I.C., 3207
Miles, D., 3340
Milio, N., 2871, 3398
Minde, K.K., 3060
Minott, K., 2989
Moin Shah., 2837
Moliha C., R., 3458
Monckosso, G.L., 3422
Mora, J.O., 3485
Morales, E., 3414
Morley, D., 3134, 3136, 3137
Morou, M., 3138
Morton, J., 3243
Mount Carmel International Training Centre for Community Services, Haifa, Israel., 3061
Moussa, W.A., 3460
Mousseau-Gershman, Y., 3250, 3422
Mujica L., H., 3458
Muller, M., 3062
Murthy, A.K., 2843
Mutiso, D., 3112
Mwabulambo, D.J., 3244

N

Nair, S.S., 3427
Najarzadeh, E., 3249
Nanna, P., 3477
National Academy of Sciences, Washington, D.C., 3063, 3064
National Family Planning Coordinating Board, Jakarta., 3293
National Fund for Research into Crippling Diseases, Arundel, UK., 3124
Nchinda, T.C., 3422

Neumann, A.K., 3296
Newell, K.W., 2938
Nguyen-van-Dan., 3002
Nguyen-van-Huong., 3002
Nguyen-xuan-Nguyen., 3486
Nhonoli, A.M., 2865
Nicholas, D.D., 3296
Nicholson, K.G., 3157
Nightingale, K.W., 3065
Noamesi, G.K., 3057
Noguer, A., 3066
Novaro, S., 2896
Nugroho, G., 3139
Nursing Journal of India, New Delhi., 3283
Nyirenda, F.K., 3067
Nzita, M., 3341

O

Oanh, B.X., 3479
Oberg, K., 3487
Ofosu-Amaah, S., 3296
Olugbile, A., 3068
Ordonez Carceller, C., 3423
Ormerod, W.E., 2982
Oshin, T.A., 3140
Oyemade, A., 3068
Ozguner, O., 2935
Ozigi, Y.O., 3003, 3245

P

Pakistan, Planning Commission., 3424, 3425
Pakshong, D.I., 3284
Palm, M.L., 3399
Palpai, P., 3477
Pam, R., 2810
Pan American Health Organization, Washington, D.C.,
    2936, 2937, 3188, 3400
Papua New Guinea, Department of Public Health.,
    3246, 3342
Paranagua Santana, J.F., 2851
Paredes Manrique, R., 2883
Parker, A., 2938
Parker, R.L., 2843
Patil, N.M., 3141
Paul, B.D., 3454
Paul, M.P., 3255
Pazos, A., 3069
Pelaez, J.E., 2880
Penchaszadeh, V., 3070
Peradze, O., 2872
Pereda F., C., 3079
Pereira, S.M., 3071
Peru, Ministerio de Salud., 2939
Pettifor, J., 3083
Pettit, J.H., 3142
Philippines, Department of Health., 2940, 2974, 3437
Phoon, W.O., 3208
Pibouleau, R.F., 2818
Pielemeier, N.R., 3072
Pillsbury, B.L., 3455
Pinto, V.A., 3488
Pio, A., 3073
Piper, D.W., 3343
Plovnick, M.S., 3365

Pradhan, P., 3004
Primary Health Care Programme Formulation
    Committee, Khartoum., 2941, 2942
Prince Leopold Institute of Tropical Medicine, Antwerp,
    Belgium., 3074
Puschel, J., 3011
Putsep, E.P., 2943

Q

Quadros, F.C., 3430

R

Radebaugh, J.F., 3122
Raimbault, A.M., 2838
Ram, E.R., 2839, 3456
Ramakrishna, V., 3175
Ramasamy, T.P., 3255
Rao, N.P., 3489
Rau, B., 3331
Rault, J., 3034
Rawitscher, M., 3445
Razavi-Farvar, C., 3472
Reader, G., 3164
Rebello, L.M., 3490
Redfield, D.L., 3213
Reilly, Q., 3344
Reitzes, D.C., 3438
Renshaw, A., 3157
Retel-Laurentin, A., 3075
Rey, M., 3491
Reyna-Barrios, J.M., 3474
Richards, R., 3164
Richardson, B.D., 3083
Richter, H.B., 2944
Rideout, J.M., 3157
Rifka, G., 3392
Rifkin, S.B., 3247, 3248
Riley, C., 2873
Rios, J.A., 3487
Ritchie, J., 3076
Rodriguez A., C., 2975
Rodriguez Guerra, E., 3198
Rodriguez Hernandez, P., 3198
Roemer, M.I., 2874
Rogoff, M., 3345
Rohde, J.E., 3260
Romano Santoro, J., 3492
Ronaghy, H.A., 3249, 3250, 3251, 3252
Roodkowsky, M., 3005
Roosman, R.S., 2875
Roscin, A.V., 3433
Rosenfield, A.G., 3401
Ross, W.F., 3346
Rossler, H., 3143
Rotsart de Hertaing, I., 3144, 3170, 3172, 3253, 3278,
    3285, 3319, 3320, 3321, 3334, 3335, 3337, 3341,
    3347, 3348, 3349, 3350, 3351, 3352, 3353, 3354,
    3355, 3356, 3357, 3358, 3359, 3360, 3361, 3362,
    3363, 3377, 3378, 3388, 3389, 3390, 3391, 3451
Rowland, M.G., 3077, 3078, 3096
Rowley, J., 3145
Roze, D., 2876
Rubiano, L.M. de, 3364
Rubin, I.M., 3365

Rueda S., B., 3366, 3367, 3368, 3369
Ruggill, J., 3212
Russel, S.S., 3249

S

Sabers, D., 3212
Sabers, D.L., 3213
Sabol, J.B., 3414
Sadjimin, T., 3260
Said, H.M., 3006
Saied, A., 2945
Sakdisawat, O., 3477
Salazar Bucheli, J.M., 2877
Salfield, J., 3493
Sanchez R., H., 3079
Sanders, R.K., 3113
Sandhu, S.K., 3080
Sangal, S.P., 3439
Sankale, M., 3146
Santos, A.T., 3494
Sartorius, N., 3081
Saunders, D.J., 3370
Schifini, J.P., 3082
Schneider, R.E., 3495
Scholl, T.O., 3025
Schuenyane, E., 3083
Schwartz, T.A., 3249
Schweser, H., 3176
Schweser, H.O., 3177, 3178, 3179, 3180, 3181, 3182,
    3183, 3184, 3185, 3209, 3254, 3286, 3301, 3307, 3371
Sebai, Z.A., 2840
Segall, M., 2983
Sekou, H., 3084, 3210, 3297, 3426, 3434
Seoul National University, School of Public Health,
    Seoul., 3085, 3308
Seoul National University, Seoul., 2984, 3147, 3298
Sethu, S., 3255
Shamsuddin, M., 2946
Shehan, M., 3164
Sheriff, M.P., 2947
Shiffman, M., 3495
Shrivastava, N., 3149
Shutt, M.M., 2948
Sich, D., 3256, 3257, 3258, 3289
Sidel, V.W., 2852
Siegmann, A.E., 3086
Simmons, O.G., 3186
Singapore, Ministry of Health., 2841, 3087, 3496
Sjoerdsma, A., 2881, 3420
Skiff, A., 3164
Smilkstein, G., 3211
Solomon, M.J., 2949, 2950
Solter, S., 3249
Sood, S.K., 3148
Sorkin, A.L., 2985
Spillmann, R.K., 3187
Srikantarumu, N., 3427
Standard, K.L., 3259
Stanley, F., 2886
Steiner-Freud, J., 3287
Stephen, W.J., 2878
Stephens, B., 3428
Stewart, G.T., 2951
Stillman, P.L., 3212, 3213

Stipek, J., 2952, 3435
Stulhman, L., 2896
Sudan, National Health Programming Committee.,
    2842, 2953, 2954, 2955
Sutherland, R.D., 2873
Suyadi, A., 3260
Swift, C.R., 3372
Swinkels, W., 2881
Swinscow, T.D., 3261

T

Tabibzadeh, I., 2849
Taiyang Production Brigade Party Branch of Chishan
    County, Shansi, China PR., 2986
Takulia, H.S., 2843, 3439
Taljaard, L.T., 3303
Tandon, B.N., 2879
Tanzania, Ministry of Health., 3373
Taylor, C.E., 3214, 3439
Thailand, Ministry of Public Health., 2844, 3262
Thapa, R., 3299
Third World First, Oxford, UK., 2980
Thomas, A., 3402
Tichy, M.K., 2819, 2820
Timmappaya, A., 2971
Titus, J.B., 3416
Torfs, M., 2938
Tribhuvan University, Institute of Medicine, Kath-
    mandu., 3088
Tribhuvan University, Kathmandu., 2956
Turizo, A., 2880

U

Uberoi, I.S., 3374
UNICEF, International Union of Nutritional Sciences,
    New Delhi., 3089
UNICEF, Nairobi., 3090
Universite Catholique de Louvain, Brussels., 3091, 3092
University of Indonesia, Faculty of Public Health,
    Jakarta., 3293
University of Indonesia, Faculty of Social Sciences,
    Jakarta., 3293
University of the West Indies, Department of Social and
    Preventive Medicine, Mona, Jamaica., 3263
Urrutia, J.J., 3050, 3051, 3497
USA, Agencia Internacional para el Desarrollo, Depart-
    mento de Estado., 3415
USA, Agency for International Development, Depart-
    ment of State., 2867, 2957, 3188
USA, Department of Health, Education, and Welfare.,
    3332
USA, Department of the Army., 3375, 3376

V

Vahlquist, B., 3199
Valdivia Dominguez, A., 3189
van der Heyden, A., 3350, 3358, 3377, 3378
Vargas Martinez, H., 2975
Varma, S.K., 3148, 3149
Vasco, A., 2880
Vaughan, A.B., 3379
Velez Gil, A., 3313
Venezuela, Ministerio de Sanidad y Asistencia Social.,
    3093
Venkataswamy, G., 3158, 3264

Verma, S.P., 3490
Viau D., A., 2845
Vieira, S., 3498
Vijayaraghavan, K., 3489
Villarreal, R., 3215
Vindu Kiama, M., 3170
Vivas, A., 2913
Vogel, L.C., 2881, 3126, 3429, 3430
Vohra, S., 3374
Voluntary Health Association of India, New Delhi., 2821

W

W'Oigo, H., 2881
Wachira, J., 3114
Wachter, E., 3380
Wade, M.A., 2882
Walker, G., 3442, 3446
Wallace, N., 2889
Walsh, D.C., 3409
War on Want, London., 2980
Watt, D.G., 3381
Watts, G., 3265
Welty, T.K., 3266
Wen, W., 3094
Werner, D., 3095
Werner, D.B., 2958
Western, K., 3073
Wey Moreira, B.H., 3498
Whitehead, R.G., 3077, 3078, 3096, 3328
WHO, Brazzaville., 2846, 2959, 2960, 3097, 3098, 3190, 3309, 3382

WHO, Geneva., 2822, 2823, 2936, 2961, 2962, 2963, 2964, 2965, 2966, 2967, 2968, 2969, 3099, 3100, 3101, 3267, 3383, 3384, 3499
Wicht, C.L., 3102
Williams, A., 3164
Wilson, T.D., 3271
Wintrob, R.M., 2847
Woigo, H., 3420
Wone, I., 3146
Wood, C.H., 3268, 3385
World Neighbors, Oklahoma City., 3269
Wray, J., 2889

Y

Yassur, S., 3103
Yassur, Y., 3103
Yemba, K.P., 3191
Yepes Lujan, F.J., 2883
Yepes Parra, A., 2883
Yoder, P.T., 3159
Yokogawa, M., 3500

Z

Zachs, U., 3103
Zaifrani, S., 3103
Zalessky, G., 3206
Zeighami, B., 3249, 3403, 3404
Zeighami, E., 3403, 3404
Ziegler, J.P., 3104
Zilkah, E., 3461
Zimmer, S., 3404

Geographic Index

(figures refer to abstract numbers)

A

Afghanistan, 2827, 2853, 2890, 2891, 3193, 3221, 3222, 3223

Africa *See also: regional name(s), e.g., East Africa and specific country name(s);* 2811, 2830, 2834, 2846, 2849, 2897, 2924, 2959, 3008, 3019, 3052, 3059, 3075, 3076, 3098, 3170, 3190, 3287, 3296, 3309, 3329, 3483, 3491

Argentina, 3100

Asia *See also: regional name(s), e.g., Middle East and specific country name(s);* 2810, 3247, 3448

Australia, 2886, 2914, 2915, 2997, 3001, 3277

B

Bangladesh, 2919, 2927, 2978, 3074, 3128, 3280, 3292

Barbados, 2829

Belize, 2933

Bolivia, 2858, 3291

Botswana, 3072, 3274, 3393, 3428, 3446, 3447, 3471

Brazil, 2829, 2851, 3011, 3291, 3454, 3487, 3492, 3498

Burundi, 2834

C

Cameroon, 2830, 2836, 2919, 3168, 3422, 3475

Canada, 2894, 2994, 3039, 3073, 3100, 3263, 3417, 3418, 3454

Caribbean *See also: Latin America, West Indies, and specific country name(s);* 2893, 2920, 2934, 3019, 3021, 3036, 3043, 3176, 3177, 3178, 3179, 3180, 3181, 3182, 3183, 3184, 3185, 3209, 3254, 3259, 3286, 3301, 3307, 3339, 3371

Central America *See also: specific country name(s);* 2832, 3013

Chile, 2829, 2852, 2858, 2878, 3079, 3082, 3186, 3291, 3454, 3458, 3469

China PR, 2832, 2855, 2856, 2973, 2986, 3006, 3048, 3094, 3291, 3332, 3397, 3455

China R, 3450, 3454, 3455

Colombia, 2808, 2829, 2858, 2877, 2880, 2883, 2898, 2913, 3024, 3081, 3187, 3229, 3263, 3291, 3313, 3364, 3366, 3367, 3368, 3369, 3470, 3485

Comoro Islands, 2860

Costa Rica, 2975

Cuba, 2824, 3125, 3189, 3195, 3198, 3230, 3263, 3291, 3412, 3423, 3499

D

Dahomey, 2834

Dominican Republic, 3291

E

East Africa *See also: specific country name(s);* 3090, 3372, 3379

Egypt, 2876, 3460

El Salvador, 2829

Equador, 2829, 2858, 2903, 2904, 3157, 3197, 3291

Ethiopia, 2919, 3074, 3159, 3291, 3339

F

Far East *See also: specific country name(s);* 3247

Finland, 3100, 3167

France, 2860, 3032, 3413

G

Gambia, 2888, 2921, 3077, 3078, 3096

Ghana, 2991, 3111, 3145, 3296, 3473

Guatemala, 2809, 2845, 2957, 2988, 2996, 3013, 3050, 3051, 3069, 3091, 3096, 3188, 3218, 3291, 3400, 3415, 3454, 3459, 3474, 3476, 3495, 3497

Guyana, 3018, 3021

H

Haiti, 3015, 3091, 3220, 3407, 3462

Honduras, 2916, 3225

Hong Kong, 2895, 3277

I

India, 2821, 2839, 2843, 2868, 2879, 2900, 2908, 2917, 2918, 2919, 2927, 2971, 2981, 2992, 3000, 3005, 3016, 3017, 3027, 3029, 3030, 3039, 3040, 3048, 3071, 3080, 3081, 3113, 3115, 3117, 3141, 3148, 3149, 3152, 3155, 3158, 3162, 3169, 3174, 3175, 3214, 3231, 3255, 3264, 3265, 3280, 3283, 3324, 3327, 3333, 3339, 3374, 3386, 3397, 3402, 3408, 3427, 3439, 3452, 3454, 3456, 3483, 3489, 3490

Indonesia, 2875, 2919, 3135, 3260, 3269, 3280, 3280, 3293, 3295, 3325

Iran, 2884, 2919, 2927, 2972, 3022, 3039, 3167, 3217, 3249, 3250, 3251, 3252, 3392, 3395, 3403, 3404, 3472

Israel, 2850, 2863, 3133, 3207, 3287, 3461

Ivory Coast, 3156

J

Jamaica, 2912, 2995, 3021, 3041, 3224, 3259, 3263, 3464, 3465

Japan, 3046, 3280, 3500

Java, 3139

Subject Index

(figures refer to abstract numbers)

A

Aborigine *See also: Minority Group;* 2886, 2914, 2915, 2997, 3001

Abortion *See also: Birth Control;* 2907, 3048, 3075, 3292

Abstracting Journal *See also: Mass Media;* 2868

Administration, Disease Control, 3494

Administration, Emergency Health Services, 2879, 3084

Administration, Environmental Health Services, 3098

Administration, Family Planning Programme, 3048

Administration, Health Centre, 2848, 2872, 3122, 3258, 3282, 3344, 3428

Administration, Health Manpower, 3394

Administration, Health Services, 2853, 2858, 2862, 2865, 2869, 2873, 2875, 2876, 2882, 2883, 2888, 2889, 2890, 2893, 2914, 2923, 2945, 2953, 2964, 2966, 2970, 3072, 3116, 3126, 3154, 3180, 3193, 3214, 3226, 3227, 3232, 3279, 3331, 3395, 3397, 3405, 3406, 3407, 3410, 3415, 3417, 3424, 3425, 3429

Administration, Hospital, 3282

Administration, Mass Campaign, 3408

Administration, Maternal Child Health Services, 3032, 3282, 3289, 3393

Administration, Nursing Services, 3402

Administration, Nutrition Programme, 2934, 3084

Administration, Rehabilitation Services, 2912

Administrative Aspect, 2832, 2848, 2853, 2858, 2859, 2862, 2865, 2872, 2873, 2875, 2876, 2879, 2882, 2883, 2888, 2889, 2893, 2912, 2921, 2923, 2934, 2945, 2953, 2964, 2966, 2970, 2994, 3084, 3098, 3116, 3122, 3126, 3154, 3180, 3193, 3214, 3222, 3226, 3227, 3228, 3232, 3236, 3266, 3272, 3282, 3289, 3329, 3331, 3340, 3342, 3344, 3393, 3394, 3395, 3397, 3402, 3407, 3408, 3410, 3417, 3424, 3425, 3428, 3429, 3430, 3494

Administrator *See also: Health Manpower;* 2840

Agricultural Sector *See also: Food Production;* 2805, 2814, 2899, 2900, 2902, 2904, 2921, 2931, 3010, 3015, 3021, 3046, 3055, 3063, 3065, 3089, 3122, 3128, 3177, 3183, 3218, 3371, 3445, 3471, 3483, 3487

Aid Post Orderly *See also: Auxiliary Health Worker;* 3116, 3226, 3246, 3253, 3344

ALERT, 3346

Anaemia *See also: Nutrition;* 2886, 3157, 3355, 3356, 3473

Anaesthesia, 3379

Annual Report, 3091, 3092, 3128

Antenatal Care *See also: Clinic, Antenatal; Maternal Child Health; Pregnancy;* 2815, 3126, 3154, 3156, 3289, 3350, 3387, 3389, 3390, 3391, 3420, 3477

Anthropometric Measurement *See also: Evaluation, Nutrition; Nutrition;* 3025, 3027, 3050, 3051, 3078, 3079, 3083, 3092, 3096, 3136, 3137, 3220, 3224, 3314, 3318, 3324, 3328, 3464, 3465, 3482, 3493

Appropriate Technology, 2805, 2807, 2810, 2884, 2885, 2889, 2892, 2906, 2930, 2935, 2938, 2944, 2952, 2962, 2968, 3031, 3033, 3052, 3054, 3055, 3064, 3069, 3076, 3082, 3090, 3105, 3109, 3119, 3134, 3137, 3140, 3141, 3149, 3327, 3338, 3370

Ascariasis *See also: Parasitic Diseases;* 3378

Attitudes *See also: Survey;* 2819, 2824, 2829, 2834, 2842, 2907, 2917, 2921, 2926, 2950, 2971, 2972, 2973, 2987, 2988, 2989, 2993, 2995, 2999, 3000, 3006, 3017, 3035, 3043, 3062, 3067, 3083, 3088, 3119, 3141, 3150, 3160, 3181, 3186, 3194, 3205, 3212, 3214, 3229, 3249, 3254, 3269, 3296, 3320, 3337, 3359, 3360, 3394, 3395, 3399, 3403, 3404, 3405, 3411, 3421, 3431, 3436, 3439, 3444, 3448, 3450, 3452, 3453, 3454, 3455, 3456, 3468, 3480, 3481, 3490, 3492

Audiovisual Aid *See also: Film; Teaching Aid;* 2803, 2804, 2821, 3003, 3087, 3166, 3171, 3174, 3188, 3286, 3333, 3336, 3348, 3349, 3370, 3377, 3378, 3484

Auxiliary Health Worker *See also: Aid Post Orderly; Basic Health Worker; Barefoot Doctor; Behdar; Community Health Aide; Community Health Worker; Dispen sary Attendant; Family Nurse Practitioner; Feldsher; Health Extension Officer; Health Inspector; Health Manpower; Health Visitor ; Medex; Medical Assistant; Ophthalmic Medical Assistant; Paramedic; Rural Health Promoter; Rural Medical Aid; Traditional Birth Attendant;* 2816, 2822, 2823, 2826, 2827, 2828, 2832, 2835, 2840, 2842, 2843, 2844, 2845, 2847, 2852, 2853, 2855, 2856, 2857, 2858, 2861, 2870, 2872, 2890, 2893, 2895, 2899, 2902, 2911, 2926, 2936, 2940, 2943, 2958, 2979, 2985, 2999, 3003, 3011, 3016, 3030, 3036, 3045, 3081, 3089, 3108, 3114, 3115, 3116, 3118, 3120, 3122, 3127, 3128, 3130, 3133, 3134, 3138, 3139, 3143, 3151, 3167, 3169, 3170, 3177, 3184, 3193, 3196, 3202, 3203, 3205, 3208, 3213, 3216, 3217, 3218, 3219, 3220, 3221, 3222, 3223, 3224, 3225, 3226, 3227, 3228, 3230, 3231, 3232, 3233, 3234, 3235, 3236, 3237, 3238, 3240, 3241, 3242, 3243, 3244, 3245, 3246, 3247, 3248, 3250,

3251, 3252, 3253, 3254, 3255, 3256, 3257, 3258, 3259, 3262, 3265, 3266, 3267, 3268, 3272, 3274, 3278, 3279, 3286, 3287, 3289, 3290, 3292, 3294, 3298, 3299, 3300, 3301, 3302, 3303, 3304, 3305, 3307, 3313, 3314, 3319, 3322, 3325, 3331, 3332, 3343, 3345, 3364, 3366, 3367, 3368, 3369, 3372, 3373, 3374, 3375, 3379, 3383, 3385, 3387, 3389, 3392, 3393, 3394, 3395, 3396, 3398, 3400, 3401, 3404, 3406, 3411, 3416, 3421, 3436, 3440, 3459, 3464, 3471, 3472, 3474, 3482, 3488, 3490, 3492

Auxiliary, Anaesthetist, 3379, 3440

Auxiliary, Child Health, 3134, 3440

Auxiliary, Dental *See also: Dental Manpower;* 2822, 2844, 3300, 3301, 3302, 3303

Auxiliary, Family Planning *See also: Family Planning Manpower; Lady Health Visitor; Traditional Birth Attendant;* 3048, 3292

Auxiliary, Health Education, 2835, 3170, 3278

Auxiliary, Health Educator *See also: Health Educator;* 3177, 3184, 3254, 3393

Auxiliary, Laboratory *See also: Laboratory Technician; Medical Technologist;* 2823, 3243, 3304, 3345

Auxiliary, Maternal Child Health, 2835, 2911, 3030, 3118, 3241, 3393

Auxiliary, Mental Health, 2847, 2895, 3081

Auxiliary, Midwife *See also: Midwife; Traditional Birth Attendant;* 2816, 2857, 3401

Auxiliary, Multipurpose, 2853, 3196, 3220, 3231, 3242, 3255, 3265, 3394

Auxiliary, Nurse *See also: Nurse;* 2816, 2845, 2870, 2899, 3156, 3272, 3279, 3286, 3313, 3400, 3469, 3474

Auxiliary, Nurse-midwife *See also: Nurse-midwife; Traditional Birth Attendant;* 2826, 2918, 3016, 3017, 3374, 3389, 3489

Auxiliary, Nutrition, 3464, 3482

Auxiliary, Orthopaedic *See also: Physiotherapist;* 3045

Auxiliary, Pharmacy *See also: Pharmacist;* 2979

Auxiliary, Sanitation *See also: Sanitation Manpower;* 3375, 3488

Auxiliary, Single-purpose, 3486

Auxiliary, Statistician, 3036

Auxiliary, Surgical, 3292, 3379

B

Bantu *See also: Tribes;* 3281, 3447

Barefoot Doctor *See also: Auxiliary Health Worker;* 2832, 2855, 2856, 3094, 3332, 3396

Basic Health Worker *See also: Auxiliary Health Workers;* 3490

BCG Vaccination *See also: Tuberculosis Programme; Vaccination;* 3093, 3132, 3348, 3499

Bedouin *See also: Tribes;* 2863

Behdar *See also: Auxiliary Health Worker;* 3251

Bibliography, 2801, 2802, 2803, 2805, 2807, 2810, 2811, 2813, 2814, 2815, 2818, 2819, 2820, 2855, 2868, 3040, 3059

Birth Control *See also: Abortion; Family Planning; Intrauterine Device; Oral Contraceptive; Tubal Ligation; Vasectomy;* 2907, 3030, 3048, 3163, 3289, 3290, 3292, 3295, 3332, 3387, 3388, 3401, 3404

Birthrate *See also: Demography;* 2815, 2826, 2839, 2990, 3022, 3030, 3075, 3316, 3388, 3403

Blindness *See also: Eye Diseases;* 3071, 3103, 3151, 3152, 3155, 3158, 3486

Brain Drain *See also: Migration;* 2876, 2985, 3167

Breast-feeding *See also: Infant Feeding;* 3007, 3029, 3042, 3062, 3118, 3324, 3339, 3352, 3391, 3457, 3460, 3464, 3465, 3473, 3476

Burns *See also: Emergency Medical Care;* 3313, 3357

C

Cataracts *See also: Eye Diseases;* 3151, 3152, 3155, 3158

Child *See also: Child Health; Family; Infant; Maternal Child Health; School Health;* 2804, 2826, 2831, 2882, 2904, 2918, 2920, 2989, 2995, 3007, 3015, 3025, 3027, 3029, 3032, 3045, 3050, 3051, 3060, 3071, 3079, 3083, 3103, 3121, 3136, 3137, 3144, 3151, 3155, 3181, 3224, 3312, 3315, 3317, 3318, 3324, 3328, 3333, 3334, 3341, 3349, 3351, 3352, 3362, 3461, 3463, 3465, 3467, 3473, 3474, 3476, 3477, 3484, 3492, 3493, 3497, 3498

Child Care *See also: Social Services;* 2917, 2920, 2986, 3094, 3178, 3485

Child Health *See also: Child; Clinic, Child Health; Infant Feeding; Maternal Child Health; Pediatrics;* 2804, 2811, 2815, 2826, 2838, 2882, 2904, 2918, 2920, 2989, 2995, 3004, 3010, 3016, 3025, 3027, 3029, 3032, 3032, 3040, 3042, 3043, 3045, 3050, 3051, 3053, 3060, 3062, 3067, 3070, 3071, 3077, 3078, 3079, 3089, 3094, 3096, 3103, 3118, 3132, 3134, 3134, 3135, 3136, 3137, 3144, 3151, 3155, 3156, 3158, 3178, 3181, 3182, 3224, 3275, 3289, 3312, 3314, 3315, 3317, 3318, 3324, 3328, 3333, 3334, 3336, 3341, 3349, 3350, 3351, 3352, 3362, 3374, 3413, 3420, 3457, 3460, 3461, 3462, 3463, 3464, 3465, 3467, 3471, 3473, 3476, 3477, 3478, 3482, 3484, 3492, 3493

Cholera *See also: Infectious Diseases;* 2864, 2978, 3097, 3104, 3121, 3173, 3304

Clinic *See also: Construction, Clinic; Health Centre;* 2817, 2857, 2881, 2888, 2890, 2984, 3018, 3018, 3040, 3106, 3118, 3125, 3130, 3132, 3135, 3141, 3156, 3179, 3198, 3218, 3222, 3274, 3283, 3331, 3341, 3346, 3420, 3423, 3429, 3430, 3463, 3475, 3481

Clinic, Antenatal *See also: Antenatal Care;* 3135, 3420

Clinic, Child Health *See also: Child Health;* 3027, 3067, 3132, 3135, 3156, 3324, 3341, 3420, 3464, 3492

Clinic, Family Planning *See also: Family Planning;* 3420

Clinic, Maternal Child Health *See also: Maternal Child Health;* 2857, 2918, 3040, 3118, 3130, 3191, 3220, 3289, 3331, 3463, 3475

Clinic, Outpatient *See also: Outpatient Care;* 2853, 2881, 2984, 3018, 3122, 3141, 3218, 3346, 3429, 3430

Communications, 2818, 2868, 2921, 2954, 2955, 2968, 2993, 3174, 3188, 3386, 3417, 3431, 3442

Community, 2809, 2825, 2914, 3045, 3133, 3167, 3178, 3179, 3184, 3191, 3197, 3247, 3273, 3320, 3339, 3398, 3415, 3423, 3436, 3470, 3482

Community Development, 2809, 2810, 2831, 2836, 2874, 2889, 2902, 2906, 2909, 2917, 2918, 2919, 2941, 2949, 2962, 2992, 2999, 3001, 3033, 3057, 3061, 3089, 3128, 3138, 3139, 3159, 3168, 3169, 3177, 3178, 3184, 3191, 3218, 3227, 3238, 3247, 3260, 3269, 3299, 3330, 3371, 3395, 3471, 3472, 3481, 3487

Low-Cost Rural Health Care and Health Manpower Training

Community Diagnosis, 2886, 2956, 3035, 3133, 3248, 3339

Community Health, 2824, 2851, 2858, 2867, 2871, 2886, 2897, 2914, 2926, 2945, 2958, 2962, 3008, 3035, 3054, 3055, 3061, 3095, 3125, 3133, 3136, 3180, 3181, 3182, 3191, 3197, 3211, 3247, 3256, 3259, 3273, 3274, 3284, 3285, 3294, 3320, 3344, 3398, 3412, 3418, 3423, 3436

Community Health Aide, 2839, 2886, 2940, 3223, 3224, 3243, 3259, 3263, 3298, 3418, 3464

Community Health Worker, 2853, 2891, 2926, 2958, 3011, 3089, 3095, 3115, 3120, 3122, 3128, 3133, 3134, 3138, 3139, 3169, 3203, 3216, 3217, 3221, 3227, 3232, 3234, 3235, 3236, 3237, 3238, 3239, 3244, 3245, 3247, 3248, 3249, 3250, 3252, 3254, 3256, 3257, 3258, 3260, 3262, 3265, 3266, 3268, 3269, 3294, 3299, 3314, 3385, 3392, 3395, 3396, 3398, 3400, 3403, 3404, 3405, 3426, 3431, 3471, 3472

Community Medicine, 3133, 3197, 3200, 3205, 3211, 3285, 3423

Community Nurse, 2886, 3061, 3114, 3156, 3270, 3271, 3273, 3282, 3284

Conjunctivitis *See also: Eye Diseases;* 3143

Construction, 2805, 2810, 2818, 2885, 2892, 2901, 2916, 2924, 2935, 2943, 2944, 2947, 2952, 2964, 3031, 3052, 3054, 3055, 3098, 3105, 3112, 3129, 3140, 3141, 3149, 3191, 3327, 3340, 3363, 3366, 3378, 3433

Construction, Equipment *See also: Equipment;* 3052, 3105, 3140, 3141, 3149

Construction, Health Centre *See also: Health Centre;* 2885, 2892, 2899, 2901, 2935, 2941, 2942, 2943, 2947, 2952, 2957, 3112, 3129

Construction, Hospital *See also: Hospital;* 2818, 2885, 2892, 2901, 2924, 2935, 2943, 2944, 2947, 2964, 3112, 3433

Construction, House *See also: Housing;* 2805, 3055, 3191

Construction, Sanitary Facilities *See also: Sanitary Facilities;* 2885, 3031, 3054, 3055, 3191, 3327, 3363, 3366, 3378, 3426

Construction, Water Supply *See also: Water Supply;* 3031, 3054, 3055, 3098, 3191

Continuing Education *See also: Training;* 2827, 3192, 3231, 3261, 3267, 3439

Cost Measures *See also: Health Economics;* 2908, 2968, 2979, 2985, 3148

Cost-benefit Analysis *See also: Health Economics;* 2815, 2913, 2923, 2930, 2966, 2985, 3026, 3153, 3398, 3417, 3442, 3443, 3444, 3446

Costs and Cost Analysis *See also: Health Economics;* 2871, 2899, 2912, 2914, 2941, 2942, 2947, 2948, 2949, 2950, 2953, 2963, 2984, 2985, 3007, 3013, 3055, 3124, 3141, 3149, 3235, 3259, 3392, 3400, 3437, 3441, 3443, 3444, 3446, 3474, 3482

Cultural Aspect, 2825, 2842, 2895, 2900, 2906, 2909, 2912, 2914, 2915, 2926, 2956, 2990, 2991, 2994, 2995, 2996, 2997, 2999, 3001, 3003, 3004, 3005, 3008, 3017, 3043, 3053, 3076, 3081, 3116, 3118, 3122, 3124, 3128, 3134, 3141, 3149, 3150, 3163, 3167, 3182, 3196, 3232, 3236, 3248, 3249, 3254, 3256, 3257, 3261, 3269, 3277, 3370, 3371, 3386, 3387, 3418, 3419, 3431, 3447, 3448, 3450, 3451, 3453, 3455, 3468, 3473, 3485, 3492

Cultural Change *See also: Culture;* 2825, 2842, 2886, 2895, 2906, 2909, 2921, 2972, 2987, 2991, 2992, 2995, 2997, 2999, 3001, 3003, 3006, 3062, 3081, 3083, 3167, 3248, 3359, 3418, 3419, 3431, 3452, 3454

Culture *See also: Cultural Change; Ethics; Folklore; Social and Cultural Anthropology; Tradition; Traditional Medicine;* 2892, 2987, 2988, 2989, 2992, 2993, 2997, 2998, 3006, 3012, 3028, 3058, 3059, 3072, 3075, 3150, 3159, 3163, 3167, 3196, 3247, 3293, 3337, 3386, 3404, 3411, 3447, 3448, 3449, 3451, 3452, 3453, 3454, 3455, 3468, 3480, 3492

Curative Medicine, 2898, 2984, 3414, 3447, 3475

Curriculum *See: specific health worker. See also: Training Course;* 2816, 2822, 2823, 2830, 2832, 2834, 2835, 2862, 2876, 2970, 3167, 3190, 3195, 3197, 3199, 3201, 3210, 3211, 3215, 3219, 3221, 3225, 3230, 3241, 3242, 3246, 3249, 3250, 3251, 3252, 3254, 3270, 3275, 3277, 3278, 3279, 3288, 3303, 3303, 3304, 3308, 3309, 3392, 3492

Curriculum, Aid Post Orderly, 3246

Curriculum, Auxiliary, 2816, 2832, 2835, 2862, 3167, 3241, 3242, 3254, 3263

Curriculum, Behdar, 3251

Curriculum, Community Health Worker, 3221, 3249, 3250, 3252

Curriculum, Community Nurse, 3156, 3270

Curriculum, Dental Auxiliary, 2822, 3303

Curriculum, Health Education, 3278

Curriculum, Health Educator, 2830, 3190

Curriculum, Health Extension Officer, 3344

Curriculum, Health Manpower, 2834

Curriculum, Laboratory Auxiliary, 2823, 3304

Curriculum, Laboratory Technician, 2823, 3230

Curriculum, Laboratory Technologist, 3304

Curriculum, Medical Assistant, 3219

Curriculum, Medical Technologist, 2823

Curriculum, Midwife, 3288

Curriculum, Nurse, 3156, 3199, 3275, 3277, 3278, 3279

Curriculum, Nurse Auxiliary, 3279

Curriculum, Physician, 2876, 2970, 3195, 3197, 3199, 3201, 3203, 3210, 3211, 3215, 3308, 3492

Curriculum, Rural Health Promoter, 3225

Curriculum, Sanitary Engineer, 3309

D

Dai *See also: Traditional Birth Attendant;* 2839, 3027, 3265, 3292

Danfa Project, 3296

Data Collection *See also: Information System; Survey;* 2837, 2868, 2891, 2946, 2948, 2960, 3018, 3022, 3035, 3036, 3049, 3078, 3095, 3099, 3131, 3148, 3200, 3298, 3315, 3316, 3339, 3394, 3405, 3412, 3414, 3417, 3441

Deafness, 2969

Demography *See also: Birthrate; Life Expectancy; Migration; Mortality; Population; Population Increase; Statistical Data;* 2876, 2886, 2890, 2898, 2990, 3012, 3030, 3032, 3035, 3072, 3316, 3412, 3413, 3469, 3470

Dental Health, 2937, 3099, 3301, 3302, 3303, 3381, 3412, 3461, 3498

Dental Manpower *See also: Auxiliary, Dental; Dentist; Dentistry; Health Manpower;* 3300, 3301

Dental Services, 3099, 3300

Dentist *See also: Dental Manpower;* 3300, 3301
Dentistry *See also: Dental Manpower;* 3381
Dermatology, 3142
Developed Country, 2976, 2985, 3039, 3042, 3123
Developing Country, 2810, 2811, 2814, 2815, 2817, 2818, 2828, 2832, 2833, 2838, 2854, 2859, 2867, 2873, 2884, 2885, 2889, 2894, 2909, 2911, 2912, 2924, 2926, 2928, 2936, 2943, 2944, 2947, 2948, 2949, 2951, 2952, 2962, 2963, 2964, 2968, 2969, 2976, 2979, 2980, 2982, 2983, 2985, 3006, 3026, 3039, 3042, 3045, 3056, 3063, 3064, 3074, 3089, 3090, 3098, 3112, 3119, 3124, 3142, 3166, 3167, 3177, 3178, 3179, 3180, 3181, 3182, 3183, 3184, 3185, 3192, 3201, 3205, 3207, 3209, 3227, 3232, 3236, 3247, 3287, 3302, 3315, 3325, 3336, 3345, 3370, 3371, 3379, 3383, 3385, 3401, 3406, 3410, 3435, 3442
Diagnosis *See also: Screening;* 2922, 3036, 3060, 3267, 3310, 3322, 3332, 3339, 3343, 3347, 3385, 3475
Diarrhea *See also: Infectious Diseases;* 3025, 3050, 3077, 3078, 3096, 3118, 3121, 3196, 3384
Diet *See also: Food; Nutrition;* 2811, 2904, 3010, 3013, 3016, 3021, 3027, 3029, 3043, 3053, 3061, 3071, 3072, 3076, 3077, 3078, 3085, 3096, 3103, 3113, 3314, 3324, 3328, 3339, 3349, 3352, 3358, 3380, 3457, 3460, 3463, 3464, 3467, 3473, 3478, 3489, 3495, 3497
Directory, 2804, 2812, 2816, 2821, 2822
Directory, Auxiliary Training Centre, 2816, 2822, 2823
Directory, Nursing School, 2816
Directory, Public Health School, 2816
Disaster, 2927, 3007, 3074, 3091, 3092
Disease Control *See also: Epidemiology; Infectious Diseases; Immunization; Mass Campaign, Disease Control; Pest Control;* 2801, 2802, 2805, 2808, 2811, 2835, 2860, 2861, 2863, 2864, 2887, 2908, 2925, 2940, 2959, 2963, 2967, 2969, 3014, 3018, 3019, 3023, 3034, 3036, 3037, 3038, 3044, 3049, 3056, 3057, 3066, 3071, 3073, 3080, 3087, 3093, 3097, 3104, 3115, 3120, 3121, 3127, 3132, 3143, 3144, 3169, 3171, 3173, 3183, 3184, 3189, 3228, 3246, 3255, 3285, 3307, 3310, 3319, 3321, 3331, 3344, 3347, 3348, 3350, 3353, 3354, 3360, 3362, 3367, 3368, 3374, 3375, 3377, 3378, 3384, 3385, 3407, 3408, 3427, 3462, 3466, 3486, 3490, 3491, 3494, 3496, 3499, 3500
Dispensary *See also: Health Centre;* 2810, 2862, 2887, 2888, 2946, 2954, 3191, 3253, 3319, 3350, 3413
Dispensary Attendant *See also: Auxiliary Health Worker;* 2862, 3191, 3216, 3319
Distribution, 2834, 2851, 2854, 2858, 2875, 2876, 2877, 2878, 2882, 2887, 2888, 2910, 2956, 2967, 2970, 2972, 2973, 2974, 2975, 2983, 2998, 3012, 3121, 3124, 3146, 3158, 3226, 3242, 3262, 3268, 3271, 3272, 3437, 3438, 3439
Distribution, Health Centre, 3146
Distribution, Health Manpower, 2834, 2858, 2877, 2878, 2882, 2922, 2973, 3108, 3242, 3262, 3397, 3412
Distribution, Health Services, 2851, 2854, 2871, 2875, 2877, 2878, 2887, 2888, 2910, 2911, 2922, 2953, 2956, 2967, 2972, 2973, 3108, 3121, 3124, 3158, 3226, 3268, 3412, 3414, 3417, 3418, 3421, 3436, 3437
Distribution, Hospital, 2974, 3437

Distribution, Nurse, 3271, 3272
Distribution, Physician, 2876, 2970, 2975, 2998, 3012, 3421, 3425, 3438, 3439
Drugs *See also: Medicinal Plant; Pharmacy;* 2801, 2802, 2804, 2846, 2869, 2907, 2922, 2941, 2942, 2968, 2979, 2980, 2981, 2982, 2983, 2986, 3002, 3006, 3038, 3062, 3072, 3093, 3108, 3113, 3121, 3142, 3143, 3150, 3158, 3199, 3280, 3317, 3319, 3321, 3334, 3341, 3346, 3348, 3353, 3359, 3363, 3374, 3376, 3378, 3379, 3429, 3430, 3450, 3486, 3499
Dukun *See also: Traditional Birth Attendant;* 3293, 3295

E

Ecology, 2990
Economic Aspect, 2805, 2859, 2903, 2906, 2911, 2912, 2918, 2920, 2921, 2926, 2930, 2933, 2948, 2951, 2973, 2978, 2979, 2980, 2982, 2983, 3016, 3017, 3021, 3026, 3053, 3062, 3105, 3108, 3134, 3147, 3177, 3182, 3183, 3269, 3300, 3358, 3398, 3418, 3421, 3431, 3445
Economic Development *See also: Health Economics; Planning, Development; Socioeconomic Development;* 2815, 2921, 2985, 2998, 3021, 3026, 3063, 3064, 3177, 3191
Education *See also: Student; Teacher; Training Centre;* 2803, 2804, 2806, 2809, 2821, 2831, 2836, 2848, 2863, 2886, 2891, 2894, 2895, 2900, 2902, 2904, 2906, 2912, 2931, 2940, 2951, 2954, 2969, 2995, 3003, 3008, 3011, 3017, 3021, 3029, 3030, 3043, 3047, 3062, 3067, 3068, 3076, 3080, 3083, 3087, 3115, 3116, 3118, 3127, 3144, 3145, 3146, 3147, 3155, 3161, 3162, 3163, 3164, 3165, 3166, 3167, 3169, 3170, 3171, 3172, 3173, 3175, 3176, 3177, 3178, 3179, 3180, 3181, 3182, 3183, 3184, 3185, 3186, 3187, 3188, 3189, 3190, 3191, 3201, 3206, 3209, 3218, 3219, 3223, 3224, 3225, 3245, 3248, 3254, 3258, 3259, 3285, 3286, 3287, 3298, 3301, 3307, 3314, 3320, 3321, 3326, 3328, 3331, 3333, 3335, 3341, 3348, 3349, 3351, 3352, 3354, 3356, 3357, 3358, 3359, 3360, 3361, 3362, 3363, 3370, 3371, 3378, 3380, 3382, 3386, 3388, 3390, 3391, 3399, 3421, 3443, 3453, 3463, 3464, 3465, 3473, 3475, 3478, 3484, 3487, 3490, 3493, 3495, 3500
Education, Disease Control, 3494
Education, Environmental Health, 3011, 3176, 3184, 3191
Education, Family Planning, 3115, 3386, 3391
Education, Health, 2803, 2804, 2806, 2809, 2821, 2830, 2831, 2835, 2836, 2848, 2853, 2863, 2864, 2891, 2894, 2904, 2906, 2918, 2931, 2932, 2940, 2945, 2951, 2954, 3003, 3006, 3008, 3016, 3017, 3023, 3027, 3047, 3068, 3080, 3083, 3087, 3115, 3116, 3122, 3127, 3135, 3144, 3145, 3146, 3147, 3152, 3155, 3161, 3162, 3164, 3165, 3169, 3170, 3171, 3172, 3173, 3174, 3175, 3176, 3177, 3178, 3179, 3180, 3181, 3182, 3183, 3184, 3185, 3186, 3187, 3188, 3189, 3190, 3191, 3206, 3209, 3218, 3219, 3223, 3224, 3225, 3245, 3248, 3254, 3258, 3259, 3278, 3285, 3286, 3287, 3294, 3298, 3301, 3307, 3320, 3321, 3331, 3333, 3334, 3335, 3341, 3348, 3349, 3350, 3351, 3352, 3353, 3354, 3355, 3356, 3357, 3358, 3359, 3360, 3361, 3362, 3363, 3370, 3371, 3377, 3378, 3380, 3382, 3390, 3391,

Evaluation, Mass Campaign, 3018, 3104, 3132, 3148, 3173, 3220, 3408, 3462, 3486, 3491, 3494, 3496, 3500
Evaluation, Maternal Child Health, 3051, 3497
Evaluation, Maternal Child Health Services, 2872, 2913, 3413, 3458, 3469
Evaluation, Medical Assistant, 3114, 3233, 3261, 3430
Evaluation, Medical Records, 3154, 3428
Evaluation, Medical Technologist, 3305
Evaluation, Mental Health, 3060
Evaluation, Mental Health Services, 3081
Evaluation, Methodology, 3498
Evaluation, Midwife, 3288
Evaluation, Mobile Health Unit, 3446
Evaluation, Nurse, 3114, 3233, 3271, 3272, 3399
Evaluation, Nursing Services, 3274, 3402
Evaluation, Nutrition *See also: Anthropometric Measurement;* 2891, 2904, 2934, 2962, 3010, 3015, 3024, 3025, 3026, 3027, 3040, 3051, 3062, 3071, 3074, 3078, 3079, 3083, 3091, 3092, 3136, 3137, 3220, 3224, 3314, 3315, 3328, 3349, 3457, 3460, 3463, 3464, 3465, 3467, 3474, 3475, 3478, 3485, 3489, 3493, 3495, 3497
Evaluation, Nutrition Education, 3245, 3465, 3473
Evaluation, Nutrition Programme, 2934, 3465, 3473, 3474, 3478, 3482, 3483, 3489, 3493
Evaluation, Outpatient Care, 3186
Evaluation, Outpatient Clinic, 2881, 3429, 3430
Evaluation, Physician, 3194, 3450
Evaluation, Planning, 2929, 2932, 3392, 3425, 3425, 3432, 3433, 3435, 3472
Evaluation, Project, 2839, 2988, 3017, 3040, 3084, 3145, 3176, 3187, 3269, 3392, 3395, 3400, 3403, 3404, 3406, 3416, 3422, 3425, 3459, 3471, 3472, 3481, 3487, 3494
Evaluation, Rural Health Promoter, 3095, 3218, 3229
Evaluation, Sanitation, 3023
Evaluation, Screening, 3018, 3060
Evaluation, Student, 3213
Evaluation, Survey, 3316, 3417
Evaluation, Teaching Aid, 3273, 3382
Evaluation, Teaching Method, 3187
Evaluation, Traditional Birth Attendant, 3290, 3293
Evaluation, Traditional Medicine, 2996, 3002, 3450, 3468
Evaluation, Traditional Practitioner, 3449, 3468
Evaluation, Training, 3212, 3215, 3236, 3273, 3279, 3295, 3305, 3383, 3392, 3394, 3400, 3472
Evaluation, Vaccination Programme, 3093, 3132, 3499
Evaluation, Waste Disposal, 3069, 3082
Evaluation, Water Supply, 2925, 3097, 3488, 3495
Eye Diseases *See also: Blindness; Cataracts; Conjunctivitis; Infectious Diseases; Trachoma;* 2969, 3071, 3103, 3143, 3151, 3152, 3155, 3158, 3207, 3287, 3467, 3486

F

Family Health *See also: Maternal Child Health;* 2824, 2850, 2853, 2890, 2891, 2918, 2937, 2965, 3008, 3122, 3178, 3188, 3221, 3225, 3256, 3268, 3274, 3393, 3471
Family Nurse Practitioner *See also: Auxiliary Health Worker;* 2899, 3263, 3284
Family Planning *See also: Birth Control; Clinic, Family Planning; Family Planning Manpower; Family Plan-*
ning Programme; Mass Campaign, Family Planning; 2815, 2821, 2835, 2857, 2890, 2891, 2907, 2916, 2951, 2978, 3012, 3017, 3022, 3040, 3041, 3048, 3072, 3085, 3088, 3115, 3128, 3135, 3145, 3163, 3217, 3249, 3255, 3258, 3260, 3262, 3268, 3274, 3280, 3289, 3290, 3292, 3293, 3294, 3298, 3336, 3352, 3361, 3386, 3387, 3388, 3389, 3391, 3393, 3397, 3401, 3403, 3404, 3406, 3420, 3469, 3471, 3477
Family Planning Manpower *See also: Auxiliary, Family Planning; Family Planning; Health Manpower;* 3048, 3200, 3292, 3393, 3401
Family Planning Programme *See also: Family Planning;* 3048, 3145, 3163, 3386, 3387
Federation of Cuban Women, 3189
Feldsher *See also: Auxiliary Health Worker;* 2861
Filariasis *See also: Parasitic Diseases;* 3056, 3080
Film *See also: Audiovisual Aid;* 2803, 2821, 3087, 3109, 3171, 3336
Financial Aspect *See also: Health Economics;* 2805, 2832, 2859, 2866, 2870, 2871, 2878, 2885, 2899, 2909, 2914, 2916, 2920, 2923, 2924, 2939, 2941, 2942, 2944, 2945, 2947, 2948, 2949, 2950, 2953, 2955, 2957, 2968, 2969, 2976, 2977, 2978, 2979, 2980, 2981, 2983, 2984, 3006, 3007, 3011, 3013, 3017, 3026, 3033, 3043, 3055, 3062, 3066, 3073, 3088, 3091, 3098, 3107, 3108, 3109, 3122, 3124, 3128, 3139, 3141, 3148, 3149, 3151, 3153, 3158, 3182, 3183, 3188, 3197, 3227, 3228, 3229, 3232, 3235, 3243, 3259, 3262, 3264, 3268, 3271, 3336, 3340, 3353, 3371, 3398, 3406, 3411, 3413, 3437, 3438, 3440, 3441, 3442, 3443, 3444, 3446, 3450, 3459, 3477, 3479, 3482, 3491, 3494, 3495
First Aid *See also: Emergency Medical Care;* 3313, 3341, 3364, 3471
Flying Doctor Service *See also: Mobile Health Unit;* 2899, 3028, 3261, 3442, 3446
Folklore *See also: Culture;* 3004, 3118, 3196, 3386, 3447, 3449, 3450, 3452
Food *See also: Diet; Hygiene; Nutrition;* 2805, 2900, 2904, 2918, 2927, 2934, 2937, 2940, 3010, 3013, 3015, 3016, 3017, 3020, 3021, 3024, 3029, 3040, 3043, 3052, 3053, 3054, 3063, 3064, 3071, 3076, 3077, 3314, 3324, 3328, 3339, 3349, 3351, 3352, 3358, 3367, 3380, 3445, 3457, 3460, 3463, 3464, 3465, 3467, 3473, 3478, 3485, 3489, 3497
Food Inspector, 3306
Food Production *See also: Agricultural Sector;* 2805, 2889, 2899, 2900, 2904, 3010, 3015, 3016, 3017, 3020, 3021, 3052, 3054, 3055, 3063, 3064, 3065, 3089, 3090, 3139, 3169, 3177, 3183, 3191, 3339, 3445

G

Gastroenteritis *See also: Infectious Diseases;* 3055, 3078, 3096, 3117, 3121, 3495
Geriatrics, 3102
Government, 2877, 2955, 3118, 3174
Government Policy *See also: Planning, Development;* 2849, 2852, 2855, 2856, 2865, 2868, 2870, 2871, 2886, 2888, 2897, 2898, 2900, 2903, 2904, 2911, 2914, 2916, 2921, 2930, 2934, 2939, 2945, 2951, 2953, 2954, 2955, 2978, 2979, 2980, 2983, 2991, 2994, 3002, 3006, 3011, 3047, 3048, 3081, 3108, 3116, 3197, 3230, 3235, 3244, 3245, 3299, 3303, 3414, 3415, 3417, 3418, 3421, 3424, 3431

Government Project *See also: Pilot Project;* 2813, 2843, 2844, 2845, 2867, 2934, 2957, 2958, 3024, 3057, 3084, 3143, 3259, 3262, 3268, 3290, 3392, 3403, 3406, 3416, 3422, 3425, 3466, 3469, 3471, 3494

Guinea Worm *See also: Parasitic Diseases;* 3434

Gynaecology *See also: Maternal Child Health; Obstetrics;* 2801, 2802, 2857, 3030, 3342, 3373

H

Handbook *See also: Teaching Aid;* 2804, 2805, 2812, 3095, 3144, 3172, 3310, 3311, 3312, 3315, 3317, 3318, 3319, 3321, 3323, 3325, 3326, 3327, 3332, 3333, 3334, 3335, 3338, 3340, 3341, 3342, 3343, 3345, 3346, 3347, 3348, 3349, 3350, 3352, 3353, 3354, 3356, 3357, 3358, 3359, 3360, 3361, 3362, 3370, 3372, 3374, 3375, 3376, 3377, 3378, 3379, 3380, 3384, 3387, 3388, 3390, 3391

Handbook, Auxiliary, 3325, 3332, 3374, 3379

Handbook, Child Health, 3312, 3317, 3318, 3333, 3341, 3374

Handbook, Dental Health, 3381

Handbook, Dispensary Attendant, 3319

Handbook, Environmental Health, 3375

Handbook, Family Planning, 3387, 3388

Handbook, Health Education, 3144, 3172, 3321, 3326, 3334, 3341, 3348, 3350, 3352, 3353, 3354, 3356, 3357, 3359, 3360, 3361, 3362, 3370, 3377, 3378, 3380, 3388, 3391

Handbook, Health Extension Officer, 3342

Handbook, Hygiene, 3311

Handbook, Laboratory, 3338

Handbook, Laboratory Technician, 3345, 3347

Handbook, Leprosy, 3310, 3346

Handbook, Maternal Child Health, 3390

Handbook, Medical Assistant, 3372

Handbook, Mental Health, 3335, 3372

Handbook, Midwife, 3387

Handbook, Nurse, 3172, 3323, 3342, 3376

Handbook, Nutrition, 3324, 3339, 3349, 3352, 3358, 3380

Handbook, Paramedic, 3343

Handbook, Physician, 3342

Handbook, Physiology, 3343

Handbook, Sanitation, 3327

Health Centre *See also: Clinic; Construction, Health Centre;Dispensary; Hospital; Mobile Health Unit; Rural Health Post; X-ray Unit;* 2828, 2848, 2850, 2853, 2855, 2869, 2870, 2872, 2881, 2885, 2887, 2888, 2890, 2892, 2899, 2901, 2925, 2935, 2941, 2942, 2943, 2944, 2947, 2950, 2952, 2954, 2971, 3029, 3031, 3107, 3112, 3114, 3116, 3121, 3123, 3128, 3129, 3133, 3135, 3146, 3147, 3162, 3186, 3191, 3217, 3222, 3253, 3258, 3261, 3265, 3269, 3282, 3283, 3289, 3308, 3344, 3379, 3420, 3425, 3428, 3435, 3446, 3475, 3478

Health Economics *See also: Cost Measures; Cost-benefit Analysis; Costs and Cost Analysis; Economic Development;* 2813, 2815, 2832, 2839, 2845, 2849, 2859, 2862, 2871, 2875, 2878, 2882, 2885, 2887, 2889, 2892, 2898, 2900, 2903, 2908, 2910, 2914, 2916, 2923, 2924, 2928, 2929, 2930, 2937, 2938, 2939, 2941, 2943, 2944, 2945, 2947, 2948, 2950, 2951, 2952, 2953, 2957, 2976, 2977, 2979, 2980, 2981, 2982, 2983, 2984, 2985, 3011, 3024, 3026, 3032,

3042, 3043, 3073, 3085, 3112, 3113, 3123, 3134, 3135, 3142, 3153, 3164, 3229, 3232, 3235, 3260, 3268, 3329, 3336, 3353, 3398, 3409, 3411, 3413, 3415, 3418, 3419, 3424, 3425, 3433, 3434, 3440, 3442, 3444, 3446, 3456, 3495

Health Educator *See also: Auxiliary, Health Educator; Health Manpower;* 2830, 3003, 3144, 3175, 3179, 3181, 3182, 3183, 3184, 3185, 3190, 3209, 3245, 3286, 3286, 3334, 3371

Health Extension Officer *See also: Auxiliary Health Worker;* 3116, 3240, 3342, 3344, 3440

Health Indicators *See also: Epidemiology; Evaluation, Health; Health Status;* 2898, 2903, 2922, 2933, 2965, 3086, 3136, 3137, 3324, 3414, 3415, 3458

Health Inspector *See also: Sanitation Manpower;* 2816, 3306, 3307, 3488

Health Insurance *See also: Social Security;* 2866, 2914, 2917, 2923, 2976, 2984, 2985, 2986, 3123, 3128, 3139, 3147, 3260

Health Manpower *See also: Administrator; Auxiliary Health Worker; Dental Manpower; Family Planning Manpower; Health Educator; Health Team; Medical Technologist; Midwife; Nurse; Nurse-midwife; Pharmacist; Physician; Physiotherapist; Psychologist; Sanitation Manpower; Social Worker; X-ray Technician;* 2803, 2805, 2809, 2819, 2820, 2828, 2830, 2833, 2834, 2836, 2837, 2838, 2839, 2840, 2841, 2842, 2843, 2844, 2845, 2846, 2847, 2851, 2854, 2855, 2858, 2859, 2860, 2863, 2866, 2868, 2869, 2872, 2873, 2875, 2877, 2878, 2882, 2883, 2887, 2888, 2889, 2890, 2894, 2896, 2897, 2898, 2902, 2903, 2905, 2909, 2910, 2911, 2916, 2929, 2931, 2932, 2937, 2939, 2941, 2942, 2946, 2954, 2955, 2956, 2959, 2973, 2974, 2978, 2985, 2999, 3002, 3010, 3012, 3029, 3034, 3036, 3040, 3048, 3008, 3093, 3102, 3108, 3114, 3116, 3124, 3152, 3160, 3165, 3180, 3185, 3193, 3197, 3202, 3202, 3204, 3205, 3210, 3214, 3228, 3230, 3231, 3237, 3239, 3241, 3242, 3244, 3245, 3264, 3272, 3276, 3304, 3308, 3309, 3320, 3329, 3365, 3371, 3392, 3396, 3397, 3412, 3413, 3414, 3417, 3418, 3419, 3422, 3424, 3426, 3448, 3454, 3459

Health Services *See also: Administration, Health Services; Dental Services; Distribution, Health Services; Emergency Health Services; Evaluation , Health Services; Maternal Child Health Services; Nursing Services; Organization, Health Services; Planning, Health Services;* 2805, 2809, 2811, 2812, 2813, 2815, 2818, 2824, 2826, 2828, 2833, 2849, 2850, 2851, 2852, 2853, 2854, 2855, 2856, 2858, 2859, 2860, 2861, 2863, 2864, 2866, 2867, 2869, 2870, 2871, 2873, 2874, 2875, 2876, 2877, 2878, 2880, 2882, 2883, 2887, 2888, 2889, 2890, 2892, 2893, 2894, 2897, 2898, 2901, 2903, 2905, 2908, 2909, 2910, 2911, 2914, 2915, 2922, 2923, 2924, 2926, 2926, 2928, 2929, 2930, 2931, 2932, 2935, 2936, 2938, 2939, 2941, 2942, 2945, 2946, 2948, 2949, 2950, 2951, 2953, 2954, 2955, 2956, 2957, 2958, 2959, 2960, 2962, 2964, 2965, 2966, 2967, 2970, 2971, 2972, 2973, 2974, 2976, 2977, 2983, 2985, 2989, 2994, 2996, 2997, 2998, 3000, 3001, 3002, 3005, 3012, 3035, 3039, 3044, 3049, 3057, 3059, 3061, 3068, 3086, 3088, 3100, 3107, 3108, 3116, 3120,

3121, 3123, 3124, 3125, 3126, 3128, 3129, 3131, 3131, 3138, 3139, 3145, 3154, 3155, 3158, 3175, 3180, 3193, 3214, 3218, 3223, 3226, 3227, 3227, 3231, 3232, 3237, 3240, 3241, 3247, 3248, 3249, 3253, 3256, 3257, 3258, 3260, 3263, 3268, 3289, 3299, 3316, 3329, 3331, 3392, 3394, 3395, 3397, 3398, 3406, 3407, 3409, 3410, 3411, 3412, 3413, 3414, 3415, 3416, 3419, 3421, 3422, 3423, 3424, 3425, 3429, 3431, 3432, 3433, 3434, 3436, 3437, 3441, 3444, 3449, 3453, 3456, 3459, 3466, 3470, 3477, 3479, 3480, 3486, 3499

Health Status *See also: Health Indicators;* 2914, 2922, 2965, 3026, 3027, 3078, 3086, 3096, 3136, 3137, 3473, 3482

Health Team *See also: Health Manpower;* 2819, 2820, 2824, 2825, 2828, 2829, 2834, 2845, 2850, 2853, 2951, 3084, 3115, 3122, 3128, 3133, 3151, 3155, 3180, 3186, 3193, 3194, 3205, 3209, 3214, 3220, 3231, 3234, 3247, 3257, 3258, 3271, 3275, 3281, 3365, 3423

Health Visitor *See also: Auxiliary Health Worker; Home Visiting;* 3131

History of Health Services *See also: Traditional Medicine;* 2855, 2856, 2865, 2869, 2870, 2874, 2875, 2880, 2898, 2972, 2976, 3002, 3014, 3037, 3058, 3073, 3170, 3242, 3408, 3417, 3466

Home Visiting *See also: Health Visitor;* 2826, 2870, 3043, 3131, 3179, 3186, 3231, 3255, 3256, 3258, 3289, 3299, 3331, 3393, 3482, 3493

Hospital *See also: Construction, Hospital; Health Centre;* 2810, 2817, 2818, 2849, 2850, 2851, 2857, 2860, 2862, 2869, 2870, 2873, 2885, 2887, 2888, 2892, 2897, 2899, 2901, 2924, 2935, 2943, 2944, 2947, 2964, 2974, 2976, 2977, 2985, 2994, 3009, 3031, 3033, 3105, 3106, 3107, 3108, 3110, 3111, 3112, 3115, 3117, 3121, 3123, 3134, 3140, 3150, 3156, 3179, 3202, 3282, 3317, 3328, 3344, 3345, 3350, 3413, 3423, 3433, 3435, 3437, 3443, 3458, 3462, 3475, 3476

Hospital, Missionary, 2817, 2849, 2897, 2977, 3156

Hospital, Rural, 3009, 3156, 3218, 3345, 3462, 3475

Housing *See also: Construction, House; Living Conditions;* 2805, 2810, 2861, 2886, 3054, 3055, 3363

Hygiene *See also: Food; Living Conditions; Sanitation;* 2801, 2802, 2869, 2944, 3004, 3047, 3050, 3054, 3055, 3076, 3077, 3118, 3144, 3181, 3183, 3295, 3307, 3311, 3332, 3341, 3350, 3363, 3366, 3367, 3378, 3390, 3464, 3473

I

Immunization *See also: BCG Vaccination; Disease Control; Vaccination Programme;* 2808, 2891, 2908, 2927, 2962, 3037, 3044, 3067, 3068, 3073, 3093, 3094, 3104, 3132, 3159, 3169, 3220, 3311, 3324, 3331, 3341, 3353, 3362, 3374, 3406, 3462, 3477, 3491, 3499

Infant *See also: Child; Infant Feeding;* 2946, 2997, 3027, 3029, 3030, 3032, 3049, 3051, 3077, 3079, 3094, 3105, 3113, 3136, 3137, 3312, 3317, 3318, 3328, 3341, 3349, 3351, 3389, 3391, 3457, 3458, 3460, 3462, 3465, 3476, 3491, 3493, 3497

Infant Feeding *See also: Breast-feeding; Child Health; Infant;* 2900, 3004, 3027, 3029, 3042, 3043, 3050, 3053, 3062, 3076, 3077, 3083, 3118, 3317, 3318,

3324, 3328, 3341, 3349, 3352, 3380, 3391, 3457, 3460, 3463, 3465, 3473, 3476, 3493

Infectious Diseases *See also: Cholera; Diarrhea; Disease Control; Epidemiology; Eye Diseases; Gastroenteritis; Leprosy; Malaria; Parasitic Diseases; Rabies; Smallpox; Tetanus; Tuberculosis; Typhoid Fever; Venereal Diseases; Yellow Fever;* 2801, 2802, 2804, 2808, 2811, 2860, 2886, 2927, 2937, 2945, 2946, 2959, 2990, 3018, 3019, 3023, 3036, 3050, 3051, 3057, 3059, 3074, 3077, 3078, 3087, 3096, 3104, 3117, 3151, 3196, 3199, 3285, 3311, 3312, 3324, 3338, 3343, 3350, 3351, 3375, 3412, 3434, 3457, 3462, 3463, 3475, 3491, 3496, 3500

Information Service *See also: Information System;* 2803, 2813, 2818, 2868, 2884, 2955, 2962, 2980, 3009, 3095, 3170, 3174, 3470

Information System *See also: Data Collection; Information Service;* 2803, 2818, 2845, 2868, 2906, 2940, 2941, 2942, 2955, 2968, 3188, 3415, 3428

Inpatient Care *See also: Health Centre;* 2885, 2892, 2922, 2924, 2944, 3102, 3105, 3106, 3107, 3110, 3113, 3121, 3164, 3317, 3328, 3342, 3376, 3402, 3435

International Aid *See also: International Cooperation;* 2850, 2867, 2893, 2894, 2906, 2916, 2918, 2921, 2925, 2927, 2942, 2948, 2957, 2958, 2978, 3006, 3011, 3016, 3017, 3040, 3074, 3091, 3092, 3108, 3176, 3228, 3336, 3405, 3441, 3488, 3494

International Cooperation *See also: ALERT; International Aid; IPPF; League of Red Cross Societies; SIDA; UN; UNICEF; voluntary organization; WHO;* 2818, 2829, 2838, 2849, 2881, 2884, 2889, 2920, 2938, 2948, 2962, 2963, 2967, 2978, 2980, 2982, 2983, 3012, 3036, 3084, 3091, 3101, 3228, 3422, 3483

Intrauterine Device *See also: Birth Control;* 3048, 3388, 3391, 3401

IPPF, 3393, 3471

J

Job Description *See: specific health worker;* 2822, 2825, 2826, 2828, 2835, 2847, 2883, 2890, 2936, 2958, 2998, 3003, 3127, 3169, 3175, 3177, 3178, 3181, 3182, 3183, 3184, 3186, 3190, 3193, 3196, 3203, 3209, 3212, 3213, 3214, 3221, 3222, 3223, 3224, 3225, 3226, 3227, 3231, 3232, 3233, 3234, 3236, 3237, 3239, 3241, 3242, 3243, 3244, 3247, 3249, 3250, 3251, 3252, 3253, 3254, 3255, 3256, 3257, 3258, 3259, 3260, 3261, 3262, 3263, 3265, 3266, 3269, 3271, 3275, 3276, 3281, 3284, 3285, 3286, 3288, 3289, 3293, 3294, 3297, 3298, 3299, 3301, 3302, 3303, 3304, 3307, 3314, 3332, 3345, 3371, 3393, 3396, 3399, 3452, 3471, 3474, 3490

Job Description, Aid Post Orderly, 3226, 3253

Job Description, Anaesthetist Auxiliary, 3379

Job Description, Auxiliary, 2832, 2835, 2845, 2862, 2936, 3213, 3231, 3241, 3242, 3254, 3263, 3396, 3459

Job Description, Auxiliary Nurse-midwife, 2826

Job Description, Barefoot Doctor, 3332

Job Description, Basic Health Worker, 3490

Job Description, Behdar, 3251

Job Description, Community Health Aide, 2839, 2936, 3223, 3224, 3243, 3259, 3298, 3464

Job Description, Community Health Worker, 2936, 2958, 3089, 3122, 3169, 3203, 3217, 3221, 3227, 3232, 3234, 3236, 3237, 3239, 3244, 3247, 3249,

Low-Cost Rural Health Care and Health Manpower Training

3250, 3252, 3254, 3256, 3257, 3258, 3260, 3262, 3265, 3266, 3269, 3294, 3299, 3314, 3471
Job Description, Community Nurse, 3271
Job Description, Dental Auxiliary, 2822, 3302, 3303
Job Description, Dentist, 3301
Job Description, Health Educator, 3003, 3175, 3181, 3182, 3183, 3184, 3190, 3254, 3371
Job Description, Health Educator Auxiliary, 3177
Job Description, Health Extension Officer, 3344
Job Description, Health Inspector, 3307
Job Description, Health Manpower, 2828, 2853, 2883, 2890, 2941, 2942, 2953, 2954, 3415
Job Description, Laboratory Auxiliary, 2823, 3304
Job Description, Laboratory Technician, 2823, 3304, 3345
Job Description, Maternal Child Health Auxiliary, 3393
Job Description, Medical Assistant, 3222, 3233, 3261
Job Description, Medical Technologist, 2823
Job Description, Mental Health Auxiliary, 2847
Job Description, Mental Health Nurse, 2825, 2847
Job Description, Midwife, 3288, 3289, 3469
Job Description, Multipurpose Auxiliary, 3255
Job Description, Nurse, 2936, 2998, 3186, 3212, 3233, 3275, 3276, 3280, 3281, 3284, 3285, 3286, 3399, 3469
Job Description, Nurse Auxiliary, 3469, 3474
Job Description, Physician, 2936, 3186, 3193, 3196, 3209, 3214, 3281
Job Description, Rural Health Promoter, 3127, 3218, 3225, 3229
Job Description, Social Worker, 3178
Job Description, Teacher, 3181
Job Description, Traditional Birth Attendant, 3293, 3297
Job Description, Traditional Practitioner, 3452

K

Korea, 3310, 3483
Kwashiorkor *See also: Nutrition;* 3067, 3096, 3103, 3324, 3328, 3339, 3351, 3460, 3475, 3482, 3491

L

Laboratory *See also: Research Centre;* 2922, 3019, 3034, 3036, 3049, 3104, 3104, 3157, 3199, 3230, 3243, 3304, 3328, 3338, 3345, 3347, 3348, 3355, 3373, 3412, 3416
Laboratory Technician *See also: Auxiliary, Laboratory; Health Manpower; Medical Technologist;* 2823, 3019, 3230, 3304, 3305, 3345, 3347
Language, 2812, 2997, 3325
League of Red Cross Societies *See also: International Cooperation;* 2927, 3007, 3074, 3092, 3280
Legal Aspect, 2877, 2906, 2914, 2945, 2964, 2980, 2982, 2983, 3006, 3233, 3271, 3272, 3276, 3372
Legislation *See also: Legislation, Health;* 2871, 2874, 2900, 2904, 2906, 2907, 2964, 2973, 2980, 2983, 3006, 3044, 3062, 3097, 3233, 3307
Legislation, Health *See also: Legislation;* 2871, 2874, 2877, 2973, 3044, 3097
Leprosy *See also: Infectious Diseases;* 2869, 3018, 3044, 3087, 3119, 3124, 3132, 3310, 3346, 3360, 3496
Life Expectancy *See also: Demography; Mortality;* 2933
Living Conditions *See also: Environmental Health; Housing; Hygiene; Slums;* 2931, 3012, 3028, 3032,

3047, 3054, 3055, 3068, 3363, 3375, 3500
Local Level, 2883, 2897, 2909, 2926, 2962, 2963, 3008, 3030, 3045, 3054, 3090, 3118, 3119, 3141, 3174, 3184, 3185, 3223, 3227, 3235, 3237, 3254, 3266, 3370, 3482

M

Malaria *See also: Infectious Diseases;* 2864, 2869, 2937, 2990, 3038, 3044, 3057, 3066, 3078, 3087, 3104, 3127, 3132, 3144, 3255, 3377, 3407, 3414, 3416, 3434, 3466, 3490, 3496
Marasmus *See also: Nutrition;* 3096, 3324, 3328, 3339, 3351, 3460, 3475, 3482
Mass Campaign *See also: Disease Control; Family Planning;* 3018, 3080, 3087, 3104, 3120, 3127, 3148, 3173, 3185, 3189, 3310, 3334, 3353, 3408, 3441, 3462, 3486, 3491, 3494, 3496, 3500
Mass Campaign, Disease Control, 2869, 3018, 3080, 3087, 3104, 3120, 3127, 3132, 3173, 3220, 3310, 3334, 3353, 3408, 3462, 3486, 3491, 3494, 3496, 3500
Mass Media *See also: Abstracting Journal; Communications; Periodical; Radio Communications;* 2803, 2804, 2940, 3006, 3080, 3083, 3087, 3170, 3174, 3176, 3184, 3185, 3307, 3421
Maternal Child Health *See also: Antenatal Care; Child Health; Clinic, Maternal Child Health; Family Health; Gynaecology; Infant; Maternal Child Health Services; Obstetrics; Postpartum Care;* 2804, 2811, 2815, 2821, 2826, 2835, 2838, 2863, 2864, 2882, 2896, 2904, 2911, 2916, 2936, 2937, 2945, 2951, 2961, 2967, 2969, 2986, 2998, 3004, 3008, 3016, 3017, 3029, 3030, 3032, 3040, 3041, 3051, 3070, 3072, 3088, 3089, 3107, 3118, 3126, 3130, 3146, 3156, 3169, 3176, 3189, 3196, 3217, 3220, 3241, 3268, 3274, 3283, 3289, 3291, 3293, 3294, 3295, 3324, 3331, 3389, 3390, 3391, 3406, 3407, 3412, 3420, 3426, 3455, 3458, 3463, 3469, 3471, 3475, 3476, 3477, 3497
Maternal Child Health Services *See also: Health Services; Maternal Child Health;* 2857, 2872, 2911, 2913, 2916, 2918, 2961, 3008, 3030, 3032, 3040, 3041, 3130, 3223, 3282, 3405, 3413, 3458, 3469, 3489
Medex *See also: Auxiliary Health Worker;* 2832, 3396
Medical Assistant *See also: Auxiliary Health Worker;* 2842, 2870, 2978, 3114, 3150, 3219, 3222, 3228, 3233, 3235, 3239, 3240, 3261, 3272, 3322, 3331, 3372, 3373, 3379, 3396, 3416, 3430, 3486
Medical Records *See also: Epidemiology; Medical Records Maintenance;* 2853, 2891, 2942, 2955, 3126, 3130, 3136, 3137, 3152, 3154, 3213, 3342, 3428, 3430
Medical Records Maintenance *See also: Medical Records;* 2942, 2953, 2955, 3044, 3126, 3152, 3428
Medical Technologist *See also: Auxiliary, Laboratory; Health Manpower; Laboratory Technician;* 2823, 3305, 3345
Medical Technology, 2823, 2978, 2979, 2982, 2983, 3148, 3447
Medicinal Plant *See also: Drugs;* 2846, 2991, 2991, 3002, 3004, 3038, 3150, 3332, 3447, 3451, 3486
Mental Health *See also: Psychiatry;* 2811, 2825, 2847, 2864, 2895, 2920, 2937, 3000, 3001, 3030, 3060, 3072, 3081, 3150, 3160, 3178, 3297, 3335, 3337, 3343, 3359, 3361, 3372, 3414, 3419, 3451, 3468
Mental Health Services, 2825, 2895, 3160

Mental Retardation, 2969, 3026, 3045, 3474, 3485
Methodology, 2896, 2906, 2909, 2928, 2932, 2936, 2948, 2949, 2956, 2959, 2960, 2965, 2966, 3008, 3013, 3019, 3022, 3026, 3035, 3070, 3083, 3086, 3095, 3099, 3131, 3137, 3174, 3188, 3203, 3248, 3314, 3315, 3316, 3322, 3340, 3382, 3394, 3398, 3403, 3422, 3430, 3432, 3444, 3458, 3470, 3484, 3498
Methodology, Evaluation, 2834, 2845, 2922, 2928, 2948, 3022, 3026, 3035, 3040, 3086, 3095, 3137, 3174, 3203, 3314, 3382, 3392, 3394, 3398, 3403, 3422, 3430, 3432, 3458, 3464
Methodology, Mass Campaign, 3013
Methodology, Planning, 2849, 2891, 2896, 2932, 2936, 2949, 2959, 2960, 2966, 3008, 3422
Methodology, Research, 3070, 3316, 3422
Methodology, Survey, 2956, 2960, 3026, 3083, 3092, 3095, 3099, 3131, 3248, 3315, 3316, 3417, 3420, 3470, 3484, 3498
Midwife *See also: Auxiliary, Midwife; Family Planning Manpower; Health Manpower; Traditional Birth Attendant;* 2836, 2841, 2850, 2857, 3126, 3200, 3274, 3282, 3288, 3289, 3387, 3401, 3440, 3469
Migration *See also: Brain Drain; Demography; Urbanization;* 2877, 2973, 2997, 3047, 3059, 3177
Military, 3375, 3376
Minority Group *See also: Aborigine; Eskimo; Nomads; Tribes;* 2863, 2871, 2987, 2994, 2997, 3117, 3122, 3178, 3266, 3417, 3418, 3419, 3431, 3438
Missionary, 2817, 2849, 2854, 2897, 2977, 3011, 3146, 3156, 3159, 3447
Mobile Eye Unit, 3151, 3152, 3155, 3158, 3486
Mobile Health Unit *See also: Flying Doctor Service; Health Centre;* 2916, 3028, 3031, 3115, 3129, 3135, 3148, 3150, 3152, 3154, 3156, 3158, 3159, 3446, 3474, 3477
Mobile Vaccination Unit, 3132
Morbidity *See also: Evaluation, Health; Statistical Data;* 2826, 2839, 2874, 2876, 2900, 2914, 2922, 2933, 2997, 3015, 3025, 3029, 3032, 3044, 3049, 3086, 3088, 3096, 3316, 3324, 3413, 3417, 3436, 3458, 3469, 3473, 3476, 3491, 3497
Mortality *See also: Demography; Life Expectancy; Statistical Data;* 2808, 2815, 2826, 2839, 2874, 2876, 2922, 2933, 2946, 3022, 3026, 3029, 3030, 3032, 3044, 3049, 3051, 3086, 3088, 3094, 3113, 3316, 3351, 3403, 3412, 3413, 3414, 3417, 3458, 3463, 3469, 3491, 3497
Mortality, Child, 3012, 3032, 3051, 3351, 3463, 3497
Mortality, Infant, 2826, 2946, 2997, 3012, 3030, 3032, 3049, 3051, 3094, 3217, 3288, 3324, 3351, 3436, 3458, 3462, 3473, 3491, 3497
Mortality, Maternal, 3030, 3458

N

National Health Plan *See also: Planning, Health Services; Planning, National;* 2833, 2852, 2855, 2856, 2861, 2865, 2867, 2877, 2878, 2882, 2883, 2888, 2890, 2900, 2903, 2904, 2908, 2909, 2911, 2915, 2928, 2930, 2939, 2940, 2941, 2942, 2945, 2948, 2951, 2953, 2954, 2963, 3239, 3240, 3262, 3265, 3299, 3397, 3412, 3414, 3415, 3416, 3424, 3432, 3447, 3471, 3499
National Plan *See also: Planning, National;* 2840, 2844, 2857, 2871, 2880, 2887, 2929, 2931, 2960, 2983,

3182, 3238, 3245, 3466, 3486
Nomads, 2941, 3028, 3047, 3151, 3159, 3167
Nurse *See also: Auxiliary, Nurse; Community Nurse; Health Manpower;* 2816, 2825, 2836, 2838, 2841, 2842, 2850, 2870, 2893, 2936, 2994, 2998, 3034, 3062, 3107, 3126, 3133, 3144, 3146, 3150, 3151, 3156, 3162, 3168, 3172, 3176, 3186, 3199, 3205, 3208, 3212, 3233, 3264, 3267, 3270, 3271, 3272, 3273, 3274, 3275, 3276, 3277, 3277, 3278, 3279, 3280, 3281, 3283, 3284, 3285, 3286, 3287, 3308, 3312, 3317, 3318, 3323, 3337, 3342, 3376, 3380, 3381, 3399, 3400, 3402, 3426, 3440, 3469, 3486, 3493
Nurse Educator, 3286
Nurse, Mental Health, 2825, 2847, 3150, 3337
Nurse-midwife *See also: Auxiliary, Nurse-midwife; Health Manpower;* 3016, 3258, 3389, 3391
Nursing Services *See also: Health Services;* 2903, 3011, 3272, 3274, 3280, 3344, 3373, 3376, 3402, 3418
Nutrition *See also: Anaemia; Anthropometric Measurement; Diet; Food; Infant Feeding; Kwashiorkor; Marasmus; Nutrition Programme; Vitamin D eficiency;* 2801, 2802, 2804, 2805, 2811, 2821, 2826, 2863, 2864, 2879, 2886, 2889, 2900, 2902, 2904, 2918, 2927, 2931, 2934, 2937, 2940, 2967, 2988, 2995, 3003, 3007, 3010, 3013, 3015, 3016, 3017, 3020, 3021, 3024, 3025, 3026, 3027, 3028, 3029, 3033, 3041, 3042, 3043, 3045, 3047, 3049, 3050, 3051, 3053, 3055, 3061, 3062, 3064, 3065, 3067, 3071, 3072, 3074, 3076, 3077, 3078, 3079, 3083, 3084, 3085, 3089, 3091, 3092, 3096, 3103, 3115, 3117, 3118, 3136, 3137, 3146, 3158, 3162, 3166, 3169, 3176, 3177, 3182, 3183, 3187, 3188, 3196, 3199, 3220, 3224, 3245, 3246, 3280, 3295, 3311, 3312, 3314, 3315, 3318, 3324, 3328, 3333, 3336, 3339, 3341, 3343, 3348, 3349, 3350, 3351, 3352, 3356, 3358, 3371, 3380, 3384, 3390, 3406, 3412, 3415, 3445, 3457, 3460, 3463, 3464, 3465, 3467, 3471, 3473, 3475, 3476, 3477, 3478, 3482, 3483, 3485, 3491, 3493, 3495, 3497
Nutrition Educator, 3182
Nutrition Programme *See also: Nutrition;* 2879, 2900, 2902, 2934, 2940, 3007, 3010, 3013, 3016, 3017, 3024, 3040, 3043, 3050, 3084, 3089, 3096, 3156, 3166, 3182, 3220, 3314, 3328, 3339, 3405, 3407, 3465, 3473, 3474, 3478, 3482, 3483, 3489, 3493

O

Obstetrics *See also: Gynaecology; Maternal Child Health; Parturition;* 2804, 2857, 2962, 3030, 3107, 3126, 3156, 3288, 3342, 3373, 3376, 3385, 3389
Occupational Health, 2814, 2861, 2864, 2901, 3046, 3047, 3106, 3110, 3357, 3375, 3414
Ophthalmic Medical Assistant *See also: Auxiliary Health Worker;* 3143, 3151, 3264, 3287, 3440, 3486
Ophthalmology, 3143, 3155, 3158, 3207
Oral Contraceptive *See also: Birth Control;* 3048, 3361, 3388, 3401, 3403, 3404
Organization, 2811, 2824, 2825, 2830, 2837, 2843, 2846, 2847, 2848, 2849, 2851, 2852, 2855, 2856, 2857, 2858, 2859, 2860, 2861, 2862, 2865, 2866, 2867, 2870, 2871, 2872, 2874, 2875, 2876, 2878, 2879, 2880, 2881, 2882, 2883, 2889, 2898, 2903, 2906, 2910, 2911, 2915, 2923, 2925, 2931, 2945, 2948, 2956, 2961, 2963, 2976, 2998, 3001, 3002,

3011, 3014, 3018, 3039, 3041, 3044, 3045, 3048, 3066, 3073, 3084, 3098, 3110, 3112, 3114, 3121, 3122, 3123, 3124, 3125, 3127, 3129, 3130, 3131, 3150, 3154, 3165, 3173, 3175, 3180, 3190, 3202, 3214, 3216, 3232, 3237, 3239, 3240, 3253, 3260, 3263, 3276, 3299, 3300, 3353, 3393, 3406, 3407, 3408, 3409, 3410, 3416, 3423, 3424, 3427, 3435, 3444, 3459, 3477, 3483, 3486, 3490, 3494

Organization, Dental Services, 3300

Organization, Disease Control, 3014, 3018, 3066, 3073, 3427, 3490, 3494

Organization, Emergency Health Services, 2879, 3084, 3092

Organization, Environmental Health Services, 2925, 3098

Organization, Family Planning Programme, 3048

Organization, Health Centre, 2848, 2872, 2881, 2890, 3112, 3114, 3129, 3253, 3344, 3420, 3435

Organization, Health Education, 3165, 3173, 3175, 3190, 3371

Organization, Health Manpower, 2829, 2837, 2839, 2843, 2846, 2866, 3012, 3214, 3216, 3237, 3276, 3412

Organization, Health Manpower Training, 2830, 2855, 2890, 3011, 3202

Organization, Health Services, 2811, 2824, 2829, 2839, 2849, 2851, 2852, 2853, 2855, 2856, 2858, 2859, 2860, 2861, 2862, 2864, 2865, 2866, 2867, 2869, 2870, 2871, 2874, 2875, 2876, 2878, 2880, 2882, 2883, 2888, 2889, 2898, 2903, 2910, 2914, 2915, 2923, 2930, 2931, 2945, 2948, 2956, 2958, 2976, 2998, 3001, 3002, 3011, 3012, 3039, 3044, 3072, 3121, 3122, 3123, 3125, 3129, 3154, 3175, 3180, 3216, 3218, 3232, 3237, 3240, 3253, 3258, 3260, 3263, 3299, 3406, 3407, 3409, 3410, 3412, 3414, 3116, 3416, 3417, 3418, 3419, 3423, 3424, 3425, 3426, 3426, 3444, 3477, 3486

Organization, Health Team, 2824

Organization, Mass Campaign, 3127, 3353, 3408

Organization, Maternal Child Health Services, 2857, 2911, 2916, 2961, 3032, 3041, 3130

Organization, Mental Health Services, 2825, 2847, 3150

Organization, Nutrition Programme, 3084, 3483

Organization, Rehabilitation Services, 2912, 2963, 2969, 3045, 3110, 3124, 3131

Outpatient Care See also: Clinic, Outpatient; 2813, 2848, 2881, 2952, 3018, 3102, 3110, 3117, 3119, 3121, 3123, 3134, 3142, 3186, 3237, 3346, 3373, 3376, 3420, 3428, 3429, 3430, 3435, 3446, 3475

Outpatient Care, Rural, 3119, 3121, 3134, 3237, 3346

P

PAHO See also: International Cooperation; 2893, 2937, 3188

Paramedic See also: Auxiliary Health Worker; 3343

Parasitic Diseases See also: Ascariasis; Filariasis; Guinea Worm; Infectious Diseases; Schistosomiasis; Trypanosomiasis; 3034, 3056, 3117, 3144, 3199, 3312, 3334, 3350, 3351, 3367, 3375, 3378

Parturition See also: Obstetrics; Pregnancy; 3107, 3289, 3295, 3312, 3342, 3387, 3389, 3391

Pediatrics See also: Child Health; 2804, 3027, 3105, 3275, 3312, 3317, 3318, 3376, 3492

Periodical See also: Mass Media; 2801, 2802, 2803,

2808, 2809, 2817, 2818, 2868, 3163

Pest Control See also: Disease Control; 2892, 3052, 3057, 3063, 3066, 3363, 3366, 3367, 3368, 3375, 3377, 3378, 3494, 3500

Pharmacist See also: Auxiliary, Pharmacy; Health Manpower; 2979, 2983, 3108, 3185, 3205

Pharmacy See also: Drugs; 2907, 2979, 2981, 2983, 3002, 3430

Physical Examination See also: Evaluation, Health; 3136, 3137, 3212, 3346, 3385, 3401, 3464

Physician See also: Health Manpower; 2829, 2831, 2836, 2840, 2842, 2850, 2852, 2861, 2876, 2936, 2970, 2972, 2973, 2975, 2976, 2984, 2985, 2993, 2998, 3006, 3012, 3046, 3062, 3111, 3125, 3133, 3155, 3180, 3186, 3192, 3193, 3194, 3195, 3196, 3197, 3198, 3199, 3200, 3201, 3202, 3203, 3204, 3205, 3206, 3207, 3208, 3209, 3210, 3211, 3212, 3213, 3214, 3215, 3281, 3308, 3326, 3342, 3381, 3400, 3409, 3411, 3421, 3423, 3431, 3438, 3439, 3440, 3450, 3459, 3472, 3492

Physiological Aspect, 3078, 3096, 3343, 3343

Physiotherapist See also: Auxiliary, Orthopaedic; Health Manpower; Rehabilitation; 3045, 3124, 3134

Physiotherapy, 3102, 3106, 3134, 3140

Pilot Project See also: Government Project; 2813, 2839, 2843, 2850, 2851, 2866, 2891, 2894, 2916, 2917, 2921, 2988, 3008, 3016, 3017, 3031, 3040, 3041, 3095, 3115, 3131, 3135, 3139, 3143, 3145, 3147, 3160, 3176, 3187, 3188, 3197, 3228, 3229, 3238, 3249, 3252, 3255, 3258, 3259, 3269, 3275, 3289, 3290, 3385, 3395, 3400, 3404, 3405, 3406, 3415, 3426, 3433, 3459, 3472, 3481, 3487

Planning, 2818, 2820, 2825, 2826, 2827, 2828, 2829, 2830, 2833, 2834, 2835, 2837, 2838, 2840, 2841, 2842, 2844, 2846, 2847, 2847, 2850, 2852, 2854, 2855, 2859, 2863, 2867, 2880, 2882, 2884, 2885, 2887, 2889, 2892, 2893, 2894, 2895, 2896, 2897, 2898, 2899, 2900, 2902, 2905, 2908, 2909, 2910, 2911, 2915, 2916, 2917, 2920, 2921, 2923, 2924, 2925, 2926, 2928, 2929, 2930, 2932, 2933, 2934, 2935, 2936, 2938, 2939, 2940, 2943, 2944, 2945, 2946, 2947, 2948, 2949, 2950, 2951, 2952, 2954, 2955, 2956, 2958, 2959, 2960, 2961, 2962, 2963, 2964, 2965, 2966, 2967, 2968, 2969, 2970, 2973, 2974, 2976, 2979, 2983, 2994, 2997, 2999, 3000, 3001, 3007, 3008, 3010, 3015, 3024, 3031, 3035, 3037, 3039, 3045, 3047, 3056, 3061, 3066, 3074, 3080, 3090, 3091, 3096, 3098, 3099, 3107, 3108, 3112, 3114, 3127, 3138, 3164, 3165, 3172, 3175, 3180, 3182, 3184, 3193, 3197, 3201, 3204, 3210, 3231, 3237, 3241, 3244, 3248, 3272, 3276, 3285, 3296, 3300, 3302, 3304, 3316, 3329, 3344, 3353, 3387, 3402, 3407, 3410, 3411, 3416, 3421, 3422, 3423, 3424, 3431, 3432, 3433, 3434, 3435, 3437, 3441, 3444, 3449, 3466, 3472, 3483, 3487

Planning, Dental Services, 3099, 3300, 3302

Planning, Development See also: Community Development; Economic Development; Government Policy; Rural Development; Social Development; Socioeconomic D evelopment; 2815, 2854, 2867, 2886, 2898, 2906, 2909, 2917, 2921, 2929, 2933, 2934, 2937, 2939, 2946, 2949, 2960, 2962, 2967,

2979, 3011, 3015, 3056, 3061, 3090, 3092, 3138, 3184, 3434, 3436, 3437, 3472

Planning, Disease Control, 2887, 2959, 3037, 3066, 3353

Planning, Emergency Health Services, 2927, 3074, 3091, 3092

Planning, Environmental Health, 2959

Planning, Environmental Health Services, 2925, 3031, 3098

Planning, Family Planning Programme, 3386

Planning, Health Centre, 2885, 2899, 2935, 2943, 2944, 2947, 2952, 3112, 3344, 3435

Planning, Health Education, 2932, 2940, 3008, 3080, 3164, 3165, 3172, 3175, 3176, 3285

Planning, Health Manpower, 2826, 2828, 2829, 2833, 2834, 2835, 2837, 2840, 2841, 2842, 2844, 2846, 2847, 2859, 2887, 2888, 2889, 2896, 2897, 2905, 2909, 2910, 2911, 2919, 2929, 2932, 2937, 2941, 2942, 2953, 2954, 2959, 2985, 3114, 3116, 3193, 3204, 3210, 3231, 3241, 3244, 3272, 3276, 3304, 3329, 3424

Planning, Health Manpower Training, 2820, 2827, 2828, 2830, 2838, 2844, 2845, 2887, 2953, 2999, 3204, 3231, 3296

Planning, Health Services, 2815, 2818, 2826, 2828, 2829, 2833, 2849, 2850, 2852, 2853, 2858, 2859, 2863, 2867, 2869, 2871, 2880, 2882, 2887, 2888, 2889, 2890, 2891, 2892, 2893, 2894, 2897, 2898, 2899, 2901, 2905, 2907, 2908, 2909, 2910, 2914, 2915, 2919, 2923, 2924, 2926, 2928, 2929, 2930, 2932, 2936, 2937, 2938, 2941, 2942, 2945, 2946, 2948, 2949, 2950, 2951, 2953, 2954, 2956, 2957, 2958, 2959, 2960, 2962, 2964, 2965, 2966, 2970, 2973, 2974, 2976, 2983, 2985, 2994, 2997, 3000, 3001, 3011, 3012, 3035, 3039, 3072, 3107, 3108, 3138, 3175, 3237, 3241, 3248, 3316, 3329, 3392, 3407, 3411, 3416, 3417, 3418, 3421, 3423, 3424, 3431, 3432, 3433, 3434, 3436, 3437, 3444, 3449, 3487

Planning, Information System, 2968

Planning, Mass Campaign, 3127

Planning, Maternal Child Health Services, 2896, 2911, 2913, 2916, 2918, 2961, 3393

Planning, Mental Health Services, 2825, 2847, 2895, 2920

Planning, National See also: National Health Plan; National Plan; 2833, 2855, 2880, 2882, 2898, 2900, 2908, 2911, 2919, 2925, 2929, 2930, 2934, 2937, 2946, 2953, 2954, 2955, 2959, 2960, 2970, 3037, 3047, 3180, 3432, 3436, 3444, 3466

Planning, Nursing Services, 3272, 3402

Planning, Nutrition Programme, 2900, 2902, 2934, 3007, 3010, 3024, 3089, 3096, 3182, 3483

Planning, Project, 2891, 2916, 2958, 3008, 3197, 3425, 3425

Planning, Regional, 2919, 2934, 2941, 2953, 2955, 3392, 3410, 3472

Planning, Rehabilitation Services, 2884, 2912, 2920, 2963, 2969, 3045

Poison, 2814

Political Aspect, 2824, 2852, 2856, 2859, 2863, 2870, 2878, 2889, 2939, 2958, 2973, 2978, 2980, 2983, 2991, 2994, 3048, 3108, 3122, 3125, 3195, 3225, 3230, 3247, 3265, 3395, 3397, 3421, 3423, 3447, 3481, 3487

Population See also: Demography; 2937, 2990, 3022, 3388

Population Increase See also: Demography; 2840, 2937, 3020, 3022, 3388

Postpartum Care See also: Maternal Child Health; 2815, 3004, 3289, 3387, 3389, 3391, 3455, 3462, 3476

Poverty See also: Slums; 2886, 2985, 2994, 2997, 3065, 3083, 3469

Pregnancy See also: Antenatal Care; Obstetrics; Parturition; 3007, 3126, 3342, 3387, 3389

Preventive Medicine, 2861, 2864, 2882, 2887, 2898, 2912, 2920, 2922, 2951, 2963, 2969, 2998, 3032, 3054, 3071, 3072, 3115, 3120, 3136, 3156, 3180, 3205, 3209, 3218, 3229, 3233, 3285, 3301, 3320, 3332, 3356, 3405, 3414, 3426, 3443, 3461, 3475, 3482

Primary Care, 2824, 2828, 2832, 2835, 2862, 2905, 2940, 2941, 2942, 2951, 2954, 3095, 3122, 3133, 3194, 3229, 3239, 3241, 3260, 3261, 3298

Prosthesis, 2884, 2969, 3106, 3140, 3141, 3148, 3149

Psychiatry See also: Mental Health; 2825, 2895, 3000, 3001, 3060, 3081, 3150, 3160, 3372, 3468

Psychological Aspect, 2819, 2820, 2842, 2917, 2930, 2988, 2992, 2994, 2996, 3062, 3070, 3116, 3248, 3276, 3359, 3372, 3451, 3468, 3476, 3485

Psychologist See also: Health Manpower; 2819

Psychology, 3350

Q

Questionnaire See also: Survey; 2841, 2950, 3060, 3079, 3088, 3092, 3099, 3212, 3293, 3316, 3320, 3382, 3403, 3404, 3405, 3406, 3420, 3438, 3439, 3470

R

Rabies See also: Infectious Diseases; 3104, 3350

Radio Communications See also: Mass Media; 2957, 3442

Radiology See also: X-ray Unit; 3109

Rehabilitation See also: Physiotherapist; 2884, 2912, 2920, 2922, 2963, 2969, 3045, 3102, 3106, 3110, 3119, 3124, 3131, 3134, 3140, 3141, 3148, 3149, 3178, 3346

Rehabilitation Services, 2920, 3102, 3110, 3148

Research See also: Methodology; Statistical Analysis; Survey; 2801, 2802, 2803, 2806, 2813, 2815, 2819, 2837, 2841, 2859, 2861, 2867, 2869, 2884, 2888, 2898, 2906, 2920, 2930, 2932, 2948, 2965, 2968, 2978, 2981, 2982, 2988, 2990, 3002, 3013, 3020, 3024, 3036, 3038, 3046, 3050, 3051, 3053, 3058, 3063, 3064, 3069, 3070, 3074, 3081, 3085, 3091, 3101, 3141, 3145, 3147, 3149, 3166, 3170, 3196, 3228, 3316, 3385, 3393, 3422, 3457, 3460, 3481, 3489

Research Centre See also: Laboratory; 2803, 2806, 2884, 2978, 3036, 3170, 3305

Research, Disease Control, 3462

Research, Emergency Health Services, 3092

Research, Environmental Health, 3063

Research, Family Planning, 3145

Research, Health Education, 2803, 3145, 3166

Research, Health Manpower, 2819, 2930

Research, Health Services, 2867, 2930, 2948, 3145, 3405

Research, Maternal Child Health, 3040, 3051, 3393

Research, Mental Health, 2920, 3081

Research, Nutrition, 3013, 3026, 3050, 3051, 3053, 3064, 3074, 3457, 3460

Research, Rehabilitation, 2884, 3141, 3149

Rural Area, 2807, 2809, 2810, 2811, 2814, 2817, 2832, 2840, 2845, 2862, 2870, 2872, 2874, 2876, 2877, 2883, 2903, 2909, 2925, 2936, 2950, 2957, 2962, 2971, 2989, 2993, 3000, 3004, 3005, 3009, 3025, 3029, 3046, 3052, 3054, 3061, 3067, 3076, 3079, 3090, 3097, 3108, 3109, 3119, 3121, 3123, 3127, 3129, 3133, 3134, 3146, 3147, 3152, 3153, 3155, 3156, 3158, 3167, 3177, 3183, 3186, 3191, 3197, 3202, 3203, 3214, 3217, 3231, 3235, 3237, 3239, 3242, 3243, 3257, 3263, 3265, 3290, 3294, 3311, 3323, 3327, 3329, 3332, 3345, 3346, 3372, 3385, 3387, 3397, 3401, 3406, 3415, 3416, 3418, 3421, 3436, 3439, 3458, 3467, 3468, 3470, 3475, 3481, 3482, 3484, 3488

Rural Development *See also: Planning, Development;* 2921, 2931, 2962, 2967, 3090, 3128, 3184, 3191, 3218, 3398

Rural Health Post *See also: Health Centre;* 2845, 2860, 2957, 2974, 3146, 3226, 3239, 3242, 3244, 3253, 3344, 3415, 3437

Rural Health Promoter *See also: Auxiliary Health Worker;* 2845, 3095, 3127, 3218, 3225, 3229, 3263, 3364, 3366, 3367, 3368, 3369, 3415

Rural Medical Aid *See also: Auxiliary Health Worker;* 2840, 2844, 3235, 3373, 3396, 3416

S

Sanitary Engineer *See also: Sanitation Manpower;* 3069, 3309

Sanitary Facilities *See also: Construction, Sanitary Facilities; Sanitation;* 2807, 2885, 3023, 3031, 3054, 3055, 3327, 3363, 3366, 3378, 3426, 3488

Sanitary Inspector *See also: Sanitation Manpower;* 3306

Sanitation *See also: Environmental Health; Hygiene; Sanitary Facilities; Waste Disposal;* 2805, 2807, 2861, 2863, 2864, 2894, 2969, 3012, 3023, 3031, 3033, 3047, 3057, 3061, 3068, 3069, 3080, 3082, 3085, 3098, 3139, 3168, 3217, 3246, 3260, 3307, 3309, 3327, 3331, 3363, 3366, 3375, 3375, 3378, 3395, 3405, 3414, 3488, 3495

Sanitation Manpower *See also: Auxiliary, Sanitation; Sanitary Engineer; Sanitary Inspector;* 2807, 3309

Sanitation Services, 2807, 3069, 3366

Schistosomiasis *See also: Parasitic Diseases;* 2864, 3044, 3056, 3057, 3061, 3132, 3171, 3434, 3494, 3500

School *See also: Training Centre; University;* 2816, 2831, 2840, 2904, 2905, 2943, 2994, 3167, 3176, 3179, 3181, 3183, 3192, 3201, 3202, 3204, 3210, 3211, 3279, 3283, 3334, 3350, 3354, 3440, 3492

School Health *See also: Child; Student; Teacher;* 2804, 2904, 3144, 3181, 3334, 3350

School, Medical, 2840, 2943, 3192, 3201, 3202, 3204, 3210, 3211, 3440, 3492

School, Nursing, 2816, 3277, 3279, 3282, 3283, 3286

School, Public Health, 2816, 2905

Screening *See also: Diagnosis;* 2908, 2922, 2940, 2961, 2962, 3018, 3060, 3143, 3154, 3212

Self-care, 2907, 2930, 3119, 3161, 3164, 3175, 3321, 3341, 3443, 3472

Skin Diseases, 3142

Slums *See also: Living Conditions; Poverty; Urbanization;* 3047

Smallpox *See also: Infectious Diseases;* 3014, 3104, 3132, 3255, 3408

Social and Cultural Anthropology *See also: Culture;* 2886, 2915, 2988, 2990, 3001, 3058, 3075, 3386, 3447, 3449, 3452, 3454

Social Aspect, 3102, 3423

Social Change *See also: Social Development;* 2810, 2854, 2895, 2906, 2911, 2958, 2997, 3001, 3145, 3167, 3182, 3194, 3247, 3394, 3397, 3419

Social Development *See also: Planning, Development; Social Change;* 2815, 2854, 2996, 3006, 3145, 3434, 3436, 3437

Social Participation *See also: Community Development;* 2809, 2810, 2815, 2819, 2831, 2832, 2836, 2852, 2853, 2855, 2856, 2865, 2866, 2871, 2874, 2890, 2891, 2897, 2905, 2906, 2909, 2911, 2917, 2918, 2919, 2920, 2921, 2926, 2930, 2931, 2937, 2941, 2942, 2945, 2954, 2958, 2961, 2973, 2984, 2994, 2996, 2999, 3001, 3003, 3008, 3016, 3017, 3018, 3033, 3040, 3054, 3080, 3089, 3090, 3095, 3115, 3116, 3118, 3128, 3139, 3145, 3147, 3161, 3164, 3168, 3173, 3175, 3175, 3176, 3178, 3179, 3180, 3184, 3185, 3187, 3189, 3218, 3223, 3225, 3227, 3234, 3235, 3238, 3242, 3247, 3248, 3257, 3258, 3260, 3269, 3307, 3334, 3355, 3400, 3406, 3418, 3431, 3436, 3443, 3454, 3472, 3482, 3487

Social Sciences, 2819, 3195

Social Security *See also: Health Insurance;* 2858, 2914, 3413

Social Services *See also: Child Care;* 2831, 2895, 2917, 2920, 3032, 3178, 3437

Social Structure, 3080, 3186, 3247, 3436, 3487

Social Theory, 3058, 3436, 3481

Social Worker *See also: Health Manpower;* 2917, 3102, 3131, 3133, 3178, 3371

Socialism, 3397

Socioeconomic Aspect, 2842, 2871, 2900, 2912, 2914, 2915, 2920, 2939, 2956, 2958, 2963, 2969, 2973, 3027, 3030, 3043, 3065, 3070, 3079, 3083, 3108, 3124, 3138, 3167, 3215, 3229, 3230, 3232, 3371, 3387, 3419, 3431, 3436, 3456, 3470, 3479, 3485, 3492

Socioeconomic Development *See also: Economic Development;Planning, Development;* 3015, 3026, 3229

Sociology, 3058, 3059, 3086, 3479

Statistical Analysis *See also: Research; Statistical Data;* 2891, 2908, 2932, 2953, 2965, 3022, 3026, 3078, 3085, 3100, 3200, 3308, 3315, 3316, 3441, 3479

Statistical Data *See also: Demography; Morbidity; Mortality; Statistical Analysis; Survey;* 2808, 2826, 2839, 2863, 2871, 2888, 2890, 2896, 2898, 2901, 2903, 2925, 2932, 2933, 2939, 2945, 2953, 2960, 2963, 2965, 2971, 2974, 2975, 3010, 3022, 3023, 3024, 3025, 3026, 3027, 3044, 3049, 3057, 3071, 3078, 3079, 3085, 3087, 3100, 3131, 3136, 3137, 3151, 3153, 3197, 3200, 3217, 3308, 3316, 3375, 3377, 3385, 3397, 3401, 3403, 3404, 3412, 3414, 3415, 3428, 3434, 3441, 3458, 3466, 3467, 3470, 3477, 3478, 3491, 3496, 3498, 3499, 3500

Student *See also: Education; School Health;* 2831, 3144, 3181, 3185, 3201, 3202, 3213, 3330, 3334, 3388, 3498

Student Selection, 2816, 2822, 2823, 2830, 2835, 2862, 3203, 3210, 3217, 3218, 3227, 3239, 3242, 3243, 3244, 3249, 3251, 3252, 3257, 3259, 3275, 3277, 3294, 3300, 3306

Supervision, 2835, 2844, 2847, 2862, 2903, 2936, 2973, 3193, 3203, 3221, 3222, 3226, 3231, 3232, 3234, 3239, 3241, 3243, 3250, 3252, 3254, 3256, 3262, 3267, 3271, 3288, 3289, 3297, 3299, 3373, 3416, 3431

Supervision, Auxiliary, 2835, 2844, 2845, 2847, 2853, 2862, 2936, 3089, 3193, 3203, 3217, 3218, 3221, 3222, 3226, 3231, 3232, 3234, 3239, 3241, 3243, 3250, 3252, 3254, 3258, 3262, 3267, 3299, 3303, 3373, 3400

Surgery, 2801, 2802, 3106, 3111, 3113, 3152, 3158, 3355, 3373, 3379, 3486

Survey *See also: Attitudes; Data Collection; Demography; Epidemiology; Evaluation; Questionnaire; Research; Statistical Data;* 2829, 2837, 2839, 2841, 2842, 2863, 2886, 2891, 2907, 2925, 2929, 2950, 2956, 2960, 2971, 2975, 2984, 2989, 2994, 2995, 3000, 3004, 3010, 3025, 3026, 3027, 3031, 3035, 3038, 3049, 3050, 3051, 3060, 3061, 3068, 3071, 3073, 3079, 3083, 3085, 3088, 3091, 3092, 3093, 3095, 3099, 3100, 3103, 3111, 3131, 3132, 3136, 3137, 3138, 3147, 3148, 3160, 3163, 3173, 3174, 3187, 3188, 3206, 3212, 3214, 3217, 3220, 3248, 3255, 3269, 3287, 3290, 3291, 3296, 3305, 3308, 3315, 3316, 3394, 3399, 3401, 3402, 3403, 3404, 3405, 3406, 3417, 3420, 3438, 3439, 3441, 3450, 3453, 3455, 3456, 3458, 3462, 3463, 3466, 3467, 3469, 3470, 3474, 3476, 3479, 3480, 3482, 3484, 3488, 3489, 3490, 3495, 3496, 3497, 3498

T

Teacher *See also: Education; Health Manpower; School Health;* 2831, 2902, 3016, 3144, 3167, 3172, 3176, 3181, 3204, 3205, 3213, 3278, 3326, 3330, 3334, 3335, 3370, 3371, 3393

Teaching Aid *See also: Audiovisual Aid; Handbook; Teaching Method; Textbook; Training Method; Training Manual;* 2803, 2804, 2821, 3003, 3087, 3095, 3172, 3174, 3219, 3273, 3278, 3315, 3320, 3321, 3325, 3326, 3329, 3333, 3334, 3335, 3336, 3337, 3341, 3344, 3348, 3349, 3350, 3351, 3354, 3355, 3356, 3357, 3358, 3359, 3360, 3362, 3363, 3365, 3373, 3377, 3378, 3381, 3382, 3383, 3385, 3386, 3390, 3484

Teaching Aid, Child Health, 3341

Teaching Aid, Dental Health, 3381

Teaching Aid, Disease Control, 3321, 3334, 3354, 3377, 3378

Teaching Aid, Environmental Health, 2821, 3363

Teaching Aid, Family Planning, 2821, 3386

Teaching Aid, Health Education, 2803, 2821, 3003, 3172, 3176, 3188, 3278, 3320, 3326, 3334, 3350, 3355, 3356, 3357, 3359, 3360, 3362, 3380

Teaching Aid, Maternal Child Health, 2821, 3333, 3390, 3484

Teaching Aid, Mental Health, 3335, 3337

Teaching Aid, Nutrition, 3188, 3333, 3339, 3358

Teaching Method *See also: Teaching Aid;* 2832, 2845, 3003, 3090, 3162, 3166, 3167, 3171, 3172, 3176, 3187, 3188, 3192, 3204, 3206, 3207, 3208, 3210, 3219, 3230, 3248, 3267, 3273, 3295, 3314, 3326,

3329, 3330, 3344, 3348, 3349, 3350, 3365, 3370, 3377, 3378, 3383, 3386, 3392, 3400, 3461

Tetanus *See also: Infectious Diseases;* 3104, 3113, 3220, 3350, 3462, 3491

Textbook *See also: Teaching Aid;* 3273

Trachoma *See also: Eye Diseases;* 2869, 3143, 3151, 3486

Tradition *See also: Culture;* 2842, 2886, 2906, 2991, 3004, 3006, 3167, 3386, 3447, 3451, 3468

Traditional Birth Attendant *See also: Auxiliary Health Worker; Auxiliary, Family Planning; Auxiliary, Midwife; Auxiliary, Nurse-midwife; Dai; Dukun; Midwife ; Traditional Practitioner;* 2845, 2907, 2998, 3089, 3265, 3290, 3292, 3295, 3296, 3297, 3405, 3426, 3462

Traditional Medicine *See also: Culture; History of Health Services; Medicinal Plant; Traditional Practitioner;* 2811, 2815, 2837, 2843, 2846, 2855, 2856, 2869, 2870, 2907, 2950, 2972, 2987, 2989, 2991, 2992, 2993, 2995, 2996, 3002, 3004, 3005, 3006, 3028, 3038, 3059, 3117, 3118, 3141, 3155, 3196, 3265, 3297, 3332, 3337, 3397, 3447, 3449, 3450, 3451, 3453, 3454, 3455, 3467, 3468, 3472, 3480

Traditional Practitioner *See also: Traditional Birth Attendant; Traditional Medicine;* 2815, 2828, 2843, 2846, 2855, 2907, 2972, 2987, 2989, 2991, 2992, 2993, 2995, 2998, 2999, 3000, 3002, 3005, 3006, 3088, 3089, 3133, 3223, 3229, 3238, 3297, 3397, 3405, 3447, 3449, 3450, 3451, 3452, 3454, 3456, 3468, 3480, 3481

Training *See: specific health worker. See also: Continuing Education;* 2803, 2807, 2819, 2820, 2822, 2823, 2827, 2828, 2830, 2831, 2834, 2835, 2836, 2837, 2838, 2840, 2842, 2843, 2844, 2847, 2850, 2851, 2854, 2855, 2856, 2862, 2863, 2872, 2873, 2875, 2876, 2883, 2889, 2894, 2899, 2902, 2903, 2905, 2909, 2916, 2931, 2946, 2951, 2954, 2955, 2958, 2970, 2976, 2979, 2991, 2999, 3002, 3005, 3010, 3029, 3034, 3036, 3046, 3048, 3069, 3081, 3093, 3102, 3108, 3111, 3114, 3120, 3125, 3134, 3138, 3151, 3155, 3160, 3165, 3169, 3170, 3175, 3180, 3181, 3190, 3192, 3193, 3194, 3197, 3198, 3199, 3200, 3201, 3202, 3203, 3204, 3205, 3206, 3207, 3208, 3209, 3210, 3211, 3212, 3213, 3215, 3216, 3219, 3220, 3221, 3222, 3223, 3227, 3228, 3229, 3230, 3231, 3233, 3234, 3235, 3236, 3237, 3239, 3240, 3241, 3242, 3243, 3244, 3245, 3246, 3248, 3249, 3250, 3251, 3252, 3253, 3254, 3257, 3259, 3260, 3261, 3262, 3263, 3264, 3265, 3266, 3267, 3268, 3269, 3270, 3271, 3272, 3273, 3274, 3275, 3276, 3277, 3278, 3279, 3282, 3283, 3285, 3286, 3287, 3288, 3290, 3292, 3293, 3294, 3295, 3296, 3297, 3298, 3300, 3301, 3302, 3303, 3304, 3305, 3306, 3308, 3309, 3313, 3326, 3330, 3337, 3371, 3373, 3383, 3385, 3394, 3395, 3396, 3399, 3409, 3416, 3423, 3424, 3438, 3439, 3440, 3459, 3471, 3472, 3492

Training Centre *See also: Education; School; University;* 2816, 2822, 2823, 2827, 2828, 2830, 2853, 2884, 2907, 2918, 2943, 2978, 2991, 3228, 3240, 3241, 3283, 3300, 3308

Training Centre, Auxiliary, 2816, 2822, 2827, 2943, 2957, 2991, 3228, 3241

Training Centre, Health Education, 2830
Training Centre, Health Manpower, 2853
Training Centre, Laboratory Auxiliary, 2823
Training Centre, Maternal Child Health, 3283
Training Centre, Medical Assistant, 3240
Training Course *See also: Curriculum;* 2991, 3170, 3199, 3207, 3212, 3242, 3257, 3279, 3282, 3306, 3448
Training Course, Auxiliary, 2991, 3170, 3242, 3257
Training Manual *See also: Teaching Aid;* 2805, 3095, 3265, 3312, 3313, 3317, 3318, 3323, 3331, 3332, 3345, 3364, 3365, 3366, 3367, 3368, 3369, 3370, 3372, 3373, 3374, 3376, 3379, 3383, 3387, 3389
Training Manual, Auxiliary, 3372, 3374, 3379, 3379, 3383
Training Manual, Barefoot Doctor, 3332
Training Manual, Community Health Worker, 3265
Training Manual, Family Planning Manpower, 3387
Training Manual, First Aid, 3364
Training Manual, Health Extension Officer, 3344
Training Manual, Laboratory Technician, 3345
Training Manual, Medical Assistant, 3331, 3373
Training Manual, Midwife, 3387
Training Manual, Nurse, 3312, 3317, 3318, 3323, 3376
Training Manual, Nurse Auxiliary, 3313
Training Manual, Nurse-midwife, 3389
Training Manual, Nurse-midwife Auxiliary, 3389
Training Manual, Rural Health Promoter, 3364, 3366, 3367, 3368, 3369
Training Manual, Rural Medical Aid, 3373
Training Method *See also: Teaching Aid;* 3275
Training, Administrator, 2840
Training, Aid Post Orderly, 3246, 3253
Training, Anaesthetist Auxiliary, 3379
Training, Auxiliary, 2828, 2832, 2835, 2840, 2845, 2862, 2891, 2893, 2957, 2985, 3072, 3120, 3138, 3202, 3208, 3216, 3230, 3231, 3241, 3242, 3248, 3254, 3263, 3267, 3274, 3383, 3394, 3396, 3400, 3405, 3406, 3440, 3459, 3472, 3492
Training, Barefoot Doctor, 2832, 2856
Training, Behdar, 3251
Training, Community Health Aide, 2839, 3223, 3243, 3259, 3298, 3418
Training, Community Health Worker, 3011, 3169, 3203, 3217, 3221, 3221, 3227, 3234, 3236, 3237, 3239, 3244, 3245, 3249, 3250, 3252, 3257, 3258, 3260, 3262, 3265, 3266, 3268, 3269, 3294, 3385, 3392, 3395, 3400, 3426, 3472
Training, Community Nurse, 3270, 3282
Training, Dental Auxiliary, 2822, 2844, 3300, 3302, 3303
Training, Dental Manpower, 3300
Training, Dentist, 3300, 3301
Training, Family Nurse Practitioner, 2899
Training, Family Planning Manpower, 3048, 3200
Training, Health Education, 3170, 3278
Training, Health Educator, 2830, 3175, 3190, 3371
Training, Health Inspector, 3306
Training, Health Manpower, 2803, 2819, 2820, 2827, 2829, 2837, 2838, 2839, 2842, 2851, 2854, 2855, 2863, 2869, 2872, 2875, 2883, 2888, 2889, 2890, 2894, 2898, 2902, 2903, 2905, 2907, 2916, 2931, 2946, 2953, 2954, 2955, 2999, 3002, 3012, 3029, 3036, 3040, 3093, 3102, 3114, 3121, 3160, 3165,

3180, 3193, 3205, 3210, 3228, 3230, 3231, 3245, 3308, 3309, 3397, 3412, 3424
Training, Health Team, 2834
Training, Laboratory Auxiliary, 2823, 3304
Training, Laboratory Technician, 2823, 3304, 3305
Training, Maternal Child Health Auxiliary, 3393
Training, Medex, 2832
Training, Medical Assistant, 2957, 3219, 3222, 3233, 3240, 3261, 3373, 3416
Training, Medical Technologist, 2823, 3305
Training, Mental Health Auxiliary, 2847, 3081
Training, Mental Health Nurse, 3337
Training, Midwife, 2957, 3200, 3274, 3282, 3288
Training, Multipurpose Auxiliary, 3220
Training, Nurse, 2838, 2850, 2893, 2951, 3072, 3199, 3205, 3208, 3233, 3264, 3271, 3272, 3273, 3274, 3275, 3276, 3277, 3278, 3279, 3282, 3283, 3285, 3286, 3287, 3308, 3337, 3399, 3426
Training, Nurse Auxiliary, 2957, 3279, 3313
Training, Ophthalmic Medical Assistant, 3151, 3264
Training, Physician, 2831, 2840, 2850, 2876, 2951, 2970, 2976, 3046, 3072, 3111, 3125, 3155, 3192, 3194, 3197, 3198, 3199, 3200, 3201, 3202, 3203, 3204, 3205, 3206, 3207, 3208, 3209, 3210, 3211, 3212, 3213, 3215, 3308, 3326, 3409, 3423, 3438, 3439, 3440, 3459, 3492
Training, Physiotherapist, 3134
Training, Rural Health Promoter, 2957, 3218, 3229
Training, Rural Medical Aid, 2844, 3373, 3416
Training, Sanitary Engineer, 3069, 3309
Training, Sanitation Manpower, 2807, 3309
Training, Statistician Auxiliary, 3036
Training, Teacher, 2957, 3181
Training, Traditional Birth Attendant, 2839, 2907, 3290, 3292, 3293, 3295, 3296, 3297, 3426
Training, Traditional Practitioner, 2843, 2991, 3005
Transport, 2921, 2954, 2957, 3153, 3196, 3338, 3345, 3418, 3426, 3431, 3442
Tribes *See also: Bantu; Bedouin; Minority Group; Zulu;* 3004, 3028, 3159, 3266, 3419, 3447, 3463
Tropical Medicine, 2982, 3111, 3199
Tropical Zone, 2892, 2901, 3491
Trypanosomiasis *See also: Parasitic Diseases;* 3104
Tubal Ligation *See also: Birth Control;* 3048, 3292
Tuberculosis *See also: Infectious Diseases; Tuberculosis Programme;* 2864, 2869, 2908, 3037, 3044, 3073, 3087, 3093, 3117, 3120, 3132, 3196, 3220, 3348, 3353, 3414, 3427, 3496, 3499
Tuberculosis Programme *See also: BCG Vaccination; Tuberculosis;* 3037, 3073, 3426, 3427
Typhoid Fever *See also: Infectious Diseases;* 2864

U

UN *See also: International Cooperation;* 2927, 2962, 2978, 3074
UNICEF *See also: International Cooperation;* 2838, 2927, 3090, 3174, 3229
University *See also: School; Training Centre;* 2830, 2851, 2883, 2903, 2982, 3197, 3201, 3215, 3300, 3404
Urban Area, 2883, 2895, 2917, 2918, 2974, 2989, 3067, 3097, 3133, 3187, 3229, 3421, 3450, 3458, 3488
Urbanization *See also: Migration; Slums;* 3006, 3047
US Indian Health Service, 3266
Utilization Rate, 2877, 2913, 2950, 2951, 2956, 2971,

2973, 2976, 2989, 2994, 2997, 3005, 3061, 3068, 3088, 3100, 3131, 3160, 3186, 3233, 3249, 3264, 3421, 3425, 3428, 3453, 3456, 3469, 3479, 3480

I have been unable to obtain a copy of the following work through my local library or bookshop. I request the help of the IDRC in procuring this material. Address coupon to: **SALUS Bibliography, c/o Micrographics Project, IDRC, Box 8500, Ottawa, Canada K1G 3H9.** *(Please type or print)*

VOLUME NUMBER _____

ITEM NUMBER _____ PAGE _____

AUTHOR/EDITOR _____

TITLE _____

I prefer ☐ microfiche ☐ photocopy (only of documents of less than 30 pages).

NAME & TITLE: _____

ORGANIZATION: _____

ADDRESS: _____

_____

_____

I have been unable to obtain a copy of the following work through my local library or bookshop. I request the help of the IDRC in procuring this material. Address coupon to: **SALUS Bibliography, c/o Micrographics Project, IDRC, Box 8500, Ottawa, Canada K1G 3H9.** *(Please type or print)*

VOLUME NUMBER _____

ITEM NUMBER _____ PAGE _____

AUTHOR/EDITOR _____

TITLE _____

I prefer ☐ microfiche ☐ photocopy (only of documents of less than 30 pages).

NAME & TITLE: _____

ORGANIZATION: _____

ADDRESS: _____

_____

_____

I have been unable to obtain a copy of the following work through my local library or bookshop. I request the help of the IDRC in procuring this material. Address coupon to: **SALUS Bibliography, c/o Micrographics Project, IDRC, Box 8500, Ottawa, Canada K1G 3H9.** *(Please type or print)*

VOLUME NUMBER _____

ITEM NUMBER _____ PAGE _____

AUTHOR/EDITOR _____

TITLE _____

I prefer ☐ microfiche ☐ photocopy (only of documents of less than 30 pages).

NAME & TITLE: _____

ORGANIZATION: _____

ADDRESS: _____

_____

_____